Handbook of Research on ICT-Enabled Transformational Government:

A Global Perspective

Vishanth Weerakkody
Brunel University, UK

Marijn Janssen
Delft University of Technology, The Netherlands

Yogesh K. Dwivedi
Swansea University, UK

Information Science REFERENCE

INFORMATION SCIENCE REFERENCE

Hershey · New York

Director of Editorial Content: Kristin Klinger
Senior Managing Editor: Jamie Snavely
Managing Editor: Jeff Ash
Assistant Managing Editor: Carole Coulson
Typesetter: Michael Brehm
Cover Design: Lisa Tosheff
Printed at: Yurchak Printing Inc.

Published in the United States of America by
Information Science Reference (an imprint of IGI Global)
701 E. Chocolate Avenue
Hershey PA 17033
Tel: 717-533-8845
Fax: 717-533-8661
E-mail: cust@igi-global.com
Web site: http://www.igi-global.com/reference

and in the United Kingdom by
Information Science Reference (an imprint of IGI Global)
3 Henrietta Street
Covent Garden
London WC2E 8LU
Tel: 44 20 7240 0856
Fax: 44 20 7379 0609
Web site: http://www.eurospanbookstore.com

Library of Congress Cataloging-in-Publication Data

Handbook of research on ICT-enabled transformational government : a global perspective / Vishanth Weerakkody, Marijn Janssen and Yogesh K. Dwivedi, editors.
p. cm.
Includes bibliographical references and index.
Summary: "This book provides comprehensive coverage and definitions of the most important issues, concepts, trends, and technologies within transformation stage e-government implementation"--Provided by publisher. ISBN 978-1-60566-390-6 (hbk.) -- ISBN 978-1-60566-391-3 (ebook) 1. Internet in public administration. 2. Information technology. I. Weerakkody, Vishanth. II. Janssen, Marijn. III. Dwivedi, Yogesh Kumar. JF1525.A8H362 2009
352.3'802854678--dc22

2008054194

British Cataloguing in Publication Data
A Cataloguing in Publication record for this book is available from the British Library.

Dedication

To my parents and wife Ayoma

—Vishanth Weerakkody

To Daphne, Henri, and Karin

—Marijn Janssen

To Murly Jija, Sudha Didi, Shiv, Kirti, and Kishan

—Yogesh K. Dwivedi

Hans de Bruijn, *Delft University of Technology, The Netherlands*
Marco De Marco, *Catholic University, Italy*
Torgeir Dingsøyr, *Norwegian University of Science and Technology, Norway*
Marwan Elnaghi, *Brunel University, UK*
René Fitterer, *SAP Research, CEC St. Gallen, Switzerland*
Karsten Gareis, *empirica, Germany*
Katarina Giritli-Nygren, *Midsweden University, Sweden*
Ulrike Greiner, *SAP Research, CEC St. Gallen, Switzerland*
Ivaylo Gueorguiev, *European Software Institute Center Bulgaria, Bulgaria*
Umesh Gulla, *GGS Indraprastha University, India*
M.P. Gupta, *Indian Institute of Technology, India*
Cory Allen Heidelberger, *Dakota State University, USA*
Vincent Homburg, *Erasmus University Rotterdam, The Netherlands*
Tobias Hüsing, *empirica, Germany*
Mojca Indihar Štemberger, *University of Ljubljana, Slovenija*
Jurij Jaklič, *University of Ljubljana, Slovenija*
Hans Jochen Scholl, *University of Washington, USA*
Jay P. Kesan, *University of Illinois College of Law, USA*
JinKyu Lee, *Oklahoma State University, USA*
Katarina Lindblad-Gidlund, *Midsweden University, Sweden*
Peter Loos, *Saarland University, Germany*
Muhammad Mustafa Kamal, *Brunel University, UK*
Edephonce N. Nfuka, *Stockholm University, Sweden*
Sevgi Ozkan, *Middle East Technical University, Turkey*
Michael Räckers, *European Research Center for Information Systems, Germany*
Mysore Ramaswamy, *Southern University, USA*
Ashwin Rao, *Cornell University, USA*
Dibakar Ray, *National Informatics Centre, Department of Information Technology, Government of India, India*
Peter Rohner, *University of St. Gallen, Switzerland*
Knut H. Rolland, *Norwegian University of Science and Technology, Norway*
Barbara Russo, *Free University of Bolzano-Bozen, Italy*
Lazar Rusu, *Stockholm University, Sweden*
Demetrios Sarantis, *National Technical University of Athens, Greece*
Ludwig Christian Schaupp, *West Virginia University, USA*
Rajiv C. Shah, *University of Illinois at Chicago, USA*
Maddalena Sorrentino, *State University of Milan, Italy*
Florian Stroh, *SAP Research, CEC St. Gallen, Switzerland*
Giancarlo Succi, *Free University of Bolzano-Bozen, Italy*
Nasrat Touqan, *Oklahoma State University, USA*
Eileen Trauth, *Pennsylvania State University, USA*
Haiko van der Voort, *Delft University of Technology, The Netherlands*
Jing Yang, *Oklahoma State University, USA*
Benjamin Yeo, *Milken Institute, USA*
Jörg Ziemann, *Saarland University, Germany*

List of Contributors

Table of Contents

Section IV
Measuring and Evaluating for Improvement

Detailed Table of Contents

Section I
T-Government Foundations

The transformation of public sector has been limited so far and current efforts have largely resulted in reinforcing old practices. To realize transformational change, government agencies will need more radical changes in core processes across organizational boundaries. To date, few countries have excelled in reaching the transformational stage of e-government. This is due in part to the complexity of reaching this high level of maturity, as t-government has to deal with aspects ranging from institutional to business process and from strategic to technical issues. This first section discusses the fundamental aspects that need to be taken into account by governments when transforming their business processes and practices. In the first chapter the need for changing institutions to avoid reinforcement of existing structure and enabling transformation is presented. The second chapter draws the attention to the need to radically reengineer business processes and presents methodologies, instruments, and tools for this purpose. In the third chapter various transformation strategies and critical design choices are identified to concentrate services in a new organizational entity called shared service centers. The fourth chapter criticizes current efforts that look at citizens only in their role as customers and neglecting other roles, which further complicates transformation. The last chapter identifies a number of factors influencing change that need to be addressed when implementing transformational change.

Public Service Transformation initiatives are intrinsically linked with the values, norms, informal rules, and other institutional aspects taken for granted beliefs. T-government initiatives need to transform institutions, whereas at the same time, institutions, through judicial and professional norms, and through power structures and path dependencies, shape ways in which technologies are designed and used in specific practices. This chapter analyzes two case studies and contributes to knowledge by helping to better understand how to deal with the difficulties, contradictions, and sometimes mind-boggling features of t-government.

T-Government requires incremental or radical business process change often going beyond departmental or organizational boundaries. Implementation of t-government requires a high level of business process orientation and typically involves a business process change project. Non-profit organizations have characteristics, which make process renovation projects considerably different from business process reengineering (BPR) in the private sector. In this chapter an approach is presented that enables governmental institutions to move towards t-government. In this chapter the general framework for business process change methodologies, techniques, and tools is customized for their needs and extended with several other business process management elements (e.g. measurement of the level of business process orientation in an organization).

One transformation effort is the concentrating of organizational functions in 'shared service centers' (SSCs). A lot can be gained by concentrating functions, including improved services through specialization, efficiencies through standardization, and cost reductions through economies of scale. Yet transforming the public sector is a difficult endeavor and expected benefits are not gained. In this chapter, the perceptions of key stakeholders from a policy network theoretical lens are examined and some major patterns determining success or failure in transforming the public sector structure are presented. A set of critical choices for initiating a SSC and various approaches for the management of the transformation process are given.

In transformational stage, governments are viewed in their role as service provider and citizens in their role as customers, however, this neglects the other roles that are important in our democratic system. Cory Allen Heidelberger criticizes the citizen-as-consumer perspective in this chapter and argues that this approach results in citizen alienation. A theoretical model based on citizen participation to guide development of t-government systems to act as social decision support systems is presented and challenges it may face are addressed.

There is a strong desire amongst governments worldwide to provide an efficient, cost effective, and sustainable electronic service delivery environment. This chapter analyzes the motivations behind this instigated change towards transformational government systems. The authors highlight the importance of radical change and innovative approaches to provide quality services and address a variety of internal organizational and external stakeholder issues that impact t-government implementation. Successful t-government implementation requires senior executive participation and active engagement of key stakeholders for benefit realization. The main message that the chapter offers is the premise that t-government adoption is surrounded by political, cultural, organizational, technological and social issues which must be considered and simultaneously addressed to enable transformation.

Section II
Interoperability and Integration Enabling T-Government

The aim of t-government is to ensure that fragmented and distributed agencies operate in a coherent manner. T-government goes typically beyond the borders of a single department or organization and organizations and their systems need to be interoperable. Interoperability aims at connecting the various organizations at a technical, business process and organization level and enables information systems to be operated in a coordinated and meaningful fashion. T-government can only be accomplished if high levels of interoperability and integration are met. Chapter VI presents an approach for public organizations which enables loosely coupled integration with other organizations based on the concept of business interoperability interface. In Chapter VII a novel approach for semiautonomously identifying transformation opportunities in business processes is presented. A life-cycle model and factors influencing enterprise application integration (EAI) is presented in chapter eight, which help to improve decision-making concerning the adoption of EAI. In Chapter IX open standards and open formats are discussed aimed at improving the access and use of government information. The last chapter in this section presents four constituents of interoperable system and a layered architecture for interoperable governmental information systems.

In t-government, autonomous organizations need to collaborate with each other. Due to the traditional independence of public organizations as well as the need to minimize modifications of internal systems,

Assessment of the results of t-government program is difficult and there is also a widespread perception of the inadequacy of the ability to measure concrete practices. This chapter adopts an evaluation perspective and considers evaluation as a social research field requiring interdisciplinary inputs capable of shedding light not only on the results, but also on the implementation process of the public services. This chapter shows the dual role or t-government evaluation, as valuable cognitive resource and accountability tool for the policymakers.

The authors of this chapter suggest that t-government is best understood as a mythologised megatrend. They argue that it has become a symbol for the modernised government of today. A symbol which, in some sense has to be demythologized in order to be realised. The authors suggest that by analysing general and specific interpretations, the myth can be partially unravelled, which is illustrated by a large scale study based on 2,624 employees in public administration. The authors suggest a loose coupling between the general and the specific level.

The high complexity of transformational government strategy is rooted in the multistakeholder environment it is derived from. In this environment the Balanced Scorecards provide the necessary tools for effective measurement and management of the transformation of public services. In this chapter, the authors show how planning and presenting the strategy in strategic maps and creating a system of performance measures for the goals in a number of perspectives can ensure a foundation for effective management system of the transformational government at a strategic level.

Transformational government impacts the public sector by opening up new, more effective ways for achievement of goals rather than simply making existing structures and processes more efficient. This chapter focuses on use of ICT by individuals in their roles as citizens, workers, learners, patients, consumers, and so forth. It is argued that the transformational potential of ICTs is rooted in its effect in terms of

Open Source Software (OSS) has been often pointed as a promising alternative that may also render public services and the underlying business processes more transparent and accessible to citizens. In this chapter, a decision-making instrument for calculating the cost of a migration to OSS is presented. The authors also report a set of good practices used to run the migration.

Qatar is seen as one of the fastest developing nations in the Middle East. The Qatari government hopes to increase accessibility of e-government services by offering free wireless Internet access to its citizens in public places. In this way, the Qatari government aims to encourage their citizens to actively participate in the global information society with a view of bridging the digital divide. This research uses the extended unified theory of acceptance and use of technology (UTAUT) model for examining the adoption and diffusion of Internet Park services in Qatar. The chapter reports that factors such as effort expectancy, perceived technology and wireless Internet trust significantly influence intention to use electronic services in Qatar.

This chapter proposes a model of e-file adoption that integrates diffusion of innovation theory, online trust and e-government experience into a comprehensive view of e-file acceptance. The authors argue that relative advantage, compatibility, trust of the government, trust of the Internet, e-filing in the past year, and previous completion of an e-government transaction all had a positive impact on adoption of e-services.

The degree of resistance to change due to organizational, structural, and social factors varies depending upon differences in political context, transition phase, and other aspects. In postcommunist countries such as Armenia, e-transformation is sometimes considered as a second disruption, the first being the fall of the Soviet rule. This chapter presents a comprehensive framework for guiding successful implementation of e-government initiatives. This framework includes critical dimensions of e-government interactions and socio-technical aspects that are particularly relevant to the special challenges of transitioning countries.

Foreword

The various stakeholders of government have different, sometimes conflicting expectations regarding services, government's inner workings, and, in general, government's role in society. Today, governments are expected to be both citizen-centric and service-friendly, but they are also requested to improve efficiency and enhance the democratic system through stakeholder participation and involvement. Private-sector business and citizens play multiple roles as stakeholders of government. While they are recipients of government services (similar to "customers" in the private sector), they are at the same time also constituents in the democratic process.

High expectations from stakeholders put governments under enormous pressures, which increasingly facilitate a transformation in the business of government. On the one hand, government's fragmentation is purposive; that is, the division of powers is at the core of any democratic system; on the other hand, the purposive fragmentation should not render the governmental system dysfunctional. If an event occurs, which cuts across jurisdictions and across spans of control, government agencies are expected to understand and deal with the situation in a timely and effective fashion. Governments need to operate in a coherent and holistic way in their problem-solving efforts.

Further, stakeholder participation in policy-making processes is of the essence. Government of the 21st century must find ways of using stakeholder input to inform similar policy-making processes down the road, in order to avoid wasteful reduplication of efforts. In short, governments face high expectations, while they have to deal with large numbers of urgent issues at the same time. Under these circumstances the understanding of effective transformative practices is key; an overview of practice-proven instruments and tools can help governments transform and retain essential knowledge during the transformation processes.

This book provides a timely contribution to the field of transformational government. It provides a number of different views on transformation and showcases successful practices from all over the world. For researchers, this book presents a valuable overview of the field of t-government. It covers the theoretical foundations, lays out the interoperability and integration aspects and portrays knowledge management and measurements approaches, which are the basis for enabling t-government. Furthermore, the book presents several theoretical lenses on t-government and charts out a number of different research directions.

Currently few countries and governments have actually excelled in accomplishing sustainable transformation. This is due in part to the complexity and the need for dealing with a variety of institutions, organizations, business processes, and technical issues. This book addresses various aspects of transformation, which can help practitioners moving forward with transformative projects. The book further presents a number of instruments and tools, which support and enable t-government. It will not only contribute to understanding the increasing awareness and need for transformation, but will also help make the concept of t-government better understood, so that practice can avoid costly mistakes.

I wish you a pleasant reading!

Prof. Dr. Hans Jochen Scholl
The Information School, University of Washington, Seattle, WA, USA

Hans J (Jochen) Scholl *is an associate professor in the University of Washington's Information School. He teaches and conducts research on information management, process change, and organizational transformation in government and other organizations. His work has appeared in the International Journal of Public Administration, Transforming Government, Electronic Government, International Journal of Electronic Government Research, Government Information Quarterly, Action Research, and the Springer Lecture Notes in Computer Science. He is the PI of the NSF-funded Fully Mobile City Government research project. He chairs the electronic government track at the Hawaii International Conference on System Sciences (HICSS) and serves as a member of the organizing committee of the DEXA/EGOV conference. He is the president-elect of the Digital Government Society of North America and the vice chair of the IFIP TC 8.5 Working Group (Information Systems in Public Administration).*

Foreword

The background to electronic government (e-government) lies in the wider debate about technology and its contribution to social, economic, and political processes. In the last few years the focus and implementation of e-government has moved from offering basic government information towards providing more interactive services to citizens. Most developed countries have now implemented e-government portals that offer a single point of access to selected key public services. These portals offer an on-line-real-time environment that facilitates two-way, transaction level services. While the initial stages of e-government targeted changing customer facing processes, more recent initiatives are aimed at transforming back office processes in public agencies. These initiatives are commonly referred to as transformational government (or t-government for short). T-government aims to place information and communication technology (ICT) at the heart of the e-government agenda to improve services by leveraging the benefits from technological and people investment through imaginative process redesign. The current transformational agenda is seen by many as the next phase of e-government, which focuses upon cost savings and service improvements.

Research on early e-government indicates that many countries have faced major challenges in implementing services that balance the institutional and citizen perspectives. It is further complicated by the fact that citizens are not only consumers of services with an interest in added-value, but also tax payers with a concern for cost effectiveness. Transformational government, with its emphasis on integrated and seamless transactions with agencies, is fundamentally more complex. The task facing public institutions to innovate, educate, and enthuse is formidable. Likewise the accompanying technical and organizational changes will exceed those experienced in the private sector.

In this context, the Handbook of Research on "ICT-Enabled Transformational Government: A Global Perspective" is timely. The global perspective is especially welcome. In their 2007 report the World Bank singled out the potential of government agencies' use of ICT to *transform* relations with citizens, business and other arms of government. This book, through comprehensive coverage of the most important issues, concepts, trends, and technologies within t-government implementations, offers crucial insights. It provides researchers, scholars, students, and practitioners with the most recent knowledge relating to the conceptual, technical, and organizational challenges in the implementation of transformational government. As one of the first books solely dedicated to covering the topic of t-government it fills an important role in mapping out the theoretical and practical agendas. Many contributions are from leading e-government scholars worldwide. The potential advantage of a collected work, over the lone researcher, is the scope of the research which is possible and the different perspectives and disciplines which can deepen the insights. The task of the editors is to realize that potential. I believe they have achieved this and have produced a book that significantly furthers our understanding as researchers and as practitioners.

I am delighted to recommend this book.

Prof. David H. Brown
Chair in Strategy and Information Systems, Director Lancaster China Management Centre, Lancaster University Management School, UK

David Brown *is chair of strategy and information systems in the Department of Management Science and director of the China Management Centre at Lancaster University Management School. His research interests have two separate but linked strands. Firstly, strategic studies including strategic information systems and e-business, and secondly the application of these strands internationally, especially in transitional economies. The majority of his work is strongly organisationally based and includes action research and soft systems methodology. His current research, funded by EU and EPSRC grants, includes: SMEs and collaborative e-business models; e-business policy in developing economies; e-science and e-management; and e-innovation in China and Laos. He has published over sixty articles on information systems, e-business and strategy formulation, and has co-authored three books on management transition in China. In 1998 he was appointed Fellow Professor in Management Science at Renmin University of China, and in 2008 he received the Greater China Recognition Award from the Department of UK Trade and Investment for his work in fostering Sino-UK relationships, especially institutional development and research.*

Preface

THE RISE OF TRANSFORMATIONAL GOVERNMENT

...This is a time to push forward, faster and on all fronts: open up the system, break down its monoliths, put the parent and pupil and patient and law-abiding citizen at the centre of it. We have made great progress. Let us learn the lessons of it not so as to rest on present achievements but to take them to a new and higher level in the future...

—Prime Minister, Tony Blair, July 2005

The combined influence of the Internet and supporting ICTs have seen commercial enterprises reaching out to people and exploiting business opportunities that would have previously not been possible. Internet enabled e-business has also contributed to a significant increase in the speed and ease of business transactions making not only competition intense between organisations, but also requiring companies to integrate new and faster systems and adjust to new technology to meet the needs of customers. Although commercial enterprises and governments had little in common prior to the e-commerce era, government and industry e-commerce agendas have become more closely linked in recent times. Conversely, more people are now less tolerant of poor, impersonal service in the public sector as they become aware of the power of the Web and experience good services in the private sector. Therefore, it is in every government's interest to make their public services more efficient and available in order to satisfy citizens' expectations, which has often eluded many governments and political leaders in modern society.

One of the key issues that public sector managers have to face when dealing with service improvement is traditional public administration practice that have been influenced by organisational cultures and practices that date back several decades. In many countries, the public services offered are highly bureaucratic and siloed where the citizens have no choice of service provider. Information and communication technologies (ICTs) are overlaid onto existing organisational structures and processes without any consideration to how they can be improved. Consequently, changing the processes and behaviour of government organisations and establishing cooperation between government agencies is fraught with difficulty. In this backdrop, the concept of electronic government (e-government) was introduced to many countries around the world in the mid/late 1990s. The essence of e-government revolved around offering key public services on-line using a Web portal. While it was relatively easy for governments to create national Web portals to assert their e-government presence, this merely amounted to information being reorganised without any fundamental change to existing back office processes or information systems and technology (IS/IT). Moreover, from a strategic perspective, for e-government implementation to be widespread and successful, exemplary strategies and practices also need to be identified in addition to establishing and prioritising processes to be e-enabled. Furthermore, every e-government programme

Figure 1. Progress towards transformational government

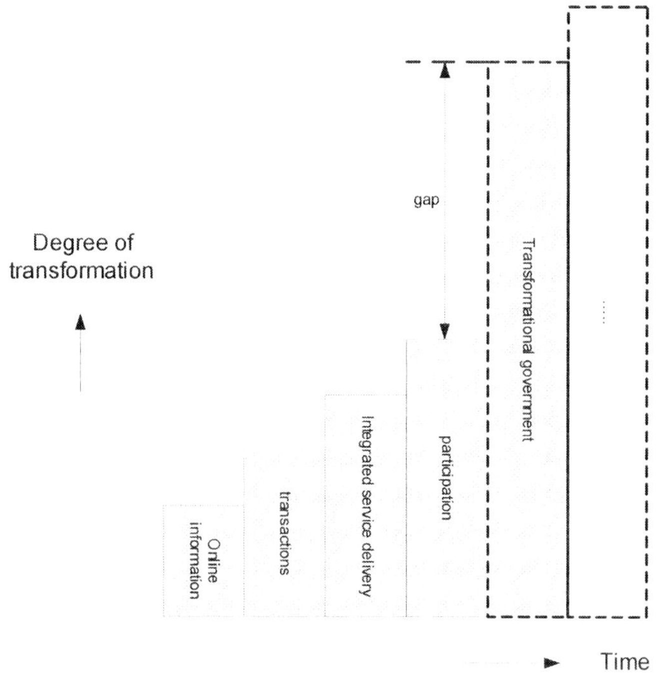

needs to have a clear idea of the proposed benefits to citizens, what challenges need to be overcome and the level of institutional change that needs to take place for it to be successful in a given context.

In the last few years e-government implementation efforts have evolved from basic information provisioning to more integrated and joined up service offerings in most developed countries. Having successfully implemented a number of transaction-based e-government services by e-enabling front office and customer facing processes, most developed countries are now working towards realising transformational government (t-government) as shown in the figure 1 below. The t-government phase is dotted as this is not accomplished yet, and might be followed by a next phase that is not known yet.

The gap between the previous phases has been relatively small, whereas the gap to the t-government phase is a bigger one. In the previous phases technology has primarily been used to reinforce existing structures. The transformational phase of e-government involves reengineering and e-enabling back office processes and information systems to enable more joined-up and citizen-centric e-government services. However, public sector transformation is a massive and complex undertaking involving distributed decision-making that requires a good understanding of the political context, culture, business processes, and technology. Transformation requires design and engineering methods for breaking through the traditional boundaries between organizational units which requires the interplay between social and technological aspects. Therefore, transformation initiatives should not only target technological issues and deliver sound enterprise architectures and business processes, but should also consider the multi-actor environment and the change of culture and even the institutional setting. The overall aim of this book is to provide an understanding and highlight some of the key challenges, issues, and complexities involved in the transformational phase of e-government. It will help to understand the strategic, organisational, technical, and social issues influencing business process and information systems change in public sector organisations in the context of t-government and the resulting overall impact of t-government upon citizens from a global perspective.

In most western countries, t-government has naturally evolved from e-government. Yet, there remains considerable confusion about t-government. The definitions offered for e-government differ according to the varying e-government focus and are usually centred on technology, business, process, citizen, or a functional perspective. These different schools of thought show there is no universally accepted definition of the e-government concept. However, we can distinguish between t-government and e-government; t-government covers a broader organisational and socio-technical dimension which involves radically changing the structures, operations, and most importantly, the culture of government. Given this context, we propose a definition for t-government that encapsulates a wider perspective of the transformational aspects of e-government. The new definition is as follows: "*t-government is the ICT-enabled and organisation-led transformation of government operations, internal and external processes, structures, and culture to enable the realisation of citizen-centric services that are transparent, cost effective, and efficient*". This definition suggests a variety of objectives that need to be realized in parallel and we propose that the creation of citizen-centric services requires considerable changes at all levels which might need radical changes, rather than incremental improvement.

OVERVIEW OF THE BOOK

This book covers theories, concepts, methods, frameworks, guidelines, technologies, and tools and techniques that are relevant to, and influence the transformational phase of e-government implementations. First, the book explores the concept of transformational government and relevant facilitators and inhibitors from a conceptual and practical perspective. Second, the book highlights the role of interoperability and integration in a t-government context. Third, the book looks at how knowledge and management support facilitates t-government. Fourth, the book highlights the significance of evaluation and measurement in e-government and t-government initiatives. Finally, the book explores adoption and diffusion related issues that influence e-government implementation and acceptance from a citizen centric angle.

The chapters that make up the book include contributions from academics, practitioners, and policymakers and thus offer a balanced perspective of the strategic, organizational, technical, and socio-cultural, as well as theoretical and practical issues that have shaped the progress of e-government and t-government. In this sense, the book is a mix of theory and practice and therefore can be useful for academia (research and teaching), as well as practice (policymakers and implementers).

The book offers readers: (a) knowledge and understanding of the content and context of ICT enabled t-government; (b) insight into public sector processes and information systems from a global perspective; (c) best practices and approaches for realizing public sector transformation; (d) overview of the key literature and theories that have shaped e-government and t-government research, and (e) the opportunity to read the contributions from leading researchers around the world in the field of e-government and t-government in one handbook of research.

We hope you will enjoy reading this research handbook as much as we did putting it together. We certainly learned much from the diverse chapters that are offered in the book.

Vishanth Weerakkody, Brunel University, UK
Marijn Janssen, Delft University of Technology, The Netherlands
Yogesh K. Dwivedi, Swansea University, UK
Co-Editors

Section I
T-Government Foundations

Chapter I
The Social Shaping of Transformational Government

Vincent Homburg
Erasmus University Rotterdam, The Netherlands

ABSTRACT

Public Sector Transformation initiatives do not exist within a vacuum. This chapter analyzes how Public Service Transformation initiatives are intrinsically linked with the values, norms, informal rules, and taken for granted beliefs (in short: institutions) that characterize the context in which the initiatives are introduced. Using two case studies (describing the Criminal Justice System in the UK and social security in Belgium and The Netherlands) it is exemplified how Public Service Transformation initiatives sometimes transform institutions, whereas at the same time, institutions, through judicial and professional norms, and through power structures and path dependencies, shape ways in which technologies are designed and used in specific practices. The chapter argues for a better understanding of the working of institutions in specific Public Sector Transformation initiatives, in order to be better able to deal with the difficulties, contradictions, and sometimes mindboggling features of Public Sector Transformation.

INTRODUCTION

Public Sector Transformation as a topic of discussion has moved from the realm of utopian thought into the realm of actual practices at the shop floors of government agencies (Borins, 2007; Dunleavy, 2006). Transformation has also become an emerging topic of study for scholars in many academic disciplines, including information systems, organization theory and public administration (Homburg, 2008).

If one discusses the topic of Public Sector Transformation, at least two questions come to mind. The first one is what exactly constitutes 'Public Sector Transformation'. What changes exactly can be discerned, what properties are important, and how does a 'transformed' public sector look like? The second one is the relation between technology on the one hand, and context in which the technology is applied. Context here refers to a set of institutions: the values, norms, rules and taken-for-granted assumptions that characterize every day practice. For instance, one of the ambitions in many transformation initiatives is to promote client orientation and efficiency, specific values that constitute the organizational context of technology. Such a line of reasoning indicates that technology, in an exogenous way, affects the structure, processes and institutions of public sector organizations (Hammer, 1996). At the same time, one can ask whether and how prevailing institutions affect ways in which technologies are applied, implemented and used. For instance, comparative studies have shown that comparable applications yield completely different effects if they are applied in various national contexts.

In this paper, a social shaping of technology perspective (Homburg, 2008; Orlikowkski & Barley, 2001; Williams & Edge, 1996) is used to answer the following research question: how are technological and institutional change in public sector transformation related and why does public sector transformation result in tensions? As such, the ambition in this chapter is to document and reflect upon the dynamics underlying the notion of Public Sector Transformation. This question is answered in a literature review of the concept of social shaping of technology, and a subsequent analysis of two transformations in the public sector, one of the criminal justice system in the UK, and one of social security reforms in the Netherlands and in Belgium.

This chapter is organized as follows. In section two, the concept of Public Sector Transformation (PST) is unraveled and analyzed. Furthermore, the social shaping of technology (SST) perspective is elaborated upon. Underlying concepts of PST and SST are used to analyze actual transformations in the UK Criminal Justice system and in the Dutch and Belgium Social Security sector in section three. Discussions and reflections are presented in section four.

BACKGROUND

What is Public Sector Transformation?

Nowadays, governments around the world enthusiastically claim that they are or are about to reengineer the apparatus of government and governance. These kinds of attempts have been coined redesign (Bekkers & Homburg, 2005), reengineering (Hammer, 1996), or reform (Pollitt, Van Thiel, & Homburg, 2006), depending on whatever seemed appropriate. Throughout this chapter, the terminology of the book as a whole will be used and changes will be referred to as Public Sector Transformation. In general, it is possible to identify two antecedents of Public Sector Transformation.

The first one is that Public Sector Transformation is an instantiation of a specific wave of managerial or administrative reforms that usually go by the name of the *New Public Management* (Pollitt et al., 2006). New Public Management marks a move away from the so-called *classic public administration paradigm,* which had remained relatively undisturbed from the late 19th century until about the 1970s. The classic public administration paradigm is generally assumed to be based on a-political public service, hierarchy and rules, permanence and stability, an institutionalized civil service, internal regulation and equality.

Since the 1970s governments throughout the Western world and beyond have been confronted with budget deficits, lack of performance of the public sector and generally public distrust in public administration. As a consequence, various waves of reforms have been carried out, emphasizing a move away from the classic bureaucratic model of organization, and emphasizing values like *results orientation, customer orientation* and *value for money.* These values were emphasized by a series of organizational and managerial changes, among others (Pollitt et al., 2006):

1. Lean and highly decentralized structures, like semi-autonomous organizations, rather than large, multi-purpose, hierarchical ministries or departments. Thus, for example, the UK, the Netherlands, Norway and Italy all had programs for separating out certain functions or activities and placing them in 'arms length' executive agencies.
2. The use of divisional structures in public service resulting in breaking down former unitary bureaucracies, as well as in inter-organizational relations with organizations in private and voluntary sectors (public-private partnerships, PPP), resulting in blurred and broadened frontiers between the public sector, the market sector and the voluntary sector.
3. A widespread emphasis on contracts (or contract-like relationships) instead of formal, hierarchical relationships. Throughout Western Europe, for example, local authorities, which had previously collected refuge or cleaned the streets using staff from their own works departments, contracted these functions out. Even if the existing unit continued to carry out the work, it now had to do so under a set of carefully-specified contractual conditions or in competition with private companies
4. A much wider-then-hitherto deployment of markets (or market-type) mechanisms (MTMs) for the delivery of public services. For example, during the 1980s UK local authorities were obliged by central government not only to use contracts but to do so through a process of mandatory competitive tendering. Other examples are found in the privatization of for example social housing, and the introduction of more competition in health care or education.
5. More attention for the management of organizations and management skills of public servants—as opposed to policy advice and legal skills which were dominant in the classic public administration paradigm. Additionally, changes in attitudes were aimed for, for example the introduction of a customer (rather than citizen) orientation, or in other words a focus on providing high quality services that serve narrower (less universal, more individualistic) interests of citizens. Finally, there was the introduction of performance-related systems for recruiting, promoting and paying staff and in general increased flexibility in hiring and firing staff.
6. A shift in the focus of management systems and efforts from inputs like staff or buildings, and processes (for example teaching, inspecting) towards outputs (test results, inspection reports) and outcomes (safety, health, standards of literacy in the community). This performance orientation is combined with an increased emphasis on accountability for performance by decentralized or even privatized units to principals and other stakeholders, but also horizontally, that is in comparison with peer organizations through benchmarking.
7. A shift towards more measurement and quantification, especially in the form of systems of performance indicators and/or explicit standards. Instead of just 'trusting the doctor' measures are developed that show how often the doctor prescribes drugs, how often patients develop post-operative complications, the length of waiting lists and the degree of compliance with the best practice protocols, and so on.

The second antecedent of Public Service Transformation is not so much managerial in nature, but more anchored in technological developments. It has been observed that information and communication technologies could be used to actually instrument some of the organizational changes that were put forward by proponents of the New Public Management. Especially since the late 1970s, new generations of technologies have become available that began to eliminate the architecture of bureaucracy. Personal computers (PCs) and especially Internet technologies are supposed to have distinct transformative powers that, in specific societal and organizational dynamics, can be used to accelerate changes inside and around governments. The aims to which these technologies are put to use differs enormously: better delivery of government services to citizens, improved interactions with business and industry, citizen empowerment through access to information (Edmiston, 2003), or more efficient government management in general.

Resulting from both managerial as well as managerial reforms in the public sector, a transformed public sector is beginning to take shape. The following characteristics of PST can be discerned:

- the blurring of traditional boundaries between organizations (Bekkers, 1998; Dewett & Jones, 2001);
- an overall process orientation and a focus on the needs of citizens; and
- the vilification of structure as a primary medium for control, accountability and knowledge dispersion, and the rise of the information infrastructure as a rival medium for structure for the purpose of achieving these ends (Groth, 1999; Zuurmond, 1998).

The image that is beginning to take shape here, as a result of both administrative reforms as well as technologically-induced changes, is that specific ideas and technologies alter specific norms and practices (or in general: institutions) in and around public sector organizations. Such a view, however, is susceptible to the criticism that the underlying line of reasoning is overly rational and technologically, economically or managerially determined. In this view, simplistic determinism is evident in the sense that technology and managerial fads and fashions (Pollitt et al., 2006) are assumed to influence the operations and underlying principles of government in an independent, objective and inevitable way. There is reason to believe, however, that technology and institutions are, in a much more complex way, embedded in each other and that the artificial separation of technology and its context is perhaps elegant but neither plausible nor workable.

Technology and Institutions: Epistemological Quarrels and Questions

Wanda Orlikowski (2001) has argued that technology and institutions are intrinsically linked to one another. Institutionalism holds that organizations, and the individuals that populate them, are suspended in a web of values, norms, rules, beliefs and taken for granted assumptions, which are at least partially of their own making. Institutionalists view organizations not as passive entities controlled by the demands of their objective environments (such as, in more or lesser degree, is assumed in contingency theory), but as active players that may strategically respond to environmental pressures. Moreover, it is assumed that technology affects the institutions of public administration, but at the same time prevailing institutions (norms, values, and agreed-upon assumptions of how to enact reality) filter technologies, and determine which technologies are implemented in specific ways, supporting specific values. Homburg (2008) provides four examples in this respect.

1. Transparency and Law Enforcement

Internationally, national and federal tax agencies have championed the race for the most successful 'wired' government services. For example, in 2004 the American Internal Revenue Service (IRS) was cited as most reliable government web site, and throughout the world tax agencies are seen as frontrunners of efficient, responsive and customer-oriented government agencies. Many agencies have both reorganized their internal structures and information systems, as well as redesigned the ways in which they communicate with the outside world. Contacts with citizens now take place using advanced, customer-friendly websites, while government agencies are cooperating more and more for the purpose of cross-checking citizens' data and fighting fraud. For citizens, this implies that the processes of requesting rebates and submitting personal information has been simplified, and there is less need to submit information that has already been supplied to tax agencies. Furthermore, through websites, tax agencies are able to offer customized information about tax laws, regulations, et cetera. The Dutch Tax Agency, for example, claims that all the background dossiers and materials that a professional Tax Inspector needs are on-line and available to citizens. In short, one could conclude that Tax Agencies have, over the past years, embraced ICTs and that these ICTs have yielded organizational transparency, customer orientation and efficiency.

There is, however, a limit to the technologically-enabled customer orientation of Tax Agencies. In the past some Tax Agencies have experimented with personalized web services, with which individual taxpayers could monitor the progress and status of tax filings. Comparable 'track & trace' services exist on almost every e-commerce application (for instance, e-banking services), and at first sight they appear desirable for Tax agencies since they would be conducive to transparency and personalized customer orientation. This ignores the 'involuntary services' and enforcement role that Tax Agencies also provide. They are both public service organizations, as well as law enforcement agencies and the balancing of these functions provides a compelling argument against the use of 'track and trace' services. In their role of law enforcement agency, Tax Agencies try to maximize the citizen's *perceived* chance of being caught while trying to submit forged income figures or other kinds of information. A fully personalized service would reveal the actual checks and countermeasures available to Tax Agencies to fight fraud. Such a service could entice citizens to maximize calculative behaviour, which is of course not in the direct interest of Tax Agencies. This provides an example of the importance of how the specific context of ICT application shapes and interacts with the way that ICTs are implemented.

2. Client Orientation vs. Good Citizens

Throughout the world, national and local governments are implementing web services to increase citizen orientation, reduce red tape, create one-stop-shops, decrease the administrative burden on citizens and corporations, and increase citizens' trust in government. By increasing the quality of public service delivery, it is hoped to bridge the often-felt gap that exists between corporations and citizens on the one hand, and government agencies and administrations on the other hand.

Although it seems reasonable that citizens' trust increases as the level of quality of services increase, Fountain (2001) argues that the opposite might be the case. She notes that public organizations are not solely concerned with service delivery and points to the multifaceted (policy making and executive) character of many public sector organizations. Addressing citizens as consumers and defining government as a production company ignores the inherent political character of public service delivery. Public organizations delivering services are not only supposed to be to responsive to the needs of customers, but also accountable to good citizens (Schudson, 1998) or 'citoyens', and to voters (Bekkers & Homburg, 2005). According to Fountain, emphasizing service delivery and ignoring notions of citizenship, other than being a customer of public service, will eventually jeopardize legitimacy and citizens' trust in government.

3. Efficiency vs. Einzelfallgerechtigkeit

Many public sector services—for example specific benefits, permits or rebates—require some sort of interaction between public servants and citizens, at least until recently. Traditionally, human public service workers have been involved in applying regulations and routines to specific requests. Many of these workers can be qualified as *street level bureaucrats:* public sector workers that interact directly with citizens and have considerable discretion in the way they organize the interaction, allocate facilities and possibly impose sanctions (Bovens & Zouridis, 2002; Lipsky, 1980). Being street-level bureaucrats, workers are both policy executors (they apply rules) as well as policy makers. Lipsky has argued that "the decisions of street-level bureaucrats, the routines they establish, and the devices they invent to cope with uncertainties and work pressures, effectively become the public policies they carry out. With others, I argue that it is a misconception to conceive of public policy as made in legislatures or top-floor suites of high-ranking administrators, because this neglects the important ways the policy gets made in the crowded offices and daily encounters of street level workers" (Lipsky, 1980: xii). Not withstanding that the discretionary powers of street-level bureaucrats are curtailed by generally prevailing laws, but also by material principles of sound administration, (principle of careful preparation, and prohibition on abuse of power), that can be used by the judiciary to correct behavior by street-level bureaucrats.

Many executive organizations have implemented form processors, decision support systems and expert systems to automate the processes of issuing administrative orders, thereby replacing or disciplining street level bureaucrats, and squeezing their discretionary margins (Bovens & Zouridis, 2002). Some executive processes have been fully automated. This transformation of execution can in part be seen as a process of rationalization, with which the predictability and control of executive processes have improved. Moreover, Bovens and Zouridis identify a new issue that has to do with the transfer of discretionary powers from street-level bureaucrats to system designers. With the emergence of fully automated executive processes, system designers have obtained the discretionary power to transform legal frameworks, regulations and organizational procedures into automated processes and programs (Bovens & Zouridis, 2002). It is an empirical question how this shift of discretionary powers in executive organizations is to be translated into new forms of accountability and checks & balances. Bovens and Zouridis also ask the question whether a fully automated execution of laws can protect justice, since although digital rigidity may be a bureaucratic ideal, the absence of *Einzelfallgerechtigkeit*[1] can lead to absurd, downright hazardous, and, therefore undemocratic situations.

4. The Dynamics of Requirements

In the beginning of the 1990s, academics from Twente University in the Netherlands recognized that street level bureaucrats working in social administration had severe difficulties with the administration of welfare programs. They developed an expert system (Tessec2) to assist street level bureaucrats. Studies showed that the quality of decisions could be increased with promising possibilities for the application of the system in the execution of the National Assistance Act, and in the administration of housing allowances. However, actual implementation was never achieved (apart from a few pilot projects), since the Tessec system never reached the status of an operational system in the standing organization of municipal social service organizations. Much to the surprise (and possibly frustration) of the developers, during the 1990s a commercial developer (MRE) introduced an expert system that got a foothold in the market and grew within a few years to become the market leader. The MRE expert system functionally resembled the Tessec system. While the marketing strategies of MRE and technological proficiency of the system outperformed the Tessec approach, this is not sufficient to explain why MRE proved to be so successful and Tessec failed in practice. Svensson (2002) has demonstrated that the failure of the Tessec system, and acceptance of the comparable MRE system a few years later, had everything to do with the institutional context and rapid changes that occurred in this context. In the 1990s, fighting fraud and preventing abuse was put on the public agenda (see also Homburg, 1999). Following various reports, the formal requirements for the administration of welfare provision had been tightened. The municipalities were required from that moment on to comply with rules and validation procedures set by accountants and national inspectorates, and these actors, particularly accountants, strongly advocated the application of expert systems. Municipalities that opted for manual administration ran the risk of very thorough and intensive reviews of individual material files, with the likelihood that errors would be found and sanctioned. In conclusion, the actual use of expert systems in social administration can only to a limited degree be explained in terms of the purely technological properties of either Tessec or the MRE system. Decisive was the change in the socio-political climate with respect to how the National Assistance Act should be executed, and the rising dominance of accountants who favored the use of expert systems. In other words, the institutional context served as a filter for technological innovation.

The above examples make a number of things clear. First and foremost, the examples confirm Orlikowski's claim that technology does not exist in a vacuum. Technology and technological innovation affect both in a desired as well as in an unforeseen way, specific institutions. At the same time, institutions determine or at least shape ways in which technologies are or are not put to use in specific contexts. Therefore, technologies are indeed embedded in complex interdependent social, economic and political webs, and are *shaped* by such broader institutional influences.

Second, it can be shown that technologies are simultaneously social and physical artifacts. They are physical in the sense that they are designed to constrain and afford specific uses, and with that, emphasize specific values, assumptions or in general organizational or societal practices. But artifacts are also social in the sense that their design and uses reflects choices and taken-for granted assumptions of designers, and that institutions influences the design, use and consequences of technologies in public administration.

The study of how technology shapes and is shaped by the broader institutional context is studied in specific branches of social studies of technology and the philosophy of technology (Williams & Edge, 1996). This field of study usually goes by the name of 'social shaping of technology' (SST), and, although SST constitutes a broach church, a common denominator is that technology and its institutional context are hard to distinguish. The lines of reasoning, and the relevance of SST for Public Sector Transformation, is furthermore exemplified in the next section, with a reflection on two case studies of transformation in the public sector in the United Kingdom, the Netherlands and Belgium.

SOCIAL SHAPING OF PUBLIC SECTOR TRANSFORMATION INITIATIVES

Introduction

In the preceding section, it has been argued that PST consists of a series of more or less technologically induced administrative and organizational changes (blurring of boundaries, process and citizen orientation, and the vilification of structure), and that in the process of these changes, because technology and context are hardly separable and are both subject to a variety of norms, values and assumptions, tensions may occur. In the subsections below, it is analyzed in two specific cases how,

Criminal Justice System in the UK as a PST Initiative

By the mid 1980s, several law enforcement agencies, prison service agencies police services and magistrate courts had begun to develop a joint information system for keeping track of subjects in the penal law enforcement chain (Bellamy &

Taylor, 1997). The introduction of the Criminal Justice System (CJS)—and the intention to more fully develop information sharing behavior between police services, magistrates' courts, prison services, et cetera—strongly affected the routines, rules and practices of information sharing between public sector organizations, for instance by modifying access to information. The development and implementation of the system is therefore not only to be understood as a technical intervention, but also as a case of information politics.

In practice, the CJS was deliberately both highly compartmentalized and decentralized, for at least two specific reasons. First, the separation of executive and judicial powers prevented a full exchange of information between for instance the Home Office, the Lord Chancellor's Department and the Crown Prosecution Service. Second, the compartmentalization is seen as a safeguard as to sustain and defend the rights and interests of individual citizens. As a result, several so-called information domains have appeared. With information domain, Bellamy and Taylor refer to a sphere of influence over which a specific organization can claim (legitimate) control, which is demarcated in terms of ownership and conventions to safeguard ownership: standards, formats and interpretations of results.

In the case of CJS, domain structure stem from constitutional and civil rights, (prohibiting sharing of information across specific boundaries) and professional paradigms (conventions held by magistrates, attorneys, police, probation service social workers, et cetera, making it difficult to assimilate information across domains). Bellay and Taylor show that the furthered attempts to expand the system, more profound stewardship over specific domains occurred. For instance, probation service professionals found it increasingly inappropriate to share personal files with police officers. Exchange of information increasingly took place under the condition that conditions of use were controlled by originating organizations.

Introduction: PST Initiatives in Social Security

One of the defining characteristics in many PST initiatives is the collapsing, or blurring, of interorganizational boundaries. Sharing information across organizational boundaries is far from an operational, neutral issue, neither in the private sector (Webster, 1995) nor in the public sector (Homburg, 2000). The issue of back office interorganizational information exchange is addressed in the public management literature by using the term joined up government (JUG). Joined-up government refers to the aspiration to achieve horizontal and vertical coordination ('cross-cutting approaches') in and among organizations (Ling, 2002; Pollitt, 2003). Both the information systems literature as well as the public management literature report formidable difficulties in actually achieving interorganizational information integration and joined up government. A recent European study has shown that there is in practice a large divergence in ways in which joined-up government and integration among agencies is actually achieved (Millard, Iversen, Kubicek, Westholm, & Cimander, 2004), and that JUG and integration are far more contextually bound than is apparent at first sight. The authors compared JUG implementations in several service clusters: income tax, car registration, citizen certificates, family allowances, student grants, social benefits, building permissions, enrolment in higher education, citizen portals, social contributions for employers, corporation taxes, customs declarations, business registration, environmental-related permits and business portals in Austria, the Benelux countries, Finland, France, the UK, Greece, Iceland, Ireland, Italy, Norway, Portugal, Spain and Sweden, and found a large variety of mechanisms with which interoperability and joined-up government was actually enforced (Millard et al., 2004: 27-44):

- by means of digitization of organizationally unchanged back-offices;

- by means of fundamental redesign of back-offices;
- by means of centralization of back-offices;
- by means of simultaneous centralization and back-offices and decentralization of front-offices;
- by means of modularizing common back-office components over broad areas, while retaining flexibility and possibilities to adapt to specific requirements; and
- by means of clearing houses that enable the exchange of information from various sources without the need to necessarily integrate data sources.

The authors conclude that "One of the clearest conclusions emerging from the present study is that state structures, and institutional, legal, regulatory and cultural factors, can be extremely important in determining the nature, cost and success of eGovernment. (...) Different countries across Europe need to develop their own paths as each has unique identities, cultures, legal systems and institutional structures" (Millard et al., 2004: 61).

The importance of institutional context is exemplified in a study on integration and joined-up government in the back office of social security in the Netherlands and Belgium (Homburg, 2007). Although the Netherlands and Belgium are, seen from a distance, rather comparable nation states (in terms of size, geographic location, et cetera) and the specific sector of social insurance has been confronted with comparable issues (fiscal crises since the 1970s, reforms of welfare state regimes, et cetera), and hence, one would expect a certain amount of resemblance of technological solutions to integrate these sectors. In practice rather different solutions were implemented.

In general, the Netherlands can be classified as being a unitary, communitarian decentralized state (Adler & Henman, 2005). Its legal model resembles the Napoleonic model, with some influences from the Constitutional State model (Steen, van den Berg, van der Meer, Overeem, & Toonen, 2005). The political system is rather consensual: almost every sector of policy consists of a myriad of consultative and advisory councils, which are deeply intertwined with government and form an 'iron ring' around ministerial departments (Pollitt & Bouckaert, 2000)

Belgium, on the other hand, can be typified as a federal, corporatist state. Its legal model is a combined Napoleonic/Latin model (encompassing a relatively strong central state, hierarchical structures and a civil service system that enjoys a high level of prestige) (Steen et al., 2005). In Belgium, in contrast to the Netherlands (see above), policy preparation is predominantly the domain of the ministerial cabinets (and not the civil service, in consultation with the 'iron rings' of consultative councils). Belgium has a tradition of political appointments of senior civil servants (Steen et al., 2005).

PST in Social Security in the Netherlands

In the Netherlands, Child Allowances and State Pensions are administered by an independent administrative body Social Insurances Bank (Dutch: Sociale Verzekeringsbank). Social Assistance, on the other hand, has been carried out by public, municipal social assistance agencies on behalf of the Ministry of Social Affairs. Until about 1995, semi-autonomous Industrial Insurance Boards had executed insurance schemes on behalf of trade unions and associations of employers. The state only had a supervisory role (Fenger, 2006). The functioning of the rather heterogeneous system of social security severely criticized in the 1990s by the Netherlands Court of Audit, a subsequent Parliamentary Research Commission (that focused on the execution of Social Insurance Acts) and a Research Committee that scrutinized implementation practices of the Social Assistance Act (the Van der Zwan Committee).

As a result of these (and other) investigations, the execution of Acts in the fields of Social

Security was reorganized. Discussions about privatization emerged (especially in the field of Social Insurances), but eventually, in 2002, the Industrial Insurance Boards merged into a independent administrative body known as the *Uitvoeringsinstituut Werknemersverzekeringen* (Executive Organization of Social Insurances). This marked a more prominent role of the state as principal in the field of social security; execution of schemes and Acts, however, still takes place in a rather divergent field of hundreds of municipal social assistance agencies, the Social Insurances bank, and the Executive Organization for Social Insurances.

In 1996, representatives from various quasi-autonomous executive agencies teamed up and developed ideas and concepts to fight fraud and to foster interorganizational cooperation. Partly, these initiatives can be understood as a genuine concern to prevent and/or fight fraud. Partly, the initiatives can be understood as pre-emptive action that allowed executive organizations to preserve and defend their autonomy against initiatives that were at that time prepared by central levels of government (more precisely: the Ministry of Social Affairs and Employment). With these initiatives, the Ministry attempted to impose standards and practices for information exchange in the sector of social security, and this was seen by executive organizations as an unwanted breach of their (informational) autonomy (Homburg, 1999).

In various talks and meetings, the RINIS concept was developed. RINIS is an abbreviation of the *Routeringsinstituut voor (Inter)nationale Informatie Stromen* (Router Institution for International Information Flows). The term RINIS both refers to:

- a relatively small (seven members of staff) bureau, which is controlled by a Board. The Board consists of representatives of organizations that participate in (and finance) the RINIS bureau; and
- an infrastructure that enables information exchange across participating organizations.

The RINIS concept started from the core of the Social Security Sector, but throughout time it has expanded and currently, the following organizations are involved:

- the Executive Organization of Social Insurances (UWV);
- the Social Insurances Bank (SVB);
- the Organization for Collecting Alimonies (LBIO);
- the Office for Enquiries in the Social Assistance domain (IB; an umbrella organization of municipal social assistance agencies);
- The Office for Granting Student Loans (IB-Group);
- The Association of (Private) Care Insurance Companies (ZN);
- The Office for Judicial Institutions (DJI);
- The National Dutch Tax Agency (Belastingdienst) and
- The Association of Bailiffs (SGN).

Characteristic for the RINIS concept of cooperation is that each of the participating organizations is a so-called authentic source of data. An authentic source of data is an organization that is responsible for the operational maintenance, content, quality and verification of a data element. For example, an executive organization is always the authentic source for a data element that results from its executive process (for example, the Social Insurances Bank is the authentic source for decisions on the basis of the National Old Age Pensions Act). But organizations may also be regarded as authentic source for other data elements; for example, the citizens' registration office is an authentic source for a client's name, date of birth and domicile. A study in 1995 revealed that most of the data elements (about sixty) are 'claimed' by one organization. About thirteen are not claimed by any organization and one data element is claimed by more than one organization (see Homburg, 1999).

PST in Social Security in Belgium

Until the second half of the 1980s, the Belgian National System for Social Security was heavily fragmented and supply-oriented. It has involved a mixture of public and private sector organizations, and, as had been the case in the Netherlands, both administratively as well as in terms of execution involved 'tripartite' parties (state, labor unions, employers' associations). The Belgian Social Security System covers seven social risks (incapacity for work, industrial accident, occupational disease, unemployment, retirement, child care and holiday pay—the so-called social security branches), and four social support systems (allowances for the disabled, guaranteed family allowance, minimum income and income guarantee for the elderly), which grant people specific minimum services after verifying their subsistence resources. The system covers 10,000,000 citizens and 200,000 employers (Deprest & Robben, 2003).

The following organizations can be discerned:

- National Illness and Disability Insurance Office (Rijksinstituut voor ziekte- en invaliditeitsverzekering);
- National Office of Social Security (Rijksdienst voor Sociale Zekerheid)
- National Old Age Pensions Office (Rijksdienst voor pensioenen);
- National Child Allowances Office (Rijksdienst voor kinderbijslag voor werknemers);
- National Fund for Work-related Disabilities (Fonds voor de beroepsziektes);
- National Fund for Work-related Accidents (Fonds voor arbeidsongevallen);
- National Employment Office (Rijksdienst voor arbeidsvoorziening) and
- National Holiday Premium Office (Rijksdienst voor jaarlijke vakantie).

A study conducted in 1986 (Viaene, Robben, Lahaye, & Van Steenberge, 1986) reported the following problems and shortcomings in the cooperation in the field of executive organizations:

- the existence of paper-based information flows;
- poor information requirements analyses by Offices (in the presence of changing legislation);
- repeated information request by various agencies regarding comparable or even similar topics; and
- in general, lack of focus on ways in which companies register data, and lack of citizen orientation.

Following the above analysis, and the recommendations of a National Committee on the Codification, Harmonization and Simplification of Legislation in the field of social security, an Act was drafted (15 January 1990) in which the so-called Cross Point Bank for Social Security (*Kruispuntbank* or *Banque Carrefour de la Securité Sociale)* was announced. Although the term 'bank' might indicate that the organization has databases by itself, it primarily (but not exclusively) functions as a referral index that allows for information exchange between various organizations, based on the principle of authentic sources of information. There is one important difference with the Dutch connotation of authentic sources, though: if the participating organizations fail to reach agreement on the articulation of authenticity of specific sources or data, or if participating organizations are not able to meet information requirements by the sector as a whole, it is the responsibility of the Cross Point Bank to provide for that information by means of setting up dedicated databases.

The infrastructure of the Cross Point Bank connects public authorities that act as core participants (like the National Illness and Disability Insurance Office and the National Office of Social Security), and auxiliary members (like labor union's insurance companies) that connect through core participants.

Goals of the Cross Point Bank for Social Security can be stated as follows: reduction of administrative burden, increased focus on needs of citizens and corporations and stronger support for the social security policy in general (Snijkers, 2005). In order to do achieve this, harmonization of legislation and implementation practice is explicitly addressed. For instance, legislation allows for assistance from Cross Point Bank to executive organizations in the development and implementation of e-government strategies (art. 3bis Act on Establishment of the Cross Point Bank, 15 January 1990). Furthermore, although it is recognized that the Cross Point Bank should not interfere with existing tasks and responsibilities in the field of executive organizations, it is explicitly acknowledged that tasks that are not carried out by existing executive organizations can or should be performed by the Cross Point Bank.

Overall, the Cross Point Bank focuses heavily on the reduction of administrative burden of citizens and corporations through improvement of intergovernmental exchange of information. At present, the Cross Point Bank for Social Security processes hundred millions of exchanges every year (2004: 339,1 million messages).

CONCLUSION

In this chapter, a social shaping of technology perspective on public sector transformation initiatives was introduced. It was demonstrated how, in specific situations, norms, values and assumptions of public sector (1) interact with, (2) filter, (3) determine and (4) are determined by specific technological applications.

So then, what are these specific institutions that are embedded in PST?

First of all, more or less strictly constitutional or judicial norms shape and are shaped by technological opportunity. Note that in the UK CJS case, compartmentalization occurred because of the principle that judicial and executive branches of government ought to be separated.

Second, it is possible to identify professionally demarcated boundaries, again in the CJS example, that partly determine how PST initiatives in practice take shape, and that sometimes constitute compelling boundaries of the applicability of specific technological solutions.

Third, practices that have to do more with power structures and path dependent institutionalized practices, such as have occurred in the implementation of social security schemes in the Netherlands and in Belgium, interact with Public Sector Transformation. The historically developed structures of vested interested proved to be decisive in shaping eventual form of technological support for information exchange and organizational practice.

The pattern that emerges from these observations perhaps is an overly conservative picture of faltering PST initiatives: initiatives that result from contradictions and tensions between various values that are never completely resolved. This, however, is not an entirely convincing image of a social shaping perspective on PST. Note that institutions are not so much a set of norms that put a constraint on technological opportunity, but are, as much as technological artifacts, the result of the making of individuals or groups of individuals. As has been demonstrated in the case of TESSEC, it can be observed that institutions change over time and that at one moment in time, institutions can constrain specific PST initiatives, whereas at other moments in time, institutions can be compelling enablers of the same PST initiatives.

The line of reasoning set out in this chapter is a plea for a better understanding of the working of institutions in specific public sector transformation initiatives, and serves to illustrate the difficulties, contradictions and sometimes mindboggling features of institutions. It can only be hoped that in the long run, both social scientists as well as developers will come to terms with the idea of institutions and how institutions and technologies are enmeshed in public sector transformation initiatives.

REFERENCES

Adler, M., & Henman, P. (2005). Computerizing the welfare state: An international comparison of computerization in social security. *Information, Communication, and Society, 8*(3), 315-342.

Bekkers, V. J. J. M. (1998). Wiring public organizations and changing organizational juridisctions. In I. T. M. Snellen & W. B. H. J. v. d. Donk (Eds.), *Public administration in an information age* (pp. 57-77). Amsterdam: IOS Press.

Bekkers, V. J. J. M., & Homburg, V. M. F. (Eds.). (2005). *The Information Ecology of E-Government*. Amsterdam: IOS Press.

Bellamy, C., & Taylor, J. (1997). Transformation by stealth: The case of the UK criminal justice system. In J. Taylor, I. T. M. Snellen & A. Zuurmond (Eds.), *Beyond BPR in public administration*. Amsterdam: IOS Press.

Borins, S. F. (2007). *Digital state at the leading edge*. Toronto, Canada: University of Toronto Press.

Bovens, M., & Zouridis, S. (2002). From street-level bureaucracy to system-level bureaucracy: How information and communication technology is transforming administrative discretion and constitutional control. *Public Administration Review, 62*(2), 174-184.

Deprest, J., & Robben, F. (2003). *E-government :the approach of the Belgian federal administration*. Brussels, Belgium: FEDICT.

Dewett, T., & Jones, G. R. (2001). The Role of Information Technology in the Organization: A Review, Model, and Assessment. *Journal of Management, 27*(3), 313-346.

Dunleavy, P. (2006). *Digital era governance : IT corporations, the state, and e-government*. New York: Oxford University Press.

Edmiston, K. D. (2003). State and Local E-Government. *American Review of Public Administration, 33*(1), 20-45.

Fenger, H. J. M. (2006). Shifts in welfare governance: The state, private, and non-profit sectors in four European countries. In P. Henman & H. J. M. Fenger (Eds.), *Administering welfare reform* (pp. 73-92). Bristol, UK: The Policy Press.

Fountain, J. (2001). *Building the virtual state*. Washington, DC: The Brookings Institute.

Groth, L. (1999). Future organizational design. In L. Groth (Ed.), *Future organizational design* (pp. 325-344). Chicester, England: John Wiley & Sons.

Hammer, M. (1996). *Beyond reengineering: How the process-centered organization is changing our work and our lives*. London: HarperCollins Business.

Homburg, V. M. F. (1999). *The political economy of information management: A theoretical and empirical analysis of decision making regarding interorganizational information systems*. Capelle aan de IJssel, The Netherlands: Labyrinth.

Homburg, V. M. F. (2000). Politics and Property Rights in Information Exchange. *Knowledge, Policy, and Technology, 13*(3), 13-22.

Homburg, V. M. F. (2007). A Comparative Account of Joined-Up Government Initiatives in Dutch and Belgian Social Security. *International Journal of Cases on Electronic Commerce, 3*(2), 1-12.

Homburg, V. M. F. (2008). *Information systems and public administration: Understanding e-government*. London: Routledge.

Ling, T. (2002). Delivering Joined-up Government in the UK: Dimensions, Issues and Problems. *Public Administration, 80*(4), 615-642.

Lipsky, M. (1980). *Street-level bureaucracy: Dilemmas of the individual in public services*. New York: Russell Sage Foundation.

Millard, J., Iversen, J. S., Kubicek, H., Westholm, H., & Cimander, R. (2004). *Reorganisation of government back-offices for better electronic public services—European good practices (back-office reorganisation).* Brussels: EU DG Information Society.

Orlikowkski, W. J., & Barley, S. R. (2001). Technology and Institutions: What Can Research on Information Technology and Research on Organizations Learn From Each Other? *MIS Quarterly, 25*(2), 145-165.

Pollitt, C. P. (2003). Joined-up Government: A Survey. *Political Studies Review, 1*(1), 34-49.

Pollitt, C. P., & Bouckaert, G. (2000). *Public Management Reform: A Comparative Analysis.* Oxford: Oxford University Press.

Pollitt, C. P., Van Thiel, S., & Homburg, V. M. F. (2006). *The New Public Management in Europe: Adaptation and Alternatives.* Basingstoke, England: Palgrave MacMillan.

Schudson, M. (1998). *The good citizen: A history of American civic life.* New York: The Free Press.

Snijkers, K. (2005). *E-Government in een interbestuurlijke context. Casestudie: OCMW's en de kruispuntbank van de sociale zekerheid.* Leuven: Steunpunt Beleirdsrelevant Onderzoek Bestuurlijke Organisatie Vlaanderen.

Steen, T., van den Berg, C., van der Meer, F., Overeem, P., & Toonen, T. (2005). *Modernising Governments in other countries.* The Hague, The Netherlands: Modernising Government Project, Ministry of the Interior and Kingdom Relations.

Svensson, J. S. (2002). Legal Expert Systems in Social Administration: From Fearing Computers to Fearing Accountants. *Information Polity, 7,* 143-154.

Viaene, J., Robben, F., Lahaye, D., & Van Steenberge, J. (1986). Algemene schets van een rationele informatieverwerking in de sociale zekerheid. *Belgisch Tijdschrift voor de Sociale Zekerheid, 4*(5), 399-473.

Webster, J. (1995). Networks of Collaboration of Conflict? Electronic Data Interchange and Power in the Supply Chain. *Journal of Strategic Information Systems, 5*(1), 31-42.

Williams, R., & Edge, D. (1996). The Social Shaping of Technology. *Research Policy, 25,* 865-899.

Zuurmond, A. (1998). From bureaucracy to infocracy. In I. T. M. Snellen & W. B. J. H. van de Donk (Eds.), *Public Administration in an Information Age* (pp. 259-272). Amsterdam: IOS Press.

KEY TERMS

Institutions: Values, norms, normative frames of reference, taken for granted assumptions and practices.

New Public Management (NPM): Management ideology with which private-sector business management techniques, performance management systems, benchmarking, autonomization) are introduced in the public sector.

Social Shaping: Perspective indicating bilateral causal relations between technology and institutions (e.g., allowing for the study of how technology affects institutions, as well as how institutions affect ways in which technologies are designed and used)

ENDNOTES

1 Justice in the eyes of specific, individual and/or particular cases

2 **Tessec:** Twente Expert System for Social Security, an expert system to be used in the administration of municipal social service departments.

Chapter II
Towards T-Government by Increasing Process Maturity in Public Sector

Jurij Jaklič
University of Ljubljana, Slovenija

Mojca Indihar Štemberger
University of Ljubljana, Slovenija

ABSTRACT

A successful e-government implementation cannot do without some kind of business process change, not only of the front-office parts of processes, but the entire processes, which often flow through several departmental units or even several government agencies. Further advances of e-government that lead to t-government, are not possible without an integration of business processes. The implementation of t-government requires a high level of business process orientation and typically involves a business process change project. Non-profit organisations have some specifics, which make process renovation projects considerably different. The purpose of this chapter is to present an approach that enables governmental institutions to move towards t-government. The general framework for business process change methodologies, techniques and tools is customised for their needs and extended with several other business process management elements, e.g. measurement of the level of business process orientation in an organisation. The relationship between business process orientation levels and the sophistication of online services is shown through a case study of one of the Slovene ministries, where the proposed adapted methodology has been successfully employed.

INTRODUCTION

Information technology has a potential to transform governmental structures and to improve the quality of governmental services. However, to be able to take advantage of those technologies, the organisations have to understand and overcome several challenges. Technological complexity and incompatibility are neither the only, nor the most difficult challenge to be overcome. T-government particularly demands a greater customer oriented focus of government agencies and is clearly tied to the improvement of performance and process integration. It requires an organisational change. Therefore, a successful t-government implementation cannot do without some kind of business process change, not only of the front-office parts of processes, but the entire processes, which often flow through several departmental units or even several government agencies.

Non-profit organisations such as public sector organisations have some specifics, which make renovation projects considerably different. Governmental organisations have a unique culture and face many challenges due to their social obligations and higher legislative and public accountability (Kumar et al., 2002). Some of the main e-government challenges are (Hendrick, 1994; Gil-Garcia & Pardo, 2005; Cats-Baril, W. & Thompson, R., 1995; Thompson, 2000): the objectives of the government are less clear, clients and stakeholders are more diverse and numerous, and concepts such as quality are more complex; the existence of multiple, sometimes conflicting, goals, and of individual interests and associated behaviours that cause reluctance to change and internal conflicts; the lack of alignment between organisational goals and the IT project; a higher level of interdependence across organisational boundaries; more constraints (compared to the private sector) imposed by red tape; a higher level of extra-organisational linkages; the turnover of top level administrators, a difficulty to implement a change is increased, and the management tends to have less authority than its private sector counterparts.

Several EU countries have made a significant progress in their online services sophistication. For example, Austria and Portugal have made major progresses since 2006. Malta, Slovenia and Estonia stand out as the countries that have embraced e-government and advanced online service delivery to levels in advance of many 'old' member states (Capgemini, 2007). However, further advances of e-government that lead to t-government are not possible without an integration of business processes, which are performed inside and between government agencies. Such approach requires a certain level of business process orientation and typically involves a business process change project.

The purpose of this chapter is to present the approach that enables public sector organisations to migrate towards t-government. The approach is based on the general framework for business process change (BPC) methodologies, techniques and tools (Kettinger et al., 1997) and is customised for governmental institutions due to their above-mentioned specifics. The methodology presented in (Indihar Štemberger & Jaklič, 2007) has been extended with several other business process management elements, e.g. measurement of the level of business process orientation in an organisation, which is extremely important for success of every process transformation initiative. It has been employed in some process improvement projects, e.g. in a BPC project in one of the Slovene ministries and this project has been used in the book chapter as a case study.

BACKGROUND

While t-government is a widely used term in public in the last few years, clear models for t-government benefit realisation and strategies for migration have not yet emerged. Public agencies and local authorities are left with practical problems of deciding on a migration approach (Irani et al., 2007). Several topics that are integral to t-government are shared with the process orientation concept already known and used in organisations of private sector. Therefore it seems promising to use the approaches that are known and proved for the business process orientation improvement for the transformation from e-government towards t-government. Clearly, there are some differences between government and business that have to be taken into account.

From E-Government Towards T-Government

E-business is becoming extremely important both in the private sector and in governmental institutions as well: here it is named e-government and is not uniquely defined. In (Hernon et al., 2002) e-government is defined as a technology, particularly the Internet, that is used to enhance the access to and delivery of governmental information and services to citizens, businesses, government employees, and other agencies. More recent definitions already emphasise the transformational component of e-government. An example is given in (Gil-Garcia & Pardo, 2005), where e-government has been conceptualised as an intensive use of information technologies for the provision of public services, the improvement of managerial effectiveness and the promotion of democratic values and mechanisms. Furthermore, Beynon-Davies (2005) denote the term e-government as the use of information and communications technology to change the structures and processes of government organisations. In the e-government Strategy of the Republic of Slovenia for the Period 2006 to 2010 (SEP-2010) of the Slovene Ministry of Public Administration (2006) the following definition is used: "e-government, or electronic public administration, is a form of carrying out business processes in public administration authorities, which is based on the use of modern information and communications technologies and is oriented towards end users".

Even though all the definitions share ICT as the underlying element of e-government, it is clear that understanding and emphases of e-government have evolved over time. In the European Union (EU) an emphasis is currently on user satisfaction, transparency, a lighter administrative burden, efficiency, and effectiveness. In this context, the Slovene e-government Strategy SEP-2010 identifies four main objectives (Ministry of Public Administration, 2006): (1) high-quality and efficient operations, i.e. rationalisation of administrative operations, (2) open and transparent functioning of public administration, (3) efficient system of public employees and efficient management of human resources, and (4) user orientation of public administration. Modern electronic services should enable better quality of services and give administration a more friendly face in contacts with users.

The framework for measurement of the progress of online public service in the scope of e-government context, which has been used in the past, has a four-level scale, where the lowest level corresponds to simple publishing of information on web pages, and the fourth, the highest level, represents full electronic handling of an administrative process. It is clear that this scale is not adequate any more as a means for achieving the above mentioned main objectives as it fails to consider quality, efficiency, and effectiveness issues of business processes strongly enough. Consequently the 5th level was added in the year 2007. This level "provides an indication of the extent, to which an online services is based on new models of front and back-offices integration, the reuse of available data and to what degree the idea of pro-active service delivery is embedded" (Capgemini, 2007).

The focus has moved from ICT enabled automation of activities of gathering customer's data towards a business process change and management enabled by modern ICT. The terms, which are usually used in the business process management and e-business frameworks, such as reducing 'red tape', proactivity, customer orientation, process measurement, process change (improvement and reengineering), efficiency, effectiveness, process quality etc., are now slowly getting more often introduced in the e-government setting as well.

Capgemini (2007) gives an example of proactive service delivery: "the government warns the user that action could be required, the government pre-fills the data in the application form that are already available in governmental databases to the extent permitted by law." These examples clearly show that the 5th level of online services sophistication concerns a high level of business process maturity and a business process change. Both examples represent a significant change in the process, enabled by ICT and improve the efficiency and effectiveness of business processes. Effectiveness as a measure of process output also includes customer satisfaction as a result of customer orientation.

In 2005, UK launched its new strategy Transformational Government Enabled by Technology (Cabinet Office, 2005). However, this change is broader than national level, thus the term t-government is used more widely around Europe and stands for "the transformation of government structures and services using technology" rather than simply putting services on the Internet. There are three distinctive topics in the t-government framework: customer-centric services, shared services, and professionalism. Again, the idea of process integration, renovation, and structural changes, which are necessary for improvement of process and services performance, can be noticed. The process integration requires managing the flow and processing of customer information using ICT from the initial customer contact to completed transaction.

T-government requires a significant shift from the current e-government practices, including a high level of service sophistication, transformation of government through IT, business process management methods like process change, automation, measurement, improvements, structural changes, supply chain integration, strategic governance etc. In other words, process orientation is heavily emphasised.

Business Process Orientation and Business Process Change

Key literature on business process management and business process change suggests that organisations can improve services to their customers and enhance their overall performance by adopting a process view of business (e.g. Davenport, 1993; Hammer and Champy, 1993; Hammer, 2004; Harmon, 2007). It has also been proved that business process orientation (BPO) has a positive impact on customer satisfaction and business performance (McCormack and Johnson 2001), (Škrinjar et al., 2006). While the BPO concept is relatively well known in the private sector, it is quite new and unknown in the public sector. However, we believe that a higher level of BPO can be the key to accomplish t-government, especially for transition form two-way interaction to transactional on-line services.

Although definitions of the BPO vary, we adopt McCormack's and Johnson's (2001) definition of process orientation: an organisation that, in all its thinking, emphasises a process as opposed to hierarchies with a special emphasis on outcomes and customer satisfaction. It becomes evident that all organisations are composed of business processes, even though they have not adopted the formal process organisational structure. Therefore, the BPO approach can be applied to each organisation and the level of process orientation can be determined.

The levels of process orientation are often presented by a process maturity concept. There is no scarcity of process maturity models (Škrinjar et al., 2006). They serve as reference models of the stages that organisations go through as they move from being immature to mature in their process orientation. The business process maturity models are based on concepts developed by researchers over the past two decades and imply that a process has a lifecycle that is assessed by the extent to which the processes are explicitly defined, managed, measured and controlled.

To analyse an organisation's understanding of its processes i.e. to measure its current position in becoming business process oriented, to compare (benchmark) to other organisations, to analyse changes to the process understanding, and consequently a BPC project's success, the BPO maturity model developed by McCormack and Johnson (McCormack & Johnson, 2001) can be very useful. The BPO maturity model was designed as a reference model of the evolutionary stages that organisations go through to become business process oriented. BPO maturity is measured by the following individual dimensions:

- **Process view** involves a focus on the workflows and processes across an organisation. It means that processes and activities are documented using process modelling techniques. It is very important that process maps represent the real process flow and that they are used for different purposes in the organisation. It allows people in different job functions and companies to communicate by using the same vocabulary. This dimension includes a broad understanding of the processes across the organisation, not just their documentation.
- **Process structure**, which does not necessarily mean the process organisational structure, but a mixture of a functional organisation with some elements of process organisation. These elements are horizontal teams, process owners - leaders who are responsible and accountable for the operation and improvement of entire processes, process management teams and chief process officer - a person who is responsible for processes and occupies a high position in the organisational hierarchy.
- **Process Jobs**, which means that job descriptions are horizontal rather than vertical. People participate in and take ownership of the entire process. Along with process owners, process teams become the main building element of an organisation. Titles such as "Order Fulfilment Team Member", "Procurement Process Owner" and "Global Supply Chain Manager" serve as examples.
- **Process Measurement and Management Systems**. This dimension includes process efficiency and process outcome measures, measurement systems, rewards for process improvement and other management practices.
- **Customer-focused Process Values and Beliefs**. These are the values and beliefs that energise an organisation. For instance, they might include organisational culture that puts customer's satisfaction in the first place in every activity or commitment of employees to process improvement.

In other process maturity models there are additional dimensions. For example in (Willaert et al., 2007) dimensions of process orientation are: customer-orientation, process view, organisational structures, process performance characteristics, culture, values and beliefs, people management; information technology and supplier perspective. One should notice the goals and dimensions which are shared between BPO and t-government concepts.

A BPO maturity model identifies five levels or steps that describe how an organisation typically evolves from a functionally strong organisation with barely visible processes stage to the integrated processes inside the organisation and with its vendors and suppliers. The initial four-stage model described in (McCormack & Johnson, 2001) is extended in (Lockamy & McCormack,

2004) with the fifth stage related to the supply chain management. The following maturity stages are defined:

- **Level 1—Initial**: Processes are unstructured and ill-defined. Processes, activities and organisational structures are not based on horizontal processes, process performance is un-predictable. Processes costs are high, customers satisfaction low, functional co-operation is also low.
- **Level 2—Defined**: Basic processes are defined and documented, but activities and organisation basically remain traditional. Processes costs remain high, customer satisfaction has improved, but is still low.
- **Level 3—Linked**: This level represents a breakthrough. Cooperation between company departments, vendors and customers is established. Broad process jobs and structures are put in place. Customer satisfaction begins to show a considerable improvement.
- **Level 4—Integrated**: The organisation, its vendors and suppliers take cooperation to the process level. Organisational structures are based on processes, process performance measures and management systems are applied. As a consequence, processes and supply chain management costs are dramatically reduced.
- **Level 5—Extended**: Competition is based on supply chains. Collaboration between companies is on the highest level, multi-organisational supply chain management teams with common processes, goals, and broad authority take shape.

In the case of government, the term supply chain denotes a sequence of public agencies that are involved in a process. Cooperation among different departments and agencies is one of the most evident obstacles for efficient government processes.

Although the BPO maturity model was initially designed for organisations in the private sector, it can be applied to the public sector as well. It has to be noted that the principle objective of government business processes is not the creation of a revenue stream (Irani et al., 2007) and that public agencies have several specifics in terms of management. Nevertheless, the same principles of performance and process management should and can be used, because the primary goal of process oriented organisations is customer satisfaction.

Climbing up the scale of maturity stages, including the improvement and integration of business processes, is not smooth. On the contrary, it is difficult because integrated business processes usually develop as "chained pairs" of activities at the beginning and are later broadened to multistage or fully integrated chains. The activities, processes, risks, and costs are often differentially defined by each activity.

A business process change (BPC) is a strategy-driven organisational initiative to improve and (re) design business processes to achieve a competitive advantage in performance through changes in the relationships among management, information, technology, organisational structure, and people (Harmon, 2003). It integrates radical change methods of business process reengineering (Hammer & Champy, 1993) and a more progressive method of continuous process improvement with adequate information technology (IT) and e-business infrastructure strategies. The main difference of both groups of methods is between the approaches. In the case of continuous process improvement, the emphasis is more on problem-solving and making minor improvements frequently. However, in the case of business process reengineering, business processes are reconceptualised. Most process change projects fall between these extremes (Harmon, 2003).

The need for a business process change in the public sector had been recognised before. In 1990, during the period of many business process reengineering (BPR) projects, e.g. US government organisations went through the reform initiative named National Performance Review (Thompson, 2000), the main intention of which was an organisational change. It is particularly important when companies introduce ERP systems (Davenport, 1998), (Al-Mashari & Zairi, 1999), e-business (Bosilj-Vuksic et al., 2002) or SCM systems (Trkman et al., 2005).

Although a decade old, we found the observation of Cats-Baril, W. and Thompson, R. (1995) still topical, namely that the concept of redesigning processes opposes the common culture in many public sector organisations, but on the other side taxpayers increasingly compare the public sector to the private sector, demanding better customer service. But do public institutions have some specifics, which make renovation projects significantly different?

While the differences between business and government are blurred, several differences that are crucial to be considered in BPC projects are ascertained in literature. Governmental organisations have a unique culture and face many challenges due to their social obligations and higher legislative and public accountability (Kumar et al., 2002).

In the literature review of e-government challenges and success strategies (Gil-Garcia & Pardo, 2005) report - among organisational and managerial challenges - of the lack of alignment between organisational goals and the IT project, the existence of multiple, sometimes conflicting, goals, and of individual interests and associated behaviours that cause reluctance to change and internal conflicts. Government institutions also often act as independent and autonomous units without taking into account what other public organisations do.

Among others, Cats-Baril, W. and Thompson, R. (1995) observed the following specifics of the government: more constrains imposed by red tape, a higher level of interdependence across organisational boundaries, a higher level of extra-organisational linkages, greater interdependence across organisational boundaries, the turnover of top level administrators, the increased need to convince employees to change the existing organisational processes, the difficulty to implement a change is increased, and management tends to have less authority than its private sector counterparts.

This is in accordance with the Thompson's research (2000) on the National Performance Review (NPR) success, the main objectives of which were: downsizing, reducing administrative costs, reforming administrative systems, decentralisation of authority within agencies, empowerment of front-line workers, cultural change, quality of services improvement, and efficiency of agency work practices improvement. The research showed that some of the demands of the NPR, such as the decentralisation of authority and cultural change, were difficult to enforce. Although the business process reengineering plan envisioned dramatic improvements in service and efficiency, the project ended up with less radical, incremental changes.

There are four major characteristics that should be considered in planning a business process change (BPC) (Kettinger et al., 1997): (1) project radicalness; (2) process structuredness; (3) customer focus; and (4) the potential for IT enablement. By analysing a typical BPC project in the public sector according to the above mentioned criteria, the following characteristics can be observed:

1. Although it would be possible to radically change some (or most) of the processes in the public sector, readiness for such radical changes is currently low in many public institutions. The organisational structures are often rigid, project resources scarce, the ingenuous senior management commitment is usually difficult to achieve, several processes are predominantly intra-functional, culture supports status quo etc. All these

characteristics support the belief that radical changes impose high risks.

2. Processes are mostly well structured; some of them are even governed by laws (e.g. administrative processes). However, many of them are partially semi-structured or not structured and they vary greatly in comparison with business, for example some professional activities, judgements.
3. Customer focus is more emphasised in the public sector as it had been in the past. Customer friendliness and simplification of procedures is the imperative of the government and administration. Very often this is the main motive for business process change in the public sector. However, in most cases the goal is not to attract new customers and keep the current ones. Customers are very often obligated to use these services, e.g. when someone wants to found a sports society it has to be registered by the state.

Customer focus is more emphasised in the public sector as it had been in the past. Customer friendliness and simplification of procedures is the imperative of the government and administration. It is clear that radical changes in the execution of business processes and in the organisational structures are not suitable for the public sector because they are not possible for many, also political reasons. Therefore classic business process change methodologies have to be adapted.

MAIN FOCUS OF THE CHAPTER

As the process orientation is heavily emphasised in the t-government topics, an increase in BPO can be used as part of a migration strategy from the current state of e-government towards t-government. The model that can be used for such transformation is shown in Figure 1.

The t-government concept has three dimensions and each of them include several elements (Irani et al., 2007). Climbing up the scale of BPO maturity stages positively influences several elements of t-government: leadership, performance driven management, information management, infrastructure integration, process integration, procurement/service level management, and service transformation delivery. Such increase in BPO can be realised trough BPC projects with carefully planned and realised change management, which is one of the critical success factors of a project of this type.

The use of a formal and robust methodology that takes the above analysed specific of public sector into account is necessary for BPC projects. Many methodologies for BPC are known, some are described in (Harmon, 2007) and can be

Figure 1. Increase of BPO as a mean for migration towards t-government

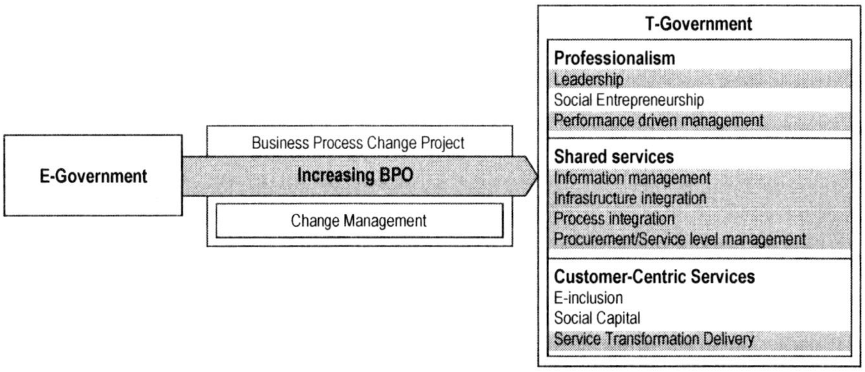

customised for the public sector (see e.g. Indihar Štemberger & Jaklič, 2007).

In (Kettinger et al., 1997) a composite Stage-Activity (S-A) framework for BPC methodologies, techniques and tools were derived. The framework is based on the description of 25 BPC methodologies practiced by the leading process change consulting firms. The methodologies in BPC projects are tailored to clients' unique needs. A framework consists of six stages that are subdivided into major activities. The six stages can be categorised as to containing the following activities:

1. **Envision:** This stage typically involves the establishment of management commitment and vision, a review of business strategy and IT opportunities, and identification and selection of key business processes.
2. **Initiate:** This stage encompasses setting of project goals, project planning and organising a project team.
3. **Diagnose:** In this stage the existing processes are documented and analysed. The processes are decomposed to sub-processes and modelled with different techniques. The models of the existing processes are named AS-IS models. Many modelling tools also allow for some type of quantitative analysis in the sense of activity-based costing or simulation analysis depending on the sophistication of the underlying modelling technique. The processes are analysed by qualitative methods as well, because many inefficiencies and drawbacks can be observed from the model alone.
4. **Redesign:** In this stage a new process design is developed. This is accomplished by evaluating different alternative processes (TO-BE models) through brainstorming and creativity techniques and also by conducting simulation and other types of quantitative analysis that is also supported by modelling tools. The new design should meet strategic objectives. This stage also encompasses proposing changes in organisational structures, management, people and information management. IS for the automation of redesigned processes are planned.
5. **Reconstruct:** This stage has to ensure migration to new processes and requires much change management. During this stage IS are implemented and users go through training.
6. **Evaluate:** The last stage of the BPC methodology includes evaluation of process performance to determine whether the project met its goals. Often it involves a linkage to a firm's TQM programmes and business process management.

The customisation of the framework based on unique project characteristics, like the project radicalness, is suggested in (Kettinger et al., 1997).

BPC projects in the public sectors have some common characteristics with the projects in the private sector; however, it is necessary to customize the S-A framework for public sector BPC projects due to the above observations and specifics. Since the radicalness of the projects in the public sector is low, the emphasis should be on documenting the existing and analysing processes as proposed by Kettinger et al. (1997). Table 1 shows activities, techniques, and tools of the proposed methodology categorised by stages of a typical BPC project as proposed and validated by Kettinger et al. (1997).

The proposed methodology is illustrated with a case study of a BPC project from one of the Slovene Ministries. The goal of the project was to do away with inefficiencies in business processes, to change the organisational structure, and to improve information system. As academic consultants we provided a methodology and assisted the project group members from the Ministry to carry out each phase of the project. To make the description of each phase clearer, each subsection explains how this phase was implemented at the Ministry.

Table 1. Stages, activities, techniques, and tools of the proposed methodology

Stage	Activities	Techniques	Tools
Envision	Defining goals, purpose, and scope of the project Establishing management commitment		
Initiate	Project planning Organising a project team Organising workshops for top and middle management Informing employees Evaluating BPO maturity Identifying key business processes Identifying limitations and constraints	Gantt chart Brainstorming Critical success factors method Structured and semi-structured interviews	Project management tools
Diagnose	Organising workgroups Documenting processes Business processes modelling Confirming models Verifying models Analysing the modelled business processes, organisational structures and IS	Structured interviews BPMN or similar process modelling technique Process documentation form Activity documentation form Discrete event simulation	Business process modelling and simulation tools
Redesign	Identifying groups of processes of the same type Proposing processes improvement and unification Proposing organisational changes Modelling renewed processes AS-IS and TO-BE processes mapping Proposing IT projects Verifying and changing proposals Determining processes owners	BPMN or similar process modelling technique Process change proposals form Current and renewed processes mapping tables Organisational chart	Business process modelling and simulation tools
Reconstruct	Implementing change Planning and implementing IT projects	Change management methods IS modelling techniques	Project management tools CASE tools
Evaluate	Implementing process monitoring system and process management Evaluating BPO maturity	Structured and semi-structured interviews	Business process management tools

Envision

In this stage, the goals, purpose and scope of a BPC project are to be set.

Sincere commitment of the top management is considered to be the most important achievement of this stage and the critical success factor of the project. As ascertained by Thompson (2000) the sustained, demonstrated commitment of its top leadership to initiate and insist on the use of results-oriented management practices is necessary. In the public sector this could be one of the major problems due to the fact that this commitment is more of a formal nature, a consequence of public opinion pressure and not the truthful awareness of a need for a change. As BPC in the public sector are very often strongly constrained and related to the changes of laws, by-laws, regulations, the commitment of top management should include a will to make the necessary changes in the regulations which fall under their competence and sometimes also to propose changes of laws and by-laws.

At this stage process values and beliefs, like customer focus, trust, need for integration etc., should begin to be developed. This growth of process values and beliefs should last for the entire project duration and should continue even afterwards, along with the continuous improvement activities. It is essential that the top management is the first with the strong process orientation understanding and then these beliefs should be spread to all levels of the organisation. Process values and beliefs among all employees are a prerequisite for achieving the latter levels of BPO maturity, beyond the level Defined.

In the case of the Ministry the main purpose was to make the processes as customer friendly (not cumbersome, short etc.) as possible. This has also been the main factor in redesigning the processes. As the key to delivering quality services is decreasing, variability, unification and standardisation of processes were strongly emphasised. The awareness of the necessity to change the processes has been achieved, also because of the lucky coincidence: at the time when the project started, the Slovene government also started the so-called anti-bureaucratic program.

By adopting the "Strategy of E-commerce in Public Administration for the Period 2001-2004" in February 2001 the Government of Slovenia defined the primary strategic orientations for the next essential phase of informatisation of public administration, which is the development of e-government. As a result, Slovenia follows a number of most developed European countries, which are approaching the accelerated development of e-government in a similar way (SEP-2004, 2001). Although, as a result, Slovenia has started a new development cycle of technological modernisation of administration and has launched a number of new projects, we have concluded that development is not progressing as planned and anticipated. This is not only a problem in Slovenia. Based on the analyses carried out in the EU, this is a problem in nearly all other countries as well (Jaklic et al., 2003). After a few years we can see that in most countries it was relatively easy to achieve earlier stages, published information, one- and sometimes two-way interactions, as these steps do not require essential changes in internal operations of administration and in business processes and procedures. The Ministry recognised that development changes in internal business processes are required for the next stage of e-government.

Initiate

In this stage the project is initiated, which includes project planning (time, finance, outcomes), organisation of the project team, and identification of the key business processes, which will be analysed and redesigned.

In some organisations key business processes are already identified and listed, but in others they are identified in a series of meetings by using discussion and brainstorming techniques. Usually there are 5 to 10 key business processes (Harmon, 2007) that can be decomposed into several sub-processes.

Top management commitment for process changes at this stage should be transformed in a way that the employees of all levels understand the goals of the project. Resistance to changes should be diminished and full participation of employees in the project ensured. As the public sector organisations are usually more rigid than profit organisations, we propose that related activities should be even more emphasised in a public sector BPC project. We propose that several workshops for top and middle management should be organised and all employees be informed about the project, its goals, and the expected outcomes. Besides that BPO maturity is evaluated by using questionnaires for managers and other structured or semi-structured interviewing techniques.

As noted earlier, one of the obstacles for a radical business process is the limitations of the current regulations, constraints of the common organisational rules and procedures on the governmental level etc. The project team has to be familiar with these limitations and constraints and with the realistic possibilities to change these regulations, rules, procedures as well.

In the case of the Ministry the project group consisted of members from the Ministry and academic consultants. A workshop for the ministry project group was conducted, in which the participants were acquainted with project goals and the methodology used. The workshop identified the key processes, which fall into the following five groups, as well: (1) Strategic planning, (2) Working program preparation, (3) Preparation of laws and provisions, (4) Financial processes, and (5) Administrative processes.

The identification of the key processes was a three-phase process. Firstly, it was necessary for the project team members from the Ministry to fully understand the business process concept. Secondly, the list of all processes was prepared, and the last step was the selection of the processes to be renovated. The brainstorming technique was used in the second and the third step. Several criteria have to be used for the selection of processes. For example a process for which the renovation benefits are promising but has a very low frequency (e.g. once a year) was not considered for a change. A very useful technique at this point is identification of critical success factors (CSF) of the project.

Diagnose

The activities at this stage can be divided into two groups or phases. Firstly, the processes are modelled, and secondly they are analysed. As radicalness of BPC projects in the public sector is usually low and the current processes will be improved, documentation and analysis of the existing processes are important and should be detailed.

Business Process Modelling

Business process modelling is an enabler for the second level of BPO, i.e. Defined, at which processes are defined and documented. Although procedures in the public sector (agencies) are very often defined and regulated by laws and other regulations, most often the regulation prescribes only a part of a process, which should be managed in its entirety from the event that starts the process to the final output for the customer. As a consequence the same process is usually run in a different manner in different agencies, gaps in the process flow between units are evident, and finally this is a major drawback for the efficient process automation. Nevertheless, process documenting should not only be considered as a means for process analysing, improvement, and standardisation. Most often, also in the case of the Ministry, this stage represents a major shift in the understanding of the process. At this point most employees start to truly comprehend the processes when they first see their models.

Before the modelling of processes is conducted, workgroups for different organisational units or areas are organised. These workgroups consist of process actors, process modellers, and middle management. Since the understanding of the process concept is usually low at this stage, all the actors are not yet known, so the workgroups can be expanded later. In our experience, actors and middle management usually fully understand the concept of processes, which flow through different organisational units after the process models are developed and presented, although workshops had been organised in earlier stages.

Workgroups document the processes by means of structured interviews with activity actors. For documentation purposes two different forms are developed: the process documentation form and the activity documentation form. In this way all the (sub)processes and activities are documented in the same manner. The process documentation form consists of the following elements: (sub) process name, (sub)process number, process trigger(s) – events, inputs, detailed description, outputs, additional comments, proposals for improvements, evaluation (cycle time, frequency, splits and decision points frequencies for each output etc.). And the activity documentation form consists of: organisational unit, process name, activity number, activity name, protagonists and other required resources, inputs, detailed description, outputs, evaluation (average/min/max time, number of available resources, costs), additional comments and proposals for improvements, attachments. The documentation also includes organisational structure documentation and IS support documentation (description and additional comments).

Processes are usually modelled in several iterations. Designed models are presented to workgroup members, who change them according to their observations. It is essential for each process model and process description to be confirmed at the end of the modelling phase by a responsible person (usually a middle manager) to avoid possible misunderstandings in the future stages of the project.

For business process modelling we suggest to use a technique that supports development of models, which are very clear and easily understood by non-specialists. Business Process Modelling Notation (BPMN) is becoming the de-facto standard technique for business process modelling and is supposed to be easy to use and understand, but also to provide the ability to model complex business processes.

In the case of the Ministry the processes were modelled by interviewing the protagonists and middle management. The iGrafx Process tool, which supports the Enhanced Process Maps (EPM) modelling technique, was used for business process modelling. The EPM technique was selected, as at the time of the project planning the BPMN was not as well recognised as it is now. Yet, it has all the required properties, such as simplicity and expressiveness, sufficient for the BPC type of projects and is very similar to BPMN.

This phase of the project was utterly resource consuming and lasted for almost six months. Models had to be changed several times based on the comments of the workgroup members and verification made by the consulting team. A number of ambiguities were discovered and removed in the modelling activity and the actors were acquainted with the "process way of thinking". It was difficult to evaluate the duration for some activities. During verification several inconsistencies in the models have been discovered, e.g. when the activity durations were multiplied by the process frequency the result was much higher than the number of working hours of the available resources.

Analysis of Key Business Processes on the Basis of their Models

In this phase, a qualitative and a quantitative analysis of the current (AS-IS) processes is conducted. Very often, the same processes are implemented in a different way for different organisational units. People are usually not aware of these differences, so the BPC project is a good opportunity to acquaint them with this problem and unify the processes of the same type. The unification can lead to the improvement of customer orientation.

The analysis results can be presented at different levels. In case of a group of similar processes there are findings for the group as a whole, and then for each process. Apart from the findings of the analysis some data from the models and process documentation, which might be of interest in the redesign phase, are presented in the analysis report.

At this point several processes were analysed at the Ministry by use of simulation as well. Processes for such detailed analysis were selected by using the criteria such as. frequency of process execution, quantity of consumed resource, level of observed problems, etc.

Redesign

At this point the most sensitive phases of a BPC project emerge. Redesign intervenes into the existing ways of work, structures, and power distribution. On the other side, the last phases of the BPC project enable shifts to the higher levels of process maturity, and consequently create circumstances for t-government or higher levels of sophistications of online services. Process owners should be appointed at the process redesign stage, as this enables process management methods in the latter stages. Efficiency and effectiveness of processes are increased with process optimisation.

Process redesign based on the findings of the analysis calls for the application of creative thinking techniques (such as brainstorming). Firstly, groups of similar processes that can be defined as one TO-BE process are identified and then new, renovated processes are designed.

As mapping between AS-IS and TO-BE processes is not 1:1, proposed new processes are relabelled. Usually one TO-BE process corresponds to several unified AS-IS processes. Two tables, which present mapping between the current and the renewed processes (and vice versa) are built. The existing-to-the-renovated-process mapping is not just about relabelling, regrouping and unification. The main achievement of different classification (and consequently different labelling) is a completely changed view on business processes. Before the change the processes had been grouped by departments (e.g. higher education department processes, sports department processes etc.). After the changes were introduced the employees started to understand that the process view is horizontal (process flows through several departments), and that processes are cross-departmental. This was one of the main breakthroughs in the employees understanding of business processes.

Proposals of new processes are described by using standardised forms. Like for the findings of the current processes analysis, proposals for changes are presented in two levels: for each process group and then for each individual process. Proposals were made on the basis of the analysis of the process models, descriptions, simulation, regulations etc. The standardised form for proposals consists of the following elements: (sub) process name, (sub)process label, corresponding processes labels, process owner, process model, event(s), input, description, output, changes by activities, other findings and proposals, resources, and findings, relevant to information management improvements.

In the case of the Ministry the main guidance in the redesign stage was the goal to simplify the processes, improve information management and provide better services for customers (institutions, citizens etc.). Secondary goals were shorter cycle times, relieving of employees, and lower costs.

There were several cases of the same process carried out differently in different areas. For instance the process "Promotion of the Employees to a Higher Professional Title" had been executed in a different way in the sports department (labelled as 5.10.6) and in the educational department (5.8.5). The renovated process labelled 5.C (see Figure 2) is only one for both departments. Of course, the substantial activity Professional Consideration (5.C.13) is specific in both departments and requires different professionals with specific knowledge.

An important suggestion for improvement of this process was providing consultation in the field of application preparation (activity 5.C.1). The percentage of incomplete applications is expected to be much lover in this way. Another important suggestion for a change is as follows: in case an incomplete application is detected, the first official at the Ministry tries to look for additional information in the existing government databases (activity 5.C.8). Should it not be found, the customer is to be notified. Different forms of notification are now possible. Besides notification by mail that was the only way before the BPC project, notification by e-mail or phone was suggested (activities 5.C.11 and 5.C.12).

Another problem regarding the process was that the information on the current status of an application was not available in the information system. It is very important to have this information, especially for t-government. Therefore the status of an application and other information related thereto are recorded several times in the process execution in activities 5.C.2, 5.C.4, 5.C.7, 5.C.10, 5.C.16, 5.C.18, 5.C.19 and 5.C.20.

From the point of view of process flows several processes were unified and this fact makes the

Figure 2. Redesigned process promotion of employees

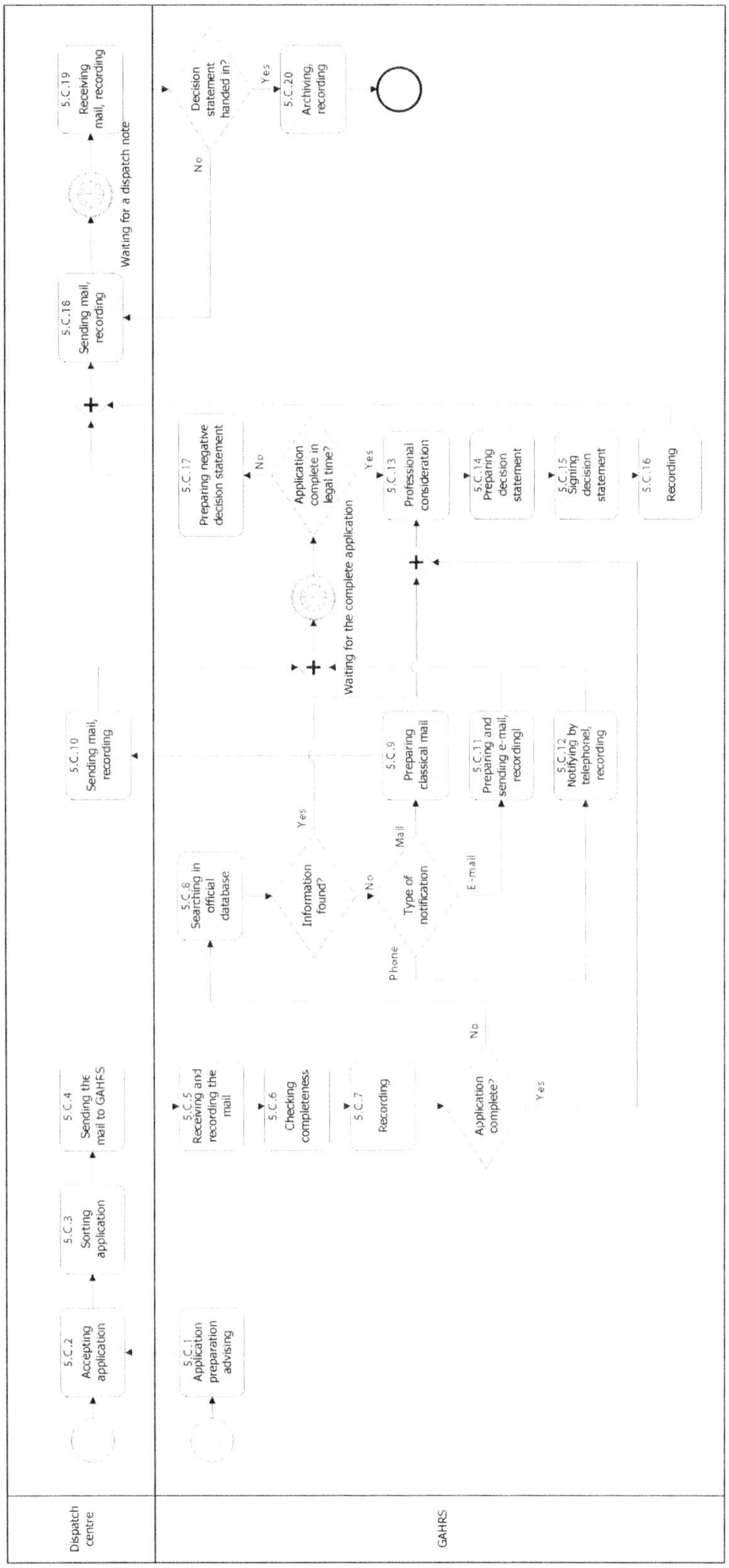

whole administrative function of the Ministry less complex in the eyes of the customers. Additionally, one stop shop in the form of service centre shared by different departments was proposed. The shared service centres can be helpful for avoiding long-lasting search processes and avoid the confusion about responsibilities to the users (Janssen & Joha, 2006).

Reconstruct and Evaluate

In the last two phases of a BPC project the proposed changes have to be implemented. The reconstruction also encompasses IS projects planning and implementation. Continuous improvement requires that processes be monitored continuously to identify changes in overall quality level, therefore a process-monitoring system (or process management system) is to be implemented at a later stage. After the changes are implemented, BPO maturity can be evaluated again to asses the progress.

The use of change management methods should be considered as the critical success factor for the entire project. Organisational structures in the public sector are hierarchical and they can hardly be expected to radically change in the pure process organisation due to regulation and political interests. Therefore a process aspect should be introduced in the existing jobs and organisational structures. Together with the process redesign, as defined in the Redesign phase, and process measurements and continuous process management, this enables a real breakthrough of BPO and should be considered as t-government.

The Ministry has started a phase of reconstruction. It is quite limited in planning and implementing IS projects, because it depends on the internal regulation for all governmental institutions in Slovenia. However, the project has certainly brought about many benefits for them. One of the main benefits is that the processes are now known and performed in a much more uniform way than before. To make the new way of work easier and to acquaint people with new renewed business processes the models are published on the internal web pages of the Ministry. Is simplifies change management and also provides an unambiguous way of process implementation.

FUTURE TRENDS

Irani et al. (2007) have identified several major research areas related to further t-government development. The model proposed in this chapter offers possibilities to contribute to several of these areas, mostly to the following:

- reengineering for process integration across the silos of public administration,
- organisational models of integrated service delivery,
- government supply chain management,
- quality assurance in government supplier management,
- comprehensive models of benefit realisation, etc.

All these topics are closely related to the business process orientation and maturity concepts. Moreover, a t-government transformational model will have to address the BPO elements (process view, process structure, process jobs, process measurement and management systems, customer-focused process values and beliefs) as these are inherently part of the t-government concept. It is important that the government understands that t-government is not possible without a high level of BPO maturity. Therefore the proposed model could be used as a starting point for developing a comprehensive model for the transformation from e-government towards t-government. Certainly, when adopting the BPO maturity model for t-government migration, the limitations of the public sector (e.g. rigid structures and political barriers) have to be taken into account.

As shown in Figure 3, process maturity level of a public agency can be increased through a BPC project. Improvements in process maturity are a prerequisite and further facilitate transformation from simple online services through more sophisticated services, up to the 5th level of sophistication of online public services with the proactive and integrated service delivery. Integration of processes through several departments or even through a sequence of public agencies requires structural changes. However, in the case of a large BPC project, e.g. for a chain of public agencies, the potential for IT enablement is quite high, as such project would allow for the highest (Extended) level of BPO and consequently integrated level of e-services.

Yet not all steps of sophistication of online services from one stage to another require the same level of increase in the BPO. For example, advancement to the transactional from the two-way interaction stage requires a significantly higher increase in BPO maturity compared to other steps. Since this is a breakthrough level of sophistication of online services that is extremely important in the way to t-government, this is probably the point where government agencies should carry out a BPC project. In our opinion such transition is not possible without it.

As e-government and moreover t-government measurement clearly lags behind the measurement of e-business and the Information Society (Booz Allen Hamilton, 2005), BPO maturity model can also be used as a foundation to develop a measurement model for t-government. Besides, measuring efficiency, benefits and maturity of t-government have to be evaluated with more problematic qualitative indicators (Irani et al., 2007). These measurements have to include not only the lag indicators, but also the lead indicators, which enable understanding of processes that ensure effectiveness. Process measurement and management is an essential part of the BPO framework that addresses the above-mentioned problems as well.

CONCLUSION

The presented methodology for BPC projects in the public sector has been employed in some process

Figure 3. Process maturity, sophistication of online services, and BPC project phases

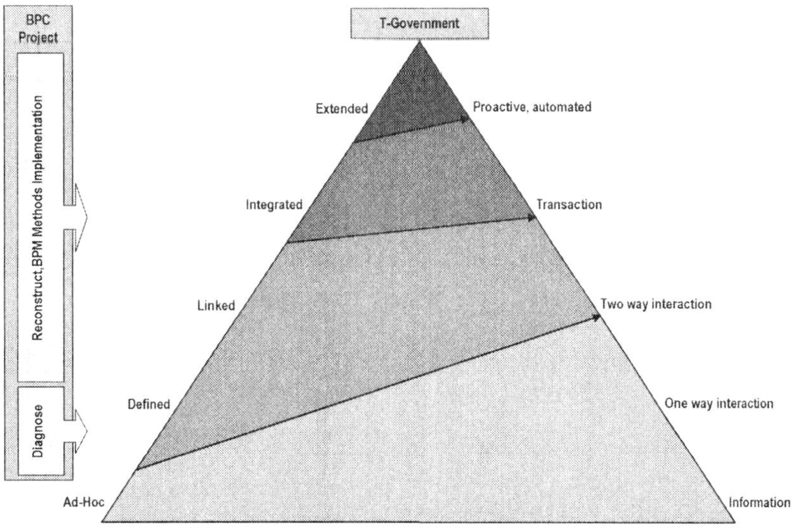

improvement projects, e.g. in a BPC project at one of the Slovene ministries. Before this project the Ministry was clearly at the first level of business process orientation. Processes at the Ministry were neither documented nor defined. Jobs were organised strictly by traditional functions. Departments that should be the owners of processes (e.g. financial department) had no influence on the performance of these processes (e.g. financial processes) in other departments.

Now the Ministry has moved from the first level to the second level of business process maturity with some elements of the third level. Among other benefits, the processes are documented, known and performed in a much more uniform way than before, models are published on the organisational internal web pages and process managers are appointed. The process managers have responsibility to harmonise all the necessary future changes in all departments, so changes to the processes must now go through a formal procedure. The financial department for instance is the owner of all financial processes and now has cross-departmental jurisdiction. The crucial achievement is that the way of thinking has been changed and as a consequence information management and sharing has improved. The results of the project also directly influence the e-government initiatives of all forms; more complex transactional e-services and other features of t-government, such as performance driven management, information management and standards, are now possible.

Even though it is not a real breakthrough, this change at the Ministry is an important step. The crucial achievement is that the way of thinking has been changed. Employees now understand the concept of the business process and this is a good foundation to proceed with the process of growing in the sense of BPO and consequently in the direction of realising transformational government.

As a consequence, some elements of t-government are now improved to some extent. In the dimension of shared services process integration, information management and infrastructure integration are essentially better. Procurement/service level management and Service transformation delivery are improved as well. Therefore we can conclude that the BPC project at the Ministry enabled a more successful implementation of t-government through increased BPO maturity.

It can be concluded from the experience described in the case study that it is currently the right moment to increase business process orientation in the European Union public sector at least to the level 3 or 4. On the one hand this is a reasonable and realistic expectation and on the other a necessary condition to achieve higher levels of online services. The case of the Ministry shows that all possible and necessary changes in the framework of BPO are difficult to implement. Nevertheless, much can be done if top management is sincerely involved in such project.

REFERENCES

Al-Mashari, M., & Zairi, M. (1999). BPR implementation process: An analysis of key success and failure factors. *Business Process Management Journal, 5*(1), 87-112.

Beynon-Davies, P. (2005). Constructing electronic government: The case of the UK inland revenue. *International Journal of Information Management, 25*, 3-20.

Bosilj-Vuksic, V., Indihar Stemberger, M., Jaklic, J., & Kovacic, A. (2002). Assessment of e-business transformation using simulation modelling. *Simulation, 78*(12), 731-744.

Booz Allen Hamilton (2005). *Beyond e-government: The world's most successful technology-enabled transformations* (Report). Retrieved March 20, 2008 from http://www.boozallen.com/media/file/151607.pdf

Cabinet Office (2005). *Transformational Government Enabled by Technology*. London: The Stationery Office, Crown Copyright.

Capgemini (2007). *The User Challenge Benchmarking: The Supply Of Online Public Services, 7th Measurement*. Retrieved March 20, 2008 from http://ec.europa.eu/information_society/eeurope/i2010/docs/benchmarking/egov_benchmark_2007.pdf

Cats-Baril, W., & Thompson, R. (1995). Managing information technology projects in the public sector. *Public Administration Review*, *6*(55), 559-566.

Davenport, T. H. (1993). *Process innovation: Reengineering work through information technology*. Boston: Harvard Business School Press.

Davenport, T. H. (1998). Putting the Enterprise into the Enterprise System. *Harvard Business Review*, *76*(4), 121-131.

Gil-Garcia, J. R., & Pardo, T. A. (2005). E-government success factors: Mapping practical tools to theoretical foundations. *Government Information Quarterly*, *22*, 187-216.

Hammer, M. H., & Champy, J. (1993). *Reengineering the corporation: A manifesto for business revolution*. New York: Harper Business.

Hammer, M. (2004). Deep Change. *Harvard Business Review*, *82*(4), 84-93.

Hendrick, R. (1994). An Information Infrastructure for Innovative Management of Government. *Public Administration Review*, *6*(54), 543-550.

Harmon, P. (2007). *Business process change: A guide for business managers and BPM and six sigma professionals, 2nd ed.* Amsterdam: Elsevier/Morgan Kaufmann Publishers.

Hernon, P., Reylea, H. C., Dugan, R. E., & Cheverie, J. F. (2002). *United States government information: Policies and sources*. Westport, CT: Libraries Unlimited.

Indihar Štemberger, M., & Jaklič, J. (2007). Towards e-government by business process change-a methodology for public sector. *International Journal of Information Management*, *27*(4), 221-232.

Irani, Z., Sahraoui, S., Ozkan, S., Ghoneim, A., & Elliman T. (2007). T-Government for benefit realisation. In *Proceedings of European and Mediterranean Conference on Information Systems 2007 (EMCIS2007), June 24-26* (pp. 22-1-22-11). Polytechnic University of Valencia, Spain.

Jaklič, J, Groznik, A., & Kovačič, A. (2003). Towards e-government: the role of simulation modelling. In: Verbraeck, A., Hlupic, V. (Eds.). *Simulation in industry: October 26-29, 2003, Delft, Netherlands. Delft: SCS, 2003* (pp. 257-262). Delft, The Netherlands: SCS – Europe BVBA.

Janssen, M., & Joha, A. (2006). Motives for establishing shared service centers in public administrations. *International Journal of Information Management*, *26*, 102–115.

Kettinger, W.J., Teng, T.C., & Guha, S. (1997). Business process change: A study of methodologies, techniques, and tools. *MIS Quarterly*, *21*(1) 55-81.

Kumar, V., Maheshwari, B., & Kumar, U. (2002). ERP systems implementation: Best practices in Canadian government organizations. *Government Information Quarterly*, *19*, 147–172.

Lockamy, A., & McCormack, K. (2004). The development of a supply chain management process maturity model using the concepts of business process orientation. *Supply Chain Management: An International Journal*, *9*(4), 272-278.

McCormack, K., & Johnson, W. (2001). *Business process orientation: Gaining the e-business competitive advantage*. Delray Beach, FL: St Lucie Press.

Ostroff, F. (1999). *The horizontal organization*. New York: Oxford University Press.

SEP-2004 (2001). *Strategy of E-commerce in Public Administration for the Period 2001-2004*.

Ljubljana, Slovenia: Ministry of Information Society. Retrieved September 10, 2003 from http://mid.gov.si/

SEP-2010 (2006). E-Government Strategy of the Republic of Slovenia for the period 2006 to 2010 Ministry of Public Administration, Ljubljana, Slovenia: Ministry of Public Administration. Retrieved March 20, 2008 from http://e-uprava.gov.si/e-uprava/

Škrinjar, R., Dimovski, V., Škerlavaj, M., & Indihar Štemberger, Mojca (2006). Process maturity and organizational structure as a framework for performance improvements. In Nilsson, A. et al. (Eds.), *Bridging the gap between academia and industry, Vol. 1.* (pp. 95-106). New York: Springer.

Thompson, J. R. (2000). Reinvention As Reform: Assessing the National Performance Review. *Public Administration Review*, *6*(60), 508-521.

Trkman, P., Indihar Stemberger, M., & Jaklic, J. (2005). Information transfer in supply chain management. In *Informing Science and IT Education Conference 2005 (InSITE 2005)*, Vol. 2, (pp. 559-573). Santa Rosa, CA: Informing Science Institute.

Willaert, P., van der Bergh, J., Willems, J., & Deschoolmeester, D. (2007). The process-oriented organisation: A holistic view, developing a framework for business process orientation maturity. In Alonso G., Dadam P., Rosemann M. (Eds.), *Proceedings of 5th International BPM Conference, Brisbane, September 24-27* (pp. 1-15). Berlin, Heidelberg: Springer-Verlag.

KEY TERMS

Business Process Change: A strategy-driven organisational initiative to improve and (re)design business processes to achieve competitive advantage in performance through changes in the relationships among management, information, technology, organisational structure, and people.

Business Process Management: Aligning processes with a organisation's strategic goals, designing and implementing process architectures, establishing process measurement systems that align with organisational goals, and training and organising managers so that they will manage the processes effectively.

Business Process Orientation: An organisation is business process oriented if, in all its thinking, it emphasises a process as opposed to hierarchies with a special emphasis on outcomes and customer satisfaction.

E-Government: The use of information and communications technology to change the structures and processes of government organisations.

Process Jobs: Job descriptions are horizontal rather than vertical. People participate and take ownership of the entire process.

Process View: Involves a focus on the workflows and processes across an organisation.

Sophistication of Online Services: A framework for measurement of the progress of online public service.

Chapter III
Transformation Strategies for Shared Service Centers in the Public Sector

Haiko van der Voort
Delft University of Technology, The Netherlands

Hans de Bruijn
Delft University of Technology, The Netherlands

Marijn Janssen
Delft University of Technology, The Netherlands

ABSTRACT

This chapter presents a set of critical choices for initiating a Shared Service Center (SSC) in a large public organization and the management of the transformation process towards it. A move to concentrating organizational support functions in SSCs in public administration is encouraged by successes in the private sector. There is a lot to gain by concentrating functions including improved services through specialization, efficiencies through standardization, and cost reductions through economies of scale. Yet the transformation process does not resemble the simplicity of the concept of SSC and many challenges need to be bridged. In this chapter, the complexities of transformation processes of the introduction of a government wide SSC for human resource management are studied. By analyzing the perceptions of key stakeholders from a policy network theoretical lens, we found some major patterns determining success or failure in both designing and implementing SSCs. By listing these, we aim to clarify the complexities of transformation processes towards SSCs in public administration and provide some strategic suggestions for these transformations.

INTRODUCTION

A recurring complaint in public administration is that governmental organizations are big, inefficient, not -customer centric and bureaucratic. Haunted by these complaints reorganization and change operations are regularly announced. In their continuous pursuit for ways to reduce costs while maintaining existing service standards, several concepts and theories appeared and disappeared. A relatively new, and promising, concept is called 'Shared Service Centers'(SSC) (Accenture, 2006; Bergeron, 2003; Ulbrich, 2006) or 'Shared Service Organizations' (Grant, McKnight, Uruthirapathy, & Brown, 2007). SSCs are types of semi-autonomous business units providing services to many users, i.e. agencies, business units and departments. They ideally have management structures that promote efficiency, cost savings and high service levels in a manner akin to companies competing in an open market (Bergeron, 2003). Many private companies have already implemented this concept (e.g. Bergeron, 2003; Strikwerda, 2005). By unbundling supportive local and central functions, like IT-support and human resource management (HRM), and concentrating them in semi-autonomous business units, such companies have cut costs considerably. Yet gaining the benefits is more difficult and benefits might be gained in other field than expected (Janssen & Joha, 2006).

Several governments are in the process of introducing shared services, among them are the USA, UK, Canada and the Netherlands (Accenture, 2006). In public administration the SSC business model seems to be promising for several reasons. Services often cannot be provided cost effectively and can be implemented only on a local level, as budgets and expertise are limited. Smaller public organizations cannot develop all the services desired or the information systems needed. Moreover, both small and large organizations have all kinds of expertise in-house that cannot be assessed outside the borders of their own organizations. In this way SSCs might provide access to expertise else out of reach. Finally, theory promises imply much more than just cost efficiency and improved service levels. Claimed advantages of SSCs include focus on core tasks, they would contribute to transparency, create possibilities to build up and share expertise, help increasing strategic flexibility and speed up decision making (Bergeron, 2003; Strikwerda, 2005).

The introduction of shared SSCs, however, is a complex and massive transformation process which might make it hard to accomplish the promises (Janssen & Joha, 2006). Ulbrich (2006) stated that the introduction of SSC requires an extensive business process (re)engineering approach. The formation of a SSC requires that agencies transfer the development, maintenance and control of their information systems to a different organization and abandon their existing information systems. Such major changes are hard to accomplish. A large number of stakeholders are involved, with complex, interdependent relationships (Janssen, Joha, & Weerakkody, 2007). We call this web of multiple actors and interdependent relations a *policy network* (or a 'network'). In this chapter we take a policy network theoretical lens on the design and implementation of SSCs. *Policy network theory* stresses the importance of the creation (and retention!) of support for major changes in networks (Bruijn & Heuvelhof, 2000; Chisholm, 1989; Kenis & Schneider, 1991; Powell, 1990). It suggests that the best design from a technical point of view doesn't necessarily lead to its support and, eventually, to its implementation.

This takes us to the main challenge addressed in this chapter. The introduction of SSCs requires a whole series of interrelated decisions for which it might turn out very hard to reach consensus within the heterogeneous types of organizations involved. At the same time the introduction of SSCs in public administration requires a good design of an organizational arrangement able to improve both efficiency and service levels. Therefore in this chapter we question if *both the quality of the organizational design of a SSC can be guaranteed and at the same time sufficient support for a SSC arrangement can be created.*

BACKGROUND: POLICY NETWORK PERSPECTIVE ON COMPLEX TRANSFORMATION PROCESSES

Individual government bodies are often relatively autonomous units. They are often free to design their own information systems. As a result, they have various degrees of expertise and knowledge and different information systems. Furthermore, their objectives and needs might differ from one organization to another organization. As they can use their knowledge to influence organizational decisions, organizations might be seen as systems (or configurations) that are partly the result of a multitude of organizational units using their power in decision making (Jaffee, 2001; Mintzberg, 1983; Morgan, 1986). So on the one hand, the units are parts of a formally hierarchical structure, on the other hand they resemble so-called 'networks': a multitude of interdependent organizations (Bruijn & Heuvelhof, 2000; Chisholm, 1989; Kenis & Schneider, 1991; Powell, 1990).

The typical network characteristics—variety and interdependence of actors—seriously hamper hierarchical management strategies. Treating these units as hierarchical subordinates that should obey commands from a single authority and accept detailed controls of implementation—fails to respect the interdependencies of the actors: the authority has the power to decide, but the quality of its decision depends upon the knowledge and relations of the other actors (Axelrod, 2006; Bruijn & Heuvelhof, 2000; Hofstadter, 1983). The subordinates won't feel incentives to provide the information the authority needs to steer adequately. A hierarchical approach therefore leads to qualitatively inferior decisions and serious implementation problems. (Bruijn, Heuvelhof, & in 't Veld, 2002).

Major changes in networks often are the result of a bargaining process between the different (semi-)autonomous stakeholders within and outside the organization (March, 1989). Or as Powell (1990, p. 303) puts it: "(...) transactions occur neither through discrete exchanges nor by administrative fiat, but through networks of individuals engaged in reciprocal, preferential, mutually supportive actions." Decision making in networks therefore often follows an unstructured pattern. It is hard to distinguish clear decision making phases beforehand. In decision making literature one often speaks of 'rounds'. In a round, actors reach a decision during a fight, or rather try to prevent doing so. A round will finish at some time and produce a provisional result, including winners and losers. This might seem to conclude the decision making, but a new round may suddenly present itself (Bruijn, Heuvelhof, & in 't Veld, 2002; Teisman, 1992).

The network theoretical perspective draws the attention for the need for analyzing stakeholders and their dynamic interaction processes. Major changes, as is the transformation to SSCs, occur in such an unstructured, dynamic interaction process. Network theory stresses the need for support to such a process and, of equal importance, the retention of that support.

The introduction of SSCs requires a whole series of interrelated decisions for which it might very hard to reach consensus within the heterogeneous types of organizations involved. For example: Which services should be shared and concentrated in the SSC? How do you retain a certain level of control? How should services be standardized? What are requirements on information systems and governance processes? How to maintain the necessary freedom and flexibility for the clients of the new SSC to customize the services to their own specific situation?

Creating and retaining support, however, won't automatically result in an optimal design of a SSC. The introduction of SSCs implies some obvious risks if the organizational model is ill-designed.

For example: The gaining of efficiency might be at the expense of service levels or giving a SSC autonomy without providing them incentives to reach some service level could lead to monopolistic (non-customer oriented) behavior of the SSC. Another example: putting too much effort on standardization and the economies of scale might lead to an inefficient, bureaucratic SSC. So, as mentioned in chapter 1, the challenge is to both design a good SSC and at the same time get support for it in a networked context.

RESEARCH APPROACH

This chapter is a result of a study of a large SSC-project in the Netherlands named P-direct (e.g. http://www.sharedservicesbijdeoverheid.nl). The objective of this project was the creation of a SSC Human Resource Management in the Dutch central government organization aimed at providing administration services for a majority of the Dutch central departments. The project was coordinated by one of those departments, the Dutch Ministry of Internal Affairs. We started conducting a literature study on the SSC- concept. As literature on SSCs in the public sector is limited and the concept is relatively unexplored (Singh & Craike, 2008), we first conducted four exploratory interviews with managers already experienced with SSCs. This literature study and exploratory interviews provided the structure for an extended series of 57 interviews we conducted with key players in this project and key players from other SSC initiatives within local governments (Bruijn, Wagenaar, Voort, & Wendel de Joode, 2004; Wagenaar, Matthijsse, Bruijn, Voort, & Wendel de Joode, 2006). We concluded this part of the study by organizing a validation workshop with public servants to get more insight into the organizational and technical aspects of the design and implementation of SSCs.

For the 57 interviews we have chosen for qualitative unstructured interviews, organized around four descriptive and two prescriptive questions, based on the literature study and explorative interviews mentioned before. They are:

1. What are the main potentials of SSCs at the Dutch central government organization?
2. What are the main risks of SSCs at the Dutch central government organization?
3. What are the main organizational and technological conditions for successful SSCs at the Dutch central government organization?
4. What are the main implementation issues at the Dutch central government organization?
5. How should the SSCs at the Dutch central governmental organization be designed?
6. How should the SSCs at the Dutch central governmental organization be implemented?

This chapter is organized along these six questions. In section 4 the main potentials and risks are discussed. Section 5 provides insight in the organizational and technological feasibility aspects (questions 3 and 4). The prescriptive design issues are discussed in section 6, while the suggestions for implementation are described in section 7. In section 8 we combine our findings and draw some main strategies for introduction of SSCs in the public sector. In section 9 conclusions are drawn.

We have chosen to present a qualitative discussion of the findings of the 61 interviews to feed a conceptual discussion on this matter. The descriptive sections (4 and 5) are careful enumerations of the suggestions by the interviewees. However, the prescriptive issues (section 6 and 7) have been structured by the authors as 'critical choices' regarding design and implementation of SSCs. The study of P-Direct is not a case study in the traditional sense. The case served only as a reference for the interviewees. In this way the use of this case study avoided potential confusion about what a SSC actually constitutes. P-Direct was in an early stage of development during our interviews. This means that the respondents could not use many observations on concrete P-Direct issues for their answers. These answers were perceptions of the respondents about what would come and what should come.

SHARED SERVICE CENTERS: CONCEPTIONS, POTENTIALS, RISKS

What Constitutes a SSC?

Despite the relatively short existence of the concept, numerous definitions of SSCs are to be found in literature (Bergeron, 2003; Janssen & Joha, 2006; Singh & Craike, 2008; Strikwerda, 2005). They also show some variety, according to the focus of the studies involved. Also different organizational models of SSCs co-exist, like the SSC as internal 'joint-venture', as a separate organizational division, as a central staff department or as a staff department within a division (Strikwerda, 2005). Two characteristics recur in every definition: 1) SSCs are a result of a concentration of services and 2) SSCs are suppliers of a service to a client.

The variety of SSC arrangements is notable. Figure 1 is derived from the interviews and shows this variety based on the organizational and process scope. SSC projects can differ in terms of (a) the type of processes that the SSC will support and/or realize, and (b) the organization(s) to which the services will be provided. For example, a SSC may be set up for the provision and support of secondary and/or supporting processes to a single department. A different SSC may provide primary, policy-making processes for several departments within a single sector (e.g. education) or within several sectors (e.g. education and health care).

Figure 1. Scope of a shared service center

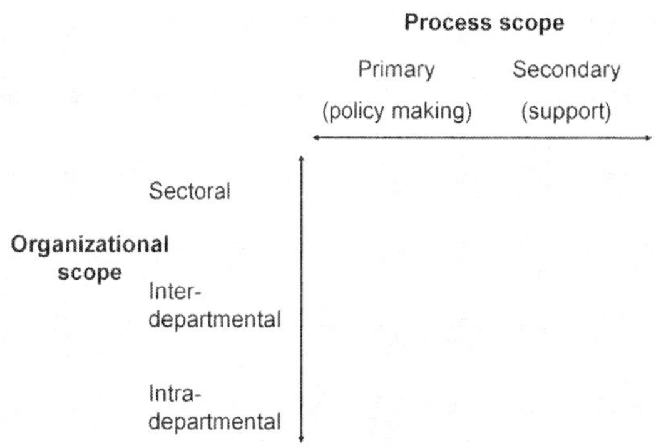

Expected Potentials and Risks

Expectations among most of the interviewees concerning the potentials of SSCs were quite high. A vast majority predicted cost reductions and better service quality. The interviews resulted in the following characteristics may lead to potential benefits for an organization.

- SSCs provide opportunities to *focus on core tasks*. A government that delegates tasks which are not policy-related to SSCs will be able to concentrate on its core tasks. Consequently, it creates room to focus more clearly on the development, implementation and enforcement of policy, since organizational complexity within public services or departments will decrease as a result of the establishment of SSCs.
- SSCs contribute to *transparency*. The use of a SSC creates distance between the clients and the provider. Distance always forces one to be explicit about and agree on orders, prices, delivery conditions, account identification, etc. Such explicitness can increase the transparency of management activities within government.
- SSCs make it possible to *build up and share expertise*. Single agencies are too small to have all expertise in-house. Because a SSC is dedicated to the design of only a single

or a few functions at most, it gathers all expertise on these functions. This compilation of expertise allows faster and better use of new developments on the function concerned. In this way, one prevents a continuous reinventing of the wheel within each individual unit of public services. Moreover, the compilation of expertise fits in with the objective of further professionalization of the various management functions.

- SSCs increase *strategic flexibility.* Shared services make it possible to distinguish between core activities and supporting activities which are adaptable, independently of one another, to strategic, organizational, political, economic or technological changes. The ability to adapt to dynamics and specific changes increases.

In the end SSCs would lead to better efficiency both at the SSC itself and at the departments that are now released from the supportive activities they used to do. The shared expertise and explicit requirements for the SSC would lead to improvement of service quality.

In contrast with these potentials a dominant risk is that *the incentives for SSCs to achieve are insufficient.* The environment of a SSC is not very competitive. It is unlikely that an organization will prefer a competitor if a SSC does not perform its job efficiently, because the costs of rebuilding trust and knowledge are very high. Usually achievements of a SSC are made explicit in Service Level Agreements (SLAs), but again it is unlikely that a SLA will provide enough incentives to improve achievements. That's because an enforcing capability of an SLA assumes a flexibility of a SSC that is common in competitive markets but rare without credible competitors. If this flexibility is absent, SSCs could easily become monopolistic.

A second risk is *bureaucratization of service provision*, both at the SSC- side and at the side of the client organization. The introduction of SSCs is efficiency driven. It is however unclear what will happen with the remaining 'old' staff departments. It is possible that these departments will grow after the SSC-operation. First, an SSC delivers standardized services, while the departments demand tailor made services. The need for translation of the standardized services could lead to extra staff service at the divisions. Second, the greater the distance between SSC and department, the bigger the chance that the processes of the SSC will be duplicated within the department. The need could be felt to let a local staff bureau create 'checks and double checks'. The overall result could be an aggregated growth of staff departments and bureaucracy.

Table 1 shows a summary of the main benefits and risks as found in the interviews.

Table 1. Overview of the main benefits and risks of SSCs

Benefits	Risks
Cost reductions Better service quality Transparency Build up and share expertise increase strategic flexibility	Insufficient incentives for SSCs performance Bureaucratization of service provision Standardization dominates over customization

ORGANIZATIONAL AND TECHNOLOGICAL ASPECTS OF FEASIBILITY

Organizational and Technological Conditions

In the previous section we discussed the consensus about the potentials of SSCs. However, during our interviews it became clear that these potentials were often subject to certain conditions and circumstance. We asked under what managerial conditions could one profit from the main potentials? From the interviews we deduced the following conditions. We found tensions between the different answers, leading to the question how one could meet *all* conditions at the same time.

Corporate governance. A clear executive board at corporate level, common in the business community, does not exist in public administration. The thirteen departments of the Dutch government can be looked upon as separate groups with partly conflicting and overlapping objectives. SSCs, on the other hand, would benefit from an unequivocal group steering. This requires the development of a new organization model, in which the property of the SSC is undivided yet in which users can exercise enough influence on the SSC. Since both the implementation and the functioning of a SSC are hedged with uncertainty, a permanent political and administrative commitment to SSCs is necessary. If such commitments do not exist and the support for SSCs would evaporate, it is deemed to fail.

Administrative organization: a shared information infrastructure. Efficiency and professionalization are frustrated by the fact that each agency stores, processes and distributes its information in its own, unique way. This makes it hard to achieve scale benefits and to exchange knowledge. A shared information infrastructure is a prerequisite for efficient provision of services, with or without SSCs. The parties should indeed be willing to fine-tune data structures unequivocally. This does not mean that autonomy of decision-making on the basis of shared data sources needs to be sacrificed.

Standardization and tailor-made services. Efficiency can be gained through standardization. A uniform supply to all departments can save costs. However, departments will ask for tailor-made services, referring to their specific characteristics and circumstances. Without the supply of tailor-made services the staff of the departments will perhaps hardly decrease, as a result of which the efficiency advantages get lost. The costs of tailor-made services are to be made transparent.

ICT as a lever. It is important to recognize the role of ICT as a lever for major organizational changes and, possibly, to anticipate such changes. New web-based technologies in ICT allow a more flexible response to the question whether services should be 'tailor-made or standardized'. In particular one sees the industry moving towards modularization of large information systems: instead of one integrated software package we see that applications are more often developed as separate modules that can be 'clicked' together with the help of standardized interfaces. More specifically, it promises to mitigate the fear for "one size fits all", by allowing customized functionalities to be included on top of a common ICT infrastructure base. However, the adoption of this trend by the major ERP systems vendors in their products is still rather slow, let alone their installed base. Since the central governmental departments were using different ERP systems, this created the need for a new system that would allow migration of the existing HRM systems to one centralized system. The scale and scope of the shared functionality of this newly to be built system triggered so much discussion and as a result changing specifications that the single remaining vendor in the tendering process finally decided to withdraw.

Implementation Issues

So far we have discussed potentials of SSCs *if they would have been implemented already.* To complement these 'end-state issues' we have asked our respondents about the implementation process. What are the main risks of failure in the implementation process? From what actors do you expect much resistance? From the interviews we could deduce the following list of implementation risks. Please note that the list is the result of a qualitative analysis. It is a clustering of considerations by respondents conceptualized by the authors.

Resistance against power concentrations during implementation. The implementation of a SSC affects the organization as a whole, from the boardroom to the work floor. If not all are convinced of the necessity of the project, many people are very likely to wage a fight to preserve their autonomy and identity. Often it is only during such large-scale processes that it becomes clear how the dependency relations are actually structured. They may turn out to be completely different from the formal responsibility structure. For the same reason, others may fear a hardly predictable concentration of power in the hands of a group which resorts to obstruction and blocking.

Emerging resistance at a later stage of the process. The widespread fear is that objectives and consequences will remain unclear. This would certainly be so if the management was to part with the control of the process either by allowing a coincidental, trial-and-error process or by giving the process a participatory style. In that case, the process would be vague and follow a chaotic course. However, there will be a point in time when consequences become evident and a separate cost benefit analysis can be made. This often occurs at a later stage of the process. This point in time entails a risk, for resistance may then intensify and may continue until the SSC actually enters the operational phase.

Resistance influencing implementation costs. Cutting costs is an important reason to introduce a SSC. However, there are frequent warnings against high implementation costs. The question is whether the benefits will balance these costs. Implementation costs not only pertain to the project costs themselves but also to the necessary conditions preceding a project, for example the costs of reorganizations. Moreover, resistance may imply that a choice will be made for a less beneficial model, with the result that the actual reduction in costs will, also on the long term, be less than expected.

Knowledge drain. Any reorganization leads to an outflow of staff. The people concerned often feel that their interests are harmed beyond reason. These are likely not the people who perform poorly; indeed, those who are valuable to the organization often have a strong position on the labor market. The outflow of such employees poses a risk, for it implies a drain of essential knowledge.

Environment: the friction of time. Many large-scale projects in public services are time-consuming and encounter an impatient environment. It is difficult to satisfy the environment with a long-term project that, moreover, does not appeal to the imagination. Primary processes often receive more attention. If the project route is not properly explained, the impression may be created that the project is failing. This negative perception by the environment can adversely affect the implementation and may be detrimental.

Political intervention. As referred to above, a minority among the interviewees argues that SSCs are only an administrative hype. All the same, administrative commitment is essential to the success of a SSC. Administrative commitment will rapidly disappear if the enthusiasm of politicians wanes. Politicians are very sensitive to the environment, with all the usual dynamics associated. That explains why respondents turned out to be particularly afraid of political interventions and/or waning commitment of politicians.

CRITICAL CHOICES FOR DESIGN

During the interviews a number of critical design decisions emerged. The views, opinions and ideas given in the interviews were abundant, but also ambiguous. Moreover, respondents disagreed about a number of critical choices to be made in the design phase and during the process of change. Based on the interview results, we identified a number of such critical choices. We will represent these choices in the form of management dilemmas: values (or design alternatives) that are seemingly contradicting (or competing) each other (see: Quinn 1988). By doing so, both the rationality of individual responses and the contradictions between responses are incorporated. The main choices for organizational design will be described first, the choices for the implementation and change process thereafter (section 6).

Process Scope: range of tasks, comprehensive or limited? The first design choice is about the question which tasks should be transferred to a SSC. Some respondents suggested transferring only completely standardized tasks that are policy-neutral and unrelated to departments. A classic example is the salary payment. Other respondents took the view that ambition should be higher: some tasks are less policy-neutral, less standardized and more department-specific. For those tasks it's hard to determine whose performance could be more efficient and perhaps more substantive. For example, legal research efforts could be shared by several departments.

Geographical location: concentration or dispersion? SSCs can be physically concentrated whereby SSCs' staff are separated from departments and accommodated in different locations, away from the client departments. Physical concentration improves the identity of SSCs and prevents old routines from dominating the SSC. Another option is to formally organize a SSC as a separate virtual entity, but to de-concentrate its staff: they remain at the department as a SSC outpost. The advantage thereof is that the SSC employees may become more sensitive to the client's needs; but the risk is here that loyalty will not be with the SSC, but with the client department.

Relations between SSC and client: professional or involved? Closely connected with the previous issue is the question of shaping the relations between SSC and client. Some respondents advocated strictly professional relations. There must be distance between the SSC and the client and a SSC must be strictly impartial towards its clients. This will provide transparency and therefore comparability and manageability. Others pleaded a close involvement between client and SSC. The fact is that clients differ, they have distinct wishes and sometimes a distinct culture, and they may attribute a different role to management, and all this requires an intensive interaction between SSC and client. Relations that are too formal or too professional are counterproductive in such situations.

Rendering of services by a SSC: supply steering or demand steering? What must be the supply of the SSC? Some respondents pleaded total uniformity where differentiation between clients is not to be permitted. Uniformity is essential since standardization must be realized to get the benefits of scale required to cut costs: differentiation of services would pose a threat to the economies of scale. However, others pleaded differentiation. They wanted the SSC to provide tailor-made services, since cost savings will be minimal for the client after implementation of a SSC if the SSC can provide only standard services.

Based on these dilemmas we draw up a typology of two opposing 'end state' SSCs. For some respondents an ideal SSC is a *'big and compelling'* one. It is a comprehensive and geographically concentrated SSC that maximizes the opportunity to build up and share expertise. Because of this ever growing expertise the SSC can improve performance and deliver a broad portfolio of services that works as a shop for their customers.

The opposite of this big and compelling SSC is a *'small and flexible'* one. Some respondents state that small SSCs also can gain 'economies of scale'. A smaller, geographically dispersed SSC is more flexible and therefore better able to provide 'tailor made' services according to both their professional knowledge and the special requests from their clients.

An overview of these two extremes and their characteristics is shown in Table 2.

CHOICES REGARDING IMPLEMENTATION

Our respondents considered attention to the implementation process to be essential, but opinions

Table 2. Overview organizational design choices

	Big and compelling	Small and flexible
Process scope	Comprehensive range of tasks	Small range of tasks
Geography	Concentrated	Dispersed
Relation to clients	Professional	Involved
Rendering of services	Supply steering	Demand steering

diverged on how this process must be realized. The interview results gave a varied and rather diffuse picture. As with the previous section, the differences will be presented in the form of dilemmas.

Decision-making: centralized or decentralized? How to make the decisions about implementing a SSC? This is the classical dilemma of centralization versus decentralization. Many respondents prefer central decision-making, for which they gave a number of reasons. First of all, complex projects like SSCs require some central coordination. A process like the separation of policy and implementation or the realization of a common ICT infrastructure will hamper without central orchestration. A second reason is that the development of central directives makes commitment of the top visible. Many respondents find commitment and clearness about objectives and consequences essential for a successful implementation of a SSC.

An important argument for decentralization is the need for support of the user organizations. Without this support, the implementation process will drag on and the result will be disappointing. Support can be gained by making decision-making participatory, in this way ensuring involvement. Another argument for decentralization is the impossibility for the central management to oversee the whole organization, including all different environments. So, according to some respondents, a certain degree of decentralization is necessary to adapt the SSC concept to the conditions at a lower level.

Implementation: radical or gradual? The second dilemma is about the pace of implementation. Where some interviewees advocated a one-time, dramatic change, others favored a gradual introduction. Usually, the one-time strategy of change is goal-oriented: the ideal SSC is delineated on paper and implemented in practice as quickly as possible. This radical change has the advantage that those concerned get a clear picture of the form and way of implementation in advance. The second strategy is a gradual implementation which allows parties to regularly adjust the design to the specific organization. This has the advantage that objections can be handled and overcome during all stages of the implementation project, with room for negotiation and accommodation.

Respondents mentioned various forms of gradual implementation: 1) start with assigning a number of services, especially policy-neutral services, to a SSC and subsequently extend the package of activities, 2) start with a flexible interpretation of principles and subsequently tighten the rules. For example, one can initially allow a voluntary usage of the services from the SSC based with a low tariff to stimulate adoption, followed later with forced supply in favor of the SSC. 3) Start with giving the Service Level Agreements a 'soft status', using an SLA as a guideline, and give it more binding force in the course of time.

Timing: conditional implementation or 'over the wall-engineering'? A number of respondents reasoned that 'the house must be in order' before a SSC can be successfully implemented. Processes must first be mapped out and the ICT infrastructure must be standardized. Only if this is in order one can take a well-considered decision about which processes must be assigned to the SSC.

However, others held a different opinion and think one should not wait until such complex standardization processes have taken place. They trust that standardization can be a result of the implementation of a SSC. Only when the SSC is a fact, it will be in the interest of many parties to fine-tune processes, and the process of change will encounter less resistance and therefore pass more quickly and smoothly.

Management of expectations: open or closed attitude? The key question is what kind of expectations must the organization create in its environment? This is especially relevant for large public SSC-projects as the one under study. By creating high expectations, the organization opens itself to the environment. The advantage of this is that the organization commits itself and, possibly, that the environment will generate valuable knowledge and ideas. Yet an open attitude towards the environment also involves risks, such as undesired media and government interventions. The fear of running such risks can easily lead to the decision to adopt a less open approach towards the environment and to try a low-profile implementation of the changes.

The interviewee responses represent two schools of thought, as can be found in literature (Lindblom 1959, Cohen c.s. 1972, De Bruijn c.s. 2002). The first advocates implementation *as a project*. The rationale behind this approach is that the right time window to introduce a SSC is *now*, and that if not promptly implemented, one would miss the opportunity. Many respondents liked this idea of a top-down approach: "maintain the stated objectives and make as few concessions as possible". They prefer "a tough approach from the very highest level", after the example of the English Cabinet's Office. The radical implementation implies a blueprint with which one gives little opportunities to potential opponents to frustrate the implementation.

The second school adheres to a *process-oriented* approach in change management. Here the idea is that implementation should follow a more gradual pattern, with the participation of as many stakeholders as possible, because stakeholders are allowed to put in their conditions in the process. The process is incremental, so shortcomings of these SSCs will be recognized during the process, and the stakeholders can be invited to bring in suggestions how to remove these. In a sense, the 'order in the house' will get more attention. A 'point of no return', such as an irrevocable administrative decision, is not created. Moreover, this approach creates room to get support for SSCs. Many interviewees considered this support essential. The typical expressions often used by interviewees were: "Go with the flow", "organic process of organization development", "Whatever you do, don't exert pressure" and "Create an evolutionary process as a result of a shared problem'.

Table 3 summarizes the dilemmas about decision-making and implementation, grouped as two distinct yet consistent approaches.

FUTURE TRENDS: INTEGRATIVE STRATEGIES

The sharing of services requires considerable design choices and has a long term impact on

Table 3. Decision-making and implementation choices

	As a project	As a process
Decision-making	Central	Decentral
Implementation	Radical	Gradual
Timing	'Over the wall engineering'	Conditional implementation
Management of expectations	Closed	Open

organizations. The analysis shows that there seems to be no best way to introduce SSCs. Both the manager and the it-expert cannot claim a certain way to successful introduction. The transformation process, as an interaction process between managers, experts and users determines the outcomes. Therefore we expect that the development of integrative transformations is necessary for creating a sound design and commitment at the same time. Our main question was how to guarantee the quality of organizational design of a SSC and generate sufficient support and commitment for it at the same time. Of course the answer to this question largely depends on the specific organization. We investigated a case study of a large interdepartmental project regarding secondary services. The SSC of Human Resource Management at the Dutch central government organization. From the interviews we have compiled a number of scenarios regarding the decision-making, timing, organization and the implementation of a SSC in government agencies. By contrasting these scenarios, each of course with their own pros and cons, two main implementation strategies can be formulated: the *Big Bang* (a 'big and compelling' SSC implemented as a project) and the *soft pressure* (a small and flexible SSC implemented as a process).

Strategy 1: *Big Bang (a big and compelling design, implementation as a project)*

A large-scale SSC is set up at once. This prevents resistance from getting a chance as it creates an accomplished fact. Departments will then admit that the SSC is a fact of life. As it was created as an impressive organization with many departments as clients, there is an incentive for these departments to commit themselves to the SSC and to make it a success. Hence a large SSC creates its own 'countervailing powers' and has constant powers that counter the risks of SSCs.

However, this strategy also carries a great risk factor. As the SSC is realized in a short time, problems become evident only afterwards. Then the SSC belongs to nobody except to the initiator, who must do some hard labor to create a new commitment. Hence there is the risk of underperformance when problems occur.

Strategy 2: *Soft Pressure (a small and flexible design; implementation as a process)*

In this strategy, implementation is a process in which the departments are involved. Support of the departments for the SSC is considered essential for ensuring its quality. During the process, there is the opportunity to learn (for example about the optimal arrangement or the degree of standardization), which eventually will result in a SSC with more chance of success. More SSCs will develop creating room for departments to choose their own SSC, and departments will feel it as if they are the owner of a SSC. This ownership is essential, for potential problems are then shared problems. Implementation should run 'as a matter of course', but this is only possible when the above-mentioned support, the learning and the ownership is addressed. This strategy carries an underperformance risk. The process may proceed slowly which increases the chance of resistance. This resistance may make the process vulnerable, and the change process may get bogged down.

These two strategies can be viewed as extremes and will seldom be used successfully in their pure shapes. However, the question is: how to use the potential advantages of these strategies and minimize the risks of underperformance at the same time? The answer lies in the capability to combine both strategies cleverly. The manner in which this combination is to be realized depends strongly on the circumstances of the project, such as the stage it is in, relevant power centers and the administrative context. Below we describe 4 of these combinations.

Combination 1: *Decision-making as soft pressure, realization as a Big Bang*

Decision-making is designed as a process and realization takes place as a project. Decision-making will start as an incremental process. In this stage of decision-making, the form of the SSC is still uncertain. When the SSC begins to take shape, the time of substantive central steering has come. The principles about which there was relatively high consensus now become elements in a centrally drawn-up blueprint, which is subsequently imposed and implemented. The advantage of this combination is that the project remains contained since it is still a blueprint. Moreover, in this case a 'point of no return' is also created, with more chance of support than the Big Bang strategy in its pure shape. Yet the moment of central intervention is the critical point. An interactive process creates many expectations. The main risk is that if too few expectations are met, this combination may raise serious resistance instead of taking it away.

Combination 2: *Decision-making as a Big Bang, realization as soft pressure*

The SSC is designed and imposed centrally. Moreover, it is a 'grand and compelling' SSC. Yet the realized principles are initially not strictly enforced: the departments and the SSC are given some room to bend the design to their will. For instance, the SSC can slightly adjust its own organization and procedures, and can further determine its range of duties in consultation with departments. There may be a need and room for tailor-made services. The advantage of this combination is the ability to convert resistance into action during the realization. The precondition is that the shared goal remains more attractive than individual goals. However, there is the difficult question about management: what degree of liberty can be allowed without seriously affecting the rationale of SSCs?

Combination 3: *Big Bang as the story, soft pressure as the practice*

Officially, the SSC is designed and imposed centrally. Once again it is a 'big and compelling' SSC, but practically, the design is the result of fine-tuning to and between departments. Moreover, there is room to readjust the design during the implementation. This combination is especially useful in a dynamic environment. In politics and media, the 'Big Bang-language' is better understood than the language of long-term processes. It is, after all, a clear design and decisive realization. Thus, Big Bang as a story lends legitimacy to the processes that actually take place.

Combination 4: *A momentum for a Big Bang*

This combination is a supplement to the strategy of soft pressure, but it puts more emphasis on the temporal component. The possibility of central intervention is intentionally kept open, for instance when the decision-making process drags on for too long (the process as a reason) or when SSCs threaten to disintegrate (a substantive reason). Hence the strategy of soft pressure is used 'in the shadow of hierarchy': all parties realize that central intervention is one of the possibilities. Making use of a momentum for central intervention requires commitment. Indeed, exact knowledge of the course of the process and of the interests currently at stake is indispensable for determining this momentum.

The quest towards sharing services has just been started and has been limited to easy-to-standardize services. In the future, the scope might be expanded and public agencies might share complete back-office functions and processes. This will even put more emphasis on effective transformation strategies.

CONCLUSION

The quest towards shared service centers has just started and there remain many research questions to be solved. In this chapter we explored the various perceptions on SSCs using interviews and a validation workshop. We found that a great variety of SSC-concepts exists. There is a variety of opinions about what makes up a SSC and which models fit best within the public administration. It is difficult to align these concepts with different organizational parts of government services. There is no agreement in literature on what characteristics make up a shared service arrangement. There is consensus about that it concerns an internal arrangement providing services to many users. There is some consensus among interviewees about some of the potential advantages of SSCs, including reduction of costs and better service quality. The same respondents, however, also mentioned the risks of monopolistic behavior and bureaucracy. This might result into the failure and discontinuation of the implementation project. A great variety of relevant managerial and technical aspects have been mentioned by our respondents. Some of these aspects are conditional. Some conditions, like a common information architecture have been mentioned manifold, but have not been worked out very well. Therefore these conditions might be sources of unexpected complications. The respondents vary in their perceptions of how these critical aspects should be tackled.

During the decision-making and implementation process many trade-offs need to be made which requires a carefully designed transformation strategy. We have formulated two extreme change management strategies derived from the perceptions about both the design and the implementation of SSCs: the 'Big Bang'- strategy using a project managerial style to introduce a large and formalized SSC and the 'Soft Pressure'- strategy combining an adaptive, decentralized organizational design with a process managerial approach. Of course it is very hard to predict which strategy will be effective. This will depend on many factors, like the specific characteristics of the organization and its environment, the people involved, and the type of SSCs. Our results indicate that making a SSC tailor-made requires a careful thought-out analysis and strategy. The critical choices and strategies formulated in this chapter should be addressed in these strategies.

Our research was focused on assessing opinions to derive critical design choices and change management strategies. Now that governments are progressing with the implementation of SSCs, further empirical research should investigate the effectiveness of change management strategies and the implications of organizational design and implementation decisions.

REFERENCES

Accenture. (2006). Shared Services: Government shared services model for high performance. Retrieved June 23, 2006, from http://www.accenture.com/Global/Services/By_Industry/Government/R_and_I/DrivingServices.htm.

Axelrod, R. (2006). *The evolution of cooperation*. New York: Perseus Books Group.

Bergeron, B. (2003). *Essentials of shared services*. New York: John Wiley & Sons.

Bruijn, J. A. d., & Heuvelhof, E. F. t. (2000). *Networks and decision making*. Utrecht, The Netherlands: Lemma.

Chisholm, D. (1989). *Coordination without hierarchy*. Berkeley, CA: University of California Press.

de Bruijn, J. A., ten Heuvelhof, E. F., & in 't Veld, R. J. (2002). *Process management: Why project management fails in complex decision making processes*. Boston: Kluwer Academic Publishers.

de Bruijn, J. A., Wagenaar, R. W., van der Voort, H. G., & van Wendel de Joode, R. (2004). *Shared services in de overheid*. Report Atos KPMG.

Grant, G., McKnight, S., Uruthirapathy, A., & Brown, A. (2007). Designing governance for shared service organizations in the public service. *Government Information Quarterly, 24*, 522-538.

Hofstadter, D. R. (1983). Computer tournaments of the prisoner's dilemma suggest how cooperation evolve. *Scientific American, 248*(5), 14-23.

Jaffee, D. (2001). *Organization theory, tension, and change*. Singapore: McGraw-Hill International Edition.

Janssen, M., & Joha, A. (2006). Motives for establishing shared service centers in public administrations. *International Journal of Information Management, 26*(2), 102-116.

Janssen, M., Joha, A., & Weerakkody, V. (2007). Exploring relationships of shared service arrangements in local government. *Transforming Government: People, Process, & Policy, 1*(3), 271-284.

Kenis, P., & Schneider, V. (1991). Policy networks and policy analysis: Scrutinizing a new analytical toolbox. In B. Marin & R. Mayntz (Eds.), *Policy networks, empirical evidence and theoretical considerations* (pp. 26-59). Frankfurt am Main, Germany: Campus Verlag.

March, J. G. (1989). *Decisions and organizations*. Oxford, UK: Blackwell Publishers.

Mintzberg, H. (1983). *Structure in fives: Designing effective organizations*. Englewood Cliffs, NJ: Prentice Hall.

Morgan, G. (1986). *Images of organizations*. London: Sage.

Powell, W. (1990). Neither market nor hierarchy: Network forms of organization. In B. M. Staw & L. L. Cummings (Eds.), *Research in organization behavior*. Greenwich, CT: JAI Press.

Singh, P. J., & Craike, A. (2008). Shared services: towards a more holistic conceptual definition. *International Journal of Business Information Systems, 3*(3), 217-230.

Strikwerda. (2005). *Shared service centers. Van kostenbesparing naar waardecreatie*. Assen, The Netherlands: Van Gorcum-Stichting Management Studies.

Teisman, G. R. (1992). *Complexe besluitvorming: Een pluricentrisch perspectief op besluitvorming over ruimtelijke investeringen*. Den Haag, The Netherlands: Vuga.

Ulbrich, F. (2006). Improving shared service implementation: Adopting lessons from the BPR movement. *Business Process Management Journal, 12*(2), 191-205.

Wagenaar, R. W., Matthijsse, R., Bruijn, J. d., Voort, H. v. d., & Wendel de Joode, R. v. (2006). Implementation of shared service centres in public administration: Dilemmas and trade-offs. In *Information and Communication Technology and Public Innovation* (Vol. 12, pp. 141-158). Amsterdam: IOS Press.

KEY TERMS

Big Bang: A transformation strategy in which an ambitious organizational design is implemented top down.

Implementation: The road to the organizational design.

Network Theory: A theory concerning the involvement of multiple stakeholders by the creation and retention(!) of support for major changes in the interorganizational networks.

Organizational Design: The purposed end-state of the total organization after the transformation process.

Shared Service: Shared services are services that are shared by multiple users and provided by one service provider.

Shared Service Centers: Semi- autonomous organizational entity in which supportive functions have been concentrated.

Service Level Agreements: An agreement between two or more parties concerning the delivery of IT-services.

Soft Pressure: A transformation strategy in which a pragmatic organizational design is implemented bottom up.

Transformation Process: The change from the current situation to the achievement of the implementation of a shared services model.

Chapter IV
Citizens, Not Consumers

Cory Allen Heidelberger
Dakota State University, USA

ABSTRACT

E-government and t-government programs too often see government as service provider and citizens as customers. T-government should view government and citizens as one decision-making entity. This chapter (1) critiques the citizen-as-consumer perspective as a cause of citizen alienation, (2) contributes a theoretical model based on citizen participation to guide development of t-government systems to act as social decision support systems, (3) highlights examples of e-government systems that encourage citizen participation, (4) sketches one possible t-government implementation of the model, and (5) addresses challenges the model and systems based on it may face.

INTRODUCTION

The idea of reengineering through technology is critical. We didn't want to automate the old, worn processes of government. Information technology (IT) was and is the great enabler for reinvention. It allows us to rethink, in fundamental ways, how people work and how we serve customers.

—*U.S. Vice President Al Gore, 1997*

During the 1990s, Vice President Gore promoted the expansion of e-government capabilities and the Internet in general. Like many public officials, he recognized the potential of the Internet to transform the way government serves its citizens.

As Vice President Gore introduced the 1997 report on the Access America Initiatives to reinvent government, he used language that indicated another transformation, a conceptual transformation in the view of citizens. Twice in this 1200-word document on e-government, Gore

(1997) refers to the *customers* e-government will serve. Nowhere in this opening statement does the word *citizens* appear.

Vice President Gore did not invent the concept of viewing citizens as customers. He was not the first nor the last government official to apply the language and paradigm of e-business to e-government. Gore's statement is but one instance of a perspective very common among government officials, IT professionals, and researchers: that e-government is just a subset of e-business.

This chapter will identify the prevailing misconception in e-government programs of citizens as mere consumers of services provided by government and the harm that incomplete conception can do. This chapter will explain that t-government—application of information systems to support all functions of government, including the function of citizens as participants—should move away from that incomplete conception to a genuinely citizen-centered social decision support model. Applying the emancipatory and participatory ideals of neohumanism to e-government can form the axiological basis for the creation and implementation of web-based computer-mediated communication systems in regional and nationwide parliaments and legislatures connecting legislators, citizens, lobbyists, and organizations in social decision support systems (SDSS). Such a paradigm shift will truly transform e-government by increasing government transparency, citizen participation, and citizen sense of "ownership" of government information and decisions.

PROBLEM: E-GOVERNMENT AS PROVIDER–CLIENT RELATIONSHIP

Foundational Perspective: E-Government as a Subset of E-Business

In a democracy, the government is "us." However, that conception of government appears largely absent from the literature and practice of e-government. When determining how to incorporate information systems into government, researchers and policymakers alike apply the template of e-business. They view government and citizens as separate entities: the government is the service provider, and citizens are customers. E-government literature portrays citizens not as participants in government but as consumers of government services.

The citizen-as-consumer mindset starts in e-government's pedigree as an offshoot of e-business. The Americas' Conference on Information Systems (AMCIS) 2008 e-government mini-track is listed under the E-business/E-commerce track. The mini-track description defines e-government as follows (italics added here and in all subsequent quotes to highlight the e-business, citizen-as-consumer mindset):

> *E-Government is an emerging paradigm to deliver government services to citizens, businesses, and other stakeholders through the use of Internet and information and communication technologies (ICTs). E-Government is an extension of e-business applications to the public sector. Increased adoption and application of e-Government across countries is being propelled by its potential to offer not only a convenient service to citizens but also related benefits such as reduced transaction costs and enhanced operational efficiency* (AMCIS, 2008)

This treatment of e-government as a subset of e-business arises from various strands of business thinking applied to efforts to improve government. In the 1960s and 1970s, the technocratic approach to government fostered a "service-delivery" perspective that often had the effect of "leaving democratic participation as an afterthought" (Keating, 1995, p. 128). The 1980s and 1990s brought an emphasis at many levels of government in many countries on market solutions, on privatizing various services and making government compete (Ryan, 2001). This movement was based on the idea that government could improve its performance by acting like business. Further reinforcing this notion was the New Public Management (NPM) movement. Given impetus by Osborne and Gaebler (1992) in their book *Reinventing Government: How the Entrepreneurial Spirit Is Transforming the Public Sector*, NPM gained popularity across Western democracies and fostered a focus in government on "market operations and management of customer service" (Butler & Collins, 2004, p. 135).

Resulting Perspective: Citizens as Consumers

Thinking of e-government as e-business has led e-government researchers to restrict their attention to government in its role as service provider and, accordingly, citizens in their role as consumers. The citizen-as-consumer paradigm is evidenced in the various taxonomies generated by e-government literature. Researchers frequently break down e-government into three types of relationships: government to citizen (G2C), government to business (G2B), and government to government (G2G) (see, for example, Affisco & Soliman, 2006; Reddick, 2004; Chen, 2003; Makolm, 2002; Fountain, 2001). "Gartner's Four Phases of E-Government" model adds government to employee (G2E) to this categorization (Baum & DiMaio, 2000), although such functions may be viewed as an element of G2G [5]. Some researchers note the US Office of Management and Budget's separate categorization of internal efficiency and effectiveness (IEE) measures (Belanger & Hiller, 2006), but these measures may be viewed as implicit aspects of G2C, G2B, and particularly G2G (Lee et al., 2005). The G2C-G2B-G2G categorization of e-government applications appears to be the most conventional, working its way even into basic IS textbooks (Turban et al., 2005, p. 781).

Tellingly absent from this conventional categorization of what e-government does is a category that recognizes the existence of or need for a citizen-to-government (C2G) set of functions. The C2G categorization is out there (Fang, 2002), but it appears in only a lesser cited1 seventh—136 out of 945—of the research documents produced in a Google Scholar search of "egovernment G2C G2B G2G" (as of April 28, 2008).

G2C taxonomies that do not include C2G may be criticized for the simple use of the word *to*, which implies a one-way relationship. Challenging this prevailing formulation, Belanger and Hiller (2006) use the preposition *with* in their five-part categorization of e-government types. They create two categories of government relationship *with* citizens, in service provision and in political process. With the latter category, Belanger and Hiller (2006) acknowledge that "the relationship between the government and its citizens as part of the democratic process... is perhaps the most essential relationship between a government and any entity" (p. 50).

If the political-process relationship is "the most essential" carried out by government, evolutionary models of e-government do not appear to reflect it. At best, e-government researchers acknowledge the importance of citizen participation in the political process, but then often shove that function to the far end of their e-government models as an advanced stage to be reached much later. Gartner's Four Phases (Baum & DiMaio, 2000) progresses from web presence, to interaction, to transaction, and ultimately transformation. An alternative model, from Balutis, envisions e-government evolving from disseminating information, to providing forms, to facilitating end-to-end electronic transactions, to ultimately "transforming government... to provide seamless services transparent to citizens" (Balutis, 2001). A third four-stage model, from Layne and Lee, establishes a progression from cataloguing, to supporting transactions, to integrating vertically and finally horizontally (Layne & Lee, 2001). Each of these models primarily views government and citizens as separate entities, with government primarily a producer of services and information and citizens merely consumers, at least in the initial stages. Discussion of the "essential" political process and citizen participation does not appear in either the Baum and DiMaio or the Balutis model until the fourth transformational stage. Even in that ultimate stage, both models focus on the "seamless" and "single-point" provision of services (Affisco & Soliman, 2006, p. 15). The Layne and Lee model acknowledges the potential for the second stage to promote citizen interaction with officials and active participation in public hearings; however, Layne and Lee (2001) remain locked in the language of "citizen-customers" (p. 129) for whom e-government's ultimate goal is to provide "one-stop shopping" (p. 124, 125).

If e-government research does occasionally recognize the C2G (or, perhaps following Belanger and Hiller [2006], C*with*G) relationship and the role of citizens as participants in the social decision-making process, e-government implementations persist in treating citizens almost exclusively as customers. An analysis of the 2002 International City/County Management Association Electronic Government survey found little movement beyond the information dissemination stage (Reddick, 2004).

A survey of e-government practices worldwide (Lee et al., 2005) finds that "E-government is mainly concerned with providing quality public services and value-added information to citizens," and acknowledges that "e-government serves a similar purpose to customer relationship management (CRM) in the business world" (pp. 99–100). Belanger and Hiller (2006), who characterize citizen participation as the most advanced stage of e-government, find very few governments using information systems to support this most vital relationship.

This e-government–as–e-business mindset reveals itself in the language chosen by the implementing government agencies at all levels. The 2002 "E-Government Strategy" published by the United States Office of Management and Budget bears the subtitle "Simplified Delivery of Services to Citizens" (E-Government Task Force, 2002). The plan business case aims to "*improve customer service*," "*generate several billion dollars in savings by reducing operating inefficiencies, redundant spending and excessive paperwork,*" and "*provide service to citizens*" (E-Government Task Force, 2002, p. 2). The document uses the term "citizen-centered" eleven times but makes no mention of initiatives that would move citizens from the receiving end of the government service pipeline to the genuine center of government decision-making.

In the United Kingdom, which originated the term *transformational government*, the service provider–client approach to e-government remains dominant. While touting his government's "bold strategy" to "transform" e-government, Prime Minister Blair still refers to the *services* the UK will *provide* to its *customers* (Blair, 2007). The farthest the UK t-government plan appears to venture into genuine citizen participation is permitting its "customers" to participate in designing some services (Chief Information Officer Council, 2007).

On a smaller scale, the South Dakota Bureau of Information and Telecommunications describes *government* itself as a consumer product: "By building a secure infrastructure *to serve their clients*, the state of South Dakota *provides* more responsive and *efficient government to its citizens*" (Newman, 2003). The Bureau goes on to describe the Service Direct e-government initiative as a portal "to serve as *one-stop shopping*" for South Dakota households and businesses seeking state forms (Newman, 2003). Absent from this document is any conception of the citizen as an equal participant in government activities.

Even at the county and city level, where government is closest to citizens, implementing agencies pursue policies and systems that cast citizens as consumers. Analyzing the 2000 and 2002 International City/County Management Association Electronic Government surveys along with data from 37 focus groups consisting of American city and county officials, Norris (2005) identified more evidence of the customer-service mindset that belies the words typically used to describe e-government goals:

> ...[P]*articipants continually spoke of citizen-centricness as a central purpose and important outcome of e-government. E-government, in their view, is* ***all about*** *benefitting citizens by* ***putting governmental services and information on the web*** *for them in ways that they could* ***easily access and use*** *(emphasis added; p. 3).*

Norris (2005) appears to find a greater focus among government officials on automating and improving efficiency of existing services and internal operations than increased participatory engagement with citizens. One respondent sees the biggest "bang for the buck" coming from "not the public web site, but the Intranet" (p. 3).

Citizens as Consumers: So What?

What harm is done by treating citizens as customers and, more broadly, e-government as the public-sector version of e-business? Butler and Collins (2004) cite retorts like "How could anyone not want better service?" (p. 140) and "We should run government like a business" (p. 143). Butler and Collins note that such common-sense assessments of e-business approaches to e-government are hard to oppose.

Indeed, e-government activities based on the e-business mindset do produce some positive outcomes. The American Consumer Satisfaction Index (ACSI) measures customer perceptions of performance of a variety of private and public institutions on a 100-point scale. The ACSI 2007 survey found that while the United States federal government in general earned a customer satisfaction rating of 67.8, federal e-government services in the U.S. scored higher, at 73.4. This score is just shy of the 74.0 rating earned by all private sector services combined (Fornell, 2007). We might conclude from these scores that focusing on businesslike customer service has allowed the federal government to create online environments where citizens feel they receive better service than in traditional government interactions. And what complaint can citizens have if being treated like customers by their governments means they can get their tax refunds, forms, and drivers licenses more quickly?

Passive Citizens, Elitist Government

If such services were all that government was about, then the citizen-as-customer model would suffice. But there is much more to government than processing forms, handing out checks, and keeping customers happy. Modeling e-government after e-business may produce some benefits, but by itself, e-business provides insufficient support for the central function of government, the active participation of citizens in directing the affairs of their own communities.

The purpose of critical research is to identify and eliminate causes of alienation and domination in the status quo (Myers, 1997). The citizen-as-consumer paradigm rests on language and goals that reinforce alienation and hierarchy and do harm to democratic government. Butler and Collins (2004) contend that "Market-driven managerialism," the approach to government represented by New Public Management, "is based primarily on happy customers rather than involved citizens" (p. 144). Ryan (2001) identifies the danger in that view: treating citizens as consumers to be kept happy redefines the government–citizen relationship as a "passive commercial transaction rather than an interactive political engagement" (p. 105). Viewing citizens as consumers goes hand in hand with viewing the government as a producer. That conceptual separation creates a sense of hierarchy; as Ryan (2001) puts it, "the language of producers and consumers contributes to notions of elitist government" (p. 107). Butler and Collins (2004) also recognize the potential for e-government initiatives focused on customer service delivery to create a "separation of politics and administration" (p. 136).

Focusing on citizens merely as consumers may also weaken the sense of community among e-government users. E-government initiatives focused on customer satisfaction may undermine citizens' sense of social responsibilities and duties. Government must be "guided by objective policies aimed at meeting social rather than personal needs" (Humphreys, 1998, p. 19; quoted in Butler & Collins, 2004, p. 142). E-government should not ignore effective customer service, but an e-government that looks at citizens only as customers perpetuates a mindset inimical to community and democratic spirit.

Customer Satisfaction: An Inadequate Measure

Applying e-business principles to e-government also poses practical methodological difficulties. Consider the use of the American Customer Satisfaction Index methodology to determine the effectiveness of e-government (see Figure 1).

Under the ACSI model, one of the drivers of customer satisfaction is perceived value, "a measure of value relative to price paid" (ACSI, 2006). In a commercial transaction, perceived value is relatively straightforward: a customer can weigh the utility of specific goods and services against the purchase price. Government services, however, rarely come with an upfront price tag. When citizens seek information from a government website, how are citizens to calculate the varying fractions of their sales tax, property tax, income tax, speeding tickets, and other payments to the government that contributed to the creation of that website? How do they determine the actual price they are paying for the person-hours a staffer in the Department of Motor Vehicles takes to respond to an e-mail request or install software that will generate an automated request? Perceived value makes more mathematical sense in the marketplace than the courthouse. Perceived value in the business sense becomes even more intractable when we try to evaluate citizen-government interactions that involve not simple transactions for which a citizen must pay some price but the exercising of basic democratic rights like participation in the political process.

The ACSI incorporates another problematic element in its model: customer loyalty. The ACSI defines customer loyalty as follows:

Customer loyalty is a combination of the customer's professed likelihood to repurchase from the same supplier in the future, and the likelihood

Figure 1. American Customer Satisfaction Index methodology (©2008 American Customer Satisfaction Index/University of Michigan. Used with permission.)

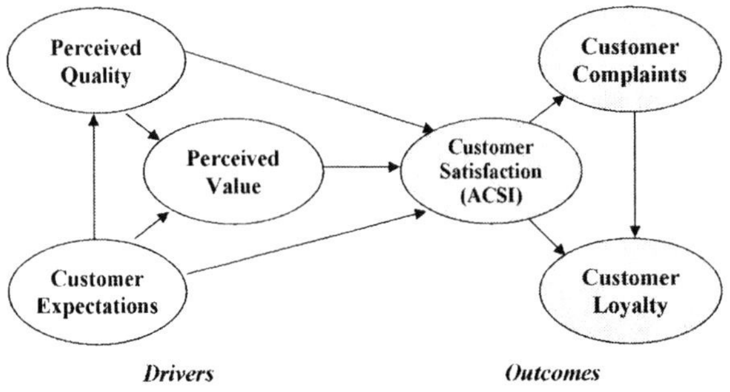

to purchase a company's products or services at various price points (price tolerance). Customer loyalty is the critical component of the model as it stands as a proxy for profitability. (ACSI, 2006)

Indeed, in the business world, customer loyalty is an excellent measure of performance. If customers walk away from a transaction and never come back, that business has clearly done something wrong.

Customer loyalty does not translate so clearly to e-government. If citizens are dissatisfied with the quality of service they receive when they apply to their county zoning officer for a building permit, they cannot walk out of the courthouse or log out of the county website and apply for a building permit in the next county. If British citizens are dissatisfied with Parliament's t-government efforts, they cannot send their taxes to the French instead. Very few citizens "comparison shop" among governments and then emigrate to obtain better government services.

Even if we view customer loyalty in the e-government context as a simple measure of a citizen's willingness to use a government website again (Stowers, 2004), the concept remains an incomplete reflection of its marketplace counterpart. A citizen who wants to buy a fishing license may apply through the state Game, Fish, and Parks website, or she may apply in person at the GF&P office; either way, she still has to deal with the same service provider. A citizen who wants to buy a book may order online through BarnesandNoble.com, she may walk into a Barnes and Noble store, or she may buy from dozens of other online and brick-and-mortar vendors. Nowhere do citizens have the sort of choice in government services that allows them to exercise or switch customer loyalty as they can in the commercial sector.

An e-business paradigm that relies on market constructs like customer loyalty, competition, and perceived value to gauge its success can capture some but not all of the aspects of the citizen-government relationship. We citizens are consumers of government information, documents, and services, but we are also producers of information, ideas, and political positions. Our relationship with government has elements of power, legitimacy, and responsibility not paralleled by any aspect of our relationship as consumers to businesses. Even the business-shareholder relationship is not as intricate as the government-citizen relationship (Klein, 2008): we are bound to our local, state, and national governments (and they to us) and to our fellow citizens by constitutional, legal, and moral obligations and rights that find no counterpart in the interactions of corporations and investors. A full understanding of the potential and purpose of e-government thus cannot restrict itself to the AMCIS (2008) definition of e-government as a subset of e-business (see Table 1).

A review of research and practice reveals the predominance of a business-world, service-provider approach to e-government. Viewing e-government as e-business reinforces and perpetuates the undemocratic misconception that government is separate from its citizens. Government officials come to see themselves as service providers. One-stop web portals may bring the government-as-service-provider closer, but

Table 1. Government and citizen roles supported by citizen-as-consumer paradigm

	Government Roles	Citizen Roles
Served by e-business, citizen-as-consumer model	• service provider • information source	• consumer of services • consumer of information
Not served by e-business, citizen-as-consumer model	• policy maker • decision maker • representative of popular will	• participant in elections • participant in legislative process

they also may make government-as-policymaker seem comparatively more distant. Citizens come to see themselves as consumers of government services rather than collaborative producers of decisions and policies. The predominant status quo approaches to e-government see only a fraction of the democratic organization and shut out a majority of stakeholders from democratic participation.

CITIZENS AS PARTICIPANTS: SYNTHESIZING A NEW-OLD PARADIGM

The idea that all of us ought to have some say in shaping government is at least as old as Greek democracy. E-government is not completely blind to that concept: it has spun off subfields that recognize and promote citizen participation: e.g., e-participation, e-democracy, and e-rulemaking. But if considerations of citizen participation are segregated to side fields while the overarching discipline continues to view citizens and consumers, the problem remains. E-government as a whole should ground its work in a truly transformational paradigm—not one centered around the misapplied concept of customer satisfaction and giving consumers what they want, but an approach focused on drawing citizens into participation and collaboration with their elected officials and public agencies. Following are the components of such a transformational paradigm for e-government.

Applying Neohumanist Ideals to E-Government

In their language of efficiency and effectiveness, the above information systems development and implementation strategies reveal an axiological basis of functionalism. The business world's drive for effective service and time- and cost-savings is relevant to government. However, functionalism forms an incomplete basis for e-government. Democracy is about more than making the trains run on time. If we value democracy, we should base the development and the goals of e-government on the participatory and emancipatory ideals of neohumanism.

Democracy demands participation. The emancipatory ideals of neohumanism lay the axiological groundwork for ensuring that social structures, including information systems, facilitate that participation. Mumford (1983) provides the seminal enunciation of the value position that "future users of computer systems at all organizational levels play a major part in the design of these systems" (ch. 1). Mumford was applying a broader democratic paradigm to the specific realm of information system development. We can both use and invert her translation of participatory ideals: we can involve citizens in the design of e-government systems, but more importantly, we should ground our e-government efforts in the idea that e-government systems, like government as a whole, should seek ways to involve citizens in the formation of the public policies that e-government systems then help to carry out. The logic of involving users in the design of a system makes as much sense in the realm of designing an office information system as it does in the broader, more important realm of creating government policy.

Hirschheim and Klein (1994) elaborate on Mumford's model, explaining that to fulfill emancipatory ideals, a social structure must make possible:

1. "individual and collective self-determination";
2. "critical self-reflection and associated self-transformation";
3. "social justice, due process, and human freedom"; and
4. "critical evaluation of claims" (pp. 87–88).

Under this paradigm, decision-making processes require emancipatory discourse, communication where the participants deceive neither themselves nor others. In other words, emancipatory discourse takes place in an environment free from distortions (Hirschheim & Klein, 1994). Among the distortions that must be removed from the discussion and development of e-government systems is the incomplete conception of citizens as mere service consumers. More broadly, e-government practitioners can work more to put information technology to work in supporting emancipatory discourse that involves all citizens as participants in the political process, not merely passive recipients of information.

Lessons from the Business Paradigm: Shifting from Vertical to Horizontal Integration

Using e-government to facilitate emancipatory discourse and citizen participation in the political process requires looking outside the e-business paradigm that casts citizens as consumers. Nonetheless, the business paradigm can provide another pillar of support for the model of participatory e-government. Businesses have pushed and been pushed by a trend from vertical to horizontal integration. Popularized by Friedman (2005), this trend has been taking place for over a decade. Barua et al. (1996) found hierarchical organization and silo-like division of business functions within firms giving way to collaboration and cross-functional teams. Outsourcing is further flattening organizational monoliths into many-tentacled creatures reaching out to far-flung partner firms and distributed work teams to achieve their goals. Information technology plays a central role in this trend, making it possible for workers, departments, and companies to create, use, organize, and share information to increase productivity and responsiveness to market conditions.

Just as information technology facilitates horizontal integration in the business world, participatory e-government can support a similar transformation in the political world. The conventional approach to e-government follows a vertical model: government provides, citizens consume. Decisions take place within the silos of the bureaucracy, with occasional, very controlled interfaces for public input such as formal hearings and annual elections. Layne and Lee (2001) speak of horizontal integration as the fourth and final stage of e-government development, though from their strictly service-provision perspective, they refer solely to horizontal integration among government agencies, not between government and the citizens. Information technology provides the means to involve citizens much more actively in the regular course of political decision-making, not simply in a flood of e-mails from activists and voters with individual complaints, but in e-government systems that can support public collaboration among citizens and between them and their elected officials. Information technology also provides the means to organize all the information generated in that collaboration into a manageable form for the ultimate legal decision makers, be they specific councils, agencies, executive officers, or the general electorate.

Social Decision Support Systems

Governments, like businesses, have complicated decisions to make, and businesses and governments alike can seek support from decision support systems (DSS). Unlike businesses, governments find their decisions further complicated by the fact that the "customers" for whom governments make decisions—i.e., *us*—are also entitled to participate in that decision-making process. DSS for government thus faces the challenge of giving information and voice to a much wider range of participants, i.e., the entire voting age population of a city, state, or nation. Turoff et al. (2002)

address this challenge with the concept of social decision support systems (SDSS), the extension of decision support systems from the scale of a single manager, project team, or firm to the scale of a community or society.

Turoff et al. (2002) do not use the term *e-government* to describe social decision support systems, but their formulation of SDSS offers a framework for the development and implementation of participatory e-government. They see information technology as a means not merely to facilitate government-to-citizen transactions but to integrate "diverse views into a growing knowledge base" and "to enhance the democratic process and truly bring people together" (p. 81). Bringing people together is not simply a matter of putting public opinion surveys and official ballots online where citizens are permitted to mark their preference among pre-determined options (Turoff et al., 2002). SDSS should involve citizens in the initial stages of decision-making, in gathering information, presenting ideas, and formulating the options that would eventually appear on legislative agendas or general election ballots.

We need not think of e-government strictly in terms of supporting the decisions of elected officials. From an SDSS perspective, the straightforward provision of information (e.g. census and economic data, hearing schedules) becomes an exercise in supporting the decisions of other society members, i.e., citizens. Even if the raw act of information provision still looks the same (e.g., a website prompting users to "Click here for city sales tax revenue for the last 12 months"), e-government developers should be ever mindful that they are creating tools for fellow participants in decisions that affect the community, not merely external agents.

E-Government Perspective for Researchers and Developers

Creating a participatory e-government system to support social-scale decision-making poses all sorts of practical challenges, many of which will be unique to the communities and cultures for which such systems may be designed. E-government researchers and developers also face an important methodological challenge. Venturing into participatory e-government means engaging with perhaps the richest and most important nexus of all the elements of information systems: information technology, people, and institutions. To fully understand the purpose and functioning parameters of a participatory e-government system, researchers and developers must "engage in interdisciplinary experimentation" informed by political scientists, sociologists, public management specialists, and other experts in political and social affairs (Rehg et al., 2005, p. 205).

This interdisciplinary approach also calls for the incorporation of researchers' and developers' own experiences in their political systems to build better e-government systems. They must remind themselves regularly that the end users they serve are not a separate clientele or population, but citizens—*us*. Where an e-government system is designed to foster public discourse, researchers must participate in that system themselves (Rehg et al., 2005). Political discourse can only be fully understood from context, and that means talking to the participants, on their terms, in the forum where that discourse takes place. Truly transformative e-government research will be as interdisciplinary and participatory as the discourse it is meant to facilitate.

Figure 2 shows these elements in a unified paradigm for researchers and developers of transformative e-government. To implement t-government applications, developers should bring together the principles of neohumanism, the lessons of horizontal integration, and the goals of social decision support systems. Viewing this combination of elements through the lenses of interdisciplinary and participatory research will transform e-government from a conventional service-provider–consumer relationship to a fuller, more democratic citizen–government relationship.

Figure 2. Theoretical model for transformative e-government

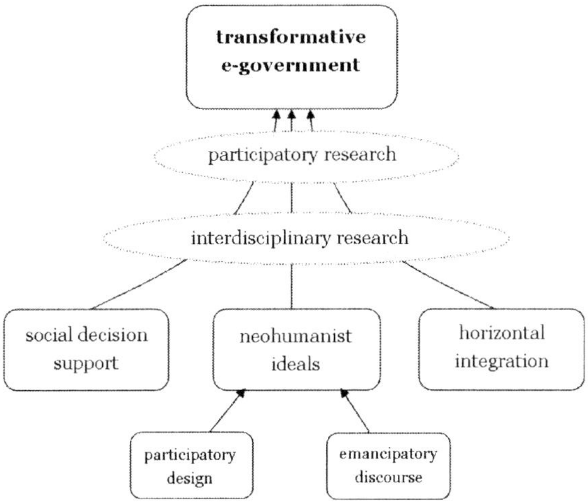

IMPLEMENTATION: PUTTING PARTICIPATORY E-GOVERNMENT TO WORK

Most official e-government initiatives follow the e-business paradigm and view citizens as consumers. Still, various online projects—some governmental, some from private or volunteer organizations—embody at least some of the participatory principles outlined in the above research and offer at least glimpses of what transformative e-government could do.

South Dakota Horizons

South Dakota Horizons is a public-private partnership between the South Dakota State University Cooperative Extension Service and the Northwest Area Foundation South Dakota Horizons, 2008). SD Horizons currently supports leadership training and community revitalization in 21 small rural towns in South Dakota. SD Horizons maintains a central blog for the parent organization and establishes separate blogs for each of the participating communities. SD Horizons coordinators and participating residents in each community use the blogs for basic informational purposes, such as announcing meetings and paperwork deadlines. They also use the community blogs to archive notes and resources from local meetings.

Another purpose of the community blogs is to encourage information flow among the participating South Dakota communities, some of which are over 600 kilometers apart (South Dakota Horizons–Fruechte, 2007). This knowledge sharing is as important among communities as within communities. SD Horizons encourages its local participants to use the blogs for active public discourse, to talk about what they see happening in their communities so they can learn from each other. The blogs are open for anyone to read and comment on; local blog administrators can also give anyone in their towns permission to post and edit articles. To give all residents an opportunity to interact online, SD Horizons encourages communities to hold monthly blog nights at schools and libraries with Internet access (South Dakota Horizons–Jacobs, 2007).

While technically not e-government, these community blogs offer the opportunity for public discourse among not just leaders but all community members. It can put all citizens on an equal participatory footing as consumers and creators of information. Citizens can discuss their plans for and progress toward improving their communities. That discourse also persists as a public record, available to any citizen for review and comment. That combination of discourse and memory can be useful in supporting participatory e-government.

OpenCongress.org

OpenCongress.org is a private project started in 2007 by the Sunlight Foundation and the Participatory Politics Foundation. It describes itself as "a free, open-source, non-profit, and non-partisan web resource with a mission to make Congress more transparent and to encourage civic engagement" (OpenCongress.org, 2008). A more vivid description (Miller, 2007) compares Open

Congress to Thomas, the official Web portal of the United States Congress: "Think of it as a user-friendly Thomas, on steroids." The website aggregates information about the members and pending legislation of the United States Congress. The site offers pages for each piece of legislation before the Congress, complete with links to related news and blog stories, an online poll, a comments page, and bill status widget that users can download to their own webpages to monitor bills that interest them. The Open Congress blog features one writer who offers regular commentary on various Congressional issues. Blog posts are open for public comment, and the blog accepts and posts tips from readers about news items of interest.

Like the Horizons community blogs, Open Congress fosters public discourse, in this case on a nationwide scale on official government activities. It couples information provision with citizen commentary. Creating and maintaining such a website is a valuable public service and an admirable volunteer effort in the absence of a comparable official participatory e-government effort. However, as an unofficial e-government project, Open Congress perhaps suffers a disadvantage in drawing users. As a private organization, it is not accountable to citizens the way government is. Citizens may also seek the official "brand" of the government agency they are dealing with for assurance that they are dealing with an "authentic" government website (Department of Information Resources, 2000) and that their voices will be heard.

Pandemic Flu Blog

The US Department of Health and Human Services used a blog to conduct a five-week forum open to health care practitioners and the general public to discuss pandemic preparedness. This blog, in conjunction with a one-day conference, precipitated a lively discussion among participants, including government officials. HHS Secretary Leavitt acknowledges the "passion" of the participants and indicates that his experience with this form of e-government "created an appetite for more" (Leavitt, 2007). One participant, though, warns that this model of citizen participation will produce plans that are "fatally flawed (figuratively and literally)" if the government focuses solely on making citizens "feel like we are 'in the loop' without actually placing us 'in the loop'" (Jensen, 2007). Emancipatory discourse only takes place when there is no deception, when citizen–legislator discourse is not merely a feel-good exercise but true participation in collaborative decision-making. Assistant Secretary of Health Admiral John O. Agwunobi (2007) notes the value of social media like the Pandemic Flu Blog in "providing and facilitating sharing of information." We may interpret this statement as a recognition of the value of citizen participation in disseminating information from the government to carry out policy, but it is unclear whether the government in this interaction recognizes the transformative role of citizens in providing information to the government to guide policy.

British Parliament eConsultations

Since summer 2007, the British Parliament has conducted six "eConsultations," efforts to solicit public input through online discussion forums. Topics thus far have included two pieces of legislation, drafts of the Climate Change and Human Tissue and Embryo bills. Three eConsultations have sought general public input on the issues of military medical care, military recruitment and retention, and domestic violence. One eConsultation dealt with creating another form of participatory e-government, a system to create an online counterpart to written citizen petitions (United Kingdom Parliament, 2008).

Parliament here makes explicit its intention to use the citizen comment it gathers to shape policy. These discussion forums serve as online, asynchronous, extended committee hearings. The eConsultations expand access to such hearings to any corner of the U.K. with Internet access. Public testimony becomes interactive, enabling citizens to not only respond to questions from MPs but to question each other and their lawmakers.

New Zealand Police Act Review

The New Zealand Police sponsored perhaps the most daring official transformative e-government experiment to date. As part of its drive to review national policing regulations, the New Zealand police opened a wiki (http://www.policeact.govt.nz) in September 2007 where the public was invited to participate in drafting a new policing act. For thirty days, citizens could access the wiki to write, revise, delete, and comment on sections of a draft policing act. Comment was not restricted to New Zealanders; officials openly embraced commentary from Internet users around the world. Said New Zealand Police Superintendent Hamish McCardle, "The wonderful thing about a wiki is we can open it up to people all around the world—other academics and constitutional commentators interested in legislation—and make the talent pool much wider" (Ramachandran, 2007). This draft was submitted to the New Zealand Parliament as a starting point for discussions in crafting the final legislation.

Designing Future Systems: A Citizen-Legislator Discourse System

The preceding examples of tentative first steps toward online citizen participation and social decision support systems all offer some guidance for the design of future transformative e-government systems. A full-fledged official implementation of participatory e-government might take the following form.

A Citizen-Legislator Discourse System (CLDS) could act as a social decision support system at the local, state, or federal level. Such a system would implement participatory and emancipatory ideals in e-government by facili-

Figure 3. Citizen–legislator discourse system architecture

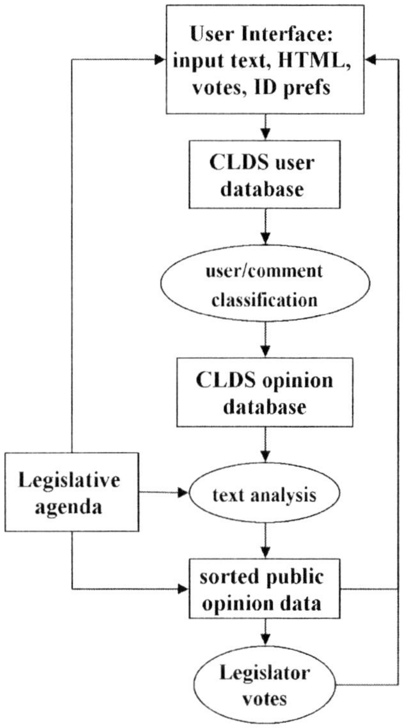

tating instant citizen participation in legislative research and deliberation. Processing information as outlined in Figure 3, the CLDS would present a common interface for all users: legislators, general citizens, registered lobbyists, and any other interested Web user. Some specific user groups (e.g. legislators, lobbyists) would be required to log in by assigned user name. General citizens could log in anonymously or as registered users.

The CLDS would incorporate numerous features to gather, categorize, and present information to users. The primary "providers" of information would be citizens, who can use the CLDS interface to reply to polls and submit opinions, news items, related laws, and research relevant to specified items of the current legislative agenda. Citizens would also use this same interface to provide commentary on submissions from other citizens, carry out public deliberations and debates, and direct questions to their legislators and each other. Lobbyists and legislators could participate in this process as well. All information would be public, transparent, and subject to commentary, much like the information presented on OpenCongress.org.

User inputs, automated routines, and human moderators would process the information within the CLDS. Users provide simple inputs—e.g. check boxes to mark submitted information as Pro, Con, or Neutral—that allow categorization of citizen input. Text analysis routines, including algorithms based on appearance of proper nouns (based on a reference list in the CLDS opinion database and on identification of sequences of capitalized words surrounded by lowercase words) and relative frequency of terms (e.g., see Gruhl et al., 2004), would allow the CLDS to further categorize discussion inputs and even flag and quarantine off-topic inputs. Human moderators—e.g., legislative staffers approved by a bipartisan committee, or even citizen nominated by users of the system—would provide further categorization and research, as well as quality control on CLDS processes.

We might consider legislators the primary "consumers" of the information compiled by the CLDS, as they would use the outputs to inform their legislative votes. Nonetheless, any user may access the outputs of the CLDS. Figure 4 displays a sample output interface that displays items currently on the legislative agenda plus an RSS feed of related news items. The close-up in Figure 4 shows a sample agenda item with simple statistical data appended by the CLDS to summarize public interest in a bill and to alert the legislator to questions and comments about the bill. Legislators and other users could click on the different areas of this opening interface to access more detailed information about each agenda item.

Figure 4. Citizen–Legislator Discourse System Dashboard: possible configuration

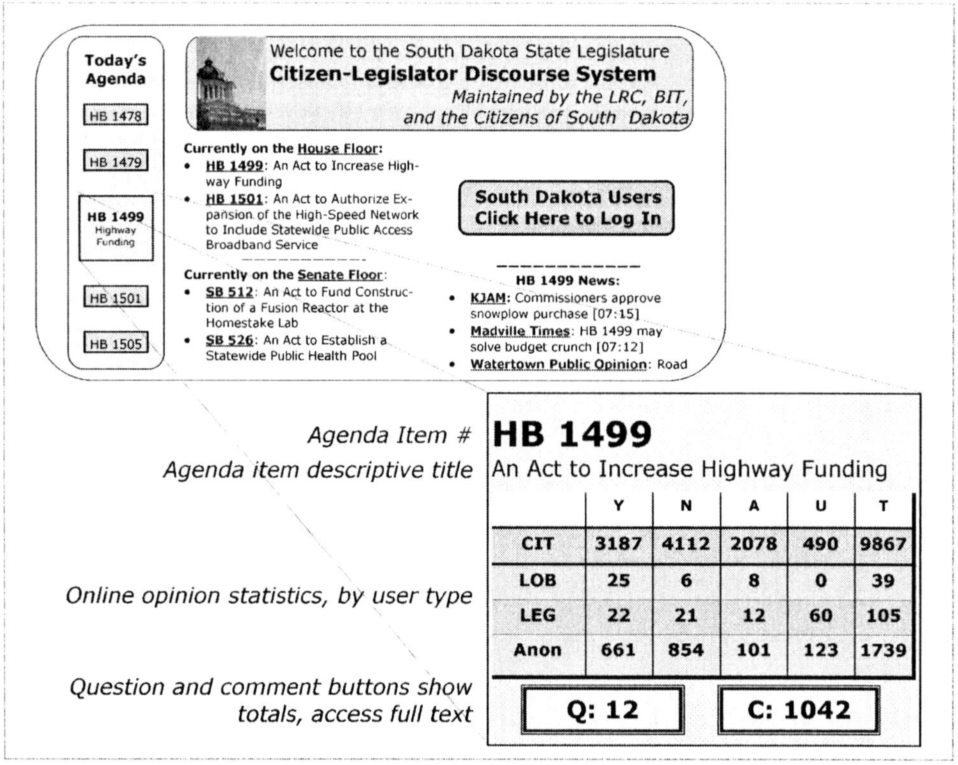

	Y	N	A	U	T
CIT	3187	4112	2078	490	9867
LOB	25	6	8	0	39
LEG	22	21	12	60	105
Anon	661	854	101	123	1739

The CLDS would provide all users with access to a wider range of organized information, especially citizen input, than is made available by any current legislative information system, computer-based or otherwise. The CLDS would instantly log and add to its public database all official legislator votes as well as CLDS-use statistics. Citizens could then easily monitor the voting records and performance of their legislators. This system would qualify as truly transformative e-government by putting all users on an equal footing as consumers and contributors of information.

Transformative E-Government Design: User Involvement

It would be an immense irony for an e-government researcher to claim the neohumanist values of Mumford (1983) and Hirschheim and Klein (1994), only to impose a complete, pre-determined design for an e-government system without seeking the input of the intended users. Citizen participation should be as much a part of the design of a transformative e-government system as an intended result. The above system sketch and the examples that inform it are less a blueprint for design than a starting point for discussion and development. Researchers and developers should interview potential users—citizens, elected officials, government IT personnel, etc.—to discover what functions and goals they would envision in a t-government system.

OpenCongress.org seeks exactly this sort of user input on its front page, asking users, "How do you use this site? What would make it more useful? Have you found a bug?" The site encourages volunteers with technical and creative skills to share their ideas and join the organization. Official "branding" may be important for establishing a t-government site's authenticity, but engaging citizen users to the point of bringing them on board to design and manage system features may prove essential in establishing citizen "ownership."

Hirschheim and Klein (1994) list several ways that information systems facilitate emancipatory discourse. Their suggestions apply as much to designing information systems as to forming public policy:

- "Computer-based networks could help overcome the limitations of space and time....
- "Electronic meeting systems could motivate people to contribute their expertise by advertising agendas and making it easy to append comments and suggestions....
- "Highly interactive, user-friendly designs could help overcome educational and skill differences of the systems development participants....
- "Proper security controls could protect individual rights through anonymity, motivating people to communicate criticisms and radical chance proposals by shielding them from the threats of those in power, as is emphasized in the group decision support literature" (p. 91).

Transforming e-government can be as much about transforming the *e-* as about transforming *government*. The process of developing e-government systems should exemplify openness to citizen participation. If the citizen-as-consumer mindset in e-government design poses a threat to democracy, a citizen-as-participant mindset in e-government design, manifested in user-generated content and technology, may just as powerfully support democracy.

CHALLENGES

As President Kennedy (1962) said of his decision to prioritize sending Americans to the Moon in the 1960s, we accept challenges "not because they are easy, but because they are hard." Transforming e-government is certainly hard. Transforming e-government to support citizen participation poses technological, social, and methodological challenges for government IT personnel and e-government researchers.

Technological Feasibility

A state government website with tens of thousands of citizens contributing content right alongside dozens of blogging elected officials is more complicated than a standard state government website with ten authorized administrators approving and publishing all content. Asked about reinventing government at the national level, Anthony Williams (in Klein, 2008) optimistically says today's Web 2.0 technology is up to the task:

Software developers have already figured out how to scale up collaboration technologies to support global business enterprises, so I see no reason why Web 2.0 could not support hundreds of thousands of people in a real-time policy debate.

Williams acknowledges the challenge of security, as do Belanger and Hiller (2006). Consumers will trust their credit card numbers to online applications, but when citizens act (and are treated as) participants in the political process, they may take a different view of security. Standards of security that work in the business realm may not satisfy participants in the political realm.

Even if the technology can handle the information, we must find ways for the technology to help humans use the information. A citizen's desire to find sales tax information does not equal a desire to read several dozen comments in a running debate on revising the sales tax formula. Even citizens interested in policy questions may not be able to afford to pay attention to a lengthy, unstructured, multi-party debate on the issue conducted on an online t-government forum. As mentioned in the description of the CLDS, t-government systems that give citizens the power to provide information must also look for technological means and human moderation (including moderation from the citizen-users themselves) to give that information useful structure.

Digital Divide

On face, the idea of using t-government to provide another avenue for participation in the political process seems positive. But what if that avenue excludes a certain group? Suppose we could divide the population of a certain jurisdiction into a class of likely t-government users and a class of likely t-government non-users. The latter group might consist of lower-income families or rural families with fewer Internet access options. A t-government system facilitates an increase in political participation among the likely users. The likely non-users make no change in their level of political participation. Have we increased the negative impacts of the digital divide by further enfranchising one group without bringing the other along? Would such negative impacts outweigh the benefits of expanding the number of voters who have increasingly easy access to their elected officials and participation in the political process (not to mention transforming the e-government paradigm away from the citizens-as-consumers mindset)?

Whichever way that political calculus may be resolved, governments seeking to transform their e-government implementations will have to seek ways to make those applications available to as many citizens as possible. Information systems initiatives may have to be coupled with broader policy initiatives to expand IT infrastructure to underserved areas. Efforts to transform e-government may also require efforts to educate citizens about the opportunities for participation those systems will make available.

Evaluation

One challenge for researchers will be determining how to evaluate the performance of transformational e-government systems. If the goal is citizen participation, then a simple criterion of "If we build it, will they come?" might not be sufficient. Researchers can count numbers of users and comments, but they will also have to find ways to measure the quality alongside quantity of participation.

If the goal of transformative e-government is social decision support, evaluation of the system may become even more challenging. How do we measure the effectiveness of a government's decision-making processes before or after the implementation of any e-government system? Rehg et al. (2005) recognize the problem in the context of decision support for urban planning decisions: "The precise problem that interests us here, however, is the lack of an inherent, or independently accessible, standard of truth or correctness" (p. 212). The quality of social decisions is inherently bound up with the changing political and economic conditions of the society making those decisions as well as the political biases and agendae of the citizens (and that includes researchers) trying to evaluate them. Return on investment, efficiency, and other business-world criteria for effective commercial decision support systems may not translate well to justice, opportunity, and other criteria for effective political decision-making. Transformative e-government applications that support social decision-making will involve more inclusive inputs and more extensive outputs that will challenge the best evaluative models.

CONCLUSION: PUTTING THE TRANSFORMATION IN TRANSFORMATIONAL GOVERNMENT

Vice President Gore was but one of myriad government officials who recognize the power of information technology to transform the way government does business. But transforming government into a business and transforming citizens into customers is not the complete model we should seek.

While the e-business paradigm fails to capture the full government–citizen relationship, current changes in e-business may exemplify the direction e-government can take in its own transformation. Collaborative Web technologies are changing the way business operates (Tapscott & Williams, 2006). When such technology can give consumers more voice in the marketplace, it makes even more sense to put that technology to work in transforming e-government to facilitate the most important collaboration of all: the collaboration of citizens in guiding the affairs of their government.

Truly transformational e-government should create systems that are not strictly provider–consumer, "them versus us" services, but open collaborations that dissolve barriers between citizens and their government, exactly like the democracy t-government systems should support. T-government systems should fulfill emancipatory ideals. They should create forums for emancipatory discourse. They should provide a social decision support system that expands participation in legislative policy-making. T-government should put the *demos* back in *democracy* and make government a collaborative, community effort.

REFERENCES

ACSI. (2006). ACSI methodology. About ACSI. American customer satisfaction index. Retrieved April 26, 2008, from http://www.theacsi.org/index.php?option=com_content&task=view&id=48&Itemid=41

Affisco, J. F., & Soliman, K. S. (2006). E-Government: A strategic operations management framework for service delivery. *Business Process Management Journal, 12*(1), 13–21.

Agwunobi, Adm. J. O. (2007). Ideas are welcome. *Pandemic Flu Leadership Blog, United States Department of Health and Human Services, May 22–June 27, 2007.* Retrieved April 27, 2008, from http://blog.pandemicflu.gov/indexc728.html?cat=7

AMCIS. (2008). E-Government: Past, present, and future. Conference mini-track description. Retrieved April 26, 2008, from http://www.business.mcmaster.ca/amcis2008/MT/amcis-pr-069-2008-File001.pdf

Balutis, A. P. (2001). E-Government 2001, part I: Understanding the challenge and evolving strategies. *The Public Manager, 30*(1), 33–37.

Barua, A., Sophie Lee, C. H., & Whinston, A. B. (1996). The calculus of reengineering. *Information Systems Research, 7*(4), 409–428.

Baum, C., & DiMaio, A. (2000). Gartner's four phases of e-government model. Gartner, Inc. Research Note (Tutorial TU-12-6113).

Belanger, F., & Hiller, J. S. (2006). A framework for e-government: Privacy implications. *Business Process Management Journal, 12*(1), 48–60.

Blair, T. (2007). Chief information officer council: Foreword. *Transformational Government: Enabled by Technology.* Retrieved April 26, 2008, from http://www.cio.gov.uk/ transformational_government/strategy/contents/foreword.asp

Butler, P., & Collins, N. (2004). Citizen as consumer. In N. Collins and T. Cradden (Eds.), *Political issues in Ireland today* (pp. 135–148). Manchester, UK: Manchester University Press.

Chen, H. (2003). Digital government: Technologies and practices. *Decision Support Systems, 34*(4), 223–227.

Chief Information Officer Council. (2007). Strategy: Citizen and business centred services. *Transformational Government: Enabled by Technology, created 01 Nov 2005, updated 23 May 2007.* Retrieved April 26, 2008, from http://www.cio.gov.uk/transformational_ government/strategy/contents/strategy_2.asp

Department of Information Resources (2000). Seamless government issues: State of Texas. Updated Apr 17, 2003, http://www.dir.state.tx.us/egov/report/seamless.htm. In M.H. Fagan. (2006). Exploring city, county, and state e-government initiatives: An east Texas perspective. *Business Process Management Journal, 12*(1), 101–112.

E-Government Task Force (2002). E-government strategy: Simplified delivery of services to citizens. *Office of Management and Budget, United States Federal Government.* Retrieved April 26, 2008, from http://www.whitehouse.gov/omb/inforeg/egovstrategy.pdf

Fang, Z. (2002). E-Government in digital era: Concept, practice, and development. *International Journal of the Computer, the Internet, and Management, 10*(2), 1–22.

Fornell, C. (2007). Government satisfaction scores: ACSI scores and commentary. Retrieved April 26, 2008, from http://www.theacsi.org/index.php?option=com_content&task=view&id=176&Itemid=62

Fountain, J. (2001). The virtual state: Transforming American government? *National Civic Review, 90*(3), 241–251.

Friedman, T. (2005). *The world is flat: A brief history of the twenty-first century.* New York: Farrar, Straus & Giroux.

Gore, A. (1997). Introduction: Access America: Reengineering through information technology. *Report of the National Performance Review and the Government Information Technology Services Board.* Retrieved April 30, 2008, from http://govinfo.library.unt.edu /accessamerica/docs/intro.html

Gruhl, D., Guha, R., Liben-Nowell, D., & Tomkins, A. (2004). Information diffusion through blogspace. *WWW Conference* (pp. 491–501). New York: ACM. Retrieved April 27, 2008, from http://citeseer.ist.psu.edu/cache/papers/cs2/24/

http:zSzzSzwww.www2004.orgzSzproceeding-szSzdocszSz1p491.pdf/gruhl04information.pdf

Hirschheim, R., & Klein, H. K. (1994). Realizing emancipatory principles in information systems development: The case for ETHICS. *MIS Quarterly, 18*(1), 83–109.

Humphreys, P. C. (1998). Improving public service delivery. *Committee for Public management Research, Discussion Paper 7.* Dublin: Institute of Public Administration. Retrieved April 27, 2008, from http://www.cpmr.gov.ie/publications/discussion-papers/improving-public-service-delivery.pdf/

Jensen, J. (2007). Comment #3, under P. Omidyar (2007). Thank you for the conversation. *Pandemic Flu Leadership Blog, United States Department of Health and Human Services, May 22–June 27, 2007.* Retrieved April 27, 2008, from http://blog.pandemicflu.gov/?p=109#comments

Keating, M. (1995). Size, efficiency, and democracy: Consolidation, fragmentation, and public choice. In D. Judge, G. Stoker, & H. Wolman (Eds.). *Theories of urban politics* (pp. 117–134). Thousand Oaks, CA: Sage Publications.

Kennedy, President J. F. (1962). The space effort. *Speech at Rice University, Houston, TX.* Rice Webcast Archive. Retrieved April 30, 2008, from http://webcast.rice.edu/speeches/19620912kennedy.html

Klein, P. (2008). How Web 2.0 can reinvent government (interview with Anthony Williams). *CIO Insight Weekly Report.* Retrieved April 21, 2008, from http://www.cioinsight.com /c/a/Expert-Voices/Web-20-Reinventing-Democracy/

Layne, K., & Lee, J. (2001). Developing fully functional e-government: A four-stage model,. *Government Information Quarterly, 18*(2), 122–136.

Leavitt, M. O. (2007). Closing thoughts. *Pandemic Flu Leadership Blog. United States Department of Health and Human Services, May 22–June 27, 2007.* Retrieved April 27, 2008 from http://blog.pandemicflu.gov/?p=8

Lee, S. M., Tan, X., & Trimi, S. (2005). Current practices of leading e-government countries. *Communications of the ACM, 48*(10), 99–104.

Makolm, J. (2002, September). Best practice in e-government. In R. Tranmüller & K. Lenk (Eds.), In *Proceedings of the First International Conference on Electronic Government, EGOV 2002, Aix-en-Provence* (pp. 370–374). Berlin, Germany: Springer.

Miller, E. (2007, February). OpenCongress.org. *SunSpots: The Sunlight Foundation blog.* Retrieved April 27, 2008, from http://www.sunlightfoundation.com/node/2202

Mumford, E. (1983). *Designing human systems for new technology: The ETHICS method.* Manchester, UK: Manchester Business School. Retrieved April 27, 2008, from http://www.enid.u-net.com/C1book1.htm

Myers, M. D. (1997). Qualitative research in information systems. *MIS Quarterly, 21*(2), 241–242. MISQ Discovery, archival version, June 1997, http://www.misq.org/discovery/MISQD_isworld/. Retrieved September 21, 2008, from http://www.qual.auckland.ac.nz.

Newman, J. (2003). Issue brief: Electronic government. *Bureau of Information and Telecommunications, State of South Dakota, Nov 2003.* Retrieved April 26, 2008, from http://www.state.sd.us/bit/Services/MGMTInfo/IssueBriefs/documents/Egovt-issue-brief.htm

Norris, D. F. (2005). E-government at the American grassroots: Future trajectory. *Proceedings of the 38th Annual Hawaii International Conference on System Sciences.* Retrieved 2008.09.19 from http://www.umbc.edu/mipar/documents/HICSSpaper.pdf

OpenCongress.org (2008). About Open Congress. Retrieved April 27, 2008, from http://www.OpenCongress.org/about

Osborne, D., & Gaebler, T. (1992). *Reinventing government: How the entrepreneurial spirit is transforming the public sector.* Reading, MA: Addison-Wesley.

Ramachandran, A. (2007, September 26). Write your own laws. *Sydney Morning Herald.* Retrieved April 27, 2008, from http://www.smh.com.au/news/web/write-your-own-laws/2007/09/26/1190486375202.html

Reddick, C. G. (2004). A two-stage model of e-government growth: Theories and empirical evidence for U.S. cities. *Government Information Quarterly, 21*(1), 51–64.

Rehg, W., McBurney, P., & Parsons, S. (2005). Computer decision-support systems for public argumentation: Assessing deliberative legitimacy. *AI & Society,* (19), 203–229.

Ryan, N. (2001). Reconstructing citizens as consumers: Implications for new models of governance. *Australian Journal of Public Administration, 60*(3), 104–109.

South Dakota Horizons (2008). About. Retrieved April 27, 2008, from http://southdakota.communityblogs.us/about/

South Dakota Horizons–Fruechte, K. (2007, August). Horizons sets up individual community blogs. Retrieved April 27, 2008, from http://southdakota.communityblogs.us/2007/08/16/horizons-sets-up-individual-community-blogs/

South Dakota Horizons–Jacobs, C. (2007, October). Ideas... host a monthly blog night in your community. Retrieved April 27, 2008, from http://southdakota.communityblogs.us/2007/10/08/ideashost-a-monthly-blog-night-in-your-community/

Stowers, G. N. L. (2004). Measuring the performance of e-government. *E-Government Series, IBM Center for the Business of Government.* Retrieved April 27, 2008, from http://www.businessofgovernment.org/pdfs/8493_Stowers_Report.pdf

Tapscott, D., & Williams, A. (2006). *Wikinomics: How mass collaboration changes everything.* New York: Penguin Group.

Turban, E., Aronson, J. E., & Liang, T. (2005). *Decision support systems and intelligent systems, 7th edition.* Upper Saddle River, NJ: Pearson/PrenticeHall.

Turoff, M., Hiltz, S. R., Cho, H.-K., Li, Z., & Wang, Y. (2002). Social decision support systems (SDSS). *Proceedings of the 35th Hawaii International Conference on System Sciences, 2002* (pp. 81–90). Retrieved April 26, 2008, from http://www.hicss.hawaii.edu/HICSS_35/HICSSpapers/PDFdocuments/CLCSC03.pdf

United Kingdom Parliament. (2008). eConsultations. Retrieved April 27, 2008, from http://forums.parliament.uk/html/index.html

KEY TERMS

E-Government (Conventional Definition): application of information systems to "deliver government services to citizens, businesses, and other stakeholders" (AMCIS, 2008).

Emancipatory Discourse: Conversation in which "distorting tendencies" have been removed, primarily by giving all participants equal opportunity to speak, question, argue, respond, etc. (Hirschheim & Klein, 1994, pp. 89–90).

Emancipatory Ideals: Principles focused on realizing "the full creative and productive potential of individuals" and replacing inequitable control structures with organizational democracy (Hirschheim & Klein, 1994, p. 85).

Horizontal Integration: Replacement of monolithic organizational structures and silo-like functional divisions (vertical integration) with collaboration and cross-functional teams.

Neohumanism: Paradigm seeking "emancipation and the realization of human potential" (Hirschheim & Klein, 1994, p. 109).

Social Decision Support System (SDSS): Information system designed to help citizens and policymakers gather information and make decisions on societal-scale issues.

T-Government (Transformational Definition of E-Government): Application of information systems to support all functions of government, including the function of citizens as participants in government.

ENDNOTE

1 Searching "egovernment" produces results containing "egovernment" and "e-government". The first 40 articles resulting from the search terms "egovernment G2C G2B G2G" had an average of 7.53 citations. The first 40 articles resulting from the search terms "egovernment G2C G2B G2G C2G" had an average of 2.33 citations.

Chapter V
Instigating Transformational Government at a Municipality Level:
A Case Study

Marwan Elnaghi
Brunel University, UK

Sarmad AlShawi
Brunel University, UK

Vishanth Weerakkody
Brunel University, UK

Wael Aziz
Dubai Municipality, UAE

ABSTRACT

This empirical research chapter focuses on the findings and the potential value of instigating a transformational government (t-government) at a municipality level. The emerging literature indicates that there is a strong desire amongst governments worldwide to provide an efficient, cost effective, and sustainable electronic service delivery environment, and Dubai Municipality in the UAE is no exception. This research aims to investigate the motivations behind this instigated change towards t-government systems. In order to achieve this transformation in services, there is a need for a radical change and an innovative approach to provide quality services. In this paper the authors report some of the findings from an in-depth case study of transformational effort in the municipality of Dubai. The study seeks to offer insights into organisational and managerial aspects surrounding the complex phenomenon of t-government evolution. The chapter concludes that successful t-government implementation requires senior executive participation and active engagement of stakeholders for benefit realisation; whereby t-government adoption is surrounded by political, cultural, organisational, technological, and social issues which must be considered and treated carefully to enable this transformation.

INTRODUCTION

The recent United Nations e-government Survey (UN, 2008) results indicate that governments are moving and progressing forward in e-government development around the world. However, given the high demands placed by e-government on a multitude of foundational pillars which include prerequisites of infrastructure, appropriate policies, capacity development, Information Communications and Technology (ICT) applications and relevant content that need to be in place to fully implement e-government services, the progress is very slow. Only a few governments have made the necessary investment to move from e-government applications per se to a more integrated connected government transformed stage (Devados et al., 2002; Irani et al., 2007; Weerakkody et al., 2008). Transformational government (t-government) is defined as radically changing the way government conducts its business internally and externally (Murphy, 2005; Montagna, 2005). In essence therefore, t-government is about the transformation of internal and external processes of government using information and communication technologies to provide efficient and user focused services to citizens, businesses and other stakeholders (Basu , 2004; Evans, 2003; Gupta and Jana, 2003; Gandhi and Cross, 2001; Stoltzfus, 2005).

In an opening address to the Organisation for Economic Co-operation and Development (OECD, 2006) Forum Secretary-General Donald Johnston States:

Globalisation, propelled by trade and investment liberalisation, and rapid technological change, is believed to have delivered prosperity and reduced poverty for millions of people in recent decades. We have learned, however, that reaping the full benefits of globalisation requires many elements including good public and corporate governance; policies that promote structural adjustment and social cohesion; greater access to education; efficient financial markets; and sound policies for research, innovation and development. Balancing all these elements while promoting globalisation and delivering prosperity require an open inclusive dialogue involving businesses, government agencies, and working groups.

In addition, e-government strategy change to enable government departments and agencies to interact with private sectors sharing a common concern of security and cost reductions in transactions and speed of delivery (Heeks, 2001; McClure, 2000). Therefore, the complexity surrounding transformational government requires at times drastic measures in order to achieve its desired output. This has lead Dubai Municipality senior executive management to take an innovative approach, and make a serious decision to initiate the Online Week. Whereby, six main departments were each completely shut for a week for any manual transactions over a period of three months (September-December 2007). This was conducted while the online system was still live and running.

Therefore, the research questions guiding this chapter are:

1. what does t-government mean to Dubai Municipality; and
2. what process related challenges do they need to overcome in order to successfully implement a one-stop shop t-government.

To explore these questions, the Dubai Municipality undertook a case study approach and instigated an Online Week where all transactions were done online. The authors analyse the initial empirical findings from this study. The case study examines a core public service process that is executed at local government level and highlights key process and information systems challenges and consequent realities of implementing a transformational stage of e-government in Dubai.

In order to investigate the aforementioned issues, this chapter is structured as follows: the next section offers a contextual background of the motivation to a t-government single channel strategy; this is followed by an outline of the innovative way for the implementation of t-government strategy; then followed by a summary of the empirical data collection strategy; thereafter some key empirical findings are presented; finally the paper concludes by providing a discussion of the issues that were encountered, future trends and answering the research questions set out above.

MOTIVATION FOR CHANGE FROM E-GOVERNMENT TO T-GOVERNMENT: A LITERATURE PERSPECTIVE

The academic and government literature on t-government are growing and include a number of papers that start to discuss methodological and conceptual frameworks for undertaking implementation and evaluation (Irani et al., 2007; Weerakkody, 2007). In the UN survey (2008), for instance, the United Arab Emirates (UAE) jumped into the top 35 countries (see table 1). According to the report, the UAE went up mostly due to the strength of three of their ministries' websites, namely: Social Welfare, Labour and Finance. These three ministries provide electronic signatures; they have a formal time frame by which to respond to online queries and e-mails; they allow for the creation of online accounts; and the submission and payment by credit card as

Table 1. E-government readiness for Western Asia (UN, 2008)

Country	Index		Ranking	
	2008	2005	2008	2005
Israel	0.7393	0.6903	17	24
United Arab Emirates	0.6301	0.5718	32	42
Cyprus	0.6019	0.5872	35	37
Bahrain	0.5723	0.5282	42	53
Jordan	0.5480	0.4639	50	68
Qatar	0.5314	0.4895	53	62
Kuwait	0.5202	0.4431	57	75
Saudi Arabia	0.4935	0.4105	70	80
Lebanon	0.4840	0.4560	74	71
Turkey	0.4834	0.4960	76	60
Oman	0.4691	0.3405	84	112
Azerbaijan	0.4609	0.3773	89	101
Georgia	0.4598	0.4034	90	83
Armenia	0.4182	0.3625	103	106
Syrian Arab Republic	0.3614	0.2871	119	132
Iraq	0.2690	0.3334	151	118
Yemen	0.2142	0.2125	164	154

part of their transactional model. Table 1 below shows the e-government readiness for Western Asian 17 countries with the position of the United Arab Emirates (ranking 32, index 0.6301), where the Emirate of Dubai, where Dubai Municipality is located, is the second largest amongst seven Emirates that constitute the UAE.

The pace of change in the UAE over the last decade in general and Dubai in particular is rather impressive. This small emirate, which is mainly a barren desert, is establishing itself as a business hub in the Gulf region. Perhaps the unique nature of Dubai historical trading culture and the government ruling systems have contributed to its success in this digital age.

Cultural Dimension and Innovation for Change

Historically speaking, in some public works decision times to get from concept to start of construction can run into several decades. For example in the late 1980s London Transport and British Rail advocated, on economic grounds, the construction of a new rail link in London–Crossrail. In 1990 the project was formally discussed in parliament (Hansard, 1990) and restraints were placed on property development along the proposed route. Although the company to manage the development was established in 2001 (Crossrail 2006), parliament has only just given approval to proceed with the work on 22 July 2008 (Hansard 2008). The decision making process has taken 30 years and completion is not expected until 2017.

In contrast, the proposal to equip the city of Dubai with over 50 miles of fully automated light rail transport system was raised in 2000 and by 2006 construction had commenced (Anon, 2006). Dubai, of course, is smaller than a city like London but this alone cannot account for the vast differences in the time scale decision make process to adopt a major public project. To gain some insight, perhaps there is a need to shed some light into this aspect of cultural dimension. The results of Hofstede's studies of cultural differences around the world show that the Asian region is very much different from the US or UK (Hofstede, 2003). For example, the power distance index of 80 for the UAE compared with 35-40 in the US and UK indicates a society that expects and accepts the authority of those in power. Combined with a high uncertainty avoidance index of 68 for the UAE (compared with 35-46 for the West) there is an expectation of an organised society with rules and regulations that are, in the main, obeyed. The individualism index, which is a low (38) for UAE when compared to about 90 for the West, also leads to a more collective behaviour with a high degree of loyalty. Thus, the nature of culture and the governance of Dubai permit decisions to be taken more rapidly and with greater certainty that they will be carried out. There is no need for the debate and consensus building that occurs in the UK or US and much less willingness to challenge the public authorities1. Adding to the motivation that since the mid 1990s ICT has played an important role in incrementally changing and shifting traditional and bureaucratic government models into the current e-government model where services are delivered according customers' needs, citizens focus, and business focus (Burn and Robins, 2003; Wassenaar, 2000; Wimmer, 2004).

E-Government Innovation and Change

E-government innovations were classified and categorized in many ways, and according to Poon and Huang (2002), e-government can be classified into five segments according to their application domains, which are: E-democracy, E-services, E-commerce, E-management, and E-decision-making. Burn and Robins (2003) have their managerial perspective of e-government, where they stated that e-government is not just about electronic service delivery, it should provide the opportunities to evaluate and transform the management processes of government organization, rethink how government provide services in order to rebuild and link these services in a way that is tailored to citizen's need, and finally be able to incorporate governance itself and change the way political and social power are organized and used.

In the implementation of e-government applications, governments are seeking efficiency, effectiveness, and data quality improvement gains (Danziger & Andersen, 2002). After more than thirty years of use of IT in the public sector, these benefits are, however, self-evident and government should move beyond these benefits focusing more on streamlining core processes and reaching customers in a more efficient manner (Andersen and Henriksen, 2006).

Dubai Municipality (DM) has noted that not all services are amenable to being put online, and not all online services are useful to citizens and businesses. In order for e-government initiatives to be effective, management leaders with an innovative approach can take steps to evaluate customer demand of e-government services, and work closely with citizens and businesses to provide users with the services that are most useful to them. Those Leaders can also promote the value of services and help implement migration and take-up strategies for online services (Elnaghi et al., 2007)

Another challenge is that those channels that involves the re-orientation of government to make it more customer-focused. Where leaders are aware of the importance of restructuring organisations and processes in order to maximise value to the user, but must overcome considerable internal resistance when implementing change. While governments have different approaches, most OECD countries agree on the importance of incentives to ensure co-ordination and to promote a sense of ownership and accountability for decentralised initiatives (OECD, 2003). The following table 2 shows the migration from e-government to t-government with brief description. There are critical variables differentiating e-government from t-government and the consequent actions that are required for an effective migration process (Irani et al., 2007).

In response to the changing business environment, governments are turning to business process reengineering (BPR), involving significant investments in information technology (IT). The concept of BPR advocates the radical redesign of business processes using enabling IT to bring about a quantum leap in value realisation and performance of government services. While reengineering can be done with proper planning, resources and commitment, more research is needed to focus on exploring ways to improve interoperability

Table 2. Differentiation between e-gov and t-gov and migration strategy (Irani et al., 2007)

	e-government (e-gov)	t-government (t-gov)	Migration from e-gov to t-gov
Focus	Putting government services on line	Making the government transformational through IT	Transformational leadership
Citizen involvement	Access & Accessibility	Build Social capital	Citizen focus
Business involvement	On-line transacting	Supply chain integration	Transformational business
Evaluation	Stage model growth	Benefit realisation	
Service delivery	Push-model	Pull-model	
Resource management	Resource allocation	Professionalism	
Integration	Shared service platform	Shared service culture	
Business model	Technological capability	Strategic governance	
IT role	Enabling online delivery	Enabling the transformation of the business of governmnet	Transformational IT

and integration between different government agencies in the context of e-government. In this context, the emerging concepts of Service Oriented Architectures (SOA) and Web Services are areas that need further exploration (Davenport, 1990; Davenport, 1993; Hammer, 1990; Hammer, 1993; Weerakkody et al., 2006).

The transfer of a service to online delivery reduces the demand on these traditional channels and holds out the potential for savings through reduction in the resources required to support them. Complete closure of a traditional access channel may well be contemplated. Ex-ante cost benefit assessments such as these depend upon significant assumptions about the number of citizens who will move to an online service delivery channel. For example the UK Inland Revenue service online taxation project estimates a 50% take up with staff savings of 1,300 posts (NAO 2002). In several cases complete transfer of the service to electronic interaction may not be possible under existing statutory and regulatory frameworks. Notwithstanding European Directives on the validity of electronic signatures (EU 1999) there are still situations where the agency needs to have physical signatures or to be able to inspect physical documents (IPS 2008). As a case in point, Australian's federal government adopted a comprehensive online strategy for the adoption of e-government (DCITA, 2000). This strategy specifically excluded closure of traditional access channels (Australian Government, 2005). However, based on the experience of other tax collectors the Australian Taxation Office did expect to make direct cost savings in its planning for there 'ETax' online system. In practice the take-up fell behind the ATO targets (Chamberlain and Castleman, 2005). The drivers for e-government broadly include improving internal cost and management efficiencies, encouraging citizen participation, promoting economic development and improving overall governance (Schware et al., 2003; Gandhi and Cross, 2001; Lee et al., 2005).

This prompts the debate about the motivation behind citizen take-up of services and the need to create incentives for citizens to switch to online services. Studies in this area identify a variety of barriers perceived by citizens. These include lack of online experience, trust and visual appeal as well as poor information quality and the degree of stress (Gilbert et al., 2004; Carter and Belanger 2005; Horst and Gutteling, 2007). However, many of these barriers lead to citizens not even trying to use the service. The extended technology acceptance model (Venkatesh and Davis 2000; Venkatesh et al., 2003) highlights the importance of social influences and hence the need encourage potential users to try out the technology by creating incentives for citizens is important. Various incentives have been tried, for example direct cash incentives, focussed advertising of online channels, social networking (Phippen et al., 2006) and co-development of services (Alford 1998). However, many of these raise issues of sustainability, appropriate use of public funds and equality of opportunity where citizens cannot gain the benefit through no fault of their own. Most of the evidence remains anecdotal and motivating citizens to adopt e-government services remains problematic (Irani and Elliman 2007; Irani et al., 2007).

The transformation phase encompasses redefining the delivery of government services by providing a single point of contact to citizens' that makes the government completely transparent to citizens and businesses (Affisco and Soliman, 2006). The transformation stage of e-government will only be achieved when the different participating agencies collaborate, streamline their business processes and integrate systems that have been historically fragmented (Hu et al., 2006; Weerakkody et al., 2007). In the UK, for instance, the Transformational Government Strategy was introduced in 2005 and sets out a six-year improvement task for public services (Cabinet Office, 2006). The UK target for reaching the transformational stage of e-government is 2011 (ibid).

CASE STUDY OF DUBAI MUNICIPALITY: A HISTORICAL BACKGROUND

There is a wide range of reasons of why Governments around the world want to go digital. Each government should have its own agenda for implementing e-government. In looking at various statements and definitions of those countries it can be seen why some they see a need to establish a digital economy. As a point in case, the United Arab Emirates in general and the government of Dubai in particular has embarked on a modernization program that has never been witnessed before. In a dialogue with the nation outlining his strategic ambitious plan and what he is aiming to achieve (Alnaqi, 2003), the Ruler of Dubai Sheikh Mohammed Bin Rashid Al Maktoum states:

our aim is for Dubai to be recognized as a leading centre in the new economy involving close co-operation with leading edge companies specialized in the development and creative applications of technology. To accomplish our aim, we need to redefine and transform our understanding of the role of government. Our e-wisdom is an asset and I shall personally lead this transformation." He further added "I want Dubai to develop a unique commercial economy in this digital age. Just as Dubai was a unique example with its trade in those bygone days when our traders have achieved fame far and wide.

In line with Dubai Government strategic directive and ambitious plan, Dubai Municipality has embarked on the digital route with the intention to move all of its services online and via a single channel. Historically, citizens would access ser-

Figure 1. Dubai Municipality strategy to move from Multichannel to single channel service delivery system

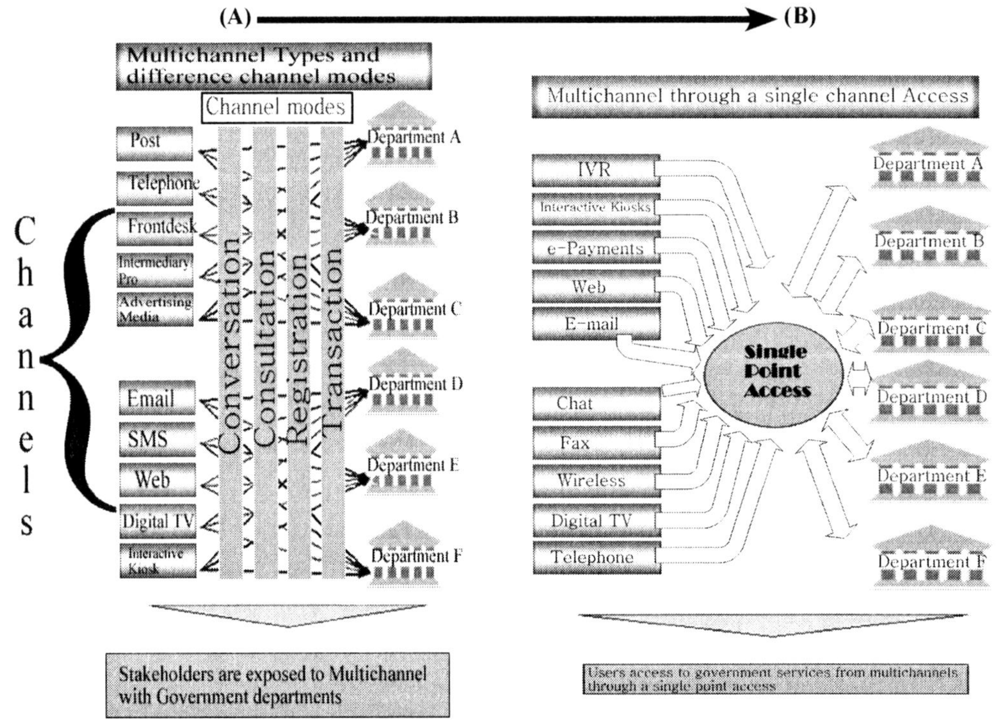

vices by: visiting local or regional offices, paper and postal communications and telephone interactions. The different channels (Post, Telephone, Interactive Voice Response (IVR), Front desk, E-mail etc.) that are being used for stakeholders to interact, using different channel modes (Conversation, Consultation, Registration and Transaction) with Dubai Municipality in contacting different departments are shown in figure1 below. It is the strategic management plan for Dubai Municipality to move from an (A) type multi-channel system of interaction to a (B) type single interaction with stakeholders.

Dubai Municipality has developed a special website to create awareness and educate the public on the use of online services. It is worth noting that there are more than 100 nationalities residing in Dubai. However, as the majority speak English, DM has a dual website with Arabic as the default language as shown in Figure 2.

Transformational Government at Dubai Municipality

Dubai Municipality offers 520 online services. The percentage of online usage of these services varies from 100% for some services to 0% for other services. Reasons behind this difference include department's commitment, customers' awareness, customers' readiness, technical complexity, and customer support activities.

As part of the "zero visit" initiative, and with a vision to "do all transactions at DM electronically with ease and confidence", Dubai Municipality conducted an "Online Week" campaign during the period from 23 September 2007 to 13 December 2007 (see Table 3), aiming to encourage its customers to use online services, decrease physical visits to the main building of the municipality and to gain more insights about what does it take to reach 100% usage of online services.

The idea of the campaign was to stop all manual transactions, for one week each, for the 6 biggest departments which provide between them 262 services, and are responsible for about 77% of all DM transactions. Full integrated media coverage and internal training sessions were designed and implemented. Certain key measures were calculated before and after execution of the campaign. Key findings and insight assortments were analyzed, identifying the key obstacles, and directions for full e-transformation and adoption.

Marketing Awareness Plan

The Online Week has followed an extensive awareness plan to DM customers. Newsletters

Figure 2. Dubai Municipality Portal is in two languages, Arabic and English, where the default one is Arabic

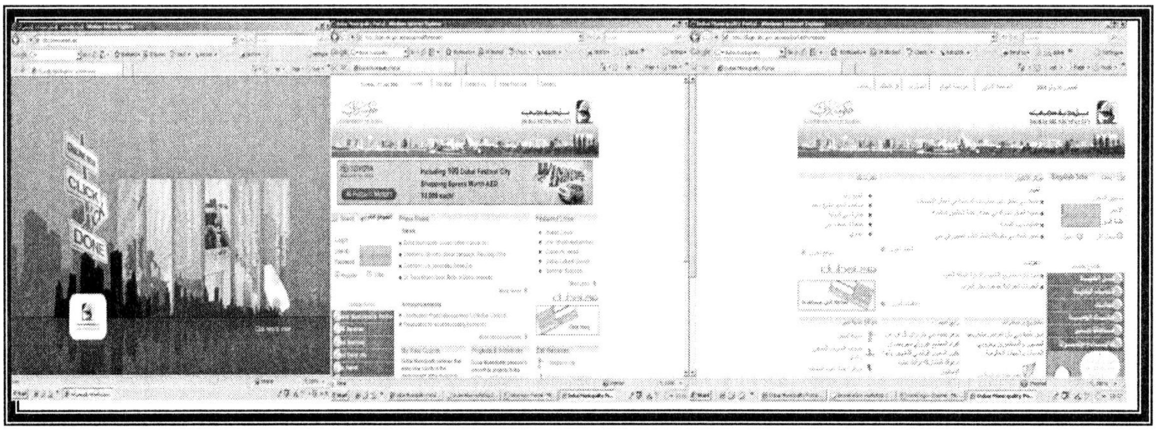

Table 3. Online Week campaign timetable with those departments involved in the study

Involved Department	Online Week
Environment	23/Sep/2007
Public Health	07/Oct/2007
Drainage and Irrigation	21/Oct/2007
Planning and Surveying	04/Nov/2007
Studies and Pre-Qualification Section–Building	18/Nov/2007
Building Permits Section - Building	09/Dec/2007

and SMS have been sent to registered customers. News articles were published in many national newspapers, online news websites and magazines. Newspapers advertisements were spread among different newspapers in Arabic and English. Radio spots were announced in different radio stations in Arabic, English, and Urdu as well, web banners were provided in some websites like DM, Dubai Police and Al Bayan newspaper. Roll up Banners were distributed in DM, Dubai Chamber of Commerce, Dubai Economic Department, and Dubai Land Department. Brochures, flyers, and CDs were also distributed. The PixMan system, which is a new technology (see Figure 3), was also implemented to promote the project and in the same time to conduct e-surveys. The PixMan systems were available at DM and in some malls like Burjman Shopping Centre and Ibn Batoota Shopping Mall. A special stand was constructed in DM to support the customers and train them on e-services. In order to assist in the successful implementation and management of the event five teams were set up

Figure 3. Dubai Municipality uses the PixMan technology to publicise the Online Week

Online Week Teams

There were five teams working together during the Online Week, where each team had specific tasks to accomplish as shown in Table 4.

DISCUSSION

This research found that during the Online Week there was direct value realisation, which included increased online transactions, e-payments, users' registration, cost savings, improved customer satisfaction, a decrease in DM main building visits and manual transactions. Overall, about 25% increase of the number of online transactions in year 2007 compared to 2006. In general, the fourth quarter of 2007 i.e. the Online Week showed about 7.5% increase in number of online transactions over the average number of the quarterly transactions of the same year. It is interesting to note that for the first time in DM history it was able to reach 100,000 monthly transactions in October 2007, compared to an average of 91,000 monthly transactions in 2007, and 73,000 monthly transactions in 2006. However, it was reported that during the same period online e-payments didn't show any noticeable increase.

The case study findings indicate that more new companies/businesses registrations have taken place which was a good indication on the effectiveness of the campaign. During the Online Week, on average about 1423 new companies and 1533 new individuals were registered to use online services. This in itself represents a remarkable increase over the monthly average registrations (for companies: 38%; company users: 33%; and individuals: 56%).

Table 4. Online Week teams with their role descriptions and responsibilities

Team name	Description of role and responsibilities
Technical Support	Provide training for counter employees, receive complains and technical problems and solve it on spot, make sure to provide network and e-services with best performance.
Media	Set goals for advertising plan, coordinate with concerned company for implementing project, measure effectiveness of marketing and communication tools to accomplish main goals.
Research and Communication	Direct contact with DM customers who are coming to DM, conduct interviews to know the reasons for not using e-services and e-pay, get customer's suggestion to improve and support services, provide reports for research results and necessary advices.
Concerned Department	Work on solve all issues related to the e-service, and provide workshops and awareness for e-services.
Online Week	Construct the general plan, state the main goals, Key Performance Indicators (KPIs) to measure the performance of all sub teams, make sure that tasks are well accomplished, to take decisions and corrective actions based on the direct follow up.

On average, it was reported that a total cost savings of about 9,384,470 AED only for the transactions of the participated departments. There was about 91% of customers who participated in the survey (1009 customers) reported that their satisfaction is either great or good. It was also reported that the total number of visitors to the DM main building was decreased by 27%.

Though this initiative has produced tangible results, it has also produced intangible benefits which may have future strategic implications. It was reported that through random interviews and meetings the Online Week managed to break the ice between different stakeholders in the e-government initiative. It was for the first time in years that business users, technical team staff, and customers have sat together and focused on specific issues, and discussed areas of mutual concerns for improvement. During the Online Week there were some e-services used for the first time (Building Studies and Prequalification section in building department), while others were used heavily but they require physical attendance after submission; both were clearly identified and rectification plans were set accordingly. A case in point, this make DM internal users more aware of the capabilities and constraints of their services, where customer support team has established a more in depth knowledge of the issues facing their customers. Senior management became more committed to the e-transformation primitives; and more importantly DM image was enhanced as a professional e-services provider for citizens and foreign investors. A summary of some of the general statistics occurred during the Online Week campaign is shown in Table 5.

E-Services Analysis

After the implementation of the Online Week, each department was asked to provide a daily report on total no of calls, and visits received at the department's counter. Table 6 below shows the statistics for a selected week. These statistics will identify the areas that DM and concerned department need to focus on to improve the quality of service provided to customers.

E-Payment

The results of all six departments with regard to e-payments are shown in the graphs (see Appendix, Figure 5). They show all concerned departments that identify the e-payment and manual payment levels before Online Week, during Online Week, and after Online Week. The triangle line indicates the Online Payment and the cross line indicates the Manual Payment. The Environment Department graph, for example, shows that e-payment have been increased from 38 to 48. The overall manual payments are not so high compared to the e-payment and most of the manual payments are for payment of hygiene fines service.

Table 5. General statistics occurred during the Online Week

Item	Total
No. of customers visited Online Week Stand	1,179
No. of Trained customers	458
No. of newly registered users	1,852
No. of newly introduced services	27
No. of online Transactions	294,646
No. of online Transactions of the involved departments	224,747
No. of online Payments amount	47,081,637
No. of online Payments amount of the involved departments	2,416,434
No. of online Payments	14,051
No. of online Payments of the involved departments	13,451
No. of e-surveys.	1009
No. of visitors to Online Week website	2,459
No. of involved departments	5
No. of involved online services	262

Table 6 Customer's visits per week

Department	Service Name	Total Visits
Public Health	Consignment Follow up	215
Planning and Surveying	Site Plan	97
Public Health	Item/Barcode Registration	58
Drainage and Irrigation	Drawing discussions	41
Drainage and Irrigation	Request for application for fees	38
Public Health	Health Certificates and e-Payment	30
Public Health	E-Service Registration Related Inquiries	29
Drainage and Irrigation	Request for application for house connection	26
Planning and Surveying	Demarcation	25
Environment	Importation of Dangerous Goods	23
Drainage and Irrigation	Request for Application for Irrigation Connection	19
Planning and Surveying	Planning Permits	6
Drainage and Irrigation	NOC Inquiry	5
Drainage and Irrigation	Request for application for ground water primmest	4
Drainage and Irrigation	Temporary Connection	4
Environment	Clearance for Industrial Products	2
Environment	Waste Disposal Services	1

Table 7. Issues with e-payment

Issues using e-Payment / Departments	Environment	Health	Drainage	Planning	Building Studies	Building Permits	Total
I have no issues with e-payment	37	53	13	30	35	121	**271**
e-payment is not available to my e-service	13	28	7	23	14	50	116
I don't have a credit card	7	10	7	12	9	15	**38**
e-payment is not trustable	6	7	6	5	5	14	**20**
e-dirham is difficult to get	19	29	14	47	33	91	**207**
I prefer to pay in cash	34	76	14	70	38	153	**368**
Total	**95**	**186**	**35**	**168**	**116**	**411**	

As a result of the analysis in the previous section with regard to payment the following analysis was produced to further focus on the core of the problem. The results are shown in Table 7 which lists the number of customers with the issues concerning e-Payment and the corresponding department.

The online user registration graph in Figure 4 represents the trend of the newly registered customers every three months compared with the Online Week period. This snap shot is taken roughly over a year, starting from January 2007 to December 2007. The graph in figure 5 on the right shows that an increase from 2924 to 4846 which is almost a 40% increase.

The Online Week provided DM senior management with different strategic insight, that made this interactive process more rewarding and provided deeper understanding to know exactly what does it take to bring government to people, and reach 100% adoption rate. The major obstacles and barriers that were identified toward for a full e-transformation are: the lack of knowledge of customers on how to use the e-service, the frequent slow down in DM portal, the difficulty in sending large attachments, the lack of integration and missing links between DM portal and other departments, the lack of awareness of the existence of new e-services, insufficient and unreliable support from call centre, some un-user friendly e-services procedures, and some specific e-payment issues.

Figure 4. Trend of online user registration

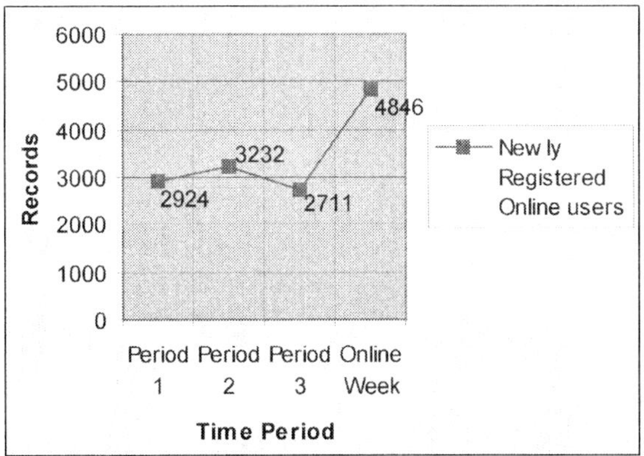

The e-payment was clearly identified as a main and critical barrier to the use of online service. There were about 30% of customers who had no issues with e-payment, about 12% of the users were not aware that they could pay online, 21% found it difficult to get e-dirham cards, and 37% preferred to pay in cash. It was rather unfortunate that the Online Week didn't have a remarkable impact on e-payment since, and perhaps due to cultural dimension, the majority preferred to pay by cheque or cash and not willing to use e-payment.

The benefit of this online week has brought to the forefront the financial matter of e-payment. This issue need to be studied and looked at carefully in a different perspective. Whereby, a strong incentives and innovative ideas need to be introduced with the cooperation of management executive office, banks, and media. The promotion of payment by direct debit need to be more fostered and implemented in more banks with massive advertisement campaign; by making the e-dirham machine more flexible with the customer's requirements, and DM need to find a way to replace the cheque payment method for future transactions. During the Online Week a considerable experience was gained on the type of needs those customers were facing when using the online services. Unlike the normal counter windows, the Online Week stand also succeeded in helping the department's employees to orient and introduce the customers to the un-used e-services. Some customers would prefer to use the express service where they can simply submit their request and pay an extra charge to get all transaction filled for them and done with a short limited time. However, this should be phased out gradually in order to encourage more use of online services.

The Dubai Municipality with its commitment for a digital future continued measuring the performance of the e-services well after the campaign period. Unfortunately after the Online Week not all the departments were committed to discourage manual transactions. However, DM continued with its determination in monitoring the type of services that got the most visits and calls, and has produced a ranked list of them for expected re-engineering (high physical visits), or providing online help (high phone calls). The customer centred approach was achieved in essence by tying the customers and employees to online services. The results in Table 8 provide a summary of total savings for customer and DM benefits.

In achieving the aim for understanding and encouraging a move from e-government to t-government, the Online Week could be seen as a successful pilot study to realize the "Zero Visit" vision. Motivating online usage of e-services should be seen as a continuous process not an occasional endeavour. Based on those achieved results and findings, it could be concluded that a 100% e-adoption is possible, over time, and a 50% target of e-payment could be reached within one year time plan. However, this requires a considerable effort and dedication from different teams that goes beyond the responsibilities and capabilities of one single department within DM.

Table 8. A Summary giving the total cost savings during the online week period

Department	Online Week Transactions	DM Saving/ Transaction	Customer Saving / Transaction	DM Savings	Customer Savings	Total Savings
Environment (29 e-services)	23,168	24	22	556,032	509,696	1,065,728
Public Health (62 e-services)	174,638	22	18	3,842,036	3,143,484	6,985,520
Drainage and Irrigation (9 e-services)	1,422	24	20	34,128	28,440	62,568
Planning and Surveying (61 e-services)	6,339	20	16	126,780	101,424	228,204
Building Studies (26 e-services)	8,917	24	25	214,008	222,925	436,933
Building Permits (75 e-services)	10,263	32	27	328,416	277,101	605,517
Total Savings				**5,101,400**	**4,283,070**	**9,384,470**

FUTURE TRENDS

The change from e-government to t-government requires a major shift in paradigm thinking and strategic direction. It requires a new style of leadership that will be able to foster this transformation and provide the appropriate management and IT infrastructure to support that dynamic and critical change.

It is anticipated that the effective use of Customer Relationship Management (CRM) system track that will be responsible mainly for managing media plans, and internal awareness sessions. Activities may include: updating customer's contacts, promoting un-used e-services, engaging departments, activating friendly online help, educating customers, better utilization of the number 700040000 for the call centre, and measuring customers' satisfaction. Furthermore, it is anticipated to run some CRM related initiatives and activities regarding loyalty programs, e-delivery, e-payment, and Public-Private Partnerships.

The improved use of web technology and channels that will facilitate in redesigning the portal for better linkage between the services to information, and re-design some e-services based on the recommendations from departments and customers as identified in the meetings and focus groups. Dubai Municipality (DM) portal slowness needs to be tracked and solved. The payment system, such as the E-Dirham machine, need to be improved to accept the amounts required by customers. Service integration within DM departments and other organizations such as Department for Economic Development should be implemented.

As e-government advances towards maturity and t-government, the role of executive management and leader continue to change. Leaders are beginning to appreciate that e-government is more about modernisation and reform than about technology. Other challenges included looking beyond electronic service delivery to ensure links with other service delivery channels, with overall public sector modernisation efforts and with the legislative and regulatory frameworks in which e-government changes are taking place.

Hence, t-government initiatives should refocus attention on a number of issues: how to collaborate more effectively across agencies to address complex, shared problems; how to enhance customer focus and involvement; and how to build relationships with private sector partners. Public administrations and municipalities must address these issues if they are to remain responsive. Notwithstanding the fact that is that front office and back office operations need to be seamlessly integrated into one system for effective transformational government.

CONCLUSION

The main positive outcome of the electronic Online Week was to enable better policy outcomes, higher quality services and greater engagement with citizens and stakeholders. Governments and public administrations will, and should, continue to be judged against these established criteria for success. The Dubai Municipality instigated transformational government initiatives refocused attention on a number of issues: how to collaborate more effectively across departments and agencies to address complex, shared problems; how to enhance customer focus; and how to build relationships with private sector partners. Public administrations must address these issues if they are to remain responsive and more competitive, which is the aim of DM in particular and Dubai Government in general.

The campaign succeeded to send a clear message to all stakeholders that DM is serious, committed and capable of providing integrated e-services. Many customers have expressed their interest in using the electronic channels as the preferred choice for submitting applications. However, a long path is expected to reach 100% usage, or adoption. This is not only in the submission phase but also throughout the entire application process. There is a set of strategies that need to take place in order to overcome all weakness and problems discovered during the Online Week campaign. Users during the Online Week stand have been categorized as the following, starting with Normal Users: they resemble any new user who is willing and can use the online services. These new users need to get the adequate training on the online usage, where concerned department employee need to inform them with all services they need to register for, and then let them to do the submission by themselves to experience the e-services. The second type is the Computer illiterate users who don't know how to use the Internet and not willing to work with online services. Usually most of those users are old people who use public services, they don't agree with the idea of registration and prefer to finish any transactions manually. The last group are those who prefer to use the express service and be treated as VIPs. At this point, the e-government section has created this group especially for those users who are willing to pay extra amount and would like to finish their transaction fast.

It is interesting to report that during the planning and surveying Online Week, it was found a user who rejected the usage of online services and asked for special and quick operation, this user lately went to the Director Office to get his transaction done quickly. So the e-government section found the necessity of treating this particular group specially and provide all DM customers with all possible satisfying treatment. Hence, keeping some channels open similar to other countries such as Australia, for example.

In addition to the training and awareness that needed to take place, it was also found it is essential for DM to use the Online Week stand as a place to advertise and start all the e-activities available at DM, such as the e-complain system where the opening was through the Online Week stand. It was recommended that the e-government committee plays major role in sponsoring such an "e-adoption" program, with direct support from the Director General office. It should be empowered to impose new policies, rules, and incentives that can get the recommended plan implemented with ease and success. Furthermore, the implementation of quality management to cater for the e-service catalogue, with the proper required changes based on the new DM organization structure. Also the designing of a complete information data-bank should be in place to incorporate all e-services with all reporting facilities.

Finally, the Dubai transformational effort has posed many questions and raised many issues where senior managements need to address. The benefit realization of transformed services gives rise to redesign those processes and implement Business Process Reengineering (BPR) as well as consider benchmarking for future development. Future research could attempt to investigate, some of the issues raised in this study, and new issues surrounding the t-government implementation.

REFERENCES

Australian Government. (2005). *'Australians' use of and satisfaction with e-government services.* Barton, Australia: Commonwealth of Australia.

Andersen, K. V., & Henriksen, H. Z. (2006). E-government maturity models: Extension of the Layne and Lee model. *Government Information Quarterly, 23*(2), 236–248.

Alford, J. (1998). A public management road less travelled: Clients as co-producers of public services. *Australian Journal of Public Administration, 57*(4), 128-137.

Anon. (2006). *Traffic and transport: Metro rail taking shape.* Dubai, UAE: Al Nisr Publishing LLC. Retrieved on July 28, 2008 from http://archive.gulfnews.com/indepth/dubaimetro/more_stories/10050775.html, accessed 28 July 2008.

Affisco, J., & Soliman, K. (2006). E-government: A strategic operations management framework for service delivery. *Business Process Management Journal, 12*(1), 13-21.

Burn, F. & Robins, G. (2003). Moving towards e-government: A case study of organisational change processes. *Logistics Information Management, 16*(1), 25-35.

Basu, S. (2004). E-Government and developing countries: An overview. *International Review of Law Computers, 18*(1), 109-132.

Cabinet Office. (2006). Retrieved from http://www.cio.gov.uk/documents/annual_report2006/trans_gov2006.doc

Chamberlain, J. & Castleman, T. (2005). Moving personal tax online: The Australian taxation office's e-tax initiative. *International Journal of Cases on Electronic Commerce, 1*(3), 54-70.

Carter, L. & Belanger, F. (2005). The utilization of e-government services: Citizen trust, innovation, and acceptance factors. *Information Systems Journal, 15*(1), 5-25.

Crossrail. (2006). *About us*. London: Cross London Rail Links Limited. Retrieved on July 28, 2008, from http://www.crossrail.co.uk/pages/aboutus48.html, accessed 28 July 2008

DCITA. (2000). GovernmentOnLine—The commonwealth government's strategy. *The Australian Government Information Management Office, Canberra, Australia April 2000*. Retrieved on July 24, 2008, from http://www.agimo.gov.au/archive/publications_noie/2000/04/govonline#Contents, accessed 24 July 2008

Davenport, T. H. (1998). Putting the enterprise into the enterprise system. *Harvard Business Review, 16*(4), 121-131

Davenport, T. H. (1993). *Process innovation: Reengineering work through information technology*. Boston: Harvard Business School.

Davenport, T. H., & Short, J. E. (1990). The new industrial engineering: Information technology and business process redesign. *Sloan Management Review, 31*(4), 11–27.

Devados, P. R., Pan, S. L., & Huang, J. C. (2002). Structurational analysis of e-government initiatives: A case study of SCO. *Decision Support Systems, 34*, 253– 269.

Danziger, J. N., & Andersen, K. V. (2002). Impacts of IT on politics and the public sector: Methodological, epistemological, and substantive evidence from the Golden Age of transformation. *International Journal of Public Administration, 25*(5), 591–627.

EU. (1999). eEurope: An information society for all-Communication on a commission initiative for the special European Council of Lisbon, 23 and 24 March 2000, Commission of the European Communities, Brussels. COM/99/0687 final. 2002. Retrieved from http://europa.eu.int/information_society/eeurope/news_library/pdf_files/initiative_en.pdf.

Elnaghi, M., AlShawi, S., & Missi, F. (2007). A leadership model for e-government transformation. *Proceedings of European and Mediterranean Conference on Information Systems* (EMCIS2007). June 24-26, Polytechnic University of Valencia, Spain.

Evans, G. (2003). *Implementing e-government: An executive report for civil servants and their advisors*. Hampshire, England: Gower Publishing Limited.

Gupta, M. P. & Jana, D. (2003). E-Government evaluation: A framework and case study. *Government Information Quarterly, 20*, 365-387.

Gandhi, S., & Cross, C. (2001). E-Government initiative at city of Orlando: Current trends and future directions. *Proceedings of the URISA conference, October 1-12.*

Grant, G., & Chao, D. (2005). Developing a generic framework for e-government. *Journal of Global Information Management, 13*(1), 1–30.

Gilbert, D., Balestrini, P. & Littleboy, D. (2004). Barriers and benefits in the adoption of e-government. *The International Journal of Public Sector Management, 17*(4), 286-301.

Horst, M., Kuttschreuter, M. & Gutteling, Jm. (2007). Perceived usefulness, personal experiences, risk perception, and trust as determinants of adoption of e-government services in The Netherlands. *Computers in Human Behavior, 23*(4), 1838-1852.

Heeks, R. (2001). *Reinventing government in the information age*. New York: Routlage.

Hu, P., Cui, D., & Sherwood, A. (2006). Examining cross-agency collaborations in e-government initiatives. *Proceedings of the 39th Hawaii International Conference on System Sciences.*

Hofstede, G. (2003). *Geert Hofstede™ cultural dimensions*. Stockholm: ITIM International. Retrieved on July 28, 2008, from http://www.geert-hofstede.com/hofstede_dimensions.php, accessed 28 July 2008

Hansard. (1990). Lord Brabazon of Tara in response to the Queen's speech. *The Parliamentary Debates (Hansard) House of Lords Official Report Monday, 12th November 1990. Fifth Series-Volume DXXIII: col 122.* Retrieved from http://www.hansard-archive.parliament.uk/The_Official_Report,_House_of_Lords_1909_to_2004/S5LV0523P0.zip.

Hansard. (2008). Mr. Deputy Speaker (Sir Alan Haselhurst) notice of royal assent. *Hansard (House of Commons Daily Debates) 22 July 2008. 479 Part No. 133: col 761.* Retrieved from http://www.publications.parliament.uk/pa/cm200708/cmhansrd/cm080722/debtext/80722-0019.htm#08072274000781.

Hammer, M. (1990). Reengineering work: Don't automate, obliterate. *Harvard Business Review, 68*(4), 104–112.

Hammer, M. & Champy, J. (1993). *Reengineering the corporation: A manifesto for business revolution*. New York: Harper Collins Publishers, Inc.

IPS. (2008). IPS online passport pre-application site. *UK Home Office: Identity and Passport Service (IPS)*. Retrieved on July 24, 2008 from https://www.ips.gov.uk/epa1rla/about.aspx, accessed 24 July 2008.

Irani, Z., Elliman, T. & Jackson, P. (2007). Electronic transformation of government in the UK: A research agenda. *European Journal of Information Systems,* (October).

Irani, Z., Ozkan, S. G. A., & Elliman, T. (2007). T-Government for benefit realisation. *Proceedings of European and Mediterranean Conference on Information Systems (EMCIS2007) June 24-26.* Polytechnic University of Valencia, Spain.

Layne, K., & Lee, J. W. (2001). Developing fully functional e-government: A four stage model. *Government Information Quarterly, 18*(2), 122–136.

Lee, S. M., Tan, X., & Trimi, S. (2005). Current practices of leading e-government countries. *Communications of the ACM, 48*(10), 99-104.

Murphy, J. (MP Parliamentary Secretary Cabinet Office Report). (2005). Beyond e-government the world's most successful technology-enabled transformations, executive summary. *INSEAD the business school for the world* (pp.1-124). Retrieved from www.localtgov.org.uk

Montagna, J. M. (2005). A framework for the assessment and analysis of electronic government proposals. *Electronic Commerce Research and Applications, 4*, 204-219.

NAO. (2002). E-Revenue. *The National Audit Office, London, UK. HC 492 14 February 2002.* Retrieved on July 24, 2008 from http://www.nao.org.uk/publications/nao_reports/01-02/0102492es.pdf, accessed 24 July 2008

OECD Forum. (2006). *Balancing globalisation*. Retrieved from http://www.oecd.org/site/0,3407,en_21571361_35842076_1_1_1_1_1,00.html

OECD. (2003). Checklist for e-government leaders. Retrieved from http://www.oecd.org/publications/pol_brief

Phippen, A., Land, F. & Ward, A. (2006). Community information line – an evaluation of citizen engagement in local e-government. *E-Government Workshop '06 (eGOV06), Brunel University, West London, UB8 3PH [accessed September 11 2006].*

Stoltzfus, K. (2005). Motivations for implementing e-government: An investigation of the global phenomenon. In *Proceedings of the 2005 National Conference on Digital Government Research, ACM* (Vol. 89, pp. 333–338). Atlanta, Georgia.

Schware, R. & Deane, A. (2003). Deploying e-government programs: The strategic importance of "i" before "e." *Emerald research, 5*(4), 10–19.

United Nations. (2008). *UN e-government survey 2008: From e-government to connected governance*. New York: United Nations. Retrieved August 2008, from http://unpan1.un.org/intradoc/groups/public/documents/UN/UNPAN028607.pdf

Venkatesh, V. & Davis, Fd. (2000). A theoretical extension of the technology acceptance model: Four longitudinal field studies. *Management Science, 46*(2), 186-204.

Venkatesh, V., Morris, Mg., Davis, Gb., & Davis, Fd. (2003). User acceptance of information technology: Toward a unified view. *MIS Quarterly, 27*(3), 425-478.

Watson, E. E., & Schneider, H. (1999). Using ERP systems in education. *Communications of the Association for Information Systems*, February 1, 9.

Wassenaar, A. (2000). *E-Governmental value chain models* (289-293). DEXA, IEEE Press.

Wimmer, M. (2004). A European perspective towards online one-stop government: The eGov project. *Electronic Commerce Research and Applications*, 92-103.

Weerakkody, V., Baire, S. & Choudrie, J. (2006). E-Government: The need for effective process management in the public sector. In *Proceedings of the 39th Hawaii International Conference on System Sciences.*

Weerakkody, V., Janssen, M. & Hjort-Madsen, K. (2007). Realising integrated e-government services: A European perspective. *Journal of Cases in Electronic Commerce, 3*(2), 14-38.

Yang, K. (2003). Neoinstitutionalism and e-government: Beyond Jane Fountain. *Social Science Computer Review, 21*(4), 432–442.

KEY TERMS

E-Government: A term that emerged in the late 1990s out of the Internet boom, but the use of computing technologies in government organizations can be traced back to the beginnings of computer history (Grönlund, 2004)

eTransformation: The process organisations undertake to move from old ways of carrying out process to new ways of conducting these activities

Globalization: The "process by which the experience of everyday life ... is becoming standardized around the world." (The Encyclopedia Britannica) While some scholars and observers of globalization stress convergence of patterns of production and consumption and a resulting homogenization of culture, others stress that globalization has the potential to take many diverse forms.

Government: A body that has the power to make, and the authority to enforce rules and laws within a civil, corporate, religious, academic, or other organization or group.

Key Performance Indicators (KPI): Financial and non-financial metrics used to help an organization define and measure progress toward organizational goals. KPIs are frequently used to "value" difficult to measure activities such as the benefits of leadership development, engagement, service, and satisfaction. KPIs are typically tied to an organization's strategy.

Pixman: A marketing research tool using the latest technology and media promotion systems that depend on direct interaction with the targeted public. It consists of a wearable audiovisual unit with a flat-screen suspended above a brand ambassador's head. (http://www.pixman-usa.com/index.htm).

ENDNOTE

1 It is not the purpose of this chapter to comment on the merits or morality of these cultural factors but simply to recognise that these differences exist and they significantly impact what can be achieved.

APPENDIX: E-PAYMENT

The results of all six departments with regard to e-payments are shown in the graphs below (see Figure 5). They show all concerned departments that identify the e-payment and manual payment levels before Online Week, during Online Week, and after Online Week. The triangle line indicates the Online Payment and the cross line indicates the Manual Payment.

Figure 5. E-Payment pre-online week, during online week, and post-online week

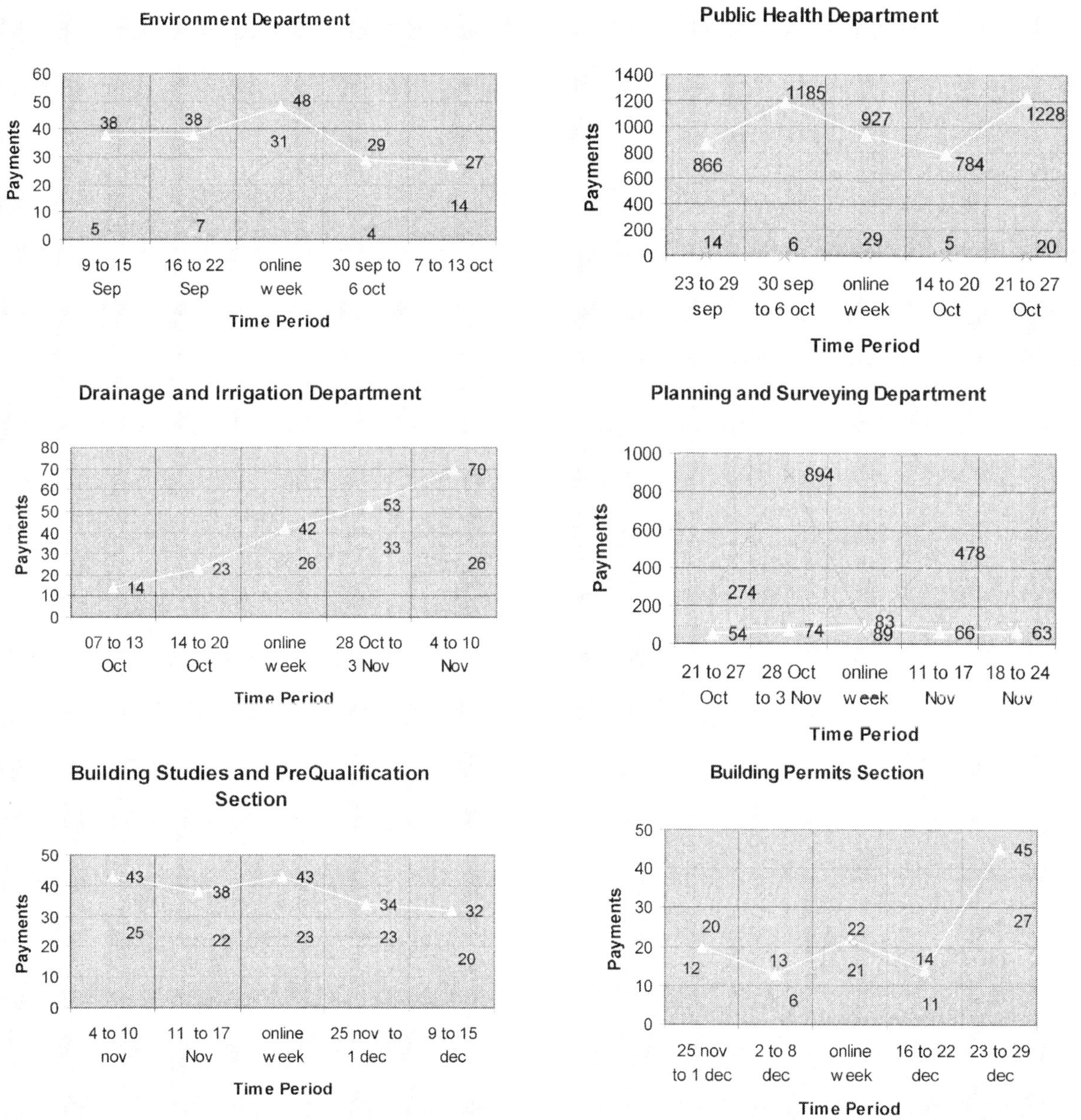

Section II
Interoperability and Integration Enabling T-Government

Chapter VI
Transforming Cross-Organisational Processes between European Administrations:
Towards a Comprehensive Business Interoperability Interface

Jörg Ziemann
Saarland University, Germany

Peter Loos
Saarland University, Germany

ABSTRACT

New legal settings, the need for improved quality of service, and technological advances increase the pressure on public administrations to cooperate in order to modernize and innovate procedures. Thus, the automation of cross-organisational processes is a clear objective. But due to the traditional independence of administrations, as well as the need to minimize modifications of internal systems, a loose coupling rather than tight system integration is desired. In this vein, a method is required that enables public administrations to create comprehensive interfaces they can publish to collaboration partners. This chapter presents the concept for a Business Interoperability Interface that describes the externally visible behaviour of administrations and supports the design and execution of loosely coupled, cross-organisational processes. Requirements for this interface are derived from the Europol-Eurojust collaboration, and the development and application of the Business Interoperability Interface are illustrated with the same scenario.

INTRODUCTION

Needed: Automated But Loosely Coupled Collaboration Between Public Administrations

Due to the increasing heterogeneity and dynamics of the European Union, more and more Public Administrations (PA) within Europe are challenged to work together and to adapt continuously to rapid technological changes. New legal settings, modernization, the need for improved quality of service, the search for competitive advantages and innovations as well as rapid technological advances create a new dynamic and complex administration environment, which requires flexibility and mobility from European public administrations. For these reasons, different governments have to cooperate in order to modernize and innovate public administrations. To avoid redundant manual work, to increase speed of process execution as well as process transparency, the IT systems of different PA should support the execution of joint, collaborative processes.

Nonetheless, due to the traditional independence of different administrations and differences in regulations, it is unrealistic to expect a tight integration of PA and their technical systems. Thus, the objective should rather be a loose coupling of organisational systems that requires only minor changes of internal systems but still supports the automation of cross-organisational processes. An analysis of related work reveals that current E-Government interoperability frameworks focus on the descriptive rather than the constructive aspects of interoperability, e.g. by providing standards and technical recommendations for selected aspects of IT system development. They only offer limited support when it comes to methods for systematically implementing cross-organisational processes (CBP), e.g. by providing a procedure model or an architecture of how to put the various standards involved in a CBP together (cp. Schmidt et al., 2007).

This raises the necessity for extending existing interoperability frameworks regarding constructive aspects that support the design and implementation of CBP in the public sector. Descriptive aspects define, for example, which specific E-Government data specifications, interfaces, process models or open standards ought to be used in different local, regional and international public administrations. Constructive aspects describe on a more generic level the methods to be applied for creating interoperable software systems of public administrations. While the descriptive aspects focus on static elements, e.g. a certain standard needed for the collaboration of two public administrations on the national level, the constructive aspects aim at the dynamics of establishing interoperable information systems, e.g. the various steps necessary to develop such a system. Note that we presume the existence of mechanisms to ensure syntax compatibility among the collaborating Public Administrations, e.g. the mapping of heterogeneous language formats is not in the scope of this work.

Research Objective: A Method to Describe Organisational Interfaces

To transform cross-organisational processes into loosely coupled, yet frictionless flows, it is not sufficient to provide PA with a selection of technical standards that they must support. Instead, tangible architectures are needed that explain which parts of internal systems can be used in cross-organisational processes and how they can be used. In this vein, we propose a method for developing comprehensive interfaces that each PA can publish to its partners. In order to also support stakeholders from a business process perspective, such an interface should not only focus on technical matters but provide conceptual information as well. Note however, that this approach does not focus on "soft" interoperability barriers like different cultures of enterprises which might hinder cooperation, but presumes that involved stakeholders are able to specify a valid cross-organisational scenario with semi-formal process models. From a technical perspective, in the context of cross-organisational business process automation and in the related field of service-oriented architectures (SOA), various methods for a suitable design of interactions between organisations have been discussed in the last years. Taking these developments into account, this article formulates requirements and a proposal for a framework that can be used to realize cross-organisational processes between public administrations. The core of this framework is the *Business Interoperability Interface* (BII) which describes the externally visible behaviour of an organisation with its collaboration partners. Similar to the well known and practice proven Architecture of Integrated Information Systems (ARIS), the interface distinguishes various enterprise dimensions – e.g. processes, information items and organisational structures – as well as different levels of technical detail (a requirement, a technical and a code level).

To provide a basis for the concept development, first requirements for the development of an interoperable system are derived from a current cross-organisational scenario: the Europol-Eurojust collaboration. Building on this, a list of objectives is defined which have to be fulfilled by the solution. In section 2, the basis of the BII is laid: a composition of state-of-the-art concepts is presented which fulfil the requirements established before. In section 3, these core concepts are combined into the BII and the position of the BII as a cornerstone of an interoperability architecture is laid out. In section 4, these concepts are illustrated in detail on the Eurojust-Europol case. Section 5 compares the BII method with related research and section 6 concludes the article with a summary and an outlook on future research.

USE CASE AND REQUIREMENTS

Example Scenario: Collaboration Between Europol and Eurojust

In the context of the R4eGov Project[1] recently various scenarios of interactions between European Public Administrations were described and evaluated to identify interoperability barriers and prepare the way for corresponding solutions. Five scenarios were investigated in detail (Boujraf & Noble, 2007; Matheis, Diedrich, Schmidt, & Wimmer, 2007; Diedrich et al., 2007) comprising 1. the German Supreme Court (Bundesgerichtshof – BGH) scenario, 2. a scenario related to the issuing of visa for international students coming to the EU, 3. the Austrian Federal Chancellery (Bundeskanzleramt – BKA) and exchange of documents with related administration, 4. an eProcurement scenario involving the Trade Register of the Paris Business Court (GTCP) and 5. the collaboration between Europol, Eurojust and related administrations. In this article we focus on the Europol-Eurojust scenario.

The Eurojust/Europol collaboration represents a European cross-border collaboration and the area of law enforcement. Europol is the European Police Office and Eurojust the European Judicial Cooperation Unit, enabling for example the collaboration of public prosecutors from the 27 member states of the EU. A closer collaboration between Europol and Eurojust is a political objective, also a higher interaction efficiency through the replacement of manual by electronic interactions. Since the main objective of the agencies consists in supporting cross-organisational collaboration between different European authorities, interoperability is an essential aspect of their overall strategy. Their collaboration is constrained and determined by a legal framework which explicitly defines the boundaries of the interactions between those agencies.

Figure 1. Overview of actors involved in the Europol-Eurojust collaboration (adapted from Boujraf & Noble, 2007)

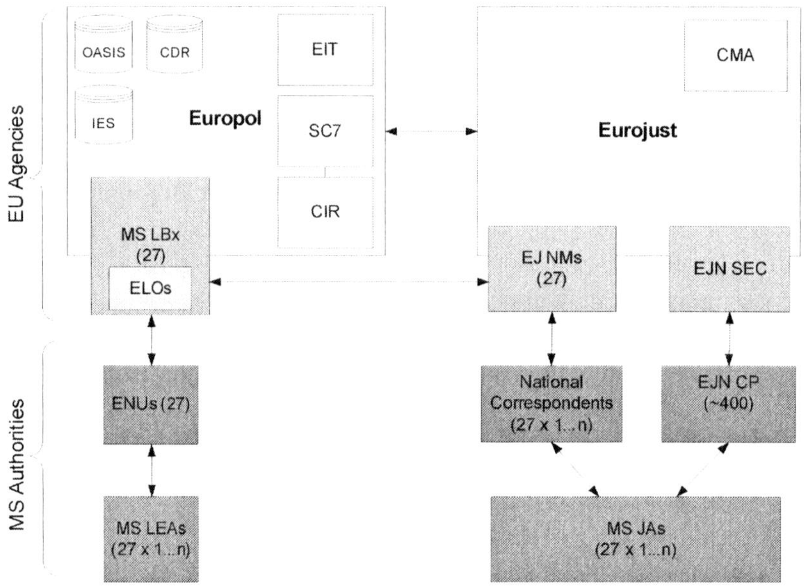

Figure 1 provides a high-level view of the collaborative workflow presented in the Eurojust-Europol case study and the actors involved in it. The collaborative scenario involves 27 actors from five countries, ten different document types being exchanged through seven different IT systems in ten different ways (Boujraf & Noble, 2007).

On the upper left hand side, Europol with comprised organisational units (EIT, SC7, CIR), IT system (OASIS, CDR, IES) and related organisational roles (Europol Liasion Officer, ELOs) are depicted. Below, Authorities related to Europol but distributed over the various EU Member States (MS) are illustrated: Europol National Units (ENU) and MS Law Enforcement Authorities (LEA). On the upper right hand side, Eurojust is depicted. It comprises the Case Management Analyst (CMA), 27 EJ National Member (EJNM) and the European Judicial Network Secretariat (EJN SEC). They are related to roles on the national level: 27 Correspondents, Contact Points (CP) and Member States Juridical Authorities (MS Jas).

In the following we provide a fictional process to illustrate this setting:

1. A French prosecutor (MS JA) discovered a case of arms smuggling, involving organized crime from various EU countries. To gather more information about this from other countries, he writes a corresponding petition to the French national corresponded.
2. The French national corresponded forwards this to the French EJ National Member (EJNM France). He analyses the petition and decides to ask EJNM from other countries about the incident. Therefore, he describes the case in a standardized document and forwards it to them.
3. After consultation with the other EJNM, it is decided that the EJNM from Germany should gather information about related incidents in Germany.
4. Therefore EJNM Germany contacts the German Europol Liaison Officer (ELO) and sends him the case description.

5. Apart from contacting the police agencies in his country (MS LEA Germany), the ELO Germany also searches in Europol IT systems for information regarding the case.
6. The Germany ELO sends the corresponding parts to the German EJNM.
7. The Germany EJNM communicates this to the group of EJNM related to the case, including the French EJNM.
8. The French EJNM communicates the relevant data to the French prosecutor who initiated the process.

In this process different means of communication might be used, e.g. telephone, personal meetings, email and postal mail. To guarantee the privacy of the sensitive information, all communications are highly secured. Therefore, all information items transferred are classified to be used only by certain roles. Though also the interaction between organisational units inside of Europol (EP) and Eurojust (EJ) need to be regarded by an interoperability solution, in the following we concentrate on the interaction across the boundaries of EJ and EP: In the example process, these are the steps 4 and 7.

Objectives of the Interoperability Solution

The evaluation of the Europol-Eurojust and the other R4eGov scenarios resulted in the definition of various requirements for developing interoperable systems (Matheis et al. 2007, Diedrich et al. 2007, Spadone, 2006, Schaad 2007, Boujraf & Noble, 2007). Based on these requirements and taking into account the current state of the art regarding methods to achieve interoperability the following objectives and principles were derived, that a corresponding interoperability architecture should support:

Enabling cross-organisational business processes. Technical interoperability (e.g. agreement on SOAP messaging) should be seen only as an enabler for organisational interoperability, e.g. the execution of a purposeful sequence of activities spanning various organisations. For this it is necessary to go beyond supporting disconnected, technical interactions and to support the execution of interactions sequences both on execution and on design level.

De-central enactment of processes. No central party should be needed to coordinate and enact cross-organisational processes. Instead, the parties should be seen as loosely coupled organisations interacting in pre-defined collaboration spheres.

Avoiding changes to partners' internal systems; Inside-Out approach. To agree on cross-organisational processes, two general methods can be followed: Outside-in means that collaborating organisations adapt their internal systems to a pre-defined, cross-organisational process. Inside-Out means that the cross-organisational process is composed from the processes of the individual partners, thus the parties have less obligations to adapt their internal systems. An approach is sought for, which enables cross-organisational processes requiring as few adaptations on internal (legacy) systems as possible.

Secure interactions. All interactions are subject to high security requirements. The interoperability solution should tackle this requirement on conceptual and technical level.

Compliancy and analysability. The processes executed at run-time should correspond to the restrictions defined at design-time (compliance) and running cross-organisational processes should be analysable, both at run-time and ex-post. The scope of this area to be analysed varies, though most important are the direct interaction partners, for example: Which activities are executed, and does their security levels correspond to the security level demanded? But similar to supply-chain scenarios such information might also be sought from indirect interaction partners, e.g. the partners of the partners.

Flexible processes. Since many actors with various behavioural options are involved for example in the Europol-Eurojust scenario, these processes have so many variants that it would be hardly feasible to capture all of them in form of classic end-to-end process models. To avoid large amount of such process variants, instead of long process chains the aim should be to describe small process chunks that are re-usable in various process variants. Optimally pre- and post-conditions of these chunks would be described in a way that allows to string them together (semi-) automatically at run-time.

FOUNDATIONS OF A BUSINESS INTEROPERABILITY INTERFACE

Methods Proposed to Realize These Objectives

A selection of state of the art methods from the field of cross-organisational business process development were chosen to realize these objectives. Those comprise high level principles (like adherence to certain SOA characteristics) but also concrete measures, e.g. the implementation of a secure messaging infrastructure.

SOA as the guiding principle. SOA means loosely coupled services via coarse grained, conceptual interfaces and the possibility to publish and discover such interfaces via distinguished repositories. In a SOA also the principle of business process orientation should be followed, e.g. the separation between a process and the services comprised in it. To foster interoperability of SOA implementations, widespread standards of the Web Service Stack should be used, including XML-based standards for description of services (e.g. the Web Service Description Language WSDL), processes (e.g. the Business Process Execution Language, BPEL), transactions (e.g. WS-atomicTransaction) and non-functional characteristics (e.g. the WS-Reliability standard).

Specification of stakeholders via public views. Following the SOA paradigm, actors will publish their behavioural possibilities and constraints to the collaboration partners. This supports a de-central approach to collaboration, where partners first publish their possibilities and expectations and optionally might adapt their interfaces to optimize a collaboration with partners. Interfaces should be provided both on a conceptual and on a technical level.

Distinguished collaboration spheres. The possibilities to participate in certain cross-organisational processes will be restricted to members of a previously defined collaboration sphere, for example all organisations that need to participate in the Europol-Eurojust collaboration. Each member will have its own public interface as well as the list of partner interfaces, which it can query for available services.

Publish and discovery via distributed repositories. Each partner in a collaboration sphere will publish its public views to distinguished collaboration partners, enabling the partners to discover required services inside the collaboration sphere. Note, that the provision of conceptual models will also support the publish and discovery functionalities: In the BII the externally relevant processes, services, organisational structures etc. will be described via conceptual models, thus enabling other organisations to search for business level concepts rather technical artefacts. Thus, instead of one central service directory as foreseen in the traditional SOA approach, various partner-specific repositories will be implemented.

Preparing interoperability at design time. If different parties want to communicate, at some point of time their interaction style must be harmonized. This might either happen at runtime (example: before a discussion starts, two parties agree to use one lingua franka) or during execution of the interaction (example: they speak Chinese and French but hire a third party as a translator). To minimize disruptions and avoid misunderstandings during design and execution of cross-organisational processes confessions have to be made for the sake of a practically achievable interoperability solution, e.g. certain agreements should exist among the partners of a collaboration sphere. These comprise:

- **Agreement on allowed syntax**. All partners in a collaboration sphere have to agree to a common syntax. This comprises the technical level (e.g. network protocols) but also the design level (e.g. standards for business process modelling). Nonetheless, to extend the possibilities of including heterogeneous partners, communication should rely on a choice of alternative standards. For example, partners in a collaboration sphere could agree to use either UML activity diagrams, Event-driven process chains or BPMN to model business processes. In case one partner only uses BPMN, it could be automatically translated to the alternative standards.
- **Shared vocabulary**. Interacting partners should have a common understanding of terms, defined in a small, comprehensive and domain specific ontology. All terms used in the ontology should be agreed upon between the collaboration partners during design time. Thus it should not be necessary that the ontology (explicitly) supports reasoning, e.g. allowing the definition of new artefacts during run-time of CBP. The vocabulary should be seen as instances of metamodels as known from enterprise modelling. E.g. an Enterprise Architecture like ARIS (Scheer, 1998) could serve as an upper ontology, providing concepts like "organisational unit", or "function" to an ontology for the domain "Europol-Eurojust and related interactions"—which could comprise for example the concept "attorney of the state" or the concept "issue arrest warrant" as instantiations of the concept "organisational unit". Thus organisations are able to map their internal terms to a common metamodel for organisational units and roles, enabling to a common definition of what the term "state attorney" means, what services he offers and what his rights are.

Model-Driven Interoperability. To support the publishing and discovery functions as well as to provide compliancy and analysability of executed cross-organisational processes, a model-driven approach will be followed. This will be ensured through semi-automatic model transformations and corresponding sustainable correlation between conceptual models and executable models. Other than compliancy, this correlation supports monitoring functionalities since it enables visualization of run-time activities via conceptual models.

Messaging infrastructure and security architecture. Both points focus on the implementation side of non-functional parts of the cross-organisational processes and are complementary to the solution tackled here, since we focus on functional aspects that have a counterpart on the business design level.[2]

Note that the requirement for flexible processes is not tackled explicitly by the measures described above. It is supported implicitly though, since SOA and the description of externally visible process in distributed repositories constitute the basis for the flexible composition of distributed process chunk into one process. The description of the exact nature of the pre- and post-conditions of the process chunks as well as the algorithm to connect them is left for future research.

Since they represent the cornerstone of the BII, in the following we will describe in more detail the concepts of public views, the various enterprise dimensions of concern for the collaboration and model-driven interoperability.

Private, Public and Global Views on a Process

If organisations want to interact they have to understand each other, e.g. know what they can expect from their partners and what their partners expected from them in a cross-organisational process. Cross-organisational processes can be described either from a central or de-central perspective. Due to the traditionally autonomous position of large public administrations and the large amount of possible global processes (that would be needed in case of a centrally described process landscape) and also to be aligned with the idea of loosely coupled services, we follow a de-central approach: Each public administration will describe the interactions it can be a part of in its own interface. As Figure 2 illustrates, this interfaces must at least be visible to the directly related partner organisations, e.g. those organisations with which messages are exchanged.

In the last decade, the area of cross-organisational processes was investigated intensively, e.g. Van der Aalst[3], Petri Nets[4], workflow research[5] and has been studied by various research Projects, e.g. ArKOS[6], ATHENA[7] and Interop NOE[8]. Recent research efforts in CBP design were accompanied by the upcoming of new SOA standards and related concepts like Web Service Choreography and Web Service Orchestration. As an outcome, three major types of models supplementing cross-organisational businesses can be observed: First, a "big picture" of the overall CBP, also called *global process model*, that displays all organisations involved in the CBP and their interactions. Second, models of so-called *private processes* which are executed inside an individual organisation and should not be published (completely) to collaboration partners; nonetheless, they contain some activities that contribute to the CBP. And third, *public processes* (also called business process stubs, process interfaces or view processes) that display only those parts of the private processes relevant for the interaction with the other organisations. The same model types are, however, described differently depending on the research community that uses the model type. For example, Schulz & Orlowska (2004) also proposed a 3-tier workflow model for cross organisational workflow that captures private partner workflows, workflow-views and coalition workflows.

During the evaluation of the use cases it became evident, that the private-public-global concept

Figure 2. Organisations publish their interfaces to relevant partners

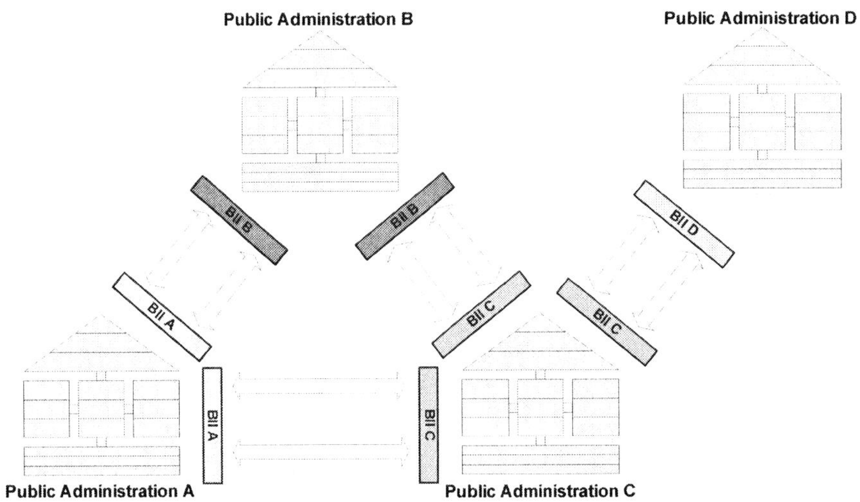

Figure 3. Relations between private, public and global systems

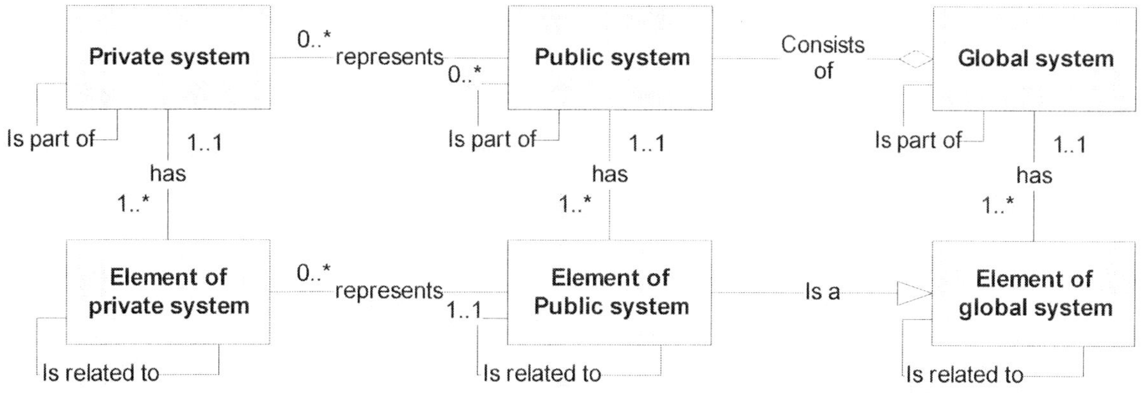

should not be restricted to processes, but should be applied explicitly to other artefacts forming part of the collaboration, also. In the case of the EP-EJ use case for example, internal rights and roles have to be mapped to globally accepted rights and roles. Therefore a generalization of the private-public-global concept was created: Figure 3 displays the relations between private, public and global systems. A public system can be seen as the interface of a private system. It only display those parts of the private system, that are of relevance to collaboration partners e.g. send and receive command, exchanged documents, or organisational roles involved in an interaction. It does not contain any secret information contained in the private system. A collection of complementary public systems constitutes a global system, for example, the public systems "A sends document X to B" and "B receives document X from A" could represent a valid global system.

Different Enterprise Dimensions to be Published

Former research focused on the process dimension and accordingly how to separate internal processes from their external counterpart. But akin to processes, also from data internal and external views can be derived, as well from organisational roles. For example a cross-organisational workflow could refer to the role "assistant" (external representation) while inside of an organisation the term "clerk" (internal representation) is used. Depending on the context of the interoperable systems, the importance of individual dimensions varies. Since the R4eGov case studies showed a high need for security, the public view of the organisational dimension is of special importance, where the rights and role of actors involved in collaborations are described. Figure 4 illustrates that other enterprise dimension can be relevant to design cross-organisational processes, also. To provide a comprehensive system for capturing other dimension relevant for cross-organisational processes, the five enterprise dimensions of the ARIS House are used.

The ARIS House (Scheer, 1998) describes a concept to model different aspects of an organisation. It covers five views necessary to model an integrated information system. The main goal of the different views is to reduce the complexity of a business process model and thereby to simplify the development of information systems. The data view comprises the description of messages (e.g. messages that trigger functions or are produced by functions) and other environmental data related to specific functions. The organisation view describes the organisational structure of an organisation and indicates the organisational units which execute the functions. The function

Figure 4. Multi-dimensional interfaces describe the public view of each organisation

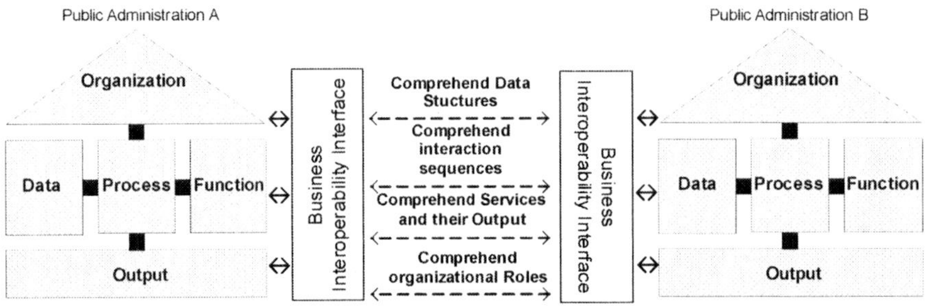

view describes the processes that transform input into output. The output view describes various the input types going into functions as well as the produced outcome. While the static structure of a system is captured by the data, organisation, function and output view, the dynamic aspect is described by the process view (also called control view); this view describes the relationships between the other views and composes them into one integrated business process. Note that there are a number of other frameworks for categorizing and modelling organisational elements (Zachmann, 1987; Vernadat & Kosanke, 1992). ARIS was chosen due to its suitability to conceptually prepare service-oriented Architectures (Ziemann, Leyking, Kahl, & Werth, 2006) and the fact that it is one of the few enterprise modelling methodologies proven to be applicable in practice—also in public administrations, e.g. it applied in many "Landesverwaltungen" of the different federal states of Germany (Scheer, Kruppke, & Heib, 2003).

Different Levels of Technical Detail to be Published

The collaborating parties should not only agree on the design of CBP, but also on the technical realization. Thus, beside the public views on design level, the BII should also contain public views on a technical level. Naturally, the technical counterparts of the design models should be compliant with those. Therefore, the concepts of Private Process, Public Process and CBP described above for the aim of modelling CBP on a conceptual level can be correlated to their counterparts on the Web Service level: conceptual private processes can be mapped to BPEL executable processes, conceptual public processes to BPEL abstract processes and conceptual global models can be mapped either to WS-CDL or to a set of complementary BPEL abstract processes (Ziemann, Kahl, & Werth, 2007). Since such interactions should be controlled by business analysts, we propose an EPC based design of the Web Service interactions. As figure 5 illustrates, we propose a two step transformation from the EPC level to the Web Service level. On the upper level, private and public processes are modelled by business analysts. Afterwards, these EPC are enriched with Web Service specific information and shaped according to conventions for compliance with BPEL processes. These models contain the Web Service invocations (also describing the message exchanged between collaborating administrations) and all control flow information relevant to specify the sequence of interactions. Note that this type of EPC processes can also be used as a visualization of BPEL processes. In the second step these technical EPC processes are further enriched by BPEL programmers, e.g. with variables used in a BPEL process to realize the control flow specified by the technical EPC process, and annotated in XML.

Following a procedure model as described below, the conceptual models should be derived

Figure 5. Adjusting organisational interfaces on three vertical levels

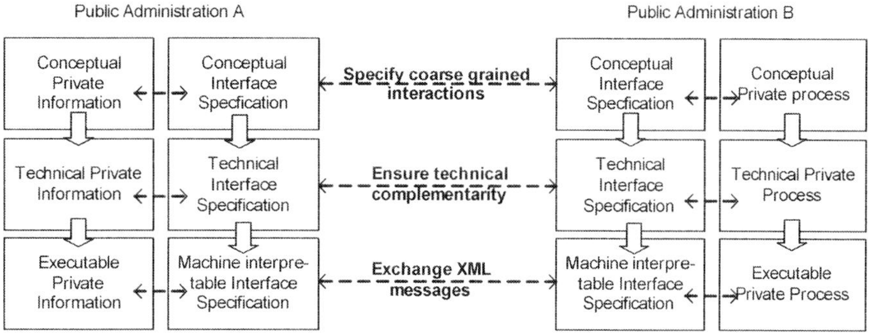

in a coherent way, ensuring that the public processes of collaborating parties are complementary. Following a model driven approach ensures that the implementation of the CBP is compliant to the conceptual model. Nonetheless, since the technical model contains further information (e.g. the name of Web Services to be invoked), the technical public process models have to be synchronized as well.

Figure 5 illustrates three vertical levels and distinguishes between internal view and an external/interface view of the processes on all three levels. The external view of Pubic Administration A shows how Public Administration B can interact with A without revealing classified knowledge of A. This kind of layering allows an incremental adoption and refinement of models which is commonly applied in IT development and is similar to the Model Driven Architecture approach of the Object Management Group. It also allows the correlation of technical models with conceptual model, e.g. for monitoring purposes technical events could be displayed inside a conceptual business process model.

THE BII AS CORE OF AN INTEROPERABILITY ARCHITECTURE

The aim of our approach is to support interoperability between large European public administrations, making use and extending the possibilities that modern information technology offers. Many different definitions of interoperability exist (Peristeras & Tarabanis, 2006), the IEEE Standard Computer Dictionary defines Interoperability as "the ability of two or more systems or components to exchange information and to use the information that has been exchanged"[9]. Nonetheless, in case of homogenous environments where "interoperability" is implicitly given due to the same language used by the involved components, no problem or research challenge exists. Accordingly, Klischewski & Scholl (2006) stress that systems and applications which interoperate are characterized by the following aspects: independency, heterogeneity, and control by different jurisdictions/ administrations or by external actors; yet also cooperation in a predefined and agreed-upon fashion. This leads to the following definition: *An interoperable software system consists of loosely coupled software components which might be heterogeneous and owned by different jurisdictions. A predefined and agreed-upon method for the description of the system elements allows implementing the interactions between the components as intended by their owners.*

In our context, an interoperability architecture aims at software development, and the term architecture refers to a software architecture. As for the term interoperability, also for the term software architecture many different definitions exist.

The most important characteristics of software architecture can be described as follows (Bass, Clements, & Kazman, 2006):

- Architecture is *high-level* design
- Architecture is the overall *structure* of the system
- A Software Architecture describes a software system comprising its *components and their interrelations* as well as the principles and guidelines governing their design and evolution over time.

This also corresponds to the often cited architecture definition of the IEEE 1471-2000 standard[10], which states that an architecture is the fundamental organisation of a system, embodied in its components, their relationships to each other and the environment, and the principles governing its design and evolution. Further, an architecture can be divided into a description view, describing the various levels and views contained in architecture models, and into a construction view[11], which provides a guide for the development of the models comprised in the architecture (Heutschi, Österle, Winter, & Brenner, 2007).

Combining the characteristics of both terms described above leads to the following definition: *An Interoperability Architecture describes the overall structure of an interoperable software system from a high level perspective. It describes the components comprised in the system and their relationships as well as the principles and guidelines governing their design and evolution over time.*

Combining the methods described above (model-driven interoperability, coverage of all enterprise dimensions, public-private-global views on systems) we define the BII as follows: *The Business Interoperability Interface of one organisation represents the sum of all models this organisation has to publish to collaboration*

Figure 6. Usage of the BII to describe the boundaries of Public Administrations on a conceptual level

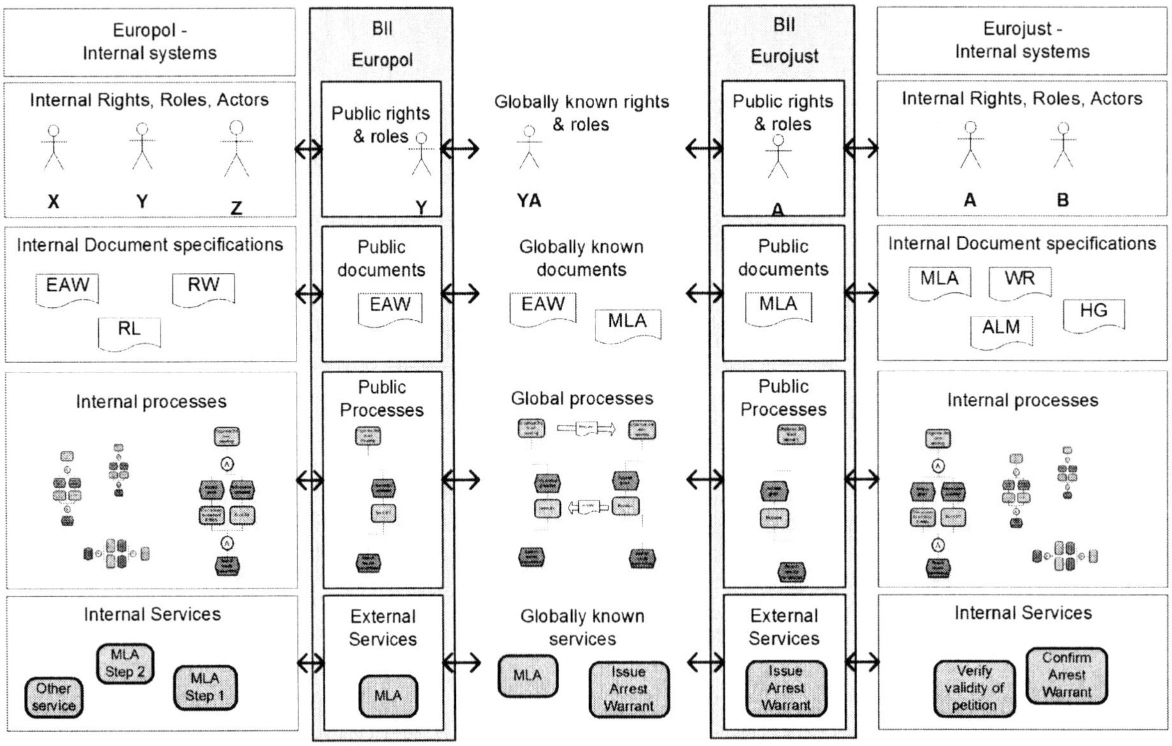

partners to enable a cross-organisational process with them. These models should cover the relevant enterprise dimensions and should be given in a conceptual, technical and code level.

Since the BII describes the boundaries of the interacting components and also the knowledge on how the components interact[12], the BII provides the essential elements of an interoperable software system and thus can be seen the core of an interoperability architecture.

To enable the agreement on cross-organisational processes during design time and to support the cross-organisational discovery of interaction elements, the interfaces of individual organisational will be described and published in the Business Interoperability Interface. The BII will describe the various dimensions relevant for cross-organisational interactions, including public views on internal processes as well as on services, organisational structures and documents. Accordingly, Figure 6 illustrates these elements between EJ and EP via the BII. Both parties display their internal systems given as the sum of processes, documents, actors and services. Correlated to the internal models are the externally visible views, which aggregate into the BII. In between the public views of both parties are the global system views, which can be seen as a sum of complementary public views. For example, a valid global process is made of two complementary view processes. Note that—though the public views are the main content of the BII—the BII might also contain global system views to indicate which public views are complementary to each other; e.g. the EP BII might store a global process which contains both the public view of EP and EJ which are verified to be complementary. Note also that in the graphic above aspect of model-driven interoperability is not illustrated: as shown in the example (see below), the conceptual models will be accompanied by their technical counterparts, e.g. apart from a conceptual business process displayed in EPC, the BII of Europol will also contain the representation of this process in machine-interpretable format like BPEL.

Correspondingly in the R4eGov project an "Interoperability Gateway" is responsible for the secure, well performing message exchange, which is complementary to the Business Interoperability Interface described here.

While the BII focuses on functional aspects, non-functional aspects will be covered by an *interoperability gateway* that provides runtime functionalities for sending, receiving, evaluat-

Figure 7. Business interoperability interface vs. technical interoperability gateway

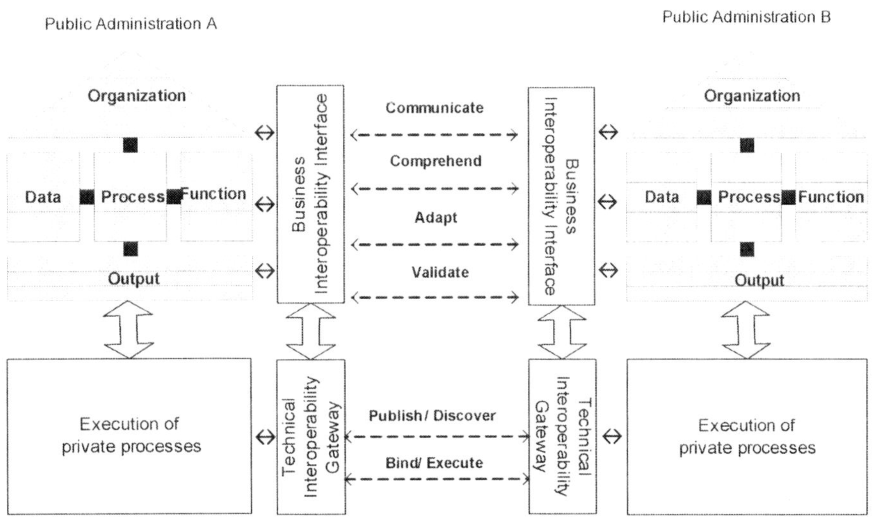

ing and judging messages and is responsible for secure data transmission and routing during runtime (Plate & Huys, 2007). Note, that although the BII focuses on conceptual information it will provide the technical versions of the conceptual information contained in it, e.g. conceptual process descriptions in form of Event-driven process chains but also their corresponding BPEL versions. But more fine grained technical information, e.g. security information going beyond the description of organisational roles, will be tackled by separate repositories comprised in the technical interoperability gateway. Correspondingly, Figure 7 displays the main elements of the overall interoperability architecture, to be implemented by each organisation: a business interoperability interface, focusing on design time, and the (technical) interoperability gateway, enabling the run-time message exchange. Note, that each dimension of the ARIS house is divided into three layers, illustrating that the BII contains conceptual (e.g. EPC), semi-technical (e.g. BPMN or technically enriched EPC) and executable models (e.g. BPEL).

In general, two cases of process automation can be distinguished that should be supported by the interoperability architecture:

1. *Automation of strongly coupled processes.* In this case a predefined unique correlation between the conceptual models comprised in the CBP description exists. For example, such a description would contain the information that at a certain point of time service A sends message X to service B; no other kind of interaction could be executed, no other party could be addressed. In this case, the process automation can be realized similarly to MDA approaches, transforming conceptual models into levels of higher technical detail.
2. *Automation of flexible processes.* In collaborative scenarios as observed in real life, often CBP are not rigid, completely predefined at design-time but rather flexible, allowing for different combinations of process parts and actors involved in a CBP. For example, service A could be followed by service B, but also by other services which fulfil the requirements description as given by service A. Thus, process automation should support scenarios where no predefined, unique CBP execution sequence is defined explicitly at design time, but instead a group of weakly coupled process parts and their pre- and post conditions allow for the execution of different CBP variants.

In the case of tightly coupled process, collaboration partners will use the BII information only at design time, to agree on the characteristics of a cross-organisational process, and to derive technical models corresponding to the conceptual levels. In the case of flexible processes, the content of the BII repositories can be queried during run time to discovery process parts which would logically follow the currently executed process part and thus prolong the collaborative process.

If the BII is used at design time, collaboration partners can exchange their model parts in order to agree on a joint CBP. For example: Europol describes an interface that if offers to Eurojust for retrieving information about minor criminal occurrences. Eurojust can access this interface and develop a complementary interface. In case that Eurojust has difficulties in implementing this complementary interface (e.g. because Eurojust does not support a certain document type), it can propose a deviation from the interface Europol offered and ask for another document type. Therefore, Eurojust would modify the model of Europol's interface and send this modified model to Europol, asking if Europol would be able to implement this. Instead of directly sending a complex technical interface description, Europol would send in a first step a conceptual model of the interface, illustrating interaction sequences, document types and organisational roles comprised in the interface. Only after both organisations agreed on the design level, they would further specify the interface description on the technical level, e.g. by publishing XML Schema definitions for the documents and WSDL descriptions for the service offered. After this agreement process, both organisations would publish in their own BII repository both the conceptual model and the technical description to relevant partner organisations

THE BII APPLIED TO THE EJ-EP SCENARIO

Since this article focuses on the automation of strongly coupled processes, in the following we present a scenario how the BII can be used to develop such processes, e.g. how the different models to be comprised in the BII of each organization are derived. Using the EJ-EP use case introduced above, it is first explained how private, public and global process models are created on a conceptual level. Since in the BII also execution level models are stored, it is explained how, based on the public process models, abstract BPEL processes for each party can be derived. To tackle beside the process- also the organisational dimension of the BII, an outlook is given on how organisational elements can be published there.

Deriving Conceptual Public Processes

In Figure 1 the simplified global process of the Europol-Eurojust interaction is illustrated. In

Figure 8. Private and public parts of the processes from Eurojust and ELO Germany

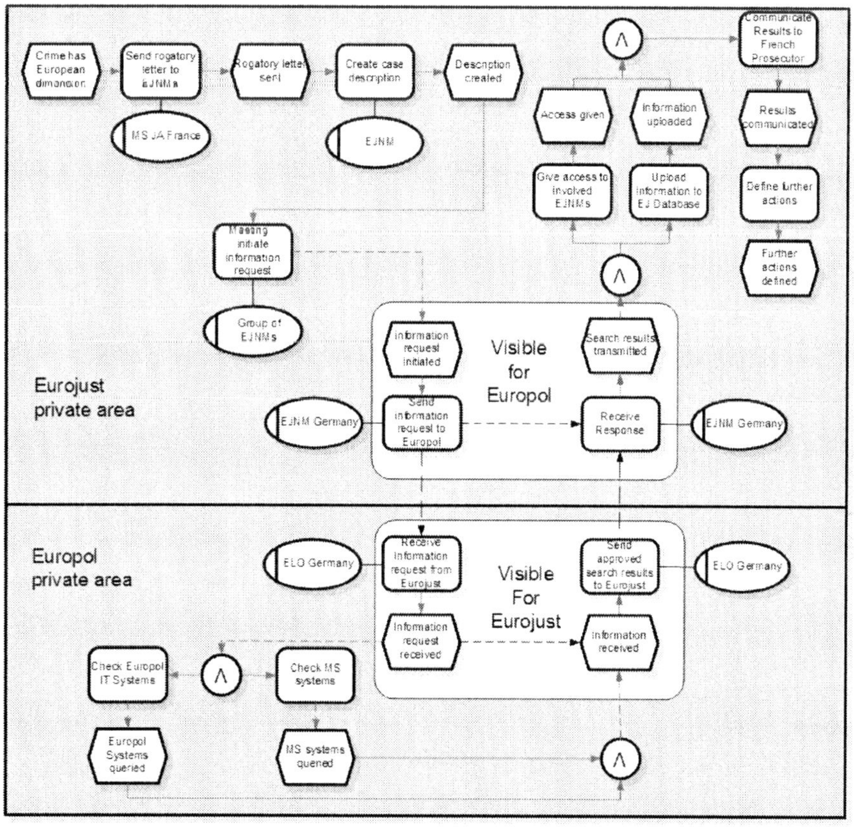

general, for developing fine grained CBP models, two approaches can be applied: an outside-in or an inside-out procedure. The inside-out procedure starts from existing private process, derives corresponding public processes and based on this establishes global processes. The outside-in approach starts from a fixed global model, derives the public interfaces and forces the collaboration parties to adapt their internal processes to the given global model. In reality, often a mix of both approaches can be observed, which involves various loops of adaptations between global, public and private processes. Thus, in the example scenario, a coarse grained global process exists. Coming from there, EP and EJ each create a refined process model of those private processes which supposedly are connected to the interaction. In this private process, they identify and detail those elements that should be visible to the partner: the public process. In a next step, EP and EJ have to verify that their public processes fit together.

Figure 8 shows the two private processes of EP and EJ, each one having distinguished public areas, which the partner can access. The public process areas should show to the direct interaction partners in which sequence what type of messages are exchanged. All other parts of the private process may stay invisible for the partners. Accordingly, the public areas in Figure 8 are restricted exactly to these information exchanges. On the other hand, even if functions are not directly involved in interactions, they might provide the collaboration partner with a better understanding of the process and also allow their own party to adapt its private processes better to the public process. If public processes are derived from a fine grained global process model, the global process normally indicates the organisational units responsible for an interaction and the public process can be derived accordingly: Each function of a global process that is annotated with organisation A must appear in the public process of organisation A. If more than one party is annotated to be responsible for this function, it has to be decided how this function is split up between these parties. In this case, an additional exchange of messages between these parties has to be integrated in the process.

Deriving Technical Public Processes

Based on the public processes shown in Figure 8, now technical EPC models are derived that contain the BPEL syntax necessary to specify the interactions between both parties. Since BPEL can represent both a graph based and a block-oriented control flow, nearly all control flow elements of EPC can be transformed to BPEL. If the EPC functions represent interactions (e.g. "receive message", "send message" etc.), they can be transformed to corresponding BPEL orders, if an EPC functions represents activities not captured by the BPEL syntax, an individual Web Service has to be created that will be invoked by the BPEL process. In Ziemann & Mendling (2005) further details regarding the transformation of EPC to BPEL are described. The result of the transformation from the EPC in Figure 8 to the BPEL aligned EPC is illustrated in Figure 9.

The whole interaction takes place between two Web Services: one offered by Eurojust, and one by the Europol. The source and destination services are attached to the interaction activities, e.g. "Invoke Async request Information from EITa" sends a message called "Request for information" to the corresponding operation of the Europol Web Service ("EP Web Service"). Again, these abstract processes only contain the information necessary to describe the interaction with the other Web Service, but not internal activities that may precede or succeed the externally visible activities.

Deriving Public Views on Organisational Elements

Similar to concepts for describing private and collaborative processes on the conceptual level, concepts have to be created to communicate organ-

Figure 9. EPC-based visualization of two complementary BPEL abstract processes

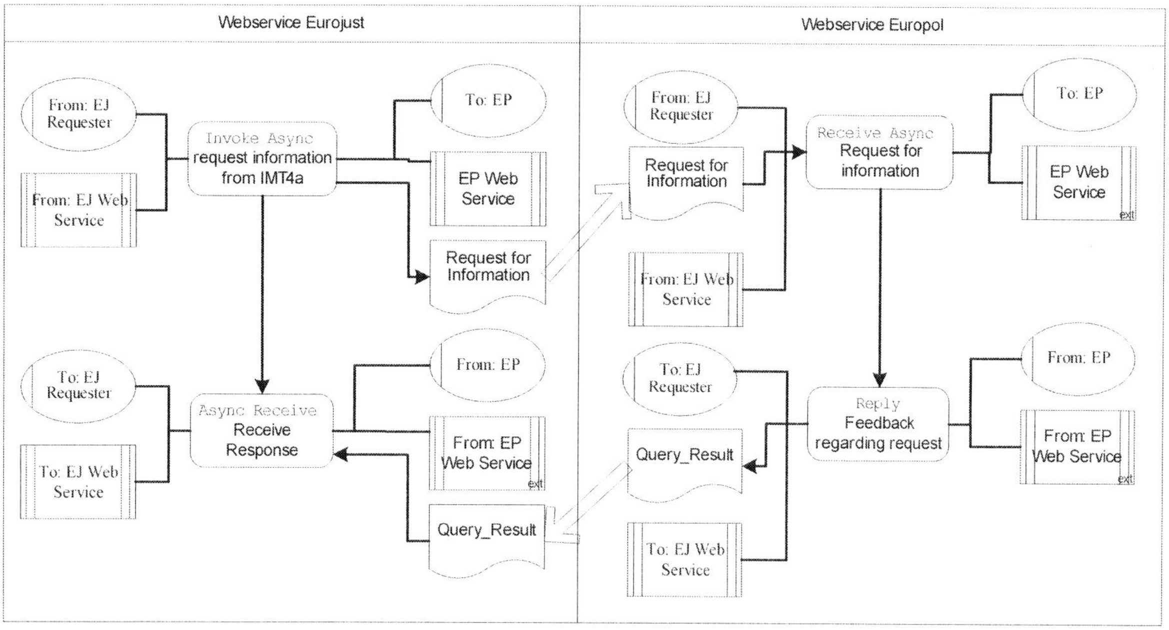

isational roles to partners in a cross-organisational process. This description should tell partners (e.g. organisation B and C), which rights certain roles in organisation A have, enabling them to judge for example if they can send this role documents having a certain degree of privacy. Such descriptions are especially important in scenarios like the EP-EJ use case, where transactions are security sensitive and fixed classifications for document secrecy and rights of stakeholders to access documents are specified. Accordingly, the private/public/global concept is applied to the organisational dimension of enterprise modelling[13].

Relation to work from the security area Though this work is originating from the enterprise modelling area, the result can be seen as closely related to work from the security area, e.g. role based access control (RBAC) for collaborative purposes (Lee & Luedemann, 2007). In comparison to RBAC models used in the security area, the models in the BII are not as technically detailed but still provide a bridge between enterprise modelling and security concepts: The typically more coarse grained models stemming from enterprise modelling can serve as an input to derive technical models needed in distributed RBAC implementations.

Private, public and global views on organisational elements in the EP-EJ scenario. Not taking into account the different levels of detail, two different kinds of organisational models were used in the EP-EJ scenario depicted by Boujraf & Noble (2007): internal models, describing organisational elements for internal stakeholders, and externally visible models, where collaboration partners describe for each other which organisational elements will be involved in the collaboration. The latter are specified in form of global models: the partners create one shared, agreed upon model that contains all elements relevant for the collaboration. In the case of just two collaborating organisations those two model types suffice. But in case that one organisation would collaborate with various changing partners, it would be more efficient to have a description of the externally relevant organisational units that could be offered to the different partners, and thus be a part of various global processes.

Therefore the use of an explicit public view for organisational elements from each organisation should be supported, constituting a part of the BII of each organisation participating in the collaboration.

Figure 1 illustrated the collaborative organisational meta-model on the Europol-Eurojust 1c) scenario which is now adjusted for the usage in the BII (compare Figure 10). EIT is a Europol organisational unit, with the right to receive an information request from Eurojust, transfer this internally and send a corresponding result to Eurojust. In order to disclose as little internal information as possible and to present collaboration partners with an expressive organisational name that corresponds to certain functionalities in a cross-organisational scenario, Europol creates a public visible proxy of this organisational unit called "EP information provider". This role has the right to execute two functions: "Receive EJ Information Request" and "Transmit EP Information", both functions have corresponding documents attached. These public visible roles can now be accessed by Eurojust, e.g. Eurojust knows to whom it could send an information request and from whom it could expect an answer. Eurojust itself creates a public visibly proxy of its "EJ NM" role, which can send out information requests to Europol and has the authorization to handle information coming from Europol. Note that all elements inside the area of "globally visible rights and roles" should be seen as public elements, also the functions and documents. Thus the function "Receive EJ Information Request" should be part of a public process and the specification (e.g. in form of an XML Schema Definition) of the "EJ Info Request" document should be public to the relevant collaboration partners also.

RELATED WORK

The BII can be seen as a consistent refinement and combination of well established concepts: Enterprise modelling, current SOA related concepts—like providing private, public and global views on services—and model-driven engineering. The proposed measure to implement the BII are based on wide spread, open source standards; thus SOA standards like WS-BPEL are supported instead of ebXML standards which do not have a comparable support. Related methods and frameworks for the design and implementation of cross-organisational business process comparable to the BII stem from various research areas as described in detail in the following.

Interoperability frameworks. To increase the cooperation between public administrations and to connect the corresponding software systems the European Commission has launched various research and development programs in the area of interoperability. Examples are the Interchange

Figure 10. Example instance of the metamodel for organizational structures in collaborations

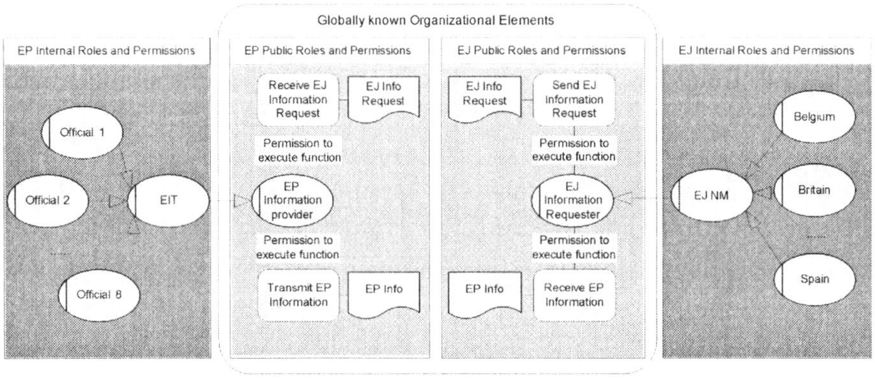

of Data between Administrations, Businesses and Citizens (IDABC, 2005) or the MODINIS program (MODINIS, 2005). The European Interoperability Framework (EIF) (European Commission, 2004) was developed within the Interchange of Data between Administrations (IDA) program (eEurope, 2005) as a framework for a common understanding of interoperability. The objective of the EIF is to support the delivery of European E-Government services to citizens and enterprises. Based on general principles like accessibility, security or the use of open standards, EIF gives recommendations and guidelines for E-Government services in order to enable the interaction of administrations, enterprises and citizens across borders. According to EIF interoperability frameworks should consider three levels of interoperability: organisational interoperability focuses on the interoperability of business processes and information architectures beyond the borders of different administrations. The semantic interoperability level aims at establishing a common meaning of the exchanged data, process models or used procedures. The linking of systems and the definition of corresponding technical standards in order to enable a seamless communication is addressed by the technical interoperability level (European Commission, Commission of the European communities, 2003). Recent analyses of current E-Government interoperability frameworks regarding their support to develop interoperable systems indicated that focus they on the descriptive aspects of interoperability by providing standards and technical recommendations for selected aspects of IT system development, but insufficient support the constructive aspects, for systematically implementing cross-organisational processes, e.g. by providing a procedure model of how to put the various standards involved in a CBP together (Cp. Matheis et al., 2007; Schmidt et al., 2007).

Service-oriented computing. The core idea of SOA is the loose coupling of services based on service description that enables their discovery in a service repository. To enable such a query and discovery, a suitable service interface description is essential. Correspondingly Overhage & Turowski (2007) state, that a specification framework to describe the externally visible characteristics of services must be the central element of a service development method. Also Heutschi et al. (2007) name interface-orientation as a design principle of SOA and cite six levels a service interface should provide. In difference to our work, their system for describing the interface does not explicitly facilitate a model driven approach. The three vertical levels of the BII allow for a systematic requirements modelling of all enterprise dimensions and a corresponding model driven refinement of the interface. But the six levels described by them do not allow such a systematic development since they represent a mixture between levels of technical detail and organisational dimensions. For example, their level 1 and 2 describe operations and thus would correspond to the ARIS function view on different level of technical granularity. Their level 3 corresponds to the ARIS process view, but the level of technical detail is unclear, e.g. if this process is on the technical level (e.g. in form of a UML activity diagrams) or on the code level (e.g. BPEL). Plus, their system does not comprise a requirements modelling level—which is essential for SOA, since to foster loose coupling, services should be described rather conceptual than technical.

E-Business protocol suites. Since protocols describe the sequence and nature of messages to be exchanged with an actor, protocols can be seen as technical interface descriptions. Various standards exist to describe protocols, including the Business Process Specification Schema (BPSS) of ebXML (Clark et al, 2001), the Partner Interface Processes (PIPs) of RosettaNet (http://rosettanet.org), WS-CDL and the abstract processes of BPEL (Business Process Execution Language for Web Services), which are also called BPEL protocols (Andrews et al, 2003). To establish an E-Business conversation, several components are necessary: interfaces published in a network, interaction descriptions and partner roles, a standard vocabulary and an environment of security and trust (Masud, 2003). RosettaNet, being a prominent example for E-Business protocols, contains all of the components listed above, but comprises only a predefined list of interaction patterns (called Partner Interface Processes, PIP) described with UML activity diagrams, text tables and XML documents. To provide more specific and technical process descriptions, Masud (2003) and Khalaf (2005) propose to transform PIPs, which represent proven well established reference models for CBPs, to BPEL processes. Other than PIP, the models in the BII are not restricted to pre-established interaction patterns, but allow also for the development of individual CBPs. The development of BII content starts from a thorough requirements modelling method by using EPC, which is originally destined for requirements modelling, other than similar approaches—as for example UN/CEFACT Modelling Methodology—which rely on originally technically notations like UML.

Frameworks for automation of cross-organisational business processes. Greiner et al.'s (2006) work describes the designing and implementing of cross-organisational business processes including different levels of technical detail: the business level, technical level and execution level. They identify how the mappings and transformations are needed among private process, view process and global process among the different levels. The business level models illustrate the organisational business aspects as a pre-requisite for the successful technical integration of IT systems or their configurations. The technical model derived from the business level model secures the technical realization of the process integration and represents the bridge to the process execution. Their work can be seen as a predecessor of the work presented in this article, but it covered only the process dimension, not taking into account the other enterprise modelling dimensions, and did not focus on the interface aspect or on a corresponding architecture.

SUMMARY AND FUTURE RESEARCH

New legal settings, the need for improved quality of service and technological advances increase the pressure on Public Administrations to cooperate in order to modernize and innovate procedures. Thus, the automation of cross-organisational processes is a clear objective of PA, but due to their traditional independence and the resulting desire to minimize modifications of internal systems, a tight system integration rather than a loose coupling of PA is strived for. In this vein, a method was presented that enables a PA to develop a comprehensive interface it can publish to its partner organisations. The so-called Business Interoperability Interface describes the externally visible behaviour of an organisation in various dimensions and supports a collaborative design and execution of cross-organisational processes, enabling the loosely coupling of organisations in cross-organisational processes. Note however, that this approach does not tackle "soft" interoperability barriers like different cultures in PA, which might hinder cooperation, but presumes that involved stakeholders are able to specify a valid cross-organisational scenario based on semi-formal process models.

The requirements for the development of an interoperable system were derived from current cross-organisational processes between European PA, namely the Europol-Eurojust collaboration. Correspondingly, a list of objectives that this solution should fulfil was defined, including a de-central enactment of processes, an inside-out approach and the agreement on a shared vocabulary. In section 2, the foundation of the BII was described: a composition of state-of-the-art concepts was proposed to fulfil the requirements gathered before. The most important concepts comprise the dissection of cross-organisational processes in a) various enterprise dimensions, b) different levels of technical detail and c) in private, public and global elements. In section 3, the core concepts were joined into a method to create the BII and the position of the BII as a cornerstone of an interoperability architecture. In section 4, these concepts were applied to the previously introduced Eurojust-Europol case study. Section 5 compared the BII method with related research, which was divided in four areas: interoperability frameworks, Service-oriented computing, E-Business protocol suites and business process automation.

Though the BII concept was motivated, described and illustrated, this work is to be seen mostly as a starting point for detailed future research: it is necessary to detail, complement, validate and implement the outlines given here. This article concentrated on the process dimension, where most research exists regarding the public-private-global concept. Nonetheless, in the process dimension, work still needs to be done regarding the correlation of the horizontal models (e.g. how to map public views to existing private views?) likewise in the correlation of vertical models, e.g. how does a EPC public process map to a BPEL abstract process? The other dimensions—organisational elements, documents, services and their output—need to be tackled correspondingly.

As described above, the BII is supposed to support two cases of process automation: Automation of strongly coupled and automation of flexible processes. This article focused on the first case, e.g. a tightly coupled CBP on the conceptual level is transformed to a tightly coupled process in BPEL. But it can be expected, that the BII represents a good foundation to achieve flexible processes: Following the SOA concept, the mechanism to achieve loose coupling is the discovery and binding of conceptually described services. The major obstacle to realizing this remains a suitable description of services that would allow for such a discovery. But since the different horizontal (enterprise dimensions) and vertical (technical granularity) dimensions of the BII represent a broad description and cover all enterprise dimensions relevant for a collaboration, the BII description should form an effective means to discover a needed service. Future work will consist in defining the public views on the different ARIS dimensions in such a way that they can serve as an upper ontology used by collaboration partners to describe the services available in a collaboration sphere.

ACKNOWLEDGMENT

The work published in this article is (partly) funded by the European Commission through the R4eGov project. It does not represent the view of European Commission or the R4eGov consortium, and authors are solely responsible for the article's content.

REFERENCES

Andrews, T., Curbera, F., Dholakia, H., Goland, Y., Klein, J., Leymann, F., Liu, K., Roller, D., Smith, D., Thatte, S., Trickovic, I., & Weerawarana, S. (2003). *Business Process Execution Language for Web Services – Version 1.1.* Retrieved April 28, 2006 from http://dev2dev.bea.com/techtrack/BPEL4WS.jsp

Bass, L., Clements, P., & Kazmann, R. (2006). *Software Architecture in Practice. Second Edition.* Addison Wesley.

Boujraf, A. D. A., & Noble, M. (2007). *Delivery of final master case study. Towards e-administration in the large (R4eGov).* Deliverable WP3-D7. R4eGov—Towards e-Administration in the large (Proposal/Contract no.: IST-2004-026650).

Clark, J., Casanave, C., Kanaskie, K., Harvey, B., Clark, J., Smith, N., Yunker, J., & Riemer, K.

(2001). *ebXML business process specification schema version 1.01.* UN/CEFACT and OASIS.

Diedrich, E., Wimmer, M., Schmidt, D., Mondorf, A., Matheis, T., Ziemann, J., & Freiheit, J. (2007). *Analysis of R4eGov scenarios for interoperability.* Deliverable WP4-D3. R4eGov—Towards e-Administration in the large (Proposal/Contract no.: IST-2004-026650).

E-Europe. (2005). *An information society for all: E-Government.* Retrieved August 14, 2006, from http://europa.eu.int/information_society/eeurope/2005/all_about/action_plan/index_en.htm

European Commission. (2004). *European interoperability framework for pan-European e-government services. European communities.* Retrieved August 14, 2006, from http://europa.eu.int/idabc

European Commission, Commission of the European Communities. (2003). *Linking-up Europe: The importance of interoperability for e-government services.* Staff Working Document.

Greiner, U., Lippe, S., Kahl, T., Ziemann, J., & Jaekel, F. (2006). *Designing and implementing cross-organisational business processes – description and application of a modelling framework.* I-ESA Conference, France, Bordeaux.

H. Lee, H., & Luedemann, H. (2007). *A lightweight decentralized authorization model for interdomain collaborations.* ACM Workshop on Secure Web-Services.

Heutschi, R., Österle, H., Winter, R., & Brenner, W. (2007). *Serviceorientierte architektur: Architekturprinzipien und umsetzung in der praxis.* Berlin, Germany: Springer.

IDABC. (2005). *The IDABC program (2005-2009).* Retrieved on August 14, 2006, from http://europa.eu/scadplus/leg/en/lvb/l24147b.htm

Khalaf, R. (2005). *From RosettaNet PIPs to BPEL processes: A three level approach for business protocols.* 3rd International Conference, BPM 2005, Nancy, France.

Klischewski, R., & Scholl, H. J. (2006). Information quality as a common ground for key players in e-government integration and interoperability. In *Proceedings of HICSS'06.*

Masud, S. (2003). *Use RosettaNet-based Web Services, Part 1: BPEL4WS and RosettaNet, 2003.* Retrieved April 28, 2006, from http://www-128.ibm.com/developerworks/webservices/library/ws-rosel/

Matheis, T., Ziemann, J., Diedrich, E., Schmidt, D., & Wimmer, M. (2007). *Methodical interoperability requirements for e-government.* Deliverable WP8-D1. R4eGov—Towards e-Administration in the large (Proposal/Contract no.: IST-2004-026650).

MODINIS. (2005). *MODINIS program: Follow-up of e-Europe 2005 action plan.* Retrieved on August 14, 2006, from http://europa.eu/scadplus/leg/en/lvb/l24226c.htm

Overhage, S., & Turowski, K. (2007). Service-orientierte architekturen – konzept und methodische herausforderungen. In V. Nissen, M. Petsch, H. Schorscht (Hrsg.), *Service-orientierte architecturen – chancen und herausforderungen bei der flexibilisierung und integration von vnternehmensprozessen.* Deutscher Universitätsverlag.

Peristeras, V., & Tarabanis, K. (2006). The connection, communication, consolidation, collaboration interoperability framework (C4IF) for information systems interoperability. *IBIS – Interoperability in Business Information Systems, 1(1).*

Plate, H., & Huys, D. (2007). *Specification and design of an extensible execution environment for collaborative e-government processes.* Deliverable WP5-D8. R4eGov—Towards e-Administration in the large (Proposal/Contract no.: IST-2004-026650).

Schaad, A., & Rahaman, M. (2007). *Extended requirements analysis of a collaborative, interoperable, and secure document exchange system*. Deliverable WP3-D9. R4eGov—Towards e-Administration in the large (Proposal/Contract no.: IST-2004-026650).

Scheer, A.-W. (1998). *ARIS – Vom Geschäftsprozess zum Anwendungssystem. 3. Edition*. Berlin: Springer.

Scheer, A.-W., Kruppke, K., & Heib, R. (2003). *E-Government. Prozessoptimierung in der öffentlichen Verwaltung*. Springer.

Schmidt, D., Wimmer, M., Mondorf, A., Herborn, T., Dietrich, L., Matheis, T., & Ziemann, J. (2007). *Critical state of the art report on interoperability in the public sector*. Deliverable WP4-D2. R4eGov—Towards e-Administration in the large (Proposal/Contract no.: IST-2004-026650).

Schulz, K., & Orlowska, M. (2004). Facilitating Cross-Organisational Workflows with a Workflow View Approach. *Data & Knowledge Engineering, 51*, 109-147.

Spadone, P. (2006). *Collaborative workflow requirements for e-government*. Deliverable WP5-D1. R4eGov—Towards e-Administration in the large (Proposal/Contract no.: IST-2004-026650).

Vernadat, F., & Kosanke, K. (1992). CIMOSA: A reference architecture for CIM. In *Proceedings of the IFIP TC5/WG5.3 eight international PROLAMAT conference on human aspects in computer integrated manufacturing, FIP Transactions (Vol. B-3)*. North-Holland.

Zachman, J. A. (1987). A framework for information-systems architecture. *In IBM Systems Journal, 26*(3), pp. 276-292.

Ziemann, J., & Mendling, J. (2005). *Transformation of EPCs to BPEL – A pragmatic approach*. 7th International Conference on the Modern Information Technology in the Innovation Processes of the industrial enterprises, Genoa, Italy.

Ziemann, J., Kahl, T., & Werth, D. (2007). Using view process models in collaborative business processes. In Putnik, G. D., Cunha, M. M. (Eds.), *Encyclopedia of networked and virtual organisations*. Hershey, PA: Idea Group Inc.

Ziemann, J., Leyking, K., Kahl, T., & Werth, D. (2006). Enterprise model driven migration from legacy to SOA. In R. Gimnich, & A. Winter (Eds.), *Workshop software-reengineering und services*. Passau, Germany: MKWI.

KEY TERMS

Business Interoperability Interface: The Business Interoperability Interface of one organisation represents the sum of all public and global process models it must publish to partners to enable a cross-organisational process with them. To enable both design and execution of cross-organisational processes, these models should cover the relevant enterprise dimensions and should be represented in a conceptual, technical and code level.

Business Process: A Business process is a sequence of activities executed to reach a business objective.

Global Process: A global process describes the interactions between two or more organisations from a neutral perspective, capturing all allowed interactions between all partners.

Interoperable Software System: An interoperable software system consists of loosely coupled software components which might be heterogeneous and owned by different jurisdictions. A predefined and agreed-upon method for the description of the system elements allows implementing the interactions between the components as intended by their owners.

Interoperability Architecture: An Interoperability Architecture describes the overall structure of an interoperable software system from a high level perspective. It describes the components comprised in the system and their relationships as well as the principles and guidelines governing their design and evolution over time.

Private Process: A private process is a Business Process which is designed for internal purposes; its elements are private in the sense that they are not public to other organisations unless declared to be so.

Public Process: The public process of party A contains those parts of the private processes needed by its collaboration partners (e.g. party B and C) to understand how they can interact with party A. It is an interface to the outside-world which extracts only that kind of information which is necessary for the interaction with one or more potential partners. Unlike statically interfaces it describes not only the operations offered by an organisation but also the sequence in which operations are executed.

ENDNOTES

1 www.r4egov.eu

2 Correspondingly in the R4eGov project an "Interoperability Gateway" is responsible for the secure, well performing message exchange, which is complementary to the BII described here.

3 http://is.tm.tue.nl/staff/wvdaalst/

4 http://www.informatik.uni-hamburg.de/TGI/PetriNets/

5 http://www.workflow-research.de/

6 http://www.arkos.info/

7 http://www.athena-ip.org/

8 http://www.interop-noe.org/

9 Another interesting definition aiming in the same direction defines interoperability as "the capability to communicate, execute programs, or transfer data among various functional units in a manner that requires the user to have little or no knowledge of the unique characteristics of those units" (Source: ISO/IEC 2382-01, http://old.jtc1sc36.org/doc/36N0646.pdf).

10 IEEE Standards Association: Std 1471-2000 Recommended Practice for Architecture Description of Software-Intensive Systems. http://standards.ieee.org/reading/ieee/std_public/description/se/1471-2000_desc.html, 2004.

11 In other work, the terms "methodical" and "functional" are used instead of "constructive" and "descriptive". Compare Matheis et al. (2007).

12 Since public processes and global processes describe not only operations but also the sequence in which operations have to be executed.

13 Note that we refer to the structural aspect of an organisation, e.g. organisational elements and their relationship, not including dynamic aspects which describe timely relationships between enterprise elements. In German this difference is expressed by the terms "Ablauforgansation" (flow-oriented organisation) vs. "Aufbauorganisation" (structural organisation).

Chapter VII
ICT-Enabled Optimization of Government Processes

Lars Baacke
University of St. Gallen, Switzerland

Jörg Becker
European Research Center for Information Systems, Germany

Philipp Bergener
European Research Center for Information Systems, Germany

René Fitterer
SAP Research, Switzerland

Ulrike Greiner
SAP Research, Switzerland

Florian Stroh
SAP Research, Switzerland

Michael Räckers
European Research Center for Information Systems, Germany

Peter Rohner
University of St. Gallen, Switzerland

ABSTRACT

The public sector is facing an increased service level demand from citizens and companies which comes along with reduced financial scope. Higher process efficiency as well as time and cost savings are required to cope with this challenge. However, own experience shows that reorganization projects in public administrations which are based on established generic process modeling methods can only identify limited reorganization potential for ICT support in single processes and just lead to small local improvements (Algermissen et al., 2005). Therefore, we have created the modeling and analysis methodology PICTURE. The PICTURE methodology first applies the domain vocabulary to efficiently capture the process landscape of a public organization. It then analyses semiautomatically the processes and points at business processes with reorganization potential. Thus, PICTURE creates process transparency and supports decision makers in developing a holistic ICT investment and transformation strategy for the entire administration.

INTRODUCTION

Nowadays public administrations (PA) are characterized by fragmented processes with distributed responsibilities and decentralized service delivery as well as highly specialized and poorly integrated line-of-business applications. Several factors put an increasing pressure on public administrations to transform and integrate their processes as well as to improve quality of public services. These factors comprise but are not limited to the following:

- external directives (e.g. EU, law concerning digital signatures, guidelines for electronic data exchange between public administrations, financial accounting),
- external expectations (from business organizations, society and politics, citizens, other administrations),
- and internal needs such as cost reduction, cycle times, process orientation, interfaces to other external (or international) organizations.

However, process-oriented reorganization projects have shown that especially the storage, retrieval, and transport times within processes have a great impact on the reorganization potential (Algermissen et al., 2005). Related weaknesses occur in a number of processes (e.g. media breaks in the internal mail system or paper-based archiving). As a result, cross functional ICT (Information and Communication Technology) such as workflow or document management systems promise much potential as they are created to support many processes in a standardized way.

However, decision makers in public administrations face more than one thousand public services and several thousand underlying processes which are not documented in a structured way (PICTURE Consortium, 2006). Additionally, they face a large ICT market with manifold systems providing a wide range of application areas and functions which are not transparent. Thus, it is difficult to analyze where an ICT should be used and to calculate its (positive and negative) impacts on the existing or transformed processes. These difficulties result in uncertainty and hence discourage investments.

This chapter presents an approach to exploit existing reorganization potentials in public administrations by supporting decision makers through a methodology that makes the effects of ICTs on administrational processes measurable. It supports guidance and control in transformation projects and thus enables decision makers in European public administrations to develop successful ICT investment strategies. The methodology has been developed and prototypically implemented in a web-based prototype within the EU-funded research project PICTURE (http://www.picture-eu.org). The research method used to develop the PICTURE approach corresponds to the design research paradigm (Hevner et al., 2004) and is based on the work of Takeda et al. (Takeda et al., 1990), Song and Osterweil (Song, Osterweil, 1994), and Avison et al. (Avison et al., 1999).

The chapter is structured as follows: after a brief discussion of related work in the area of public administrations, process modeling, and process analysis we present and discuss in detail the three major parts of the PICTURE approach:

- **Model** the as-is situation of processes and ICT infrastructure in a strictly end-user driven approach. This is achieved through collaborative modeling by administrational staff using pre-defined process building blocks (a detailed description of the procedure for identifying such building blocks can be found in (Baacke et al., 2009)). These ensure usage of a common, syntactically and semantically comparable terminology by all involved participants.
- **Analyze** the impact of ICT components on the process landscape in a quantitative,

qualitative, and monetary dimension. This includes finding potential sources for inefficiencies and error-prone process parts and identifying appropriate ICT functionalities to resolve them. It also includes identifying possible process enhancements through ICT.
- **Visualize** the results in a set of reports which provide the decision makers with a sound foundation for their investment decisions.

After that we will discuss the results of the design of the PICTURE methodology in section 4 recapitulating the requirements conducted from related work and will finish with a conclusion which outlines further research.

RELATED WORK

Process Modeling in Public Administrations

Public administrations differ from the private sector in their structure, their spectrum of tasks and their set of objectives (cf. for example the results of the ICTE-PAN project, funded by the European Commission in 2002-2005 (Villa, 2005))[1]. The subject of business process management, process modeling and analysis stems from the private sector (Becker et al., 2003; Green, Rosemann, 2000; Shanks et al., 2003). In contrast to public administrations, such industries act in a more market-oriented way and are continuously adjusting their products and services to differentiate from competitors. As a result the private sector is very heterogeneous in the way of performing activities striving to produce in a faster and more efficient way than the competitors. This is reflected by the conducted activities or processes and the basic principles of operations. Generic process modeling notations such as Event-driven Process Chains (EPC) (Scheer, 2000) and Business Process Modeling Notation (BPMN) (Karagiannis, 1995; Mayer et al., 1995; Object Management Group, 2006; Schaffroth, 2005) have been primarily designed for usage in the private sector and therefore have to cope with this heterogeneity. A further examination of process modeling notations reflecting the public sector domain can be found in Brain et al. (Brain et al., 2005). However, generally, they are not specialized for certain types of enterprises or certain domains.

Public administrations though have specific challenges with respect to process modeling: (1) A single public administration offers a great variety of heterogeneous products and services which leads to a great number of underlying administrative processes (Algermissen et al., 2005). (2) Despite this large number, the administrative processes delivering these services are similar in structure due to the fact that the outcome of public administration processes is typically determined by law (Baacke et al., 2007). Therefore similar weakness points and modernization potential can be found in all public administrations. (3) Administrative processes often involve different departments (Villa, 2005). Therefore domain experts from different organizational units have to be involved when modeling processes. (4) The workflow of administrative processes is normally semi-structured (Knaack, 1999). An appropriate method to capture all processes in a semantically standardized way to allow for semi-automatic analysis for finding weaknesses and reorganization potentials has to consider the following requirements.

(R1) The modeling language facilitates capturing the entire process landscape: Experiences from reorganization projects in the public sector domain show, that in order to disclose reorganization potentials, it is important to capture more than a single process. A medium-sized municipal administration has more than 1,000 different processes (Algermissen et al., 2005). To fully identify the modernization potential in a public administration as much of these processes as pos-

sible should be considered in the analysis phase. However, it is also possible to analyze only a part of the administration, e.g. a specific department. The level of granularity of the process models for a complete overview has to be rather coarse to allow capturing them in a reasonable time frame. However, existing process modeling approaches lack an easy possibility to fix the level of abstraction of the created models which often leads to very detailed models.

(R2) The modeling language allows for efficient modeling: For budget reasons, efforts should be kept as small as possible when capturing the process landscape. However, in public administrations, the process knowledge is distributed over the whole administrations. To minimize the need for external consultants and reduce the modeling effort per person, the domain experts should be included in the modeling process. This leads to the requirement, that the modeling methodology must provide mechanisms to distribute the modeling tasks across the organization. Only distributed modeling involving as many domain experts as possible will ensure that enough relevant information for the analysis of a landscape of processes can be captured.

(R3) The modeling language is easy to understand for a domain expert: To ensure that domain experts can contribute to the modeling of processes the modeling language should exhibit a minimal and intuitive set of elements and constructs (Opdahl, Henderson-Sellers, 2002). This can be achieved by using domain specific constructs in the modeling language (Guizzardi et al., 2002; Kelly, Tolvanen, 2000). Universal modeling languages however lack these domain specific constructs.

(R4) The models are syntactically and semantically comparable: One reason why employees cannot improve their processes on their own is that not all of them have detailed knowledge about other employees' processes. To allow for an automated analysis of the process landscape it has to be possible to identify similar patterns in the processes which can be supported by the same ICT solutions. Therefore it has to be possible to identify similar or deviating structures in process models (Kashyap, Sheth, 1996) which is only possible if the models are syntactically and semantically comparable. However, if modelers can freely choose the level of detail, the naming, and the attributes type conflicts, naming conflicts and structural conflicts can arise (Batini et al., 1986; Lawrence, Barker, 2001; Pfeiffer, Gehlert, 2005). In an EPC, for example, one modeler might call a function which approves an application "Approve application" while another modeler names it "Accept application" (Synonym Conflict). Further, one modeler could use the functions "Check application formally" and "Check application contextually" to describe the steps necessary to check an application while another modeler just uses a function called "Check application". When using existing universal approaches, such conflicts can occur and so hamper an efficient analysis of the data (Hardar, Soffer, 2006; Pfeiffer, 2007).

Following these requirements it can be stated, that it will be hard to address them by generic modeling methods and notations. Therefore it is necessary to create a new process modeling approach to ensure that sufficient processes for a meaningful analysis can be captured in a public administration with the appropriate amount of information.

Existing ICT Value Analysis Concepts

Although a large number of ICT evaluation methods have been developed for the private sector (for example 65 ICT methods have been identified by Renkema & Berghout in 1997 (Renkema, Berghout, 1997)), only a few methods have been designed specifically for application in public sector organizations. These have emerged during the last decade in line with the initiatives for Public Administration reform across Europe and the world.

ICT evaluation methods and concepts addressing the public sector have been developed recently both by private organizations (e.g. Gartner, IBM, Accenture) as well as governmental organizations (US Federal Government, French Government, and Australian Government Information Management Office (AGIMO)). Moreover, there are initiatives by the European Commission such as the development of pan-European measurement frameworks (e.g. eGEP Measurement), the identification of pan-European benchmarking indicators (e.g. UNDERSTAND project (http://www.understand-eu.net/)) and the promotion of good practices (e.g. eGovernment Good Practice Framework (http://www.egov-goodpractice.org/)).

According to (Walter, Spitta, 2004) the value of ICT investment consists of positive impacts (benefits) and negative impacts (sacrifices or costs). These impacts are commonly divided into:

- **Qualitative impacts:** these are impacts that cannot be quantified or measured in monetary terms e.g. employee satisfaction, quality of services, process improvement etc.
- **Quantitative impacts:** these are further categorized into **monetary impacts** (e.g. cost of labor, operational costs such as consumables, printing, service transactions etc.) and **non-monetary impacts** (e.g. time of service execution, number of errors etc.)

We have analyzed twelve ICT value analysis methods and concepts which (i) consider qualitative and quantitative aspects, (ii) assess the impact of introducing ICTs in an organization and (iii) target public sector organizations (or are highly relevant for the public sector although having been developed for a different domain) (PICTURE Consortium, 2007c).

The key finding was that although a significant number of ICT evaluation concepts/ methods exists, these focus primarily on the impact of ICT on the end-users (citizens) rather than the back-office environment and the processes of a public administration. A few methods consider the impact of ICT on the back-office (e.g. operational efficiency measures), however they do not address the impact of ICT on the processes of a public administration in the desired detail. Additionally, the majority of methods focuses on the impact of E-Government (i.e. the electronic/web-based delivery of government services), whereas we address the impact of a broader spectrum of ICTs for the public sector that support administrational processes (such as document management or workflow systems).

Although parts of the various existing methods could have been reused, for the purposes addressed by PICTURE, a new measurement approach had to be developed.

THE PICTURE APPROACH

PICTURE Usage Scenario

The aim of PICTURE is to support decision makers in public administrations in their ICT investment decisions. This is achieved by illustrating and quantifying the effects these investments have on the process landscape of a public administration. Figure 1 illustrates a possible scenario how PICTURE can be applied in a reorganization project in public administrations.

One possible trigger for applying PICTURE is that management and *decision makers* in public administrations want to improve the quality of their services for the citizens (1). That endeavor is supported by a *PICTURE expert* who is typically a specially trained person in the IT department. This person is responsible for configuring the PICTURE tool according to the goals of the reorganization project (this relates to process modeling as well as to the process analysis) and serves as the advisor in the public administration (2).

The actual PICTURE project is conducted in three phases. In the first phase, the modeling phase, the processes of the public administrations are captured. As the decision makers and the PICTURE expert typically do not have an overview over all relevant processes, *modeling coordinators* from all involved departments assist them in identifying these processes (3). The modeling coordinators then assign modeling tasks to the actual *modelers*. These modelers are domain experts from the public administrations who model exactly those parts of the processes they are familiar with (4). This allows for a distributed modeling of the whole process landscape of the public administration (cp. requirement 2 discussed in section 2.1).

In the next phase, the analysis phase, a semi-automated process analysis is performed and inefficiencies are identified, based on the information captured in the process models. The impact of different ICT investments on these inefficiencies is measured in quantitative, qualitative, and monetary terms (5).

In the last phase, the visualization phase, the analysis results are presented to the decision makers in form of consolidated reports. The decision makers can use the results to derive the appropriate reorganization steps and reasonable ICT investments (6).

Model

In the following, the modeling methodology of the PICTURE approach is presented. The purpose of this methodology is to facilitate the capturing of all processes of a given public administra-

Figure 1. A usage scenario for the PICTURE approach

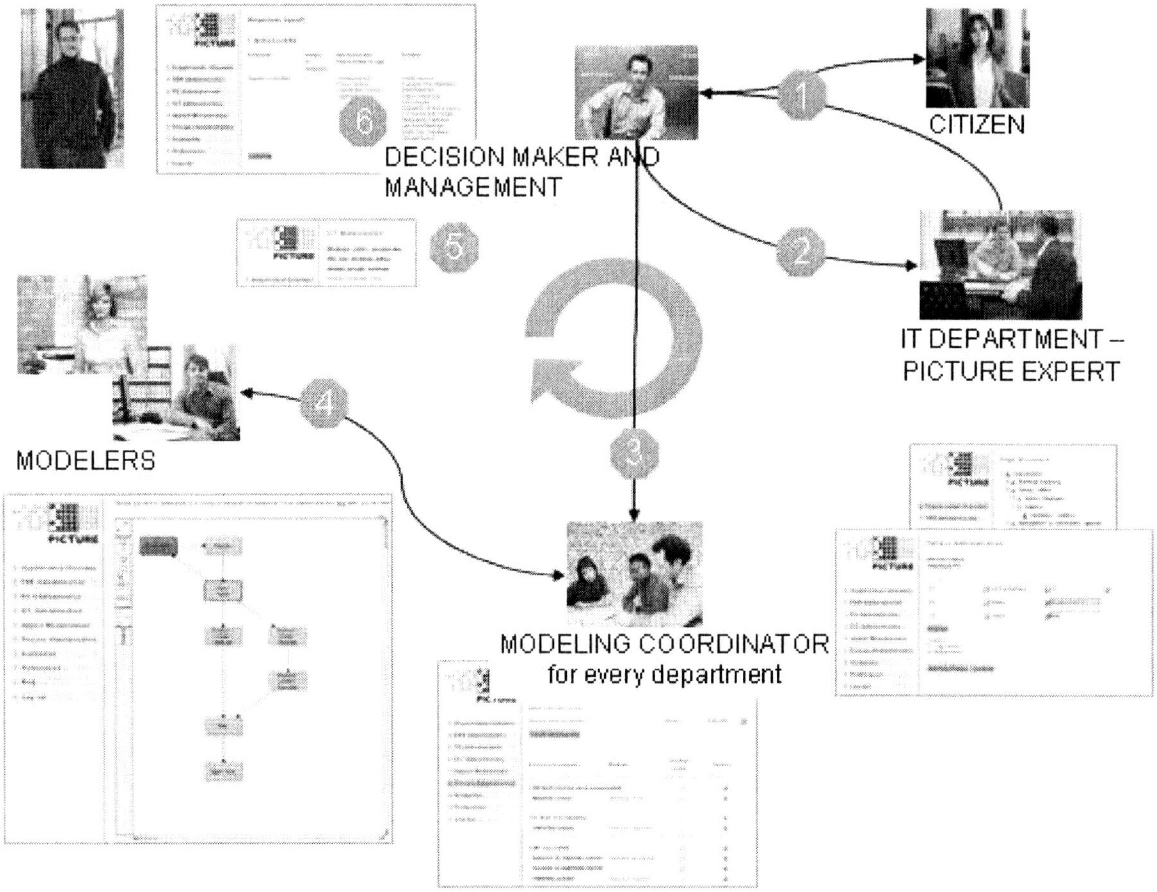

tion to provide a broad basis for the subsequent semi-automatic ICT impact analysis. Therefore, the modeling methodology must allow for an efficient and semantically standardized modeling of the process landscape. This is achieved by using a domain specific modeling method based on predefined Process Building Blocks (PBBs), which capture a set of common activities from the domain of public administrations (cp. section 3.2.4).

The PICTURE modeling methodology consists of four views: a Process view, an Organizational view, a Processed Object view and a Supporting Elements view. Figure 2 shows an example, how the different views work together. In the following, the views are described in detail.

Organizational View

The organizational view depicts the organizational structure of a public administration. Thereby, it is possible to capture two aspects: who executes a process or part of a process, and who is responsible for a process.

Capturing the people who are involved in a certain process is central for further analysis as it builds the foundation for deriving personnel costs from specified processing time. Additionally, other cost rates, for example printing costs, depend on the organizational unit associated with a process. Furthermore, capturing the organizational unit allows identifying processes with many organizational breaks.

The organizational view comprises the following elements:

Figure 2. Views of the PICTURE modeling methodology

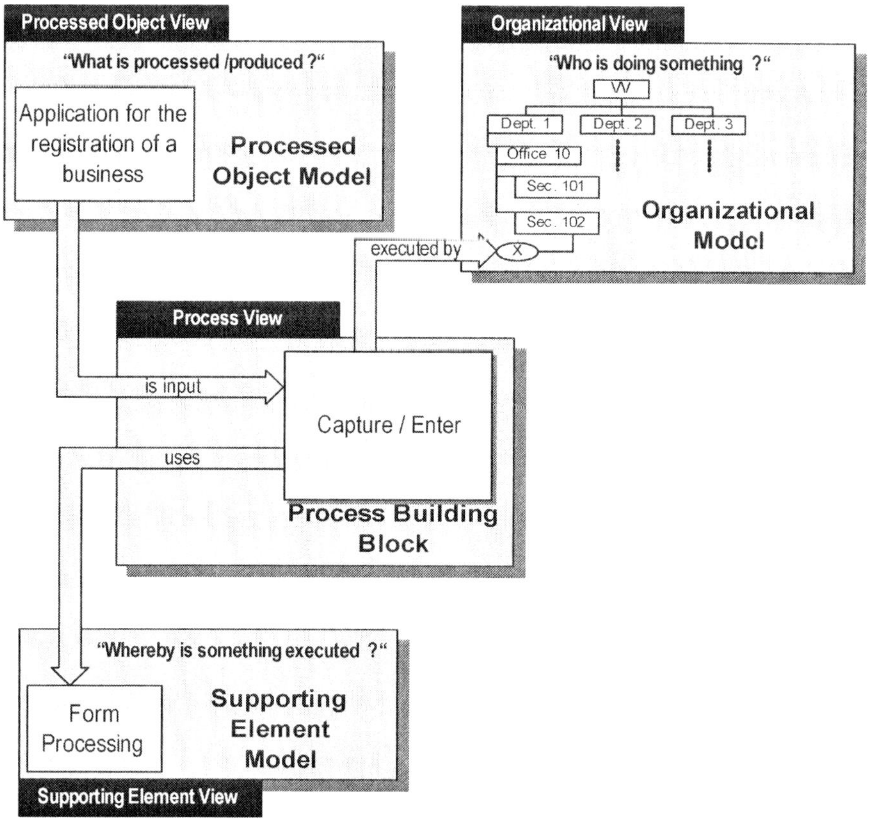

Organizational Units: Organizational units encapsulate a number of positions with similar tasks. As most public administrations are organized in a functional manner units can be modeled hierarchically. Typical organizational units are departments or offices.

Positions: A position is responsible for performing a certain set of tasks. This set of tasks is constitutive for the position. Therefore, a position is an abstract concept, which exists independently of the persons assigned to the position. One or more persons can be assigned to a position and one person can be assigned to one or more positions. Each position is associated with its respective organizational unit.

Persons: A person depicts an actual official of a public administration. As described above, a person can be assigned to one or more positions.

Processed Object View

The Processed Object view describes "what" is dealt with and what is produced in the administrative processes. In administrative behavior, typically information from different information carriers is consumed and other information is produced, e.g. a paper form or an oral transmission. Besides information, in a few cases physical objects can be the subject of processing, e.g. car license plates that are invalidated. The Processed Object view consists of the following elements:

Processed Object (PO): A Processed Object describes the information, document, message or any other object that is processed by the corresponding activity. Examples for POs are applications or permits.

Processed Object Category (PO Category): POs can be classified using PO Categories. These categories are organized hierarchically in a tree structure. This allows for the standardization of POs and therefore facilitates retrieval by the domain experts during modeling and analysis through standardization.

Supporting Element View

In an analogous manner to the Processed Object view, the Supporting Element view describes objects, which support domain experts during their activities. This view consists of the following elements:

Supporting Element: Supporting Elements depict those utilities that support an activity. They cover technical as well as physical information systems such as electronic and paper-based files, archives, etc.

Supporting Element Category: Similar to POs Supporting Elements are categorized in a hierarchical structure. This simplifies the selection, extension, and maintenance of Supporting Elements. Supporting Element Categories might e. g. be Software Systems or Hardware Devices.

Process View

The Process view depicts the process structure of the public administration. Its core constructs are the PBBs which represent single activities within the process. Main principle of the modeling approach is the differentiation between activities (PBBs) and the respectively processed objects (POs, such as documents, messages, etc.). PBBs (e.g. <send>, <sign> and <print>) as well as POs (e.g. "application form" and "approval") can be specified in more detail by the modeler using respective attributes such as "processing time", "communication channel", "medium" (of documents), etc. An initial list of PBBs and attributes identified in the project can be found in (Baacke et al., 2008). Furthermore, PICTURE uses constructs such as Processes, Sub-Processes, Alternatives, and Connections to structure the process landscape of a public administration. The Process view also integrates the other views via PBB attributes. A "global view" on the process describes thereby the flow of sub-processes within a certain process and hence shows connections between different organizational units/positions. On a more detailed level the "local view" describes the control and data flow within a sub-process using the concepts of alternatives and PBBs.

Process: In the modeling view of PICTURE a process consists of a combination of an object (e.g. a passport) and a specific action, which is performed on the object (e.g. to issue, to extend, or to change). Citizens or any other party inside or outside of a public administration can demand that object, (driver's license, passport etc.). A process consists of the activities (PBBs), which are necessary to perform a certain action.

A process as defined above can span several organizational units of a public administration and can therefore involve several employees. When those processes are captured in interviews with employees involved in a modeling project two strategies can be used: (1) Employees can provide information about the processes they actually perform or (2) about the processes they have some knowledge about. Most employees have relevant knowledge about many more processes than they actually execute. Collecting all this information from the employees corresponds to a *"Model what you know"* approach. The advantage of this approach is that only few employees have to be involved in a project to capture the desired processes. However, by following this approach one faces the risk of overlooking relevant information as the knowledge of each employee about specific details is limited. To avoid this, a strict *"Model what you do"* approach can be applied. Following this approach every employee only describes what he or she is doing without stating any other information. Especially, if the processes span multiple organizational units with many dependencies between them this option provides a more efficient approach. To facilitate this distributed capturing of processes the construct of a *sub-process* is introduced.

Sub-Process: Processes are further divided into sub-processes. Each process has at least one sub-process. A sub-process is a process section carried out within a single organizational unit by a single position. The officials associated with this position are familiar with the activities that have to be performed during the sub-process. Thus, a single official or a small group of officials can model a sub-process on their own without much need for any further enquiries.

Besides this organizational scope, a sub-process also has certain characteristics regarding its content. A sub-process should be performed in one block of work without any major interruptions. Ideally a sub-process fulfils a clearly defined task in the context of the service that is delivered by the overall process. Thus, the sub-process concept allows also for a content-based structuring of processes.

Alternatives: The basic idea of PICTURE is to model sub-processes in a sequence of PBBs. This is due to the fact that officials usually perform their tasks in a sequential way. Therefore there are no parallel activities in a sub-process. If the sequence of a certain set of tasks is not fixed, the most common sequence should be modeled. Capturing all possible sequences would bring no further insights for the analysis of the processes.

However, in order to model complex processes there is the need to allow for control flow mechanisms to depict alternative process flows. This kind of process flow corresponds to the logical XOR (exclusive or) operator. Alternative flows are needed to express decisions within sub-processes (e.g. accept or decline an application) or differences in the delivered product (application for a small or a large building). In PICTURE, this is realized by using alternatives. An alternative is an additional sequence within a sub-process. It only contains PBBs, which are different from the standard process flow. A percentage value indicates the probability of the different alternatives. Alternatives can—but do not have to—be merged back into the standard flow at some point.

Connections: The second kind of process control structures needed in PICTURE is parallel process flows. A parallel process flow means that different activities are performed at the same time. Parallel flows correspond to the logical AND operator. As a sub-process in PICTURE is performed by a single person, parallel process flows are not possible within one sub-process. However, between different sub-processes (which are performed by different persons) parallel processing is possible, i.e. two different sub-processes can be performed in parallel.

In PICTURE, parallel process flows are realized using connections. Connections combine two PBBs from different sub-processes. In addition to the incoming and outgoing PBB, the connection also contains the POs, which are sent between the PBBs. Both PBBs involved in a connection need to have the same POs. Only a certain subset of the PBBs is allowed to be the incoming or outgoing PBB in a connection.

Example

The following example illustrates the main constructs of the PICTURE modeling methodology. The example describes the process of promoting an official to a higher position. Figure 3a) shows the different sub-processes in this process. In the first sub-process the applications for the positions are received and sorted by the personnel office. Then, they are evaluated in parallel by the personnel board and the equal opportunities commissioner. Based on those evaluations the personnel office either sends letters of refusal or accepts the application for processing. In the second case the approval procedure is initiated. In that case an approval by the personnel board and the equal opportunities commissioner is necessary. Afterwards the personnel office publishes the decision.

Figure 3b depicts the sub-process in which the letters of acceptance and refusal are sent. It shows the Process Building Blocks and the concept of an alternative, as in 90% of the cases refusals are sent and the process terminates and only in 10% an acceptance is sent.

Based on this formalized process documentation, the second part of the PICTURE methodology—the analysis of the processes—is now able to identify and evaluate appropriate cross-functional ICT. The analysis methodology is presented in the following section.

Analyze

Main objective of the measurement methodology is the analysis of the semantic, building block-based process models in order to identify potential supporting ICTs as well as to evaluate and quantify their impact on the process landscape of a public administration. The analysis part of

Figure 3. Process "promotion of internal staff" in a global and a local view

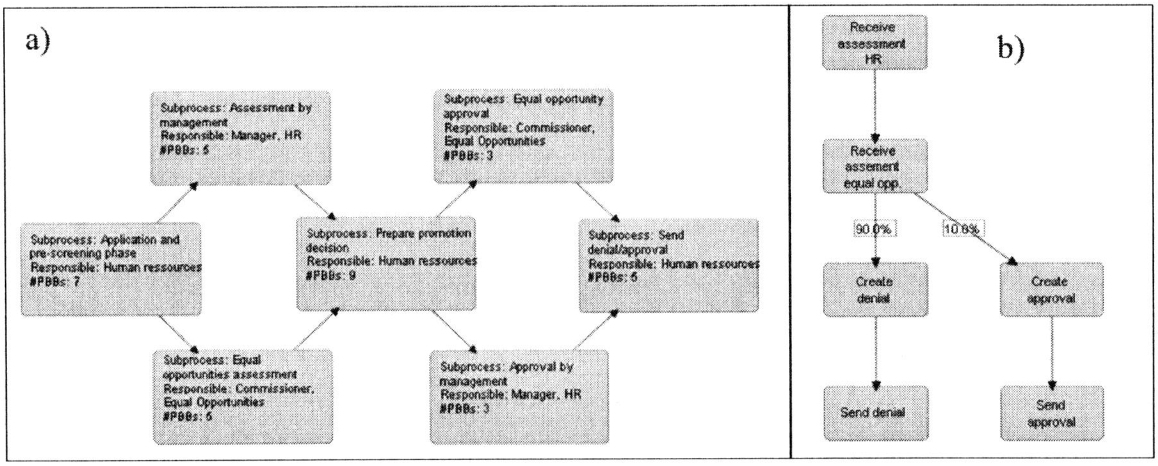

the PICTURE approach will deliver answers to the following two questions:

- Which ICT functionality groups (ICT FGs) can contribute to reduce organizational and procedural inefficiencies?
- How will the introduction of an ICT have impact on the process landscape (including qualitative as well as quantitative aspects)?

Answering these questions implies a weakness-based approach, as in the first step ICT related inefficiencies have to be identified within the modeled process landscape of a public administration. Subsequently, positive but also negative impacts of ICT have to be analyzed in order to evaluate the effects from a qualitative and quantitative perspective.

Methodological Approach

Starting point for the analysis is the process information formalized in respective models which are based on semantically standardized process building blocks (cp. section 3.2.4). The modeled semantics are the foundation for analyzing the process flow not only from a syntactical but also (in particular) from a semantic view. This enables a precise and automated identification of specified weaknesses, which is the first step of the developed methodology.

In the second step, identified weaknesses can be related to deficiency-reducing or deficiency-eliminating ICTs. This step implies that the focus is set on weaknesses that can be addressed by ICT. Although the project indeed concentrated on ICT-related weaknesses, the generic methodology as such, also allows for the identification of non-ICT-related deficiencies.

Having identified a weakness and its related ICTs, the third step contains the linkage of potential impact which will be quantified in step four by considering specific characteristics, such as number of cases per year, sum of cycle times or sum of cost reduction. The whole approach is illustrated in Figure 4.

If applied not only to one process but to the whole process landscape of a public administration this procedure delivers valuable information about

- existing deficiencies (in order to initiate and prioritize modernization projects),
- ICTs which enable reduction or elimination of the deficiencies (in order to conceptualize

Figure 4. Structure of the analysis approach

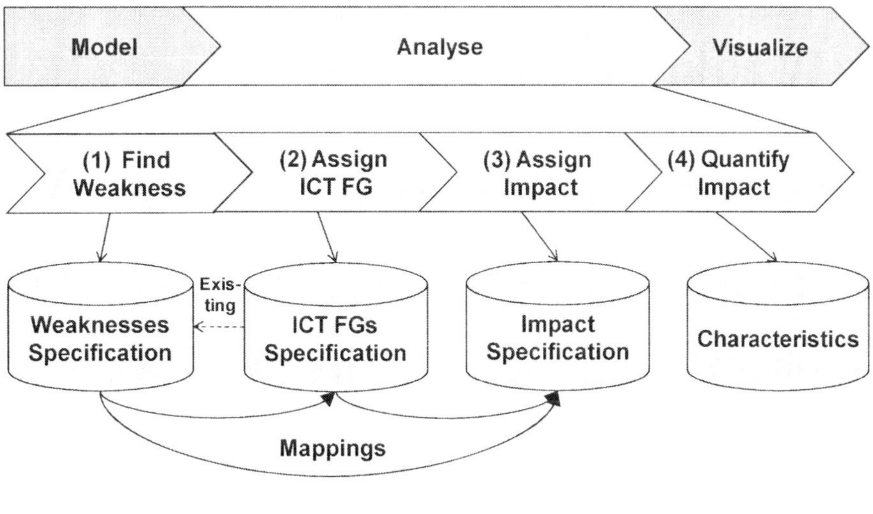

investment strategies for new ICT based on substantiated information),
- how the introduction of new ICT will impact the process landscape of a public administration (in order to argue towards decision makers and to support a holistic change process including organizational development).

The different steps of the methodology presented above are designed rather flexible in order to be customized to specific needs of a public administration. According to these steps, concrete process characteristics, weaknesses, ICT functionality groups (ICT FGs), and impact dimensions as well as their correlations had to be defined initially. These components and their interrelations constitute the analysis framework described in the subsequent section.

Analysis Framework

The analysis framework shown in Figure 5 formally describes the different components and their interrelations using the Unified Modeling Language class diagram notation (Jacobsen et al., 1999).

Starting point for the analysis is the process description modeling the as-is situation (top part of the framework). Each model consists of standardized elements such as Core Activities represented in PBBs, POs, attributes, organizational responsibilities, and supporting elements such as (existing) ICT functionalities.

The focus of the methodology lays on the identification of weaknesses (cp. first step in Figure 4) within these semantic process models and their elimination through the support of new ICT functionalities. Based on the state of the art described in section 2.2 a number of potential weaknesses (A) have been specified (cp. Table 1). A weakness describes conditions which are considered as inefficient (e.g. media breaks or the use of expensive and time-consuming communication channels).

Each weakness is formally described by a so called weakness pattern (B) that represents how the deficiency constitutes itself within the building block-based and attributed process models. Simple weakness examples are media breaks. They can be

Figure 5. Framework for ICT impact analysis (adopted from Baacke et al., 2008)

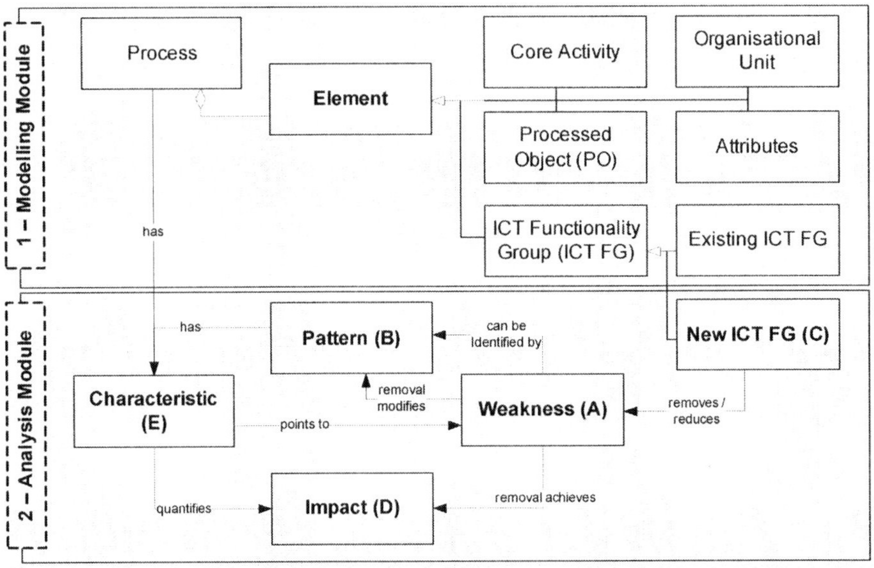

Table 1. List of weaknesses (following PICTURE Consortium, 2007b, pp.13) ©2008 Institute of Information Management, University of St. Gallen, Switzerland. Used with permission

Weakness	Description
Media break	Change in medium or channel of processed object e.g. from electronic format to paper
Redundant use of documents	Many printed / electronic copies of documents are created
Redundant templates (lack of standard.)	Different templates are available for the same document or activity
Unclear storage location of documents	It is not clear where the original document is stored. As a result, civil servants spend much time searching for documents.
Use of inefficient communication channels (efforts) for output	Inefficient communication e.g. via mail typically results in long transport times and causes higher costs and media breaks
Integration of different input channels	Applications and requests can be triggered via a vast amount of different channels (e.g. personally in municipalities' office, mail, email, internal mail, internet, fax). Their integration causes manual efforts (resulting in longer cycle time and higher costs) and media breaks.
Redundant use of IT applications	Different IT systems are used to perform the same process activity in different departments/by different people.
Lack of integration between systems	Many different applications are used in one process in the Public Administration that often are not well integrated.
Lack of transparency and traceability	No systems are available that can be used to track the progress of a process and to find out who is currently working on a particular request. Also, the hand-over of tasks between civil servants is not ensured / cannot be tracked. This might result in longer idle times and reduced information availability/ response time
Redundant data sets	It is not clear who maintains the master data set and what data sets are replications within the public administration.
Multiple format/ medium of information	The same information is stored in multiple formats/media e.g. printed paper, floppy disks etc.
Multiple redundant signatures required	Many signatures (not required by official legislation) are requested for single documents.

identified by locating the building blocks <Print> or <Scan>, or by detecting a change of medium (e.g. from electronically to paper-based) which is a mandatory attribute of each processed object.

As the project aims at the identification of potentially supporting ICTs (C), a set of ICT FGs was specified which address specific weaknesses (PICTURE Consortium, 2007a). ICT FGs are defined as granular clusters of technical services which belong together from a functional and business-driven perspective and are considered more suitable than business applications such as content management systems or document management systems. The wide range of differing functionalities per vendor within a certain application type on the one hand and the wide range of similar functionalities in different application types on the other hand have been recognized. This results in business applications not being at the appropriate level of detail for ICT impact assessment. The final set of ICT FGs contains 24 services grouped in three categories. The following list shows the categories and the related services:

- **Core ECM/BPM Services:** Catalog Services / Classification Services / Search Services / Forms Services / Decision Management Services / Object Management Services / Publishing Services / XML Management Services / Workflow Services / Auditing Services / Library Services / Content Federation Services / Event Services / IDARS Services / Retention Management Services / Distribution Services / Lifecycle Management Services / Interoperability Services / Optimization Services

- **Supporting Services:** Input, Presentation, and Output Services / Data Services / Storage Services
- **Surrounding Services:** Security Services / Integration Services

If related to a weakness, ICT FGs will have impact on the existing process landscape. Such impacts (D) can be categorized into a quantitative and a qualitative dimension. The subsequent table lists the initially defined set of impacts in the respective category.

If activities within the process models are not sufficiently supported by recommended ICT FGs the methodology provides a proposal of relevant FGs. The missing usage of ICT FGs can be defined in the weakness profiles (e.g. "weakness XY exists if a document is sent manually in a paper-based way if it is not mandatory that the document is paper-based"; cp. section 3.4).

In order to quantify the identified impacts (cp. step 4 in Figure 4), additional information is required about the characteristics (E) of a process (e.g. number of cases per year), a process alternative (e.g. probability of its occurrence) and its elements and relations (e.g. number of PBBs, number of document transports or the sums of transport and cycle times). If an ICT FG can be recommended that eliminates a weakness by substituting a manual activity, the duration of this activity will also be reduced. This time reduction (multiplied with the number of cases per year and the probability of the respective variant which are other specified characteristics) can be quantified based on the above mentioned parameters and represents one specific impact of the ICTs' introduction.

The overall impact analysis correlates the previously described framework components. The mappings assign one or more ICT FGs to a weakness, and the weakness reduction or elimination realizes qualitative and quantitative impacts. Both mappings have been developed together with the user partners of the research project and are formalized with concrete rules. A complete analysis rule then consists of three components (Figure 6).

The application of the analysis framework is exemplified in the subsequent section.

Example

Within the example process sequence shown in Figure 7 two potential weaknesses can be identified. The first weakness is a media break represented by the PBB <Print>. The costs of

Table 2. List of ICT-related impacts (following PICTURE Consortium, 2007b, pp 15) ©2008 Institute of Information Management, University of St. Gallen, Switzerland. Used with permission

Quantifiable impacts (Reduction of ...)	Quality-related impacts (Improvement of ...)
Processing time	Legal compliance
Idle time	Traceability / Audit trail
Transport time	Calculation results
Number/probability of errors	Integrity of information/data
Need for consumables	External service and information availability
Storage space	External service and information accessibility
System redundancy (software licenses)	Internal information availability
	Internal information accessibility
	Privacy
	Data Protection

Figure 6. Components of an analysis rule

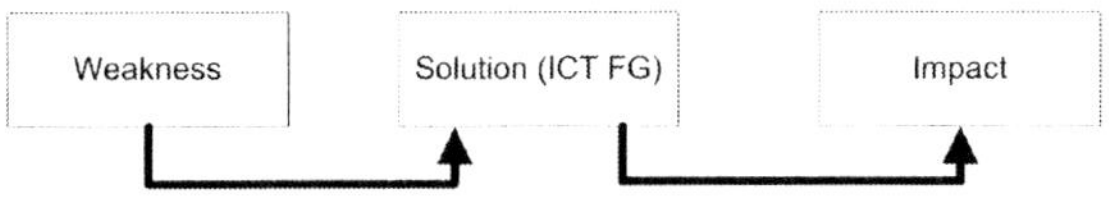

this inefficiency can be well quantified based on the specified number of copies for this PBB, the specified number of pages of the respective PO, the probability of the process alternative and the number of process cases per period. Thus, an ICT FG that is able to avoid this media break would eliminate or reduce these costs. This example is limited to the description of a single process. However, if scaled to an organization context, the fragmented process knowledge requires the involvement of different modelers. These modelers have diverse levels of expertise and views on process models that vary in the degrees of abstraction and detail, which needs to be considered when capturing the process landscape of a public administration. As a result the described approach of process analysis, if to be applied to a whole public administration requires semantic process modeling and analysis using weakness patterns as exemplified in the following.

The reason for this media break is—in most cases—the second weakness recognizable within this sequence: the use of mail which is considered as an inefficient communication channel (since costs are high and transport times are long). This weakness can be identified by analyzing the attribute "communication channel" of the communication-related PBBs such as <Send|Give> and <Receive>.

As described in section 3.3.2, each defined weakness can be addressed by one or more ICT FG(s). The inefficient communication channel "mail" can be substituted by the more efficient communication channel "e-mail" using the respective ICT FG. This means: The ICT FG "e-mail" can be recommended to be introduced in the public administration. The impacts of this ICT FG can be quantified by transport time reduction which is an attribute of the communication-related PBBs (multiplied by the number of affected PBBs in the processes, the probabilities of the respective variants and the number of cases of the processes) and lower costs for the communication (postal charges, costs for paper and printing, etc.—also multiplied by the affected number of copies, pages, postal items, etc.). In this scenario, the inefficient (paper-based) communication channel is substituted by its digital counterpart. This suggests that the need for a paper-based PO—and the media break itself—is removed. Thus, a reduction of costs caused by the related media break can also be calculated for the impact analysis of an e-mail introduction.

An example for a possible negative impact in this scenario is the digital divide issue (Johnson,

Figure 7. Characteristic PBB sequence

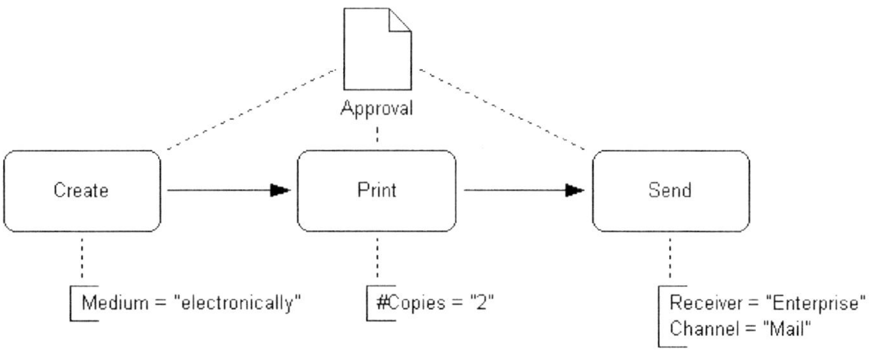

2002). As not all recipients are able to communicate digitally, the number of respective electronic cases has to be adjusted and prorated scenarios can be drawn. To address this issue, the weakness component of the analysis pattern can be refined by adding the restriction that only those mail communications should be digitized by the ICT FG e-mail which relate to internal parties or external business parties, such as business organizations or governmental organizations (which is also specified by an attribute of the respective PBBs).

Tool-Based Realization

In order to evaluate the PICTURE methodology in practice it has been implemented in a web-based prototype. The five cities from different European countries acting as user partners of the research project used this prototype for evaluating both the method as well as the prototype. The focus of the following description of the implementation is on the process analysis as this part represents the major research contribution. We first briefly sketch the modeling part which is based on the concepts described in section 3.2 and then describe the analysis part which implements the concepts described in section 3.3.

Based on the "model what you do" approach explained in section 3.2, the modelers in public administrations who are non-experts in modeling use a dialog-oriented capturing and management of semantic process models. Through the web-based approach the overall modeling effort can be easily distributed between the modelers.

To realize this approach, the presentation of processes is separated into two views. As described in section 3.2.4 the "global view" describes the flow of sub-processes within a certain process. On a more detailed level the "local view" describes the control and data flow within a sub-process.

Modelers capture the process information on the sub-process level. The modelers are thereby guided through a wizard-approach that ensures description of the activities within sub-processes in a consistent and analyzable way. Each activity is described in a three-step approach addressing PBBs, POs as well as their respective attributes (cp. section 3.2.1) including information about the interfaces between sub-processes. The two views described in this paragraph support navigability and sustain the approach of modeling analog to the execution of the real-world processes.

The process models captured are subsequently analyzed using the impact measurement module. To analyze processes for weaknesses (see step "find weakness" in section 3.3.1), the PICTURE expert first has to define patterns representing these weaknesses. For this purpose the PICTURE tool enables the user to define patterns in a flexible and unrestricted way. These patterns comprise all relevant objects used in the process modeling such as PBBs, POs, ICT FGs, and organizational units. Figure 8 shows the definition of a pattern representing a media break that can be identified by the following sequence of PBBs occurring in processes: Print—Send—Receive. In addition to the pattern definition all relevant functionality groups addressing the respective weakness (step "assign ICT") as well as potential savings for the impact measurement of ICT components (step "assign impact") can be specified (for the sake of simplicity not included in Figure 8). All this information is subsumed within one view—the weakness profile.

Having defined a set of weakness profiles, the decision maker can run the analysis of the process landscape based on these profiles. As decision makers in public administrations have different information needs, the PICTURE tool provides several kinds of reports covering the specific requirements. These information needs are derived from the overall goal of having more and better data for decisions about IT investments and improvement of processes. Therefore, the final information displayed to the decision maker will always relate to one or several processes that are

Figure 8. Pattern definition of a weakness profile

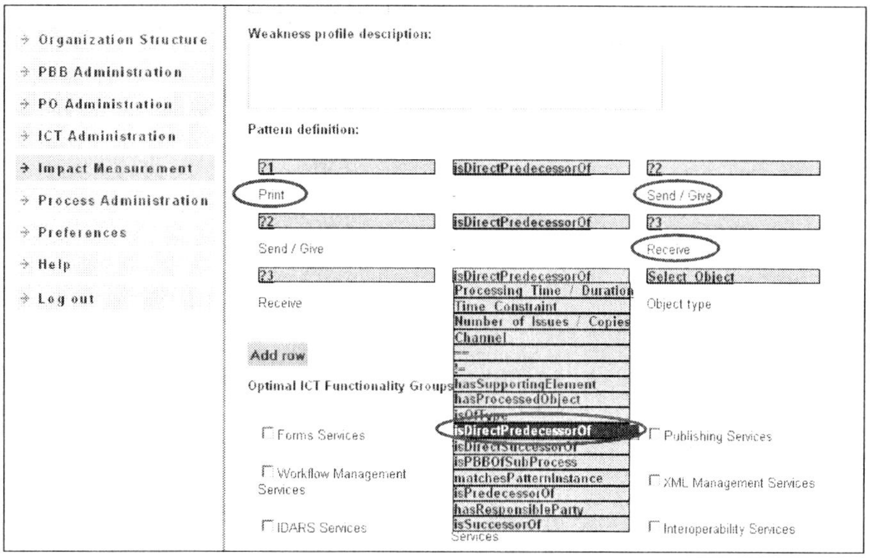

Figure 9. From information need to detailed report

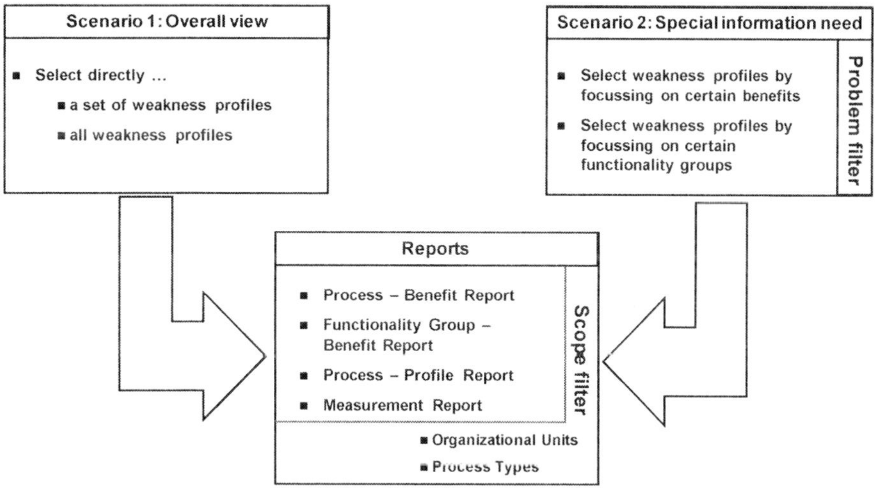

executed in the public administration. We distinguish two basically different information needs a decision maker has when starting the analysis:

- the decision maker intends to see the overall situation for the processes in a public administration with respect to weaknesses that can be improved through application of ICT and other re-organization measures or
- the decision maker intends to analyze the process landscape with a particular problem or ICT functionality in mind.

Starting from these entry points the user will then drill down further into the results until reaching the report that provides the required information. Figure 9 shows the two alternative ways to gain information from the reports as stated above.

In the first usage scenario the decision maker wants to get the general overview about the situation in his public administration or in particular organizational units of it (see left side of Figure 9). Therefore, the user can chose between single weakness profiles for which the processes should be analyzed or alternatively an analysis of the complete predefined profile set can be carried out.

The second scenario (problem filter) supports a decision maker who has a particular problem in mind, that needs to be addressed, a particular benefit that should be achieved or a particular ICT functionality group whose potential and impact on the processes should be evaluated (e.g. a functionality group proposed by the IT department or offered by a vendor). Therefore, this scenario does not present the overall impact situation of all weakness profiles but only a set of profiles that are related either to benefits or to functionality groups. Thus, the user either selects a particular benefit to be realized, respectively the problem to be addressed, or the particular ICT functionality to be analyzed with respect to potential benefits from its implementation. With this information the report is triggered and displayed to the user.

In the reports view that will be displayed after the user has made the selections, several types of reports are provided:

- *Process-Benefit Report:* shows for each process affected by one of the pre-selected weakness profiles the number of weakness profile occurrences *related to benefits*. The decision maker can derive from that report which processes have the highest potential for improvements for a certain benefit (e.g. faster process).
- *Functionality Group-Benefit Report:* for each functionality group the numbers of addressed weakness profiles related to benefits are shown, i.e. which functionality group will benefit the most processes. For instance, if the IT department has suggested several ICT to be implemented the decision maker can check with the tool, how many processes and organizational units can benefit from this ICT. The information from this report also allows the decision maker to get an idea which ICT functionality group could be beneficial and should be evaluated in detail by the IT department.
- *Process-Weakness Profile Report:* shows for each process the number of weakness profile occurrences. The decision maker gets a comprehensive overview of weaknesses occurring in the overall process landscape.
- *Measurement Report*: shows for each process affected by one of the pre-selected weakness profiles the potential savings in quantifiable values such as time or resources (for each weakness profile). This report provides the decision maker with the measurement of the impact of ICT components (step "quantify impact").

In addition to drill-down functionality (from dimensions of benefits to single benefits) a scope filter is provided for the process-benefit report as well as the functionality group–benefit report. This can be applied by the user to limit the amount of information:

- Show only results for processes executed in a particular organizational unit. This view helps the user to concentrate the effort on particular organizational units.
- Show only results for processes of a certain type (e.g. encash process). This view helps the user to concentrate the effort on processes of a specific type.

DISCUSSION

In section 2 several requirements for creating a new methodology which fits the special needs of public administrations were listed. These requirements were deducted from the goals of the PICTURE approach—model, analyze, and visualize—as well as from the envisioned modeling scenario, in which the domain experts from the public administrations model their activities themselves. This section will first evaluate how the presented distributed modeling methodology meets these requirements. Second, we discuss experiences from the application of the process analysis methodology.

Process Modeling Methodology

(R1) The modeling language facilitates capturing the entire process landscape: The PBBs of the process landscaping methodology have a fixed level of detail which allows for the desired coarse granular capturing of the process landscape. Furthermore, the presented process landscaping methodology allows for a distributed modeling methodology. This is realized through the differentiation between the local view and the global view. Through this distributed modeling methodology domain experts are able to model their activities themselves. Thereby it is possible to model the whole process landscape as the effort is distributed over a large number of modelers.

(R2) The modeling language allows for efficient modeling: In the presented process landscaping methodology the effort of the domain experts is minimized by two means. The distributed modeling methodology allows involving a large number of officials in the modeling activities. This minimizes the effort for a single domain expert and the need of external modeling experts. Additionally, the domain experts only model the parts of the processes they are familiar with, thus further accelerating the modeling. Furthermore, the fixed coarse granular level of detail guaranteed by the PBBs avoids too detailed models and minimizes the modeling effort as well.

(R3) The modeling language is easy to understand for a domain expert: The domain-specific process modeling constructs are easily understood by domain experts. The PBBs which form the core of the modeling language have fixed semantics and describe specific activities of the public administration domain. If necessary, new PBBs can be defined flexibly. In order to maintain an unambiguous set of PBBs, which is a prerequisite for meaningful analysis, the methodology needs to be designed so that semantic overlapping of PBBs is avoided. Addressing the different understanding of PBBs by domain experts (individual terminology) the provision of extensive explanations and synonyms for the PBB names has been included in order to avoid creation of redundant PBBs. Other language constructs are also designed to be easily understandable for the domain experts, e. g. the sub-process definition which is based on the organizational structure of the public administration or the processed object categories which use vocabulary of the public administration domain. The sequential modeling of the process landscaping methodology also minimizes the options to connect the language constructs. Guided modeling techniques for the use of alternatives, connections, and cross-sectional processes also ensure that these constructs are used correctly.

(R4) The models are syntactically and semantically comparable: The central concept to guarantee comparable process models for the process landscaping methodology are the process building blocks. They provide a fixed level of detail and specific semantics. The fixed semantic avoids type conflicts (i.e. a fact from the application domain is modeled differently by different persons). Furthermore, naming conflicts cannot occur as the type of a PBB is fixed and individual names specified by the modeler are only used for better readability but not for analysis. Finally, structural conflicts (i.e. real-world objects are modeled at different levels of abstraction) are also avoided through the PBBs as they fix the level of abstraction. Additionally, the simple syntactic constructs and the guided modeling techniques lead to processes which are structured similarly.

Impact Measurement Methodology

The brief examples presented in section 3 give an overview of the potentials that are realizable by this analytic part of the PICTURE approach.

The benefits for ICT value measurement (from a qualitative as well as a quantitative perspective) and ICT investment analysis are easily visible. In addition to such ICT related questions, the methodology allows also to identify deficiencies with no reference to new ICTs (e.g. mere organizational inefficiencies) by defining respective weakness patterns. The PICTURE expert can define arbitrary search patterns as long as they are constructed from PBBs which also make up the process models. Therefore, it is possible to create new specific search patterns to find non-ICT related inefficiencies.

During the application phase one specific problem appeared: the overlapping of weakness patterns. Although weakness patterns can be defined very exactly, there are cases (e.g. PBB sequences) where e.g. two or more weaknesses are found. It is possible, that the introduction of a specifically recommended ICT FG for one of the weaknesses influences the modeled sequence and potentially the recommended ICT FGs for the other weakness becomes unnecessary. Two questions come up: Which of the ICT FGs should be recommended first (e.g. selection by impact)? How often should the analysis be iterated in order to identify the optimal combination of new ICTs?

Although these cases did not occur often so far, additional evaluation is required to increase the maturity level of the analysis component. Furthermore, the initial specifications have to be elaborated and completed.

CONCLUSION AND OUTLOOK

As stated in section 2.1, public administrations possess many characteristics that differentiate them from enterprises. A reorganization approach must take these particular characteristics into account in order to be applied successfully in the public sector. The objective of our research has been to develop an approach for efficiently capturing and semi-automatically analyzing processes in order to provide sound data for decisions on ICT investments. Based on capturing process knowledge of the current as-is situation, weaknesses and ICT impact potential is identified. Successful application of this approach helps decision makers to build a coherent ICT investment strategy which will contribute to the key areas of transformational government (Chief Information Officer Council, 2007):

- the "transformation of public services for the benefit of citizens, businesses, taxpayers and front-line staff",
- the "efficiency of the corporate services and infrastructure of government organisations, thus freeing resources for the front-line",
- the "steps necessary to achieve the effective delivery of technology for government".

Through the integrated analysis of processes, organizational structure as well as IT infrastructure PICTURE addresses the impact of the change of business processes and information systems in the public sector.

To verify the applicability of the approach several workshops have been conducted with the partner cities of the project consortium. The workshops focused on the evaluation of the different phases of the PICTURE approach—the modeling as well as the analysis. For the modeling part a couple of indicators have been measured such as the duration of the modeling preparation and the modeling of the processes by city employees. The average effort for one process is about 70 minutes. Compared to the generic modeling approach of event-driven process chains clear efficiency gains could be identified (Algermissen et al., 2005). These can primarily be attributed to the simple, structured and domain-specific modeling concept. Hence, with the PICTURE approach we have presented a domain specific approach that addresses an economic modeling, analysis and visualization of administrational processes.

In order to enhance their knowledge about their

processes, analyze them and gather data for future investment decisions in their administrations the partner cities also evaluated the analysis module of the PICTURE prototype. They considered the provided reports as a comprehensive and valuable resource for creating development plans and supporting annual ICT investment plans.

ACKNOWLEDGMENT

The work published in this paper is (partly) funded by the E.C. through the PICTURE STREP. It does not represent the view of E.C. or the PICTURE consortium, and authors are solely responsible for the paper's content.

REFERENCES

Algermissen, L., Delfmann, P., & Niehaves, B. (2005). Experiences in process-oriented reorganisation through reference modelling in public administrations: The case study regio@KomM. In *Proceedings of the 13th European Conference on Information Systems (ECIS 2005)*. Regensburg, Germany.

Avison, D., Lau, F., Myers, M., & Nielsen, P. A. (1999). Action research. *Communications of the ACM, 42*(1), 94-97.

Baacke, L., Fitterer, R., Mettler, T., & Rohner, P. (2008). A methodology for ICT impact analysis based on semantic process models. In *Proceedings of the 7th International EGOV Conference*. Torino, Itay.

Baacke, L., Rohner, P., & Winter, R. (2007). Aggregation of reference process building blocks to improve modeling in public administrations. In A. Grönlund, H. J. Scholl, & M. A. Wimmer (Eds.), *Proceedings of the Electronic Government, 6th International EGOV Conference* (pp. 149-156).

Baacke, L., Rohner, P., Winter, R., & Fitterer, R. (2009). Component-based distributed modeling of collaborative service processes: A methodology for the identification of reference process building blocks. In *Proceedings of the Forty-Second Annual Hawaii International Conference on System Sciences (HICSS-42)*.

Batini, C., Lenzerini, M., & Navathe, S. B. (1986). A comparative analysis of methodologies for database schema integration. *ACM Computing Surveys, 18*(4), 323-364.

Becker, J., Kugeler, M., & Rosemann, M. (2003). *Process management: A guide for the design of business processes*. Berlin, Germany: Springer.

Brain, D., Seltsikas, P., & Tailor, D. (2005). Process modelling notations for e-government: An assessment of modelling notations for identity management. In *Proceedings of the BLED 2005*.

Chief Information Officer Council. (2007). Transformational government. Retrieved on September 9, 2007, from http://www.cio.gov.uk/transformational_government/strategy/

Green, P., & Rosemann, M. (2000). Integrated process modeling: An ontological evaluation. *Information Systems, 25*(2), 73-87.

Guizzardi, G., Pires, L. F., & Sinderen, M. J. v. (2002). On the role of domain ontologies in the design of domain-specific visual modeling languages. In *Proceedings of the 2nd Workshop on Domain-Specific Visual Languages, 17th ACM Conference on Object-Oriented Programming, Systems, Languages and Applications (OOPSLA 2002)*. Seattle,WA.

Hardar, I., & Soffer, P. (2006). Variantions in conceptual modeling: Classification and ontological analysis. *Journal for the Association of Information Systems 7*(8), 568-592.

Hevner, A. R., March, S. T., Park, J., & Ram, S. (2004). Design science in information systems research. *MIS Quarterly, 28*(1), 75-105.

Jacobsen, I., Booch, G., & Rumbaugh, J. (1999). *The unified software development process.* Boston: Addison-Wesley.

Karagiannis, D. (1995). BPMS: Business process management systems. *ACM SIGOIS Bulletin 16*(1), 10-13.

Kashyap, V., & Sheth, A. (1996). Semantic and schematic similarities between database objects: A context-based approach. *The International Journal on Very Large Data Bases (VLDB), 5*(4), 276-304.

Kelly, S., & Tolvanen, J.-P. (2000). Visual domain-specific modelling: Benefits and experiences of using metaCASE tools. In J. Bézivin, & J. Ernst (Eds.), *Proceedings of the 1st International Workshop on Model Engineering. 14th European Conference on Object-Oriented Programming (ECOOP 2000).* Cannes, France.

Knaack, I. (1999). *Die Einführung von vorgangsbearbeitungssystemen in der öffentlichen verwaltung als IT-organisatorischer gestaltungsprozeß.* Berlin, Germany.

Lawrence, R., & Barker, K. (2001). Integrating relational database schemas using a standardized dictionary. In *Proceedings of the 16th ACM Symposium on Applied Computing.* Las Vegas, NV.

Mayer, R. J., Menzel, C. P., Painter, M. K., deWitte, P. S., Blinn, T., & Perakath, B. (1995). *Information Integration for Concurrent Engineering (IICE) IDEF3 Process Description Capture Method Report.*

Object Management Group. (2006). BPMN Final Adopted Specification 1.0. Retrieved on April 30, 2006, from http://www.bpmn.org/Documents/OMG%20Final%20Adopted%20BPMN%201-0%20Spec%2006-02-01.pdf

Opdahl, A. L., & Henderson-Sellers, B. (2002). Ontological evaluation of the UML using the Bunge–Wand–Weber model. *Software and Systems Modelling, 1*(1), 43-67.

Pfeiffer, D. (2007). Constructing comparable conceptual models with domain specific languages. In H. Österle, J. Schelp, & R. Winter (Eds.), *Proceedings of the European Conference on Information Systems (ECIS 2007).* St. Gallen, Switzerland.

Pfeiffer, D., & Gehlert, A. (2005). A framework for comparing conceptual models. In *Proceedings of the Workshop on Enterprise Modelling and Information Systems Architectures (EMISA 2005)* (pp. 108-122). Klagenfurt, Austria.

PICTURE Consortium. (2006). *Report on current practice of process modeling projects & techniques in European public administrations* (Deliverable 1.1).

PICTURE Consortium. (2007a). *ICT functionality groups specification* (Deliverable 2.6).

PICTURE Consortium. (2007b). *PICTURE Impact measurement methodology* (Deliverable 3.4).

PICTURE Consortium. (2007c). *Study on ICT value analysis concepts for European PA* (Deliverable 3.1).

Renkema, T. J. W., & Berghout, E. W. (1997). Methodologies for information-systems investment evaluation at the proposal stage: A comparative review. *Information and Software Technology, 39*(1), 1-13.

Schaffroth, M. (2005). Paradigmenwechsel bei der Gestaltung von e-government-Prozessen? / Das generische Geschäftsmodell der Vorgangsbearbeitung—Ein Diskussionsbeitrag aus der Schweiz. In R. Klischewski, & M. Wimmer (Eds.), *Wissensbasiertes Prozessmanagement im E-Government.* Münster, Germany: LIT.

Scheer, A.-W. (2000). *ARIS—Business process modeling.* Heidelberg, Germany: Springer Publishing.

Shanks, G., Tansley, E., & Weber, R. (2003). Using ontology to validate conceptual models. *Communications of the ACM, 46*(10), 85-89.

Song, X., & Osterweil, L. J. (1994). Experience with an approach to comparing software design methodologies. *IEEE Transactions on Software Engineering, 20*(5), 364-384.

Takeda, H., Veerkamp, P., Tomiyama, T., & Yoshikawa, H. (1990). Modeling design process. *AI Magazine, 11*(4), 37-48.

Villa, M. (2005). Process modelling in the public administrations & e-government gateways: ICTE-PAN. In *Proceedings of the eGovInterop'05 Conference*. Geneva, Switzerland.

Walter, S. G., & Spitta, T. (2004). Approaches to the ex-ante evaluation of investments into information systems. *Wirtschaftsinformatik, 46*(3), 171-180.

KEY TERMS

Process Building Block (PBB): A business process typically consists of a number of activities producing a specific process result. Although public administrations have a huge variety of collaborative service-processes, core activities within these processes recur commonly. PBBs represent such recurring activities which can be combined to complete workflows. They can be specified by attributes, supporting ICT and related POs (see below). Due to their standardized semantics, PBBs enable distributed modeling based on common terminology and semi-automated, pattern-based analysis.

Processed Object (PO): A PO describes the information, document, message or any other object that is processed by the corresponding activity. Examples are applications or permits.

Supporting Element: Supporting Elements are technical or physical information systems (electronic and paper-based files, archives, etc.) that support an activity.

ICT Functionality Group (ICT FG): FGs are defined as granular clusters of technical services which belong together from a functional and business-driven perspective and are considered more suitable than business applications such as content or document management systems. They allow for ICT impact measurement as they bridge the gap between the wide range of differing functionalities per vendor within a certain application type and the wide range of similar functionalities in different application types on the other hand.

Pattern Definition: A pattern contains a certain combination of PBBs, POs and their attributes. It represents a specific weakness and can be used for the automatic identification of weaknesses in the process landscape.

Weakness Profile: In addition to the pattern definition all relevant functionality groups addressing the respective weakness as well as potential savings for the impact measurement of ICT components can be specified in a weakness profile.

ENDNOTE

1 For more information please visit: http://www.eurodyn.com/icte-pan/

Chapter VIII
Mapping Factors Influencing EAI Adoption on the Adoption Lifecycle Phases in LGAs

Muhammad Mustafa Kamal
Brunel University, UK

ABSTRACT

Literature indicates several private and public organisations have adopted Enterprise Application Integration (EAI), however its application in the Local Government Authorities (LGAs) is limited. Although, there exist few EAI adoption models, these models mainly focus on a number of different factors (e.g. benefits, barriers, cost) influencing the decision making process for EAI adoption. Moreover, these models do not illustrate factors influencing the decision making process for EAI adoption on the adoption lifecycle phases. Literature indicates that the adoption process involves a sequence of phases an organisation passes through before taking the decision for adoption. This exemplifies that LGAs may also have to pass through several adoption phases before taking the decision to adopt EAI. However, due to the multiplicity of factors it may not be easy for LGAs to take decisions to adopt EAI by merely focusing on different factors. This may impede the decision making process for EAI adoption in LGAs. Notwithstanding, the implications of EAI have yet to be assessed, leaving scope for timeliness and novel research. Thus, it is of high importance to investigate this area within LGAs and result in research that contributes towards successful EAI adoption. This chapter makes a step forward as it: (a) presents four adoption lifecycle phases, (b) tests the adoption lifecycle phases, and (c) mapping the factors influencing EAI adoption on the adoption lifecycle phases, through three case studies. Hence, it significantly contributes to the body of knowledge and practice. In doing so, provides sufficient support to the decision makers for speeding up the decision making process for EAI adoption in LGAs.

INTRODUCTION

Literature indicates that several researchers have proposed EAI adoption models e.g. Themistocleous (2004) proposed EAI adoption model in multinational organisations, Khoumbati (2005) followed the stream by evaluating and proposing a model for EAI adoption in healthcare organisations, Mantzana (2006) utilised Khoumbati (2005) EAI adoption model and extended the research area in healthcare sector, by identifying the healthcare actors involved in EAI adoption process and the causal relationships among the healthcare actors and factors that influence EAI adoption. In the area of LGAs, Kamal *et al.*, (2008); Kamal and Themistocleous (2006, 2007) proposed and tested an EAI adoption model. Chen's (2005) model differs from other existing EAI adoption models, as Chen (2005) did not specifically research on EAI; instead Chen (2005) identified the significant differences in the way Small and Medium Enterprises (SMEs) and large companies approach integration technologies.

These models mainly focus on a number of different factors (e.g. benefits, barriers, costs) influencing the decision making process for EAI adoption. In addition, there are differences indicating that the factors that influence the decision-making process for EAI adoption differ from one type of organisation to the other depending among others on the nature and size. For instance, one set of factors is used to support EAI adoption in SMEs and another in large organisations, whereas, there are differences among influential factors that are used in private sector, healthcare organisations and the local government authorities. The aforesaid EAI adoption models do not: (a) address the adoption lifecycle phases and (b) illustrate which factor(s) influence the decision making process for EAI adoption on the adoption lifecycle phases. Rogers, (1995) suggests that adoption process involves a sequence of phases an organisation passes through before taking the decision to adopt a technological solution(s). In the context of technology adoption, several researchers propose diverse phases in their technology adoption processes e.g. Kamal (2006), Frambach and Schillewaert (2002), Gallivan (2001) and Darmawan, (2001). On the contrary, in the context of EAI implementation, several researchers put forward different phases in their EAI implementation process e.g. Lam and Shankararaman (2004), Themistocleous and Irani (2006) and Reiersgaard *et al.,* (2005). Technology adoption process illustrates several phases that focus on both the pre- adoption and post- adoption phases, whereas, EAI implementation process exhibits post- adoption phases. Despite their contribution to the technology adoption and EAI implementation area, the authors do not cover these phases in the context of this research.

The reason is that the current research investigates on the adoption lifecycle phases and mapping of factors influencing the decision making process for EAI adoption in LGAs on adoption lifecycle phases and not on EAI implementation phases or beyond. In the area of mapping the factors influencing EAI adoption, Khoumbati and Themistocleous, (2007) proposed a modelling technique i.e. Fuzzy Cognitive Mapping (FCM) simulation to evaluate EAI adoption in healthcare organisations. Nevertheless, their research merely demonstrates the causal inter-relationships between the EAI adoption factors (Khoumbati and Themistocleous, 2007) and does not interpret the mapping of the factors influencing EAI adoption on the adoption lifecycle phases. Thus, it can be argued – despite the fact that the private and public organisation's decision to adopt EAI may in fact be the most important development for integrating their heterogeneous IT infrastructures. Nonetheless, to the best of the authors' knowledge, there is lack of broad-based theoretical and empirical research on mapping the factors influencing the decision making process for EAI adoption in LGAs on the adoption lifecycle phases. Thus, given the increasing attention to EAI adoption by academics (Mantzana, 2006; Khoumbati, 2005; Themistocleous, 2004), the authors attempt to further investigate on the adoption lifecycle phases and mapping of factors on adoption lifecycle phases in the local government domain. The necessity for relatively similar research is highlighted in the literature (Somers and Nelson, 2001; Prescott and Conger, 1995).

ENTERPRISE APPLICATION INTEGRATION OVERVIEW

Enterprise application integration has emerged to overcome integration problems at all levels (e.g. data, object and process). According to Linthicum (2000, p. 354) EAI is the: "*unrestricted sharing of information between two or more enterprise applications. A set of technologies that allow the movement and exchange of information between different applications and business processes within and between organisations*". EAI is a generation of software that combines a variety of integration technologies e.g.: (a) message brokers, (b) adapters, and (c) application servers etc, to build a centralised integration infrastructure (Themistocleous, 2004). It incorporates functionality from a diversity of systems and results in the development of flexible, and maintainable integrated IT infrastructures (Serian, 2002). EAI also allows the organisations to simplify interactions among organisation applications by adopting a standard approach to integration, replacing hundreds or thousands of ad hoc integration designs (Ruh *et al.*, 2000).

Literature indicates that for "*x*" applications a total of "*(x*(x-1)/2)*" interconnections are needed when each application is interconnected with the rest of the applications (Themistocleous, 2004). This can be explained as e.g. when an application is interconnected (through traditional integration) to several other Information Systems (IS) requires any change, it affects all other applications because it has equivalent number of interconnections with those applications. On the other hand, when the same application that is integrated through EAI architecture requires some changes; the rest of the system is rarely affected. The reason is that these systems are not directly interconnected with the application that requires those changes. Thus, this way only those applications that require changes are altered, resulting in a reduced maintenance effort and increased flexibility with few interconnections among the applications (Themistocleous, 2004). Figure 1 illustrates the differences in the number of connections when traditional integration approaches and enterprise application integration are adopted.

Organisations that integrated their IT infrastructures with EAI have reported benefits (Bass and Lee, 2002). Themistocleous and Irani (2001) analysed and explained the benefits that derive from the use of EAI technology and classified them into: (a) organisational (e.g. results in more organised business processes), (b) managerial (e.g. achieves return on investment), (c) operational (e.g. reduces cost), (d) strategic (e.g. increases collaboration among partners), and (e) technical (e.g. achieves data, objects and process integration). Literature also indicates another significant EAI business benefit i.e. the reduction of overall integration cost and the reason for this is due to the decrease in both integration time and maintenance costs (Linthicum, 2000). In addition, EAI provides a flexible, manageable and maintainable IT infrastructure that supports the changing business and technical requirements (Themistocleous *et al.*, 2005). Based on an EAI based integrated organisation-wide architecture, organisations can increase their productivity and provide better services for their customers and improve their relationships with their clients (Ruh *et al.*, 2000).

However, the high investment costs associated with EAI have caused much concern for many organisations (Chen, 2005). Sanchez *et al.*, (2002) argues that although the initial cost

Figure 1. Traditional integration approaches[1] vs enterprise application integration[2]

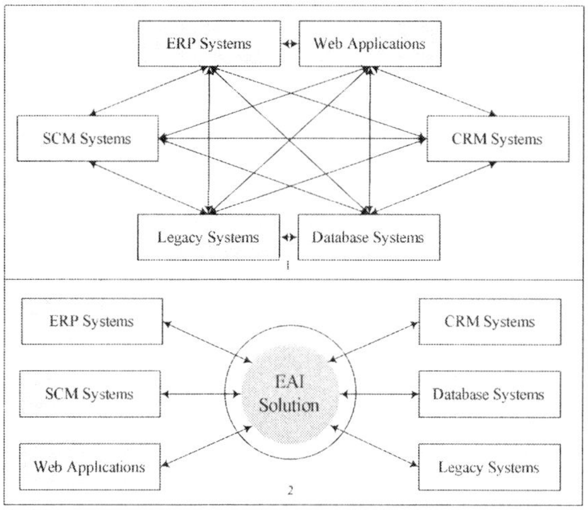

of investing in EAI technological solutions may be daunting to several sector organisations, the cost of integration are in fact more extensive when EAI technological solutions not adopted. The authors report here that on prolonging the integration problem is likely to be more costly than an initial EAI investment, especially when long-term plans including new technologies and IS into the IT infrastructure. The reason may be that while not taking integration into consideration, each application that is initially developed based on own requirements, may have its own meaning of organisational objects (e.g. citizens). Thus, each application that has data (with own meaning) may overlap with data in other applications. This data redundancy and inconsistency generates significant data integrity problems and increases the maintenance and integration cost. As the literature indicates that EAI is based on a set of integration technologies, each EAI package differs from other EAI package to package. The reason is that each EAI vendor configures its EAI package using a different subset of integration technologies. Thus, during the selection process organisations need to evaluate their EAI technologies to meet their organisational and integration problems.

FACTORS INFLUENCING EAI ADOPTION IN LGAS

LGAs are complex organisations that have developed their own structures and systems according to their requirements (Senyucel, 2005). Nye (1999) states that such LGA structures have been based traditionally on a bureaucratic model that emphasizes decentralisation and specialisation in a mechanical and pre-planned approach. LGA service delivery and administration has also tended to be organised in the same bureaucratic manner (Senyucel, 2005). Due to the bureaucratic nature and the culture, LGAs have experienced from what may be termed as – IT lag time (Beaumaster, 2002). The authors indicate that LGAs have experienced approximately ten years of lag time between the adoption of new technologies and IS and its acceptance and routinisation across the organisations (Danziger *et al.,* 1986). This shows that LGAs have been laggards in adopting new technological solutions (Kamal and Themistocleous, 2007). The authors report that laggards can be summarised as those who adopt a technology only when they have no choice. In fact, many laggards do not explicitly adopt technologies at all, but rather acquire them accidentally when a particular technology is a component of a packaged solution (Rogers, 1995). Sometimes LGAs are forced to adopt new technologies, as other LGAs may require them to adopt as well (Kamal and Themistocleous, 2006). Thus, LGAs may be categorised in the late majority group. There might be an exceptional case where LGAs might be considered as innovators, such as cases where LGAs (Singapore) that have proactively adopted sophisticated information technologies to boost their economy (Devadoss *et al.,* 2002). Whereas, in other cases, LGAs wait till a technology becomes mature and then push the private sector to adopt this technology (Themistocleous *et al.,* 2004). The authors report that EAI adoption by LGAs does not significantly differ from other information technologies adopted within LGAs.

However, literature indicates limited published research case studies for EAI adoption in LGA (most of them discuss EAI in healthcare, SMEs and multinational organisations). The lack of published cases can be interpreted in many different ways. Some explanations may be that: (a) LGAs adopt new IT reactively compared to private organisations (Themistocleous, 2004), (b) lack of skilled staff and reluctant to adopt new technologies, lack of understanding and knowledge of EAI in LGAs (Kamal and Themistocleous, 2006), (c) LGAs have been very slow or even unprepared for technological transformations (Devadoss *et al.,* 2002), and (d) LGAs are unable to react proactively as technologies constantly change and evolve around them (Beaumaster, 2002). Additionally, several LGAs consider that the uncertainty about the costs and benefits of adopting EAI is a central problem (Janssen and Cresswell, 2005). The reason is that the information needed about costs and benefits may be incomplete or inaccessible to several LGAs. Carter *et al.,* (2001) argues here that the access to information can be limited by organisational and functional boundaries that distribute knowledge of value-added activities such that no one, including top management, has complete knowledge of the processes. Due to the lack of insight LGAs are still reluctant to adopt EAI unless they are forced to do so (Janssen and Cresswell, 2005).

Other reason may also be that LGAs do not know whether and to what extent they should invest in EAI and they are unable to assess the return on these investments. The decisions taken in one LGA can have a profound influence on the activities, costs and benefits of other LGAs. Often the implications for other LGAs are not clear, consequently these other LGAs do not want to invest or change their processes to profit from EAI. There is a debate about how costs are divided and how benefits should be distributed over LGAs. The authors report that these barriers may impede the adoption of EAI in LGAs. However, in taking this issue as a literature gap, Kamal and Themistocleous (2006, 2007) proposed an EAI adoption model in their previous research. The model presents several factors influencing EAI adoption in LGAs. These factors have been well investigated and tested in the literature. Kamal *et al.,* (2008) and Kamal and Themistocleous (2007) also tested these factors in several LGAs. The analysis and applicability of these factors that cover a broad scope of the organisation provide sufficient support to the authors to build an understanding for the development of EAI adoption model in LGAs. Table 1 illustrates the factors influencing EAI adoption in LGAs.

EAI ADOPTION LIFECYCLE PHASES AND MAPPING OF FACTORS INVOLVED IN LGAS

Research conducted in the enterprise application integration area highlighted including among others: EAI adoption models with each model exhibiting several factors influencing EAI adoption (Table 1) in the private and public domain (Mantzana, 2006; Khoumbati, 2005; Themistocleous, 2004). Literature indicates that factors can be viewed as sited exemplars that help extend the boundaries of process improvement, and their effect can be characterised as much richer if viewed within the context of their importance in each phase of the implementation process (Somers and Nelson, 2001). In the context of EAI implementation, Lam and Shankararaman (2004) were the first who proposed a methodology for EAI named as Enterprise Integration Methodology (EIM) with five stages: (a) understand the end-to-end business process, (b) map the process onto components, (c) derive the requirements, (d) produce the architecture and (e) plan the integration. EIM methodology has contributed to the enterprise application integration area as it underlines the importance of understanding business processes

Table 1. Factors influencing EAI adoption in LGAs (Adapted: Kamal et al., 2008)

Factor Category	EAI Adoption Factors	References
Pressure Factors (PF)	Project Champion	Kamal, (2006); Kamal, (2004); Garfield (2000); Norris (1999).
	Citizen's Satisfaction	Benynon-Davies, (2005); Benynon-Davies and Williams, (2003).
	Critical Mass	Akbulut, (2002); Bouchard (1993).
	Market Knowledge	Hong and Kim, (2002); Johannessen (1994).
Technological Factors (TF)	Evaluation Frameworks	Themistocleous *et al.*, (2005)
	Technological Risks	Ebrahim and Irani, (2005); Gil García and Pardo, (2005)
	IT Infrastructure	Norris (1999); Perry and Danziger (1980).
	Personnel IT Knowledge	Akbulut, (2002); Perry and Danziger (1980).
	IT Sophistication	Akbulut, (2002); Perry and Danziger (1980).
	Data Security and Privacy	Signore *et al.*, (2005); Lam, (2005); Kamal, (2004).
Support Factors (SF)	Top Management Support	Ngai and Gunasekaran, (2004); Beath, (1991).
	IT Support	Themistocleous *et al.*, (2005)
	Higher Administrative Authority	Kim and Bretschneider (2004); Moon and Bretschneider, (1997).
Financial Factors (FF)	Return on Investment	Lam (2005); Janssen and Cresswell, (2005).
	Cost	Themistocleous *et al.*, (2005)
Organisational Factors (OF)	Centralisation	Ebrahim *et al.*, (2004); Melitski, (2003).
	Managerial Capability	Senyucel (2005); Kim and Bretschneider, (2004).
	Barriers	Songini, (2004); Themistocleous *et al.*, (2005).
	Benefits	Themistocleous *et al.*, (2005); Bradford and Florin (2003).
	Formalisation	Ebrahim *et al.*, (2004); Lee *et al.*, (2003).
	Size	Akbulut (2002); Brudney and Seldon, (1995).

when integrating systems and stressing the need to map processes on existing software solutions.

According to Themistocleous and Irani (2006), EIM has limitations that it does not cover issues like systems' restructuring or the new software solutions that need to be developed, thus, in doing so, proposing an EAI methodology for the development of integrated IT infrastructures consisting of eight stages. These stages are: (a) planning, (b) scenarios building and evaluation, (c) business process reengineering, (d) systems restructuring, (e) requirements analysis, (f) filling the gap – new systems development, (g) integration and testing and (h) operation and maintenance. On the other hand, Reiersgaard *et al.*, (2005) also proposed a framework for EAI implementation process that is based on the enterprise experience cycle model with four stages such as: (a) chartering, (b) project, (c) shakedown and (d) onward and upward phase. The analysis of the EAI methodology and EAI framework illustrate several stages that specifically discuss on the implementation stages beyond the adoption phase.

Despite their contribution to the EAI area, the authors do not cover up these stages in the context of this chapter. The intent is to map the factors influencing EAI adoption on different phases of the adoption lifecycle and not beyond the adoption phase. In the area of mapping EAI factors, Khoumbati and Themistocleous, (2007) proposed a modelling technique i.e. FCM simulation to evaluate EAI adoption in healthcare organisations. Nevertheless, their research merely demonstrates the causal inter-relationships between the EAI adoption factors (Khoumbati and Themistocleous, 2007) and does not map the factors influencing EAI adoption on different adoption lifecycle phases.

Thus, it can be argued – despite the fact that the private and public organisation's decision to implement EAI may in fact be the most important development for integrating their heterogeneous IT infrastructures. To the best of the authors' knowledge, there is lack of broad-based theoretical and empirical research on mapping the factors influencing the decision making process for EAI adoption on different phases of the adoption lifecycle in LGAs. Integration is indeed a concern within the area of Electronic Government (e-Government) and perhaps particularly challenging for local government authorities (Lam, 2005; Janssen and Cresswell, 2005). Thus, given the increasing attention to EAI adoption by academics (Mantzana, 2006; Khoumbati, 2005; Themistocleous, 2004), the authors attempt to investigate the adoption lifecycle phases and mapping of factors on different adoption lifecycle phases in the local government authorities. The necessity for relatively similar research has been highlighted in the normative literature (Janssen and Cresswell, 2005; Somers and Nelson, 2001; Prescott and Conger, 1995).

INVESTIGATING ADOPTION LIFECYCLE PHASES

Paul *et al.*, (2000) suggests that technology adoption can be considered as an organisation's decision to acquire a specific technology and make it available to target users for their task performance. On the contrary, technology adoption involves a sequence of phases an organisation passes through before taking the decision for adoption (Frambach and Schillewaert, 2002; Gallivan, 2001). Rogers (1995) explains that adoption is the process through which an individual or other decision-making unit passes from first knowledge of an innovation, to forming an attitude toward the innovation, to a decision to adopt or reject, to implementation of the new idea, and to confirmation of this decision. Several researchers proposed adoption lifecycle phases e.g. Kamal (2006) proposed a novel taxonomy of IT innovation adoption with eight phases, Gallivan (2001) proposed three innovation adoption and implementation phases, whereas, Darmawan, (2001) proposed four phases of innovation adoption process. With regards to organisational adoption, Gopalakrishnan and Damanpour (1997) also reported two main distinguishable stages: initiation and implementation of innovation. The actual adoption decision occurs between the initiation and implementation stage. In the initiation stage, the organisation becomes aware of the technology, forms an attitude towards it acceptance and evaluates the technology (Gopalakrishnan and Damanpour, 1997). In implementation stage, the organisation decides to purchase and make use of IT. Nevertheless, such organisational adoption decision marks merely the beginning of the actual implementation of technology.

From this point onwards, the acceptance or assimilation becomes vital in the organisation. Gopalakrishnan and Damanpour (1997) and Rogers (1995) point here that technology adoption process can only be considered a success to the extent that technology is accepted and integrated into the organisation and the target individual adopters demonstrate commitment by continuing to use the technology over a period of time. The aforesaid research studies illustrate important adoption phases, however, these adoption studies also discuss on phases beyond the adoption phase i.e. focusing on both the pre-adoption and post- adoption phases. However, it is not the intent of this research to investigate on phases beyond the adoption phase. The reason is that as the current research investigates on EAI adoption not on EAI implementation and beyond as reported earlier. The authors attempt to move this research a step forward and present four

Figure 2. Adoption lifecycle phases (Adapted from Kamal, 2006)

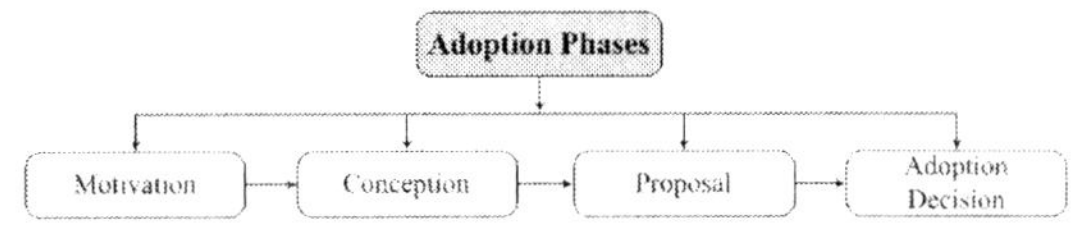

adoption lifecycle phases and map the factors influencing the decision-making process for EAI adoption in LGAs on adoption lifecycle phases (motivation, conception, proposal, and adoption decision) in Figure 2.

Motivation Phase

Motivation signifies the state when an organisation becomes aware of a specific technology and attempts to acquire knowledge about the technology, further leads to motivating the organisation in ascertaining an attitude towards its adoption (Kamal, 2006; Becker and Whisler, 1967). Frambach and Schillewaert (2002) and Darmawan (2001) have described this state as initiation phase in their respective models. Rog ers (1995) reports this stage as knowledge and states that knowledge occurs when an individual or (decision-making unit) is exposed to innovation's existence and gain some understanding of how it functions. Thus, it can also be said that motivation is a natural phenomenon i.e. when any organisation realises a problem that may be solved by a specific technology, the organisation is motivated to attain knowledge about how the technology may resolve their problem.

Conception Phase

Conception phase refers to a plan of action that the organisation should pursue. In highly innovative organisations presumably this phase (conception) is exhibited by a number of organisational members such as creating an attitude towards technology adoption (Kamal, 2006; Becker and Whisler, 1967). Agarwal and Prasad (1998) refer to this stage as *perception*, towards technology adoption. Rogers (1995) refers this stage as persuasion. Persuasion occurs when an individual (or a decision-making unit) forms a favorable or unfavorable attitude towards innovation adoption (Rogers, 1995). Thus, it appears that conception phase is directly related to the motivation phase. For instance when if an LGA is motivated to invest in EAI, the decision makers may indeed attempt to acquire the details i.e. to develop some views as to how EAI may assist them in solving their problems.

Proposal Phase

Proposal refers to making a formal proposition for technology adoption to rest of the organisation (Kamal, 2006; Becker and Whisler, 1967). The researcher asserts that proposing the innovative idea to the rest of the organisation is very crucial for making technology adoption decision. At this phase, the departments making decisions to adopt technology need to provide substantiated reasons for approval from the organisation, besides this the departments need to analyse their requirements and assess their capabilities for acquiring a technology. Dixon (1999) reports that analysing the fit of technology is an influential factor for technology adoption. In several organisations, a formal justification proposal is prepared and accepted by decision-makers, prior to any investment or expenditures (Irani *et al.*, 2002). Whereas, Paul *et al.*, (2000) signifies proposal submission as the commencement of a formal technology adoption process i.e. opting to move towards the adoption decision. Thus, it can be said that the probability of an organisation's adopting a technology will increase as its current adoption stage moves up the adoption continuum. For instance, an organisation that has already submitted a formal adoption proposal under organisational funding is more likely to adopt the technology than organisations that have thought about potential adoption but decided not to pursue it at present (Paul *et al.,* 2000).

Adoption Decision Phase

Adoption Decision is the actual phase where organisations take the decision to adopt a specific technology (Kamal 2006; Frambach and Schillewaert, 2002). Darmawan (2001) analysed adoption phase at two levels: (a) at organisational level adoption i.e. when an organisation begins to realise the need for strategic change and decides to adopt technology, thus, the decision ends with the acquisition of technology, and (b) the individual level adoption, commences with the acquisition of technology, and finishes when technology is utilised. Karahanna *et al.,* (1999) reports that the phases leading the adoption decision as pre- adoption phase (where the target behaviour is technology adoption), and the phases following the adoption decision collectively as post- adoption phase (where the target behaviour is the continuous technology usage). The current research only covers the pre- adoption phases, not the post- adoption phases.

The earlier sections highlighted factors influencing EAI adoption in LGAs and in this section, the authors presented adoption lifecycle phases. Kamal and Themistocleous (2006; 2007) tested the factors (Table 1) through several case studies in their previous research; nevertheless, the adoption lifecycle phases and mapping of factors on the phases are tested through one case study (Kamal *et al.,* 2008). Thus, the authors take into consideration the adoption lifecycle phases as a *research issue* and attempt to test them through another case study in the subsequent sections. The research issue is as follows:

Research Issue 1-adoption lifecycle phases: *LGAs can pass through several phases while adopting EAI.*

Mapping EAI Adoption Factors on the Adoption Lifecycle Phases

The research conducted hitherto indicates that the process of EAI adoption and use in different sectors such as multinational, healthcare and SMEs has been significant to deriving the benefits of enterprise application integration (Mantzana, 2006; Khoumbati, 2005; Chen, 2005; Themistocleous, 2004). The existing studies on EAI adoption have investigated on factors, actors and the causal relationship among and between them. Yet from a conceptual and empirical point of view, none of the existing studies related to EAI adoption has investigated the mapping of the factors influencing EAI adoption process on different phases of the adoption lifecycle. The researcher considers this as a literature gap and reports that it is important to understand and manage the EAI adoption process in LGAs. This can be attributed to several reasons (both in the areas of EAI and LGAs) including among others: (a) EAI is very often considered as high-risk project (e.g. Janssen and Cresswell, 2005), (b) proliferation of EAI technologies (Linthicum, 2000) etc.

On the other hand, LGAs are characterised as laggards and often resist to the technological changes, however, these changes should therefore be managed as their importance in bringing change in the organisation is vital (Themistocleous *et al.,* 2004; McIvor *et al.,* 2002). With such aforesaid evidences, the researcher points out that it does worth to study the mapping of factors influencing EAI adoption in LGAs on different adoption lifecycle phases. Along with the proposed factors influencing EAI adoption in LGAs, the mapping of factors influencing EAI adoption in LGAs on different phases of the adoption lifecycle also make a novel contribution at conceptual level. Nevertheless, the actual mapping of factors on different phases of adoption lifecycle will be carried out after conducting empirical research. Hence, the researcher suggests that while adopting EAI, realising the factor(s) that influences the decision making process for EAI adoption in LGAs on different phases of the adoption lifecycle may provide much deeper comprehension on EAI adoption process. Therefore, the researcher proposes the following research issue for further investigation:

Research Issue 2-Mapping EAI Adoption Factors: *The influential factors for EAI adoption can be mapped on different adoption lifecycle phases to support the decision makers while adopting EAI.*

RESEARCH METHODOLOGY

The role and the applicability of EAI in developing integrated IT infrastructures remains under investigation within LGAs. This chapter attempts to study EAI to understand how public organisations use EAI technology to develop integrated IT infrastructures. The authors have followed an interpretive, qualitative case study approach to conduct this research. Interpretitivism stance was adopted, as the aim of this chapter is to understand how LGAs integrate their IT infrastructures. An interpretivism stance allows the authors to navigate and better explain this phenomenon. Also, the authors suggest that in the context of this research a qualitative approach is more appropriate as such approach can be used to: (a) investigate little-known phenomena like EAI, (b) examine organisational and support factors, (c) examine the phenomenon in its natural setting and, (d) learn from practice.

In addition, the authors used a case study strategy to explore and understand the development IT infrastructures in LGAs. In doing so, various data collection methods such as interviews, documentation, and observation were used. The bias that is considered to be a danger in using qualitative research approach is overcome by data triangulation. The use of multiple data collection methods makes the triangulation possible, which provides stronger substation of theory (Eisenhardt, 1989). For the purpose of this chapter, three types of triangulation are used namely: (a) data (b) methodological and, (c) interdisciplinary triangulation.

CASE ORGANISATION

For confidentiality reasons, the authors use the names LGA_AB (**D**epartment_A), LGA_ABC (**D**epartment_B) and LGA_XY to refer to the case organisations. **D**epartment_A and **D**epartment_B are two different departments within LGA_AB. This case organisation provides its services through various service areas including social and environmental services, property, housing, education, health etc. In the past, each department developed their own IT infrastructures. As a result, LGA_AB consisted of numerous heterogeneous information systems that were based on a diversity of platforms, operating systems, data structures and computer languages. Most of these systems were legacy information systems that still today run on mainframe environments. Since there was a lack of common IT infrastructure, and a lack of central coordination of IT, the majority of LGA_AB departments adopted their own applications to support their business activities. These individual applications were not developed in a coordinated way but in stead evolved as a result of the latest technological innovation. This has led to incompatible systems with integration problems. LGA_AB has attempted to overcome this problem by integrating their systems. For example, the LGA_AB turned to Enterprise Resource Planning (ERP) implementations in an attempt to overcome the Year 2000 (Y2K) problem and automate its business processes. Although ERP systems have addressed the Year 2000 (Y2K) problem they only provide a partial solution for the integration problem. This is because ERP systems were not designed to integrate disparate systems but rather to replace them to achieve integration.

The need for an integrated and flexible IT infrastructure has been necessitated with the existing infrastructure causing numerous problems. These problems became an obstacle for them as they prevented it from implementing its business goals. For instance, LGA_AB could not support its goal of closer collaboration and coordination of inter-organisational business processes due to the non-integrated nature of its applications. This held LGA_AB back from achieving an integrated IT infrastructure and cost reductions.

Similarly, LGA_XY faced a number of challenges in meeting its internal performance targets whilst also addressing the modernising government agenda. LGA_XY developed a number of different systems e.g. for finance, human resources, and payroll and purchasing that were provided by different suppliers, with distinct data repositories and network infrastructures and were no longer able to meet the needs of a modern, dynamic authority. This illustrates that LGA_XY's IT infrastructure has been considered as highly fragmented and outdated, with almost 100 separate systems in place. In addition the financial control and the actual administration were spread out among the organisation, so different parts of the organisation looked at different parts of the IT. For instance, like other departments adult services department also had their own programme of work implementing various IT systems and services. It was dependent on ageing mainframe systems that delivered neither the necessary functionality nor the capacity. In addition, the mainframe financial system could only be accessed by accountants that used it to open and close the annual accounts and complete government returns, but budget and management information was out of date and difficult to obtain. LGA_XY used a general ledger system that did not address the strategic or operational management needs of the organisation. There was no strategic procurement focus and no corporate procurement system, and the whole borough did not operate a commitment accounting system. Operational inefficiencies were prevalent and management information was late and unreliable. For example, the operational issues in procurement and finance were constraining the performance of the borough. LGA_XY had no overall visibility of its budgets, payment commitments and suppliers. Critically, management information was spread across multiple systems, and it took an average of eight weeks to provide key management information. The way LGA_XY was doing business with their partners was costing too much, due to which there was no productivity. There was no control over the systems from data security point of view. It was clear that a single, integrated solution was required if the borough was to achieve the major business transformation involved in modernising its services. The borough therefore took the decision to update its key corporate IT infrastructure.

The interviews were conducted with the *(a)* Head of ICT (HICT), Senior Development Support Engineer (SDSE), Service Delivery Manager for Applications (SDMA) from LGA_AB Department_A, *(b)* Head of IT (HIT), Project Manager (PM) and the Web Manager (WM) from LGA_AB Department_B and *(c)* Head of IT (HIT), Project Manager (PM) and Senior Systems Developer (SSD) from LGA_XY. After conducting interviews, it illustrates that their IT infrastructures has been underdeveloped and not integrated and thus, several limitations existed in their IT infrastructures. The interview discussions illustrate that the limitations of the IT infrastructure led LGA_AB Department_A, Department_B and LGA_XY to take a decision to significantly advance in the delivery of their services by adopting EAI technological solution to develop an integrated IT infrastructure. Individual meetings were conducted to initially test the factors (Table 1) influencing EAI adoption and assessing the importance of the factors. In doing so during the meetings the authors discussed and shared views on different EAI adoption factors (Table 1) with the interviewees. Some factors had similar views from all the interviewees e.g. project champion was reported as important personnel for both the case organisations for taking lead in their respective projects. Similarly, full support from top management in the case organisations, interviewees ranked this factors as most important and similarly for barriers, the interviewees considered it as most important factor, whereas, other factors had dissimilar views. This may be attributed to the precincts of their responsibilities in their respective projects. However, each interviewee was asked to exemplify the importance of each factor. Table 2 illustrates the importance of factors using Miles and Huberman (1994) scale of less important (○), medium important (◉) and most important (●) and where the interviewees did not respond, the authors used "×" symbol to illustrate as no response.

Factors as presented in Table 1 have influenced the decision makers at LGA_AB Department_A, while adopting EAI except two i.e. Table 2 highlights the importance of formalisation and evaluation frameworks factor as less important or even with no comments (×) from one interviewee. The reason regarding the evaluation framework factor as mutually agreed by interviewees is that: "*... selection of technology has not always been done very well and it's been ad hoc look at the system often by the people that do not have sufficient technological skills and no techniques applied to evaluate the technology...*". This factor is related to the formalisation factor. The reason is

Table 2. Testing of factors influencing EAI adoption in the case organisations

		LGA_AB Department_A			LGA_AB Department_B			LGA_XY		
	EAI Adoption Factors	**HICT**	**SDSE**	**SDMA**	**HIT**	**PM**	**WM**	**HIT**	**PM**	**SSD**
PF	Project Champion	●	●	●	●	●	●	●	●	●
	Citizen's Satisfaction	●	●	○	●	●	◉	○	○	○
	Critical Mass	◉	●	●	◉	◉	●	○	○	◉
	Market Knowledge	◉	◉	●	◉	◉	◉	●	●	●
TF	Evaluation Frameworks	○	○	×	◉	◉	●	◉	◉	◉
	Technological Risks	◉	●	●	●	◉	●	○	○	○
	IT Infrastructure	●	●	○	●	●	○	●	●	●
	Personnel IT Knowledge	●	●	◉	●	◉	◉	●	●	●
	IT Sophistication	◉	◉	◉	◉	●	◉	◉	●	●
	Data Security and Privacy	●	●	●	●	◉	●	●	●	●
SF	Top Management Support	●	●	●	●	●	●	●	●	●
	IT Support	◉	●	◉	●	◉	◉	●	●	●
	Higher Administrative Authority	●	◉	●	●	●	●	●	◉	●
FF	Return on Investment	●	●	●	○	◉	○	●	●	◉
	Cost	◉	●	●	●	◉	●	●	●	●
OF	Centralisation	◉	●	●	●	●	●	●	●	●
	Managerial Capability	●	●	●	●	◉	●	●	●	●
	Barriers	●	●	●	●	●	●	◉	●	●
	Benefits	●	●	◉	●	●	●	●	●	●
	Formalisation	○	○	○	●	●	●	◉	●	●
	Size	◉	◉	●	●	●	●	●	◉	◉

that within LGA_AB Department_A there were no clear procedures, norms and formal processes for selecting and assessing EAI software and thus ended in taking the decision to select EAI software without assessing by relying on their software vendor. For LGA_AB Department_B, the financial capability was improved i.e. cost fell because quality data reduced the form rejection rates and received e-Forms that did not need to be manually keyed-in, whereas, return on investment was not tested. The interviewees reported that: "*... due to silo mentality we were not able to prove the return on our investment in this project...*", whereas at LGA_XY three factors were not tested e.g. as the EAI project conducted in LGA_XY was related to employees and managers of the organisation, citizen's satisfaction factor was reported as not relevant and was not tested. For critical mass factor, LGA_XY consider themselves as front runners among the other London boroughs in terms of adopting technologies. The head of IT reported that: "*... we have an alliance with other boroughs but we consider ourselves as front runners in area of integration/IT solutions, thus, we follow a proactive approach while adopting IT solutions and aim to be the leaders in what we do ...*". Third factor that was not tested is technological risks. The interviewees mutually agreed that "*... we did not face any risks for relying on software vendor for the EAI solution, as we selected them for our integration project after a rigorous search and evaluation of integration solution suppliers... in addition, we relied on them as they had great experience on IT projects and clear view regarding the integration of EAI solutions ...*".

The overall results depict relatively mixed views from the interviews. However, with the conformity of several factors as highly and moderately important, the authors assert that the factors (Table 1) are tested through these case organisations. Nonetheless, the extracted results in Table 2 may not seem sufficient as they are just based on the understanding of the interviewees. The authors argue here that merely by discussing on different factors and attaining the verbal results during the interview sessions, it may not be possible to identify that precisely which factor(s) influences EAI adoption on different phases of the adoption lifecycle. Due to this reason and to further enhance the research, the authors asked the interviewees to map the factors based on their importance on different phases of the adoption lifecycle for EAI adoption in the case organisations.

FINDINGS FROM THE CASE ORGANISATIONS

The main issues derived from LGA_AB Department_A, LGA_AB Department_B and LGA_XY presented earlier are summarised and described below along with the comments from the interviewees:

Testing Adopting Lifecycle Phases

The interviewees were asked to comment and illustrate the importance of the adoption lifecycle phases. All the interviewees agreed that these phases are very important. For example the senior development support engineer and service delivery manager for applications at LGA_AB Department_A mutually agreed that: "*... these phases are vital with a perfect breakdown ... however, for adoption phase we call it an investment phase ...*". Whereas, the head of ICT reported that: "*... the proposal and adoption decision phases are vital and are physical aspects whereas motivation and conception are not necessarily physical aspects ...*"

The interviewees from CICTD also reported new phases. For example, the head of IT and service delivery manager for applications reported that before the *motivation* phase, they passed through another phase i.e. *external driver* and/or *driving force* phase for their EAI project. They further added that in this phase, CICTD was driven by some external influences e.g. pressure from the central government, peer pressure and other stakeholder's (internal and external) influence to improve the service delivery. Due to this, CICTD was motivated to run an EAI project. In addition, the senior development support engineer stated that the project team also passed through another phase before the *proposal* phase i.e. *discussion phase* and/or *research phase*. The interviewee reported that in this phase, CICTD had to do some research on the EAI solution and discussions were carried out with other colleagues before preparing a final proposal. The interviewee further added that we had to analyse our resources that were needed to actually enable to run the project.

After analysing the interviews from CICTD, the authors note that external driver and/or driving force phase can be the same as motivation phase. The reason is that an organisation may be motivated to take a step when it is either influenced internally due to some problem or externally through some stakeholders influence. Whereas, the discussion and/or research phase may also be the same as proposal phase. The rationale is that in proposal phase, the departments may need to do some evaluation and provide valid reasons for approval from the organisation, besides this the departments need to analyse their requirements and assess their capabilities for acquiring a technology. Interviewees from LGA_AB Department_B and LGA_XY did not report any new phase; nevertheless, they highlighted the importance of these phases and pointed out that they came across these phases during their projects. For example, the project manager from LGA_AB Department_B reported that: "*... there is a definite attempt to thing about what the problem is and there is definitely a proposal for how to get there and definitely there are some senior people in the department to take the decision. So I think it is a fair lifecycle and does reflect the adoption phases at LGA_AB Department_B for EAI project ...*". Whereas, the web manager from LGA_AB Department_B stated that: "*... I think it is a reasonable lifecycle and does reflect the adoption processes at LGA_AB Department_B for our EAI project ...*". The head of IT and the project manager at LGA_AB Department_B mutually agreed that: "*... motivation is developing a business case i.e. when we identified our business needs, conception is the phase where we determined the technology and platform for us to go forward, proposal is the phase where we made a formal case for EAI adoption and forward it to the decision makers and adoption decision is the phase what we actually call as the investment phase, we took the decision and signed the contract. Thus, it does reflect the adoption phases for EAI project ...*". The senior systems developer at LGA_XY also further added that: "*... I consider them as fair adoption lifecycle phase's pattern and it does illustrate the adoption processes for the EAI project at LGA_XY ...*".

Thereafter, the interviewees were asked to illustrate the importance of the adoption lifecycle phases using Miles and Huberman (1994) scale as aforesaid. The importance of each phase is presented in Table 3.

The aforesaid empirical findings test the adoption lifecycle phases and fulfill the purpose

Table 3. Importance of adoption lifecycle phases in the case organisations

	LGA_AB Department_A			LGA_AB Department_B			LGA_XY		
Adoption Lifecycle Phases	**HICT**	**SDSE**	**SDMA**	**HIT**	**PM**	**WM**	**HIT**	**PM**	**SSD**
Motivation	⊙	●	●	●	●	●	●	●	⊙
Conception	⊙	●	●	●	●	●	●	●	●
Proposal	●	●	●	●	●	●	●	●	●
Adoption Decision	●	●	●	●	●	●	●	●	●

Table 4. Mapping factors influencing EAI adoption on different phases of the adoption lifecycle in the case organisations

		LGA_AB Department_A											
		HICT				SDSE				SDMA			
	Factors	M	C	P	AD	M	C	P	AD	M	C	P	AD
	Project Champion	✓	✓	✓	✓	–	–	✓	–	✓	–	–	–
	Citizen's Satisfaction	–	–	✓	–	✓	✓	✓	✓	✓	–	–	–
	Critical Mass	✓	✓	✓	–	✓	✓	–	–	✓	✓	–	–
PF	Market Knowledge	–	–	✓	✓	✓	✓	–	–	–	✓	–	–
	Evaluation Frameworks	–	–	–	✓	–	–	–	–	–	–	✓	–
	Technological Risks	–	–	✓	✓	–	✓	✓	✓	–	✓	✓	✓
	IT Infrastructure	✓	✓	✓	–	–	✓	✓	✓	–	✓	✓	–
	Personnel IT Knowledge	–	✓	✓	✓	✓	✓	✓	✓	–	✓	–	–
	IT Sophistication	✓	✓	✓	–	✓	✓	✓	✓	–	✓	–	–
TF	Data Security and Privacy	✓	✓	✓	–	✓	✓	✓	✓	–	✓	–	–
	Top Management Support	✓	–	✓	✓	–	✓	✓	✓	✓	–	–	✓
	IT Support	–	✓	✓	✓	✓	✓	✓	✓	–	✓	✓	✓
SF	Higher Administrative Authority	✓	–	✓	✓	✓	✓	✓	✓	✓	✓	–	–
	Return on Investment	–	–	✓	✓	✓	✓	✓	✓	✓	✓	✓	✓
FF	Cost	–	–	✓	✓	–	–	✓	✓	✓	✓	✓	✓
	Centralisation	–	–	✓	✓	✓	✓	✓	✓	–	✓	–	–
	Managerial Capability	–	–	✓	✓	–	✓	✓	✓	–	✓	✓	✓
	Barriers	–	–	✓	✓	–	✓	✓	✓	✓	–	✓	✓
	Benefits	–	–	–	✓	✓	✓	✓	✓	✓	–	✓	✓
	Formalisation	–	–	✓	–	✓	✓	✓	✓	–	–	✓	–
OF	Size	✓	✓	✓	✓	✓	✓	✓	✓	✓	✓	–	–

continued on following page

of *research issue 1 - Adoption Lifecycle Phases: LGAs can pass through several phases while adopting EAI.* Subsequently, the authors present the mapping of factors influencing EAI adoption on the adoption lifecycle phases.

Testing the Mapping of EAI Adoption Factors on the Adopting Lifecycle Phases

The interviewees were asked to map the factors influencing EAI adoption on different phases of the adoption lifecycle. Horizontally, Table 4 illustrates the adoption lifecycle phases e.g. Mapping (M), Conception (C), Proposal, (P) and Adoption Decision (AD), whereas, vertically Table 4 represents the factors influencing EAI adoption in the case organisations. The mapping of factors on different phases of the adoption lifecycle is based on the importance of each factor influencing EAI adoption in the case organisations.

Table 4 displays varied results for the mapping of factors on adoption lifecycle phases by the interviewees. This mapping of factors is based on the interviewees observation and understanding of factors and its impact on their decision making

Table 4. continued

		LGA_AB Department_B											
		HIT				PM				WM			
	Factors	M	C	P	AD	M	C	P	AD	M	C	P	AD
PF	Project Champion	✓	✓	✓	✓	✓	–	✓	✓	–	–	✓	✓
	Citizen's Satisfaction	–	–	✓	–	✓	–	–	–	✓	–	–	–
	Critical Mass	✓	✓	✓	–	✓	✓	–	–	✓	–	–	–
	Market Knowledge	–	–	✓	✓	–	✓	–	–	–	–	✓	–
TF	Evaluation Frameworks	✓	–	–	✓	–	–	✓	–	–	✓	–	–
	Technological Risks	–	–	✓	✓	–	✓	✓	✓	–	–	✓	✓
	IT Infrastructure	✓	✓	✓	–	–	✓	✓	–	✓	✓	–	–
	Personnel IT Knowledge	–	✓	✓	✓	–	✓	–	–	–	–	✓	✓
	IT Sophistication	✓	✓	✓	–	✓	✓	–	–	–	✓	–	–
	Data Security and Privacy	✓	✓	✓	–	–	✓	✓	–	✓	–	✓	–
SF	Top Management Support	✓	–	✓	✓	✓	–	–	✓	✓	–	–	✓
	IT Support	–	✓	✓	✓	–	✓	✓	✓	–	✓	✓	–
	Higher Administrative Authority	✓	–	✓	✓	✓	✓	–	–	✓	–	–	✓
FF	Return on Investment	–	–	✓	✓	✓	–	✓	–	✓	–	✓	–
	Cost	–	–	✓	✓	✓	✓	✓	✓	–	–	–	✓
OF	Centralisation	–	–	✓	✓	–	✓	–	–	✓	–	–	✓
	Managerial Capability	–	–	✓	✓	–	✓	✓	✓	✓	–	–	–
	Barriers	✓	✓	✓	✓	✓	–	✓	✓	–	–	✓	–
	Benefits	–	–	–	✓	✓	–	✓	✓	–	–	✓	–
	Formalisation	–	–	✓	–	–	–	✓	–	–	–	✓	✓
	Size	–	–	✓	✓	✓	✓	–	–	–	–	–	✓

continued on following page

process at each phase of the adoption lifecycle for each case study. For example, in the case of project champion as a factor for EAI adoption in LGA_AB Department_A, the head of IT reported that: "... *involvement of the project champion is important in all the adoption lifecycle phases because project champions provide: (a) senior lead, (c) take responsibility and (c) supervise throughout any project* ...".

The senior development support engineer reported that: "... *involvement of the project champion is vital only at the proposal phase because depending on the information from the project manager, the project champion is in a position whether to get investment from the top management* ...". The service delivery manager for applications had a different opinion and said that: "... *from a 'driver force' point of view, the project champion typically influences on getting the project started, whilst in subsequent phases they can keep motivation going, especially where there a doubts raised about continuing, the conception, proposal and adoption phases usually deliver their required outcomes by process and not an individual's energy* ...". For LGA_AB Department_B, the web manager reported that: "... *project champion - a key motivator that influences on getting the project started, not particularly*

Table 4. continued

		LGA_XY											
		HIT				PM				SSD			
	Factors	**M**	**C**	**P**	**AD**	**M**	**C**	**P**	**AD**	**M**	**C**	**P**	**AD**
PF	Project Champion	✓	✓	✓	✓	✓	✓	✓	✓	✓	✓	✓	✓
	Citizen's Satisfaction	–	–	–	–	✓	–	–	–	–	–	–	–
	Critical Mass	–	–	✓	✓	✓	✓	–	–	✓	✓	✓	–
	Market Knowledge	–	✓	–	✓	✓	✓	–	–	–	✓	✓	–
TF	Evaluation Frameworks	✓	–	✓	✓	–	–	✓	–	✓	✓	✓	–
	Technological Risks	–	–	✓	–	–	✓	✓	✓	–	✓	✓	✓
	IT Infrastructure	–	✓	–	✓	–	✓	✓	✓	–	✓	✓	–
	Personnel IT Knowledge	–	✓	–	–	✓	✓	✓	✓	✓	✓	✓	–
	IT Sophistication	–	✓	–	✓	✓	✓	✓	✓	✓	✓	✓	–
	Data Security and Privacy	–	–	✓	–	–	–	✓	✓	–	✓	✓	–
SF	Top Management Support	–	✓	–	✓	–	✓	✓	✓	✓	–	–	✓
	IT Support	–	–	✓	–	–	✓	✓	–	–	✓	✓	–
	Higher Administrative Authority	✓	–	–	✓	✓	–	✓	✓	✓	–	✓	✓
FF	Return on Investment	✓	–	✓	✓	✓	✓	✓	✓	✓	–	✓	✓
	Cost	✓	–	✓	✓	–	–	✓	✓	✓	✓	✓	✓
OF	Centralisation	–	✓	✓	✓	✓	✓	✓	✓	–	✓	✓	✓
	Managerial Capability	–	✓	–	✓	–	✓	✓	✓	✓	✓	✓	–
	Barriers	✓	–	✓	–	–	✓	✓	✓	✓	✓	✓	✓
	Benefits	–	✓	–	✓	✓	✓	✓	✓	✓	✓	✓	✓
	Formalisation	–	✓	–	–	✓	✓	✓	✓	✓	✓	✓	–
	Size	✓	–	–	–	✓	–	–	–	✓	–	–	–

involved in conception phases, whilst in subsequent phases they can keep motivation going until decision taken to adopt the solution ..."

Whereas, for LGA_AB Department_B, the head of IT reported that: "*... project champion - a key motivator that influences on getting the project initiated, according to my knowledge, champion was not particularly involved in the conception and proposal phases during this project, whilst in the adoption decision phase the champion was indirectly involved merely to represent the department as the final decision to adopt was from the head of the department and other top management ...*". The difference in opinion on mapping the factors can be attributed to the understanding, observation and participation of each interviewee in their respective EAI projects. However, based on the empirical findings, the authors note that the identification of adoption lifecycle phases and mapping of factors on adoption lifecycle phases may support in better realising and understanding EAI adoption in LGAs. This is important as it may support the management decisions and actions during the introduction of EAI solutions. The analysis also reflects different ways of working and performing their functions even within the same organisation. This can be attributed to the staff members with different cultural backgrounds and different abilities of observing and understanding different phenomenon. Thus, the aforesaid empirical findings test the mapping of factors on adoption lifecycle phases and fulfill the purpose of *research issue 2 – Mapping EAI Adoption Factors: Factors can influence EAI adoption in LGAs on different phases of the adoption lifecycle*.

CONCLUSION

This chapter attempts to move the research a step forward to improve the decision-making process in *LGAs* while adopting EAI. In doing so, in the earlier sections the authors briefly discussed on how EAI may benefit the organisations in overcoming their integration problems. Thereafter, the authors explained on the current research conducted on EAI in the local government domain and highlighting factors influencing EAI *adoption* in *LGAs*. The factors presented in Table 1 are based on the EAI *adoption* model proposed in their earlier publications by (Kamal and Themistocleous, 2006, 2007). Yet again, the case study presented in this chapter tests these factors and highlight their importance (Table 2). In the subsequent section, the authors highlight the current research conducted in the area of *adoption* lifecycle phases and mapping of factors on *adoption* lifecycle phases. However, the main strength of this chapter is validating the *adoption* lifecycle phases through the case studies by mapping the factors (from Table 1) influencing EAI *adoption* on the *adoption* lifecycle phases. The case studies conducted in LGA_AB Department_A, LGA_AB Department_B and LGA_XY test the *adoption* lifecycle phases.

Interviewees also highlighted the factors influencing their decision on the different *adoption* lifecycle phases (however, due to the length of the chapter, authors just mentioned about the importance of project champion factor on *adoption* lifecycle phases with comments from the interviewees). The interviewees also mentioned four new phases that the authors explained as similar to the existing phases e.g. the head of IT and service delivery manager for applications from LGA_AB Department_A reported that before the motivation phase; they passed through another phase i.e. external driver and/or driving force phase for their EAI project. It can be said that these phases may exist in other local government authorities; however the new phases need validation. The authors present the revised *adoption* lifecycle phases in Figure 3.

The rationale for undertaking this research is that EAI is a relatively a new research area in the local government domain. Due to this, LGA officials are reluctant to make investments in EAI. This can be attributed to: (a) lack of skilled staff and disinclined to adopt new technologies, (b) lack of understanding and knowledge of EAI in the *LGAs*, (c) *LGAs* have been very slow or even

Figure 3. Revised adoption lifecycle phases

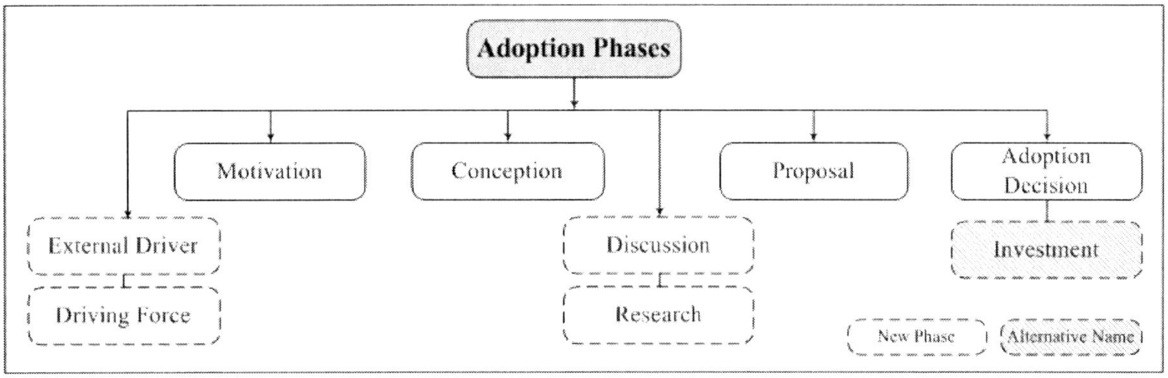

unprepared for technological transformations (Devadoss *et al.*, 2002; Beaumaster, 2002), (d) *LGAs* are unable to react proactively as technologies constantly change and evolve around them (Beaumaster, 2002). Therefore, the process of identifying factor(s) influencing the decision-making process for EAI *adoption* on *adoption* lifecycle phases may assist *LGAs* while taking the decision for EAI *adoption*. The authors claim that the process of mapping the factors on *adoption* lifecycle phases has not been applied for the analysis of EAI *adoption* factors in *LGAs*. The authors suggest that it is mostly appropriate to use this process while adopting EAI, especially for high-risk EAI based project.

REFERENCES

Agarwal, R., & Prasad, J. (1998). The antecedents and consequents of user perceptions in information technology adoption. *Decision Support Systems, 22*(1), 15-29.

Akbulut, A. Y. (2002). An investigation of the factors that influence electronic information sharing between state and local agencies. In *Proceedings of the 8th Americas Conference on Information Systems*, (pp. 2454-2460). Dallas, TX.

Bass, C. & Lee, J. M. (2002). Building a business case for EAI. *EAI Journal*, 18-20.

Beath, C. M. (1991). Supporting the IT champion. *MIS Quarterly, 15*(3), 355-72.

Beaumaster, S. (2002). Local government IT implementation issues: A challenge for public administration. In *Proceedings of the 35th Annual Hawaii International Conference on System Sciences*, (pp. 1725-1734). IEEE Computer Society.

Benyon-Davies, P. (2005). Constructing electronic government: The case of the UK inland revenue. *International Journal of Information Management, 25*(1), 3-20.

Benyon-Davies, P. & Williams, M. D. (2003). Evaluating electronic local government in the UK. *Journal of Information Technology, 18*, 137-149.

Becker, S. N., & Whisler, T. L. (1967). The innovative organisation: A selective view of current theory and research. *The Journal of Business, 40*(4), 462-469.

Bouchard, L. (1993). Decision criteria in the adoption of EDI. In *Proceedings of the 14th International Conference on Information Systems*, Orlando, Florida, USA (365-376).

Bradford, M., & Florin, J. (2003). Examining the role of innovation diffusion factors on the implementation success of ERP systems. *Inter. JAIS*, *4*(3), 205-225.

Brudney, J. L., & Seldon, S.C. (1995). The adoption of innovation by smaller local governments: The case of computer technology. *American Review of Public Administration, 25*(1), 71-87.

Carter, F. J., Jambulingham, T., Gupta, V. K., & Melone, N. (2001). Technological innovations: A framework for communicating diffusion affects. *Information and Management, 38*, 277-287.

Chen, H. (2005). *Adopting emerging integration technologies in organisations*. Unpublished doctoral thesis, Brunel University, London, UK.

Danziger, J. N., & Kraemer, K. L. (1986). *People and computers: The impacts of computing on end users in organisations*. New York: Columbia University Press.

Darmawan, I. G. N. (2001). Adoption and implementation of information technology in Bali's local government: A comparison between single level path analyses using PLSATH 3.01 and AMOS 4 and multilevel path analyses using MPLUS 2.01. *International Education Journal, 2*(4), 100-23.

Devadoss, P. R., Pan, S. L., & Huang, J. C. (2002). Structural analysis of e-government initiatives: A case study of SCO. *Decision Support Systems, 34*, 253-269.

Dixon, R. D. (1999). The behavioural side of information technology. *International Journal of Medical Informatics*, *56*(1-3), 117-23.

Ebrahim, Z., & Irani, Z. (2005). E-Government adoption: Architecture and barriers. *Business Process Management Journal*, *11*(5), 589-611.

Ebrahim, Z., Irani, Z., & Sarmad, S. (2004). Factors influencing the adoption of e-government in public sector. *European & Mediterranean Conference on Information Systems*, Tunis, Tunisia.

Eisenhardt, K. M. (1989). Building theories from case study research. *Academy of Management Review*, *14*(4), 532-550.

Frambach, R. T., & Schillewaert, N. (2002). Organisational innovation adoption: A multi-level framework of determinants and opportunities for future research. *Journal of Business Research*, *55*(2), 163-76.

Gallivan, M. J. (2001). Organisational adoption and assimilation of complex technological innovations: Development and application of a new framework. *The DATABASE for Advances in Information Systems*, *32*(3), 51-85.

Garfield, M. (2000). Critical success factors for the state telemedicine policy. In *Proceedings of the 6th Americas Conference on Information Systems*, Long Beach, California, USA (pp. 1573-1578).

Gil-García, J. R., & Pardo, T. A. (2005). E-Government success factors: Mapping practical tools to theoretical foundations. *Government Information Quarterly*, *22*(1), 187-216.

Gopalakrishnan, S., & Damanpour, F. (1997). A review of innovation research in economics, sociology, and technology management. *Omega*, *25*(1), 15-28.

Hong, K. K., & Kim, Y. G. (2002). The critical success factors for ERP implementation: An organisational fit perspective. *Information and Management*, *40*(1), 25-40.

Irani, Z., Sharif, A., Love, P.E.D., & Kahraman, C. (2002). Applying concepts of fuzzy cognitive mapping to model: The IT/IS investment evaluation process. *International Journal of Production Economics*, *75*, 199-211.

Janssen, M., & Cresswell, A. (2005). Enterprise architecture integration in e-government. In *Proceedings of the 38th Hawaii International Conference on System Sciences*, Hawaii, USA (pp. 1-10).

Johannessen, J. A. (1994). IT and innovation: Identifying critical innovation factors. *Information Management & Computer Security*, *2*(2), 4-9.

Kamal, M. M., Themistocleous, M., & Elliman, T. (2008). Extending IT infrastructures in the local government authorities through enterprise application integration. In *Proceedings of the 14th Americas Conference on Information Systems – AMCIS'08*, Toronto, Canada.

Kamal, M. M., Themistocleous, M., & Elliman, T. (2008). Mapping factors influencing EAI adoption in the local government authorities on different phases of the adoption lifecycle. *European and Mediterranean Conference on Information Systems*, Dubai, UAE.

Kamal, M. M., & Themistocleous, M. (2007). Investigating EAI adoption in LGAs: A case study based analysis. In *Proceedings of the 13th Americas Conference on Information Systems*, Keystone, Colorado (pp. 1-13).

Kamal, M. M., & Themistocleous, M. (2006). A conceptual model for EAI adoption in an e-government environment. *European and Mediterranean Conference on Information Systems (EMCIS)*, Costa Blanca, Spain (pp. 1-11).

Kamal, M. M. (2006). IT innovation adoption in government sector: Identifying the critical success factors. *Journal of Enterprise Information Management*, *19*(2), 192-222.

Kamal, M. M. (2004). Integrating e-government through EAI. In *Proceedings of the 10th Americas Conference on Information Systems*, New York, USA (pp. 1143-1149).

Karahanna, E., Straub, D. W., & Chervany, N. L. (1999). Information technology adoption across time: A cross-sectional comparison of pre-adoption and post-adoption beliefs. *MIS Quarterly*, *23*(2), 183-213.

Khoumbati, K., & Themistocleous, M. (2007). Application of fuzzy simulation for the evaluation of enterprise application integration in healthcare organisations. *Transforming Government: People, Process, and Policy*, *1*(3), 230-241.

Khoumbati, K. (2005). *Evaluating the adoption of enterprise application integration in healthcare organisations*. Unpublished doctoral dissertation, Brunel University, London, UK.

Kim, H. J., & Bretschneider, S. (2004). Local government information technology capacity: An exploratory theory. In *Proceedings of the 37th Annual Hawaii International Conference on System Sciences* (pp. 121-130).

Lam, W. (2005). Barriers to e-government integration. *The Journal of Enterprise Information Management*, *18*(5), 511-530.

Lam, W., & Shankararaman, V. (2004). An enterprise application integration methodology. *IT Professionals*, *6*(1), 40-48.

Lee, C. S., Chandrasekaran, R., & Thomas, D. (2003). Examining IT usage across different hierarchical levels in organisations: A study of organizational, environmental, and IT factors. In *Proceedings of the 9th AMCIS* (pp. 1259-1269).

Linthicum, D. (2000). *Enterprise application integration*. Massachusetts: Addison-Wesley.

Mantzana, V. G. (2006). *Investigating the adoption of enterprise application integration in healthcare organisations using an actor-oriented approach*. Unpublished doctoral dissertation, Brunel University, London, UK.

McIvor, R., McHugh, M., & Cadden, C. (2002). Internet technologies supporting transparency in the public sector. *The International Journal of Public Sector Management*, *15*(3), 170-187.

Melitski, J. (2003). Capacity and e-government performance. *Public Performance and Management Review*, *26*(4), 376-390.

Miles, M., & Huberman, A. (1994). *Qualitative data analysis: An expanded sourcebook*. Newbury Park, CA: Sage.

Moon, J., & Bretschneider, S. (1997). Can state government action affect innovation and diffusion. *Technology Forecasting and Social Change*, *54*, 57-77.

Ngai, E. W. T., & Gunasekaran, A. (2004). Implementation of EDI in Hong Kong: An empirical analysis. *Industrial Management & Data Systems*, *104*(1), 88-100.

Norris, D. F. (1999). *Leading edge information technologies and their adoption: Lessons from US cities*. Hershey, PA: Idea Group Publishing.

Nye, Jr., J. (1999). *Information technology and democratic governance: Governance in networked world*. NH: Hollins Publishing Company.

Paul J-H. H., Chau, P. Y. K., & Sheng, O. R. L. (2000). Investigation of factors affecting healthcare organization's adoption of telemedicine technology. In *Proceedings of the 33rd Annual Hawaii International Conference on Systems Sciences* (pp. 1-10).

Perry, J. L., & Danzinger, J. N. (1980). The adoptability of innovation: An empirical assessment of computer applications in local governments. *Administration and Society*, *11*(4), 461-492.

Prescott, M. B., & Conger, S. A. (1995). Information technology innovations: A classification by

IT locus of impact and research approach. *The DATA BASE for Advances in Information Systems, 26*(2/3), 20-41.

Reiersgaard, N., Salvesen, H., Nordheim, S., & Päivärinta, T. (2005). EAI implementation project and shakedown: An exploratory case study. In *Proceedings of the 38th Annual Hawaii International Conference on System Sciences (HICSS'05)*, (pp. 1-10).

Rogers, E. M. (1995). *Diffusion of innovations, 4th ed.* New York: Free Press.

Ruh, W., Maginnis, F., & Brown, W. (2000). *Enterpriser application integration* (A Wiley Tech Brief). New York: John Wiley & Sons Inc.

Sanchez, E., Beery, D., & Shehab, J. (2002). EAI systems bring IT together. *Network Computing.*

Senyucel, Z. (2005). Towards successful e-government facilitation in UK local authorities. *E-Government Workshop '05 (Egov05)* (pp. 1-16).

Serian, D. (2002). *Middleware and enterprise application integration.* London: Springer Verlag.

Signore, O., Chesi, F., & Pallotti, M. (2005). E-Government: Challenges and opportunities. *CMG Italy – XIX Annual Conference*, Florence, Italy.

Somers, T. M., & Nelson, K. (2001). The impact of critical success factors across the stages of enterprise resource planning implementations. In *Proceedings of the 34th Annual Hawaii International Conference on System Sciences* (pp. 1-10).

Songini, M. L. (2004). Australian firm faces ERP implementation woes. *Computerworld.*

Themistocleous, M., & Irani, Z. (2006). Towards a methodology for the development of integrated IT infrastructures. In R. J. Sprague (Ed.), *Proceedings of the 39th Annual Hawaii International Conference on System Sciences (HICSS'06)* (pp. 4-7). Hawaii, USA: IEEE Computer Society.

Themistocleous, M., Irani, Z., & Love, P. E. D. (2005). Developing e-government integrated infrastructures: A case study. In *Proceedings of the 38th Annual Hawaii International Conference on System Sciences (pp. 1-10)*, Big Island, HI: IEEE.

Themistocleous, M., Irani, Z., & Kuljis, J. (2004). Extending the information system lifecycle through enterprise application integration: A case study experience. In *Proceedings of the 37th Annual Hawaii International Conference on System Sciences (HICSS'04)(pp. 1-8) –Track 8*, Big Island, HI: IEEE.

Themistocleous, M. (2004). Justifying the decisions for EAI implementations: A validated proposition of influential factors. *Journal of Enterprise Information Management, 17*(2), 85-104.

Themistocleous, M., & Irani, Z. (2001). Benchmarking the benefits and barriers of application integration. *Benchmarking An International Journal, 8*(4), 317-331.

KEY TERMS

Adoption Process: It is a process through which an individual or other decision-making unit passes from first knowledge of an innovation, to forming an attitude toward the innovation, to a decision to adopt or reject, to implementation of the new idea, and to confirmation of this decision.

Electronic Government (e-Government): E-Government (from electronic government, also known as e-Gov, digital government, online government or in a certain context transformational government) refers to the use of internet technology as a platform for exchanging information, providing services and transacting with citizens, businesses, and other arms of government. E-Government may be applied by the legislature, judiciary, or administration, in order to improve internal efficiency, the delivery of public services, or processes of democratic governance.

Enterprise Application Integration (EAI): Unrestricted sharing of information between two or more enterprise applications. A set of technologies that allow the movement and exchange of information between different applications and business processes within and between organisations.

Information Technology Infrastructure: The term IT infrastructure refers to the part of the infrastructure of an organisation that forms a platform for the IT applications.

Local Government Authorities (LGAs): LGAs are administrative offices that are smaller than a central government and are in direct contact with the community. The term is used to contrast with offices at nation-state level, which are referred to as the central government or national government. The pattern of LGAs is complex, with the distribution of functions varying according to the local arrangements.

Chapter IX
Improving Access to Government Information with Open Standards for Document Formats

Rajiv C. Shah
University of Illinois at Chicago, USA

Jay P. Kesan
University of Illinois College of Law, USA

ABSTRACT

An important element of transformational government is improving the access and use of government information. Effective use of government information requires government to move beyond traditional proprietary document formats because these formats limit access and use of information stored digitally. In this chapter, we show how document formats based on open standards and the Extensible Markup Language (XML) can revitalize citizens' access and use of government information. We also offer an improved definition of open standards to assist governments in selecting which document formats to adopt. A critical part of this new definition is an emphasis on multiple implementations of an open standard, which is also known as running code.

INTRODUCTION

The rise in the use of digital media by governments has created vast amounts of digital information. Much of this information is stored in various document formats, such as DOC, XLS, and PPT. The developers of these formats hold proprietary control over them and therefore limit users' widespread access to them. A new set of document formats, however, based on open standards and the Extensible Markup Language (XML) has the potential to allow easier dissemination and access to this information. In this chapter, we explain how these formats function and provide governments with guidelines for selecting document formats that will allow a greater level of access and use of government information.

Document formats are specifications for storing electronic information. A myriad of document formats exist for various tasks from word processing to architectural drawings. Most citizen interaction with digital government is with documents formatted as Web pages. While the Web has greatly enhanced citizen interaction, government Web pages cover only a small portion of the information developed and collected by government. Virtually every piece of information on a Web page began in another document format. As such, most of the existing document formats make it difficult to search for this information as well as repurpose it for other uses.

The next generation of document formats are based on open standards. Open standards refer to specifications that are publicly available and developed through a public process. They stand in contrast to standards that are proprietary and restricted to certain parties. A significant benefit of open standards is that anyone can implement the standard. The result may be a proliferation of competing implementations that leads to economic and technological benefits for adopters.

This next generation of document formats is based on XML. XML uses markup tags to add structure to documents. The power of these tags is that it fosters more powerful searching and the ability to access and manipulate information within documents. For example, the U.S. Patent and Trademark Office (USPTO) uses an XML-based system for processing applications. By receiving XML-based documents, the USPTO can avoid the cumbersome process of scanning in paper documents, especially because the submittals to the USPTO start as electronic documents. The XML format uses a set of tags to mark aspects of the documents' procedural data (names, addresses, fee data, title of invention, etc.) and application data (abstract, description, claims, figures, patent citations, and drawings). With this information "marked" in a document, the patent office can automatically process a document. For example, the patent office could extract information manually regarding the inventor and document. Without an XML-type format, it would be necessary to read each document and then "cut and paste" the relevant information.

The first section of this chapter provides background on various documents formats, including the most widespread formats developed by Microsoft, two next generation XML-based document formats, ODF and OOXML. The second section reviews the benefits of open standards, which are a critical reason why governments are moving to document formats based on open standards. The final section focuses on the criteria which government should use in the selection of the next generation document formats.

BACKGROUND ON DOCUMENT FORMATS

The most recognized document formats are Microsoft's Word DOC format for word processing, Excel's XLS for spreadsheets, and Powerpoint's PPT format for presentations. However, there are countless other formats that are used by government. Information produced and used within government is created and modified within document formats. The ability to edit, search, and analyze this information directly can transform how government manages itself as well as its relationship with its citizens. Consider the example of Thailand:

December 26, 2004. 7:58 am. A thirty-foot-high wall of water—a tsunami—slams into the famed resort islands off Thailand's southern coast. In one tragic moment, thousands of lives are lost, and thousands more are missing.

In the race to identify victims and assist survivors, Thailand's government hits its own wall. Responding agencies and non-governmental groups are unable to share information vital to the rescue effort. Each uses different data and document formats. Relief is slowed; coordination is complicated. The need for common, open standards for disaster management was never more stark or compelling. The Royal Government of Thailand responded by creating a common website for registering missing persons and making open file formats in particular an immediate national priority (Berkman Center for Internet & Society at Harvard Law School, 2005).

This section focuses on the ability of document formats to share and repurpose information. The latest developments in document formats will allow government and citizens alike to capture a significant portion of the information created within government that is currently hidden away in various documents and spreadsheets. New tools are emerging within new document formats that allow users to quickly find and reuse this information, without time-consuming searches or relying on laborious cut and paste functions to transfer documents to a new format. This section begins by highlighting the domination of Microsoft's proprietary formats and their limitations. The section then focuses on the advantages of XML and the two leading document formats based on XML, the OpenDocument Format (ODF) and Office Open XML (OOXML).

Microsoft's document formats are the primary formats used by governments. This reflects Microsoft's overall domination of the market for office productivity software. It has maintained a market share of at least 95% for its Office suite for many years ("Rivals Set Their Sights on Microsoft Office: Can They Topple the Giant?," 2007). While other document formats are available, most information produced and used within government is stored in Microsoft's document formats. Microsoft's document formats, such as DOC, have a long history. Microsoft has used the DOC format in Microsoft Word 95 to 2003. It has kept the document format code from the public (until recently) as a way to stem competition. Microsoft's control of the DOC file format has imposed a high barrier to entry for competitors. Any rival word processor needs to be able to read Microsoft's DOC format because of its ubiquity. A number of companies have tried to develop various filters and converters, but without the knowledge of Microsoft, they are unable to deliver a 100% high fidelity conversion.

One of the key problems with Microsoft's DOC format arises from a technical decision made many years ago. The DOC format is a binary format. Binary formats store information in the language of ones and zeros. This makes it easier and faster for computers to read, write, process, and save information (Hyde, 2003). This was important in the early days of computing when computers had 1 MB of RAM on a processor running at 20 MHz. Computers today have a 1000 times more memory and processing speed. This has removed the pressing need to use binary formats. Having recognized this development, Microsoft is moving to the next generation of document formats based on Extensible Markup Language (XML).

XML as the Next Generation Document Format

The origins of XML go back to IBM's Generalized Markup Language (GML) to format documents in the 1960s. Various tags or markups would describe parts of the document such as chapters, headings, and paragraphs. This idea would lead to the development of Standard Generalized Markup Language (SGML). SGML would eventually become an international standard in 1985. While SGML is not well known to most users, two of its descendants, HTML and XML, have become ubiquitous.

The free availability of SGML made it popular at CERN and the official markup language for the laboratory. When Tim Berners-Lee developed the World Wide Web while at CERN, he was inspired by SGML in the creating a markup language for Web documents (Gillies & Cailliau, 2000). This language is the Hypertext Markup Language (HTML) and is the established document format for the Web.

XML was created as another subset of SGML. It was designed as a middle ground between HTML and SGML. HTML was focused largely on the presentation of content and considered too limiting for representing structured data. SGML, on the other hand, was considered too complex. XML arose not only as a markup language like HTML, but also as a specification for defining markup languages. XML allows users to define markups and thus store almost any kind of data in a way that other applications and users can then easily access, edit, and process that data.

XML markup tags are human-legible. Ideally, a set of tags should be meaningful by just reading the document. Here is a sentence in XML:

```
<sentence><clause>Benedict Arnold didn<punctuation type="apostrophe"/>t cross the Delaware<punctuation type="semi-colon"/></clause><clause>he crossed his country<punctuation type="period"/></clause></sentence>
```

The use of markup tags ensures that XML differentiates between content and presentation. Moreover, by using more specific tags, it is possible for documents to contain more structured data. Consider this example:

```
<CONTACT>
<NAME>Sally Smith</NAME>
<ID>001</ID>
<COMPANY>ACME International</COMPANY>
<EMAIL>ssmith@acme.com</EMAIL>
<PHONE>555-1234</PHONE>
<STREET>10 Elm St.</STREET>
<CITY>New York</CITY>
<STATE>New York</STATE>
<ZIP>Zip: 10024</ZIP>
</CONTACT>
```

A document with this contact information in a structured format allows for easier searching and manipulation. A user could search hundreds of documents to quickly find contacts with a zip code of 10024. Or a process could be setup to automate adding in contact information for incoming documents for a mailing list. The use of tags in XML makes it easy for a computer to generate data, read data, and manipulate data. As a result, XML serves as useful way for computers to interchange data at various levels, from databases to documents to metadata (Salminen, 2005).

In sum, the value of XML is that the tags and structured data allows for a transformative reuse and repurposing of data. These attributes and abilities have led to a consensus that XML is the wave of the future, and there is considerable movement in a variety of domains to move toward storing more information in XML schemes (Bangeman, 2007). While this chapter focuses on document formats, XML has much wider applicability.

Open DocumentFormat

The benefits of XML led StarOffice, a competitor to Microsoft Office, to develop a document format based on its code. The OpenDocument Format (ODF) standard began as an XML interchangeable file format for the StarOffice application. The ODF standard is built upon many other existing open standards. This decision had several implications. First, it helped the standard remain vendor neutral and implementation agnostic. Second, by relying on XML, ODF avoided reinventing the wheel, which meant it would not have to go through the lengthy development and vetting process for these functions. It could instead rest the standard on the shoulders of other standards. Specifically, ODF incorporates open standards, such as XHTML,

SVG, XSL, SMIL, XLink, XForms, MathML, and Dublin Core (Organization for the Advancement of Structured Information Standards, 2007).

ODF is now developed by a technical committee under the auspices of an industry consortium called the Organization for the Advancement of Structured Information Standards (OASIS). In 1998, OASIS enlarged its focus to include the increasingly popular XML. This was a natural move for OASIS; it originated with vendors promoting SGML. As a result of moving the development to OASIS, ODF is considered an open standard as explained in the next section.

ODF is making significant strides in establishing itself as a viable document format (and alternative) to Microsoft's formats. Once ODF was approved as an OASIS standard in May 2005 and as an ISO standard in May 2006 under the name, ISO/IEC 26300:2006, a number of software applications began supporting it. OpenOffice.org, a free open source office suite, used ODF as well as the related StarOffice, which is sold by Sun Microsystems. Some other adopters of ODF include KOffice which is for Unix and Linux platforms, Abiword, Wordperfect, and in TextEdit on the Mac. The rise of ODF has also led to plug-in products to incorporate support for ODF within Microsoft Office. And in 2008, Microsoft announced it would incorporate support for ODF in the next update to Microsoft Office.

OOXML

The growth of ODF led Microsoft to formally announced a move to an XML-based document format with its Office Open Extensible Markup Language (OOXML) format in 2005. It later submitted the standard to Ecma in November 2005 to pursue an open standards development path for OOXML. Ecma has a long history of developing standards for information technology firms (Ecma International, 2006). Ecma published the OOXML standard in December 2006 and it was approved by the ISO in April 2008 under the name, ISO/IEC 29500.

OOXML was designed to move away from the DOC binary formats to an XML standard. OOXML's design clearly reflects its lineage as a Microsoft document format in light of how the standard is based upon past proprietary design decisions. The OOXML standard is very complex and fully of subtle design choices in an effort to maintain backward compatibility with older DOC formats. Unlike ODF, which started on a blank slate, OOXML carries the weight of maintaining compatibility with legacy formats. In the ECMA's "Office Open XML Overview" it states, "OpenXML was designed from the start to be capable of faithfully representing the pre-existing corpus of word-processing documents, presentations, and spreadsheets that are encoded in binary formats defined by Microsoft Corporation" (Ecma International, 2007).

OOXML was first implemented by Microsoft in its release of Microsoft Office 2007. A number of other applications have begun to implement OOXML including Apple's iWorks and Corel's WordPerfect. Novell has created a plug-in for Openoffice.org office suite so it may use OOXML.

THE SIGNIFICANCE OF DOCUMENT FORMATS BASED ON OPEN STANDARDS FOR GOVERNMENTS

A crucial feature of both ODF and OOXML is their emphasis on being an open standard. Yet the definition of open standards has never been absolute; instead, the term sometimes refers to various characteristics of standards used in software (Krechmer, 2006; West, 2007). Open standards are generally defined based on three criteria (Crocker, 1993). First, the standard is publicly available to everyone at a minimal cost. Second, no entity controls the standard or the standard is licensed on "reasonable and nondiscriminatory terms." Third, the development process for creating the standard involves public participation.

Open standards should not be confused with "open source." Open source is a development model for software based on the public availability of the source code. It is one of many ways to develop software, other development models include proprietary and shareware. While open source software typically relies upon and uses open standards, they are two different concepts. For example, May suggests open source is useful for underdeveloped countries because of its cost savings and flexibility (May, 2006). This distinction is important to note because governments are choosing between vendors that rely on open source, e.g., IBM and Sun, versus vendors that offer proprietary software, e.g., Microsoft. The decision to use open standards should not affect the choice of a particular vendor, because open standards can be supported by either open source or proprietary software.

The benefits of open standards for governments are economic, technological, and socio-political. Open standards have significant economic benefits because they reduce barriers to entry, limit vendor lock-in, and decrease switching costs. As a result, open standards are often considered a public good, because of the benefits they confer not only on the immediate participants, but also for all of society (Tassey, 2005). Examples of open standards include the transmission protocols such as FTP, HTML, which serve as the language for Web pages, and the image format known as JPEG. Many observers have asserted that the growth, widespread use and popularity of the Internet is largely the result of its reliance on open standards (Kahin, 1995; Maxwell, 2006).

Open standards also offer the technical benefits of interoperability for government. According to the Institute of Electrical and Electronics Engineers, interoperability is best defined as, "the ability of two or more systems or components to exchange information and to use the information that has been exchanged" (IEEE, 1990). Interoperability allows technologies to easily interface with each other, in addition to allowing data to move transparently. Interoperability at one level ensures the ability to seamlessly swap implementations. This quality is important for adopters, because it provides them with choices. At another level, interoperability can assure users that there will not be technical barriers to collaborating with other parts of government, since the data and applications should all work seamlessly. This technological feature helps users to deal with the increasing complexity of information technology in a transparent manner (Maxwell, 2006).

DeNardis and Tam highlight several ways that open standards can have political implications (2007). First, standards can directly affect formal democratic processes. A clear example is voting. Historically, the voting process has standards that are open and transparent regarding the gathering and tabulation of votes. Considerable concern has been raised with electronic voting, because of the lack of open standards for these machines. Second, standards affect broader social conditions that affect democracy. For instance, relying on proprietary standards can deny citizens and government access to electronic information. Open standards are crucial in ensuring government and citizens have access to information that is necessary for the operation of a democracy. Third, standards themselves may be a substantive political issue. After all, a number of standards affect fundamental social values in areas such as property rights, privacy, free speech, and access to knowledge. The final point DeNardis and Tam make concerns the legitimacy of a standard development processes. They suggest that a closed development process is a deviation from basic democratic values and can raise questions of legitimacy. After all, a closed process is denying parties the chance to provide input and voice their concerns.

The benefits of open standards have been widely recognized. A number of governments and organizations, for instance in the United States (Committee for Economic Development, 2006) and the United Kingdom (Office of Government Commerce, 2004), have called for government policies that strongly encourage or mandate open standards. With regards to document formats, a number of governments have already expressed preferences for document standards based on open standards. These governments include Norway, Belgium, Japan, Germany, Malaysia, Netherlands, Brazil, Japan, Denmark, and the state of Massachusetts in the United States.

GUIDELINES FOR GOVERNMENTS IN SELECTING DOCUMENT FORMATS

This section focuses on guidance for governments in selecting document formats. It begins by providing a definition of open standards. This definition has been amended from the general definition of open standards by requiring running code. The next two sections emphasize the need for governments to focus on choosing standards and not implementations as well as supporting multiple open standards.

Defining Open Standards with a Running Code Requirement

An unclear understanding of what defines open standards can lead governments to miss out on its benefits. Our previous research on the open standards policy in Massachusetts highlighted this issue (Shah, Kennis, & Kesan, 2009). To prevent other governments from repeating the mistake, this section provides a useful working definition for open standards.

As a starting point, governments should not conflate open standards with open source. Open standards are specifications that can incorporated into either open source or proprietary software. When governments require the use of open standards, they are not choosing business models. Instead, open standards allow for competition and allow government to pick the software solution, regardless of how it was developed, that meets their needs.

A definition of open standards needs to incorporate a requirement for running code. Running code refers to the existence of multiple independent interoperable implementations of an open standard. Governments have typically defined open standard as "specifications for systems that are publicly available and are developed by an open community and affirmed by a standards body." (Commonwealth of Massachusetts, 2004) This is the widely accepted definition of open standards (Krechmer, 2006). The definition focuses on characteristics associated with the development of the open standard. The problem is that governments have conflated the definition of open standards with the consequences of standards, i.e., multiple implementations (West, 2004). The current definition does not address the desirable outcomes of open standard, it merely assumes it will flow out of an open development process.

The existence of an open standard does not ensure that a user will receive the much-touted benefits of an open standard. An open standard exists only on paper. It takes the efforts of multiple vendors to incorporate the standard for the economic and technological benefits to appear. For example, a companion to SGML during the 1980s was the Office Document Architecture (ODA). This standard was developed as a way to represent the structure of a document, including images. Unlike the more generalizable SGML, ODA focused on a fixed set of parameters that would facilitate document interchange (Fanderi, Fischer, & Kamper, 1992). The work was supported by the European Union and resulted in an Ecma standard in 1985, which was eventually finalized as an ISO standard (ISO/IEC 8613) in the mid-1990s. However, the standard never became widely used. The accepted explanations are the long standards development process and the lack of vendor support (Ditch, 2007; Veal, 2001).

The conflation of the definition of open standards and its consequences can be explained by several factors. First, there is a natural conflation between open standards and open source. They share a long history and share many of the same supporters. Most people could not distinguish the difference between them. With an open source project, it is implicit that an implementation exists; however, the same is not true for open standards. As a result, it becomes easy to forget that open standards depend upon implementations. Second, for simple open standards, implementation can be trivial and taken for granted. However, with document formats implementation cannot always be taken for granted. The ODF standard is about 700 pages, and the OOXML standard is over five thousand pages. Implementing standards of this length is very difficult, especially when interoperability between multiple implementations is a significant goal. Third, vendors may try to conflate an implementation with a standard. After all, if a government standardizes one particular implementation, then a vendor has the possibility of locking that government into using its product. It is no accident that the dominant implementations of ODF and OOXML are tied to major IT vendors.

To avoid confusion with open source and to highlight its benefits, the definition of open standards needs to incorporate a requirement for running code. Running code is a shorthand term to refer to multiple independent interoperable implementations. There needs to be multiple implementations to provide competition in the market and choice for adopters. Moreover, these implementations also need to be independent and interoperable. Independent implementations ensure that standards can be adopted by anyone (not just the party pushing for the standard). Interoperability is important, because it ensures that multiple implementations will all work together. This is essential from an adoption perspective, because it ensures minimal costs when switching between implementations. After all, the ability to seamlessly switch implementations is the key benefit of open standards.

A requirement of independent interoperable implementations is not new. The Internet Engineering Task Force requires that a standard be implemented by two independent vendors before it can be considered an open standard (Bradner, 1996). This requirement is informally known as the need for "running code" and is a requirement for all IETF open standard standards. Not all standards organizations, however, require "running code." The ISO, for example, does not require implementations during the standards approval process.

Nonetheless, it is imperative for governments to adopt open standards only when there is running code. Without running code, governments are not going to receive the enormous benefits of open standards. In 2008, there were multiple implementations of ODF and OOXML. However, there were interoperability concerns. A study found significant interoperability issues between various ODF implementations, e.g, OpenOffice.org, Wordperfect, and KOffice (Shah & Kesan, 2008). Similar problems were found for OOXML implementations. They found that the best implementations may result in formatting problems, while the worst implementations actually lose information, e.g., information found in pictures, footnotes, comments, tracking changes, and tables. As a result, the study warns that adopters of these standards may be effectively be locked-in to the dominant implementations. The study suggests governments need to push for continued progress in interoperability, before running code exists either for ODF or OOXML.

Support Standards Not Implementations

Open standards are specifications, they are not implementations. Open standards exist on paper, while implementations are software products. For example, ODF is defined by a specification set by OASIS and the ISO. It is not defined by its leading implementation, OpenOffice. Similarly, OOXML should be defined by its specification set by Ecma and perhaps the ISO. It should not be defined by its leading implementation, Microsoft Office.

Vendors may try to push governments to conflate an implementation with a standard. After all, if a government standardizes on one particular implementation, then a vendor has the possibility of locking-in a government to a certain product. However, this conflation removes the benefits of an open standard for the government.

A related concern is that the dominant implementation may try to lock-in government. This concern has been voiced in regards to OOXML, because Microsoft is the dominant implementation. Microsoft could add proprietary extensions to OOXML that make it difficult for others to interoperate. In this case, they would seek to conflate the OOXML standards with their implementation. This would help preserve the market share of Microsoft Office. Microsoft has been accused of using this strategy to gain market share in numerous areas including Web browsers (U.S. Department of Justice, 1999), java (Groklaw, 2007), and the Kerberos authentication technology (Livingston, 2000). This is often termed the "embrace, extend, and extinguish" strategy. Embrace refers to Microsoft embracing known standards or the specifications and interfaces of another company's software. Once embraced, the specifications are extended by adding proprietary extensions to the standard. The adoption of these proprietary extensions causes interoperability problems. Once the proprietary extensions are seen as de facto standards, then they are made unavailable to industry participants. This places competitors, who might have developed the standard at a competitive disadvantage. The key way for government to avert this is by requiring all vendors to adhere to the open standard. If a vendor wishes to extend the standard, they may do so, but they should also provide a suitably easy-to-use compatibility mode that adheres to the open standard.

Support Multiple Open Standards

There are numerous benefits of open standards. These benefits persist when there are multiple open standards in a similar technology area. For example, there are a number of open standards for image formats, e.g., JPEG, PNG, CGM. Similarly, there are a number of open standards for documents, e.g., HTML and TXT. Multiple standards often arise because existing standards were inadequate for a certain set of requirements.

If the standards are truly open, then governments should support all such standards. The idea here is that government should encourage open standards, but not try to pick and choose favorite standards among open standards. In the case of document formats governments should support both ODF and OOXML, but only when there is running code, e.g., multiple interoperable implementations.

Summary

The key points for government are the following. First, an open standards policy needs to incorporate a running code requirement that refers to multiple independent interoperable implementations. Second, governments need to focus on supporting standards and not implementations. Finally, governments should encourage and support multiple open standards.

CONCLUSION

Document formats control how information is stored and used. Governments should move away from the traditional proprietary Microsoft document formats to new open standard XML-based document formats for several reasons. First, the new formats offer an unparalleled ability for government and its citizens to search, analyze, and synthesize the information. These document formats will allow a transformative change in the access and use of government information as compared to the current proprietary document formats.

Second, the new XML-based formats are based on open standards. Open standards offer a wealth of economic, technological, and social benefits over proprietary standards, such as the DOC format. Open standard can reduce costs and increase competition by avoiding vendor lock-in and supporting multiple independent implementations. Open standards can also offer social and political benefits, because the open standards process is much more attuned to democratic mores than proprietary standards.

The key to unlocking these benefits is selecting document formats that are open standards. In defining open standards, governments should consider not only the origins of open standards, but also whether these standards have resulted in multiple implementations. After all, without running code, the benefits of open standards will not be realized.

REFERENCES

Bangeman, E. (2007). Adobe to make PDF an open standard. Retrieved on October 2, 2007, from http://arstechnica.com/news.ars/post/20070129-8724.html

Berkman Center for Internet & Society at Harvard Law School. (2005). *Roadmap for open ICT ecosystems.*

Bradner, S. (1996). RFC 2026: The Internet standards process—revision 3. Retrieved on February 2, 2002, from http://www.ietf.org/rfc/rfc2026.txt

Committee for Economic Development. (2006). *Open standards, open source, and open innovation: Harnessing the benefits of openness.* Washington, DC: Committee for Economic Development.

Commonwealth of Massachusetts, I. T. D. (2004). *Enterprise open standards policy* (No. ITD-APP-01).

Crocker, D. (1993). Making standards the IETF way. *Standardview, 1*(1), 48-56.

DeNardis, L., & Tam, E. (2007). *Interoperability and democracy: A political basis for open document standards.* Paper presented at the 5th International Conference on Standardization and Innovation in Information Technology. Retrieved on October 28, 2008 from http://www.krechkin.com/siit2007/program.html

Ditch, W. (2007). XML-based office document standards. *JISC Technology & Standards Watch.*

Ecma International. (2006). Ecma international approves office open XML standard.

Ecma International. (2007). Office open XML overview. Retrieved on November 1, 2007, from http://www.ecma-international.org/news/TC45_current_work/OpenXML%20White%20Paper.pdf

Fanderi, H., Fischer, K., & Kamper, J. (1992). The open document architecture: From standardization to the market. *IBM Systems Journal, 31*(4), 728-754.

Gillies, J., & Cailliau, R. (2000). *How the web was born.* Oxford, UK: Oxford University Press.

Groklaw. (2007). Expert testimony of Ronald Alepin in Comes v. Microsoft - Embrace, Extend, Extinguish—Updated. Retrieved on October 22, 2007, from http://www.groklaw.net/article.php?story=20070108020408557

Hyde, R. (2003). *Art of assembly language.* San Francisco, CA: No Starch Press.

IEEE. (1990). *IEEE standard computer dictionary.* New York: IEEE.

Kahin, B. (1995). The Internet and the national information infrastructure. In B. Kahin & J. Keller (Eds.), *Public access to the Internet* (pp. 3-23). Cambridge, MA: The MIT Press.

Krechmer, K. (2006). The meaning of open standards. *The International Journal of IT Standards and Standardization Research, 4*(1), 43-61.

Livingston, B. (2000). Is Microsoft's change in Kerberos security a form of 'embrace, extend, extinguish'?. Retrieved on September 17, 2007, from http://www.infoworld.com/articles/op/xml/00/05/15/000515oplivingston.html

Maxwell, E. (2006). Open standards, open source, and open innovation: Harnessing the benefits of openness. *Innovations: Technology, Governance, Globalization, 1*(3), 119.

May, C. (2006). Escaping the TRIPs' trap: The political economy of free and open source software in Africa. *Political Studies, 54*(1), 123-146.

Office of Government Commerce. (2004). *Open source software:Use within UK government.*

Organization for the Advancement of Structured Information Standards. (2007). Open by design: The advantages of the opendocument format (ODF). Retrieved on September 12, 2007, from http://www.oasis-open.org/committees/download.php/21450/oasis_odf_advantages_10dec2006.pdf

Rivals set their sights on Microsoft Office: Can they topple the giant? (2007). *Knowledge@Wharton*. Retrieved on October 3, 2007, from http://knowledge.wharton.upenn.edu/article.cfm?articleid=1795

Salminen, A. (2005). *Building digital government by XML*. Paper presented at the Hawaii International Conference on System Sciences, Hawaii.

Shah, R. C., & Kesan, J. (2008). *Evaluating the interoperability of software implementations for open standards: ODF and OOXML as examples.* Paper presented at the Telecommunications Policy Research Conference.

Shah, R. C., Kennis, A., & Kesan, J. P. (2009). Lessons for government adoption of open standards: A case study of Massachusetts policy. *Journal of Information Technology & Politics, 5*(4), 387-398.

Tassey, G. (2005). Underinvestment in public good technologies. *Journal of Technology Transfer, 30*, 90-94.

U.S. Department of Justice. (1999). Microsoft engaged in a predatory campaign to crush the browser threat to its operating system monopoly. Retrieved on September 5, 2007, from http://www.usdoj.gov/atr/cases/f2600/v-a.pdf

Veal, D. C. (2001). Techniques of document management: A review of text retrieval and related technologies. *Journal of Documentation, 57*(2), 192-217.

West, J. (2004, May 13). *What are open standards? Implications for adoption, competition, and policy.* Paper presented at the Standards and Public Policy, Federal Reserve Bank of Chicago, Chicago, IL.

West, J. (2007). The economic realities of open standards: Black, white, and many shades of gray. In S. Greenstein & V. Stango (Eds.), *Standards and Public Policy* (pp. 87-122). Cambridge: Cambridge University Press.

KEY TERMS

Extensible Markup Language (XML): A general-purpose specification for creating custom markup languages. It is extensible because it allows users to define their own elements.

Document Formats: Specifications for storing information, a commonly used document formats include Microsoft's DOC format or Adobe's PDF format.

Interoperability: In the context of information technology, interoperability is the ability of two or more systems or components to exchange information and to use the information that has been exchanged.

Open Standards (Typical): Open standards are generally defined based on three criteria. First, the standard is publicly available to everyone at a minimal cost. Second, no entity controls the standard or the standard is licensed on "reasonable and nondiscriminatory terms." Third, the development process for creating the standard involves public participation.

Running Code: Having multiple independent interoperable implementations of a standard. The term originates within the standards body known as the Internet Engineering Task Force.

Standards: In the context of information technology, standards are guidelines for allowing disparate devices and applications to communicate and work together.

Chapter X
Interoperability and Constituents of Interoperable Systems in Public Sector

Dibakar Ray
National Informatics Centre, India

Umesh Gulla
GGS Indraprastha University, India

M. P. Gupta
Indian Institute of Technology, India

Shefali S. Dash
National Informatics Centre, India

ABSTRACT

This chapter, based on analysis of literature, introduces a definition and a layered architecture for government information systems. It argues that the interoperability of information systems is essential in providing integrated government services, but unfortunately there is no consensus on what interoperability is and what constitutes interoperable information systems. By analysing available academic literature and government reports on interoperability, the authors have attempted to address this problem. Based on the study, a comprehensive definition of interoperability is presented here. Further, the authors have identified four constituents of interoperable system and finally, a layered architecture for interoperability of government information systems has been presented. The authors believe that an unambiguous definition and clear idea about constituent of interoperability would remove much confusion in conceptualisation, design, and development of interoperable systems in government.

INTRODUCTION

E-government all over the world are slowly graduating from Cataloguing and Information stage to integrated One-stop service provisioning. One-stop Government refers to the integration of public services from a citizen or customer of public services point of view. Ideally, online one-stop government requires that all public authorities are interconnected and that the citizen is able to access public services from a single point even if these services are actually provided by different departments or authorities. Furthermore, the citizen should able to access these services in terms of life-events and without knowledge of the functional fragmentation of the public sector (Tambouris, 2001).

But in reality we are far from the ideal situation, one reason for this is difficulty in attaining interoperability among government information systems (Landsbergen & Wolken, 2001). The difficulty in attaining interoperability is not simply technical; it includes organizational, economic, political and cultural issues. Although, most of the articles on e-government interoperability deal mainly with technical aspects, there is growing realization that interoperability is much more complex than getting the 'bits and bytes to flow properly' between two systems (Landsbergen & Wolken, 2001). At the same time Pardo & Scholl (2002) in their study indicates interdependence of social, behavioural and technical spects in success of information systems in public sector. Such a holistic view, in our opinion should be reflected in the definition of interoperability. But unfortunately there is no consensus on the definition of interoperability. Most of the definitions are mainly technology oriented with no or very little mention of the other dimensions of interoperability. In this chapter, a literature based study is done to find out various definitions available in literature. Based on the analysis of these definitions, a comprehensive definition of interoperability for government domain is presented. The detailed study of the literature is continued further to identify various facets of interoperability. At the end a layered architecture consisting of various domains of interoperability are presented.

BACKGROUND

Dawes (2002) defines e-government as "E-government is the use of information technology to support government operations, engage citizens, and provide government servics". Based on academic research and practical experience, Dawes (2002) further says that transformation from traditional program based service to integrated service would be one of the main requirements in future. According to her, future vision of e-government is that of integrated information and services.

Transformation from the very basic stage of e-government to the integrated service provisioning is not simple, but it evolves through stages, with progressively added degree of technological and organizational sophistication at each stage (Gil-Garcia & Martinez-Moyano, 2007). Although the stages of evolution are neither strictly mutually exclusive or progressive, nor there is consensus on stages and their numbers. Gil-Garcia & Martinez-Moyano (2007) give an exhaustive list of stages of e-government evolution. They are—Initial presence, Extended presence, Interactive presence, Transactional presence, Vertical integration, Horizontal integration and Totally integrated presence.

Despite difference about nomenclature of the final stage, there is agreement on the purpose of the stage, i.e. delivery of integrated service and information (Irani, AlSebie & Elliman 2006). This stage refers to a situation, where government services are integrated both vertically across different levels of government and horizontally cutting across different services and functions of government. A transformation of government so far unseen takes place at this stage, where services are arranged according to the requirements of the citizen and not according to the functional structure of government. Governments at this stage undertake major institutional and administrative reforms to fully exploit the potential of information technologies(Gil-Garcia & Martinez-Moyano, 2007).

Such an integrated environment, which Wimmer (2001) refers as " Online One-stop Government," is a single point of access to electronic services and information offered by different government authorities. Kubicek & Hagen (2000) defines a similar term 'One Stop government' as '..all of a customer business can be completed in a single contact, be it in face to face or via phone, fax, Internet or other means'. But to provide citizen access to joined up services, an online integrated view is a must, whether the citizen uses it directly or through a intermediary. So it seems 'Online One stop government' is a more appropriate terminology to express the paradigm.

Another term quite popular to represent such integrated view is 'joined-up government' (Pappa & Makropoulos, 2004). The concept is not a new one, it attempts to resolve problem faced by all big imperial bureaucracies, whether Roman, Ottoman or Chinese. Joined-up government is a convenient label for studying an old problem faced by administrations, that is coordination (Bogdanor, 2005). The 'Joined-up government approach attempts to align distinct government entities to the pursuit of the objective of the government of the day. This objective of joined-up government is generally achieved by using pooled budgets, joint teams and shared leaderships (Bekkers & Homburg, 2005). The term came to prominence again in 1999 when Tony Blair Government presented the whitepaper "Modernising Government " in order to reform the government. Joined-up government which provides an alternative approach to administrative reform (Bogdanor, 2005), is no doubt would provide a solid base for providing joined up government services and information. In rest of the chapter we would be using 'Online One stop government' to represent a single point of access to electronic services and information from government, as we believe that this term succinctly express the phenomenon.

Realising online one-stop government requires interoperability at technical level of the information and communications systems, as well as close cooperation and alignment of goals, objectives, aspiration and business processes etc. of the participating entities (Klischewski, 2004).

WHAT IS INTEROPERABILITY

There are numerous definitions of Interoperability available in academic literatures, standards and government documents. These definitions vary widely in meaning and content. Some of them covers only the technical part, some are quite comprehensive and cover both technical as well as non technical aspects. Ford et al. (2007) have identified about thirty four distinct definitions of interoperability. As interoperability is a major deciding factor in modern warfare, most of the definitions are related to armed forces and most of them concerned about technical interoperability. Another major source for definition of interoperability is different standard organisatons. Table 1 is a extended and modified list of interoperability definitions published by Ray, Gulla & Dash (2007). Definitions are classified into four domains, viz. Technical, Data, Organisational and Environmental. Technical domain deals with data communication between systems, Data domain deals with syntax and semantics, Organizational domain covers aspects like, culture, business process and personnel, Environmental domain covers aspects like policy, legality etc.

From Table 1, it is clear that interoperability at technical level is the ability of information systems to share and use information. Meaningful use of information requires that syntax and semantics of the information received should be known to the system. Exchange of information requires cooperation, coordination and support of

Table 1. Various definitions of interoperability

Definition	Source	Origin of the definition & the domains covered
The term interoperability refers to a bottom-up integration of existing systems and applications that were not designed to be integrated when they were built.	University Consortium for Geographic Information Science, (1996)	Geographical Information Systems, Academic, Technical.
"to be **interoperable**, one should actively be engaged in the ongoing process of ensuring that the systems, procedures and culture of an organisation are managed in such a way as to maximise opportunities for exchange and re-use of information, whether internally or externally."	Miller, (2000)	Academic, Technical, Organisational, Data.
...interoperability is more than getting bits and bytes to flow properly–fundamentally, the goal of interoperability is the more difficult problem of getting people and organizations to share information in an information technology environment.	Landsbergen & Wolken (2001)	Academic, e-Government, Technical, Organisational.
Interoperability is characterised by network protocols, interfaces between operating systems, the platform independence of applications and the communicability of records and fields. It is the technical support arrangements connecting organisations and often requires formally codified standards.	Kinder (2003)	Academic, Technical.
Interoperability means the ability of information and communication technology (ICT) systems and of the business processes they support to exchange data and to enable the sharing of information and knowledge.	IDABC, (2004)	Government,Technical, Organisational, Data.
a. the ability of two or more systems or elements to exchange information and to use the information that has been exchanged. b. the capability for units of equipment to work together to do useful functions. c. the capability, promoted but not guaranteed by joint conformance with a given set of standards, that enables heterogeneous equipment, generally built by various vendors, to work together in a network environment. d. the ability of two or more systems or components to exchange information in a heterogeneous network and use that information.	IEEE quoted by Morris (2004)	Standard Body, Technical, Data.
The ability of systems, units, or forces to provide services to and accept services from other systems, units, or forces and to use the services so exchanged to enable them to operate effectively together [Chairman of the Joint Chiefs of Staff, Instruction 6212.01A: "Compatibility, Interoperability, and Integration of Command, Control, Communications, Computers, and Intelligence Systems." June 1995, Joint Chiefs of Staff. "Department of Defense Dictionary of Military and Associated Terms, as amended through December 7, 1998" (Joint Publication 1-02)]. The condition achieved among communications-electronics systems or items of communications-electronics equipment when information or services can be exchanged directly and satisfactorily between them and/or their users. The degree interoperability should be defined when referring to specific cases [Joint Chiefs of Staff. "Department of Defense Dictionary of Military and Associated Terms, as amended through December 7, 1998" (Joint Publication 1-02).].	Kausnic & Anderson, (2004) p.2	Defense, Technical.
Interoperability is the ability of a system or process to use information and/or functionality of another system or process by adhering to common standards.	European Public Administration Network, (2004).	Government, Technical, Data, Organisational.
Interoperability describes the ability to work together to deliver services in a seamless, uniform and efficient manner across multiple organisations and information technology systems.	Australian Government Information Management Office, (2005a)	Government, Technical, Data, Organisational.
...interoperability is the way in which reliable data is provided and communicated in a secure, accurate and efficient way. It has to surmount barriers of national policies, culture, language, and systems of medical knowledge representation and use of ICTs.	Telemedicine Alliance, (2005)	Health,Technical, Data, Organisational, Environmental.

continued on following page

Table 1. continued

Definition	Source	Origin of the definition & the domains covered
..interoperability is a state which exists between two application entities when, with regard to a specific task, one application entity can accept data from the other and perform that task in an appropriate and satisfactory manner without the need for extra operator intervention.	CEN/ISSS eHealth Standardization Focus Group, (2005)	Health, Technical, Data.
Interoperability is operationally connecting constituencies, to provide value.	Malotaux,, van der Harst, Achtsivassilis, Hahndiek, (2007).	Government, Technical, Organisational, Data.
The ability of government organisations to share information and integrate information and businesses by use of common standards.	NZ e-GIF, (2007)	Government, Technical, Data.
Interoperability, simply put, is the ability of people, organizations and systems to interact and interconnect to efficiently and effectively exchange and use information. In today's increasingly heterogeneous information technology (IT) marketplace, technical interoperability is an important feature for IT products and services. The ability to achieve meaningful technical interoperability, however, largely depends upon the health and stability of the broader interoperability ecosystem. Thus, technical interoperability must be pursued alongside the often more complex and challenging goals of organizational, legal and public policy, and semantic interoperability. So too, a successful implementation may need to address political, economic, or cultural barriers to interoperability.	Baird (2007)	Academic,Technical, Organisational, Symantic, Environmental.
The ability of distinct systems to communicate and share semantically compatible information, perform compatible transactions, and interact in ways that support compatible business processes to enable their users to perform desired tasks. Although our definition of interoperability was derived from a technical perspective, it applies to all aspects of eGovernment, if system is interpreted broadly… this broad definition implies that an Interoperability Framework is far more than just a list of recommended standards.	Rothenberg,. Botterman & Oranje-Nassau (2008)	Academic, Technical, Organisational.

the participating agencies. Success of technical interoperability thus depends on broader interoperability ecosystems consisting of organizational, data and environmental factors (Baird, 2007). In case of government information systems environmental factors include public policies, legal and constitutional issues.

The problem of ambiguity in definitions is further complicated by interchangeable use of the terms integration, interoperation and interoperability. In order to clear the confusion, some researchers have made attempt to differentiate these concepts (Klischewski 2004; Scholl & Klischewski, 2007; Janssen. & Scholl, 2007; CEN/ISSS, 2005; Chen. & Vernadat, 2003). According to these authors integration is a broader concept related to cooperation and coordination among the organizational entities to form a close relationship, temporary or permanent, for the purpose of providing joined up services or for sharing information.

In our opinion, it is quite confusing to use multiple terms to define a phenomenon where different government departments providing a particular service are interconnected and the customer (citizen, private enterprise or other public administration) is able to access these services from a single point despite the fact that delivery of these services require cooperation of different government departments. In that regard we think the approach of Malotaux, et al. (2007) and Baird (2007) is a better one. They have used the most widely used term 'Interoperability' to cover both technical and non technical aspects. To express specifically the technical aspects of interoperability the term 'technical interoperability' is used.

In this chapter we have extended the definition given by Baird (2007). We define Interoperability as, *"the ability of people, organizations, business process and information and communications systems to interact, interconnect and work together to deliver services and information in a seamless, uniform and efficient manner across multiple organisations and systems. Technical interoperability i.e. interconnection, data integration, workflow management, security, document archiving, etc. must be pursued alongside the often more complex and challenging goals of organizational and data interoperability. A successful implementation may need to address also the environmental factors like constitutional, legal political and economic barriers to interoperability."*

WHAT CONSTITUTES INTEROPERABLE E-GOVERNMENT SYSTEM

Interoperability is multidimensional, and while defining interoperability we have touched broadly upon the important dimensions of an interoperable system. Here we would try to find out from the literature more about these dimensions and their constituents. For this study, we categorised literature pertaining to e-government into three groups: National/Regional Interoperability Frameworks, Study on barriers to e-government interoperability and Academic literature on interoperability. The collection of literature is then analysed to find out various facets of interoperability discussed there. These facets are then categorized under four broad groups Technical, Organisational, Data and Environmental.

National/Regional Interoperability Frameworks

In order to address the problem of interoperability a number of governments have come out with a set of principles, standards, best practices and methodologies for government information systems in the form of National/Regional Interoperability Frameworks. Most of these frameworks deal mainly with technical aspects of interoperability, although there are notable exceptions:

- **Australian Interoperability Framework[1]:** recognises that interoperability is about addressing mutiple domains and name them as Business Process, Information and Technical domain.

  Business Process domain deals with legal, commercial, business and political organisational issues those facilitates interaction between government agencies.

  Information domain deals with information and process elements that convey business meaning. Elements include in this domain are reference taxonomies and processes, code lists, data dictionaries and industry specific libraries.

  Technical domain comprises technology standards used to deliver content across the communication and IT infrastructure.
- **European Interoperability Framework[2]:** IDABC (IDABC stands for Interoperable Delivery of European eGovernment Services to public Administrations, Business and Citizens) published the final version 1.0 of its European Interoperability Framework (IDABC EIF) in November 2004. The framework was published to support the pan-European delivery of electronic government services. The framework defines three domains of interoperability: organisational, semantic and technical.

  Organisational interoperability deals with defining business goals, modelling business processes and bringing about the collaboration of administrations that wish to exchange information and may have different internal structures and processes.

  Semantic interoperability is concerned with ensuring that the precise meaning of exchanged information is understandable by any other application that was not initially developed for this purpose.

Technical Interoperability covers the technical issues of linking computer systems and services.

In the same line **Estonian**[3] Interoperability framework also discusses about organization, semantic and technical interoperability.

- **Danish Interoperability Framework**[4]**:** (National IT Architecture Committee, 2006) provides three overall categories of standards: technical standards, data standards and process standards to be followed by government departments.
  - *Process Standards:* concerned with how and where information is sent and processed—and how it is handled.
  - *Technical Standards:* comprises of technical aspects like data integration, interconnectivity, user interfaces, etc.
  - *Data Standards:* concerned with unambiguous definition of the terms exchanged between IT systems and their components.
- **New Zealand E-Government Interoperability Framework**[5]**:** New Zealand Interoperability Framework categorised standards using a "layer model". Constituent of the layers are:
  - *Network*
  - *Data Integration*
  - *Business Services*
  - *Access and Presentation*

  The framework also contains standards related to security, web services, best practice, e-Government services, which according to the framework is applicable to all elements of the layer.
- **Interoperability Framework–Hong Kong**[6]**:** recognizes that in order to be interoperable, two information systems needs to be based on mutually agreed on specification covering both business and the technical aspects.

  Business aspects covers interaction modalities between the entities, legal consequence of such interaction, information that are exchanged in such interactions and semantic aspects of the information exchanged. Technical aspects deals with application integration, interaction, security etc.

  The framework provides:
  - A set of technical standards and data standards that help define the interface across different systems;
  - Guidelines for project teams to work out some of the business-oriented specifications;
  - Standards documents that define infrastructure architecture, conventions and procedures.
- **Interoperability Framework–Saudi Arabia**[7]**:** (Saudi e-Government Program 2005) The framework provides specifications and policies, to enable cross-governmental integration and facilitate G2G transactions and data sharing. The framework has three components: Data Standards, Metadata Standards and Technical Standards.

  Data Standards consists of catalogue of data standards and data schemas. Data Standards define data on business and logical level and also defines how data is exchanged between systems.

  Metadata Standards consists of attributes to be used to tag electronic documents and also consists of a dictionary of these attributes.

  Technical Standards provides technical standards and policies to ensure interoperability at a technical level
- **Interoperability Framework–UK**[8]**:** In the United Kingdom the eGovernment Interoperability Framework (e-GIF) was issued in 2000, and updated to version 6.1 in March 2005. The e-GIF defines the minimum set

of technical policies and specifications for any cross-agency collaboration and for e-government service delivery. These cover interconnectivity, data integration, content management metadata and services access.

- **Interoperability Framework for E-Governance–India:** National Informatics Centre (NIC) has initiated the development of an Interoperability Framework for E-Governance (National Informatics Centre, 2004), which comprises of policies and technical standards to facilitate interaction between isolated e-governance applications.
  The IFEG has the following components:
  - *Technical Standards and Policies:* This component defines technical policies and specifications governing electronic information flow across the government. They cover interconnectivity, data integration, government electronic services access and delivery mechanisms and content creation and management.
  - *Government Data Standard:* The IFEG intends to adopt XML and the development of XML schemas as the basis of the government interoperability and integration strategy. Inherent to the development of XML schemas is a predetermined and agreed upon set of data standards. These data standards are to be used in the schemas and other interchange processes. These data standards are also to be used for data storage.
  - *IFEG Meta Data Standard:* Metadata would be used for easier management and discovery of information resources possessed by government agencies. IFEG Metadata standard would define the elements, refinements and encoding schemas for the resources.
  - *XML Schema:* IFEG envisages that a library of XML schemas would be developed for inter-organizational interchange of data.

Malotaux, et al. (2007) while recommending for second version of European Interoperability Framework (EIF), puts forward an interoperability reference model. The reference model has two layers as compared to the three layers of EIF v1.0. The layers are (1) Real world system and (2) Information system. The Real world system layer is mapped to Organizational and Semantic Layer of EIF v1.0. The Information system layer is equivalent to Technical layer of EIF v1.0. The Real world system consists of three sub layers (1) Organization, (2) Process and (3) Information. The Information system has three constituent (1) Data presentation (syntax), (2) Application (interaction) and (3) Hardware (transport).

Kubicek & Cimander (2007) after studying selected Interoperability frameworks classify four levels of Interoperability, viz. Technical Interoperability, Syntactical Interoperability, Semantic Interoperability and Organisational Interoperability

At this point, it is worth mentioning that although not very widespread, but some of the countries already have or in the process of adopting Enterprise Architecture (EA) as the basis of development of Information systems in government. Guijarro (2004, pg 38) defines enterprise architecture as ".. a comprehensive description of all key elements and relationship that make up an organization. It aims to align the business process and goals of an enterprise and applications and systems that build up the technical infrastructure'. Guijarro (2004) considers EA as the second stage of interoperability.

The fundamental purpose of EA is to harmonise individual organization's decision about ICT in order to achieve interoperability (Organisation for Economic Co-operation and Development, 2006). EA captures an organisation's core business processes and IT capabilities to achieve business standardisation and integration requirements of the organisation's operating model. On a holistic basis, EA allows Government organisations to uncover common business services and allow underlying systems and applications to interoperate to provide seamless delivery of e-services to its citizen and business. Additional benefits include common technology platforms, data exchange standards and application development standards.

USA is in the forefront of adopting Enterprise Architecture in the domain of government. In 2002, Office of the Management and Budget (OMB) of the Executive Office of the President of the United States, established Federal Enterprise Architecture (FEA) as 'a business based framework for cross agency, government-wide improvement.'

The FEA is a collection of reference models that develop a common taxonomy and ontology for describing IT resources. These include the Performance Reference Model, the Business Reference Model, the Service Component Reference Model, the Data Reference Model and the Technical Reference Model.

Some other countries, who reported to be working in this direction are Germany, Denmark, UK (Guijarro, 2007; Janssen & Hjort-Madsen, 2007). Australia have also initiated the process of developing and adopting Enterprise Architecture for government (Australian Government Information Management Office, 2005b). Guijarro (2007) in his study on Interoperability frameworks and EA in e-government across Europe and the United States suggests that FEA of US government shows the highest degree of maturity among the interoperability efforts and their chances of success in removing the organizational barrier for interoperability are high. At the end of the survey, Guijarro, suggests that government should approach interoperability issue in two phases. In the first phase government should provide technical standards and policies, in the form of Interoperability Frameworks to enable seamless flow of information between government departments in the delivery of e-services. In the next phase government should attempt to acquire organizational interoperability by, aligning administrative procedures with technical systems by means of Enterprise Architecture.

Analysis of the Interoperability Frameworks have shown that, although these documents predominantly technical in nature, they do mention about non technical aspects as well. The dimensions covered in the interoperability framework, can be categorised as follows—Organizational, Business Process, Information, Data, Semantic and Technical. Information, Semantic and Data domain deal basically with standardization of the meaning of the information exchanged among Information Systems running at various government departments. Organisational domain deals with business goals, business processes, collaboration among administrations those wish to interoperate. Australian Interoperability Framework defines Business Process as a separate domain, and is related to identifying commonality in business process so that business processes can be aligned and ultimately departments can work together. Business Process generally is treated as a sub domain with in organizational interoperability (United Nations Development Programme, 2007, pp 9). Technical interoperability domain deals technical aspects of interoperability and covers issues like Network, Systems, Applications etc. Accordingly we clubbed the findings into three major dimensions:

1. **Organisational:** business process, collaboration of administrations.
2. **Data:** semantic, semantics.
3. **Technical:** application, hardware, message format, network

Study on Barriers to E-Government Interoperability

Articles under this category covers studies on barrier to enterprise wise integration, barriers to collaboration and information sharing in government and studies on barriers to e-Government in general.

Gil-Garcia & Pardo (2005) group challenges faced by any e-government initiatives into five categories. They are (1) Information and data, (2) Information Technology, (3) Organizational & Managerial, (4) Legal & Regulatory and (5) Institutional & Environmental. Similarly Ebrahim & Irani (2005) have summaried barriers experienced by public sector organizations while implementing of e-government projects. They classified barriers into five dimensions: (1) IT Infrastructure, (2) Security and Privacy, (3) IT Skills, (4) Organisational and (5) Operational costs.

An interoperability initiative, like any other e-government system faces same challenges, but as the interoperability initiatives requires close cooperation among participating agencies and transmission of data from one system to another, complexities at each domain increases many fold.

Landsbergen & Woken (2001) in their article concludes that government has not yet achieved the desired result of use of Information Technology in government, because lack of interoperability of the information systems. They classify barriers to interoperability into four categories: (1) Political, (2) Organisational, (3) Economic and (4) Technical.

Lam (2005b) in his research on barriers to e-government integration identifies four basic categories of barriers, namely (1) Strategy, (2) Technology, (3) Policy and (4) Organisation.

Snijkers, (2006) distinguishes three dimensions in an intergovernmental e-government project. These dimensions are (1) Power dimension: refers to mutual dependencies between the participating agencies, (2) Strategic dimension: refers to convergence or divergence of strategic goals between the participating agencies, (3) Institutional dimension: refers to the degree in which conflicts are avoided and trust has been developed.

Zhang, Dawes & Sarkis (2005) while studying dynamics of knowledge sharing among government organizations, found a number of organizational factors and technological factors those have substantial influence on the knowledge sharing process.

Gil-Garcia, Chengular-Smith & Duchessi (2007) in their study on impediments and benefits of e-government information sharing projects, group impediments in to four categories. They are (1) Technological, (2) Organisational, (3) Political and (4) Legal.

While studying enterprise application integration (EAI) in health care organizations, Khoumbati, Themistocleous & Irani (2006) classify barriers to adoption of EAI under five categories. They are (1) Operational, (2) Managerial, (3) Strategic, (4) IT Infrastructure and (5) Organizational.

Janssen & Cresswell (2005) recognise that there are substantial barrier to implement interoperable systems to support information exchange and cross-agency business processes. They identify (1) Public sector structure, (2) Difficulty in getting stakeholders commitment, (3) Lack of Business and Technology knowledge at senior management level.

Lam (2005a) while investigating success factors in enterprise application integration, organised seventeen key success factors into four main categories, namely (1) Business, (2) Organisation, (3) Technology and (4) Project.

Other than the usual Organizational and Technical dimensions, literatures from this category describes about Legal, Regulatory, Institutional, IT Skills, Cost, Political, Economical, Managerial and Public Policy related factors. Most of these studies here either do not mention data/information as a separate barrier or club them with technological barriers.

Legal, Political, Regulatory, Economical factors constitute the environment within which information systems operate and these factors influence interoperability efforts and its outcome. We have clubbed these factors under Environmental dimension.

Managerial, IT Skills, Strategic issues are largely related to organization and hence are considered as factors of Organisational domain.

Academic Literature on Interoperability

Pardo, Cresswell, Dawes & Burke (2004) propose a sociotechnical framework to represent the complex causality among the factors that influence the ability of organizations to integrate information. They propose a holistic nested model having four components namely (1)Technology solutions, (2) Organisational / Business process, (3)Inter-organisational setting and (4) Policy and Social Environment. The Technology solution component resides at the center of the model, which depends on business practices of the organizations involved. Business process in tern is influenced by the inter-organisational setting, which again depends on the policy and social environment. Backhouse (2005) proposes a modified version of Technical, Formal and Informal (TFI) model for a holistic understanding of the interoperability. The model is based on research conducted at Information System Department of London School of Economics and by Stamper, et al. (2000). The basic model has three embedded layers, namely Informal (Knowledge, Experience, Socio cultural background), Formal (Bureaucracy, structure of the organization) and Technical (ICT systems), which indicates the interrelationship among the layers. The modified model incorporates a semantic layer across three layers. Janssen, M & Scholl H.J. (2007) describes a four layer architecture for interoperability. The top most layer of the architecture is (1) Pragmatic Level, which is made of Organizational and Business Process layers. Other layers of the architecture are, (2) Semantic Level, (3) Syntax level and (4) Technical level.

Baird (2007) while discussing government role in developing Interoperability Ecosystem, names five facets of the ecosystem. They are, (1) Technical Interoperability, Organizational Interoperability, (3) Legal and Public Policy Interoperability, (4) Semantic Interoperability and (5) Cultural, Political and Economic environment.

Miller (2000) classify interoperability into six categories Technical Interoperability, Semantic Interoperability, Political/Human Interoperability, Inter-community Interoperability, Legal Interoperability and International Interoperability.

Peristeras & Tarabanis (2006) proposes a interoperability framework based on some well-defined concepts from linguistics. The framework has four interoperability types, organized in three demarcated areas. The interoperability types are (1) Connection, (2) Communication, (3) Consolidation and (4) Collaboration. Connection layer corresponds to channels for exchanging signals. Communication and Consolidation layers correspond to informational aspects of interoperability, i.e. format, syntax and semantics of data. Collaboration layer corresponds to functions, actions to be performed on the data, i.e. Process.

Similar to other two categories of literature, here we find mention of interoperability aspects like technical, organizational, semantic and syntax. In this category of literature two works mention about importance of the environmental aspects like Legal, Public Policy, Political, Social and Cultural issues (Pardo etal, 2004; Baird, 2007). We found three works in this category that describe layered model of interoperability (Padro etl 2004,;Stamper, et al., 200; Janssen & Scholl, 2007) having organizational, data and technical layers.

ANALYSIS OF THE FINDINGS

Layered Architecture

Based on the analysis of literature we propose a nested layered model for interoperable Information Systems. The study shows that the dimensions discussed in the literature can broadly be of three types viz. Orgnisationl, Data and Technological. Literature also suggest about some controlling and enabling factors those influence and limit degree of interoperability. These factors are clubbed under the dimension Environmental factors. The ability to achieve technical interoperability depends on organizational and data interoperability. Environmental dimension has an overall effect on the entire underlying interoperability dimensions. Environmental dimension specially constitutional and legal factors have profound effect on the scope and degree of interoperability among government Information Systems (Jaeger, 2002). Proposed model is shown in Figure 1.

Support of these three core layers as important constituent of interoperability is available in the Interoperability Frameworks. European Interoperability Framework (IDABC, 2004) has all the three elements in their framework. Australian Interoperability Framework has also suggested almost the similar three core layers. Support of these core layers are also available in literatures (Pardo etal.,2004; Baird, 2007). Literatures on interoperability barriers also mention same factors as important barriers to interoperability (Gil-Garcia & Pardo, 2005). The support of the environmental factors are available in the works of Pardo et al.,2004; Baird, 2007; Gil-Garcia, Chengular-Smith & Duchessi, 2007; Landsbergen & Woken, 2001; Lam, 2005b; Gil-Garcia & Pardo, 2005.

Figure 1. Layers of interoperable information systems

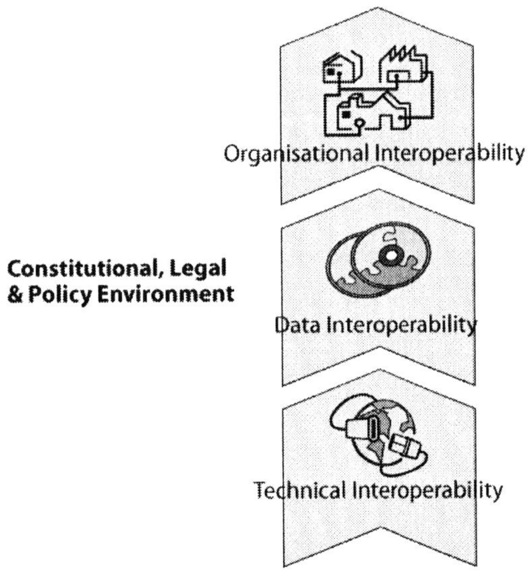

In the next few paragraphs we would describe in details these layers and the sub factors in each layer.

Factors Related to Organisational Interoperability

According to the most of the National /Regional Interoperability Frameworks, organizational dimensions mainly concerned with coordination and alignment of organizational goals, priorities, process and collaboration of administration. Organizational issues rise out of explicit and implicit difference among the participating agencies (Gil-Garcia, Chengalur-Smith & Duchessi, 2007). These issues include misaligned organizational goals, trust, overly ambitious goals, organizational culture, budgeting mechanism, problem of fixing responsibility, lack of guidelines and models to follow, leadership etc. Some of the issues are discussed here:

Alignment of Organisation goals and objectives: Achieving alignment of goals with organizations with diverse mission, objectives, culture and priorities is very difficult task (Zhang, Dawes & Sarkis, 2005). Different organizational priorities is found to be one of the major barriers of interoperation (Gil-Garcia, Chengalur-Smith & Duchessi; Lam, 2005b). Scholl & Klischewski (2007), hypothesised that interoperation between government entities is most likely to occur when missions of these entities align or converge. Scholl & Klischewski further propose that high frequency of interaction between government entities indicate higher relatedness of mission and objectives. Difficulty in aligning objectives increases many folds as the number and diversity of agencies involved in interoperation increases.

Goals of the project: Lee (2005b) and Zhang, Dawes & Sarkis(2005) have identified over ambitious goals of the interoperability project as a major barrier. Too ambitious projects with large number of participating agencies increase the complexity to a very high level. According to the authors very complex projects require higher level of process redesign and organizational restructuring and these factors make such a interoperable project more difficult to implement.

Trust: Mayer, Davis & Schoorman (1995) define trust as the willingness of a party to be vulnerable to the actions of another party based on the beliefs in the other party's ability, benevolence, and integrity. Trust has been found in literature to be an essential element of collaboration. Interoperation requires mutual respect for each others objectives and constraints. Lack of trust leads to reduced cooperation and sharing, which could be fatal for any collaborative effort. For example, say one government department uses details of citizen data collected by another department. If the first department does not have faith in the ability of the second department to collect data accurately, it would be hesitant to using that data. Personal trust builds up among individuals working together and interacting frequently to achieve a common goal. Personal trust is extendable to institutional level (Hu, Cui & Sherwood, 2006)

Funding: Generally in government funding is made agency wise. For an interagency project using such funding may create problem because one agency may make resources available for such a project, but the ultimate benefit of which may be manifested at a different place. Moreover as gestation period of such project is generally long, annual budgeting system may not be a suitable funding mechanism for interoperable project.

Leadership and management control: Importance of leadership in e-Government projects is well documented. Leadership issue becomes all the more important for an interoperable e-government project, because of the requirements of higher degree of collaboration, coordination and interoperation of diverse departments than a stand alone project. Lee (2005b) identifies two types of 'champions', one is the top level leaders, who can ensure sufficient commitment of funds and resources and another leadership is at operational level. Gil-Garcia et al. (2006) suggests that top management support would not be forthcoming when the project has conflicting goals, unrealistic time frame or due to question of turf. Management control, which is the process of testing, measuring and providing feedback with respect to a defined goal, is also an equally important issue for an inter organizational interoperability project (Hu, Cui & Sherwood 2006). A team based approach which facilitates consensus building and allow the participating agencies to negotiate the differences to reach consensus is probably a suitable one for an interoperability project over a top-down authoritative one.

Turf: Interoperability projects by integrating delivery of government services may threaten independent existence of some participating departments. Individual or agencies always try to protect their existence, programs, people and priorities (Gil-Garcia. et al., 2006). In most of the cases resistance to change come out of fear of losing control, resource and position on implementation of a project, which have potential to change organizational structure and current way of working. In an interoperability project, if individuals or organizations perceive that their turf, influence, position are under threat, they may not provide the required support to the interoperability effort.

Fixing responsibility: In government setup, responsibilities are well defined, but in an integrated environment fixing responsibility are very difficult, where operations depend on actions taken across department boundary.

Common Standards and Model: Lack of a common model, architecture or standards to follow is found to be a major stumbling block in implementation of an interoperable system (Gil-Garcia, et al., 2006; Zhang, Dawes & Sarkis, 2005). Its difficult for participating to develop an interoperable system without existence of a guideline or model to follow. Many governments now have come up with Interoperability Frameworks, which provides the technical standards and available best practices. At the same time an overarching view of what service each department provides, what are the commonalities among these services are required. To address this problem number of countries have come up with Enterprise Architecture for government.

Manpower with required knowledge: Organizational structure of government is based on hierarchical Weberian Model, which emphasises specialization, departmentalization and routinisation of the production process (Ho, 2002). As a result departments which involved in the project do not have much understanding about the process and functioning of other departments and this lack of understanding work as impediments on the overall workflow of an integrated system (Gil-Garcia et al, 2006). At another level, staff members specialise in their specific work, which result in a situation, where within an organization, program staff lack knowledge about technology and technical staff lacks knowledge about the public services. Over and above that as technology changes too fast it becomes impossible to all concerns to keep up. Adequate training may change the situation as adequate training is important in any cases which involve organizational change.

Interoperability Readiness: E-government being a relatively new concept, many government agencies are still engaged in a learning process of what e-government is and how it can be implemented within their own agencies (Cresswell, 2005). Lam (2005) argues that many e-government agencies are ill prepared for undertaking development of integrated e-Government systems. Evidence for readiness can include specific policies and procedures to support collaboration. Collaboration readiness is reflected in the provision of resources to support collaboration, including budget, staff and technology. (Cresswell, 2005). So a department want to participate in an inter departmental integration project, must put the required policies in place, arrange for resources like funding, technical and managerial manpower and technological infrastructure, before venturing into the initiative.

Business Process: Business Process deals with common methods, processes and shared services for collaboration, including work flow, decision making and business transactions. Alignment of business process is essential in order to provide integrated service. But unfortunately, with a few exceptions, coverage of Business Process Interoperability in the literature is at the best sketchy. Malotaux, et al. (2007) in their report on recommendations for EIF v 2.0 points out these shortcomings in EIF v 1.0. They, in fact added a separate layer named 'Process' in their proposed reference model and propose that business processes must be aligned to achieve the overall interoperability. The authors further suggest that these processes may be standardize according to industry specific global practices. Australian government has come out with a separate Business Process Interoperability Framework (BPIF). The BPIF provides tools and mechanism to map business process within an agency or across multiple agencies and also to find out the commonalities in business processes and to understand the flow of information across these processes.

Factors Related to Data Interoperability

To be interoperable the systems must allow agencies to effectively exchange data, combine it with other information resources, and subsequently process it in a meaningful manner. This is not possible until meaning and syntax of data is known across agencies. (European Public Administration Network, 2004). Data layer deals with organizational data, their definition, format, interrelationships with other data elements, ownership, allowed values and metadata. In most of the literature this layer is named as either information, semantic or data domain. In some cases they are clubbed under technical domain.

Ownership of data in an interoperable environment, is an important policy decision, and would encourage information sharing across departments (Landsbergen & Wolken, 2001). For a piece of data a department of government can play role of a provider, custodian or user during the lifecycle of the data (Australian Government Information Management Office, 2005). Responsibility of the data provider is to ensure quality of the collected data which would enhance trust and confidence in the system. On the other hand responsibility of the user of data is to use single authoritative source.

Two factors are very important for data interoperability: its format and structure and its content and meaning. In case organisations involved in interoperability project are fixed and predetermined, interoperability at data level can be achieved by mapping from one format to another. Semantics or meaning of the data can also be hard coded for processing by applications running at agencies different from the one which generated the data. But as the number of agencies involved number of mapping utility increases unmanageable non-linear way. Moreover any change in the format requires change in all the mapping utilities. The situation get more complicated, when an organisation provides a service which can be used by any organization interested in using it. For example authentication of a social security number or permanent account number for taxation, the consumer of the service can be consumed by other government or private organisation. In such a scenario, stnadardisation of the syntax and semantics is a must.

Syntactical interoperability: Syntactic interoperability is concerned with ensuring that data from the exchanged messages are in compatible formats. Standardisation of format and content of data provide a new e-government project with a model to follow and facilitates any future interoperability effort. Moreover use of standard data model would be of great help in an emergency situation, when government requires to pull together all available information. This standardisation process should be developed in a collaborative environment and may start with finding out the common data elements used across departments for providing important government services. These data elements can be culled out of the existing data bases, paper forms, manuals and other resources used for providing services. Data models for important objects like citizen, business, address, land records should be developed for whole of government. Data for which standardisation is not available, or where standard data is not adequate, department can develop their own standard, following a common data standardisation policy with adequate metadata for reuse and for development of translator. Appropriate metadata should be developed for each data element, to facilitate easy usage and understanding of the data element. Data dictionaries, XML Schemas, metadata standards are the tools used to overcome syntactical interoperability.

Semantic problem arises because same concept may be defined by different terms in different information systems. Semantic interoperability is concerned with ensuring that the exchanged information has the same meaning for both the sender and the receiver of the message. This is achieved by unambiguously defining meaning of data and sharing the definition among the user of the information. Although there are a few example of UML, RDF, OWL based Semantic data model developed for government (Brusa, Caliusco & Chiotti, 2007) but achieving semantic interoperability is not easy and at present there is no example of large scale semantically interoperable e-government system (Janssen & Scholl, 2007).

Factors Related to Technical Interoperability

This layer deals with technical issues of linking computer systems and services (IDABC, 2004).

Advent of Internet has reduced the problem of interoperability to a great extent. Use RDBMS, web services and Open Standards have also reduced the level of incompatibility. Information about technical issues related to interoperability is widely available in literature and Interoperability Frameworks. As mentioned earlier lot of countries have come up with Technical Interoperability Frameworks (Guijarro,2007), which depicts set of policies, technical standards and guidelines to be followed by government departments to be interoperable. These frameworks generally list of standards for information presentation, network, discovery and naming, specifications for web services, security etc.

Environmental Factors

Each government department works within legal, constitutional and political environment. Information systems of government are also bound by those requirements. These factors have profound effect on the all the three core layers of the framework. For example, Federal System of USA and the constitutional provision on division of power may restrict total integration and interoperability between and among branches and levels of government (Jaeger, 2002; Scholl & Klischewski, 2007). Such constitutional constraint may also determine the type of integration, that is information vs. process integration (Klischewski, 2004), Legal validity of Digital Signature is a must for end to end integration of some service. Countries where digital signature is not legally valid, end to end integration may not be possible (Gil-Garcia, Pardo, 2005). Legislation on security and privacy and government policy on data ownership and usage instills confidence in the user and allow government departments direction about data sharing. Existence of statutory requirements may also initiate integration. For example, in India, the central legislation on road transport, the "Motor Vehicles Rules 1989" (Government of India, 1989), requires that each state would maintain a register of driving license issued (section 23) and motor vehicles registered in the state (Section 75). Moreover under this legislation each state is required to submit a copy of each register to central ministry. This requirement initiated a data integration project for creation of digital state and central register. Another environmental factor is political pressure, which in a democracy, is a reflection of popular demand for a service. For example, citizens online experience with private business increases expectation of similar integrated service from government. Finally such popular demands get reflected into political initiatives of integrated government services.

CONCLUSION

In this chapter a literature based study is done to find out definition and constituent of interoperable information systems within public sector. In the first part of the study analysis of the available definitions of interoperability is done. Based on the analysis a comprehensive definition of interoperability is proposed. The definition covers technical as well as non technical aspects of interoperability. In the second part, a study of the literature is done to find more about the constituents of interoperability in government. Identified facets of interoperability are grouped into four broader categories, viz. Organisational, Data, Technical and Environmental. Finally based on the study of interoperability constituents, an embedded layered architecture for interoperable information system for public sector is presented. The layered architecture has three core layer of Organisational Interoperability, Data Interoperability and Technical Interoperability. These layers are embedded into Legal, Constitutional and Policy Environment.

In our opinion a holistic approach in developing interoperable information systems has more chance of success. Proposed definition and the framework would provide the practitioners a broader perspective while handling interoperable e-government systems. This framework would also provide a handy checklist of issues to be taken care while conceiving, designing and implementing interoperable e-government systems.

REFERENCES

Australian Government Information Management Office. (2005a). Australian government technical interoperability framework, version 2. Retrieved on April 3, 2008. from http://www.agimo.gov.au/publications/2005/04/agtifv2

Australian Government Information Management Office. (2005b). Australian government architecture reference models, version 1.0, June 2007. Retrieved on March 14, 2008, from http://www.agimo.gov.au/__data/assets/pdf_file/0007/57517/AGA_Reference_Models_Version_1.0.pdf

Backhouse, J. (Ed.). (2005). Structured account of approaches on interoperability D4.1 v1.0. FIDIS. Project, December 2005. Retrieved on March 12, 2008, from http://www.fidis.net/fileadmin/fidis/deliverables/fidis-wp4-del4.2.set_of_requirements.pdf

Baird, S. A. (2007, December 10—13). Government role in developing an interoperability ecosystem. In *Proceedings of the 1st international Conference on Theory and Practice of Electronic Governance, ICEGOV '07,* Macao, China (Vol. 232, pp. 65-68). New York: *ACM.*

Bekkers, V., & Homburg, V. (2005). E-Government as an information ecology: Backgrounds and concepts. In V. Bekkers & V. Homburg (Eds.), *The information ecology of e-government: E-government as institutional and technological innovation in public administration* (pp. 1-20). Amsterdam: IOS Press.

Bogdanor, V. (2005). Introduction. In B. Vernon (Ed.), *Joined-up government* (pp. 1-18). Oxford, UK: University Press.

Brusa, G., Caliusco, M. L., & Chiotti, O. (2007). Enabling knowledge sharing within e-government back-office through ontological engineering. *Journal of Theoretical and Applied Electronic Commerce Research, 2*(1), 33-48.

CEN/ISSS. (2005). E-Health Standardization Focus Group. Current and future standardization issues in the e-health domain: Achieving interoperability. Retrieved on April 5, 2008, from http://www.i2-health.org/ehealth-iop/eHealth-StandardizationExecutive%20summaryFinalversion2005-02-21.pdf

Chen, D., & Vernadat, F. (2003). Enterprise interoperability: A standardisation view. In *Proceedings of the IFIP TC5/WG5.12 International Conference on Enterprise Integration and Modeling Technique* (pp. 273-282). B.V. Kluwer.

Cresswell, A. M., Pardo, T. A., Canestraro, D. S., Dawes S. S., & Juraga, D.(2005). *Sharing justice information: A capability assessment toolkit* (p. 116). Albany, NY: Centre for Technology in Government.

Dawes, S. (2002). *The future of e-government.* Albany, NY: Center for Technology in Government. Retrieved on March 10, 2008, from http://www.ctg.albany.edu/publications/reports/future_of_egov/future_of_egov.pdf

Government of India. (1989). Central motor vehicles rules, 1989. Retrieved on March 1, 2007, from http://www.morth.nic.in/index3.asp?sublink2id=280&langid=2

Ebrahim, Z., & Irani, Z. (2005). E-Government adoption : Architecture and barriers. *Business Process Management, 11*(15), 589-611.

E-Government Unit, Cabinet Office. (2005). E-Government interoperability framework, version 6.1, 18th March 2005, London, UK. Retrieved on April 10, 2008, from http://www.gov-talk.gov.uk/schemasstandards/egif_document.asp?docnum=949

European Public Administration Network (EPAN). (2004). Key principles of interoperability. Architecture, Ireland: European Union.

Ford, T. C., Colomb, J., Grahamr, S. R., & Jacques, D. R. (2007, June). A survey on interoperability measurement. In *Proceedings of 12th International Command and Control Research and Technology Symposium*, Newport, RI.

Gil-Garcia, J. R., & Pardo, T. A. (2005). E-Government success factors: Mapping practical tools to theoretical foundations. *Government Information Quarterly, 22*(2), 187-216.

Gil-Garcia, J. R., Canestraro, D., Costello, J., Baker, A., & Werthmuller, D. (2006). Fostering innovation in electronic government: Benefits and challenges of XML for web site management. Paper presented at the 67th ASPA National Conference, organized by the American Society for Public Administration, Denver, CO.

Gil-Garcia, J. R., & Martinez-Moyano, I. (2007). Understanding the evolution of e-government: The influence of the systems of rules on public sector dynamics. *Government Information Quarterly, 24*(2), 266-290.

Gil-Garcia, J. R., Chengular-Smith, I., & Duchessi, P. (2007). Collaborative e-government: Impediments and benefits of information-sharing projects in the public sector. *European Journal of Information Systems, 16*(2), 121-133.

Guijarro, L. (2004, August 30-September 3). Analysis of the interoperability frameworks in e-government initiatives. In R. Traunmüller (Ed.), *Electronic Government: Third International Conference, E-Gov 2004*, Zaragoza, Spain (Vol. 3183, pp. 36-39). New York: Springer-Verlag Berlin Heidelberg.

Guijarro, L. (2007). Interoperability frameworks and enterprise architectures in e-government initiatives in Europe and the United States. Government Information Quarterly, 24(1), 89-101.

Ho, A. T. H. (2002). Reinventing local governments and the e-government initiatives. *Public Administration Review, 62*(4), 434-444.

Hu, P. J., Cui, D., & Sherwood, A. C. (2006, January 4-7). Examining cross-agency collaborations in e-government initiatives. In *Proceedings of the 39th Annual Hawaii international Conference on System Sciences—Volume 4 (HICSS)*. Washington, DC: IEEE Computer Society.

IDABC. (2004). European interoperability framework for pan-European e-government services, version 1.0, Brussels. Retrieved on January 3, 2008, from http://europa.eu.int/idabc/en/document/3761

Irani, Z., Al-Sebie, M., & Elliman, T. (2006, January 4-7). Transaction stage of e-government systems: Identification of its location and importance. In *Proceedings of the 39th Annual Hawaii international Conference on System Sciences—Volume 4 (HICSS)*. Washington, DC: IEEE Computer Society.

Jaeger, P. T. (2002). Constitutional principles and e-government: An opinion about possible effects of federalism and the separation of powers on e-government policies. *Government Information Quarterly, 19*(4), 357-368.

Janssen, M., & Hjort-Madsen, K. (2007). Analyzing enterprise architecture in national governments: The cases of Denmark and The Netherlands. 40th Annual Hawaii International Conference (HICSS 2007) (p. 218a). System Sciences.

Janssen, M., & Scholl, H. J. (2007, December 10-13). Interoperability for electronic governance. In *Proceedings of the 1st International Conference on Theory and Practice of Electronic Governance*

(ICEGOV '07), Macao, China (Vol. 232, pp. 45-48). New York:ACM.

Kasunic, M., & Anderson, W. (2004 April). *Measuring systems interoperability: Challenges and opportunities* (Tech Rep. CMU/SEI-2004-TN-003). Carnegie Mellon University, Software Engineering Institute.

Khoumbati, K., Themistocleous, M., & Irani, Z. (2006). Investigating enterprise application integration benefits and barriers in health care organisations: An exploratory case study. *International Journal of Electronic Healthcare, 2*(1), 66-78.

Kinder, T. (2003). Mrs. Miller moves house: The interoperability of local public services in Europe. *Journal of European Social Policy, 13*(2), 141-157.

Klischewski, R. (2004). Information integration or process integration? How to achieve interoperability in administration. In R. Traunmüller (Ed.), *Proceedings of EGOV 2004,* (LNCS 3183, pp. 57-65).

Kubicek, H., & Hagen, M. (2000). One stop government in Europe: An overview. In M. Hagen & H Kubicek (Eds), *One stop government in Europe: Results from 11 national surveys* (pp. 1-36). University of Bremen, Bremen.

Kubicek, H., & Cimander, R. (2007, September 11). *Three dimensions of organisational interoperability.* Paper presented at eGovInterop'07 Conference, Paris, France.

Lam, W. (2005a). Investigating success factors in enterprise application integration: A case-driven analysis. *European Journal of Information Systems, 14*(2),175-187.

Lam, W. (2005b). Barriers to e-government integration. *The Journal of Enterprise Information Management, 18*(5), 511-530.

Landsbergen, Jr., D., & Wolken, Jr., G. (2001). Realizing the promise: Government information systems and the fourth generation of information technology. *Public Administration Review, 61*(2), 206-220.

Mayer, R. C., Davis, J. H., & Schoorman, F. D. (1995). An integrative model of organizational trust. *Academy of Management Review, 20*(3), 709-734.

Malotaux, M., van der Harst, G., Achtsivassilis, J., & Hahndiek, F. (2007). Preparation for update European interoperability framework 2.0--final report, 4.6.2007, for the interoperable delivery of European e-government services to public administrations, businesses and citizens. Retrieved on April 1, 2008, from http:// ec.europa.eu/idabc/servlets/Doc?id=29101

Miller, P. (2000). Interoperability: What it is and why should I want it. *Ariadne, 24.* Retrieved on April 5, 2008, from http: //www.ariadne.ac.uk/issue24/ interoperability/intro.html

Morris, E., Levine, L., Meyers, C., Plakosh, D., & Place, P. (2004). Systems of systems interoperability (CMU/SEI-2004-TR-004). Software Engineering Institute, Carnegie Mellon University.

National Informatics Centre. (2004). IFEG—interoperability framework for e-governance: Technical standards, version 2.0.

National IT Architecture Committee. (2006). The interoperability framework, version 1.2.14, Retrieved on March 14, 2008, from http://standarder.oio.dk/English/

Organisation for Economic Co-operation and Development (OECD). (2006). OECD e-government studies: Denmark. OECD.

Pappa, D., & Makropoulos, C. (2004). Designing a brokerage platform for the delivery of e-government services to the public. In M. Wimmer (Ed.), *Knowledge Management in Electronic Govern-*

ment: 5th IFIP International Working Conference (KMGov 2004).

Pardo, T., & Scholl, H. (2002, January 7-10). Walking atop the cliffs-avoiding failure and reducing risk in large-scale e-government projects. In *Proceedings of the 35th Annual Hawaii international Conference on System Sciences (Hicss'02)* (Vol. 5). Washington, DC: IEEE Computer Society.

Pardo, T. A., Cresswell, A. M., Dawes, S. S., & Burke, G. B. (2004). Modeling the social & technical process of interorganizational information integration. In Proceedings of the 37th Annual Hawaii International Conference on System Sciences (p. 8). IEEE.

Peristeras, V., & Tarabanis, K. (2006). The connection, communication, consolidation, collaboration interoperability framework (C4IF) for information systems interoperability. *Interoperability in Business Information Systems (IBIS), 1*(1), 61-72.

Ray, D., Dash, S. S., & Gulla, U. (2007). In J. Bhattacharya (Ed.), *Towards next generation e-government* (pp. 12-25). New Delhi, India: GIFT Publication.

Rothenberg, J., Botterman, M., & Oranje-Nassau, C. V. (2008). Towards a Dutch interoperability framework recommendations to the forum standaardisatie. Rand Corporation.

Saudi e-Government Program. (2005). YEFI—yesser framework for interoperability. Retrieved on March 14, 2008, from http://www.yesser.gov.sa/english/YEFI.asp?id=item4

Scholl, H. J., & Klischewski, R. (2007). E-Government integration and interoperability: Framing the research agenda. *International Journal of Public Administration, 30*(8-9), 889-920.

Snijkers, K. (2006, May 11-13). *Managing intergovernmental e-government projects.* Paper presented at NISPAcee Conference, Ljubljana, Slovenia.

Stamper, R., Liu, K., Hafkamp, M., & Ades, Y. (2000). Understanding the roles of signs and norms in organizations—a semiotic approach to information systems design. *Behaviour & Information Technology, 19*(1), 15 -27.

State Services Commission. (2007). New Zealand e-government interoperability framework (NZ e-GIF), version 3.2, July 2007. Retrieved on April 7, 2008, from http://www.e.govt.nz/standards/e-gif

Tambouris, E. (2001, September 3-7). An integrated platform for realising online one-stop government: The eGOV project. In *Proceedings of the 12th international Workshop on Database and Expert Systems Applications (DEXA)* (p. 359). Washington, DC: IEEE Computer Society.

Telemedicine Alliance. (2005, November). *Towards interoperable e-health for Europe. (BR 255).* Noordwijk, The Netherlands: ESA Publ. Div.

United Nations Development Programme. (2007). *E-Government interoperability: Guide.* Bangkok, Thailand: UNDP Regional Centre.

University Consortium for Geographic Information Science. (1996). Research priorities for geographic information science. *Cartography and Geographic Information Science, 23*(3), 115-127.

Wimmer, M. A. (2001). European development towards online one-stop government: The "eGOV" project. In *Proceedings of the International Conference of Electronic Commerce (ICEC2001),* Vienna, Austria.

Zhang, J., Dawes, S. S., & Sarkis, J. (2005). Exploring stakeholders' expectations of the benefits and barriers of e-government knowledge sharing. *The Journal of Enterprise Information Management, 18*(5), 548-567.

KEY TERMS

Data Interoperability: Data interoperability is concerned about processing and interpretation of received data. Data interoperability deals with issues such as identifiers, formats and the meaning of data.

Interoperability: The ability of people, organizations and business process and disparate information and communications systems to interact, interconnect and work together to deliver services and information in a seamless, uniform and efficient manner across multiple organizations and systems.

Legal & Policy Environment: Government operates with in strict constitutional framework. Total integration and interoperability between systems may be outright unconstitutional because of the constitutional provision of separation of power among different branches of government. Thus legal, political, regulatory, economical factors constitute the environment within which e-government operates and these factors influence interoperability efforts and its outcome. For example governments come out with legal and policy frameworks to protect citizens' privacy and these frameworks in turn limit types of information that can be shared between agencies.

Organizational Interoperability: Organizational interoperability is concerned with how different organizations collaborate to achieve their mutually agreed e-government goals. Concerned organizations need detailed agreement on collaboration and synchronization of their business processes to deliver integrated government services.

Technical Interoperability: Technical interoperability deals with purely technical aspects of interoperability such as transmission protocols and data exchange formats

ENDNOTES

1 http://www.agimo.gov.au/services/framework

2 http://europa.eu.int/idabc/en/document/3761

3 http://www.riso.ee/en/information-policy/interoperability

4 http://standarder.oio.dk/English/Guidelines/

5 http://www.e.govt.nz/standards/e-gif/

6 http://www.ogcio.gov.hk/eng/infra/eif.htm

7 http://www.yesser.gov.sa/english/

8 http://www.govtalk.gov.uk/schemasstandards/egif_document.asp?docnum=949

Section III
Knowledge and Management Support

Chapter XI
Communities of Purpose: Eliminating Knowledge and Enhancing Practices in Transformational Government Programmes

Ashley Broganza
Brunel University, UK

ABSTRACT

The integration of organizational knowledge across functional communities is increasingly seen as important. The frameworks to do so are often referred to as a 'higher order set of principles' or as 'overarching architectures.' While recognizing these frameworks as a source of competitive advantage, this chapter underlines the importance of linking organizational knowledge to practice. At the operational level, actual practices are rarely aligned with canonical practices contained in manuals, training programmes, and computer systems. In this theoretical chapter we show that the divergence between actual and canonical practices is exacerbated by a number of communities of practice addressing conflicting stakeholder interests. It is the link between knowledge and actual practice that is of central interest to this chapter. Exploring this relationship necessitates a reexamination of the role of communities of practice and frameworks for bringing together conflicting stakeholder interests. Drawing upon literatures from knowledge management, communities of practice, stakeholder, and resource-based theory this chapter suggests an integrative Purposive Community metaframework. The proposed conceptual framework contributes to the resource-based view of the firm by linking organizational knowledge to actual practices and enhancing organizational capabilities by integrating diverse stakeholder interests and expectations through a shared common goal. Such a metaframework can enhance an organisation's dynamic capability to respond to and create change in its external environment.

INTRODUCTION

All transformational programmes face a common challenge: to identify the knowledge that should be retained and to eliminate the rest. The search for a solution to this challenge is not helped by the academic literature which makes the assumption that knowledge is generally useful. Identifying the knowledge to be retained is not as simple as it first appears. Knowledge is embedded in day-to-day activities, which are the practices and routines carried out by people and systems. Transformational programmes invariably affect practices and routines and consequently affect organisations' stock and flow of knowledge. The relationship between knowledge and activities has received little direct research attention.

Knowledge to be eliminated is difficult to manage in transformational programmes. One way in which internal stakeholders can preserve their activities is by ensuring knowledge they create, control and use is left unchanged. Attempts to eliminate knowledge leads to resistance to change and creates barriers to the transformational programme. Knowledge exists within the structures of functional departments or divisions. Consider the major functions in any public sector organisation – finance, delivery, operations, human resources and customer services – each has its own knowledge base. Functions value the knowledge they create and use because the people, in the silos, know how *their* knowledge and *their* practices are conjoined. Yet in many large public sector organisations the practices and knowledge of one silo are barely understood by another. Elimination of knowledge becomes virtually impossible because no one knows the knock-on effects of removing knowledge from the organisation.

Divergent internal stakeholders' interests result in tensions and disputes between people with formal and informal power. This causes dysfunctional behaviour in and between functions, which further exacerbates knowledge protectionism. The effects of differences in external stakeholders' interests and expectations also lead to internal conflicts in activities. Often internal stakeholders compete to satisfy the interests of external stakeholders. For example, the finance function of a government department might emphasise the interests of its principle stakeholder, the Treasury that requires budgets to be reduced; whereas, the customer services or service delivery functions might focus on their key stakeholders, customers, who what higher levels of service that require bigger spending budgets. Consequently, functions are more inclined to compete than co-operate.

The problem of linking of knowledge and practice is of central interest to this chapter. It extends the resource-based view of the firm by proposing a Community of Purpose (CP) meta-framework for linking knowledge and actual practices through a shared common goal. There are three parts to the meta-framework: the *purpose* is determined by the identification of a common shared goal; the *community* is a set of internal stakeholders who have common interests and influence actual practices; and *dynamic capabilities* that organisations need to develop to services to external stakeholders. A community is defined as the condition of having certain attitudes and interests in common. A Community of Purpose provides a 'space' that allows diverse interests of stakeholders and functional silos they influence to come together to achieve a common shared goal. Such a community can enhance organizational capabilities.

The objective of this chapter is to develop the Community of Practice meta-framework. In order to achieve this objective, this chapter draws upon and integrates literatures on knowledge management, communities of practice, stakeholder theory and resource-based theory. The chapter starts by laying the groundwork for a conceptual model of a Community of Purpose. It examines relevant perspectives on knowledge management in order to provide an understanding of the different types of knowledge, its dimensions and behavioural characteristics. Next, a discussion on communities of practice directs attention to its advantages and drawbacks and makes the case for an integrative meta-framework – the Community of Purpose. Finally, an exposition of the research on stakeholder and the resource-based theories develops a better understanding of the CP meta-framework.

BACKGROUND

Laying the Theoretical Foundations for a Community of Purpose

The literatures on knowledge management and communities of practice focus amongst others, most notably on the work of Polanyi (1966), Kogut and Zander (1992), Brown and Duguid (1991), Tsoukas (1996), Liedtka (1999), Wenger (2000) and Daft and Weick (1984). While the distinction between tacit and explicit knowledge is vital to our understanding of knowledge, other knowledge typologies are also considered in order to shed further light. The emphasis on the social, tacit, codified, canonical, non-canonical, and the diffusion aspects of knowledge are seen as important in developing an understanding of a purposive community.

Literatures on stakeholder theory drawn from Clarkson, (1995); Freeman (1984); Hill and Jones (1992) and Rowley and Moldoveanu (2003) amongst others provide an overview of the importance of stakeholders in the determination of organisational outcomes. This includes looking at their legitimate claim to the organisation and their power and impacts on its decisions. Also discussed is the importance of aligning resources and stakeholder expectations.

The resource-based theory has had a significant influence on both strategic and knowledge management research over the past two decades (Barney 1986, 1991; Wernerfelt 1984). Resource-based theory views the organization as a body of knowledge located in structures of coordination that organizes productive practices and routines, adds value to physical resources and matches these to the external marketplace to deliver superior performance (Grant 1997; Nelson and Winter 1982; Tsoukas 1996). Teece and Pisano (1994) further developed the resource-based theory proposing the dynamic capabilities theory as the subset of the competencies/capabilities which allows a firm to create new products and processes in response to changing market circumstances.

Underpinning Concepts of the Community of Purpose

Kogut and Zander (1992) argue that the capabilities of an organization rest in the organizing principles by which relationships among individuals, groups and organizations are structured. They introduce the concept of combinative capability to synthesize and apply current and acquired knowledge. They also suggest that organizations are social communities in which individual and social expertise is transformed into economically useful products and services by the application of a higher order set of principles.

Lave (1998) and Lane and Wenger (1990) consider learning as social construction that implicitly considers knowledge within the context that has meaning and firmly reject transfer models that separate knowledge from practice. Similar examples can be found in the works of Brown et al. (1989) and Pea (1990). Lave and Wenger's (1990) practice-based theory of learning as legitimate peripheral participation in communities-of practice indicates that separating knowledge-practice is unsound, both in theory and in practice. Daft and Weick's (1984) interpretive account of enacting organizations considers innovation in the context of changes in a community's 'way of seeing' or interpretive view. Firms create and transfer knowledge in an organizational context (Kogut and Zander 1992). Within the context of the discussion of this paper this interpretive view is influenced by stakeholder expectation and is a contributory factor to disparities in organisational practices.

Group theory focuses on groups as canonical, bounded entities that lie within an organization and organized or at least sanctioned by that organization and its view of tasks (Hackman 1990). Brown and Duguid (1991) discern that communities are, by contrast, often noncanonical and not recognized by the organization. They are more fluid and interpenetrative than bounded, often crossing the restrictive boundaries of the organization to incorporate people from the outside. In this context, the canonical organization becomes a questionable unit of analysis for managing knowledge. Communities emerge in the process of activity, as opposed to being created to carry out a task. Orr's (1990, 1987) research emphasize the need to focus on the formation of and change in the communities in which work takes place. Brown and Duguid (1991) argue that evolving communities of practice are significant sites of innovating through constant adaptation to changing membership and changing circumstances. This is of particular interest to this paper. The influence of stakeholder expectations on communities of practice is an important consideration in the proposed purposive community. It is the bringing together these varying practices through a common shared goal that can provide organisations benefits of new knowledge.

Organizations address a set of stakeholder expectations (Rowley 2003). These stakeholders can be any individual or group of individuals who have power over the achievement of the organization's strategy and can affect or be affected by an organization's activities/practices (Braganza and Lambert 2000). Stakeholders are exemplified by employees, customers, suppliers, governmental regulators, local community, business partners and investors. They place a variety of sometimes conflicting demands upon the organization to which it must respond (Meyer and Rowan 1977). The extent to which these demands are met is critical to the success of any organization. Where stakeholders' demands change in ways that require new knowledge, the organization generally and specific communities of practice, in particular, need to respond dynamically. Community members need to develop or absorb new capabilities rapidly to meet stakeholders' new expectations while concurrently maintaining or enhancing those that address stakeholders' on-going needs (Cohen and Levinthal 1990; Eisenhardt and Martin 2000). From a stakeholder perspective, the choices made, decisions taken by management and longer term organizational survival, are functions of the extent to which an organization satisfies its stakeholders on a sustained basis (Carroll 1993). From this perspective, therefore, the application of knowledge to a particular context is determined by stakeholder expectations. Differing expectations lead to disparities between practice and actual practice. Organisational knowledge therefore needs to be linked to actual practice in order to gain maximum advantage in its application and in improving dynamic capability.

Recognition of the dynamic nature of interaction and the different levels of ability in firms to generate, build and continuously renew essential competencies is linked to different levels of performance and can be traced back to Penrose (1959). Dynamic capabilities, as part of the competencies/capabilities approach (Teece and Pisano 1994), enable organizations to create new products and processes and adapt to market conditions. The dynamic capabilities approach which is considered part of the resource-based view (Barney 1986, 1991, 1995; Grant 1996; Rumelt 1984; Wernerfelt 1984) emphasizes management capabilities and inimitable combinations of resources that cut across all functions, including R&D, product and process development, manufacturing, human resources and organizational learning.

The next section of the chapter explores specific literatures that contribute to the development of the Community of Purpose. Literatures on knowledge management and communities of practice help towards achieving this understanding.

KNOWLEDGE MANAGEMENT

Developing an understanding of the 'knowledge' part of the linking of knowledge with actual practice is seen as an important step towards developing a CP meta-framework. Failure to recognise knowledge as having a number of characteristics and behaviours can lead to a simplistic view of knowledge and its management.

Polanyi (1966) observes that we know more than we can tell. Many theoretical perspectives of human knowledge draw upon the distinction he makes between tacit and explicit knowledge. Tacit knowledge develops through individual experiences, commitment and involvement (Nonaka and Takeuchi 1995). It is context sensitive and difficult to share through formal, structured communications or as structured information (Lam 2000; Zack 1999). Organizational tacit knowledge is embedded in its routines (Blackler 1993). These are coordinated behaviours that are selected automatically in an almost programmatic manner (Nelson and Winter 1982) and vary between organizations based on unique ingrained values and culture (Daft and Weick 1984). Explicit knowledge can be codified and exchanged with greater ease than tacit knowledge and is encoded in documents, manuals, standard operating procedures, and knowledge management systems (Blackler 1993).

De Long and Fahey (2000) categorize knowledge into three distinct types: human knowledge, social knowledge and structured knowledge. Human knowledge is what people know or know *how* to do and consists of both tacit and explicit characteristics. Social knowledge is largely tacit in nature, shaped by behaviours and implicit assumptions that result from working together. Cross et al. (2001) refer to this as the fabric of relationships among individuals or a network of individuals and manifests in informal networks and transactional relationships (Bhagat et al. 2002). Structured knowledge is embedded in knowledge-based systems, day-to-day practices and formal rules.

Garud and Nayyar (1994) identify three dimensions of knowledge: *the tacit-explicit dimension*, similar to the classification of Polanyi (1966); *simple-complex dimension*, complex knowledge involves greater amounts of information, facts and observations and is more difficult to communicate; whereas simple knowledge deals with less information and is more easily communicated. The third dimension is *independent-systemic*, independent knowledge is transferable and retains meaning and relevance even when taken out of the context, while systemic knowledge is context specific).

Lam (2000) identifies knowledge from an ontological perspective, the individual-collective dimension, and from an epistemological perspective, an explicit-tacit dimension. Four images of knowledge are derived from these: embrained knowledge, embodied knowledge, encoded knowledge and embedded knowledge (Blackler 1993; Millar, Demaid, and Quintas 1997). Embrained knowledge, *(individual-explicit),* is dependant on the conceptual skills and cognitive abilities of individuals. It is abstract and theoretical as it reflects the ability to recognize reason and rework taken-for-granted assumptions (Blackler 1993). Embodied knowledge, *(individual-tacit),* is action oriented and depends on practical application (Shin, Holden and Schmidt 2001). It is specific to a particular social context and is rooted in specific problems, actions and decisions (Barley 1996). Encoded knowledge, *(collective-explicit),* is often simplified and generic, and is information encoded in signs and symbols. Encoded knowledge is stored in books, codes of practice, recipes and blueprints. Embedded Knowledge, *(tacit-collective),* resides in tacit routines of the organization (Nonaka 1994). These routines are socially constructed and influence organizational capabilities (Nelson and Winter 1982).

Davenport and Prusak (1998) introduce the notions of knowledge velocity and knowledge viscosity. Knowledge velocity refers to the speed with which knowledge moves through an organization and is enhanced by knowledge-based systems. Knowledge viscosity refers to the richness and depth of the knowledge being shared or transferred and is mediated by a number of personal, cultural and organizational factors (Nahapiet and Ghoshal 1998).

The distinction between tacit and explicit knowledge, knowledge typologies and knowledge dimensions places an emphasis on the social, tacit, codified, canonical, non-canonical, and diffusion aspects of knowledge. Researchers privilege knowledge that is extant within organisations. There is an uncritical assumption that all current knowledge is good and should be preserved and managed. This assumption is untenable because knowledge has value in a specific context. As environments change so knowledge itself becomes dated and outmoded. This assumption, if left unchallenged, can lead organisations to degenerate over time.

COMMUNITIES OF PRACTICE (CoP)

Communities of practice are seen as providing valuable knowledge resources. They are an emergent but important organizational form that can radically foster knowledge sharing, learning and change and allow the free flow of knowledge (Wenger 2000). Communities of practice create strategies (Liedtka 1999), generate new approaches to problem solving (Orr 1990), create core competencies and develop skills through situated learning (Lave and Wenger 1991). They are informal and self-organizing, often with members being self-selecting (Brown and Duguid 2001; Lave and Wenger 1991).

People participate in a CoP because they are interested and passionate about a specific subject area or problem the organization is facing (Wasko and Faraj 2000; Wenger and Synder 2000), and can generate significant sources of innovation (Daft and Weick 1984). They sustain competitive advantage by managing and exploiting the organization's intellectual capital (Lesser 2004). CoPs build new capabilities or hone existing capabilities through accumulated knowledge of organizational processes that underpin the coordination of practices (Day 1994). Members of a CoP are bound together by shared concerns for outcomes achieved for stakeholders as well as the personal growth of the members themselves (Liedtka 1999). Community membership has strong social aspects and creates relationships with practices and routines, which constitute and reconstitute themselves around local experiences (Gherardi and Nicolini 2000). Knowledge embedded in a community of practice is collectively owned, ensuring its relevance and currency over time (Teigland and Wasko 2001). In this way, community-based knowledge is hard for competitors to imitate or substitute, creating a viable and sustainable source of competitive advantage (Mahoney and Pandian 1992).

Strategic communities of practice, independent of formal structures, are aimed at achieving an organization's broader strategic aims and add value in a number of ways (Storck and Hill 2000). Higher quality knowledge is achieved through membership diversity, informal reporting and learning. Secondly, through cross unit participation, knowledge diffusion and openness for conflict resolution, the number of surprises and revisions to plans are reduced. A greater capacity to deal with unstructured problems that stems from members working on super-ordinate rather than task goals adds value. Members within strategic communities of practice participate voluntarily and the motivation for knowledge sharing among business units and corporate staff is high. An outcome of this is greater internalization of learning as members begin to trust one another. Because the community is perceived to have greater external validity and exists outside formal structures there is a higher likelihood of implementing joint goals. Resilience to internal pressure develops and individual development and learning becomes reinforced by the opportunity to put learning into practice.

While these are all important strengths of individual communities of practice there are however, a number of drawbacks that needed to be highlighted. These are explored in some depth in the next section.

Drawbacks in Communities of Practice (CoP)

CoPs reside often within functional silos and as a consequence divisions in labour produce deeper structural divisions in knowledge (Brown and Duguid 1998). Knowledge is distributed across the organization and does not reside in a single department, function or division (Chesbrough and Teece 1996). Consequently, knowledge becomes difficult to manage (Wenger and Synder 2000), and from an organizational perspective, becomes invisible and therefore difficult to exploit (Chesbrough and Teece 1996). Members in a CoP can become aligned so closely with a common set of assumptions and shared beliefs. Over time, members lose a sense of perspective, often neglecting evidence that runs counter to accepted assumptions and beliefs (Garud and Rappa 1994). Cross community knowledge exchange is essential yet there are virtually no effective mechanisms for exchanging cross community knowledge (Brown and Duguid 1998; Cabrera and Cabrera 2002). The consequences are that knowledge becomes as divided as the functional silos that produce it (Denison, Hart and Kahn 1996). For example, Ford's knowledge initiatives, based upon functional communities, delivered cost savings but did not prevent the Firestone Tyre debacle (Stewart 2000). Storck and Hill (2000) found that membership of the communities they studied were defined and managed on a functional basis. Community members that are functional experts in an area of the business produce quite specialized knowledge which becomes local to the community that produces it (Brown and Duguid 1998).

Knowledge within each community of practice becomes 'sticky' (von Hipple 1994). The reasons for knowledge stickiness fall into two categories, motivational barriers and knowledge barriers (Szulanski 2003). Other examples of knowledge stickiness can be found in Boland and Tenkasi (1995); Cabrera and Cabrera (2002); Fahey and Prusak (1998); Hansen (2002); Hendriks (1999); Lippman and Rumelt (1982); Pinto and Pinto (1991); Soo et al. (2002); Szulanski (1995); Szulanski (1996).

Furthermore, restructurings, job redundancies, off-shoring functions, mergers and acquisitions all affect the ability of community and its members to be the source of new knowledge for innovation. This effectively reduces CoP effectiveness, making them vulnerable and isolated (Wenger and Synder 2000). Each community focuses on its internal competencies, formalizing them to the point of making them inflexible (Leonard 1998). Arguably, the most serious drawback is that this inflexibility can hamper the organization's ability to absorb, assimilate and exploit knowledge.

Added to this is the perspective introduced in this paper. Communities of practice are influenced by diverse stakeholder expectations and these lead to disparities in organisational practices. The result is an inefficient linking of knowledge with practice. Addressing these outlined drawbacks in communities of practice by bringing conflicting interests of stakeholders through a common shared goal is seen as an important aspect of Communities of Purpose.

MAIN FOCUS OF THIS CHAPTER

Towards a Community of Purpose Meta-Framework

Kogut and Zander (1992) describe higher-order principles as those that "facilitate the integration of the entire organization" (1992:390). They recognize that complex organizations consist of communities within which reside varieties of functional specialists and suggest that an organization's functional knowledge is 'nested' within these higher-order principles. These principles must be able to coordinate large numbers of people across varied functions. Dougherty (2001) draws attention to the need for effective cross-functional coordination because knowledge developments cannot be separated from how it is organized.

The relationship between knowledge and organizational structure is of concern. Brown and Duguid (1991) suggest that the organization should be reconceived as a "community of communities, acknowledging ... the many noncanonical communities in its midst ... and legitimize and support the myriad of enacting activities perpetrated by its different (community of practice) members" (Brown and Duguid, 1991; pp. 53). They call for a new "overarching organizational architecture" (1991:54:55), one that spans internal functional boundaries and strengthens the ways in which communities are linked together. This architecture they argue, "must stretch from the level of individual communities of practice ... to the level of the overarching organizational architecture, the community of communities" (1991: 55). Within this overarching architecture, each community of practice searches for shared meanings with other communities, which are formed and reconstituted continually.

Such an architecture advances the integration of cross-community practices and processes that deepen the organization's absorptive capacity (Cohen and Levinthal 1990), which in turn, creates dynamic capabilities that enable the organization to gain and sustain competitive advantage (Brown and Duguid 1991; Eisenhardt and Martin 2000; Raff 2000; Teece, Pisano, and Shuen 1997). These capabilities extend beyond competencies (Hamel and Prahalad 1994). They are directed towards underpinning internal changes (Zahra and George 2002). The link to internal change is vital because no single community can specify, in advance, the knowledge that will be required, be practical and relevant and where and when that knowledge will be required (Tsoukas 1996), not least because change in the external environment cannot be predicted. Furthermore, as communities of practice sense changes in the environment which requires a reconstitution of their practices or knowledge, they have to be coordinated across other communities to be fully effective (Benner and Tushman 2003).

The proposed concept of a Community of Purpose goes some way in contributing to an overarching organizational architecture or higher order principles in enhancing dynamic capabilities. The key lies in the consideration of stakeholders as an integral aspect of this framework. This is done next.

Adding the Stakeholder Perspective to a Community of Purpose

The ability of organizations to generate value and satisfy its primary stakeholder groups depends on creating and sustaining comparative advantage relative to competitors (Clarkson, 1995). Freeman (1984) inspired the development of stakeholder theory and suggested that stakeholders are any group or individual that affect or is affected by the achievement of the firm's objectives (Freeman 1984:25). Stakeholders have also been defined as having a legitimate claim on the organization (Hill and Jones 1992). Individuals and groups are deemed stakeholders because they have power to impact the organization (Carroll 1993). Risk bearers are stakeholders because they have something, in the form or financial or human capital, to gain or lose based upon the organization's actions and behaviours (Clarkson 1995; Hill and Jones 1992).

Organizations address a set of stakeholder expectations if they are to prosper and survive (Rowley and Moldoveanu 2003). Thus, the choices and decisions organizations take are, along with management perceptions, aspirations, beliefs and organisational history, also a function of stakeholders. Clarkson (1995) points out that all stakeholders are of value and consequently no one stakeholder's expectations should gain precedence or dominate. However, organizations are unlikely to address stakeholders' expectations with equal vigor or attention. Rather, expectations will be addressed in varying degrees relative to the perceived importance of the stakeholder at a particular period of time (Jawahar and McLaughlin 2001). Considering the range of stakeholders that include shareholders, banks and lending institutions, trades unions, customers, suppliers, employees, local communities, and pressure groups, it appears likely that organizations prioritize certain stakeholders over others, especially if they are likely to exercise their power and mobilize resources against the focal organization (Rowley and Moldoveanu 2003).

Thus the inclusion of the diverse interests of stakeholders and communities of practice through a common shared goal is crucial to the CoP meta-framework. Stakeholders determine and provide organizational purpose that then determines its practices. This interdependence is based upon a passion to achieve one or more of the organization's strategic aims (Liebeskind 1996). This level of coordination also enhances the strength of communities of practice by bringing together through a common shared goal the richness of reality that is not captured at the organizational level canonical rules. This is an important dynamic capability. Dynamic capabilities allow firms to create new products and processes in response to changing market circumstances. To gain a better understanding of dynamic capability the resource-based theory is discussed next.

Community of Purpose and the Resource-Based Theory

The resource-based theory has had a major influence on strategic management research (Barney 1986, 1991, 1995; Grant 1996; Rumelt 1984; Wernerfelt 1984). It argues that an organization's strategy is determined by the resources it has accumulated and that "a firm's competitive position is defined by a bundle of unique resources and relationships" (Rumelt 1984: 557).

One of the main weaknesses of the resource-base theory is that the terms used by the theory lack clarity (Bowman and Ambrosini 2003). Wernerfelt (1984) describes resources as assets which can be tangible or intangible in nature and that are possessed semi-permanently by an organization. These include assets, organizational processes, people, machines, software, brands, intellectual capital and knowledge that enables the organization to conceive and implement strategies that deliver sustainable advantage (Barney 2001a; Barney 2001b; Daft and Lengel 1996; Dierickx and Cool 1989; Lesser 2004; Lippman and Rumelt 1982).

The sustainability of delivering value for money rests on the organisation's ability implement transformation changes to its resources (Peteraf 1993) and the organization's ability to accumulate and develop new resources over time (Kogut 2000). When organizations combine and coordinate resources, they create competencies (Hamel and Prahalad 1994) and capabilities (Stalk, Evans, and Shulman 1992). A distinct competence reflects the organization's ability to perform more efficiently or more effectively than its competitors. Organizational capabilities refer to the organization's ability to deploy its competencies, and represent its ability to respond or initiate changes to embedded practices and routines within its communities of practice (Teece, Pisano, and Shuen 1997). But these communities are influenced by conflicting stakeholder interests that leads to internal conflict and competition for limited resources. Misalignment between resources and stakeholder expectations can also lead to dysfunctions in the structure, so that organizational members behave in ways that defend and develop knowledge resources that are no longer relevant (Liedtka 1999), while others refuse to share their knowledge (Lapré and Van Wassenhove 2003).

A community of purpose, through linking knowledge with actual practice, provides an organization with the prize of an inimitable resource and corresponding dynamic capability. An inimitable resource cannot be replaced by another resource that delivers the same strategic ends (Bowman and Ambrosini 2003). Resources are substitutable when they are either similar or very different (Barney 1991). Resources can be inimitable because of asymmetries in knowledge-related processes and skills (Miller, Eisenstat, and Foote 2002) and socially complex relationships (Dierickx and Cool, 1989; Tsoukas 1996). Single communities, such as a department on its own, can limit the development of dynamic capabilities, which focus on creating future resources (Eisenhardt and Martin 2000; Teece, et al. 1997) when the organization is in an environment that is turbulent, changing rapidly or high velocity (Bourgeois and Eisenhardt 1988; Laughlin 1991; Meyer, Goes, and Brooks 1995).

Resource-based theory highlights the importance of inimitable resources as a foundation of dynamic capabilities in organisations. The purposive community meta-framework adds to this capability by bringing knowledge form diverse communities of practice to bear upon actual practices through a common shared goal.

CONCLUSION

The need to bring knowledge sources into an integrated meta-framework was first proposed by Kogut and Zander (1992), Tsoukas (1996) and Brown and Duguid (1991), who referred this as 'higher order principles', 'overarching organization architecture' and 'dispersed knowledge'. Bogenrieder and Nooteboom (2004) stress the importance of looking at both knowledge sharing and knowledge production. Measures taken for supporting knowledge sharing may impose uniformity of meanings and procedures that limit the variety needed for the development of new knowledge. They suggest an alternative approach of considering intra-organizational groups for learning.

This chapter has contributed to the resource-based view of the firm by proposing the linking of knowledge with actual practice. Actual practices arise from communities of practices striving to meet differing stakeholder expectations. The identification of a common shared goal becomes the key to bringing these varying expectations onto a common platform and underpins the usefulness of such a meta-framework in developing further inimitable dynamic capabilities. These dynamic capabilities also bear a direct relationship to an organization's absorptive capacity (Cohen and Levinthal 1990), namely in its ability to recognize the value of knowledge, assimilate and evaluate it across specialist communities, and applying it to achieving strategic advantage. There is also a significant link between absorptive capacity and innovation and in creating strategic success (Zahra and George 2002).

The Community of Practice meta-framework goes some way in ensuring that dynamic capabilities are created (Eisenhardt and Martin 2000) and that conflicting stakeholder expectations continue to be addressed (Rowley 2004). The concept of a CP meta-framework also makes a significant contribution to the notion of 'higher order principles' by linking diverse stakeholder expectations to its resource strategy and execution. A Community of Purpose as an integrative part of a 'higher order principles' cuts across functional and organizational boundaries and incorporates tacit and explicit knowledge resources from diverse sources by considering the importance of stakeholders and the influence they exert upon the continual survival of an organization. It develops dynamic capabilities by increasing an organization's on-going ability to monitor, track and address current and emergent expectations though specific application of knowledge to actual practice.

There are challenges that need to be overcome in the implementation of the Community of Purpose meta-framework. The identification of a common shared goal requires making explicit organizational processes. Identifying relationships that increase value added by linking these processes comes next. This should be achieved by identifying a common shared goal. A major challenge and possible barrier would come from the differing interests of stakeholders who remain to be convinced that such linkages would increase value added. This would require the senior management support, the involvement of champions and possibly boundary spanners. This is probably the most difficult challenge in setting up a Community of Purpose with implications to restructuring of organizational structure and the relinquishing of fiefdoms.

These challenges suggest that the Community of Purpose meta-framework has limitations in terms of the organizations that might use it. In particular, the framework would be relevant to organizations going through transformational change, such as those undertaking a major restructuring, creating joint ventures or alliances and outsourcing or right-shoring practices of one or more communities. The Community of Purpose meta-framework will be of interest to public sector organizations that seek to transform themselves to meet the emergent demands of the taxpayers. These organizations will seek to redefine their stakeholders' expectations, creating new expectations or offering to satisfy emerging stakeholder interests. These organizations develop new practices and knowledge to address these stakeholders' expectations, thus, generating capabilities that are distinct in the business of government delivering value for money to taxpayers.

REFERENCES

Barley, S. R. (1996). Technicians in the workplace: Ethnographic evidence for bringing work into organization studies. *Administrative Science Quarterly, 41*(8), 404-441.

Barney, J. B. (1986). Types of competition and the theory of strategy: Toward an integrative framework. *Academy of Management Review, 11*, 791-800.

Barney, J. B. (1991). Firm resources and sustained competitive advantage. *Journal of Management, 17*(1), 99-120.

Barney, J. B. (1995). Looking inside for competitive advantage. *Academy of Management Executive, 9*(4), 49-61.

Barney, J. B. (2001a). Is the resource-based "view" a useful perspective for strategic management research? Yes. *Academy of Management Review, 26*(1), 41-56.

Barney, J. B. (2001b). Resource-based theories of competitive advantage: A ten year retrospective on the resource-based view. *Journal of Management, 27*(643), 650.

Benner, M. J., & Tushman, M. L. (2003). Exploitation, exploration, and process management: The productivity dilemma revisited. *Academy of Management Review, 28*(2), 238-256.

Bhagat, R. S., Kedia, B. L., Harveston, P. D., & Triandis, H. C. (2002). Cultural variations in the cross-border transfer of organizational knowledge: An integrative framework. *Academy of Management Review, 27*(2), 204-221.

Blackler, F. (1993). Knowledge and the theory of organizations: Organizations as activity systems and the reframing of management. *Journal of Management Studies, 30*(6), 863-884.

Bogenrieder, I., & Nooteboom, B. (2004). Learning groups: What types are there? A theoretical analysis and an empirical study in a consultancy firm. *Organization Studies, 25(2)*, 287-313.

Boland, R. J., & Tenkasi, R. V. (1995). Perspective making and perspective taking in communities of knowing. *Organization Science, 6*(4), 350-372.

Bourgeois, L. J. I., & Eisenhardt, K. M. (1988). Strategic decision processes in high velocity environments: Four cases in the microcomputer industry. *Management Sciences, 14*(816), 835.

Bowman, C., & Ambrosini, V. (2003). How the resource-based and the dynamic capability views of the firm inform corporate-level strategy. *British Journal of Management, 14*, 289-303.

Braganza, A., & Lambert, R. (2000) Strategic integration: Developing a process-governance framework. *Knowledge and Process Management, 7*, 177-186.

Brown, J. S., Collins, A., & Duguid, P. (1989). Situated cognition and the culture of learning. *Education Researcher, 18*(1), 32-42.

Brown, J. S., & Duguid, P. (1991). Organizational learning and communities-of-practice: Towards a unified view of working, learning, and innovation. *Organization Science, 2*(1), 40-57.

Brown, J. S., & Duguid, P. (1998). Organizing knowledge. *California Management Review, 40*(3), 90-111.

Brown, J. S., & Duguid, P. (2001). Knowledge and organization: A social-practice perspective. *Organization Science, 12*(2), 198-213.

Cabrera, A., & Cabrera, E. F. (2002). Knowledge-sharing dilemmas. *Organization Studies, 23*(5), 687.

Carroll, A. B. (1993). *Business and society:Ethics and stakeholder management.* Cincinnati, OH.

Chesbrough, H. W., & Teece, D. J. (1996). When is virtual virtuous? Organizing for innovation. *Harvard Business Review, 74*(1), 65-73.

Clarkson, M. B. E. (1995). A stakeholder framework for analyzing and evaluating corporate social performance. *Academy of Management Review, 20*, 92-117.

Cohen, W. M., & Levinthal, D. A. (1990). Absorptive capacity: A new perspective on learning and innovation. *Administrative Science Quarterly, 35*, 128-152.

Cross, R., Parker, A., Prusak, L., & Borgatti, S. P. (2001). Knowing what we know: Supporting knowledge creation and sharing in social networks. *Organizational Dynamics, 30*(2), 100-120.

Daft, R. L., & Lengel, R. H. (1996). Organizational information requirements, media richness and structural design. *Management Science, 3*, 554-571.

Daft, R. L., & Weick, K. E. (1984). Toward a model of organizations as interpretation systems. *Academy of Management Review, 9*(2), 284-295.

Davenport, T. H., & Prusak, L. (1998). *Working knowledge: How organizations manage what they know.* Boston: Harvard Business School Press.

Day, G. S. (1994). The capabilities of market-driven organizations. *Journal of Marketing, 58*, 37-52.

de Long, D. W., & Fahey, L. (2000). Diagnosing cultural barriers to knowledge management. *Academy of Management Executive, 14(*4), 113-128.

Denison, D. R., Hart, S. L., & Kahn, J. A. (1996). From chimneys to cross-functional teams: Developing and validating a diagnostic model. *Academy of Management Journal, 39*(4), 1005-1023.

Dierickx, I., & Cool, K. (1989). Asset stock accumulation and sustainability of competitive advantage. *Management Science, 35*(12), 1504-1511.

Dougherty, D. (2001). Reimagining the differentiation and integration of work for sustained product innovation. *Organization Science, 12*(5), 612-631.

Eisenhardt, K. M., & Martin, J. A. (2000). Dynamic capabilities: What are they? *Strategic Management Journal, 21*(10), 1105-1121.

Fahey, L., & Prusak, L. (1998). The eleven deadliest sins of knowledge management. *California Management Reveiw, 40*(3), 265-275.

Freeman, R. E. (1984). *Strategic management: A stakeholder approach.* Boston: Pitman

Garud, R., & Nayyar, P. R. (1994). Transformative capacity: Continual structuring by intertemporal technology transfer. *Strategic Management Journal, 15*, 365-385.

Garud, R., & Rappa, M. A. (1994). A socio-cognitive model of technology evolution: The case of cochlear implants. *Organization Science, 5*, 344-362.

Gherardi, S., & Nicolini, D. (2000). The organizational learning of safety in communities of practice. *Journal of Management Inquiry, 9*(1), 7-18.

Grant, R. M. (1996). Toward a knowledge-based theory of the firm. *Strategic Management Journal, 17*(109), 122.

Grant, R. M. (1997). *Contemporary strategy analysis.* Cambridge, MA: Blackwell.

Hackman, J. R. (1990). *Groups that work (and those that don't).* San Francisco: Jossey-Bass.

Hamel, G., & Prahalad, C. K. (1994). *Competing for the future.* Boston: Harvard Business School Press.

Hansen, M. T. (2002). Knowledge networks: Explaining effective knowledge sharing in multiunit companies. *Organization Science, 13*(3), 232-248.

Hendriks, P. (1999). Why share knowledge? The influence of ICT on the motivation for knowledge sharing. *Knowledge and Process Management, 6*(2), 91-100.

Hill, C. W. L., & Jones, T. M. (1992). Stakeholder-agency theory. *Journal of Management Studies, 29*, 131-154.

Jawahar, I. M., & McLaughlin, G. L. (2001). Toward a descriptive stakeholder theory: An organizational life cycle approach. *Academy of Management Review, 26*(3), 397-414.

Kogut, B. (2000). The network as knowledge: Generative rules and the emergence of structure. *Strategic Management Journal, 21*, 405-425.

Kogut, B., & Zander, U. (1992). Knowledge of the firm, combinative capabilities, and the replication of technology. *Organization Science, 3*(3), 383-397.

Lam, A. (2000). Tacit knowledge, organizational learning, and societal institutions: An integrated framework. *Organization Studies, 21*(3), 487-513.

Lapré, M. A., & Van Wassenhove, L. N. (2003). Managing learning curves in factories by creating and transferring knowledge. *California Management Review, 46*(1), 53-71.

Laughlin, R. C. (1991). Environmental disturbances and organizational transitions and transformations: Some alternative models. *Organization Studies, 12*(2), 209-232.

Lave, J. (1998). *Cognition in practice: Mind, mathematics and culture in everyday life.* New York: Cambridge University Press.

Lave, J., & Wenger, E. C. (1990). *Situated learning: Legitimate peripheral participatory* (IRL Report 90-0013). Palo Alto, CA: Institute of Research and Learning.

Lave, J., & Wenger, E. C. (1991). *Situated learning: Legitimate peripheral participation.* Cambridge, MA: Cambridge University Press.

Leonard, D. (1998). *Wellsprings of knowledge: Building and sustaining the sources of innovation.* Boston: Harvard Business School Press.

Lesser, E. (2004). *Communities of practice: Making the most of intellectual capital.* IBM Corporation.

Liebeskind, J. P. (1996). Knowledge, strategy, and the theory of the firm. *Strategic Management Journal, 17*(Special Issue), 93-107.

Liedtka, J. (1999). Linking competitive advantage with communities of practice. *Journal of Management Inquiry, 8*(1), 5-16.

Lippman, S. A., & Rumelt, R. (1982). Uncertain imitability: An analysis of interfirm differences in efficiency under competition. *The Bell Journal of Economics, 13*(2), 418-438.

Mahoney, J. T., & Pandian, R. J. (1992). The resource-based view within the conversations of strategic management. *Strategic Management Journal, 13*, 363-380.

Meyer, A. D., Goes, J. B., & Brooks, G. R. (1995). Organizations reacting to hyperturbulence. In G. P. Huber & W. H. Glick (Eds.), *Organizational change and redesign: Ideas and insights for improving performance* (pp. 66-111). New York: Oxford University Press.

Meyer, J. W., & Rowan, B. (1977). Institutional organizations: Formal structures as myth and ceremony. *American Journal of Sociology, 80*, 340-363.

Millar, J., Demaid, A., & Quintas, P. (1997). Trans-organizational innovation: A framework for research. *Technology Analysis & Strategic Management, 9*(4), 399-418.

Miller, D., Eisenstat, R. A., & Foote, N. (2002). Strategy from the inside out: Building capability-creating organizations. *California Management Review, 44*(3), 37-54.

Nahapiet, J., & Ghoshal, S. (1998). Social capital, intellectual capital, and the organizational advantage. *Academy of Management Review, 23*(2), 242-266.

Nanda, A. (1996) Resources, capabilities, and competencies. In B. Moingeon & A. Edmondson (Eds.), *Organizational learning and competitive advantage*. London: Sage.

Nelson, R. R., & Winter, S. (1982). *An evolutionary theory of economic change*. Cambridge, MA: Harvard University Press.

Nonaka, I. (1994). A dynamic theory of organizational knowledge creation. *Organization Science, 5*(1), 14-37.

Nonaka, I., & Takeuchi, H. (1995). *The knowledge creating company*. New York: Oxford University Press.

Orr, J. (1987). Narratives at work: Story telling as cooperative diagnostic activity. *Field Service Manager*, 47-60.

Orr, J. (1990). Sharing knowledge, celebrating identity: War stories and community memory in a service culture. In D. S. Middleton & D. Edwards (Eds.), *Collective remembering: Memory in society* (pp. 169-189). Newbury Park, CA: Sage.

Pea, R. D. (1990). *Distributed cognition* (IRL Report 91-0015). Palo Alto, CA: Institute for Research and Learning.

Penrose, E. T. (1959). *The theory of the growth of the firm*. New York: Wiley.

Peteraf, M. A. (1993). The cornerstones of competitive advantage: A resource-based view. *Strategic Management Journal, 14*, 179-191.

Pinto, M. B., & Pinto, J. K. (1991). Determinants of cross-functional cooperation in the project implementation process. *Project Management Journal, 22*, 13-20.

Polanyi, M. (1966). *The tacit dimension*. New York: Doubleday.

Raff, D. M. (2000). Superstores and the evolution of firm capabilities in American bookselling. *Strategic Management Journal, 21*, 1043-1060.

Rowley, T. J. (2004). Moving beyond dyadic ties: A network theory of stakeholder influences. *Academy of Management Review, 22*(2), 867-910.

Rowley, T. J., & Moldoveanu, M. (2003). When will stakeholder groups act? An interest-and identity-based model of stakeholder group mobilization. *Academy of Management Review, 28*(2), 204-219.

Rumelt, R. (1984). Towards a strategic theory of the firm. In R. B. Lamb (Ed.), *Competitive strategic management* (pp. 556-570). Englewood Cliffs, NJ: Prentice-Hall.

Shin, M., Holden, T., & Schmidt, R. A. (2001). From knowledge theory to management practice: Towards an integrated approach. *Information Processing and Management, 37*, 335-355.

Soo, C., Devinney, T., Midgley, D., & Deering, A. (2002). Knowledge management: Philosophy, processes, and pitfalls. *California Management Review, 44*(4), 129-150.

Stalk, G., Evans, P., & Shulman, L. E. (1992). Competing on capabilities: The new rules of corporate strategy. *Harvard Business Review, 70*(2), 57-69.

Stewart, T. A. (2000). Knowledge worth $1.25 billion. *Fortune, 142(*12), 120-121.

Storck, J. & Hill, P. A. 2000, "Knowledge diffusion through 'strategic communities'", *Sloan Management Review* pp. 63-74.

Szulanski, G. (1995). Unpacking stickiness: An empirical investigation of the barriers to transfer best practice inside the firm. *Academy of Management Journal, Best Papers Proceedings*, 437.

Szulanski, G. (1996). Exploring internal stickiness: Impediments to the transfer of best practice within the firm. *Strategic Management Journal, 17(*Winter Special Issue), 27-43.

Szulanski, G. (2003). *Sticky knowledge: Barriers to knowing in the firm.* Thousand Oaks, CA: Sage.

Teece, D. J., Pisano, G., & Shuen, A. (1997). Dynamic capabilities and strategic management. *Strategic Management Journal, 18(*7), 509-533.

Teece, D. J., & Pisano, G. (1994). The dynamic capabilities of firms: An introduction. *Industrial and Corporate Change, 3*(3), 537-556.

Teigland, R., & Wasko, M. (2001, August 3-8). Recombining knowledge through know-how trading: Examining the impact of informal boundary-spanning communication on individual performance. *Academy of Management Proceedings.*

Tsoukas, H. (1996). The firm as a distributed knowledge system: A constructionist approach. *Strategic Management Journal, 17*, 11-25.

von Hipple, E. (1994). Sticky information and the locus of problem solving: Implications for innovation. *Organization Science, 40*(4), 429-439.

Wasko, M. M., & Faraj, S. (2000). It is what one does: Why people participate and help others in electronic communities of practice. *Journal of Strategic Information Systems, 9*, 155-173.

Wenger, E. C. (2000). Communities of practice and social learning systems. *Organization, 7(*2), 225-246.

Wenger, E. C., & Synder, W. (2000). Communities of practice: The organizational frontier. *Harvard Business Review,* 139-145.

Wernerfelt, B. (1984). A resource-based view of the firm. *Strategic Management Journal, 5(*2), 171-180.

Zack, M. H. (1999). Managing codified knowledge. *Sloan Management Review, 40*(4), 45-58.

Zahra, S. A., & George, G. (2002). Absorptive capacity: A review, reconceptualization, and extension. *Academy of Management Review, 27*(2), 185-203.

KEY TERMS

Communities of Practice: A process of social learning that takes place and shared socio-cultural practices that emerge and evolve when people who have common goals work together as they strive towards achieving those goals.

Dynamic Capabilities: Involves an organisations ability to integrate, build, and reconfigure internal and external competences to address rapidly changing environments

Knowledge: A mix of framed experiences, values, contextual information, and expert insight that provides a framework for evaluating and incorporating new experiences and information

Knowledge Management: A process that helps organizations identify, select, organize, disseminate, and transfer important information and expertise that are part of the organization's memory.

Resource Based View (theory): A method used to determine the strategic resources available to a firm.

Chapter XII
Knowledge-Driven Project Management in Government Transformation

Yannis Charalabidis
National Technical University of Athens, Greece

Demetrios Sarantis
National Technical University of Athens, Greece

Dimitris Askounis
National Technical University of Athens, Greece

ABSTRACT

As implementation projects for transforming e-government mature, the need for successfully tackling project management emerges: without a project management method, those who commission an e-government project, those who manage it and those who work on it will not have the necessary tools to plan, organise, monitor, and reschedule tasks, responsibilities and milestones. In taking forward both the Government Modernisation and the Civil Service Reform agendas, renewed emphasis is being placed on project management approaches and techniques for achieving policy objectives more effectively and efficiently. The present chapter, after giving an overview of state-of-the-art project management methodologies, goes further in indicating the needs of the e-government domain and proposing a goal-driven way to manage all the aspects of e-government projects. Specifically designed tools support the application in a lighthouse project of the Greek public sector, leading to reusable conclusions on achievements and problems faced.

INTRODUCTION

Government transformation programmes and projects are usually shaped in a way to reduce government costs, improve delivery of public services, increase transparency, increase engagement of citizens in public matters, or achieve better outcomes in major policy areas (such as education, employment, taxation, health, or social security). The success of such large scale coordinated attempts depends on how well they are able to satisfy their objectives, usually delivering the promised quality within predicted time and calculated effort. The transformational nature, the large scale and the involvement of a large number of function-oriented officials are the key factors that usually make e-government projects more complex than usual IT projects (OECD, 2003).

The inability of governmental organisations to successfully complete public information technology projects threatens to undermine efforts to implement e-government. In parallel, an increasing number of countries formulate ambitious action plans for implementing e-government. Their aim is to move service delivery to the World Wide Web, to enhance information to citizens and to make public sector workplaces smarter for the benefit of citizens, politicians and civil servants alike. As OECD (2001) states "Unless governments learn to manage the risks connected with large public IT projects, these e-dreams will turn into global nightmares. Governments must get the fundamentals of IT right if they want to harvest the huge potential of going online".

E-government project failures are all too common - some make the headlines, but most of them are quickly forgotten. A survey of e-government projects in developing and transition economies revealed that as many as 85 percent are a partial (unattained goals) or total (abandoned implementation) failure (Heeks 2003a). The reasons for failure are many and varied. Common reasons include: lack of internal ownership, absence of vision or strategy, poor project management, inadequate technological infrastructure and obstacles to data interchange (Heeks, 2003b). Lack of a business case for the project, over reliance on technology as the main driver for e-government, and lack of sufficient administrative reform to accompany e-government are also cited (Schware, 2004).

As implementation projects for transforming government mature and tend to become closely interrelated, the need for successfully tackling project management emerges: without a project management method, those who commission an e-government project, those who manage it and those who work on it will not have the necessary tools to plan, organise, monitor and re-schedule tasks, responsibilities and milestones. In taking forward both the government modernisation and the civil service reform agendas, renewed emphasis is being placed on project management approaches and techniques, for achieving policy objectives more effectively and efficiently. High level government officials indicate though that their needs do not conclude at asking for a different systematic approach, able to realise the domain specificities, but go further in demanding a tool able to carry forward good practices in e-government transformation and support the reuse of already travelled pathways. Those involved will not be clear about how much responsibility, authority and accountability they have and, as a result, there will often be confusion surrounding the project. Without a project management method projects are rarely completed on time and within acceptable cost, especially in large e-government projects.

Knowledge is wasted moving from one government transformation project to the other. As stated in (Heeks, 2003c), failures are not exploited to point the way for a better design and lessons are not developed. Even though success cases exist, they are not properly analysed in order to capitalise the gained knowledge and utilise it in future attempts.

National governments cope with considerable challenges trying to locate the right pathway of implementing and managing successful e-government projects. Organisations begin the project implementation with a blank paper instead of having pre-defined templates for project management charts and deliverables that can be fleshed out. The management of government transformation projects is, in significant part, the management of technology, people, organisation, and knowledge. E-government requires cross-agency cooperation because of functional needs for scale, consistency, and integration.

This chapter is organised in five sections. In section two, the strong features and the gaps of the traditional project management methodologies are identified concerning government transformation projects. Next, in section three, gleaning the 'bread and butter' elements of the conventional project management and implementation methodologies and covering their gaps concerning e-government transformation projects, an e-government transformation project management (eGTPM) approach is introduced. In the fourth section, we examine how a lighthouse Greek government project, that has adopted an eGTPM approach, has coped with the challenges of novelty and cross-agency collaboration. Finally, section 5 presents conclusions and future perspectives of this work.

STATE OF THE ART

Overall View of E-Government Projects Management Challenges

The selection of the appropriate project management methodology is significant to the healthy development of e-government projects. However, up till now, the project management framework of e-government has been not been thoroughly developed, as most of the project management models put forward by authoritative organizations are generic, some of them have been applied in plain IT implementation projects, and they are not directly targeting the specificities of e-government transformation.

Most of the project and software development management methodologies follow a hard, rational approach: they focus on data (not information), technology (not people), processes (not services), management structures (not knowledge). Their point of view relates partly to the roots of project management in engineering, where the physical resources dominated and where scientific principles were needed in order to successfully implement projects. This idea continues to run through project management. It also relates partly to the dominant image of e-government systems being the image of IT, and the dominant language being the jargon of IT (Avison et al, 2008).

Government projects demand flexibility and ability to address change. Following this path, the identified gaps in the traditional project management methodologies are usually cemented with more measurement, more control and more rules (Gupta et al, 2004); hence the calls by the governments of developed countries for use in e-government projects of more planning, more measurement, and more strict methodologies (US Government, 2003).

Hard, rational 'best practice' in e-government project management does not seem to deliver, and needs to be tempered with a softer, more behavioural and knowledge centric approach: according to U.S. Office of Management and Budget Branch Chief, Daniel Chenock, as stated in (Cohen et al., 2003), "e-government is about transformation. It is citizen-centred - not program centred. It is not just a tool but part of a whole system of technology, process and organization that brings change. e-government is not in isolation of other management challenges".

Technological complexity and incompatibility are not the only, nor the most difficult, challenges to overcome in government transformation projects. Managerial, political, and legal factors have been identified as important elements to take into consideration in the design and development of e-government initiatives as well (Gil-García et al, 2005), (Dawes et al, 2002).

The adaptive challenges of e-government projects go far beyond pure technology. They call for new organizational structures and skills, process optimisation, new forms of leadership, and perhaps even a redefinition of purpose. They also call for a significant broadening and organisational transformation. The new dynamics are very far from traditional public sector projects for procuring and contracting. Yet, while the potential for a recasting of both public management and political accountability is real, the transition is fraught with dynamic uncertainties (Allen et al, 2001).

Many well established project management methods may be commonly used by public or private sector organisations that are trying to plan, organise and monitor e-government projects. Starting with the generic ones, the group of Project Management Institute (PMI) Method, PRINCE2, Goal Directed Project Management (GDPM) proceeding with the software oriented project management methodologies, sequential ones like the traditional Waterfall Model, the Structured Systems Analysis and Design Methodology (SSADM) and the Systems Development Life Cycle (SDLC), the iterative ones like Rational Unified Process (RUP), Rapid application development (RAD), Dynamic Systems Development Model (DSDM), will usually be represented towards the government and industry employees, either through a consulting, a training, a certification or a tools path. The dynamic group of software specific methodologies and tools surely contains Feature Driven Development (FDD), Extreme or Agile Programming (XP or AGP), SCRUM and other specialised methodologies like Information Technology Infrastructure Library (ITIL) and Joint Application Development (JAD). Such methods and tools are usually proposed by the software industry, sometimes in an attempt to solve the problem, providing the same tools that are used during code development.

The absolute value of some methods and tools of the above list, together with their convergence in common topics, certainly indicate that there is a solid ground. This so rich collection does not however provide a systematic answer to the question "what are the necessary steps for developing a National e-government Standardization Framework for Interoperability, especially when 25 projects are currently being planned and another 50 are in various phases of implementation"—this is left for the experts. And then the tools are used as Gantt chart creators, while methodologies take the role of management guidelines for quality, risk or conflict resolution. All the above, together with the lack that most government officials stress—and that is knowledge reuse, are paving the way for approaches that can exploit model driven design and provide domain specific ways of implementing safe, or challenging, goals.

In this section we make a selection and present an overview of the commonly used project management and software implementation methodologies in IT projects. We give a global description of each of the selected methodologies and we discuss their key points, advantages and disadvantages.

Generic Project Management Methodologies

Projects in Controlled Environments

Projects in Controlled Environments (PRINCE) is a project management methodology covering the organization, management and control of projects, developed and maintained by the UK National Computing Centre (NCC, 2005). Since its introduction, PRINCE has become widely used in both the public and private sectors and is now the de facto standard for project management in the UK. The latest version of the methodology, PRINCE2, is designed to incorporate the requirements of existing users and to enhance the methodology towards a generic, best practice approach for the management of all types of projects. PRINCE2 is a process-based approach for project management providing an easily tailored and scalable methodology for the management of all types of projects. Each process is defined with its key inputs and outputs together with the specific objectives to be achieved and activities to be carried out. The methodology describes how a project is divided into manageable stages enabling efficient control of resources and regular progress monitoring throughout the project. The various roles and responsibilities for managing a project are fully described and are adaptable to suit the size and complexity of the project, and the skills of the organization.

Project Management Institute (PMI) Method

The Project Management Institute (PMI) published the first Project Management Body of Knowledge Guide (PMI, 2001), (PMI, 2006) as a white paper in 1987 describing the sum of knowledge within the profession of Project Management (PM) in an attempt to document and to standardize generally accepted project management information and practices. Generally accepted does not mean that the knowledge and practices described in the PMBOK framework are or should be applied uniformly on all projects; the project management team is always responsible for determining what is appropriate for any given project. The Guide is process-based, meaning it describes work as being accomplished by processes. Processes overlap and interact throughout a project or its various phases. Processes are described in terms of:

- Inputs (documents, plans, designs, etc.)
- Tools and Techniques (mechanisms applied to inputs)
- Outputs (documents, products, etc.)

The PMBOK framework splits the project processes into five distinct process groups: initiating, planning, executing, controlling and closing. These groups do not imply that the project has to go through each one in this order; they are only provided in order to be able to structure and categorize the different project processes. PMBOK also identifies several project knowledge areas: integration management, scope management, time management, cost management, quality management, human resource management, communications management, risk management and procurement management.

Goal Directed Project Management

Goal Directed Project Management (GDPM) is a powerful, pragmatic approach for gaining consensus from all stakeholders on the overall objectives of a business program or project (Andersen et al, 2004). It provides a single-page, top-level view of the goals of the project (a milestone plan), which is used as a high-level communications and control tool. GDPM complements, not replaces, detailed product or activity-based approaches that project managers are used to applying. The milestone plan shows planned achievement against the key management objectives, and the activity plan shows achievement against the detailed delivery tasks.

GDPM is a management philosophy accompanied by a set of tools and principles for planning, organizing, leading and controlling projects. The method is characterized by its practical and "psychological" approach to both focusing a project group to reach common goals and on controlling the progress of each individual. The focus on results provides a direct link between the project plan and the organisation's business plan. The business plan should state the final goal for the project, and may also reflect one or more intermediate goals for the project. It is, therefore, straightforward for the organisation and project planners to ensure the project is synchronized with the organisation's needs and plans. The GDPM method allows project sponsors and team members to focus most of their attention and effort on project issues and not on project management methodologies and/or tools.

Table 1. Generic project management methodologies strengths

Title	Description
PRINCE 2	
Structured method	It is a structured approach to project management. It provides a method for managing projects within a clearly defined framework
Proven and established best-practice in project management	It embodies many years of good practice in project management and provides a flexible and adaptable approach to suit all projects
Product based and activity-oriented planning	The method identifies all the expected products and the associated work required to complete a project
Quality review	A quality checking technique with a specific structure, defined roles and procedure designed to ensure a product's completeness and adherence to standards
Common language for all participants in the project	There are often different groups of people involved in projects: the customer, one or more suppliers, and of course the user. PRINCE2 is designed to provide a common language across all the interested parties involved in a project
Useful for educative use	The essential training material and the training methodology are provided from a number of training institutions.
Regular reviews of progress	It enables projects to have regular reviews of progress to plan and to business case
Good communication channels	It provides good communication channels between the project, project management, and the rest of the organisation
Management Roles	The project management structure consists of roles and responsibilities that bring together the various interests and skills involved in, and required by, the project regarding the management of it
Management Documents	It includes descriptions of a number of standard management documents that are invoked through the methodology.
Lessons Learned	Lessons learned report bring together any lessons learned during the project that can be usefully applied to other projects.
Product Breakdown Structure	This is a deliverable oriented, hierarchical structure which seeks to define the entire scope of the project as a set of products
PMI	
Framework of generally accepted project management principles	An internationally recognised standard which provides the fundamentals of project management, irrespective of the type of project
Teaching the subject content	PMI Guide takes the best approach for purposes of teaching the subject content of each knowledge area
It provides the knowledge needed to manage the project life cycle	It states the knowledge needed to manage the life cycle of any project, program and portfolio through their processes
Stakeholder analysis in government projects	It includes all 'individuals and organizations who are actively involved in the project, or whose interests may be positively or negatively affected as a result of project execution or successful project completion
Unified project management terminology	A common terminology is provided understandable to all the participants
Tells the practitioner what to do	It provides guidance to the practitioner on what to do but not on how to do it.
GDPM	
Managing change	The top-down management approach of the methodology provides the possibility of managing the appeared changes
Collaborative approach	It is based and supports effective collaboration among the participants
Focuses project teams on common goals	The goals are clear and understandable to the entire project team
Guides the contributions of all team members & stakeholders	It assures the clear definition of roles and responsibilities. Each team member and stakeholder knows exactly what he should do during the project implementation

continued on following page

Table 1. continued

Title	Description
Alignment with the organisation's business plan	Project is in line with the organisation's business plan and there is a pre-agreed commitment to the target
Realistic plan & team commitment	The project plan is realistically designed guaranteeing team's commitment
Light methodology–Minimisation of bureaucracy	It is light-touch, non-bureaucratic and is expressed in simple terms using a language that can be understood and adopted by people who are not professional project managers. It encourages simple non-bureaucratic administration

Table 2. Generic project management methodologies weaknesses

Title	Description
PRINCE 2	
Definition of the detailed project plan at initial stage. Complicated activity diagram	Unnecessary time is spent managing and documenting the project causing significant delay.
Managing organizational change	Public administration essential organisational changes during the project implementation are not addressed efficiently
Generic - must be tailored to suit the occasion	It is method and not a cure. People who use it should tailor it efficiently to the project in hand
Bureaucratic methodology	Documentation and control may take precedence over innovation and flexibility
User should be familiar with every aspect of the methodology	It is a complex methodology and every person who works on a PRINCE2 project should be quite familiar with every aspect of PRINCE2 to know how to apply it.
Responsibilities transfer risk	Because of the various roles and responsibilities involved, participants in the project can easily blame each other when something goes wrong
Splitting up a project often results in a lack of knowledge	Splitting up a project often results in a lack of knowledge of the project by responsible persons like the Project Manager.
Project Roles	Human factors are not within the scope of the methodology
Not systematic knowledge reuse	Lessons learned are recorded but they are not exploited in future projects in a systematic manner
Goal / Milestone breakdown structure	The project is structured in a bottom-up manner, not in a top-down one
Not covering the original need, solution generating and feasibility studies	It takes the view that the go ahead has been agreed and that the project now needs organising and controlling
PMI	
Planning is an ongoing effort throughout the project	It does not cover the necessity of continuous project planning update
Not so effective to provide guidance for running a specific project	It is a descriptive approach not guiding the practitioner on how to run a specific project.
Complex for small projects.	It is a generic methodology covering a large number of management aspects, some of them not essential for small projects
Has to be adapted to the government area	In order to be efficient, it has to be adapted to the government area, project size and scope, time and budget and quality constraints
Profession independent management aspects	Covers those aspects of the project management process that are profession independent, it does not give specialised directions
Minimal coverage of various project management methodologies and techniques	It does not propose specialised methodologies and techniques

continued on following page

Table 2. continued

Title	Description
GDPM	
Not a full project management methodology	It does not cover the full project management spectrum, it is used to increase the project management effectiveness of other models or methodologies
Use of specific techniques	It demand usage of specific techniques in order to be applied
Not much support to solve complex scheduling problems	It does not provide extended support functions for complex scheduling problems

Tables 1 and 2 present the more important strengths and weaknesses of the 3 generic project management methodologies for the e-government domain (see also Wideman, 2002).

Software-Oriented Project Management Methodologies

Sequential Methodologies

Sequential methodologies are based on the waterfall model (Royce, 1987) which is a sequential software development model, in which development is seen as flowing steadily downwards through the phases of requirements analysis, design, implementation, testing, validation, integration, and maintenance.

Structured Systems Analysis and Design Methodology (SSADM) is a widely used computer application development method in the UK (Goodland at al, 1995). Like PRINCE, its use is often specified as a requirement for government computing projects. SSADM sets out the waterfall view of systems development, in which there are a series of steps, each of which leads to the next step. SSADM's steps include Feasibility Study, Requirements Analysis, Requirements Specification, Logical System Specification and Physical Design.

Systems Development Life Cycle (SDLC) is defined as a software development process, although it is also a distinct process independent of software or other information technology considerations. It is used by a systems analyst to develop an information system, including requirements, validation, training, and user ownership through investigation, analysis, design, implementation, and maintenance (Haag et al, 2003), (ISACA, 2003).

Iterative Methodologies

The Rational Unified Process (RUP) is a software development methodology where the software design process is described with high detail, hence being particularly applicable on larger software projects (Kruchten, 2003). It is a disciplined approach to assigning and managing tasks and responsibilities in a development organization. The goal of this process is to produce, within a predictable schedule and budget, high-quality software that meets the needs of its end users.

Rapid application development (RAD) is a software development process that involves iterative development, and the construction of prototypes (Martin, 1991). Traditionally the rapid application development approach involves compromises in usability, features, and/or execution speed while enabling quality products to be developed faster, saving valuable resources. RAD proposes that products can be developed faster and of higher quality by user involvement in the development prototyping and user testing of designs, or re-using software components (Kerr et al, 1993).

Dynamic Systems Development Method (DSDM) is a framework originally based upon RAD (Tuffs et al, 1999). DSDM utilizes continuous user involvement in an iterative development and incremental approach, which is responsive to changing requirements, to develop a software system that satisfies the business requirements on time and on budget. DSDM is one of a number of Agile methods for developing software and it forms a part of the Agile Alliance (Agile Alliance, 2008).

Tables 3 and 4 present the more important strengths and weaknesses of the software-oriented project management methodologies for the e-government domain.

Other Software-Specific Project Management Methodologies

Other methodologies that are used through software development and may provide partial solutions to e-business and e-government projects include:

- **Feature Driven Development (FDD),** a mixed iterative and incremental software development process focusing on management of features (characteristics or requirements) of software elements (Palmer et al, 2002).
- **Extreme Programming (XP),** a software engineering methodology targeting rapid development and quality through iterations (Beck, 1999).
- **Joint Application Development (JAD),** a popular fact-finding technique that brings users into the development process as active participants (Wood et al, 1995).

The IT Infrastructure Library (ITIL) is the most widely accepted approach to IT service management (ITIL, 2008). ITIL is a cohesive best practice framework, drawn from the public and private sectors internationally. It describes the organisation of IT resources to deliver business value, and documents processes, functions and roles in IT Service Management (ITSM).

Identifying the Gaps in Existing Project Management Methodologies

Conventional generic and software-specific project management techniques establish a solid foundation for e-business and e-government projects; yet from the specific nature of e-government transformation projects and the presented weaknesses, there are limitations and gaps that are identified and presented below:

Gap 1: Inability to Capture the Goal-Driven Nature of E-Government Projects

E-government projects are primarily goal-driven projects. Both government strategy at high level and e-government project objectives are drawn by all ranks public sector officials from employees to politicians. They apprehend the broad vision, or sometimes more specifically, they set the goals that they expect from government reorganisation or transformation projects. In such a way, their role and sometimes their knowledge does not allow them to perceive how the targeted goal should be achieved. It is the responsibility of project managers and project implementers to identify, design and implement the essential steps to achieve the final goal. It is here where we identify the first and likely the most important gap in generic project management methodologies, as they usually structure project implementation in a bottom-up manner, attempting to define the necessary activities and the analytic project plan prior to the final milestones. That approach could often lead to a very good plan to achieve the wrong objective. Our perception is that government transformation projects demand a top-down project management approach. The high level goal should be decomposed in its fundamental structural elements leaning on the one hand the responsibility of setting the goals to politicians and charging, on the other hand, the materialization responsibility to the implementers.

Gap 2: Inadequate Support of Knowledge Transfer

The nature of government transformation projects is manifold, composed of different elements. Many of the projects, if not all, include information systems development but technology factor is not the critical one. Such type of projects also includes other important dimensions, such as policy development, process reorganization or organizational change. Considering e-government projects complexity, the fact that they are relatively new type of projects and the substantial rate of e-government project failures the gap of knowledge transfer and reuse is identified in the applying methodologies. Looking through the existing project management and implementation methodologies we ascertain that even though in some cases best practices and lessons learned from already materialised government transformation projects are collected, they are not exploited systematically and adequately in order to methodologically re-use the gained knowledge. In e-government, effective gathering and reuse of lessons learned is critical to the long term success. e-government projects failure lead to public scrutiny and, more importantly, the loss of the taxpayer's money. Trust is a relationship, and like all relationships it must be nurtured carefully (Undheim, 2008).

Gap 3: Scarce Use of Patterns and Templates

Primarily because most of the methodologies are of generic use, specific project methodological patterns and deliverable templates are not proposed or supported. Thus, a deficit is detected concerning lack of piloting and reusability. Even though general directions are provided, existing methodologies do not provide structured patterns and much more they do not generate deliverable templates specialised in each category of government transformation projects.

Gap 4: Inadequacy in Capturing the Multidimensional Nature of Projects

During a government transformation project an organization is adopting new technology that is likely to trigger or require major organizational change. Markus argues that there is a significant difference between such projects and traditional IT-project management, as well as between such type of projects and traditional organizational change management (Markus, 2004). Traditional IT-project management has a technical focus but lacks adequate attention and tools for issues related to final goal and its sustainability; organizational change management has a strong people focus during a change, but has little to say about how IT alters the problem of organizational change (Markus et al, 2006). Government transformation projects nature is manifold, composed of different elements, much more complex, unpredictable and multidimensional demanding different approach than the singular one that tend to dominate in the traditional methodologies. Many of the projects, if not all, include information systems development but technology factor is not the critical one. Such type of projects also includes other important dimensions, such as policy development, process reorganization or organizational change. While implementing e-government projects, we need an integrated approach for managing organizational change in situations where IT is the main change driver.

Gap 5: Limited Support of Multiple Project Paths

Project management and implementation methodologies utilise the notion of stages or phases in order to divide methodologically a project. They also use a straightforward activity based project plan structure which does not depict the singularity of each project area. Because of the special character of the government transformation projects and the multiplicity of different factors involved in them, a gap is identified concerning the methodological structure of project planning. Grouping the essential constitutional steps which are of similar content is not covered adequately, except GDPM which is realised in some extent.

Gap 6: Poor Modelling of E-Government Stakeholders

Despite other projects, where the stakeholders are few and obvious, in governmental projects the stakeholders are numerous and sometimes they do not appear until the initiation of the project or even worse until their interests are being opposed. Common stakeholder groups in such type of projects may be citizens, enterprises, politicians, public administration managers, administrative civil servants, public sector IT staff, IT companies, business consultants, collaborating public organisations, financial institutions, etc. Consequently, a gap is identified during the precise and timely specification of the e-government project stakeholders. The intended beneficiaries of the project at various levels should clearly be identified and benefits that will accrue to each of the stakeholders should be concretized. It is only then that all the stakeholders can work harmoniously and collaboratively towards the ultimate goal (Bhatnagar, 2002).

Conscious that technological innovation cannot be analysed independently of organisational change (Markus et al, 1998), (Orlikowski, 1992) we have chosen to give priority to analytical perspectives that originate not only from the information systems field, but also from the organisational and human aspects of the project implementations. The aim of the e-government Transformation Project Management methodology is to provide a systematic, business-oriented way of implementing e-government projects involving the use of information and communication technology (ICT) to transform the way in which the public organisations deliver their services and relate to the society.

ADDING KNOWLEDGE TO TOOLS

eGTPM Methodology Features

Through reusing methodologies from the enterprise modelling domain and combining example project components (along the ideas of industry models, of the e-business area), eGTPM method provides a knowledge-rich environment for planning, organising and monitoring e-government projects—covering the identified gaps in the previous section, with the following key characteristics:

Feature 1: Top-Down, Goal-Driven Project Management Approach

eGTPM philosophy is based on the sound understanding of the final project target as well as to the precise decomposition of it in well-defined sub-goals. Decomposition of project plan into sub-goals (milestones) leads to the development of a rigorous component-based understanding of project implementation. The profound project apprehension will improve the quality of selection, implementation and continuous improvement of transformation projects, and will reduce project risks. Using the top-down approach and especially the project breakdown in milestones, the uncoupling between the targeted goals and the implementation procedure to achieve them is accomplished.

In parallel, following eGTPM, the expectations connection to one specific deadline date is avoided. If results have not been achieved by that date, there will likely be a sharp drop in motivation in the organisation. Alternatively, we recommend that intermediate results (milestones) be planned for delivery during the course of the project. In this way, a 'big day' crisis situation is defused.

Feature 2: Knowledge Reuse

Beforehand, it was detected that there is a lot of knowledge deriving from already materialised government transformation projects which remains unexploited inside project managers' minds or in project schedules, plans and reports. This accumulated knowledge varies from method steps, techniques and practices, up to systems, project deliverables and lessons learned.

Milestones, activities, deliverable templates, roles, responsibilities and other reusable items, from the already implemented e-government projects, are stored in a repository and they are available for reuse in order to build a new government transformation project. This repository could serve as the backbone of knowledge management in e-government transformation projects, making experience and best practices available for future e-government projects.

Feature 3: Patterns and Templates Exploitation

Depending on the particular type of government transformation project (National Gateway, Regional Portal, Back Office systems interconnection, e-government framework implementation etc.), eGTPM embodies the use of properly structured patterns that could provide the bedrock on which a new government project can be planned. Advancing a step more, eGTPM provides a selection of parameterized deliverable templates which are produced based on the common context and content of each deliverable. On a more practical manner, eGTPM allows different systems and projects to be exposed into the common melting pot, permitting mutually learning and easier exchange of best practice. eGTPM serves as the common language in the international e-government project implementation arena, to enable easy start-up when several parties are involved and to decrease the risk of mis-communication between these parties familiar with different project management terminology and content.

Feature 4: Project Result Paths

There is often a tendency in the specifications of e-government projects to overemphasize the technical aspects and ignore the people and organisational aspects. Most times it is easier to imagine the concrete, technical tasks rather than the abstract, organizational and human ones. People, Systems, Organization and Knowledge (PSO-K) is an important concept, part of it adapted from Goal Directed Project Management, as depicted in Figure 1. It refers to the principle that the e-government project implementations not only influence the technical aspect (Systems) but also changes in the area of People and Organization.

Figure 1. The PSO-K nature of government transformation projects

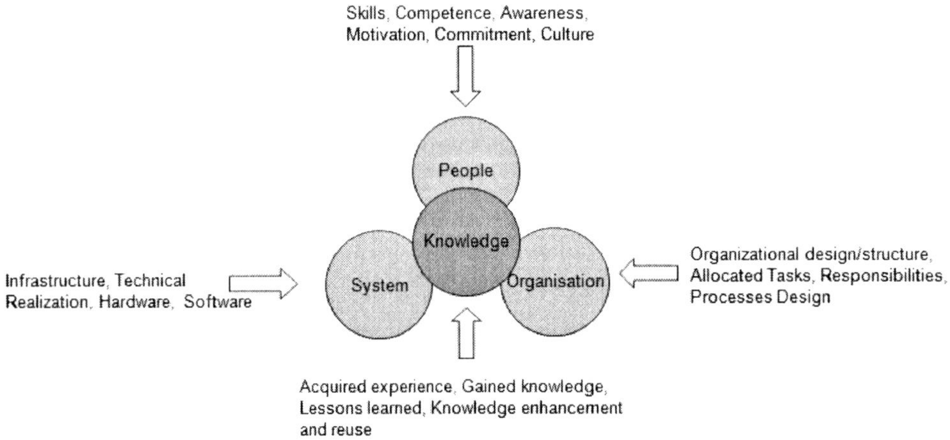

eGTPM adds another area, Knowledge management, to the essential components of structuring e-government projects. Knowledge management is a collaborative, integrated strategy and implementation approach for effective creation, capture, organization, access, use, and reuse of all organisation knowledge assets. Knowledge management component organizes and makes information available electronically in a way that is useful for decision makers, project implementers and project managers.

Feature 5: Complete Coverage of Stakeholders

Stakeholder management is a significant issue in government projects and bespeaks subtle treatment. Initially, eGTPM ensures that all the project stakeholders are identified, by providing a pre-defined set of most common stakeholders in e-government projects. The methodology advantage is not detected only in the definition of the stakeholders, but much more by specifying the expected role and responsibility of each role in each specific activity or deliverable, in order to ensure each participant's commitment to the project.

eGTPM Concepts

Having identified the existing gaps concerning project management in e-government projects and having defined the key features of eGTPM, in this section the main methodological concepts are defined. eGTPM provides a sound basis for project management in e-government area, being a results-oriented approach to project management and offering a radical departure from the more traditional project management methodologies, focusing on what must be achieved, the goals, rather than on trying to predict timescales and resources for activities. eGTPM (Figure 2) is the methodology to manage the life cycle of an e-government Transformation Project based on the principles of Dynamic Enterprise Modeling (DEM).

Concept 1: Milestone (Sub-Goal)

Successful project management of government transformation projects require bringing the disparate organizations, business processes, technologies, agendas, cultures and people together to create a harmonious and workable solution.

Figure 2. eGTPM methodology overview

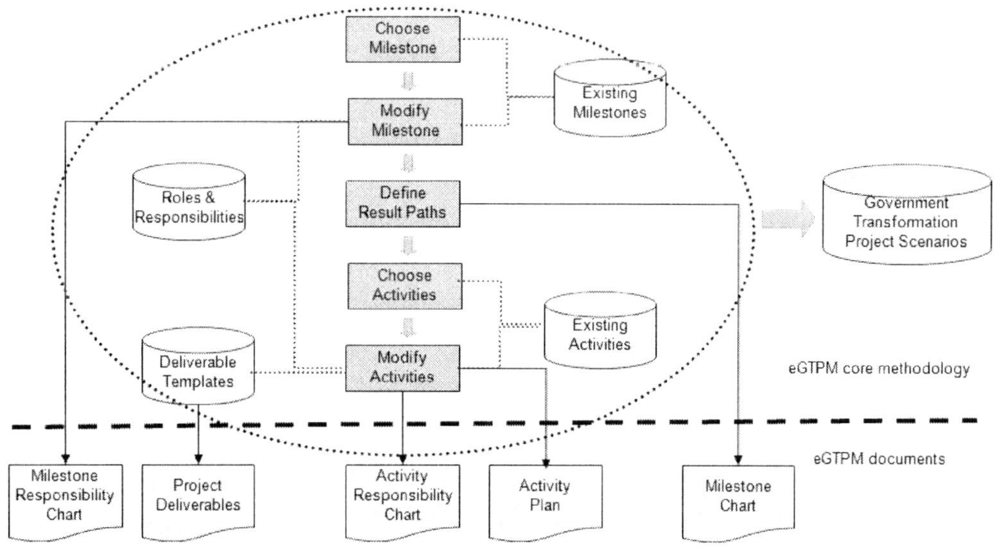

And this solution is not known in advance—the effort of going on the 'ride' is as important to the outcome as the original intent. Also government transformation projects are identified as component type projects. They usually are not one-piece projects, but they are clearly formulated objectives, divided into milestones (sub-goals). Imprecise or even incorrect goals will have harmful effects on the e-government project and sometimes people are lured to the 'fast track'. This implies that to implement the project first should be decided and then achieve the partial milestones of it. In traditional planning, milestones represent the completion of activity, not the accomplishment of a result. The focus is on "doing things" rather than on achieving real results. In eGTPM the milestone is defined as a practical and tangible step within the project described as a state, which must be reached to meet the final objective.

Concept 2: Knowledge Management Enabled by eGTPM

Existing best practices and already successfully implemented e-government projects could pave the way for approaches that can exploit model driven design and provide domain specific ways of implementing safe and challenging goals. An attractive alternative for building the project plan from scratch is the selection of an appropriate pre-configured project plan using an eGTPM e-government project scenario. Government transformation project scenarios are stored in the Scenario Repository. The project scenarios are fully compliant with the latest concepts and the terminology used in eGTPM framework. The selected project scenario serves as a basis for the public organisation specific project plan. Because every e-government project is unique, the project scenario allows removing or editing the initial scenario milestones. In the selected scenario we can also insert newly created milestones or additional milestones from the Milestone Repository.

Instead of selecting a generic e-government project scenario, the user can also select a previously customized project plan that has been created for a similar project. This previously plan can be modified and adopted as desired to serve as the basis for a new e-government project plan. In our experience the added value of the eGTPM will grow with the number of available customized e-government project plans.

Concept 3: Deliverable Templates

eGTPM exploits the fact that government transformation projects deliverables present a considerable number of common features. Based on this commonality, it proposes the generation, reuse, and customisation of deliverable templates form in the level of contents definition.

Concept 4: Project Planning

In eGTPM, by concentrating on the results, a plan is devised which is more flexible to the changes that will undoubtedly arise during the project. Furthermore, the project manager is able to build a management framework attuned to the unique demands of the specific project environment. The project team is able to describe technical goals such as system implementation, as well as objectives regarding personnel involvement and organizational restructure.

An e-government project usually addresses several needs or purposes in an organisation; it usually has a composite goal and the plan is therefore multi-dimensional. This means that several aspects of the project are worked in simultaneously. In order to bring out the multi-dimensional aspects of project work, we introduce the element of the result path. A result path is a series of milestones that are closely related to each other.

Result paths tell the readers of the plan what results the project aims to achieve, as shown in Figure 3. Goals for the project can be used as a

Figure 3. Milestone plan and result paths

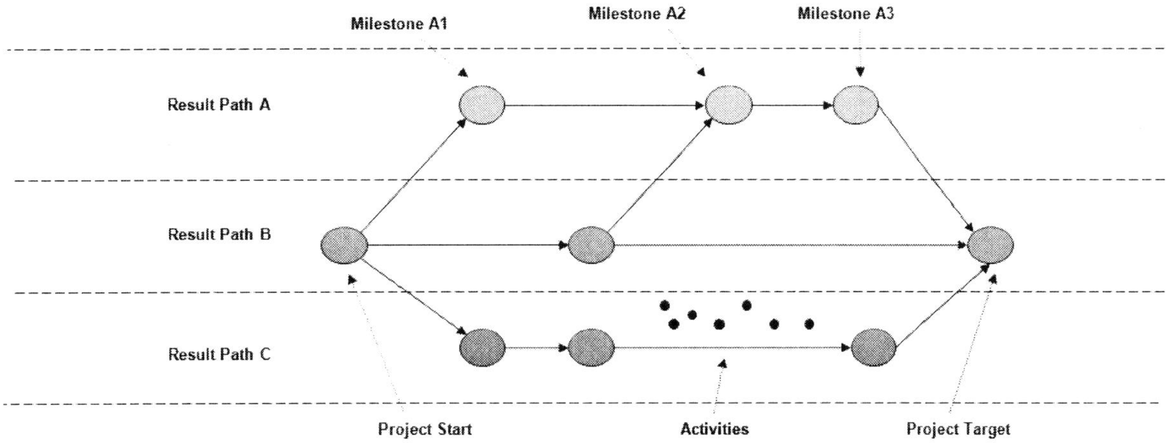

starting point to define result paths in the milestone plan. A goal expresses precisely what we want to achieve and the specific type of result. Therefore, goals are suitable as the basis for dividing the plan into result paths. These paths are the columns in a milestone plan. The placement of milestones along the result paths demonstrates the principle that changes must be met in a balanced way.

Concept 5: Stakeholder Analysis and Responsibility Planning

eGTPM identifies the project stakeholders which are affected positively or negatively from the results. During the stakeholder analysis their areas of interest, the kinds of contributions to the project, the expectations of the stakeholder, the power of the stakeholder and the appropriate strategy to work with the stakeholder are identified in the stakeholder table. In this way the project support is increased and the appropriate informative channels are discovered.

eGTPM Planning Levels

eGTPM consists of two levels: the control level and the operational level. Each of these is discussed in the following sections.

Control Level (Milestone Plan)

The planning at this level is concerned with what is to be accomplished and not how the work will be done. In other words, this level is goal oriented. In e-government project work, it is quite impractical to operate solely with final goals. It is necessary to have certain checkpoints along the way. We call these checkpoints milestones. It should be easy to ascertain whether or not a milestone has been reached. It is not always easy to formulate milestones in this way. But the easier it is to decide whether a milestone has been reached, the easier it becomes to control an e-government project. It is even better if the milestones also provide the organisation and the managers with useful results. The milestone then becomes both a checkpoint and a deliverable. We obtain what is called evolutionary development, a gradual fulfilment of project goals. The e-government project does not wait until the last milestone to deliver all the results, but rather it plans to deliver results in instalments.

A milestone is a description of a state the project should be in at a certain stage. As much as possible, a milestone should be neutrally stated in regard to ways of obtaining it. It is important for a milestone to be described in such a way that it is possible to ascertain that the desired state has been reached. This is the crux of this method of project management. It is impossible to have goal directed project management if it is not possible to check that an actual state has been reached. Project planning at control level includes the following steps:

1. The milestones or intermediate objectives are defined in terms of time, costs and quality.
2. The responsibilities for attaining the milestones are defined.
3. The (decision making) authorizations, escalation procedures and the project communication and reporting structure are described.
4. The milestones are described as situations or stages to be achieved during the project.

Milestones specify what is to be achieved, not how it is to be achieved. Once defined in this way, they are less susceptible to change throughout the e-government project. Fixed points of departure at project and milestone level are the contract between the public organisation and the project staff. This leads to predictable results, clear-cut responsibilities and prevents the principal from being submerged in details and losing sight of the overall process.

Operational Level (Activities Plan)

Project planning at operational level includes the following steps:

1. A definition is given of how (through which activities) the milestone can be attained.
2. The employees are assigned by name to each activity and the resources are defined.
3. The role and responsibility of each employee are defined.
4. The amount of work to be performed by each employee is estimated for each activity.
5. The critical path and the lead time are determined in detail. The end date in the project schedule is the desired date for the milestone.

As the activity description is developed, the employees are involved in estimating the efforts and determining the start and end dates. The activities are described in such a way as to allow for straightforward and immediate assessment of the project's progress in time. This not only commits the project manager to making the target or milestone date, but also challenges the project staff to do so.
The relation between the various eGTPM key elements is depicted in Figure 4.

eGTPM Tool Support

The proposed tool allows for easy project configuration and the use of best practice implementation scenarios when defining milestones, activities and responsibilities. In addition to similar implementation methodologies, methods and tool sets, eGTPM Tool focuses on speed as well as on the flexibility and scalability of solutions and their corresponding implementation. As shown in Figure 5, the eGTPM Tool enables easy and flexible configuration of an e-government specific project plan and its deliverables. eGTPM Tool has the following objectives:

- Efficient preparation of comprehensive and consistent e-government project documentation (milestone chart, milestone list, responsibility chart, project schedule)
- Provide e-government project configuration based on data gained through experience
- Enable Knowledge Management (by using one central place for archiving historical project data)

The basic building blocks of project plans according to eGTPM are the milestones. With the eGTPM the user can create his own specific milestones for the project plan. He can also make

Figure 4. Key elements of eGTPM

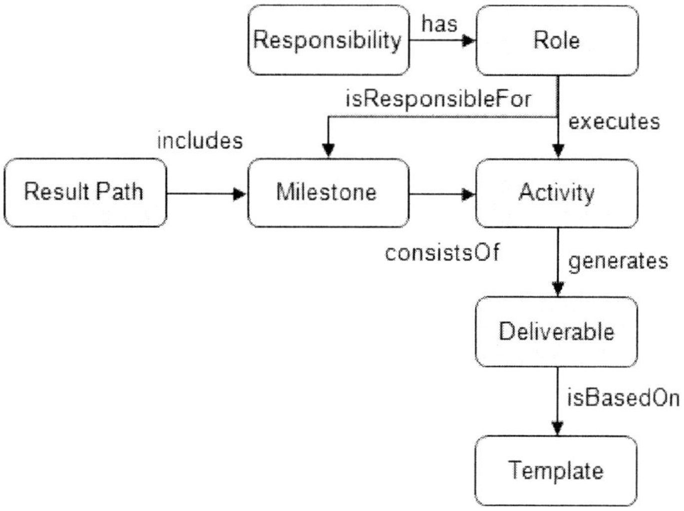

use of a large number of existing milestones for the plan. These generic milestones are stored in a Milestone Repository where he has the option of customizing the information first by editing part of the generic milestone information. The project plans that are configured with the eGTPM tool can be transferred automatically to Microsoft Office and deliver the following documents:

- Project Schedule (MS Project document) which lists the stages, milestones and supporting project activities. This becomes the starting point for detailed project scheduling
- Milestone Chart (MS Excel document) which serves as a summary chart for reporting purposes
- Responsibility Chart (MS Excel document) which depicts the basic project responsibilities at the Milestone level for different roles (i.e. contractor and public organisation)
- Milestone List (MS Word document) which describes all the milestone details for the generated plan

The tool provides the user the possibility to select a milestone from the repository and change its information (Figure 6).

eGTPM Tool user can customize almost all information. The eGTPM responsibility codes are displayed automatically once the user has positioned his pointer in the referring fields. Information inserted in the field "Comments" serves only as background information, and is only displayed in this window. This could be used as documentation by the person who created this milestone, or a warning for the usage of this milestone. Note the tab 'More', giving access to additional milestone information. Under 'More' the deliverables, completion criteria, services and additional information can be viewed. Unlike the comments in the previous screen, the additional information will be printed in the milestone list. All of these fields can be customized, if required. The user has also the option of selecting 'New', indicating that he wants to create a new milestone. If the user chooses to modify the default activities for the milestone, he should select 'Modify Activities' in the window milestone information (Figure 7).
The user has also the option of selecting 'New', indicating that he wants to create a new activity or edit if he likes to modify an activity.
After the creation and the modification of the milestone information the checkboxes indicate that the

Figure 5. Milestone and scenario eGTPM tool repository

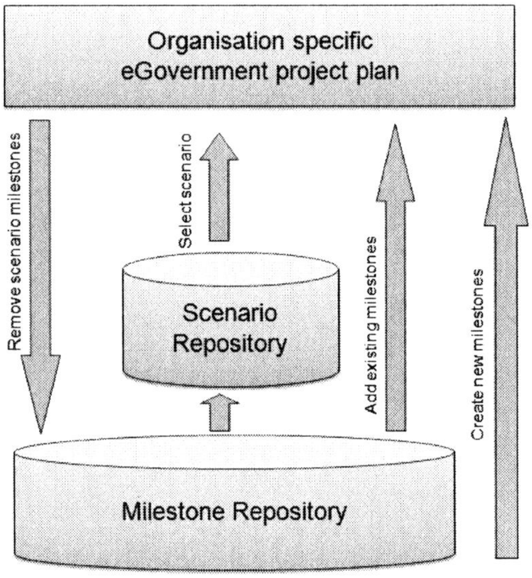

Figure 6. Milestone details

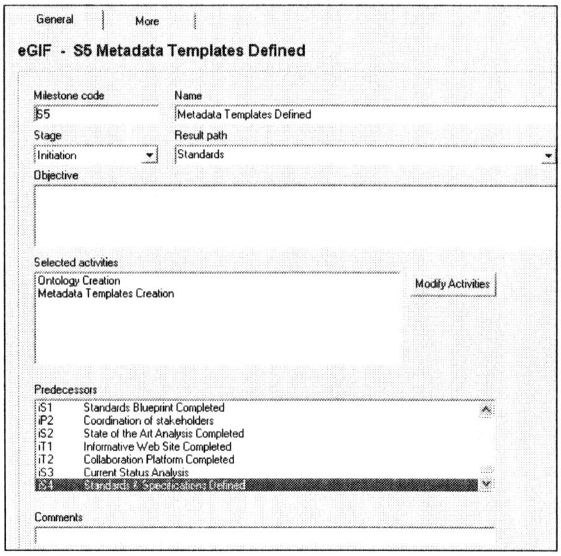

user can proceed to the third step of deliverables generation (Milestone Chart, Responsibility Chart, Project Schedule, Milestone List) further analysed in the following section.

APPLICATION IN E-GOVERNMENT PROJECTS

Project Scope

In the case of the Greek Public Administration, e-government evolution is currently addressed through a large number of ongoing projects (Central Governmental Portal, Central Local Administration Portal, National Network Infrastructure and numerous front-office Information Systems to provide electronic services) that demand a high degree of interoperability with legacy systems (Table 3). In this context, the Greek eGIF comes to facilitate the Greek Public Administration to adapt to the Digital era, ensure deployment of joined-up information systems and delivery of high quality services to the citizens and businesses and contribute to the resolution of the interoperability problem.

The existing applying implementation procedure in Greek government transformation projects is based on the bottom-up approach. Most of the projects are organised attempting to define the necessary activities and the analytic project plan prior to the final milestones. As a result most of them delay having exceeded the pre-defined

Figure 7. Activities selection

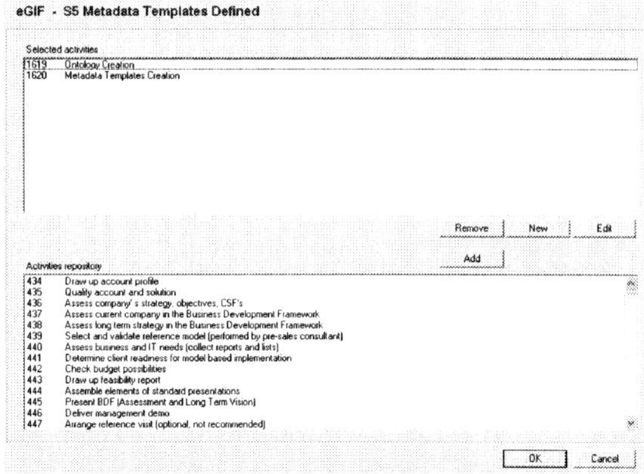

Table 3. The size of the interoperability problem in Greece

Organisational Aspect	Systems Aspect	Non-Governmental Stakeholders Aspect
20 ministries, 13 prefectures, 52 districts, 1,000 municipalities	200 Governmental Internet Portals	1,000 IT products and services companies
1,000 Governmental "Points of Service"	1,000 Municipal Internet Portals	750,000 Enterprises, SMEs and VSEs
> 3,000 non-interoperable Service Types (Government to Citizens and Businesses)	2,500 Public Administration Back Office Systems	11,000,000 Citizens
		18,000,000 Tourists per year
> 4,500 Document Types exchanged between Administrations		> 20,000,000 service requests per year (mostly non-electronic)

budget. On the top of that they do not cover the full spectrum of the stakeholders' expectations leading to incomplete results or projects that cope with sustainability issues.

Project Structure According to eGTPM

The milestones (sub-goals) with their corresponding descriptions have been selected to structure the Electronic Government Interoperability Framework milestone list. The milestones (Table 4) that have been chosen aim to cover all aspects of eGIF project. They reflect what we wish to focus on in the project. In practice we must, often, weed out some milestones to obtain an easily comprehensible plan.

Milestone List

iP1: Project File Defined
A file containing the overall plans of a project and any other important documents is defined. It includes a record of project data/documents in scheduled time basis.

iS1: Standards Blueprint Completed
A blueprint with the contents that will be included in the Standards document is predesigned. After discussions, the stakeholders conclude in a mutual agreement concerning the framework that will be followed during the Standards document implementation.

iP2: Coordination of Stakeholders
Interests Service, Improvement of the communication and coordination among project stakeholders is targeted. It articulates and formalizes the roles and responsibilities of each stakeholder improving the project effectiveness and efficiency. Benefits for each stakeholder are ensured.

iS2: State of the Art Analysis Completed
Remarkable eGIFs, other relative initiatives and projects are carefully selected, and their usefulness is evaluated. State of the art analysis of relevant frameworks at a pan-European and national level is conducted, lessons are learned and presented.

iT1. Informative Web Site Completed
A comprehensive on-line project presentation website is developed and linked to all partners' websites. It will serve as the reference point for people interested in the project itself, but will also contain reference material on all covered related fields, subscription functionalities for participation in public project events, various contact options to the project management as well as selected experts, etc. A "Partners Area" will be developed to facilitate shared editing and shared document management.

iT2: Collaboration Platform Completed
Establishment of a permanent collaboration platform, which will include all the essential tools for the project implementation and it will serve as a cross project collaboration tool for knowledge, experience and best practice sharing, as well as results consolidation and dissemination support.

iS3: Current Status Analysis
Analysis of the existing implementations for each standard, technology or methodology identified.

A review of current developing country e-government projects is implemented. Picture of the existing situation is derived.

iS4: Standards & Specifications Defined
Issues concerning the standards and specifications effectiveness, efficiency, openness, usefulness and applicability are examined and evaluated. The set of standards and specifications for achieving interoperability and information systems coherence across the public sector are defined.

iS5: Metadata Templates Defined
The essential e-government entities are defined and the exact metadata fields of them are identified. The mechanism and the templates to collect all the relevant to public services, documents, systems and organisations metadata is defined.

iS6: Services Modeling Completion
All relevant details regarding the service execution are extracted and depicted in process diagrams with the help of enterprise modeling tools. The essential service data and metadata are collected and they are exploited using the relative tools.

iS7: Documents Modeling Completion
All relevant details regarding the documents structure are extracted and depicted in data schemas with the help of data modeling tools. The essential document data and metadata are collected and they are exploited using the relative tools.

iD1: Training Completed
The training material is designed, produced and the training courses take place. Training specification and material planning is taking place according to customer needs and directions.

iP3: eGIF Version Completed
The essential steps take place in order to complete a full eGIF version cycle. This milestone is an iterative one and takes place according to the contractual agreement.

iD2: Dissemination Completed
Dissemination material is produced and dissemination activities take place. Dissemination specification and the relative material planning is taking place according to customer needs and directions.

Table 4. Project milestones (sub-goals)

Code	Title
iP1	Project File Defined
iS1	Standards Blueprint Completed
iP2	Coordination of stakeholders
iS2	State of the Art Analysis Completed
iT1	Informative Web Site Completed
iT2	Collaboration Platform Completed
iS3	Current Status Analysis
iS4	Standards & Specifications Defined
iS5	Metadata Templates Defined
iS6	Services Modeling Completion
iS7	Documents Modeling Completion
iD1	Training Completed
iP3	eGIF Version Completed
iD2	Dissemination Completed
iP4	Project Closure
iP1	Project File Defined
iS1	Standards Blueprint Completed
iP2	Coordination of stakeholders

iP4: Project Closure

The typical and substantial project termination is taking place. All the contractual commitments are met.

Milestone Plan

The milestone plan (Figure 8) is the project's global plan. The development of the eGIF milestone plan has been performed at the start of the project. The purpose was for all core project members and stakeholders to acquire a common understanding of the goals and how the project shall progress. This was essential to gain commitment from them. Moreover, project participants agree on which milestones are specifically critical to the project so that everyone understands the severe consequences if these milestones are not reached in time or are realised with poor quality.

Figure 8. Milestone Plan (automatically generated by eGTPM tool)

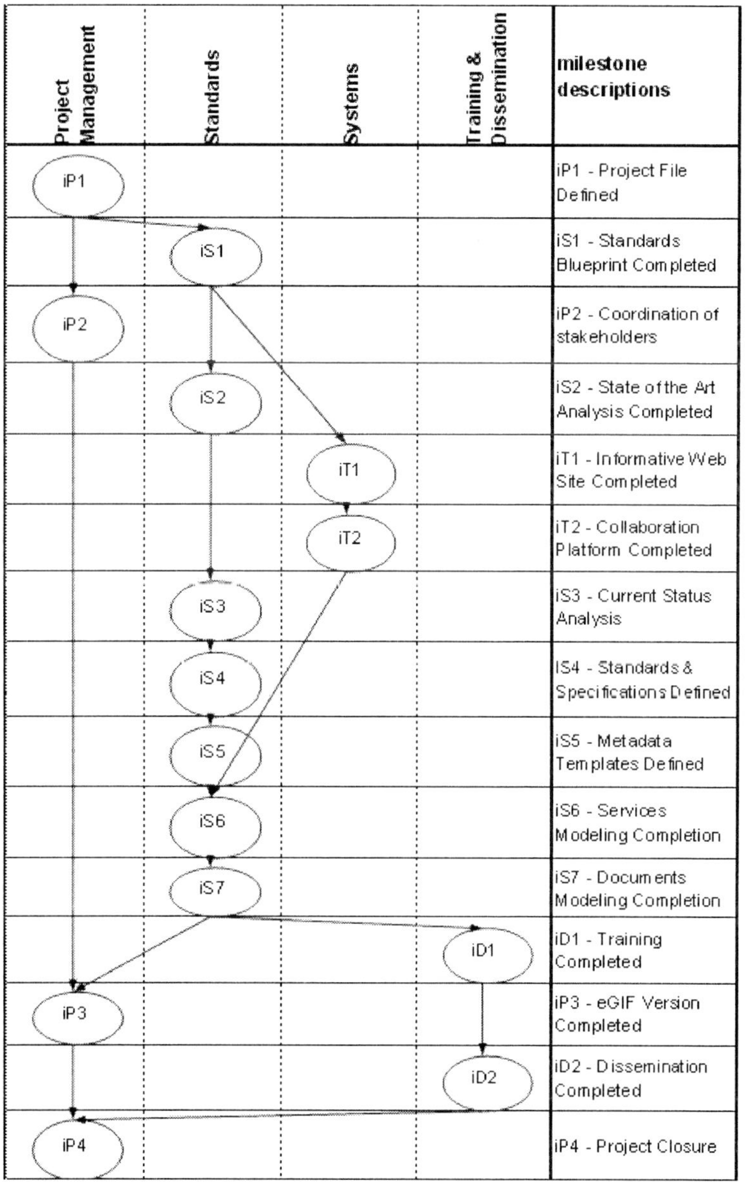

Table 5. Activity plan (extract)

Milestone Code	Milestone Title	Activity	Deliverable
iP1	Project File Defined	Project Initiation & Kick off meeting	Project Plan & Monthly Report
iS1	Standards Blueprint Completed	Stakeholders meeting	Standards Blueprint contents definition
		Standards Blueprint definition	Standards Blueprint
iP2	Coordination of stakeholders	Definition/selection of the highest priority "core organisations"	Regular Meetings & Meeting proceedings
		Definition/selection of the relative project contractors/IT companies	
		Public Organisations Working groups formation	
		External Working groups formation	
iS2	State of the Art Analysis Completed	Definition of Assessment Criteria	Assessment Methodology
		Survey of existing State of the Arts	Best Practices
		Selection of the appropriate relative frameworks(national-international) to assess them	
		Relative frameworks consideration	
		Results Consolidation & Conclusions	

Activities and Deliverables

The milestones are composed from activities that are presented using the relative activity plans. Activity planning is the drawing up of a detail plan to achieve the milestones of the milestone plan. It is through activity planning that we determine how to reach the milestones within the time limits and with the resources allocated. the activity plan includes all the project milestone information, as shown in Table 5.

Responsibility Chart and Project Schedule

A major part of project planning is performed with the help of the responsibility chart (Figure 9). The milestone responsibility chart clarifies the role of the different participants necessary to achieve the milestones. eGTPM provides a predefined pool of responsibilities (Figure 9) which can be extended-modified by the user. In order to complete the responsibility chart the following roles have been identified in the eGIF project: Management, Project Manager, Steering Committee, Working Group, Key Users, End Users, External Expert, IT Support, Service & Data Analyst, Service & Data Modeller, Security Expert, Business Consultant, Model Consultant, Application Consultant, Technical Consultant, Analyst / Programmer.

Exploiting the project data (Milestones, Activities) significant value is added to project planning producing the project schedule (Figure 10). Use of milestones allows project management to much more accurately determine whether or not the project is on schedule. By constraining the dates

Figure 9. Responsibility chart (automatically generated by the eGTPM Tool)

Responsibility Chart

Responsibility

- D - takes (final) Decision
- d - takes decision with consultation
- P - manage Progress
- T - provides Training
- C - must be Consulted
- I - must be Informed
- A - available to Advice
- X - eXecutes the work

Milestones	Management	Project Manager	Steering Committee	Working Group	Key Users	End Users	External Expert	IT Support	Service & Data Analyst	Service & Data Modeler	Security Expert	Business Consultant	Model Consultant	Application Consultant	Technical Consultant	Analyst / Programmer
iP1 Project File Defined	A	D/P	C						X	X		X	X			
iS1 Standards Blueprint Completed		D/P	A		C	C	A		X	X		X	X			
iP2 Coordination of stakeholders		D/P														
iS2 State of the Art Analysis Completed		P	A	A					X	X	A	D	X	X	X	
iT1 Informative Web Site Completed		P			D	d		X	A	A		A	A			X
iT2 Collaboration Platform Completed		P			D	d		X/T	A	A		A	A			X/T
iS3 Current Status Analysis		P		C	A	A			X	X	A	D	X		X	
iS4 Standards & Specifications Defined		P	A				A	X	X	X	X	D	C	C	C	C
iS5 Metadata Templates Defined		P			C	C	A		X	X		d	D			
iS6 Services Modeling Completion		P		C			A		X	X		d	D			X
iS7 Documents Modeling Completion		P		C			A		X	X		d	D			X
iD1 Training Completed		D/P	C		A	A		A	X	X		d	d	X	X	A
iP3 eGIF Version Completed		P	D	X	X	X	A		X	X	A	d	d			
iD2 Dissemination Completed	A	P/D	d	X	X				d	d		X	X	X	X	A
iP4 Project Closure		P/D	d						X	X		X	X			

Figure 10. Project GANTT Chart (automatically generated by the eGTPM Tool)

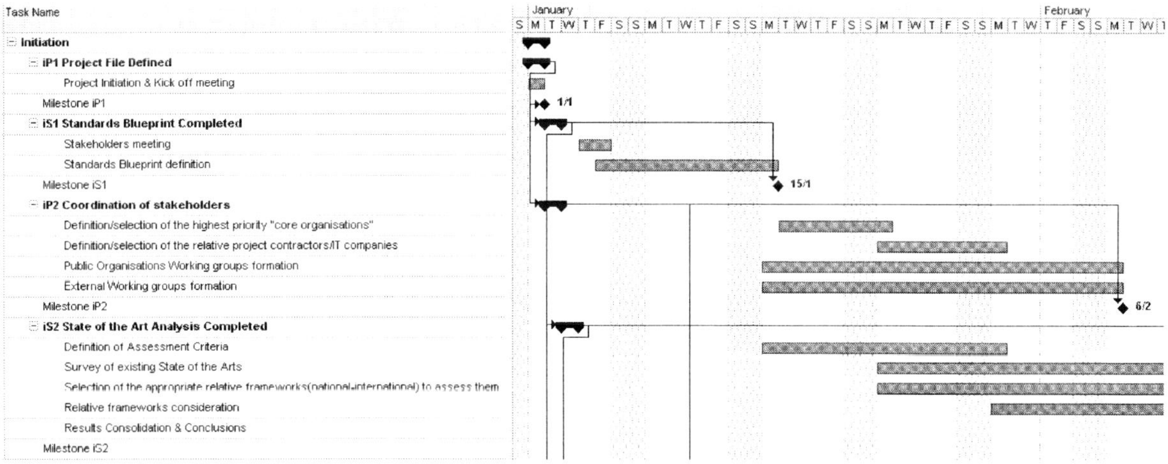

associated with milestones, the critical path can be determined for major schedule intervals in addition to the entire project. This segmentation of the project schedule into intervals allows earlier indication of schedule problems and a better view into the activities whose completion is critical to the project timeline.

eGTPM application on the specific project resulted to a project that have satisfactory covered the expectations of all the stakeholders (public administration, IT industry, government, citizens, enterprises etc.) involved in it. The goal oriented nature of the approach gave the opportunity of covering all the different aspects and issues that have arisen during the implementation in a timely and cost efficient manner. The project contractor and the contracting authority are now equipped with an amount of e-government project implementation knowledge which is easy exploitable in future projects.

CONCLUSION

Electronic government transformation projects, usually containing both ICT-related and overall Policy related goals, are posing new challenges for Project Management support, asking for the inclusion of previous knowledge as a resource that current methods and tools tend to pre-suppose. This is spotted especially when planning and controlling transformation projects at multiple levels of span, ranging from a specific Public Sector Organisation to Regional or National Planning Bodies. By basing on existing project management methods, new methods that utilise information and knowledge from common, scenario based templates are starting to appear.

E-Government-oriented and Knowledge-embodying approaches can provide substantial support in planning, organising and monitoring complex projects, especially when concerning e-government ICT Infrastructure, Policy Formulation, Standardisation or Technology Transfer. Initial applications in the Public Sector have shown that the level of guidance and reuse can ensure the positive contribution to project quality and implementation speed. Further development at tools and knowledge base population levels will certainly be important towards final adoption and effective use.

Our comparison of selected project management methodologies has provided insight into the extent to which research is reflected in guides to inform practice. The analysis highlighted the particular characteristics of the methodologies and provided a critical review of the extent to which these methodologies reflect current research. The results derived from the analysis of gaps between existing methodologies and the specific needs of e-government projects have been exploited in order to produce eGTPM methodology.

eGTPM methodology presented in this paper introduces a tool supported methodology (not just a paper-based proposal) that aims to constructively complement traditional methodologies on successfully managing government transformation projects. To this end, it attempts to cover a number of key issues concerning project management of such type of projects, such as:

- Projects goal driven nature
- Exploiting knowledge transfer
- Use of specific patterns-templates
- Multidimensional project type
- Project result paths
- Sea of stakeholders

The proposed methodology aims to support practitioners, project managers and public organisations officials at various levels towards implementing government transformation projects. Standardization is provided at the higher level for analysis of e-government projects and at the lower level for details, time is saved in setting up a schedule by building on predefined scenarios, a common language and a common base of knowledge is built through the use of knowledge repository and lessons learned from previous projects are used to improve patterns and the templates. Initial methodology showed better management of the strategic aspects of e-government projects, better management and change of project structure, as well as easier development of standardised deliverables, through the use of the predefined templates.

eGTPM methodology, after its application in a number of e-government projects, has been already populated with data, amounting to 40 milestones, more than 100 activities, 50 deliverable templates and more than 20 individual roles—thus being able to assist the structuring of a number of key e-government projects, like Interoperability Framework Development, Service Portal Creation, e-government Survey development and so on.

Reusable artefacts of the presented approach include the overall eGTPM framework and concepts, the developed milestones and activities, the developed document templates and the identified roles. Using the concept of the Scenario Repository opens very interesting opportunities for consulting public organizations and practices that are committed to Knowledge Management. These consulting organizations can build and distribute their own repository with project scenarios, depicting the common approach of that organization and including their best practice experiences.

Project implementers and practitioners applying eGTPM methodology should take into account the conditions, the technological level, the political antecedences and strategic objectives concerning e-government that prevail in each country.

Future work along the methodology includes continuation with data population, eGTPM tool refinement, further research on the existing distinct gaps and coverage of issues that have not yet been encountered such as budget management, quality management and risk assessment—currently covered through generic methods. Finally, another future goal is to communicate eGTPM methodology to practitioners through the introduction of a practical guide. The guide will provide direction to practitioners as they consider, make a case for, and implement government transformation initiatives.

REFERENCES

Agile Alliance. (2008). Retrieved on September 15, 2008, from http://www.agilealliance.org

Allen, B. A., Juillet, L., Paquet, G., & Roy, G. (2001). E-Governance & government on-line in Canada: Partnerships, people, & prospects. *Government Information Quarterly, 18,* 93-104.

Andersen, E. A., Grude, K. V., & Hague, T. (2004). *Goal directed project management.* Kogan Page.

Avison, D., & Fitzgerald, G. (2008). *Information systems development.* McGraw-Hill.

Beck, K. (1999). *Extreme programming explained: Embrace change.* Addison Wesley.

Bhatnagar, S. (2002). E-Government: Lessons from implementation in developing countries. *Regional Development Dialogue, 24.*

Cohen, S., & Eimicke, W. (2003). *The future of e-government: A project of potential trends and issues.* In *Proceedings of the 36th Hawaii International Conference on System Sciences.* IEEE Computer Society.

Dawes, S. S., & Pardo, T. (2002). Building collaborative digital government systems. In W. J. McIver, & A. K. Elmagarmid (Eds.), *Advances in digital government. Technology, human factors, and policy.* Norwell, MA: Kluwer Academic Publishers.

Gil-García, J. R., & Pardo, T. (2005). E-Government success factors: Mapping practical tools to theoretical foundations. *Government Information Quarterly, 22*(2), 187-216.

Goodland, M., & Slater, C. (1995). *SSADM version 4.* McGraw-Hill Publishing Co.

Gupta, M., Kumar, P., & Bhattacharya, J. (2004). *Government online opportunities and challenges.* Tata McGraw-Hill Publishing Company Limited.

Haag, S., Cummings, M., & McCubbrey, D. (2003). *Management information systems for the information age.* McGraw-Hill Companies.

Heeks, R. (2003a). *Most eGovernment- for-Development Projects Fail: How Can Risks be Reduced?.* iGovernment Working Paper Series, IDPM. University of Manchester, UK.

Heeks, R. (2003b). *Causes of e-government success and failure: Factor model.* Institute for Development Policy and Management. University of Manchester, UK.

Heeks, R. (2003c). *eGovernment for Development, The Impact of eGovernment Failure.* University of Manchester, UK: Institute for Development Policy and Management.

Information Systems Audit and Control Association (ISACA). (2003). *System development life cycle (SDLC) review document G23.* USA.

ITIL Website. (2008). http://www.itil-officialsite.com

Kerr, J., & Hunter, R. (1993). *Inside RAD: How to build fully functional computer systems in 90 days or less.* McGraw-Hill.

Kruchten, P. (2003). *The rational unified process: An introduction (3rd edition).* Addison-Wesley Professional Management Institute.

Markus, L., & Robey, D. (1988). Information technology and organizational change: Causal structure in theory and research. *Management Science, 34.*

Markus, L. (2004). Technochange management: Using IT to drive organizational change. *Journal of information Technology 19*(1), 4-20.

Markus, L., & Bashein, R. (2006). *Interorganizational tecnochange: How to make successful choices in electronic partner integration.* Society for Information Management, Advanced Practices Council.

Martin, J. (1991). *Rapid application development.* Macmillan Coll Div.

NCC. (2005). *PRINCE2 manual (managing successful projects with PRINCE2).*

Organization for Economic Cooperation and Development, OECD. (2001). *The hidden threat to e-government: Avoiding large government IT failures.*

Organization for Economic Cooperation and Development, OECD. (2003). *The e-government imperative.*

Orlikowski, W. (1992). The duality of technology: Rethinking the concept of technology in organizations. *Organization Science.*

Palmer, S. R., & Felsing, J. M. (2002). *A practical guide to feature-driven development.* Prentice Hall.

Project Management Institute, PMI. (2001). *The PMI project management fact book.*

Project Management Institute, PMI. (2006). *Government extension to the PMBOK guide, third edition.*

Royce, W. (1987). Managing the development of large software systems: concepts and techniques. Proceedings of the 9th international conference on Software Engineering. IEEE Computer Society Press.

Schware, R. (2004). *Seminar on e-governance: From successful pilot to sustainable implementation.* The World Bank Group, Global Information and Communication Technologies Department.

Tuffs, D., Stapleton, J., West, D., & Eason, J. (1999). Interoperability of DSDM with the rational unified process. *DSDM Consortium*, 1.

Undheim, T. (2008). Best practices in e-government: On a knife-edge between success and failure. *European Journal of E-Practice.*

US Government, General Services Administration. (2003). *Federal e-government initiatives: Are we headed in the right direction?* Washington, DC.

Wideman, R. (2002). *Comparing PRINCE2 with PMBoK.* Vancouver, Canada: AEW Services.

Wood, J., & Silver, D. (1995). *Joint application development.* John Wiley & Sons Inc.

KEY TERMS

eGIF: E-Government interoperability framework.

E-Government Transformation: The process of implementing e-government projects while transforming the way services are provided, organisational structures, systems and documents.

eGTPM: E-Government transformation project management.

eGTPM Tool: A software tool for automatically generating eGTPM project planning deliverables.

Goal-Directed Project Management: A project management methodology focusing on structuring projects around goals.

Milestone Chart: The chart illustrating the key milestones of a project, their inter-relations and their relations with result paths.

Responsibility Chart: The chart illustrating project roles and their responsibilities per activity of the project.

Result Paths: The project axes that combine several relative milestones (e.g. technology, people, knowledge).

Chapter XIII
Interorganizational Communications in Disaster Management

Jing Yang
Oklahoma State University, USA

JinKyu Lee
Oklahoma State University, USA

Ashwin Rao
Cornell University, USA

Nasrat Touqan
Oklahoma State University, USA

ABSTRACT

In response to the lessons and criticisms over the recent large-scale disasters and relief activities during the disasters, many government organizations around the world have recently launched initiatives to improve their disaster management capabilities. While a revision of disaster management capability may entail transformation of organizational structures, business processes, and technical infrastructure across multiple organizations, the field of disaster management suffers from lack of theoretical foundation. With a special emphasis on information and communication technologies (ICTs), the chapter provides a review on various issues examined in the recent disaster management literature and develops a conceptual framework of the relationships between technological properties of ICTs and multiagency collaboration in disaster management. This chapter contributes to the theoretical foundation of the field by identifying major research issues in the disaster management communications and their relationships with relevant entities and environmental factors. Discussions on future research directions are also presented.

INTRODUCTION

A large number of government agencies around the world have recently launched initiatives to improve their disaster management capabilities, in response to the lessons and criticisms over the recent large-scale disasters and relief activities during those disasters. One of the most pressing issues for the initiatives is inter-organizational communication and coordination. During the 9/11 terrorist attacks[1] (2001), the police and fire departments could not communicate with each other over the radio, and thus could not coordinate their rescue efforts in a collaborative manner. In response to Hurricane Katrina[2] (2005), New Mexico's governor offered troops to Louisiana State, but the actual dispatch was delayed by one week due to the lengthy paperwork process between the two states (Adams, 2005). Indeed, military rescue teams were not able to send helicopters into the disaster zone, in a timely manner, because the Federal Emergency Management Agency[3] (FEMA) did not have the authority to allow it. While the logistics were being worked out and permissions obtained, valuable time was wasted and many lives were lost (Adams, 2005). The lack of inter-organizational communication and holistic coordination resulted in a chaos in the emergency response and relief operations, in addition to the already devastating aftermath of the disaster. Many government organizations, whether they were actually involved in the response and relief operations or had observed the past disasters, have been trying to implement what they have learned from the very expensive lessons, especially in the area of inter-organizational communication and information sharing among disaster management organizations (DMOs).

An important lesson from past disaster management efforts is that although the response activities undertaken by official first responder agencies (e.g., police officers, fire fighters, emergency medical crews) are crucial, those activities constitute only part of the big picture. Equally significant is the manner in which those first responders interact with and obtain support from non-government relief organizations, such as the Red Cross, private companies in the telecom and building industries, and financial companies (Kapucu, 2006). In that sense, success of disaster management is dependent upon effective sharing and use of valid and timely information among a large number of stakeholders in the society, including government authorities, non-government organizations (NGOs), private sector organizations, and the public. 9/11 provided a chance, in a sense, to recognize the needs of the private sector industries in the US, and now Corporate America[4] is anticipated to communicate with their stakeholders more openly and more expediently than they would have done before 9/11 (Wright, 2002). Unfortunately, the response to Hurricane Katrina revealed that, 3 years after 9/11, DMOs were still ill-equipped with information and communication technologies (ICTs) that should have effectively supported various DMOs in times of crisis, as well as in day-to-day emergency response operations that required coordination between several different public safety agencies (Weiser, 2007).

Disaster management researchers have been working on ways to prepare for future disasters, natural or man-made. Many case studies that compare various ICTs and organizations have been conducted in order to organize the ideas about how to leverage ICTs in order to facilitate inter-organizational communication among DMOs. For example, Turoff (2002) summarized the requirements for an effective system and proposed major factors for a successful disaster management system. Moe (2006), developing a new approach to natural disaster management, highlighted the importance of having proactive and reactive strategies for natural disaster management. Weiser (2007) and Mendonca et al. (2007) examined a wide variety of ICTs to find out how ICTs are developed and used by DMOs and the challenges for them. While numerous studies have also argued that appropriate use of technology and a suitable communication infrastructure can improve the efficiency and effectiveness of relief operations in disasters, the majority of them are based on isolated case studies without overarching perspective over the related issues.

This chapter attempts to summarize the relationships between ICTs and multi-agency disaster management and builds a framework to conceptualize this research domain, by reviewing various issues examined in the recent disaster literature. It places a focus on changes in multi-organizational disaster management systems that may induce or be induced by new development of ICTs. Given the developmental stage of the field, the conceptual framework and research directions presented in this chapter will accelerate much needed theory development (Mendonça et al., 2007). The chapter also exposes disaster management practitioners to various issues that must be taken into account when improving their disaster management capability, thus providing important practical implications. The following section describes the backdrop of the recent disaster research. The current status of ICTs for disaster management is briefly presented in the next section, in order to provide a basic technological understanding of the field. Then, we discuss issues in organizational changes causing or caused by the technological elements of disaster management systems. The chapter is closed with some suggestions for future research and implications of the discussed issues.

RESEARCH BACKGROUND

In the wake of the 9/11 tragedy (2001) and following calamities such as Hurricane Katrina (2005) and the Indian Ocean earthquake[5] (2004), people realized how important effective disaster communications are, for public and private organizations alike. According to a survey on the effect of the 9/11 attacks on communications and public relations of Corporate America, 87% of the surveyed senior public relations executives in major US corporations say the attacks had an immediate impact on their organization's public relations and communications function, and more than two-thirds believe the tragedy will serve as a catalyst to change how their companies communicate, especially to employees and other strategic stakeholders (Wright, 2002). Even before the event of 9/11, some researchers advocated the importance of improving the efficiency of inter-organizational communication in disaster management organizations. For example, Drebek (1985) tried to promote Integrated Emergency Management System (IEMS) approach, pointing out the importance of explicit recognition of fundamental structural qualities that characterize emergency responses within American society. After examining the responses to a broad spectrum of large-scale disasters within the United States, he proposed four structural qualities of IEMS at that time, which were localism, lack of standardization, unit diversity, and fragmentation. Because American society was relatively decentralized, such decentralization allowed for and, to some extent, promoted a lack of standardization. With the given conditions, cross-agency communication was perceived to be the greatest weakness, and hence, the source of most difficulties. Subsequently, Drabek (1985) proposed six strategies for enhancing intergovernmental coordination in multiagency networks, which involve disaster planning based on process framework, identification of warning system functions and responsibilities, establishment of emergency operation centers, community disaster exercises, structural adaptation for centralized multiagency decision-making, and coordination of recovery decisions.

The recent large-scale disasters that devastated the communication infrastructure, including ICTs for DMOs, have drawn a strong research interest in the technological aspects of DMO communications. Subsequently, many new technologies as well as modification of existing ICT have been proposed to improve disaster management. For example, Banipal's examination of the performance of communication networks and information systems during Hurricane Katrina (Banipal, 2006) identified that breakdown of backhaul circuits, flooding of public switched telephone networks (PSTN), and disruption of electricity contributed to the mass-failure of communication systems. The study also found that wireless voice and data networks had faster recovery time and performed better than landline networks, but quick dispatch of backup generators and protection of communication hubs, circuits, and antennas from environmental hazards are challenging tasks for wireless networks. Based on the findings, he also proposed integrated disaster management strategies for coordinated response to disaster.

Weiser's work (2007) highlights the necessity of modification of public safety communication systems. He pointed out that the traditional public safety mindset about ICTs focuses on the value of a radio link that each agency can receive. Such a mindset often limits the value of ICTs to a single channel analog voice communication between members within a single organization. According to Weiser, public safety communications systems are a showcase of how not to develop an ICT for disaster management. The first problem in the current model of public safety communication systems is that they are centered on expensive single-purpose radio systems, which enforces most agencies to adopt an architecture that does not allow for evolution and dynamism. Second, despite the aspirations of the Project 25[6] effort, the model of public safety exceptionalism has left agencies isolated. This has limited the number of ICT vendors who, in turn, prepared to meet the individual agencies' needs by selling them expensive equipment. Finally, in a move that ignores the recent technological trends (e.g., WiFi network), public safety agencies generally depend on radios that have the entire communication mechanism (e.g., protocol) hardwired in physical devices. Such a rigid architecture is inferior to layered models (e.g., OSI 7 layer model, TCP/IP suite) that ensure compatibility and interoperability between different physical devices. Moreover, many of the public safety communication systems are designed for voice (and short text messaging at most) communications only, while the current level of technology can easily support multi-media communication capabilities, as seen in consumer electronics.

With the advance of new information and communication technologies, we have many new tools and ideas, at our disposal, to improve emergency mitigation, response and recovery, and organizational re-structuring of DMOs (Jennex, 2004). Some examples would be using CD/DVD based storage media for distribution of disaster information, Internet websites as a common infrastructure that provides access for disaster response teams distributed across multiple locations/organizations, and e-mails for improved communications. Geographical Information Systems (GIS) and satellite capabilities can also aid DMOs' decision-making process during an emergency. Indeed, the role of geographic information and associated technologies in an emergency response situation is now considered going well beyond the simple production of maps, to encompass operational and technological interoperability for organizing and supporting emergency responders and for contributing to homeland security (Harrison, Gil-Garcia, Pardo, & Thompson, 2006). Nevertheless, unleashing the full potential of such technologies is possible only with adequate supports from the organizational side, such as business process, norms, and interpretative schemes. Likewise, DMOs can improvise necessary reliefs during disaster management operations only when their collaborative spirits and organizational flexibility are supported by right technological elements.

As shown above, we are facing urgent and compelling needs to transform the existing disaster management systems, including the organizations, strategies, and operational processes, in order to leverage the advance of new information and communication technologies. Therefore, more research is needed for theory development and understanding of the relationships among technologies, communications, and successful emergency responses (Mendonça et al., 2007). The majority of the past research on disaster management systems can be categorized as a case study or technical design science studies, as opposed to empirical testing (e.g., survey, behavioral experiment, quantitative analysis of observed or secondary data) of interactions between ICT and DMOs. They tend to focus on technological functionality and attributes, rather than their causes or effects on the user organizations. The following section presents the current issues in ICTs involved in emergencies, and discusses how they influence the inter-organizational communication and coordination.

CURRENT ISSUES IN ICT FOR DISASTER MANAGEMENT

Previous research suggests a circular induction relationship between ICTs for disaster management and inter-organizational collaboration among DMOs. The needs for collaboration in large-scale disasters have led to the advance in ICTs for disaster management, while use of improved ICTs can improve the efficiency and effectiveness of inter-organizational communication and coordination among DMOs. In this section, we discuss the current issues in ICTs for disaster management along the line of circular influences.

Properties of ICTs for Disasters Management

Interoperability of ICT

Relief activities and decision making in a large-scale emergency responses typically involve a large number of relief organizations, and thus information must be shared across the multitude participating DMOs, and their activities must be coordinated within and across their organizational boundaries (Kapucu, 2006). Understandably, the majority of recent emergency management literature involves a large-scale disaster case or a scenario that entails collaboration among a large number of relief organizations. This is perhaps due to the successive catastrophic events that struck in different parts of the world in the beginning of the 21st century (e.g., 9/11 Attacks in 2001, Indian Ocean Earthquake in 2004, and Hurricane Katrina in 2005). As the scale of a disaster grows, ad-hoc groups are more likely to emerge, making it more difficult to inter-connect their ICTs (Quarantelli, 1997). Consequently, research on large-scale disasters places an emphasis on cross-organizational collaboration, which requires the inter-operability of ICTs in such a dreadful calamity.

During the response to 9/11, first responders such as New York Police department (NYPD) and Fire Department (FDNY) were not able to communicate with each other because they were on different radio frequencies. This became a major obstacle to their initial response and following coordination efforts to control the aftermath (Kean & Hamilton, 2004). When different agencies cannot directly communicate amongst each other, forcing them to resort to messengers and communications middlemen through a central dispatch center, significant delays will undermine the relief efforts (Banipal, 2006).

Unfortunately, the reality of today is that many emergency responders are still relying on a technological architecture designed and implemented based on 1980s technology. In the US, most public safety radio systems were using 50-year old spectrum techniques until 1995 (Weiser, 2007). With such an old spectrum technique, inter-organizational interoperability, as well as internal operability (e.g., bandwidth and adaptability), had to be severely limited (Weiser, 2007). In order to enable public safety agencies to operate in more technologically dynamic climate and to achieve far greater levels of (inter-)operability, Weiser

(2007) recommended the adoption of modular architectures, Internet-based Protocols, a new generation of communication technologies (e.g., cognitive radio[7], broadband access channel), and rights managements techniques to share information resources. Some improvements have actually been made in the interoperability of public safety radio systems in the recent past. For example, the ALMR (Alaska Land Mobile Radio)[8] system greatly improved public safety communications by enabling federal, state, and local governments to share frequencies (Weiser, 2007). Manoj and Baker (2007) also pointed out that overcoming radio interoperability issue is a pressing technological challenge and suggested adoption of dual-use technology and makeshift local area networks as a solution.

Adaptivity of ICT

In addition to the needs for interoperability, emergency responders often need to take new roles, build new structures, and adapt existing technologies to the novel situations, in order to meet emergency response goals. Fortunately, the recent advance of ICT offers a very valuable technological property that can cope with the inherent uncertainty and irregularity of emergency management: Adaptivity.

In the disaster management context, adaptivity can be thought of as a multidimensional concept, suggesting some forms of flexibility, scalability, and intelligence embedded throughout the response system[9]. While multiple aspects of the situation, such as information needs and available alternatives for a response action, continuously change during an emergency response, most ICTs for emergency response are designed for routine processes with a limited number of most likely response scenarios. In order to manage complex and dynamic emergency conditions, ICTs must include some form of adaptivity, the capability to self-organize and self-adjust according to the peculiar characteristics of the particular emergency and the constantly changing environment. Meissner et al. (2002) nominated Mobile Ad-hoc Networks[10] (MANETs) as a good candidate for hot-spot communications, especially for most affected areas in a disaster, because MANETs offer self-organizing and self-healing capabilities. An example of such an adaptive MANETs is CalMesh[11] (Manoj & Baker, 2007).

HCI & Decision Support

Jefferson (2006) emphasized that, in order for disaster management operations to succeed, all data and information collection and analysis must be inherently related to decision making and action. Unfortunately, confusion in interpretation and meaning during a disaster response cannot be resolved by simply adding more connectivity, because more access means more likelihood of greater and quicker diffusion of incorrect information, which may result in an accelerated loss of disaster relevant information (Quarantelli, 1997). In this regard, another stream of research focuses on design challenges for human-computer interaction (HCI) and human factors in emergency management systems, so that more effective and efficient interactions are achieved. For example, it is a widely accepted view of user-centric systems that the human role in emergency response information systems should not be neglected: the human being part of the system and the computer being part of the team. The computer and the human work with other people and other computer systems in other agencies, sharing information and working together to manage the crisis, mitigate effects, and support the victims after the event (Carver & Turoff, 2007). Banipal (2006) also agreed that it is critically important to design systems to enhance open and rapid communication and information sharing, for faster response times to disasters. It has been found from previous research that online moderators are often necessary for efficient information flow with discussion threads, and an online community of experts should be put together for consultation when a crisis arises that requires group-decision making (T. L. Jefferson, 2006; Turoff, 2002).

Effective Public Notification

Today's ICTs can utilize a variety of communication channels, each with different relative advantages and disadvantages. Some ICTs can allow streamlined information flow to a limited number of DMO agents, while some others allow instant distribution of short messages to a very large, yet a targeted group of audiences. As our environment become more complex (e.g., hi-tech public transportations, nuclear power plants, or high-density building complex) and the potential impact of an emergency becomes larger, how to choose an appropriate channel has becomes a relevant issue in successful disaster management operations. Apart from interactions among DMOs, the recent large-scale disasters and diffusion of new ICTs have also changed the interactions between DMOs and the general public. Experiencing the 9/11 attacks, the Indian Ocean earthquake (aka. Southeast Asia tsunami), the Hurricane Katrina, and more recently the series of shooting sprees on several US school campuses (e.g., Virginia Tech Massacre[12]), government disaster planners and business continuity managers realized that the lack of a reliable and timely mass notification system between emergency responders and civilians was one of the most damaging causes, and are now spurring the adoption of mass notification technologies (1996). In the US, the devastating impact of Hurricane Katrina also forced government agencies at all levels to at least reflect on the deficiencies in their organizational and communicational structures to effectively deal with the public.

Network Reliability

Improvements of commercial wireless telephone networks, an approach actively explored in Europe, have also often been proposed (Brito, 2006) for DMO communications. Commercial mobile networks can be referred to as what Meissner et al. (2002) call "wide-area communications." Most wide-area communications in their current forms of implementation are inappropriate for handling mission-critical disaster management communications. They often become unreliable because they lack prioritization or group call schemes (e.g., inability to reserve bandwidth for DMOs), which can create overload and "chaos in the air" during major emergency situations. Also, those networks are beyond public safety organizations' control and tend to collapse during disasters due to the overwhelming demand from private users or due to infrastructure damages. As a consequence, major improvements are required for most commercial mobile networks before they can be accepted as a reliable public safety system.

Integration into Daily Operations

In order for an emergency response system to be effective during an actual emergency, it must be used regularly (Turoff, 2002). However, the very nature of an emergency and a disaster makes it impossible for DMOs to layout a perfect plan for inter-organizational disaster management systems. The uncertainty, low frequency, and high intensity of catastrophic events often force DMOs to choose either to maintain a very expensive multi-agency network that may not work in unexpected situations or to just accept the risk that cannot be accurately predicted anyway. Even if a system is in place, it may be rarely used in everyday operation. Incident Management Systems is a set of tools specially designed for marshalling pre-identified and pre-assembled resources to respond to an emergency or disaster (Perry, 2003). Usually, all emergency planning and response begins with local capabilities and resources that later may be supplemented by extra-community capabilities and resources. While the agencies that respond to everyday emergencies are typically the same ones that initiate the response to disasters, few municipal fire and police departments regularly use such systems, except on very large incidents (Perry, 2003). Some fire services have realized that they need a common incident management system that can be used on all incidents, hoping that daily use of the system would enhance the effectiveness of the system when it is used in more rare, extremely large incidents.

Although some studies have presented successful implementation cases of ICTs for disaster management, most of them are still in an experimental stage with limited implementation, in terms of the coverage and functionality. It may take a long time to observe global improvement of inter-organizational collaboration triggered by improved ICTs. The speed of improvement in ICT-triggered inter-organizational collaboration may be slower than desirable, but one should keep in mind that it is more about changing organizations and societies, rather than replacing an old technology with a new one. In the following section, changes in organizational structure, operational processes, and socially constructed beliefs are discussed in relation to ICTs for disaster management.

Changes in Multi-Agency Disaster Management

Organizational and social challenges in emergency response involve issues that can arise from organizational structure and interactions between social factors, including DMOs, workgroups, and individuals (Manoj & Baker, 2007). When groups accustomed to a hierarchy and centralized decision making suddenly encounter an emergency situation that cannot be handled by a single group, they have to cope with a situation where they are required to work with other groups in a flatter and more dynamic multi-organizational structure that emerges during the post-disaster relief efforts. Thus, an immediate challenge for DM communities would include determining what type of (inter-)organizational structure and operational processes work best, in addition to utilizing interoperable and adaptive ICTs. A hybrid model that combines a hierarchical organizational model for accountability and a flat dynamic model for efficient communications has been suggested as an ideal solution (Manoj & Baker, 2007). One question is then how to find the sweet spot for a group of responders in the continuum between the two extremes. Disaster management also entails communications within and between ephemeral groups, such as news media, non-governmental humanitarian societies, and the public. Therefore, DMOs must consider the scope of inter-organizational network and the extent to which they are communicating within the network, when they consider redesigning their organizational structure and collaborative operational processes.

Organizational Adaptability

Comfort and Kapucu (2006) hypothesized a direct relationship between the capacity of a group to coordinate their actions and the group's capacity to process information for group decision making, which is in turn determined by the technical structure required for information search and exchange, organizational policies and procedures, and cultural openness to new information. They also presented a five-phase model of auto-adaptation that includes a non-linear flow of processes from information search, to information exchange, to sense-making, to adaptation, and finally to inter-organizational learning. Mendonca et al. (2007) identified that developing all-inclusive doctrines and procedures to guide complex responses, under a rigid, military-like hierarchical management model, is the major cause of ICT failures during past emergency response, and argued that two important factors, the degree of improvisation and the degree of combining various ICTs, are needed to support personnel in accomplishing response tasks. In a similar vine, Barosa et al.

(2008) defined information orchestration as an information architecture in which an information orchestrator adaptively matches information demand and supply across multiple disaster management groups. They found several hurdles that need to be overcome if information quality for relief workers is to be improved, and argued that adaptivity of disaster management systems can be enhanced by using information orchestrators, which in turn will improve the information quality for disaster management.

Direct Coupling

While the above mentioned research stream focuses on providing DMOs with socio-technical mechanisms that can facilitate improvisational interactions among a potentially large number of stakeholder organizations, the effects of such new technologies on organizational structure and operational processes may be viewed from the classical perspective of coordination theory (Comfort & Hasse, 2006). Rephrasing the electronic market hypothesis, will adoption of advanced ICTs lead to more direct couplings between federal and local-level government organizations, without involving of the middleman (i.e., state-level government) in disaster management? Comfort and Hasse (2006) found a striking pattern of asymmetry in the communication processes among organizations participating in an emergency response. That is, federal agencies assisting local agencies directly, leaving state agencies out. The number of potential direct couplings may also increase, because inclusion of various NGOs (e.g., red-cross, charities) and private firms (e.g., Home Depot), in addition to governmental DMOs, has been proven to be instrumental in response to a large-scale disaster like Hurricane Katrina (2006).

Incentive-Driven Control

While the additional organizations would generate a steady and trusting flow of information among DMOs, there also exists a thrust toward decentralization. Waugh and Streib (2006) argued that centralized decision making, as seen in Katrina, can delay approving and dispatching response mechanisms. Denning and Hayesroth (2006) also found that centralized decision making will not work for Hastily Formed Networks (HFN)[13]. Under a HFN, the participating federated organizations cooperate toward a single purpose, but retain their separate identities and may compete vigorously on matters outside that purpose. For example, during the relief operations in the Hurricane Katrina's aftermath, the communication and information sharing among the relief organizations were very difficult due to the different local practices, terminology, data format, and organizational culture. Because there was no common hierarchy to define an authority to set overall direction and resolve conflicts, the DMOs that formed the network quickly fell into defensive positions and did not coordinate well. Denning and Hayesroth (Waugh & Streib, 2006) argued that any attempt to make an HFN operate hierarchically, including the FEMA HFN is likely to fail, and recommended that governments adopt the best practices of hyper-networks that combine federated organizations, decentralized control, and value-based information management. In line with this recommendation, the National Performance Review also called for delegating authority, replacing rules and regulations with incentives, developing budgets based on result, exposing government operations to competition, and searching for market rather than administrative solutions (Stuver, 2006).

Joint Resource Management

Manoj and Baker (2007) identified that rapid deployment of communication systems for first responders and workers is a difficult technological challenge. One profound cause of this challenge is resource (e.g., limitations of staff capacity, financial resources) constraints (Currion, Silva,

& Walle, 2007; Moe, 2006). Lack of adequate resources and poor or no analysis of major risk factors can lead to a number of problems resulting in termination and suspension of the project. Some technologies might not be willingly adopted, because organizations are not always willing to spend money on the implementation and training of the technology that will be rarely used. A solution for this type of problems may be resource pooling. According to Currion (2007) investment in disaster preparedness remains low around the world, and thus disaster management systems should be shared, developed, and owned globally. Arens and Rosenbloom (2003) also called for an assembly of nationwide network of computation, data, and services that can support utilization of any resource needed during a response. The Free and Open Source Software (FOSS) principles and practice mesh well with the humanitarian sector on three important criteria: approach, cost, and adaptability. Van De Walle and Turoff (2007) touched upon a need in global disaster management and predicted that free and open source emergency management systems will play an increasingly important role in future humanitarian operations, given the key characteristics of an open-access approach, low-cost deployment, and easy adaptability. Establishing a standard is also a critical step towards the efficient use of limited resources. Public safety agencies have had a tendency of making their own decisions about ICT, failing to adopt technology that operates effectively and interoperates with others emergency responders (Weiser, 2007). Federal Policy needs to view disaster management communications as an integrated system and take the leadership in developing a new framework for disaster management ICT.

Involvement of Non-Gov Partners

The Internet has proven to be a powerful communication channel for government to interact directly with citizens, especially during times of crisis because of its resistance to system failure (Brito, 2006). With convergence of voice network and IP network technologies, a private enterprise could be brought into the picture to set up a commercial mobile network-based communication channel between DMOs and the public, an approach actively being explored in some European countries (2003). Arens and Rosenbloom (2007) also highlight how the current state and promising near-future of IT makes it possible to create policies, build a general-purpose infrastructure, and develop general capabilities that could be adapted instantly to respond to any threat. For example, the Internet could be used by DMOs and citizens in areas like emergency medical services, structural and wild-land firefighting, urban search and rescue, emergency evacuation simulation, emergency dispatch work, and information systems modeling for receiving a formal response by relaying information to the news media. Doing so will not only allow agencies around the country to learn what is going on and how they can help, but will also help inform non-government organizations(NGOs) and private organizations that may not be in direct contact with the primary DMOs. Also, secondary response agencies can be informed without interfering with the primary responders working under severe time pressure.

Multi-Channel Interactions

There are a number of media channels, including television, radio, newspaper, and the Internet, that the citizens can choose from, in order to find information or to communicate with their government. Quite a few researchers have explored the differences among the media channels, especially during a disaster (Lee & Rao, 2007; Quarantelli, 1996; Thomas & Streib, 2003). While the news stories from the television and radio are more filtered and simplified due to time crunch, the printed news media, such as the news paper and the Internet provide extensive coverage and information to the citizens. One of the most dramatic changes in recent decades is the growing interest in the Internet. The use of the web by the private sector has grown, the public sector has followed closely behind, and virtually all large U.S Governments and their agencies – federal, state, and local - now have their own websites and online services (Lee & Rao, 2007). Many citizens can contact and use government services online rather than waiting in long lines at government offices or being placed on hold over the phone. The magnitude of the feedback, the usage of information, and the statistical information that can be collected from the Internet are immense when compared to the other information channels. However, one of the main disadvantages of Internet usage is the missing one-to-one relationship with the government. The other barriers to the adoption of Internet include: low trust, privacy risk, loss of information, and riskier financial transactions.

We have presented some changes in (inter) organizational collaboration that have been brought or are expected to occur by adopting improved ICTs for disaster management. It must be noted, however, that achieving coordination and information sharing through improved ICTs across multiple organizations is extremely difficult in an ad-hoc fashion, especially during an extreme event. While use of enhanced ICTs may be a necessary condition to achieve a "shared common operating picture and situational awareness" (Kapucu, 2006; Mendonça et al., 2007), pre-incident planning is often the critical catalyst that actually realizes the expected improvements in inter-organizational collaboration (Theresa L. Jefferson, 2006).

CONCEPTUAL FRAMEWORK

In order to present the abovementioned issues and their underlying relationships in a meaningful and easy-to-understand structure, we developed an overarching conceptual framework of ICT for disaster management and inter-organizational collaboration (Figure 1). The framework depicts how the needs for inter-organizational collaboration in a disaster induce evolution of ICTs, and how the improved ICTs, in turn, can improve the inter-organizational communication and coordination in disaster management: the circular relationship between ICTs and the inter-organizational collaboration.

The circular relationship is influenced by two types of environments: disaster environment and institutional/organizational environment. They can be treated as the sources of exogenous forces and controllable moderators, respectively, between ICTs and intra/inter-organizational collaboration in the disaster management research context. The disaster environment refers to the conditions prompted by a disaster situation, which determine the desirable properties of ICTs or the innovations required by multi-agency disaster response. As shown in the upper half of the framework, previous research on ICTs focuses on such properties as interoperability, adaptivity, interface and decision support quality, timely mass notification, network reliability, and dual purpose ICTs in order to meet the needs for DMOs that must cope with uncertainty, low frequency, and highly intense disaster situations. The scale, time pressure, and type of hazards are also important factors considered in improvement of ICTs.

Similarly, the institutional/organizational environment refers to the conditions in which ICTs affect inter-organizational collaborations in a disaster. Some of the frequently considered institutional/organizational factors in the previous research include, but not limited to (inter)organizational structure, stakeholders and their conflicting interests, policies and regulations governing the DMOs, financial, technical, and human resources available for DMOs and their culture. These factors have important managerial implications because they are often controllable, while they can play a critical role in achieving a high level of inter-organizational collaboration when an enhanced ICT is adopted by DMOs. Past research suggests

Figure 1. A conceptual framework of ICTs for disaster management and inter-organizational collaboration

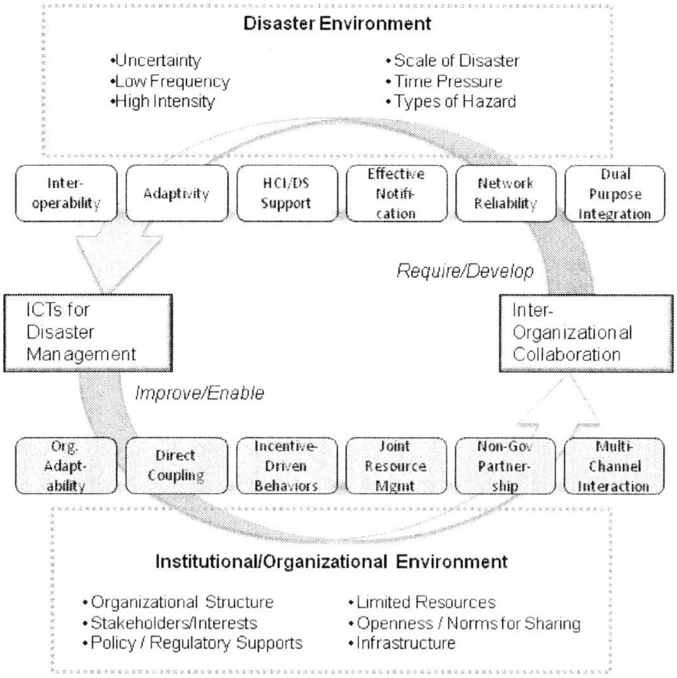

that successful inter-organizational collaboration in disaster management entails organizational changes such as increased adaptability, direct coupling, incentive-driven collaboration, cooperative resource management, involvement of more non-gov partners (e.g., NGO), and selective use of multi-channel communications.

CONCLUSION AND FUTURE RESEARCH DIRECTIONS

In this chapter, we presented a review on recent studies in the multi-disciplinary field of disaster management communication and developed a conceptual framework to understand the relationships among various issues discussed in the literature. Our review shows that inter-organizational collaborative disaster management is a challenging issue, and ICTs can play a key role in the collaboration efforts of DMOs.

The recent large-scale disasters, including 9/11, Hurricane Katrina and the Indian Ocean earthquake, have drawn a huge attention to technical requirements of ICTs, organizational structure, operational processes, and culture of disaster management communities and individual DMOs. Previous research in this area can be categorized into two groups based on the focus of the study. The first group focuses on the technological characteristics (e.g., interoperability, adaptivity) of ICTs that can enable or support inter-organizational collaboration under an extreme condition. Studies in the other group focus on identifying the institutional environments (e.g., hierarchy, stakeholders) or organizational factors (e.g., resource, culture) that can facilitate or hinder inter-organizational communication and coordination when an ICT is used in a disaster situation. These two groups of studies are actually looking at the two sides of the same coin, the circular relationship between ICTs and inter-organizational collaboration, as shown in our conceptual framework of the relationship between ICTs and inter-organizational collaboration (Figure 1).

Given a set of general (e.g., uncertainty, low frequency, high intensity) and peculiar conditions (e.g., scale, time pressure, type of hazards) in a disaster situation, the recent studies on ICTs suggest that interoperability, adaptivity, HCI/decision usability, effective public notification, reliability, and integrated functionality are some of the important technological requirements for ICTs for disaster management. On the other hand, inter-organizational collaboration is subject to more complex interactions between available ICTs and institutional/organizational environments. Some of the widely studied institutional/organizational factors include the structure of DMOs and their interests, policies and regulations, financial, technological, and human resources, organizational culture, and existing infrastructure, among others. The literature suggests that these institutional/organizational factors play a critical role in the consequences of ICT use, which include not only the performance of inter-organizational collaboration but also transformation of the inter-organizational relationships (e.g., organizational adaptability, direct coupling, incentive-driven collaboration, etc.). Nevertheless, most studies in this group have neither explicitly theorized nor empirically examined the relationships between the institutional/organizational factors and the changes in collaborative relationships. For example, organizational adaptability can be conceptualized as a condition that allows DMOs to take the advantage of adaptive ICTs (Bharosa et al., 2008), but it could also be considered as a result of successful adoption of an adaptive ICT in a right institutional/organizational environment (e.g., organizational policies and procedures, cultural openness) (L. K. Comfort & Kapucu, 2006).

We posit, based on our review, that advanced ICT can improve inter-organizational communications, which will lead to changes in the inter-organizational relationships, disaster management strategies, and the operational procedures of the disaster management community. Likewise, we also posit that political and environmental pressures to improve disaster management performance will accelerate changes in the organizational structure, strategy, and processes of a disaster management community, which will seek for new ICTs that can support the transforming organization better. Therefore, the shape as well as the performance of multi-agency collaboration in a disaster will be transformed by changes in any of the two factors (i.e., technology and organizational changes). What we need to make sure is that the changes on one side correspond to the changes in the other side. When a transformation of disaster management does not accompany appropriate changes in the battery, the system will not achieve its full potentials when the next disaster puts the system to the test.

Future Research on Transformation of DMOs

The dynamic environments and the developmental stage of the ICT research in the multi-agency disaster management field provide a fertile ground for future research. Although both disaster environment and institutional/organizational environment exert strong influence on the relationship between ICTs and inter-organizational collaboration, the institutional/organizational environment calls for more research attention, mainly due to its complex interaction with technological attributes of ICTs. Potential managerial implications that stem from the controllability of the institutional and organizational factors also add a justification for additional research in the area. As discussed in the previous sections, the current status of the research in this area implicitly suggests moderating/mediating effects of some environmental factors on the relationship between ICT adoption and successful inter-organizational collaboration. Therefore, future research should focus on clarifying the relationships among the four groups of factors: the properties of ICTs, institutional/organizational environments, transformation of collaborative disaster management structure/practices, and the performance of the ICT-enabled multi-agency collaboration. For example, some researchers have emphasized the importance of incentive mechanisms for voluntary collaboration (Stuver, 2006), but we do not know much about the effectiveness of various institutional/organizational factors that can constitute an incentive mechanism nor how DMOs would change their behaviors in response to a particular incentive mechanism, which in turn will have considerable impact on the performance level of multi-agency collaboration. Future research on this topic may examine alternative theoretical explanations that can explain observations in the previous studies.

Future Research on ICTs for DMOs

The emphasis on future research needs in the transformational aspects does not mean that there is no room left for further development in ICTs for disaster management. One particularly urgent research need is to understand the effects of disaster factors on information needs. While most of the recent studies emphasize interoperability and adaptivity for smooth coordination of a multitude of relief agencies, the criteria for information quality and the system quality to assure the information quality in various disaster environments have been relatively neglected topics in the previous research. The way data and information are collected and managed from multiple sources to provide the right information to the right DMOs in a timely fashion is especially important for effective disaster management given that disaster management operations often involve severe psychological, political, physical, and time pressures. Such pressures can significantly undermine the relief agents' ability to make the right decisions or take the right actions under extreme conditions. Therefore, ICTs for disaster management should encompass a mechanism that can assist users with information search, aggregation, summarization, filtering, and delivery at the right points in the disaster management system. Making the issue further complicated, the right mix of information quality and system quality for a disaster manager may differ from one situation to another, depending on the particular characteristics of the disaster and the role of the disaster manager – an open link to the organizational transformation research topic area. Unfortunately, little is known about the critical information quality attributes, information processing needs, and disaster conditions. Therefore, building a theoretical foundation of information dynamics in disasters will be a great direction for future research.

Our conceptual framework provides an overview of current research issues that lead to various future research directions. Streams of research projects well positioned and focused on some of the topic areas on our conceptual framework will be able to accelerate the development of sound theories and provide strong managerial implications to practitioners, all geared toward increased adoption and implementation of new ICTs and vibrant re-engineering of disaster management processes among relief agencies.

ACKNOWLEDGMENT

This research has been supported by NSF under grant #IIS-0733388 and IIS-0809186. Usual disclaimer applies

REFERENCES

Adams, S. (2005). Learning the lessons of Katrina for the unexpected tomorrow. *Risk Management, 52*(12), 24-29.

Arens, Y., & Rosenbloom, P. S. (2003). Responding to the unexpected. How IT can help prepare for the future attacks and disasters. *Communications of the ACM Journal, 46*(9), 33-36.

Banipal, K. (2006). Strategic approach to disaster management: Lessons learned from Hurricane Katrina. *Disaster Prevention and Management, 15*(3), 484-494.

Bharosa, N., Janssen, M., Rao, H. R., & Lee, J. (2008, May 4-7). *Adaptive information orchestration: Architectural principles improving information quality.* Paper presented at the 5th International Conference on Information Systems for Crisis Response and Management (ISCRAM2008), Washington, DC, USA.

Brito, J. (2006). Public safety interoperability. *Regulation, 29*(3), 6-7.

Carver, L., & Turoff, M. (2007). Human-computer interaction: The human and computer as a team in emergency management information systems. *Communications of the ACM, 50*(3), 33-38.

Comfort, & Hasse. (2006). Communication, coherence, and collective action: The impact of Hurricane Katrina on communications infrastructure. *Public Works Management & Policy, 10*(4), 328-343.

Comfort, L. K., & Kapucu, N. (2006). Interorganizational coordination in extreme events: The World Trade Center attacks, September 11, 2001. *Natural Hazard Journal, 39*, 309-327.

Currion, P., Silva, C. d., & Walle, B. V. d. (2007). Open source software for disaster management. *Communications of the ACM: SPECIAL SECTION: Emergency Response Information Systems: Emerging Trends and Technologies Table of Contents, 50*(3), 61-65.

Denning, J. P., & Hayes-Roth, R. (2006). Decision making in very large networks. *The Profession of IT, 49*(11), 19-23.

Drabek, T. E. (1985). Managing the emergency response. *Public Administration Review, 45*, 85.

Harrison, T., Gil-Garcia, J. R., Pardo, T. A., & Thompson, F. (2006). *Learning about interoperability for emergency response: Geographic information technologies and the World Trade Center crisis.* Paper presented at the Proceeding of the 39th Hawaii International Conference on System Sciences.

Jefferson, T. L. (2006). Evaluating the role of information technology in crisis and emergency management. *The Journal of Information and Knowledge Management Systems, 36* (3), 261-264.

Jefferson, T. L. (2006). Using the internet to communicate during a crisis. *The Journal of Information and Knowledge Management Systems, 36*(2), 139-142

Jennex, M. (2004). Emergency response systems: The utility Y2K experience. *Journal of Information Technology Theory and Application, 6*(3), 85-102.

Kapucu, N. (2006). Interagency communication networks during emergencies: Boundary spanners in multiagency coordination. *American Review of Public Administration, 36*(2), 207.

Kean, T. H., & Hamilton, L. H. (2004). *The 9/11 report.* New York: St. Martin's Press.

Lee, J., & Rao, H. R. (2007). Perceived risks, counterbeliefs, and intentions to use anti/counterterrorism Web sites: An exploratory study of government-citizens online interactions in a turbulent environment. *Decision Support Systems, 43*(4), 1431-1449.

Manoj, B. S., & Baker, A. H. (2007). Communication challenges in emergency response. *Communications of the ACM, 50*(3), 51-53.

Meissner, A., Luckenbach, T., Risse, T., Kirste, T., & Kirchner, H. (2002, June 24). *Design challenges for an integrated disaster management communication and information system.* Paper presented at the The First IEEE Workshop on Disaster Recovery Networks (DIREN 2002), New York City, co-located with IEEE INFOCOM 2002.

Mendonça, D., Jefferson, T., & Harrald, J. (2007). Collaborative adhocracies and mix-and-match technologies in emergency management. *Communications of the ACM, 50*(3), 44-48.

Moe, T. L. (2006). An integrated approach to natural disaster management: Public project management and its critical success factors. *Disaster Prevention and Management, 15*(3), 396.

Perry, W. R. (2003). Incident management systems in disaster management. *Disaster Prevention and Management, 12*(5), 405-412.

Quarantelli, E. L. (1996). Local mass media operations in disasters in the USA. *Disaster Prevention and Management, 5*(5), 5-12.

Quarantelli, E. L. (1997). Problematical aspects of the information/communication revolution for disaster planning and research: Ten nontechnical issues and questions. *Disaster Prevention and Management: An International Journal, 6*(2), 94-106.

Stuver, P. (2006). Maximizing emergency communication. *Risk management, 53*(5), 30-35.

Thomas, J. C., & Streib, G. (2003). The new face of government: Citizen initiated contacts in the era of e-government. *Journal of Public Administration Research and Theory, 13*(1), 83-102.

Turoff, M. (2002). Past and future emergency response information systems. *Association for Computing Machinery. Communications of the ACM, 45*(4), 29.

Van De Walle, e. a. (2007). Emergency response information systems: Emerging trends and technologies. *Communications of ACM.*

Waugh, W. L. J., & Streib, G. (2006). Collaboration and leadership for effective emergency management. *Public Administration Review, 66*(Special Issue on Collaborative Public Management).

Weiser, P. J. (2007). Communicating during emergencies: Toward interoperability and effective information management. *Federal Communications Law Journal, 59*(3), 547-573.

Wright, D. K. (2002). Examining how the 11th September, 2001 terrorist attacks precipitated a paradigm shift advancing communications and public relations into a more significant role in corporate America. *Journal of Communication Management, 6*(3), 280-292.

KEY TERMS

Adaptivity of ICT: Refers to the capability of an ICT to self-organize and self-adjust according to the peculiar characteristics of dynamic environments. It is a multidimensional concept, related to the flexibility, scalability, and intelligence embedded in an ICT for disaster management.

Disaster Management Systems: A collection of ICTs, DMOs, relationships among the DMOs, and operational procedures/business processes of the DMOs, of which objective is to prevent, mitigate, and minimize the impact of disasters.

Disaster Management Organizations (DMOs): Refer to organizations that prevent, mitigate, and recover unexpected events that adversely affect people or resources and threat the continued operation of organizations. Unexpected events include any natural or man-made disaster. DMOs are responsible for preparing for disaster before it occurs, minimizing the impacts when it occurs, and rebuilding society from the aftermath of an occurred disaster. DMOs may include government agencies (e.g. Police, Fire, Medical Services), non-government organizations (e.g. UN, Red Cross), and some private sector first responder organizations (e.g. utility, transportation, healthcare, construction firms).

Information and communication technologies (ICTs): An umbrella term that includes all technologies for the manipulation and communication of information. ICTs may encompass any technology to transmit, receive, store, and process data or information of any format. In this chapter, it refers to any technology involved in disaster management, including public/2-way radio, television, cellular phones, computer, network hardware and software, satellite systems, etc.

Inter-Organizational Communication: Refers to a process of information transmission and/or reception that occurs between two or more purposeful partners across organizational boundaries. The communication partners may be individuals, groups of people, or computerized (software) agents.

Interoperability: Refers to the ability of diverse systems and organizations to work together (inter-operate). The term is often used to refer to a technical property in an engineering sense, or alternatively in a broad sense, taking into account social, political, and organizational factors that impact system performance. Interoperability of an ICT in disaster management refers to the capability of the ICT to work with different ICTs used by various DMOs, which may involve supports for common radio frequency spectrum, communication protocols, information/message formats, etc.

Multi-Agency Collaboration for Disaster Management: Refers to cooperative endeavors of multiple disaster management organizations in an effort to coordinate their relief activities or find alternative solutions to manage the disaster situation.

Organizational Adaptability: Refers to the degree to which an organization (or a group of collaborating organizations) can adjust its structure and business processes and successfully achieve its goals, in accordance with the peculiar characteristics of dynamic environments, a process a.k.a. improvisation. An adaptive ICT may be adopted in an attempt to increase organizational adaptability, but it is neither necessary condition nor sufficient condition for organizational adaptability.

ENDNOTES

1 The September 11 attacks (often referred to as 9/11) were a series of coordinated suicide attacks that crashed commercial airliners into several iconic buildings (i.e., World Trade Center, Pentagon) in the US. The attacks were launched by Al-Qaeda on September 11, 2001.

2 Hurricane Katrina of 2005 was one of the five deadliest hurricanes in the US history (http://www.nhc.noaa.gov/pdf/TCR-AL122005_Katrina.pdf).

3 The Federal Emergency Management Agency (FEMA) is an agency of the United States Department of Homeland Security (DHS), which has the responsibility to coordinate the relief activities in a disaster that overwhelms the resources of local and state authorities.

4 Corporate America is "an informal phrase describing the for-profit world of corporations within the United States not under government ownership" (http://en.wikipedia.org/wiki/Corporate_America).

5 The Indian Ocean earthquake was one of the deadliest natural disasters in history that occurred near Sumatra, Indonesia on Dec. 26, 2004. The earthquake triggered a series of 30 meters high tsunamis that killed more than 225 thousand people in 11 countries along the coastal line of the Indian Ocean.

6 Project 25 (P25) or APCO-25 is "an interoperability suite of standards for digital two-way wireless communications products and systems. The P25 standards are created by a committee of manufacturers,

public safety agencies and state and federal communications professionals to provide detailed standards for the design of communications systems so that all purchasers of P25-compatible equipment can communicate with each other" (http://www.tiaonline.org/gov_affairs/press_publications/documents/TIAResponsetoGAOReportonP25.pdf). P25 is a TIA (Telecommunications Industry Association) standard, which is a US (functional) counterpart of TETRA (Trans European Trunked Radio) (http://www.tetra-association.com/) standardized by ETSI (European Telecommunications Standards Institute).

7 Cognitive radio is "a wireless communication network or node capable of efficiently changing its communication parameters to avoid interference with other users of the radio frequency." (http://www.fcc.gov/oet/cognitiveradio)

8 http://www.ak-prepared.com/almr/

9 http://www.iscram.org/dmdocuments/ISCRAM2008/SpecialSessionsCFP/ISCRAM2008_CFP115.pdf

10 Mobile Ad-hoc Networks is "a wireless network that transmits from computer to computer. Instead of using a central base station (access point) to which all computers must communicate, this peer-to-peer mode of operation can greatly extend the distance of the wireless network." (http://www.pcmag.com/encyclopedia_term/0,2542,t=mobile+ad+hoc+network&i=47135,00.asp)

11 CalMesh is "an ad-hoc network of small, lightweight, and easily reconfigurable nodes that quickly self-organize to form a reliable wireless mesh network… designed to be rapidly deployed at the site of a crisis to restore the communication fabric crucial to emergency response" (http://calmesh.calit2.net/)

12 The Virginia Tech massacre was a school shooting consisting of two separate attacks approximately two hours apart on April 16, 2007, that took place on the campus of Virginia Polytechnic Institute and State University (Virginia Tech) in Blacksburg, Virginia. (http://en.wikipedia.org/wiki/Virginia_Tech_massacre)

13 http://faculty.nps.edu/dl/HFN/index.htm

Chapter XIV
Competence in Transforming the Norwegian Welfare Sector:
A Case Study and Implications for Future E-Government Initiatives

Knut H. Rolland
Norwegian University of Science and Technology, Norway

Torgeir Dingsøyr
Norwegian University of Science and Technology, Norway

ABSTRACT

E-government initiatives need to take the competence involved in producing high-quality services for citizens into account. We draw on insights from a pilot project in a Norwegian municipal aiming at radically restructuring the Norwegian welfare sector and show how the competence to provide high-quality services rely on the collective achievement of individuals' knowing-in-practice when dealing with particular cases and situations. Furthermore, we show how competence in terms of 'processes of knowing' is intrinsically related to organization structure and existing information systems. Transforming the Norwegian Welfare Sector then, involves transforming a sociotechnical network of heterogeneous elements, where existing processes of knowing plays an important role. Based on this, we discuss implications for implementing e-government in local municipals, and in particular e-government initiatives that aim at introducing all-embracing integrated IT solutions across organizational and geographical borders. The chapter concludes by sketching implications for future research on e-government.

INTRODUCTION

In recent information systems and management literatures much has been written on the socio-technical challenges involved in introducing e-government solutions in different countries and contexts (e.g. Homburg, 2004; Irani et al., 2005; Jones and Hughes, 2001; Moon, 2002; Robey and Holmström, 2001; Wastell et al., 2004). A recurring finding from many of these studies indicate that many e-government initiatives do not have the expected outcomes. These multifaceted outcomes can hardly be traced back to a few easily isolated factors, but needs to be understood in a broader context of interaction between different institutions, actors, and technologies (Myers, 1994; Robey and Holmström, 2001). For example, Gil-Garcia and Pardo (2005) lists challenges for e-government initiatives, which include challenges related to information and data, information technology, organization and managerial, legal and regulatory as well as institutional and environmental.

An important part of this context—and rarely emphasized in the current discourses on e-government, is the issue of the competence involved in providing high-quality services for citizens. As e-government aims at transforming the way front-end services for citizens are delivered, this typically has important implications for individuals' existing competencies. For example, this can imply both practical and more in-depth knowledge about the consequences for reporting particular cases when using an IT-system compared to a more manual routine. Furthermore, introduction of e-government also typically implies new ways of distributing work and new ways of coordination among different units and disciplines, knowing what others know and directing particularly complex cases to relevant individuals becomes key competence. In contrast to industry that can emphasize on a specific niche of customers, the welfare sector cannot choose not to handle a huge variety of a-typical cases. In this regard, the public welfare sector is a particularly interesting example of so-called 'knowledge-intensive work'; since it has to take into account the full complexity of a huge variety in cases and local situations (Alvesson, 2004).

A relevant analytical perspective in this regard is to conceptualize learning and organizational knowledge as inherently related to practice and context. In contrast to a perspective that views **knowledge** as objective resource that can easily be codified, represented, and transferred by information technologies, this lens views knowledge in organizations as continuously in the making (Blackler, 1995), distributed across individuals and organizational units (Hutchins 1995; Tsoukas, 1996; Tsoukas 2005), deeply entrenched in practices and communities (Brown and Duguid, 1991; Lave and Wenger, 1991; Orlikowski, 2002), and thus inseparable from its broader context (Thompson and Walsham, 2004). On the conceptual level of the individual, a clear-cut distinction between tacit knowledge and explicit knowledge becomes highly artificial. As Tsoukas (1996, p. 14) reminds us, "[**Tacit] knowledge** is the necessary component of all knowledge; it is not made up of discrete beans which may be ground, lost, or reconstituted ... []... The two are inseparably related". This way of conceptualizing knowledge in organization is especially helpful for recognizing the reflexive nature of knowledge—or more appropriate processes of knowing, in terms of how knowing is produced and re-produced through individuals' actions. Rather than simply new facts, knowledge is—as Lave argues, a process: "knowledge is not primarily a factual commodity or compendium of facts, nor is an expert knower an encyclopedia. Instead knowledge takes on the character of a process of knowing" (cited in Orlikowski 2002, p. 252). Accordingly, competence or gaining competence can be perceived as "a process of developing people's capacity to enact what we may term 'useful practices'—with usefulness seen to be a necessary contextual and provisional aspect of situated organizational activity" (Orlikowski 2002, p. 253).

In this perspective, the competence for providing high-quality services hinges on the ability of the welfare service to provide processes of knowing that enact a wide range of different knowledge resources distributed across different local communities' practices and IS. Providing welfare services for individual citizens, whether in terms of digital services on the net—or through face-to-face interactions in offices in local municipals, does not simply amount to 'feeding' people with standardized information and informing them about their rights and possibilities. Our point is not that relevant information per se; as for example information on government web portals is of no use, but that such information always needs to be enacted in the particular situation and case at hand. Precisely, in the case of knowledge-intensive work, knowing is a performed achievement that typically involve a heterogeneous collection of knowledge representations comprising everything from personal networks, paper documents, and different digital representations in IT-systems. Particular mechanisms, or ways of organizing and systems of trust need to be in place for such information to become 'working knowledge' (Ellingsen and Monteiro, 2003).

By analysing e-government in this perspective, our intention is here to contribute to insights that run counter to a perspective that tends to overemphasize the blessings of large-scale integration efforts in public sector. E-government initiatives merely attempting to integrate existing typically heterogeneous collections of knowledge, can turn out to be counter-productive since integration inherently means curbing potentially rich knowledge representations into pre-defined categories and thereby limiting useful sources for cultivating useful processes of knowing. As e-government initiatives typically aim at integrating heterogeneous collections of different IS across different government levels, local agencies, and municipals, existing mechanism for enacting are transformed in both intentional and unintentional ways, risking local breakdowns and a reduction in the quality of the services. Thus, central to our argument is that the existing 'hybrid collective' of knowing and IS together tends to influence the implementation of e-government initiatives.

Empirically, this paper draws on a case study of the local implementation of a national-wide pilot aimed at re-organizing the entire Norwegian welfare sector. In Norway there has lately been numerous initiatives for 'modernizing' the welfare sector in order to transform it to a more effective and efficient organization. We studied one of these—"the Pilot" project (in Norwegian: Samordningsforsøket) which aimed at re-organizing the three departments comprising the welfare sector into one department having common work processes, IS, and local offices. This was tried out in 17 different local municipals, and our case was Saupstad, a relatively large local office in a suburb of Trondheim, Norway's third largest city. In relation to e-government initiatives our findings from Saupstad suggests that the current organization of front-end services as well as back office IS were tightly connected to the processes of knowing in terms of interactive service work of the first-line, problem solving strategies, and the general vocabulary used in discussions.

This is highly important for design of e-government as it underscores that neither re-organizing nor implementing new IS are not sufficient for providing high-quality services alone. A transformation through e-government initiatives must also take into account a change of existing processes of knowing which in many cases imply a certain degree of inertia or path-dependency for such change to take place.

The rest of the paper is structured as follows. In the following section we describe the method used for the research reported, then the basic structures and institutions that make up the Norwegian welfare sector. Next, we take a closer look at the experiences from the pilot project at the local office at Sauptad and show how re-organization is intrinsically related to processes of knowing and existing IS. Then, we discuss and theorize upon the implications for changing the existing processes of knowing and IS in the welfare sector in Norway.

RESEARCH METHOD

The case study took place between 2003 and 2005 and involved two master students in addition to one of the authors. The case of Saupstad was selected because both the previous conservative Government and the local media had presented it as a successful showcase of how the welfare sector should be organized. It was also one of the pilot projects trying out a full integration of the previous three public units.

The primary objective of the study was to uncover the implications of the current IS and work practices for providing first-line service to citizens. We were particularly interested in seeing how individuals used or failed to use other departments' IS as the three departments did not have one integrated system.

We regard our research as an 'interpretive case study' (Klein and Myers, 1999; Walsham, 1995) involving various forms of data collection. A primary source was observing the first-line consultations and the multidisciplinary teams in the back office. This gave us first hand insights into how used information and collaborated in order to provide high quality services. In addition to observations, three interviews of management were conducted regarding the work of the different departments and the implementation of the Pilot project. We also attended meetings and more informal lunch breaks. In addition, we have consulted a number of official documents from the Norwegian Government covering all aspects of the Pilot projects, plans for a new IT infrastructure in the welfare sector, as well as evaluations of pilot projects by Telemark research institute.

To reduce threats to validity (Robson, 2002) in this case study, we have relied on a prolonged involvement in the case, using triangulation both by multiple sources of data and by using multiple observers. We have used peer debriefing after observation in the case, and member checking in that employees in the case units have commented on key findings.

THE NORWEGIAN WELFARE SECTOR

The Norwegian welfare sector is comprised of three core institutions. In a major reform, these institutions will change the way they are working in order to improve a seamless service to the citizens. These departments are the Public employment service (Aetat), the Social security service (Sosialtjenesten) and the National insurance service (Trygdeetaten). We briefly describe each of these institutions, and continue by describing the motivation for and foreseen process for reform.

The national insurance service has three aims:

- Provide safety an ensure welfare for people who lack income from work.
- Contribute to levelling income and living standards throughout the life of individuals and between groups.
- Contribute to self-help in order to give individuals the ability to support themselves.

The service has about 9000 employees and was responsible for transferring 220 billion NOK in 2004 to recipients of national insurance benefits such as people who have retired. 1.3 million Norwegians have national insurance benefit as their main income, and the service provides support to around 2 million users.

The main aim of the public employment service is to provide information about vacant positions to persons seeking employment, guide persons seeking employment, qualify persons who are unable to enter the job marked by themselves, and provide economic support for unemployed. The service has about 3800 employees, and a budget of about 29 billion NOK in 2004. During 2004, more than 450.000 people were registered as users of the public employment service.

The social security service aims at advancing economical and social security, to better living conditions for disadvantaged groups, contribute to increased equivalence and equal opportunities and prevent social problems. They are further responsible for contributing to that every individual has a possibility to live by themselves and have an active and meaningful existence. The service had 4.100 employees in 2004, and had 7.2 billion NOK in expenses in 2003. In 2003, around 135.000 persons received economic support from the social security service.

The Reform

In the past, users of these public services often had to interact with all three departments. A survey from 2002 showed that 56% of the users of the Social security service also use services from one of the others units. Quite often the services have offices at different locations. A report from the Social security service at the district of Saupstad in Trondheim describes the case of "Berit"—a person with intoxication problems - who from 1977 to 2000 gets 94 decisions and interacts with 20 executive officers from all three units. According to the report this is not untypical.

The Norwegian government believes integration of these departments will give the users better service and focus resources on getting more people back to work, and less on communication between the units. This work is part of a large reform process to "modernize" the whole public sector in Norway. Integrating these departments will mean integrating much of their knowledge, knowledge management practises and information technology systems. In the near future, it also means to give the users an integrated initial contact point.

The integrated initial contact point will provide services from all three departments, and will be responsible for all internal coordination in the former departments as well as to other relevant sectors of the welfare state. The main responsibility will be to:

- Provide information and counselling, assistance on job searching, reception and registration of simple forms, and come to decisions on simple administrative matters.
- Clarify working capacity, and more complex benefit needs, make action plans for persons with social problems.

In particular, there are five requirements for the new integrated contact points.

- All users shall have one contact points easily available, which takes care of all relevant services.
- More users than today shall receive participatory processes to get back into work as soon as possible.
- Users shall get a fast and overall clarification on needs and co-ordinated service.
- Users shall have an equivalent service independent of residence, resources, competence and services located in the local contact point.
- Users shall meet a practically shaped office, technological solutions and a professional methodology which invites for participation.

Consequences for IT Infrastructure

Today, the three departments have very different **IT infrastructures**. The Public employment service has a "modern" workflow-oriented business system, which covers all present services that the department is responsible for. The National insurance service uses a range of systems, including a legacy system which requires a user to prompt for information in many different ways to get a total overview of the benefits given to a person. Efficient executive work requires good knowledge of the system. The social security service does not have a national standard system, but several solutions are in use in the different municipalities. The largest municipalities use a commercial business system tailored for the social security where clients are registered, decisions logged and action plans are registered.

This reform is expected to lead to substantial changes in the IS applied. A strategy for short-term integration of IS has been developed. A goal is to establish an integrated infrastructure as depicted in Figure 1, with a common public user portal, a common intranet and a common front-end to existing business systems to be used in the integrated initial contact points.

However, the government seeks a long-term solution in a more "fullgrown and integrated ICT-solution in the form of a business system for the whole or main parts of the welfare administration"1. In the four-stage model of e-government initiatives by Layne and Lee (2001), this represents a step from "vertical integration", where local systems are linked to higher level systems, to "horizontal integration", where systems are integrated across different functions.

But as we shall see in the next section, it is possible to define workarounds that make it possible to work in an integrated manner with the old IT-infrastructure, with a cost of extra administration.

EXPERIENCE FROM RE-ORGANIZING IN A LOCAL MUNICIPAL

The 'Pilot Project' at Saupstad, Trondheim

Saupstad is a suburb located in the southern part of Trondheim, Norway's third largest city with 157 000 inhabitants. Saupstad is a relatively large community with a more heterogeneous population in terms of a larger amount of people on the dole compared to the rest of Trondheim. In this context, a smooth functioning and accessibility of the social welfare system services is considered particularly acute.

The local Pilot project at Saupstad in the municipal of Trondheim was initiated in February 2003 by managers from all three welfare departments (Public employment service, the Social security service, and the National insurance service), and lasted out 2005. The main argument for participating on this project along with 16 other local welfare offices was to ensure a "more efficient workflow and better follow-up of citizens using the welfare services". Before the Pilot project, the different

Figure 1. Integrated infrastructure

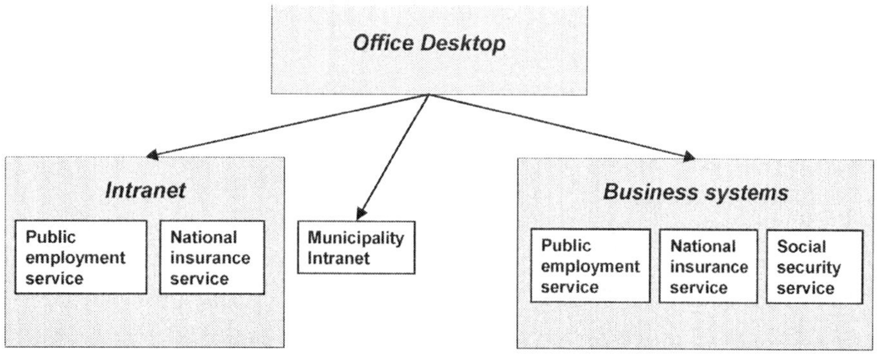

departments had their own front-end service for users and although they had frequent meetings and phone calls across departments, they were largely separated physically, culturally, organizationally, as well as disciplinary. The consequence of this was poor coordination and collaboration between departments, and bewilderment among already frustrated users, as they were often sent from door-to-door, office-to-office. Hence, a primary aim for the Pilot project was to re-structure in order to implement one common physical front-end office for users. After several common workshops the three departments moved into a new building and implemented a common front-end for consultations (see Figure 2) in August 2003.

This was referred to as "one door policy", and according to an initial survey among its users welcomed as a positive change. In addition, a common "back office" was established where individuals originally employed in different departments were put together in multidisciplinary teams for workflow management and solving particularly complex cases involving more than one department.

An evaluation of the pilot projects by Telemark research states, that "The Saupstad model is characterized by that they to a great extent have been able to combine low transactions costs, specialization and overall services. The model has been designed so that all users have been met by a multidisciplinary team, who in total possess broad competence, and have access to a wide range of instruments and decision-making power. One of the prerequisites for this work has been that the units are physically close".

Figure 2. Common front-end for citizens at Saupstad

Re-Organizing Leading to Incompetence?

However, perceived as relatively successful, the "one door policy" also had multiple unintended consequences. Whereas the Pilot project introduced a 'back office' where different departments' local processes of knowing were integrated in multidisciplinary teams, the processes of knowing in the back office became more disintegrated with the front-end consultations.

As expressed by one of the mangers: "the HR department perceives it as a big problem that it tends to be a gap between those who are working in the front-end and those who are working in the back office". The physical and organizational re-organization had generated a lack of possible ways of communicating between the back office and the front-end resulting in not only lack of coordination, but also lack of experience and knowledge sharing. This was considered particularly important since generic rules and policies within for example the social security service cannot simply be 'applied' to specific cases. In contrast, rules and policies need to be made sense of through enacting accumulated experience when giving advice and informing citizens during a consultation. Thus, although the teams in the back office had access to the relevant information through IS and paper files, the re-organization implied a detachment from practice making their work even more difficult.

This illustrates that just having access to relevant information does not necessarily mean that individuals become competent or that high quality in welfare services to citizens are ensured.

As often argued in practice-based theories of knowing, participation and access to a community is actually a prerequisite to learning (Lave and Wenger, 1991). Indeed, re-organizing can in the worst-case mean incompetence.

The Role of IS in Current Processes of Knowing

An interesting finding from our study of Saupstad office was that the Pilot project revealed how the processes of knowing in the different departments were shaped by use of IS. The existing IS inscribed different ways of **sense-making**, possible problem solving strategies, and points of focus.

The information system used by the National insurance service "InfoTrygd", includes a number of specific acronyms which represents specific functionality or status. For example in one case it was accidentally discovered that a person had moved out of the Saupstad area, which meant that the person had to be registered at a different local office. The process for doing this only partly involved the "InfoTrygd" information system, and was described through different acronyms referring to the menus and options that had to be traversed in order to accomplish the task. In this way, these acronyms are frequently used in discussions among employees in the department in order to pass on their experience or to discuss issues of ambiguity or more complex cases. In this way, the acronyms make up a community-based resource for making sense of specific cases and 'transferring' knowledge from individual to individual within the National insurance service.

Similarly, in the Public employment office where they used a more modern information system "Arena" which inscribed a specific structure for the process for how to follow up unemployed citizens, an important mechanism for understanding and generating meaning among individuals was the notion of a "folder". In short, a folder is an abstract entity that describes the status of an unemployed person, which then implies certain trajectories for further work. Thus, the information system inscribes the possible ways of dealing with unemployment persons, and thus implicitly underscores a certain point of focus and a problem solving strategy.

What turned out to be a delicate issue here, was that the Public Employment Service considered it too risky for individuals not being familiar with the departments work practices to have access to their information system. Consequently, without access to the Arena information system individuals from the departments found it difficult to understand the work flow in the Public Employment Service, since it was so embedded in the information system.

These examples underscore that it is difficult to learn the practice of a particular community just by gaining access to its information resources. Thus as noted by Brown and Duguid (1991, p. 48), "The central issue in learning is becoming a practitioner not learning about practice". In order to become a practitioner then, mundane practices and narratives such as the abbreviations in the National insurance service are crucial entry points. What our study adds to this is that in cases where work practices are increasingly intertwined with specific uses of a technology, the technology in itself becomes an essential part of communities' processes of knowing. In this way, the Arena information system becomes an 'obligatory passage point' (Latour, 1987) for becoming a practitioner in the Public Employment Office.

Sharing Experience through Awareness and Knowing-in-Practice

A generally positive consequence of the re-organization was that workers from different departments became more aware of each other's cases and ways of dealing with specific users' problems. The workers developed informal practices for sharing experience regarding specific cases and also more disciplinary specific knowing-in-practice. For example, post-it notes where used in order to give small messages and to coordinate tasks. This sharing and exchange of post-it notes was often done on the basis of overhearing a discussion between a colleague and a user, and a legitimate awareness through eavesdropping developed as a common practice.

This highlights that practices for 'knowing-the-citizen' in terms of his or her 'story' with the different departments were crucial for deciding upon further actions and guiding users to other relevant people those expertise was more relevant. On the other hand, since the back office was located in a different building, this also illustrates that a more informal communication and collaboration support is needed rather than access to different traditional IS and pre determined workflows.

SOME IMPLICATIONS FOR E-GOVERNMENT INITIATIVES

A Complex Hybrid of Processes of Knowing and IS: an Obstacle for E-Government Implementation?

Our study has important implications for introducing e-government solutions in local municipals. First, radical new ways of organizing merely based on improved access to information through IS is a strategy that is likely to have unfortunate consequences since existing work practices and coordinating mechanisms are an intrinsic part of the competence to produce high quality services. In the context of implementing e-government with a larger amount of digitalized services on the net and possibly an even greater geographical and organizational distance from practical consultations and decision-making and case handling, we argue that there is a risk that the quality of service would go down. A most important lesson here is thus that one should not assume full flexibility in re-organizing ways of working just because an e-government solution enables information to be accessible across time and space. As **encoded knowledge** (or information) in IS would always rely on being enacted in concrete practices and contexts by competent individuals and communities (Lave and Wenger, 1991; Orlikowski, 2002; Thompson and Walsham, 2004; Tsoukas, 1996), e-government 'solutions' should not solely be focused on 'improved access to information'. Rather, future e-government initiatives should focus their attention to how information technologies can facilitate individuals' ability to enact knowledge in order to produce better services for citizens. For example, in our study of the practices at Saupstad, we recognized how awareness and physical layout of the offices were important for individuals' enactment of the encoded knowledge in IS. What we argue here in not that the sharing of information across context through IS are impossible, but that it takes a lot of extra work for both the 'producers' and especially the 'consumers' of the information (Berg and Goorman, 1999). The frequent use of 'post-it' notes by the workers on the front-end illustrates this point.

Second, existing IS do not only represent **'path-dependency'** in technical terms (Ciborra et al., 2000), but also in terms of processes of knowing. Existing IS are intrinsically embedded in the different departments' processes of knowing, and hence a particular piece of information only makes sense in specific situations and on the basis of a wider historical and contextual experience. As seen in the case, long-term use of various IS in different departments seem to have influenced processes of knowing in the sense that IS constitute an important component in the different communities-of-practice in the municipal. IS can in this sense be perceived as a material structure for what is perceived as valid and relevant knowledge. Because of this strong alignment between the IS and the processes of knowing the existing IS seem to strengthen the existing processes of knowing. Thus, the technologies are an important component of the existing 'knowledge paradigm' or 'epistemic culture' (Knorr-Cetina, 1999). Processes of knowing and the related IS make up a 'complex hybrid' that cannot easily be split up and decomposed as self-contained components. Consequently, e-government initiatives should focus on both new IS and KM solutions in tandem as proposed by Newel et al. (Newel et al., 2003). However, how this should be undertaken in practice remains an important issue for future IS research.

Increased Integration of IS: A Solution or a Problem?

The **integration of existing IS** suggested in the welfare sector in Norway will obviously make it easier for employees to gather information from various existing systems. By establishing new components on top of the existing IS new services can be provided. One the other hand, there are good reasons for also expecting new kinds of problems due to the increasing socio-technical complexity of e-government solutions.

First, in order to provide an efficient seamless service for the integrated initial contact point, integrating IS is not sufficient. Providing good counselling and quick administrative decisions, clarifying working capacity, benefit needs and making action plans for people with social problems requires a broad overview of laws, regulations, similar situations and an overview of competencies in all three former departments. This becomes increasingly complicated when dealing with situations that require judgements, like most of the work performed by the social security service. In order to increase the judgement and awareness of competence in local municipalities, the sector should draw on research performed in the knowledge management field. A variety of supporting activities should be tried out, from initiatives without a technology element, such as multidisciplinary work teams, information brokers and collaborative processes (Bryson and Anderson, 2000) to systems such as collaboration technology (Munkvold et al., 2006), competence overviews (Dingsøyr et al., 2005).

Second, informed by recent empirical as well as more theoretical literature, integrated IS tend to have inherent complexities producing and re-producing unintended side effects and fragmentation (Kallinikos, 2004; Rolland and Monteiro, 2006). As argued by Kallinikos (2004, p. 13) in the case of ERP-systems, a comprehensive e-government solution would be subject to double-bind effects in that it "both enables and undermines purposeful actions". Furthermore, it is likely that e-government solutions in the attempt to increase integration also would produce increasing risk and fragmentation as an unintended side effect (Rolland and Monteiro, 2006). In order to be implemented integrated IS typically need, in various ways, to connect to and integrate with existing IS and practices that there not anticipated from the outset. Consequently, as argued by Rolland and Monteiro (2006), this increases the socio-technical complexity and risks, because systems that were never mean to be integrated are tightly coupled together. Similarly, in one way or another, existing IS in the public sector are planned to be more or less integrated by a new common system. This will, we predict, increase the socio-technical complexity and risk in the use and management of the system it self, and possibly also in the services for citizens. The question then becomes: who takes the responsibility for these risks? And who has to deal with the consequences?

CONCLUSION: SOME IMPLICATIONS FOR RESEARCH ON E-GOVERNMENT

Many governments are working to realize benefits offered by information technology in e-government initiatives. We have argued that competence involved in producing high-quality services for the citizens must be better addressed in the research literature. Knowledge management in the public sector is a field, which has not been sufficiently addressed in the research literature, but it is a field of growing interest. In a survey on knowledge management in the public sector in OECD countries1, Norway was ranked "on average" on "efforts made at improving knowledge management", and "perception of level and quality of knowledge management practises, organisational and cultural change". The OECD-report "Knowledge management in government" , states that "governments cannot afford to overlook a ground swell that is currently transforming companies, and more especially big companies."

Knowledge management is one of three prioritised areas in the strategy for information and communication technology in the public sector in Norway, which states: "to support the governments goal for the modernisation work, it is important to support development and management of the knowledge capital through a system and a function that maintains the need to identify critical knowledge areas, knowledge development, knowledge directing and spreading of knowledge". They further emphasize that "the value of knowledge management relates directly to efficiency in the sense that direction and spreading of knowledge makes the departments more able to manage today's situation and future challenges".

We believe knowledge management should be a core element of the reform of the welfare sector in Norway, and argue that it is important to reach research-based understanding of how competence influences e-government strategies. In the future, we would particularly like to focus on active experimentation with techniques and tools in the integrated contact points to foster broad competence and increase judgment through action research (Davison et al., 2004) programs. We will specifically address the following research questions:

- How can local municipals implement flexible collaboration technologies in order to cultivate communities-of-practice that cut across different disciplines?
- What mechanisms can be employed in order to develop a necessary competence in relation to e-government implementation?
- How can the socio-technical complexity in e-government solutions be reduced?

REFERENCES

Alvesson, M. (2004). *Knowledge work and knowledge-intensive firms.* Oxford, UK: Oxford University Press.

Berg, M., & Goorman, E. (1999). The contextual nature of medical information. *International Journal of Medical Informatics, 56*, 51-60.

Blackler, F. (1995). Knowledge, knowledge work, and organizations: An overview and interpretation. *Organization Studies, 7*(2), 277-300.

Brown, J. S., & Duguid, P. (1991). Organizational learning and communities-of-practice: Toward a unified view of working, learning, and innovation. *Organization Science, 2*(1), 40-56.

Bryson, J. M., & Anderson, S.R. (2000). Applying large-group interaction methods in the planning and implementation of major change efforts. *Public Administration Review, 60*(2), 143-162.

Ciborra, C. U., Braa, K., Cordella, A., Dahlbom, B., Failla, A., Hanseth, O., Hepsø, V., Ljungberg, J., Monteiro, E., & Simon, K. A. (2000). *From control to drift: The dynamics of corporate information infrastructures.* Oxford, UK: Oxford University Press.

Davison, R. M., Martinsons, M. G., & Kock, N. (2004). Principles of canonical action research. *Information Systems Journal, 14*(1), 65-86.

Dingsøyr, T., Røyrvik, E., & Djarraya, H. K. (2005). Supporting organizational learning: The contribution of a technical skills management tool. *Communications of the ACM, 12*, 96-100.

Ellingsen, G., & Monteiro, E. (2003). Mechanisms for producing a working knowledge: Enacting, orchestrating, and organizing. *Information and Organization, 13*, 203-229.

Gil-Garcia, J. R., & Pardo, T. A. (2005). E-Government success factors: Mapping practical tools to theoretical foundations. *Government Information Quarterly, 22*, 187-216.

Homburg, V. (2004). E-Government and NPM: A perfect marriage? In *Proceedings of the 6th International Conference on Electronic Commerce (ICEC'04)* (pp. 547-555). ACM Press.

Hutchins, E. (1995). *Cognition in the wild.* Cambridge, MA: MIT Press.

Irani, A., Love, P. E. D., Elliman, T., Jones, S., & Themistoleous, M. (2005). Evaluating e-government: Learning from the experiences of two UK local authorities. *Information Systems Journal, 15*, 61-82.

Jones, S., & Hughes, J. (2001). Understanding IS evaluation as a complex social process: A case study of a UK local authority. *European Journal of Information Systems, 10*, 189-203.

Kallinikos, J. (2004). Deconstructing information packages: Organizational and behavioural implications of ERP systems. *Information and Organization, 17*(1), 8-30.

Klein, H. K., & Myers, M. D. (1999). A set of principles for conducting and evaluating interpretive field studies in information systems. *MIS Quarterly, 23*(1), 67-93.

Knorr-Cetina, K. (1999). *Epistemic cultures: How the sciences make knowledge.* Cambridge, MA: Harvard University Press.

Latour, B. (1987). *Science in action: How to follow scientist and engineers through Society.* Cambridge, MA: Harvard University Press.

Lave, J., & Wenger, E. (1991). *Situated learning: Legitimate peripheral participation.* Cambridge, MA: Cambridge University Press.

Layne, K., & Lee, J. (2001). Developing fully functional e-government: A four stage model. *Government Information Quarterly, 18*, 122-136.

Moon, M. J. (2002). The evolution of e-government among municipalities: Rhetoric or reality? *Public Administration Review, 62*(4), 424-433.

Munkvold, B. E., Eim, K., & Husby, O.S. (2006). A case study of information systems decision-making: Process characteristics and collaboration technology support. *International Journal of Cooperative Information Systems, 15*, 179-203.

Myers, M. D. (1994). A disaster for everyone to see: An interpretive analysis of a failed IS project. *Accounting, Management, and Information Technology, 4*(4), 185-201.

Newel, S., Huang, J. C., Galliers, R. D., & Pan, S. L. (2003). Implementing enterprise resource planning and knowledge management systems in tandem: Fostering efficiency and innovation complimentary. *Information and Organization, 13*, 25-52.

Nonaka, I., & Takeutchi, H. (1995). *The knowledge-creating company : How Japanese companies create the dynamics of innovation.* Oxford, UK: Oxford University Press.

Orlikowski, W. U. (2002). Knowing in practice: Enacting a collective capability in distributed organizing. *Organization Science, 13*(3), 249-273.

Robey, D., & Holmström, J. (2001). Transforming municipal governance in global context: A case study of the dialectics of social change. *Journal of Global Information Technology Management, 4*(4), 19-32.

Robson, C. (2002). *Real world research.* Oxford, UK: Blackwell.

Rolland, K. H., & Monteiro, E. (2006). *When 'perfect' integration leads to increasing risk: The case of an integrated information system in a global company.*

Thompson, M., & Walsham, G. (2004). Placing knowledge management in context. *Journal of Management Studies, 41*(5), 725-747.

Tsoukas, H. (1996). The firm as a distributed knowledge system: A constructivist approach. *Strategic Management Journal, 17*(Winter Special Issue), 11-25.

Tsoukas, H. (2005). *Complex knowledge: Studies of organizational epistemology.* Oxford, UK: Oxford University Press.

Walsham, G. (1995). Interpretive case studies in IS research: Nature and method. *European Journal of Information Systems, 4*, 74-81.

Wastell, D., Kawalek, P., Langmead-Jones, P., & Ormerod, R. (2004). Information systems and partnership in multiagency networks: An action research project in crime reduction. *Information & Organization, 14*, 189-210.

KEY TERMS

Community of Practice: Groups who interact on an ongoing basis on topics they have in common. Communities may be unrecognized or recognized by the organization(s) the groups belongs to. The purpose of the community is knowledge-creation, they are usually loosely connected, self-managed and informal.

Competence: The scope of a persons knowledge.

E-Government: The use of internet technology to provide information exchange between public authorities and citizens, companies and other authorities.

Interpretive Case Study: A direction within information systems which sees knowledge of reality as gained through social constructions, focusing on the complexity of human sensemaking.

Knowledge-Intensive Work: Work which is characterized by requiring access to and manipulation of knowledge.

Legacy System: Old computer systems, potentially hard to maintain, and may be running on old hardware which can be difficult to mend. Often, legacy systems are not well understood, so extending the systems and integrating with newer systems might be difficult.

Situated Learning: Learning that takes place in the context which it is to be used.

ENDNOTE

1. Knowledge Management in Government: An Idea whose time has come, Human Resources Management Working Party, OECD, prepared by Jean-Michel Saussois, 2003.

Chapter XV
The Call for Transformational Governance in the Knowledge Economy

Benjamin Yeo
Milken Institute, USA

Eileen Trauth
Pennsylvania State University, USA

ABSTRACT

Increasingly, regions are developing initiatives towards building a knowledge economy. This change is also bringing about a transition from more static forms of information technology (IT) work to more dynamic forms of knowledge work. It follows that knowledge industries will involve more multifaceted forms of collaboration among workers and organizations using IT. In view of the complexities in knowledge work, this chapter develops an argument for a transformational approach to governance, whereby policymakers create mechanisms to continuously evaluate local social contexts so as to continuously adapt policies to unique local conditions. This argument is based on the results of three markedly different case studies of knowledge economies: San Joaquin Valley, California; Ennis, Ireland; and Singapore. These data are used to show how local and unique social conditions influence the sustainability of a knowledge economy. Given the unique characteristics of local contexts, a transformational approach represents one useful approach to governance.

INTRODUCTION

A key characteristic of the new global economy is its shift from a tangible asset-based economy to one that is reliant on intangible knowledge-based assets that depend heavily on human capital (DeVol et al., 2004). Here, knowledge-based inputs replace material inputs as the key productive forces in an economy (Stehr, 2002). These inputs are comprised primarily of human capital and innovation. The most technologically advanced economies are knowledge-based, where information and knowledge are direct productive forces that drive the economy.

The knowledge economy has resulted from the rise in knowledge-intensive work amidst increased globalization (Houghton & Sheehan Peter, 2000). Hence, governments are devoting increasing efforts to the development of knowledge-based industries, whose value chains are driven by human capital, innovation and technologies. In this chapter we refer to knowledge-based activities as knowledge work.

The knowledge economy is characterized by industries that engage in knowledge work. However, as we argue in subsequent sections, knowledge is inherently dynamic and abstract in nature. It differs from information, which is more static and easier to define. Hence, governance of knowledge work is more complex than information work.

The objective of this chapter is to develop an argument for a transformational approach to governance of a knowledge economy. We review literature on the knowledge economy and investigate regional efforts to develop a knowledge economy. We utilize findings from empirical investigations of three regions: San Joaquin Valley, California; Ennis, Ireland; and Singapore, to develop an argument for the importance of a transformational perspective towards governance at the regional level. Such policies relate to business activities that influence the development of continuous innovation. In this chapter, we discuss the call for a transformational perspective in governance to be relevant to the continuous innovation-driven knowledge economy.

This chapter is structured into four main sections. We begin by defining the concepts of governance, knowledge work, and the knowledge economy. We then present our theoretical framework, the case study method employed, and overviews of the three case study sites. In the next section, Findings, we discuss the key themes of the case studies drawn from the empirical relevant findings. In the final section, we consider the need for a transformational perspective to ensure successful governance of knowledge industries in a knowledge economy.

LITERATURE REVIEW

Governance

The Worldwide Governance Indicators Project initiated by the World Bank, defines governance as the process by which governments are selected, monitored and replaced. It is the capacity of the government to effectively formulate and implement sound policies to govern economic and social interactions among its citizens and institutions. (Daniel, Aart, & Massimo, 2008). In this chapter, we focus on the second part of the definition that looks at the initiatives of the government to formulate and implement policies and interactions with its population.

Electronic governance then, refers to the use of information and communication technologies (ICTs) to facilitate government's policies and interactions. Electronic voting and online tax filing systems are examples of technologies that facilitate these public activities. They also facilitate transparency between a government and its citizenry.

Transformational governance takes a different turn. It is concerned with context and how governments change their strategies to fit these contexts. According to the cabinet Office of the U.K. government, transformational governance is about "transforming government through technology. It is also about making government *transformational* through the use of technology—creating and retaining the capacity and capability to innovate and use technology effectively as technology advances. This is the only way in which public services can keep up with a continually changing, globalised society," (Chancellor of the Duchy of Lancaster, 2005).

For purposes of this chapter, we adapt this definition to define transformational governance as the capacity to develop initiatives that can keep up with continuously changing social contexts.

In this chapter, we make the argument that the knowledge economy, and efforts to create and sustain it, occur against a background of dynamic contexts. Effective deployment and leverage of ICTs require an understanding of these contexts. Furthermore, the concept of knowledge work itself is a dynamic entity. Therefore, a transformational approach to governance can allow policymakers to continuously evaluate these contexts to develop effective policy frameworks.

Dynamic Knowledge Work

In this section, we review literature on the information hierarchy to derive working definitions of knowledge work, and hence, the knowledge economy.

Data, information and knowledge. The information hierarchy, given in Figure 1, represents the hierarchy of data, information, knowledge, and wisdom. For the purposes of this chapter, we focus only on three of the four entities: data, information, and knowledge. Data are neutral entities that do not contain intangible values. Upon processing, they become information that informs the recipient about an entity. Further processing transcends information to knowledge, whereby the one who possesses it knows how to apply relevant information to solve problems effectively (Zeleny, 1987). Figure 1 shows the increasing relevance of the context and understanding as data becomes knowledge. The complexity of the context increases as data becomes knowledge, thus requiring higher cognitive processing skills to understand.

Knowledge creation. Knowledge can be seen as value-added information. It is internalized from five different types of information: facts, concepts, processes, procedures, and principles (Clark & Chopeta, 2004). These are defined as specific instances, groups of entities that share common characteristics, processes and activities that describe how things work, detailed steps to perform a task, and guidelines respectively. Clark and Chopeta define these five different types of information collectively as artifacts

Figure 1. Information hierarchy

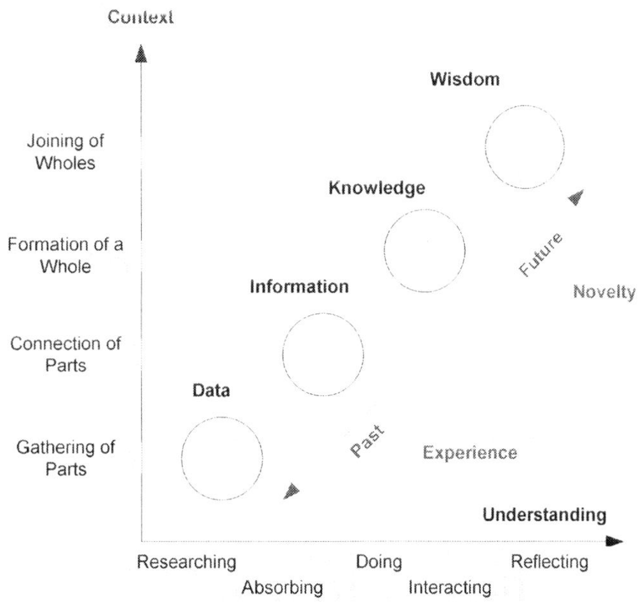

Figure 2. The knowledge creation process

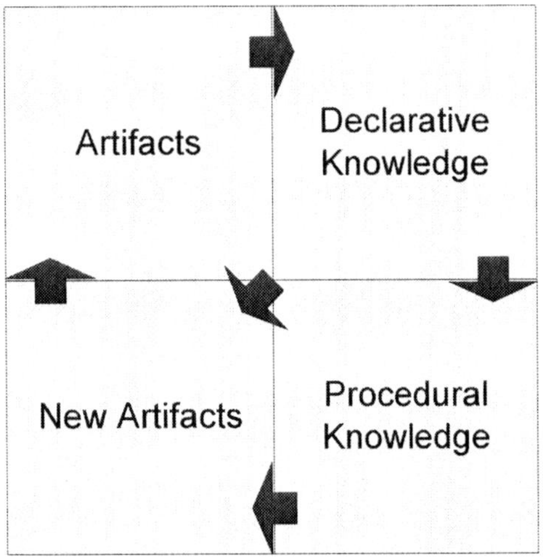

(Clark & Chopeta, 2004). According to Clark and Chopeta, artifacts form the basis for declarative knowledge, which is defined as propositions that enable an individual to represent objects based on their inter-relationships. Declarative knowledge constitutes the basis for procedural knowledge, or knowledge required to perform tasks so as to achieve a goal (Clark & Chopeta, 2004).

Figure 2 illustrates the knowledge creation process, which can be defined as knowledge work (Clark & Chopeta, 2004). Declarative knowledge is created from artifacts to provide the foundation for procedural knowledge. Thus, new artifacts are created, which in turn, become artifacts for new knowledge. According to Yeo (2007), this process highlights the dynamism of knowledge work because what is a creation today is not necessarily a creation tomorrow. The knowledge created however, can be codified and transmitted to others as information because of the loss of contextual richness. In turn, they may internalize the information (artifacts) to create new knowledge.

The preceding discussion established the dynamism, and hence the complexity involved in knowledge work. Knowledge work can occur in any industry that involves the creation of new artifacts that engages in continuous innovation. Therefore, knowledge work can occur in any society; it is not limited to a particular industry (Yeo, 2007). The concept of innovation is discussed in a subsequent section. Using this definition of knowledge work, we turn to the definition of the knowledge economy, which is characterized by industries engaged in knowledge work.

The Knowledge Economy

The knowledge economy has come to be characterized by production and services based on knowledge work (Powell & Snellman, 2004). Today, it refers to economies in which a significant part is based upon the production, dissemination, and application of knowledge and the utilization of information technology (IT) to do so. Value is placed upon the demand for and price of knowledge goods (Drucker 1993). In its economic structure, there is a gradual shift away from an economy driven by material inputs to an economy in which productive and distributive processes are increasingly oriented around knowledge inputs (Stehr, 2002).

In 1973, Bell (1973) defined the knowledge society as a post-industrial society. In his conceptualization of a knowledge society, "the sources of innovation are increasingly derivative from research and development" and "the weight of the society—larger share of employment—is increasingly in the knowledge field" (Bell, 1973, pp. 212). For purposes of this chapter, we use the terms knowledge society and knowledge economy inter-changeably.

The concept of a knowledge economy has continued to evolve. The basic conditions for the knowledge economy today are the availability and viability of information systems, innovation systems, institutional regime, and human resources (United Nations Economic Commission for Europe, 2002). Situated amidst a competitive global arena, the knowledge economy is characterized by knowledge diffusion. It is also closely related to the development of information and communication technologies (ICTs), emphasizes education and knowledge work, and focuses on knowledge creation and innovation (Drucker, 2004; Godin, 2003).

According to Yeo (2007), among more recent conceptualizations, knowledge economies refer to economies whereby the production, dissemination, and application of knowledge are based on the utilization of information technology (IT). This constitutes a significant part of the economy. Value is placed upon the demand for and price of knowledge goods (Drucker, 1993). In the economic structure of the knowledge economy, there is a gradual shift away from an economy driven by material inputs to an economy in which productive and distributive processes are increasingly oriented around knowledge-based inputs (Stehr, 2002).

Following the definition of knowledge work in the preceding section, we define a knowledge economy as one that focuses on the role of learning and continuous innovation (Yeo, 2007). Knowledge industries are based on less tangible aspects of human capital such as learning (Drucker, 1993) (Drucker, 2004). Thus, according to Godin, the knowledge economy is characterized by knowledge diffusion, closely related to the development of information and communication technologies, emphasizes education and knowledge work, and focuses on knowledge creation and innovation (Godin, 2003).

Taken together, methods for learning and competence building through education and training institutions are primary factors that facilitate the growth of a knowledge economy (Archibugi & Bengt-Ake, 2001). In an information economy, which comprises the industry sector that produces, processes, and distributes information goods and services (Yeo, 2007; Trauth, 2000), governance may be focused on developing and leveraging technological capabilities to facilitate electronically-driven processes. However, governance in the knowledge economy may focus on developing and leveraging the development of mechanisms that facilitate innovation.

The discussion thus far points to the concept of innovation as a key entity and driver of the knowledge economy. Baark emphasized the importance of innovation in the knowledge economy that involves continuous learning and creation (Baark, 2005). Since knowledge-intensive businesses are more comprehensive and organized in their approach to adapt systematically to new technological applications (Gates, 1995), the ability to continuously innovate becomes a fundamental characteristic of the knowledge economy (Yeo, 2007).

Because market development is dependent on innovation, continuous innovation will lead to a continuous cycle of knowledge creation in a knowledge economy. Since the knowledge economy is characterized by knowledge diffusion through education and innovation (Drucker, 2004; Godin, 2003), governance in the knowledge economy focuses on developing and leveraging the mechanisms that facilitate these processes.

Governance in the Knowledge Economy

Given the definitions of knowledge and the knowledge economy discussed above, information work can be seen as work that involves products and services that deliver value-added data. Knowledge work, therefore, involves continuously creating new entities. It follows that knowledge industries will invest heavily in research and development (R&D) through continuous innovation. Taken together, the knowledge economy supports R&D by providing conditions for continuous innovation.

This definition of knowledge work is complex because it represents a set of dynamic conditions rather than a static state. This argument is supported by Brint's (2001) characterization of the knowledge economy. According to Brint (2001), knowledge industries that make up the knowledge economy have three characteristics. First, the environment in which they operate is not stable and, hence, is not predictable. Next, the industries are characterized by the speed of change, where decision-making is highly dependent on fast-moving events, such as technology change. Finally, the primary service output of these industries is not commercialized as a commodity (Brint, 2001).

Therefore effective governance for sustained growth in a knowledge economy may be oriented around the ability of policies to create an environment of knowledge creation. And because knowledge is cumulative, this implies a continuous cycle of innovation. Therefore, it follows that a transformational perspective in governance may be an effective approach to ensure its sustainability. In this chapter we discuss three case studies that show the complexities involved in their social conditions despite their similar economic objective of a sustainable knowledge economy.

METHOD

In this section, we outline the research method that was executed to conduct the three case studies. The case studies were conducted as a part of Yeo's (2007) dissertation research conducted from 2003 to 2006.

Theoretical Framework

Trauth's Influence-Impact model (shown in Figure 3) was used as a framework to guide this study (Trauth, 2000). This model resulted from Trauth's study of the role of socio-cultural factors in the evolution of Ireland's information economy and is, in turn, shaped by it. Figure 3 depicts four categories of factors—infrastructure, public policy, economy, and culture—that influence the development of an information economy. Subsequently, the information economy results in societal changes in its infrastructure, public policy, economy, and cultural contexts. The Influence-Impact framework was used to guide this research because both studies sought to understand the influence of the contextual conditions in an information / knowledge economy.

The influence component of the framework (left hand side of Figure 3) was applied to three cases—San Joaquin Valley, a region in Central California, Ennis, a town in Western Ireland, and Singapore. An interpretive approach similar to that taken by Trauth's (2000) was employed to investigate the infrastructural, policy, economic, and cultural factors that contributed to continuous innovation in each context. These findings were categorized into 12 relevant themes in the development of a sustainable knowledge economy, as illustrated in Figure 4. The 12 themes were

Figure 3. Influence-Impact Model (Trauth, 2000)

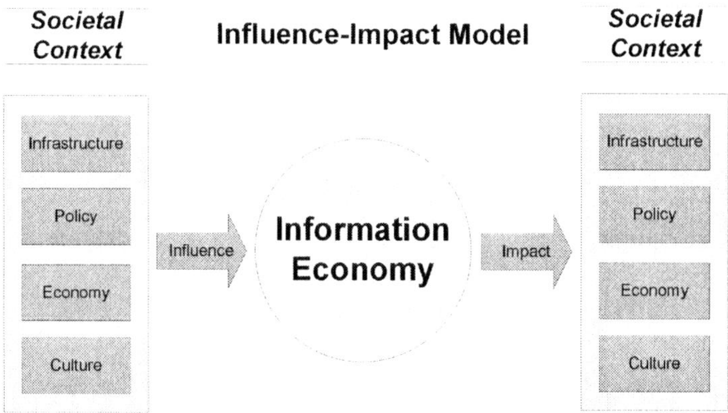

Figure 4. Contextual factors influencing a sustainable knowledge economy (Yeo, 2007)

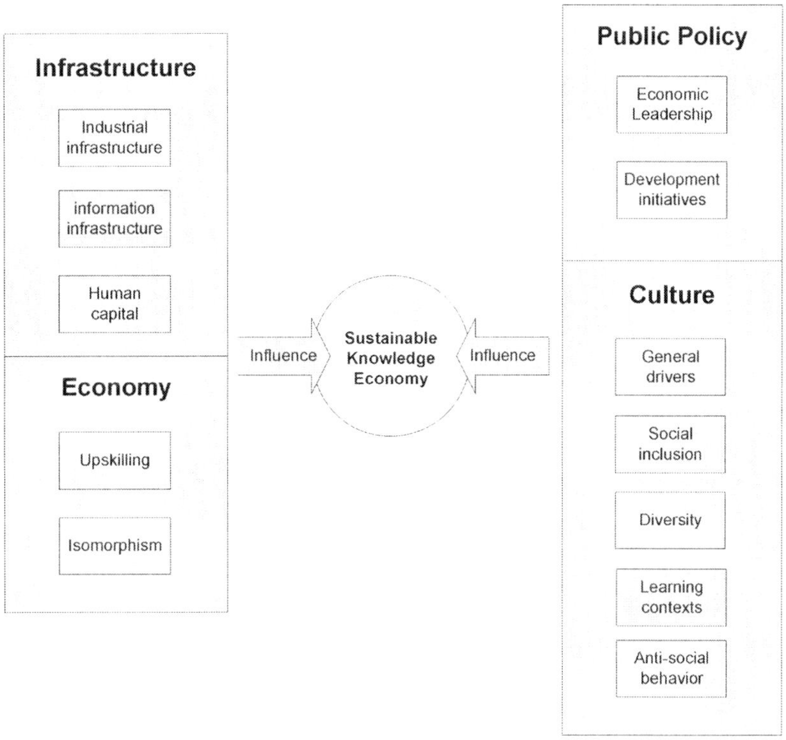

common across all three cases, but were manifested differently because of their unique social conditions.

In this chapter, we focus on two main themes—learning contexts, and information infrastructure—to argue for the need to adopt a transformational perspective in governance. Within the scope of our discussion, we bring findings related to the theme of diversity as discussion points. In Figure 4, the shaded components represent the parts of the larger study where findings were extracted and used in this chapter.

The Case Study Method

A case study is a qualitative research method. This method is ideal when a holistic, in-depth enquiry is needed (Feagin, Orum, & Sjoberg, 1991). According to Yin (1989), a case study method is most conventionally executed to analyze problems where the goal of the research is to understand why or how different phenomena occur, or can occur. It also allows the researcher to focus on the dynamics of a single setting (Yin, 1989). Case studies are designed to include details from participants' perspectives through the analysis of relevant data from different sources. Yin (1994) explained that case studies are often used because the phenomena studied are bounded to their contexts, and therefore immensely complex (Yin, 1994). Ragin (1999) argued that in these situations a more holistic approach is needed. The study must involve a triangulation of different types of evidence using different methods (Ragin, 1999).

We wanted to understand the local conditions in these three regions, and how they are relevant to governance. Hence, a case study method was appropriate because these conditions are bounded to their contexts. In addition, a bottom up approach was used because of the complexity involved in the concept of knowledge work. In this approach, the researchers used the Influence-Impact model as a guide to investigate the themes involved in creating a sustainable knowledge economy.

Case Study Sites

There were three regions used as case study sites in this research—San Joaquin Valley in California, Ennis in West Ireland, and Singapore. These regions are markedly different in terms of their social, political, and economic make-up.

Located in the U.S., San Joaquin Valley is a region targeted by the state of California's development efforts to position it as a technology-based economy. At present, agriculture is a dominant industry (Kirch Foundation, 2005). Thus, the region is an agriculture-based economy, with other industries such as manufacturing, amidst its efforts to develop a knowledge economy.

Ennis is a region within Ireland, a country that leapfrogged from an agriculture-based one to an information economy (Trauth, 1999). In the process, Ireland skipped the industrial economy to arrive at an information economy. Ennis is attempting to leverage the country's achievements to create sustainable knowledge industries. It is currently known as an information age town: an exemplary case of a small town having developed its own information technology base.

Singapore is a modern economy in Asia with no rural regions. It has well-established and well-developed information and knowledge services sectors. Singapore is attempting to sustain its competitiveness amidst intensified global competition.

These three regions are in different continents and are at different stages of development with the common goal of developing a sustainable knowledge economy. However, their experiences with infrastructural development, learning contexts, and diversity point to the need for a transformational approach to governance. A graphical representation of the research design is given in Figure 5. Each region studied is depicted by a circle. The overlapped region denotes the comparison and hence, similarities, among them. In Yeo's (2007) research, each region was covered in-depth for comparison, and common themes were extracted due to similarities across the three cases.

Data Collection

Through the course of the data collection, the first author was immersed in each region in

Figure 5. Research design

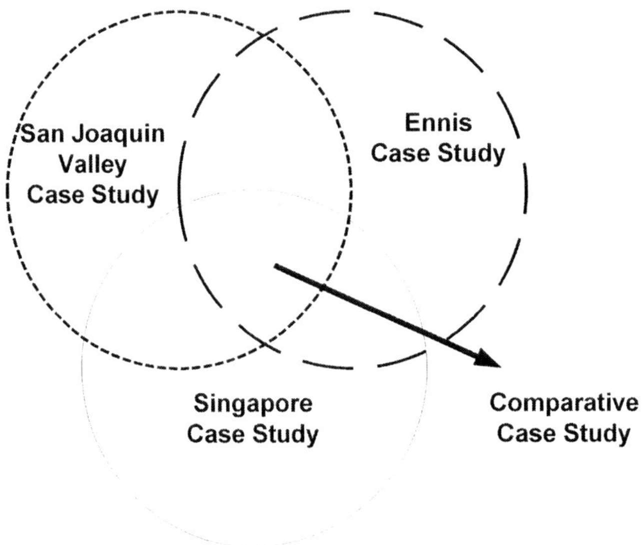

order to obtain an in-depth understanding of the local contexts. The case study findings from all three cases were compiled mainly through a combination of in-depth interviews, document reviews, and participant observation. Interviews were conducted with key informants who were well-informed about the respective regions. There were three types of interviewees: business owners or professionals, economic development personnel from government offices or non-government organizations, and academic researchers who specialized in the region. The findings were coded for similarities and aggregated to arrive at broad common themes. Publicly available documents about the economic initiatives and social conditions of each region were also reviewed. Finally, participant observations in each context were useful in supporting the interpretations. Thus, an in-depth understanding of a community's culture was developed by speaking with local residents, reading local newspapers and participating in and observing their activities.

FINDINGS

In all three case studies, the findings related to technological advancement and learning show that social contexts in the three regions are markedly different. The complex social conditions affect the development of knowledge industries and reflect the challenges they each face. These local challenges, in turn, reinforce the need for a tailored rather than a universal form of governance.

Technological Advancement

During the time of the data collection, each of the three regions had to some degree experienced technological advancements. However, despite the introduction of information technologies, the researchers found that social conditions were facilitating and restricting the adoption, and hence, leverage of these technologies. The social conditions that were very unique to each region were documented and categorized under the theme of information infrastructure as shown in Figure 4.

The authors argue for a need to take a closer look at these unique conditions so as to develop tailored approaches to governance. This is especially so given the high relevance of these social contexts to economic development efforts. The following sections illustrate the findings from each region pertaining to their respective contexts.

San Joaquin Valley. Fresno is both the main county and city of San Joaquin Valley. The county has recently experienced an influx of IT-based industries. Many organizations were adopting fast connections in their operations, and there was an increase in the use of the high-end technological services. For example, the St. Agnes Hospital, the Chamber of Commerce, and the Latino Network are among the exemplary organizations that have used video over telephony. Initiated by the local government, Fresno County was also the first county in California to deploy the GigaMAN network service. Fresno County Office of Education has utilized DS-3 and T-1 services for instructional and business services.

At the same time, some local businesses felt that they did not need organizational information systems such as large enterprise systems because it was difficult to justify the high initial investments (Yeo, 2007). Some have deployed similar systems to manage their businesses but did not appear to exploit the full potential of their capabilities. For example, many rely much more on the telephone than email. Many interviewees have explained that they prefer the telephone to email, even though email has a benefit of making one-to-many communication more efficient and effective (Yeo, 2007).

These findings suggest that the use of information technology in San Joaquin Valley might have been affected by cultural barriers. Several key informants suggested that there may be a lack of a market drive towards the use of technologies because low-skilled labor costs less. Furthermore, an often cited reason for in-migration is the low cost of living in San Joaquin Valley (Public Policy Institute of California, 2004). It can also be argued that this is the same motivation for residents to remain in the Valley. With the migration of businesses and residents, some interviewees believe that they will bring about demand for higher end IT services which will, in turn, boost the industry and the need to create more innovative products and services.

The region has had difficulty in retaining all segments of its population. Those with high school and post secondary education often leave the region because of a lack of education and employment opportunities (Public Policy Institute of California, 2004). This finding suggests that the migration pattern acts as a possible social barrier to the leverage of the information technology capabilities currently in place.

San Joaquin Valley is a case in which availability of infrastructure, alone, may not be the sole determinant of economic growth in its economy, including work in the knowledge economy. Here, cultural barriers also present challenges for this development. Thus, addressing these knowledge economy barriers requires a flexible approach that can adapt to these local conditions. Policies must encourage the use of higher value-added work, while taking into consideration the attraction of low labor costs to businesses. At the same time, it must attract, develop and maintain sufficient knowledge industries to feed the need for a highly qualified population.

Ennis. Ennis did not experience widespread industrial development before becoming a part of the Information Age Town project (McInerney, 2003). This national initiative started as a competition among Irish towns. In 1997, Ennis emerged as one of the selected towns, and received $25 million (using conversion rates in 1998) from Telecom Éireann, the Irish Telecommunications Board, to introduce and build information technological infrastructures (McInerney, 2003; eircom, 2000). The Information Age Town Project task force helped implement information infrastructures and enable businesses to apply these technologies to their operations. Information technologies were also introduced into the school curriculum to prepare students for technologically-skilled jobs (Yeo, 2007).

As a result of the project, Ennis had the highest household computer ownership in Europe in 2000. Eighty-three percent of Ennis' households have multimedia-enabled computers, and 91 percent of these have activated an Internet account. Among them, 45 percent had at least one active Internet user (eircom, 2000). Ennis is also involved in developing third generation technologies to push Ennis towards becoming a leading player in innovation (eircom, 2000).

Local residents in Ennis have access to the Internet from their homes, with reduced costs: $0.92 per hour during peak hours (8am-6pm), and less than $0.35 during off peak hours (The Clare Champion, 1998) based on the conversion rate in 1998. However, metered use of the Internet may discourage extensive use. In contrast, many other developed countries have unlimited high speed Internet access packages that allow users to remain connected. In response to this need, Ireland Offline is a voluntary organization aimed at promoting affordable un-metered Internet access to users (Ireland Offline, 2006).

On the business front in Ennis, not all businesses have access to the Internet in their offices even though they have websites. This is because much of the maintenance is often performed at their homes. Further, not all these websites are capable of e-commerce. Many serve to provide information but do not support online sales. The business owners commented that although they understand the potential of these technologies, they preferred to conduct their businesses in traditional face-to-face ways.

According to Eircom, the Information Age is "one in which economic and cultural life is critically dependent on information and communications technologies and where people get the full benefits of that technology at work, at home and at play" (Mc.Quillan, 2000). Thus, an Information Age town such as Ennis might reasonably be expected to possess such characteristics. However, the case study findings show that businesses in Ennis did not appear to be fully utilizing the technological capability that exists.

Taken together, the findings show that while infrastructure is available in Ennis, business owners might not see the value of leveraging these technological capabilities. Policies may be needed that are geared towards communicating the value of these technologies, rather than being limited to building the infrastructure.

Singapore. Singapore has one of the most developed information infrastructures in the world (Raveedran, 1998). Due to the country's emphasis on information technology development, there is ubiquitous access to advanced telecommunication networks and services. (International Telecommunication Union, 2005). Singapore first began introducing information technology planning and development in its economic strategy in the late 1970s. The strategy of the government was sought to transform the existing labor-intensive manufacturing-based economy into a high value-added post-industrial economy (Ang, 1999).

In 2003, the BackPack.NET Initiative, a five-year project, was implemented. It was aimed at, first, enhancing learning experiences through the use of emerging information technologies such as tablet personal computers and digital ink and, second, creating a framework for industry players, schools and researchers to develop software and solutions. In the first phase, students in selected schools were equipped with individual tablet PCs with wireless connectivity and digitized textbooks. Access to course materials and various Internet resources were available anywhere on campus. This allowed one-to-one teacher-student attention and increased the efficiency involved in pedagogical practices. The wireless connectivity also allowed students to participate outside school hours and engage in real-time discussions with experts in various subject areas (International Telecommunication Union, 2005).

With the level of technological integration and reliance on information services in Singapore, the Information Technology Standards Committee (ITSC) was formed to create and maintain technical standards in 1990. This industry-led effort comprises industry and government parties to ensure the neutrality and viability of these technical standards. For example, these standards include those applicable to the construction industry as well as those more tailored for integrated circuits (Information Technology Standards Committee, 2003).

Singapore can be said to be effectively leveraging the existing information infrastructure. This appears to be a key thrust of the government's IT strategies. The standardization program is an example of this strategic focus. Also, the Intelligent Nation 2015 program shows that the government is attempting to use the existing penetration to increase the quality and quantity of information services through nationwide coverage. Taken together, Singapore appears to be on the forefront of information technology infrastructure development. There is a strong push from the government to develop IT infrastructures, and at the same time, the high penetration reflects positive public responses towards IT development.

Learning Contexts

In the knowledge economy, economic growth is increasingly dependent on the investments in human capital through education, learning, and the institutions that involve continuous innovation. In these economies, investments in human capital are critical towards maintaining the mechanisms that generate innovation: institutions and industries that produce knowledge.

Empirical research in labor economics suggests that education improves productivity (Marshall, 1994), thus supporting the importance of human capital. In the cases studied, attitudes towards learning were found to be influential to the nurturing of continuous learning for the sustainability of the knowledge economy. These contexts of learning involve accounts of receptivity as well as conditions related to training (and re-training) environments.

San Joaquin Valley. The interviews suggested that some members of the local population who depend on agriculture for their living did not place a high importance on their children's education. Parents prefer their children to help out in the farms and carry on the family tradition of agriculture. Some do not think that upward social mobility is possible for them. This observation may at least partially explain the tendency for farm workers to remain at their jobs despite the availability of better wage non-farm jobs (UC Davis, 2004b). The lack of encouragement from the families facilitates possibly negative attitudes towards education among the younger generation.

Local farmers harvest different crops at different places at different times of the year. As such, their children are forced to move with them. Thus, they are unable to complete their education at the same place. This means that it is very difficult to track the needs of the children who move frequently from one school to another. Furthermore, many who manage to complete their education tend to leave San Joaquin Valley because of the lack of education and employment opportunities in the Valley (Public Policy Institute of California, 2004). Over time, this leads to a drain of human capital from the Valley to regions such as San Francisco or Los Angeles, despite their higher costs of living. Most of the farm workers had low levels of education but high levels of engagement in labor (UC Davis, 2004b). A report on the implementation of the California Partnership for San Joaquin Valley contained stakeholder comments about the importance of addressing negative attitudes towards change as a feature of facilitating regional growth (High Beam Research, 2006).

San Joaquin Valley is a largely rural region. However, the teachers tend to reside in urban areas such as Fresno City. This makes it a challenge for them to be engaged in the local learning contexts because they may not have an in-depth understanding of their students' needs. Therefore, a challenge for creating a positive learning environment for rural San Joaquin Valley includes supporting rural education initiatives. One key informant explained that a community reflects its citizenship. Therefore, having leaders to *develop* a community is different from having leaders to *live* in the community. The learning context then, becomes a key aspect of San Joaquin Valley's challenge of developing effective educational programs for continuous learning.

Ennis. A key objective in the Information Age Town Project was to develop Ennis as a center of excellence for lifelong learning (eircom, 2000). Ireland has a long tradition in education. It has one of the highest rates in the world, with 81 percent of Irish students completing second-level (secondary) and 60 percent continuing further studies (Education Ireland, 2007). According to Trauth's (2000) findings on Ireland, "education became a way of maintaining national and religious identity," (Trauth, 2000, p.60).

The eagerness to learn was observed particularly among some workers in their mid 30s. These workers lived through the hype and crash of the dot com era. According to some business owners who employ workers across a wide age range, this group of workers were quick to embrace new methods of working once they were convinced about how these methods can lead to higher productivity. This finding was similar to Trauth's (2000) that young workers in Ireland were more flexible and quicker to grasp new knowledge (Trauth, 2000, p.56). These young workers were the innovative thinkers who fueled the information economy from the 1980s and 1990s. They became this cohort of workers in their mid 30s during the time of the data collection in Yeo's (2007) study.

Among third level students (tertiary students) at the tme of the data collection, there was some fear of unemployment. This fear could have stemmed from the 1980s when it was difficult for the earlier generation of university students to get decent jobs. Following the dot com crash after the turn of the millennium, some became skeptical about the prospects of an IT career, despite the growth of the Irish information economy. The learning context in Ennis is thus, challenged by both attitudinal differences among different demographics, as well as fear and skepticism of high value technology-based industries.

Looking at Ireland as a whole, the segment of the population that has done well economically are those who have successfully generated their own income. This includes entrepreneurs and artists (McWilliams, 2006). The learning context then, is an influential factor in facilitating knowledge work. In the development of an innovative workforce, these attitudes can potentially lead to increased training costs, workload and frustrations (McQuillan, 2000).

Singapore. Singapore's education system is designed in such a way that career paths are efficiently structured and laid out. This system is called the streaming system whereby students are put into different classes and programs based on their academic performances. While there are always exceptions to these possibilities, the system and curricula are designed to facilitate this process. In this way, the labor market is efficiently filled for the growth of its economy.

It was introduced in 1984 by the government as an efficient way to tailor education programs according to the needs and abilities of each student (ThinkQuest, 2006). From a regional economic perspective, this can quickly create a labor force for the fast growing economy. Attempts to implement a similar system in the U.S. were met with opposition because it is a form of social class stratification and were perceived as unfair (ThinkQuest, 2006).

In view of the high emphasis on examinations in Singapore's learning context, exam anxiety was perceived as a major reason for unhappiness among children in Singapore. Almost 50 percent of children participating in the United Nations Children's Fund (UNICEF) survey in 2001 responded that performing lower than expectations in school would make them unhappy. Furthermore, more children fear failing examinations than their kin dying. In a survey conducted by the Singapore Press Holdings in 2000, 36 percent of the children surveyed rated failing examinations as their greatest fear, compared to 17 percent who rated family members dying as their greatest fear (Family and Community Development, 2003).

The findings from a Ministry of Children and Youth Services (MCYS) study in 2004 showed that parents place high emphases on their children's performances in school. About two-thirds want one of their children to be a university graduate and about 50 percent want all their children to hold bachelor degrees. In addition, 50 percent of parents surveyed were afraid that their children would not be able to graduate from the university (Family and Community Development, 2003).

As such, students in Singapore appear to experience pressure from both the system and their families. Policies to promote human capital development and continuous innovation may face the challenge of addressing these pressures.

DISCUSSION: A TRANSFORMATIONAL PERSPECTIVE

The findings from these case studies show that it would be difficult to apply a consistent policy framework in the governance of every region. Literature on policy fit shows the importance of developing policies that are relevant and sensitive to local conditions. With these non-static and non-universal conditions, it is even more important for policies to reflect these characteristics, so as to be continuously relevant and effective.

Governments may therefore, develop processes that continuously investigate local economic and social conditions in their transformational governance efforts. These constant and mutually adaptive discourses from the government and society reflect the transformational nature of both entities in the knowledge economy. From the government's perspective, this amounts to transformational governance where flexible policies are developed to reflect the dynamic conditions in a society.

Transformational governance differs from electronic governance. As noted earlier in this chapter, electronic governance refers to the use of information technologies to facilitate the governance process. This includes using internet-based technologies to facilitate public processes. It was also noted that information differs from knowledge in its nature. Information is static, while knowledge is dynamic. In the information economy therefore, it is possible to rely on information technologies to facilitate efficient and effective electronic governance.

However, the knowledge economy is characterized by continuous innovation, as explained in our review of the literature on the knowledge economy. The three case studies showed that each was experiencing complex social conditions that would not be easily addressed by technological innovation alone. The technological advancements in each region were influenced by their respective social contexts. Furthermore, their learning contexts were faced with challenging issues such as attitudinal barriers in San Joaquin Valley, flexibility and fear in Ennis, and social pressure in Singapore.

These different challenges call for the need to adapt policies to local conditions that may not be static. The case of Ireland shows that workers have different attitudes towards information technologies due to their different experiences. These may remain within their cohort over time.

According to Houghton and Sheehan (2000), effective development policy makers pay attention to the production structure in an economy (Houghton & Sheehan Peter, 2000). Development policies must be assessed based on their structural impact before implementation. This is to ensure that policies can contribute positively towards the increase of knowledge work (Australian Business Foundation, 1997). However, this becomes challenging because the structure of each region can be very different.

It follows therefore, that regions must find ways to adapt their development initiatives to their own unique cultural settings. According to Mukand and Rodrik, these specific cultural settings include characteristics such as history, geography, political economy, and institutions in place (Mukand & Rodrik, 2002).

On another note, there may be intended and unintended consequences resulting from these policies (Trauth, 1996). In Trauth's (2000) Influence-Impact Model, she illustrated these consequences as the impact of an economy on the societal context. In view of this, Trauth (1996) recommended that ongoing investigations for policy making are important in a region's attempt to develop its information economy. According to Trauth (1996), these assessments are not aimed to replicate experiences of another region. Instead, these assessments serve to allow regions to adapt policies to local contextual conditions strategically.

Trauth's (1996) recommendation is not restricted to the information economy alone. It can be applied to transformational governance in the knowledge economy. This is also especially relevant because knowledge work cannot be easily defined by industry types, but by the process of continuous innovation. Knowledge work also involves accumulation and collaboration. The skills acquired can be applied to a wide range of industries. Thus, it is more difficult to create and sustain knowledge industries compared to information industries. In view of this, in the knowledge economy, isolated policies are less appropriate (Houghton & Sheehan Peter, 2000).

According to Houghton and Sheehan, policies for the knowledge economy need to focus on skills, human capital, and learning competencies (Houghton & Sheehan Peter, 2000). These are dynamic entities. Branscomb and Florida argued that workforce quality, knowledge, culture of entrepreneurship and infrastructure, are interrelated and they have broad-based implications on general policy directions (Branscomb & Florida, 1997). Furthermore, technological advancement in itself is a static entity relative to technological adoption. Therefore, it is reasonable to argue that skills, human capital, and learning competencies are dependent on the unique characteristics in each region. Indeed, the findings showed that the social contexts affecting technological advancement and learning were markedly different in each region.

According to Hinsz, knowledge work requires higher-order cognitive processing based on complex, emergent, dynamic, and profuse information (Hinsz, 2001). Technological advancement comes with a gradual shift towards the softer side of IT whereby knowledge management and knowledge workers become important facets of an economy (Yeo, 2007). Collaborative knowledge work requires collaborations among groups of individuals through higher-order cognitive processing. It is comprised of the performance of an intellectual task and collaborative work of team members (Hinsz, 2001). In view of these, developing a knowledge economy becomes increasingly complex.

The Influence of Non-Homogeneous Social Contexts

As an added dimension, regional economic outcomes are closely related to social conditions that facilitate creativity and diversity (Florida, 2002b). Quigley argued that a diverse set of firms and industries benefit the regional economy (Quigley, 1998). Jacobs added that innovation and regional growth are facilitated by diversity in the population (Jacobs, 1961).

The importance of openness to immigration has been a key to innovation and economic growth. This was evidenced by the economic histories of many national economies. The high tech industries in the U.S. are competitive in part because of its openness to the participation of foreigners. In contrast, Japan and Germany experienced economic stagnation because of their relative homogeneous makeup in population (Zackary, 2000). Florida and Gates found that the concentration of the high tech industry and diversity were positively correlated with each other (Florida & Gates, 2001). Florida argued that the relationship between talent concentration and diversity is stronger than that between talent concentration and climate, cultural or recreational amenities (Florida, 2002a).

The three regions were found to have experienced diversity in their economic growth contexts. In San Joaquin Valley, one instance of diversity was the influx of the immigrant Hispanic population that joined the workforce. Many immigrants worked in farms and lived under harsh conditions. They were paid low salaries and had long working hours (UC Davis, 2004). As a result, they could not afford proper housing. Many of them lived in hazardous areas such as open spaces or unused garages.

According to Barlett and Kinney, in 2005, almost 25 percent of Hispanic children in California did not have health insurance (Bartlett & Kinney, 2005). With the high Hispanic population in California, almost 50 percent of Californian children are Hispanic (Bartlett & Kinney, 2005). According to the National health and Nutrition Examination Survey, 77 percent of first-generation Hispanic children were never insured. This stands in sharp contrast with 12 percent of non-Hispanic white children (Bartlett & Kinney, 2005). The low opportunities for medical care leads to their lower performances in schools and later on in their careers (Bartlett & Kinney, 2005).

Trauth's (2000, p.338) findings on Ireland showed that imported culture was not easily assimilated into the existing culture in the workplace. Imported culture in this case, refers to the culture that accompanied the national culture of the American multinationals in Ireland. In her interviews conducted between 1989 and 1990, her respondents explained that in Ireland, tasks were performed differently from the way they were done under an American culture. Echoing this finding, McWilliams (2006, pp.224-225) explained that Irish music became perceived as a "precious resource" in Ireland despite the influx of MTV with globalization, thus suggesting the barriers towards external cultures. In Ennis, despite the increased ethnic mix of students in schools, some business owners remarked that they preferred to employ the local Irish in higher level management positions.

In Singapore, diversity is a clear characteristic in its population. The ethnic makeup of Singapore can be divided into four groups—Chinese (76.7 percent), Malay (14 percent), Indian (7.9 percent) and others who do not fall into this category (1.4 percent). Most of the latter category comprised of Eurasians. In 2006, Singapore's population strength was 4.5 million. However, only about 80 percent were citizens and permanent residents. The rest were foreigners (Singapore Department of Statistics, 2007).

Singapore adopts an open policy towards foreign expatriates, who are deemed as assets to its global economy. Without access to natural resources, human capital becomes critical in its economic development plans. As a result, Singapore's research and development innovation policy is largely focused on recruiting and incorporating foreign talents. It adopts an open policy towards diversity at many levels of management.

The evidence of diversity in all three regions further suggests the uniqueness of their social contexts. However, this further complicates their existing contextual complexities, pointing to a need for localized and tailored governance. Feldman argued that localized knowledge creation can result in higher productivity (Feldman, 2005). Institutions also function differently in different regions (Rodrik, 2000). In view of this, local adaptation is especially important because different regions present unique challenges to governance, despite having similar economic objectives. A uniform and structured approach taken by Singapore in its learning context may not be suitable in the multi-faceted learning contexts in Ennis and San Joaquin Valley. Veugelers argued that structural reforms are complex and require consideration to many local factors (Veugelers, 2005). Therefore, a transformational perspective that is flexible and adapts to these local conditions becomes important in governance. This study has shown this importance in regions developing initiatives towards a knowledge economy.

Limitations and Future Research Directions

The use of case studies as a research method has been subject to criticisms because it is highly dependent on a single case. Therefore, this limits the ability to provide generalizations across other cases (Tellis, 1997). However, Lee and Baskerville explained that generalizations from case study findings can be made to theory and not necessarily to populations. In this way, the generalization can be done even if the findings come from an isolated case (Lee & Baskerville, 2003). Using this mode of generalization, the Influence-Impact Model provided a high level and systematic way of framing and conceptualizing observed behavior in the three cases. By using inductive reasoning, the researchers were able to generalize the findings to the theoretical level: the relevant parts of observed behavior in the three cases were situated theoretically to understand their relevance under various themes. Case study findings facilitate hypotheses formation and subsequent generation of theories based on empirical evidence (Eisenhardt, 1989). Therefore, further testing of these findings can be executed using a wide variety of approaches.

Nonetheless, the use of multiple cases can increase the robustness of the study because the results are strengthened through replication (Yin, 1994). In addition, the case studies here were guided by clear objectives and a basic standard instrument that allow generalizations across multiple cases (Yin, 1989). Under these guidelines, the case study method allowed the researchers to arrive at general theoretical conclusions from qualitative findings. While the conclusions pointed to unique transformational perspectives tailored to local conditions, they can be used to inform policy makers about the need to develop continuous investigation mechanisms so as to continuously transform governance as needed in local indigenous conditions amidst a global arena in a knowledge economy.

Indeed, the report on transformational governance by the Chancellor of the Duchy of Lancaster in the U.K., suggested that transformational governance must "systematically engage with citizens, business and front-line public servants to understand and then specify the transformational changes which service providers need to meet—learning from the best practice already within the public sector, from other governments and from the private sector"(Chancellor of the Duchy of Lancaster, 2005, p. 7). This recommendation further emphasizes the need for the transformational perspective and is consistent with our evidence of unique regional conditions for effective governance in the knowledge economy.

REFERENCES

Ang, P. H. (1999). Information highways policy and regulation: The Singapore experience. In V. Iyer (Ed.), *Media regulations for new times* (pp. 97-114). Singapore: Asian Media Information and Communication Centre.

Archibugi, D., & Bengt-Ake, L. (2001). *The globalizing learning economy*. Oxford, UK: Oxford University Press.

Australian Business Foundation. (1997). Sydney, Australia: Australian Business Foundation.

Baark, E. (2005). Innovation policy forensics: An analysis of biotechnology in Hong Kong. Systems of innovation, institutions, and public policies. *DRUID Tenth Anniversary Summer Conference 2005 on Dynamics of Industry and Innovation: Organizations, Networks and Systems,* Copenhagen, Denmark.

Bartlett, L., & Kinney, J. (2005). *Latino youths in California have lower health care coverage rates than non-Hispanic whites. UCLA study finds investing in health care for youths may lead to stronger future workforce.* California, USA: UCLA News.

Branscomb, L., & Florida, R. (1997). *Challenges to technology policy in a changing world economy. Investing in innovation: Creating a research and innovation policy that works.* USA: MIT Press.

Brint, S. (2001). Knowledge society and the professions. Professionals and the 'knowledge economy': Rethinking the theory of postindustrial society. *Current Sociology, 49*(4), 101-132.

Chancellor of the Duchy of Lancaster. (2005). *Transformational government enabled by technology* (p. 7). UK: HM Government.

Clark, R., & Chopeta, L. (2004). Graphics for learning: Proven guidelines for planning, designing, and evaluating visuals in training materials. Jossey-Bass/Pfeiffer.

Daniel, K., Aart, K., & Massimo, M. (2008). Governance matters VII: Aggregate and individual governance indicators, 1996-2007. *World Bank Policy Research Working Paper No. 4654.*

DeVol, R., Klowden, K., Collins, J., Wallace, L., Wong, P., & Bedroussian, A. (2004). *Arkansas' position in the knowledge-based economy: Prospects and policy options.* Santa Monica, USA: Milken Institute.

Drucker, P. F. (2004). The age of social transformation. *The Atlantic Monthly, 274*(5), 53-80.

Drucker, P. (1993). *Postcapitalist society.* New York: Harper Business.

eircom. (2000). *Ennis information age town: A connected community.* Ireland: eircom.

Eisenhardt, K. M. (1989). Building theories from case study research. *Academy of Management Review, 14*(4), 532-550.

Feagin, J., Orum, A., & Sjoberg, G. (1991). *A case for case study.* Chapel Hill, NC: University of North Carolina Press.

Feldman, M. (2005). *The importance of proximity and location. Knowledge and place: Proximity, mobility, clusters, and institutions: Advancing knowledge and the knowledge economy.* U.S. National Science Foundation.

Florida, R. (2002a). The economic geography of talent. *Annals of the Association of American Geographers, 92*(4), 743-755.

Florida, R. (2002b). *The rise of the creative class–and how it's transforming work, leisure, community, and everyday life.* New York: Basic Books.

Florida, R., & Gates, G. (2001). *Technology and tolerance: The importance of diversity to high-tech growth.* Washington, D.C.: Center for Urban and Metropolitan Policy.

Gates, W. (1995). *The road from here.* New York: Viking.

Godin, B. (2003). The knowledge-based economy: Conceptual framework or buzzword. *Canadian Project on History and Sociology of S&T Statistics. Working Paper No.24.*

Hinsz, V. B. (2001). A groups-as-information-processors perspective for technological support of intellectual teamwork. In M. D. McNeese, E. Salas, & M. Endsley (Eds.), *New trends in cooperative activities: System dynamics in complex environments* (pp. 22-45). Santa Monica, CA: Human Factors and Ergonomics Society Press.

Houghton, J., & Sheehan, P. (2000). *A primer on the knowledge economy.* Melbourne City, Australia: Center for Strategic Economic Studies, Victoria University.

Information Technology Standards Committee. (2003) Singapore IT standards. Retrieved on March 20, 2007, from http://www.itsc.org.sg/index.htm

International Telecommunication Union. (2005). Ubiquitous network societies. The case of the Republic of Singapore. *ITU Workshop on Ubiquitous Network Societies.* International Telecommunication Union.

Ireland Offline. (2006) Campaigning for affordable, unmetered, and broadband internet access in Ireland. Retrieved on March 9, 2007, from http://www.irelandoffline.org/

Jacobs, J. (1961). *The death and life of great American cities.* New York: Random House.

Kirch Foundation. (2005) San Joaquin Valley air quality. Retrieved on February 18, 2007, from http://www.kirschfoundation.org/who/ar2005/ar2005_04.html

Lee, A. S., & Baskerville, R. L. (2003). Generalizing generalizability in information systems research. *Information Systems Research, 14*(3), 221-243.

McQuillan, H. (2000). *Ennis information age town: A connected community.* Ireland: Eircom.

McInerney, C. (2003). Wired Ennis: Learning and technology in an informaion age town. *Information Technology, Education and Society, 4*(2), 9-34.

Mukand, S. W., & Rodrik, D. (2002). In search of the holy grail: Policy convergence, experimentation, and economic performance. *American Economic Review, 95*(1), 374-383.

Powell, W. W., & Snellman, K. (2004). The knowledge economy. *Annual Review Sociology, 30*, 199-220.

Public Policy Institute of California. (2004). *How is migration changing the central valley.* San Francisco: Public Policy Institute of California.

Quigley, J. M. (1998). Urban diversity and economic growth. *Journal of Economic Perspectives, 12*(2), 127-138.

Ragin, C. C. (1999). The distinctiveness of case-oriented research. *Health Services Research*, 1137-1151.

Raveedran, L. (1998). *ASEAN telecommunications regulations report. Media Regulations for New Times.* Bangkok, Thailand: Asian Media Information and Communication Centre (AMIC).

Rodrik, D. (2000). *Institutions for high quality growth: What they are and how to acquire them.* National Bureau of Economic Research, Inc.

Singapore Department of Statistics. (2007) *Key annual indicators.* Retrieved on March 30, 2007, from http://www.singstat.gov.sg/keystats/annual/indicators.html

Stehr, N. (2002). *Knowledge and economic conduct. The social foundations of the modern economy.* Toronto, Canada: University of Toronto Press Incorporated.

Tellis, W. (1997). Introduction to case study. *The Qualitative Report, 3*(2).

The Clare Champion. (1998) *Information age dawns in 2,500 Ennis homes.* Retrieved on March 9, 2007, from http://www.clarelibrary.ie/eolas/coclare/places/infoage/dawns.htm

Trauth, E. M. (2000). *The culture of an information economy. Influences and impact in the Republic of Ireland.* The Netherlands: Kluwer Academic Publishers.

Trauth, E.M. (1996). Impact of an imported IT sector: Lessons from Ireland. In E.M. Roche and M.J. Blaine (Eds.), *Information technology development and policy: Theoretical perspectives and practical challenges* (pp. 245-261). Aldershot, UK: Avebury Publishing Ltd.

Trauth, E.M. (1999). Leapfrogging an IT labor force: Multinational and indigenous perspectives. *Journal of Global Information Management, 7*(2), 22-32.

United Nations Economic Commission for Europe. (2002). *Concept, outline, benchmarking, and indicators.* New York & Geneva: United Nations Publications.

Veugelers, R. (2005). *Assessing innovation capacity: Fitting strategy and policy to the right framework. Measuring knowledge and its economic effects: Advancing knowledge and the knowledge economy.* Washington, D.C.: National Academies.

Yin, R. (1994). *Case study research. Design and* methods. (2nd ed.). Beverly Hills, CA: Sage Publications, Inc.

Yin, R. K. (1989). *Case study research. Design and methods.* USA: Sage Publications, Inc.

Zackary, P. G. (2000). *The global me: New cosmopolitans and the competitive edge - picking globalism's winners and losers.* New York: Perseus Books.

Zeleny, M. (1987). Management support systems: Towards integrated knowledge management. *Human Systems Management, 7*(1), 59-70.

KEY TERMS

Case Study: A qualitative research method that involves an in-depth approach to a single research problem. The goal of a case study is to understand why or how different phenomena occur, or can occur.

Electronic Governance: The use of information and communication technologies (ICTs) to facilitate government's policies and interactions

Governance: The capacity of the government to effectively formulate and implement sound policies

Information: Is categorized into five types: facts, concepts, processes, procedures, and principles. These are termed as artifacts.

Knowledge: The ability to apply relevant information to solve problems effectively

Knowledge Economy: An economy made up of knowledge industries. These are industries that engage in continuous innovation.

Knowledge Work: Defined as continuous innovation.

Transformational Governance: The capacity and capability to develop initiatives that can keep up with continuously changing social contexts.

Section IV
Measuring and Evaluating for Improvement

Chapter XVI
Developing an Interdisciplinary Approach to the Evaluation of E-Government Implementation

Maddalena Sorrentino
State University of Milan, Italy

Marco De Marco
Catholic University, Italy

ABSTRACT

Can we assess the results of an e-government program in terms of its capacity to provide solutions to problems of public import? While interest in the evaluation of public IT investments is growing worldwide, there is also a widespread perception of the inadequacy of the knowledge that informs concrete practices. This chapter adopts a perspective that centers mainly on conceptual arguments; it considers the evaluation as a social research field requiring interdisciplinary inputs capable of shedding light not only on the results, but also on the implementation process of the public services. The proposed interpretive key, which draws on contributions from organization theory, augments the significance of evaluation research. The reflections offered here have the goal of both providing further insights for the academic e-government community as a whole and helping to better inform public management praxis.

INTRODUCTION

E-government is not only growing in importance, but is increasingly put to debate across the world. The public sector's deployment of Information and communication technologies (ICT)—including internet—with objectives such as efficiency, quality of services, effectiveness of the public action, accountability, and a renewing of the political agenda (OECD, 2004) has become a key component in a set of market-driven reforms initiated by many governments since the early 1980s. Now, everyone is looking closely at the level of expectations generated by e-government (according to Lim & Tang, 2008, it 'marks a turning point in public agencies' use of IT') and the significant economic resources invested (Cresswell, Burke & Pardo, 2006; EITO, 2007).

But are the arguments in favor of e-government supported by an adequate evaluation framework? On which basis can we evaluate the success of an e-government program? At present, there are no tried and trusted common criteria capable of responding to these fundamental questions. Our knowledge to inform decisions on whether the social, economic or political effects should be realistically associated with an e-government project and what action—other than the construction of electronic services—is required, is limited (Avgerou et al., 2006).

The diffusion of e-government is documented by huge quantities of data, as attested to by the governmental reports produced on an ongoing basis (Dunleavy et al., 2002). Benchmarking exercises and international country rankings that document the development of the scenario in a comparative key receives ample media attention (Janssen et al., 2004).

In Italy, the nationwide e-government drive is guided by the ten legislative objectives defined by the Minister for Innovation in 2002 (CNIPA, 2007). Each of those goals is clearly stated and, at least on the surface, enables a rigorous quantitative comparison between the stated objective and the current situation. For example, Goal One requires that all those public services flagged as priority be made available online. Each annual report published after 2002 by CNIPA (the independent authority that assists Italy's governmental bodies with their computerization programs) maps the progress of each objective/initiative on the basis of indicators set up at the national level. In addition, some months ago the CNIPA website (www.cnipa.it) implemented a "monitoring dashboard" that enables any citizen wanting to know the up-to-date situation of the 134 e-government projects co-financed by the Italian government Action Plan to get detailed information, also in graphic format, on programs implemented by the local administrations. Another example, again in Italy, is that of the Ministry for Health, which recently published its second study with information on the times and waiting lists for hospital admission and outpatient clinics provided by the national health service. That information was gathered from a total of 367 websites belonging to the regional administrations, healthcare agencies, hospitals and other social service structures across the country.

Are we by any chance looking at examples of e-government evaluation systems? The answer can only be no: all the examples cited are at most systems of indicators useful for formalizing the end of the project/s in question or to communicate to the outside world the results achieved to date.

An analysis of the literature reveals that the debate so far has been influenced by disciplines that address e-government from an isolated and, thus, separate standpoint. For instance, a recent contribution by Chan et al. (2008) observes how the researchers who study e-government implementation generally come from the sphere of information systems. Therefore, the result is for the most part a techno-centric view of e-government (Heeks & Bailur, 2007) or, at best, draws on partial contributions by one or other of the many disciplines that have approached the theme (e.g. economics, policy studies, law, administration, sociology). Another major research current in e-government implementation evaluation is management science, for obvious reasons, given the role played by the consultancy firms that operate in the public sector and the oversight agencies.

This chapter adopts the perspective whereby the evaluation is understood as an empirical research method based on the analysis of the processes and results of public programs, aimed at broadening the cognitive scope of the policy-makers and the administrations (Lippi, 2007; Pressman & Wildavsky, 1973). In evaluation

Figure 1. Policymaking and evaluation types (adapted from: Lippi, 2007, p. 77)

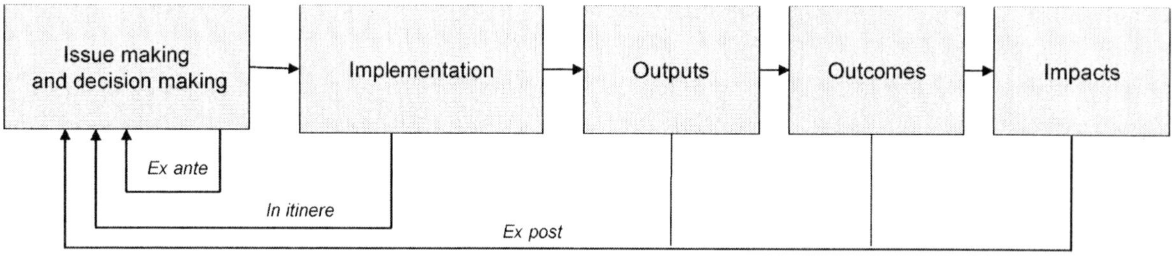

language, that operation of influencing the policymakers and administrations is expressed with the term *enlightenment* (Weiss, 1998). However, in our opinion, e-government would be more appropriately addressed by using an evaluation and not merely a measuring logic, given that this latter assumes two conditions difficult to observe in the PA: limited complexity and absence of uncertainty (Rebora, 1999, p. 16).

We will use the broadest meaning of the term "results" that encompasses not only the services and performances delivered, but also the effects it has on the larger social system. The method of classifying approaches to evaluation adopted here recognizes two dimensions. The first reflects the two macro-phases of the policymaking—i.e., on the one side, issue-making and decision-making and, on the other, implementation—that lead to intervention in the public arena. The second dimension concerns the different types of evaluation that can be adopted, which, according to the object of analysis, are: a) the immediate products (outputs) or the effects subsequent to the public policy (i.e. outcomes and impacts); b) the implementation, i.e. the process of making services operational; or c) the phase in which the agenda is defined (known as the issue-making and decision-making phase). This is how the ex-post evaluation of all the activities that *retrospectively* analyse the outputs, the outcomes, and the impacts of a public policy is defined. The ongoing (or "*in itinere")* evaluation is defined as all those techniques used to analyze performance *during* the implementation process. Ultimately, the ex-ante evaluation is defined as the retrospective analysis of the decisions taken *before* the launch of the implementation phase.

The three types of evaluation, which are separate only from an analytical viewpoint, respond to diverse cognitive needs. The ex-ante and ex-post evaluations confirm or revoke the decisions already taken. Vice versa, the ongoing evaluation—which generally responds to a more advanced cognitive question—accompanies the decision-makers during the actual implementation of the services, accounting and reporting on the situation as it unfolds. Because the ex-ante evaluation has no bearing on the aims of this chapter from hereon we will discuss prevalently the two other categories. Figure 1 outlines the proposed classification.

The discussion that follows is part of the conceptual research and seeks to examine some aspects of the debate that have so far been neglected. In that sense, we propose to help fill a gap in the current e-government literature that—let us not forget—is a nascent academic field (Scholl, 2006). Our decision to favor the conceptual aspects is linked mainly to the nature of the evaluation. Indeed, it is our belief that this latter does not equate to a *generic* study, conducted theoretically or in abstract terms on social change, but, on the other hand, consists of a *specific* study of the change traceable to *one* specific intervention and that alone (Lippi, 2007, p. 54). As a consequence, the evaluation research is initiated on the mandate of one stakeholder, who takes on the role of client; that precondition is unavoidable for the obvious reason that the study pathway and the research questions vary according to the specific needs of the recipient. Disregarding this aspect means misrepresenting the intrinsic mission of the evaluation and comparing it with any other kind of investigation on the social scenario and excluding its calling to formulate opinions aimed at influencing policymaking (Lippi, ibidem, p. 56).

In the following pages, we will seek to demonstrate how the theory of organization provides a core reference point, despite having been inexplicably ignored up to now. In particular, the studies that perceive the organization as a process of bounded rational actions and decisions offer a point of convergence for the different branches of knowledge needed to analyze and evaluate complex social phenomena, such as those connected to digital government implementation. To use a metaphor well known to scholars of public policy (Barrett & Fudge, 1981), we believe a commitment needs to be made to open the "black box" into which the evaluator cannot (or is unable) to see. Naturally, in this chapter we neither attempt to solve nor address the issue of the best frameworks, criteria, parameters, and indicators to use in dealing with the problem of e-government evaluation (although the interested reader can find useful references in: Gupta & Jana, 2004; Stowers, 2004). Indeed, in our opinion, an essential condition for laying the cornerstones of a truly interdisciplinary debate (given the nature of the problem) is a knowledge of the conceptual underpinnings of the diverse proposals and that, in time, this knowledge will help enrich the evaluation research agenda.

Opening the "black box" that comes between the implementation and the result means adopting an observation strategy with clear assumptions on what one wants to investigate compared with the type of assessment required and, therefore, the type of expected results (Stame, 2007). We are convinced that a push in this direction would prove useful and fruitful not only to researchers but also practitioners.

Therefore, in the following pages we will:

1. Provide a map that enables us to better understand the existing perspectives that have already addressed the implementation evaluation;
2. Explain why the mainstream literature does not adequately represent the phenomena related to e-government implementation; and
3. Take a first step towards an alternative interpretive proposal that incorporates and adopts the contributions from organization science.

The chapter proceeds as follows. We first explain the reasons underpinning the interest in e-government evaluation and describe the different levels of evaluation. We then illustrate why evaluating e-government is intrinsically problematic. After which we briefly review the relevant literature on this field. The next section highlights the key assumptions of the most common approaches and explains why the evaluation proposals and systems developed to date fail to fully convince. We then propose the Theory of Organizational Action (TOA) as an interdisciplinary touchpoint for analyzing e-government implementation. The following section discusses some of the possible implications related to the use of this framework for the research and practice of e-government evaluation. Ultimately, the conclusions offer some final remarks.

THE RATIONALES FOR EVALUATING

Each country shows a growing interest in the evaluation activities of public ICT investments (Dawes, 2008). Evaluation is needed to argue the case for new projects and expenditure, to justify continuing with initiatives, to allocate additional IT funds, to assess progress towards program goals and to understand impacts (OECD, 2004, p. 134). Evaluating e-government is now more important than before, especially in those contexts (e.g., Italy) where "the evaluation practice centers prevalently on the analysis of public investments in the preliminary stage, having given up the investigation of the post-implementation effects on the concrete reality of things" (Marra, 2004). The proof of the success or failure of e-government programs is far from conclusive, also because e-government is invariably associated with significant and growing expectations (OECD, 2004; Scholl, 2005; Sorrentino, 2006). But what are we learning from the e-government experiences underway?

The regular surveys carried out by authoritative institutions such as the OECD reflect the widespread perception of the inadequacy of the knowledge that informs concrete practices. In one of its latest reports, referring to Holland, which is certainly one of the most advanced countries on the digital government front (OECD, 2007, p. 17), we read: "The purpose (of the government officials, authors' note) in monitoring and evaluating activities primarily seems to be that of tracking user take-up of e-services, not determining whether overarching e-government goals of efficiency and effectiveness are being met". Even such an advanced country as Norway "a whole-of-government framework for monitoring and evaluating e-government at the ministry and agency level is still not in place" (OECD, 2005, p. 147).

We should not be surprised by the fact that many public evaluators prefer to focus on the least problematic aspects, or what is called 'delivery benchmarking' (for example, many countries have successfully set up systems of indicators for measuring progress in the development of the so-called information society). The reason for that is readily explained. Conducting an evaluation based on systems of indicators translates into using data and information that mostly exists already within the PA, which indubitably favors the diffusion of such practices. The other advantage is that the performance indicators can be presented in a selective way (i.e. 'without evidence of lack of success', Thompson, 1967, p. 93). Sometimes, the administrations do not seem concerned with correctly zooming in on the problem or the phenomenon that the indicators are meant to represent. Consequently, these are often presented as given parameters of success, while, in reality, they simply document the results obtained in the timeframe in question, such as the economic and technical investments, user categories, user satisfaction levels, level of service interaction, and compliance with international standards, etc. (for a review, we refer the reader to, for example, West, 2005; 2006). According to Rebora (1999, p. 40), in these cases, it is more appropriate to talk about pre-evaluation methods.

The case of Italy illustrates the problems of approaching e-government without the support of an adequate evaluation framework. According to Picci (2006), such a "poor" reference model for e-government policy as that of Italy offers—necessarily—a reduced whole of measuring possibilities. The benefits cited in the governmental reports published in the past few years—continues the author—are not measurable because they are not explained. Likewise, the "great leverage effect" of these benefits is not quantifiable because it is not clear about either what it deals with or from what and in what way it derives. The lack of a model stops us from identifying, among the variables deemed relevant, the cause-effect relationships that, in principle, would enable the temporal monitoring—and successive quantification—of the programs' development. Even hypothesizing a "limited" evaluation attempt in terms of the envisaged savings—Picci goes on to say—it is impossible to formulate adequate forecasts. It is not enough, for example, to multiply the cost difference between the provision of a service in the traditional way and the corresponding online service for the expected number of online service take-ups. Even if we want to follow this apparently simple road, we first need to define the number of these latter, but that data—in turn—depends on several factors, many of which are influenced by policy choices. Such an uncertain and undefined picture—concludes Picci—should induce caution when formulating any kind of savings forecast based on the take-up of online services.

THE ROLE OF EVALUATION

On its own, evaluation is a very broad area indeed, encompassing many fields of application and many of the different process phases typical of the implementation of a particular project or program (Hirschheim & Smithson, 2000). It sets out to analyze the results of a specific project or program, broadening the cognitive position of the actors involved. The aim is to offer (to those who want to know: e.g., policymakers, citizens, institutions) a founded and constructive opinion. Therefore, the evaluation is an investigation of the real situation aimed at observing its dynamics and the transformations versus an intention, by which we mean a previously specified outlook of change. Implementation and evaluation are the opposite sides of the same coin, implementation providing the experience that evaluation interrogates and evaluation providing the intelligence to make sense out of what is happening (Pressman & Wildavsky, 1973, p. xv)

Taking different cognitive positions leads to different opinions (Lippi, 2007, p. 21). The most diffused cognitive position is that of common sense. A common sense opinion, as expressed by the man on the street, translates into the approval or disapproval of the conduct of the administrators in respect of a certain service or on the principles guiding the action. That type of opinion expresses agreement or disagreement, but does not provide an evaluation on the merit and does not serve to understand the reasons for the success or lack of success. According to Lippi, it is positioned at a *zero level* of the evaluation. An example of this type of evaluation is the heated debate—reported also in Italy's leading newspapers—that has involved the various layers of public opinion following the City of Milan's introduction of a vehicle entry charge (called the Ecopass) aimed at restricting the access of polluting vehicles to the town center. The launch of the initiative (the first of its kind in Italy) required substantial investments in ICT that have led, among other things, to the installation of 43 access points manned by CCTV and other remote control devices. The new system also harnesses a complex computer network, encompassing information desks, websites, call centers, and automated teller machines, to enable applicant citizens to pay and receive the access pass. The provision in question came into force in January 2008 and, according to the mayor, is in experimental form.

In addition to the common sense-derived opinion, we have the cognitive opinion of the expert, i.e. opinions that are founded on direct experience or competence. The opinion of the stakeholders is, by definition, partisan (Lindblom, 1964). Therefore, if a stakeholder is a political body, the evaluation will be guided, above all, by its ideological orientation and interests. This latter—in the policymaking arena—is positioned at *level one*. To continue with the example of Milan, politicians and technicians from a range of disciplinary spheres have expressed opinions on the decisions taken by the city administration and on the basis of their respective political party leanings and responsibilities in the matter. A great many provincial, regional and, government institutional representatives have intervened in the debate. Citizen committees and delegates of the various business categories (e.g. retailers, professionals, companies based in the suburbs) have made suggestions. The City of Milan went ahead with the experiment and uses its "Mobility Agency" to systematically diffuse the technical reports and data derived from monitoring air quality in the Ecopass area.

The opinion above that of "level one" comes from outside the policymaking arena, i.e., it is not influenced by vested party interests. This type of opinion stems from an extraneous cognitive position, which we can class as *level two* of the evaluation. This position is ideal as it not only enables the policymakers to enrich their knowledge, but also raises the degree of accountability to the citizen-voters. In that sense, the evaluation expands the cognitive positions of the policymakers and helps to shed a new and different light on the problems in question.

The implementation of the Ecopass project was fraught with delays related to the introduction of the electronic payment systems for the permits. In addition, a malfunction in the device that automatically reads the number plates caused the issuance of c. 160,000 fines to motorists unaware that they had infringed the new regulations for driving into Milan town center. The ensuing requests for clarification by the motorists sent the municipal offices and the call center into turmoil, while the justices of the peace and the prefectures were swamped with appeals. The shifting of the responsibility between the implementers (which received much coverage in the press) and the critics of the procedures adopted for purchasing the technologies exacerbated the disputes between the supporters and the opponents of the regulation, which, however, was not modified. Most of the glitches encountered on the technological front were eventually removed, nevertheless, the experience of the January-September period revealed a substantial cognitive deficit between the actors involved: some of whom had no idea of the work done by the others, even though the implementers (traffic police, municipal transport company, information systems department, councilors) report to exclusively the same institutional subject, i.e. the City of Milan. This latter continued to issue reports on the level of air pollution in the regulated area. At the time of writing this chapter, no external evaluation had been conducted on the City of Milan's Ecopass project, at least to our knowledge.

THE METHODOLOGICAL CHALLENGES

Public administrations implement e-government while facing two uncertainties: that of successfully rolling out the projects and that of satisfying the needs that inspired them. The uncertainties of e-government are its realization on the technical level, but also the effects on the society that surrounds it. Using a classification of effects shared by several disciplinary spheres, we define e-government outputs as those immediate "products" generated by the work of the PA—e.g., the amount of IT investments, the number of e-applications processed, the number of digital signatures issued, the amount of time users spend on a website, and the permits and other documents downloaded. On the other hand, e-government outcomes are the short- or medium-term effects that emerge when the output reaches the target market—citizens, businesses, other PA (e.g., number of registered users, adoption rates within specified user groups, level of citizen satisfaction, accessibility of services, response time, trustworthiness). Ultimately, the impacts refer to the capability of the program to address the underlying problem/s; among the many examples is the reduction of social unrest, equity, greater democratic participation, the narrowing of the digital divide, and citizen perception and engagement, promoting community wellbeing, etc. Compared with the effects mentioned earlier, the impacts are more ambitious as these force administrations 'to ask what is the final significance of what they are doing" (Regonini, 2001, p. 163). The uncertainty of the effects of e-government is generally proportionate to the degree of complexity and relevance of the initiatives/services implemented.

E-government shares with other public policy sectors the presence of some methodological issues that reflect on the evaluation agenda. Gregory & Martin have conceptualized (1994, S45-49) the key issues that need to be addressed by the evaluators in order to derive reliable assessments of the success of public programs, which are:

1. time and timing (i.e., the time at which an evaluation is undertaken and the period over which the program impacts are assessed);
2. focus (i.e., the purpose of the evaluation);
3. goal specification (i.e., the extent to which policy objectives have been achieved);
4. additionality (i.e., the possibility of attributing program impacts directly to the service/s implemented);
5. choice of impact measures (i.e., the measures used to assess the progress made towards the program goals);
6. beneficiaries (i.e. policymakers, researchers/evaluators, independent funding organizations, and policy recipients or 'consumers'); and
7. success criteria (i.e., how to define success or failure).

Entering the discussions that underlie each of the above issues—which correspond to the methodological challenges—would enable us to take some great strides forward. While here we have proposed simply a list, the interested reader can refer to the original text for more in-depth information. We believe that the questions raised by Gregory and Martin drawing upon policy studies are worthy of our full attention and that they can provide useful ideas also for the reflection on e-government evaluation. In addition to the issues identified above, we can cite two other challenges on which we should also focus when formulating an opinion on the results of an intervention program.

Above all, we need to consider that only in rare cases does e-government lead to the implementation of individual, isolated projects. In fact it is far more likely that it requires a parallel number of interrelated change programs, which prompts us to examine two critical factors (Lippi, 2007). The first is whether implementation involves more than one level of government or whether it involves different forms of multilevel governance, perhaps intersecting also with other non-institutional actors. The second critical factor is whether the unit of analysis is inter-organizational, that is, if the programs need to be implemented, for instance, solely at the administrative level, by diverse public and private-sector offices and organizations. Let us take the example of the one-stop shops (i.e., single points, either geographical or electronic, in which a number of governmental departments integrate their operations to deliver the public services directly to the citizens, Petrakaki, Hayes & Introna, 2008). The implementation of this type of solution ('seamless government') from the technical viewpoint implies investing in ICT to create interfaces and connections between archives and legacy information systems, but, the most important questions regard the design, planning and implementation of new operating practices and routines to manage forms of interagency cooperation between the public administrations involved. In addition, we need to focus on the role of the organizational actors (e.g., officers, counter clerks, social workers, administrative workers), who, remaining almost totally in the dark due to their apparent role as expediters, can have an impact on the process by exercising an unpredictable discretionary power: what are called *street level bureaucrats* (Lipsky, 1980) can upset or reshape the spirit of a program or public policy. The evaluation must factor in not only the end-users, but also the system of interests (more or less organized) that surrounds it. Returning to our example of one-stop shops, the professionals (e.g., recruitment consultants, notaries, accountants, civil engineers) and the banks can put on pressure to attain or reject the new electronic services. In this sense, they play an increasingly determining role in the success of e-government initiatives (Capgemini & TNO, 2004). Evaluating therefore means entering a tangle of cause-effect relations that tends to swell and expand to infinity. Drawing the line at some point, by, for instance, excluding some of the causes and including others from the evaluation is a tough job and almost never "neutral", given that it is accompanied by many theoretical, political, and ethical implications.

The second methodological challenge in evaluating e-government is the availability of a competent workforce (Gupta & Jana, 2003). The earlier generation of computerized services launched by the public administrations mainly consisted of obligatory projects or to comply with specific legislation or to create communication infrastructures or large-scale information systems in which to deploy activities/software applications traceable directly to the institutional mission of the public agencies (De Marco & Sorrentino, 2007). We should not be surprised at the fact that, up till recently, ICT initiatives were either not evaluated at all or were assessed symbolically, based on what Schick (1971) has effectively defined "pseudo-evaluation". Given that the choices were obligatory and could not be postponed, the agencies rarely felt the need to undertake a systematic assessment and monitoring activity that shifted from the reporting and measuring of the classic parameters of IS performance evaluation. Neither should we be surprised by the fact that the bureaucrats—motivated by the lack of available resources to dedicate to the evaluation—traditionally have ranked the performance improvement of the programs mandated to them very low on their list of priorities. e-government (which cannot always be strictly considered an obligatory program environment) requires employees to move away from the traditional mindset (Gupta & Jana, 2003).

The concomitant presence in the public sector of two weak factors that feed off each other (i.e., the low level of sensitivity and the lack of the development of specific skills) seriously risks compromising the practicability and efficacy of the evaluation. In Italy, for example, the 2008 Finance Bill obliges the managers of local public services to publish a "Service Quality Charter" and to involve the consumer associations in their periodical audits of service adequacy. If there is no action to stimulate and develop the evaluation culture, then it will be reduced to a mere act of compliance with the law. Should that logic prevail, any evaluation system (not only e-government) will, at most, be able to develop only as a bureaucratic superstructure, and will find it difficult to have a real impact on the practices of the public administrations.

LITERATURE REVIEW

Evaluation research is a highly composite field. The studies that have approached evaluation from the information systems (IS) viewpoint are an obligatory reference point for those seeking to understand and assess whether ICT is used appropriately or inappropriately to achieve the specific objectives. According to some authors (Symons, 1991; Klecun & Cornford, 2005; Willcocks & Lester, 2000), any evaluative activity needs to consider the evaluation context (who is evaluating and why), the process (how), and the content (what). Another significant aspect for the purposes of the evaluation (and its results) is the choice of the time (when) to carry out an evaluation effort (Hirschheim & Smithson, 2000).

Mainstream IS literature distinguishes between formative and summative evaluation (e.g. see Kumar, 1990 and cited references). The former "produces information that is fed back during development to help improve the product under development. (...) Summative evaluation is done after the development is completed". Summative (or post-implementation) evaluation provides information about the effectiveness of the product to those decision-makers who are going to be adopting it. The decision to rely on one or another type depends on the cognitive needs of the evaluator: supervising the process of a program underway (formative); or pulling strings in view of a new program, in the case of the summative evaluation.

While we do not have room here to go into a full review of the many contributions on information systems evaluation produced over the years, historically, we can say that much of the debate has centered on identifying the criteria, methods and indicators that show how well the information system or its components operate (Alter, 1996; Heintze & Bretschneider, 2000), where the main objective is to make the software as 'reliable' as the underlying hardware. Various approaches have been developed to improve efficiency (defined as performing a particular task well in relation to given criteria). There are many proposals and recommendations for implementing computer-based information systems (IS) in cost-efficient ways, for identifying gaps in particular performance criteria (Seddon et al., 1999; Willcocks & Lester, 2000). The literature abounds with suggestions on how to measure the success of IS through methodologies and sets of indicators (Newcomer & Caudle, 1991; Stewart & Walsh, 1994).

An alternative approach to the evaluation seeks to show not only whether an information system performs, but also how it fits the people who use it and, as such, its influence on working practices. That perspective means an evaluation focused on the identification and assessment of the gaps between what the different categories of users and developers expected, and its actual performance. The studies that spotlight the social dimension of IS place actors and the respective agendas and expectations at the centre of their analysis. These contributions see the evaluation tend to lose its (presumed) ideological neutrality to instead take on a political connotation, which takes account of the competing interests, the values, the symbolic actions and the personal views of the diverse subjects (Symons & Walsham, 1991; Walsham, 1993). The basic conviction is that the power relations between the different groups represented in the evaluation affect the evaluation outcome. Critical studies also acknowledge that vested interests take an active part in constraining the evaluation process itself, since evaluation, potentially, redistributes power (Klecun & Cornford, 2005, p. 230).

Management science is another fundamental reference point in evaluating the implementation of a project or policy of any scale or scope, based on the resources brought into play. In particular, the contributions that inspire what is called New Public Management, NPM (Barzelay, 2001; Flamholtz, 1996; Hopwood & Miller, 1994) have led to the importation of ideas, techniques and organization structures from the private sector. This current of study is interested in examining the economic conditions that enable the administrations to satisfactorily meet (in terms of quantity, quality, time, and cost) the citizens' demand for goods and services. Therefore, the evaluation analyzes the resources (input) used to launch program implementation, that is, the regulatory, human, organizational, technological, and financial resources, then the processes adopted to transform those inputs into results, i.e. activities and services that can be used by the target market. Cheng, Cheng & Yang (2007) suggest the Balanced Scoreboard approach and attempt to devise a systematic e-government evaluation framework. Distinguishing the results in terms of output, outcome and impact is retained highly significant by the management scholars because it induces the administrations to surpass the self-referential criteria in the evaluation, obliging them to compare the final goals of their program. In the absence of such pressure, maintain the followers of the managerial approach to evaluation, those responsible for the implementation tend to present the data as indicators of the success of their initiatives, while these simply explain what has been done. The most orthodox of the evaluation analyses carried out in line with the dictates of management science has been the object of many critics (Regonini, 2001). But that detracts nothing from the fact that in all the countries where it is practiced, it has been a fundamental component of the public intervention at whatever level. In Italy, management control is perhaps the managerial means that has grabbed the most attention in the public administration in the past decade .

The e-government theorists have addressed the evaluation theme by using a variety of research approaches. A substantial body of literature has sought to demonstrate the presence of causal relations between particular e-government projects or initiatives and some of the intangible effects, including: accountability, transparency, citizen trust, and so on. On the subject of accountability (see: Griffin & Halpin, 2005; Gupta & Jana, 2003; Janssen, Rotthier & Snijkers, 2004), the study by Wong & Welch (2004) compares the openness of the websites of e-governments in 14 countries and tests the impact of the contextual and organizational factors on their openness. In other cases, the objective of the scholars is to identify and evaluate patterns in the development of e-services in the regional and local governments (Kaylor, Deshazo & van Eck, 2001; Irani et al. 2005; Löfstedt, 2007) or between countries (Janssen, Rotthier & Snijkers, 2004; Pina, Torres & Royo, 2007). Peters, Janssen & van Engers (2004) have tried to evaluate the current measurement instruments used by Dutch agencies to benchmark their situation. A recent study by Lim & Tang (2008) analyzed whether and how e-government and related initiatives affect the perceived performance of environmental decision-making. Each time, the research sets out to offer insights and key factors from e-government implementation efforts (Beynon-Davies & Williams, 2003; Chan, Lau & Pan, 2008; Pardo & Scholl, 2002).

Other, less numerous studies have attempted to develop frameworks to support the evaluative design of e-government projects, as in the case of Grimsley, Meehan & Tan (2005), who produced a model based on a stakeholder-centric approach. While the attempt by Fear (2007, p. 13) is highly ambitious as it proposes a useable interpretive model—according to the author—as a framework to: (a) determine which components are essential to give the policy external validity, credibility , implementability, and so on; and (b) provide a common point of reference for policymakers, stakeholders, and evaluators. Ultimately, we cite the original work by De' (2006), who placed the evaluation of e-government systems in a larger perspective that factors in the effects of the projects on the policy takers. Drawing on a dual analytical repertory—i.e. that offered by management sciences and that of the Theory of Development proposed by Nobel laureate Amartya Sen—the author has demonstrated the usefulness of approaching the evaluation theme from an interdisciplinary perspective, integrating the contributions proposed by different areas of study.

OPENING THE BLACK BOX

The above selective, but not exhaustive review confirms that evaluation is a vast field that draws on numerous contributions of interest, which naturally deserve to be recognized and appreciated. The diverse studies have been produced in a way that makes it difficult to compare the different proposals and not only because it remains still unclear as to whether e-government initiatives make a substantive contribution to public sector performance (Bertot and Jaeger, 2008; Moon, 2002; Lim & Tang, 2008). Or because mixed research findings are often presented (Avgerou et al., 2004), but also, and above all, because the authors' orientations are sharply diverse. Each time it is maintained that the technologies impose change on the public administrations. In this case, the dependent variable is the organization: "the organizations must adapt to technological change" (Cyert & Kumar, 1994, p. 333). In other cases, the dependent variable is the technology (or its pattern of diffusion within or across society), which is considered a means to attain the objectives of the public organizations that use it. According to this second perspective, the dependent variable is the technological constraint: "[technology] is the means to achieve the goals of those who use it" (Kraemer & Dutton, 1979, p. 102).

In essence, the practice of the implementation, of the products generated, or of the effects sparked by the e-government projects are still a black box in most cases. Why then do the evaluation proposals developed to date fail to fully convince? It is not easy to answer that question without referring to specific examples of techniques, tools or empirical cases. As we want to suggest a reflection of the general type, we must necessarily refer to the fundamental assumptions of the discourse, given that our interest is in highlighting which methods of reading and interpreting the organized reality underpin the contributions indicated in the earlier section. The most basic question is: what is the idea of organized setting that underpins the proposals formulated by the different authors?

In attempting to respond to that question, we will focus on two crucial aspects of our discussion: the relationship between technology and organization, and the concept of rationality. However, we must warn readers that a quick answer would mean a sharp radicalization of the positions. No evaluation theory or practice can be completely pigeon-holed into a perspective (which latter must be considered an ideal type in the Weberian sense of the word). In addition, the concrete reality presents us with evaluation practices, models, and theoretical frameworks that draw on these assumptions, often unknowingly. As a result, it is not always possible to trace a line of demarcation between one proposal and another.

The dominant rhetoric (positivist approach) on e-government includes the widespread idea that technology is always and anyhow a tool of emancipation, participation, empowerment, democratization, and so forth. Information systems functions and activities are seen as largely deterministic, rational and overt (Hirschheim & Smithson, 2000, p. 400). This view excludes from the discourse of organizational change (and its evaluation) the importance of the interests and objectives of the parties. For contrasting reasons, neither does the subjectivist approach seem capable of unveiling the illusory nature of the dominant rhetoric on e-government, given that this approach sees information systems as mostly non-deterministic, political and covert (ibidem). The subjectivist approach focuses on the participating actors and meanings, and tends to lose sight of organizational rationality as a whole, which, on the other hand, is an essential reference point for any analysis perspective that aspires to capture the sense (and evaluate) the changes that accompany the deployment of ICT in complex organizational settings.

It is not our job to establish who is 'right' or who is 'wrong' in these opposing—and, in any event, incomparable—views. The question, if approached in these terms, would be a "mis-question". Nevertheless, we can say that the polarization of the assumptions around extreme positions, or that are anyway firmly anchored to "one-way" interpretations, has borne little fruit up to now, from neither the theoretical nor the practical perspective, so we must move on (Becker & Niehaves, 2007; Scholl, 2003; 2005; 2006; Sorrentino, 2006). The concrete reality (and not only in the public administrations) is always multi-branched and difficult to assess using dichotomist readings (e.g. positivist approach vs. subjectivist approach; technological imperative vs. organizational imperative; actor vs. system; and so on), given that neither one nor the other approach is capable of capturing the nuances, the ambiguities or mixed results inside or outside the public programs (e.g. e-government) under study. In essence, the above interpretive proposals prove mostly inadequate when it comes to explaining situations—in practice, all the situations—that are not intermediate stages of a continuum, but, on the other hand, "combine" in various ways the elements of one or the other study orientation.

ORGANIZATIONAL ACTION AND E-GOVERNMENT EVALUATION

This section adopts a different approach in seeking to better clarify the role and importance of the contributions from organizational theory in evaluating e-government. The choice of using a framework based on the contributions of organizational knowledge does not equate to saying that e-government is an area of study that belongs exclusively to organizational theory. Nevertheless, there can be no doubt that this latter presides over the process logic that organizes the technical goals and technical actions in organizational settings.

The perspective (Maggi, 1990; 2003) known as the Theory of Organizational Action (TOA) translates the organization into actions and decisions and is "mindful of the individuals and the relational structures that these produce and reproduce unceasingly" (Maggi & Albano, 1997). Starting with the contributions of some classic authors (i.e., Barnard, Simon, Thompson, Giddens), Maggi has identified a common thread on which he has built his proposal. Action is a term that in social studies indicates the connection of the behavior of a human agent to a subjective meaning. The originality of this theory can be seen from several viewpoints. However, lack of space means that we will only cite those most useful to our reflection on e-government evaluation.

Let us start by indicating how this theory addresses the relationship between technology and organization. While on the one side there are perspectives that see the organization as a concrete reality, in which there are also intentional behaviors (or action), on the other, there is the processual perspective (on which the TOA is based) whereby the organization is action developing over time. Organizational action is a particular form of bounded rational behavior (Simon, 1947), given that, by definition, it is an action that tends to fit the means (i.e. human and material resources) to the ends (i.e. the attainment of the desired and the avoidance of the undesired results, Simon et al., 1991, p. 493).

Also the notion of technology is different. Technology should be understood as both the whole of the technical knowledge and the artifact, or a process component. This dual role makes ICT platforms relevant from the organizational standpoint: they might lead to constraints or opportunities of change in the action of the individual and collective actors. The idea of opportunity evokes a choice of alternatives in a scenario that is never completely closed or defined beforehand. Technology is a key factor of organizational regulation processes. Therefore, whether the ICT solutions and artifacts are more or less adequate depends on the greater or lesser capacity to achieve the expected results in that particular context.

Bounded rationality guides the organizational action and enables its evaluation. The evaluation itself is understood to be a bounded rational process intrinsic to the organizational action. Certainly, it is a limited evaluation but it can concern the processes related to the technical, structural and institutional choices, and how these unfold over time, in line with changes in knowledge and values. Therefore, the TOA framework excludes a priori the possibility of successfully maximizing the results (and thus evaluating these in terms of efficiency) because it would be like saying that the knowledge of relationship between the *means*—i.e. the technical skills, the software programs, the operating practices, and the ICT platforms developed and deployed—and the *ends*—or the problem that lies at the root of the public service program—is optimal. Realistically, then, we could say that it is possible to direct the actions and the decisions of the public administrations on the theme of e-government toward satisfactory results for the diverse relevant groups, the needs and opinions of which—we reiterate—can diverge considerably and change in time. In other words, the evaluation that is always possible is the organizational 'fitness for the future' (Thompson, 1967, p. 84).

The TOA, contrary to what is maintained by the mainstream literature—which assumes the absolute determination or, conversely, the total non-determination of the evaluation system—"reveals the heuristic nature and, at the same time, the weakness and the strength of character of the organizational process" (Maggi, 1990, p. 96). The interpretive path and thus the evaluation are based on the adequate causality opposed by—on the one side—the absolute causality needed for the positivist view, and—on the other—the denial of any causal explanation by the subjectivist view.

The evaluation cannot be extrapolated from its context because it is considered an organized activity that is necessarily manifested inside an organizational process with its own specific features. The level of detail chosen for the analysis will vary in line with the needs of the evaluator, although the real situation will always be interpreted in its elements of action and decision. A description of the whole picture is always useful, whether we are examining and interpreting large-scale organizational settings (e.g., the effects of a national e-government action plan) or whether we need to focus on one phase of a broader process (e.g., the provision of public e-services by a web portal). The analysis needs to be carried out with the aim of highlighting the expected results, the technical actions implemented to achieve them, and the effects related to regulation, i.e. the organizational coordination and control processes.

DISCUSSION AND LIMITATIONS

Evaluating e-government means using real data to concretely verify the assumptions of change contained in the action plans promoted by the public administrations. The reliability of an opinion given on a specific intervention (or part of it)—formulated in terms of 'adequate causality'- increases the more it can factor in the contextual conditions accompanying the carrying out of the diverse actions and decisions made by the administrations involved at the various levels.

The TOA, we recall, places the emphasis on the organizational dimension of the setting that is the object of analysis. In contrast, other theoretical proposals (which are also the most diffused in the public discourse) believe that dimension to be an additional and secondary element: not only do they separate technological rationality and organizational rationality, but also place the former above the latter. According to this widespread way of thinking, the public-sector manager responsible for implementing an e-government program must "do nothing except" remove the hurdles that interfere with the technical rationality encapsulated in the ICT artifacts. Wherever the implementation reveals divergences compared with the plans, due to clashing objectives or vested interests, the responsibility would be attributed to all those forces that "resist" the change (Vann, 2004).

We do not believe an alternative conceptual framework, such as that proposed, to be a silver bullet, but it can help to place e-government implementation (or, generally, any type of change in the public sector) on a more realistic and, therefore, less illusory footing. The evaluation process and its results will depend on the decisional level taken into account and on the variability of the objectives and the technical knowledge characterizing the situation observed. Further, the evaluation itself is understood to be a bounded rational process intrinsic to the organizational action. Unlike other kinds of assessment, the organizational evaluation can always be carried out. It is an evaluation of the organization's fitness for future action, and consists of evaluating the goals of the action, the process relationships, and the reciprocal congruency of all these dimensions.

Adopting the framework proposed here means avoiding the non-critical assumption of the simplified idea that the efficacy of an e-government project stems immediately from the clarification of its formal setting and from the relevance of the powers and resources attributed to the implementation activities. At the same time, it shuns the risk—which itself becomes an interpretive weakness—of taking into account the effects (directly or indirectly positive or negative) of e-government exclusively based on the stakeholders' personal views and values.

At this stage of our reflection, we believe the foundations have been laid for addressing the evaluation research on e-government from a more advanced cognitive level. But what are the advantages of adding the TOA to a toolbox that—as we have seen—is already fairly full? We suggest some aspects worthy of attention. First, placing the organizational processes of action and decision at the center of the analysis means considering time a key variable. That is compatible with the assumptions of the ongoing evaluation (defined as level two, Lippi, 2007), i.e. that which offers the policymakers and managers the highest cognitive input for correcting or reorienting the program objectives. Judgment on the effects of an e-government program are extended to the processes that have generated those effects.

Second, and as a consequence of the preceding point, shedding light on the processes helps increase the body of common knowledge available on the organization and its relationships with the environments and the diverse categories of subjects with which it relates. *Enlightenment*, in turn, is a step forward in improving organizational learning (Regonini, 2001; Weiss, 1998) and creates the conditions that favor further assimilation of a culture oriented to the evaluation of the results and external accountability.

Third, the proposed framework adopts an analysis strategy in which the effects of the interventions are traced back to organizational decisions. In e-government terms, it recognizes the need to examine the organizational processes of: *design* (i.e. the decisions on the architecture and technical standards); *adoption* (i.e. the decisions of integrating the artifacts in the activities); and *use* (i.e., of appropriation in the daily practices of the users) of ICT platforms and the relative effects on the coordination and control processes. Think how useful this interpretive key would be in evaluating the implementation of the City of Milan's Ecopass project.

Fourth, the processual vision of the TOA enables us to analyze situations in which the change goes beyond the "boundaries" of a specific institution. This factor is especially significant, given that e-government policies in all countries are acquiring an increasingly networked configuration: see, for example, the trend of sharing the delivery of e-services via intermunicipal agreements (Sorrentino & Ferro, 2008).

Our contribution to the reflection stops here for now. The evaluation of e-government continues to remain a broad and complex question and what we have presented here is solely an initial exploration of the direction indicated. The heuristic value of the TOA has already been tested in earlier studies that have sought to interpret the meaning and the extent of some experiences in the e-government arena (e.g., Sorrentino, 2006; 2007) although this theoretical framework has never been applied to the specific theme of evaluation up to now.

The chapter does not address (and, naturally, this is a limitation) what is perhaps the most critical—and certainly not a given—aspect of the discourse, that is, the moment in which the results of the evaluation are applied in practice. Then the question becomes: how is it possible to make the evaluation operational and effective? What accompanying actions are needed to ensure that the policymakers or the public-sector managers adopt the indications prompted by an evaluation? At present, we are unable to answer that question.

Of course, the validity of our proposals must be tested and developed in the field. The hope is that other scholars can take up these themes and enrich the debate with new ideas and new empirical evidence. As underscored by Christie (2003, p. 91): "Evaluation is (...) distinguished from other academic fields by the continuous interplay between the theoretical and the practical."

CONCLUSION

This chapter maintains that evaluation, by nature, is an applied research area that presents an epistemological peculiarity, that of being oriented to the construction of an opinion on the setting. The evaluator relies on a toolbox (conceptual, theoretical, methodological, technical) to ascertain—data in hand—whether the intervention has or hasn't changed "the world" compared with the initial plan. The policymaker gets a decisional rationality from the evaluation that aims to summarize the results achieved (ex-post evaluation) or to report on the intervention as it unfolds (ongoing evaluation). The intention represents the idea that is concretized in the agenda-setting and decision-making phases, the real situation is a result of the implementation practice, the products generated and the ensuing effects.

We have suggested the use of the conceptualization offered by the Theory of Organizational Action (TOA) that is intrinsically interdisciplinary and draws on the studies of several classic authors, whose contributions apply broadly across all types of organization settings. The non-deterministic view of technological change would open new interdisciplinary touchpoints where the organizational evaluation can be combined with other types of evaluation (technical, economic, political, and so on). The concept of intentional and bounded rationality could be used as a starting point from which to develop a flourishing dialogue between the diverse study spheres interested in analyzing e-government and its effects. That would certainly enrich the future evaluation agenda (Sorrentino, 2007).

From the concrete viewpoint, this study suggests that because 'implementation is the only source of experience that managers can use to test and improve their programs' (Pressman & Wildavsky, 1984, p. xviii), the significance does not lie in e-government itself but the way it is implemented. It requires the joint use of many lines of intervention and support actions. Evaluation is an integral part of the organizational action and is itself a process. The typical measuring of outputs or technological or financial effects should be integrated with the analysis of the social impacts and public policies. In the presence of interventions whose objectives are general and broad in scope (e.g. national e-government plans)—and, therefore, potential bearers of ambiguity and negotiations between the implementers (Lindblom, 1964; Lipsky, 1980)—the organizational analysis reconstructs the bounded rational processes of action and decision that have led to specific consequences. That helps the street-level bureaucrats to reflect on the nature of the problems and trace the possible negative effects or contingencies to the processes of design, adoption and use of the ICT.

Evaluation (and it couldn't be otherwise) continues to be an imprecise activity (Pressman & Wildavsky, 1984) steeped in ambiguity, even though an approach such as the one suggested can help decision makers to preventively incorporate the evaluation-related needs as early as the planning and design phase of the e-government project or program. As suggested by Simon (1947, p. 316), wherever professional practice takes place, the organizational dimension is a fundamental source of information upon which the higher levels of the hierarchy must rely heavily for their decisions.

At this point, a question springs to mind: why has the contribution of organization science only seen sporadic and relative use to date? We can advance two tentative answers. First, the organization approach is generally little used in public policy discourses, which means we must work hard at diffusing it among both the universities and the practitioners. Indeed, this contribution is an initial (and fatally incomplete) attempt in that direction. Second, up to now, different disciplines have offered separate and opposed interpretations of e-government. Significantly—and therefore worthy of recognition and encouragement—the academic world is starting to chart a course that links the knowledge generated by the different branches of learning. However, we point out that most of the cases in question see the efforts of the researchers focus more on the accumulation of different knowledge—that are and continue to be kept separate—rather than an effective meeting between the disciplines to build something new, something that goes beyond the "one-way" interpretations.

REFERENCES

Alter, S. (1996). *Information systems: A management perspective.* Menlo Park: The Benjamin/ Cummings.

Avgerou, A., Ciborra, C., Cordella, A., Kallinikos, J., & Longshore Smith, M. (2006, May). *E-Government and trust in the state: Lessons from electronic tax systems in Chile and Brazil.* LSE Working Paper Series No. 146.

Barrett, S., & Fudge, C. (Eds.) (1981). *Policy and action: Essays on implementation of public policy.* London: Methuen.

Barzelay, M. (2001) *The new public management: Improving research and policy dialogue.* Berkeley, CA: University of California Press.

Becker, J., & Niehaves, B. (2007). Epistemological perspectives on IS research: A framework for analysing and systematizing epistemological assumptions. *Information Systems Journal, 17,* 197-214.

Bertot, J.C., & Jaeger, P. T. (2008). The e-government paradox: Better customer service doesn't necessarily cost less. *Government Information Quarterly, 25,* 149-154.

Beynon-Davies, P., & Williams, M. D. (2003). Evaluating electronic local government in the UK. *Journal of Information Technology, 18,* 137-149.

Capgemini, & TNO. (2004, November). *Does e-government pay off?*

Chan, C. M. L., Lau, Y., & Pan, L. (2008). E-Government implementation: A macro analysis of Singapore's e-government initiatives. *Government Information Quarterly, 25,* 239-255.

Cheng, J., Cheng, S., & Yang, M. (2007). *Evaluating the e-government based on BSC. Integration and Innovation Orient to E-Society, Vol. 2.* Boston: Springer.

Christie, C. A. (2003). Understanding evaluation theory and its role in guiding practice: Formal, folk, and otherwise. *New Directions for Evaluation, 97*(Spring), 91-93.

CNIPA. (2007). *Linee strategiche volte ad indirizzare le amministrazioni nella predisposizione del piano triennale per l'informatica 2008-2010.* Rome.

Cresswell, A. M., Burke, G. B., & Pardo, T. A. (2006, September). *Advancing return on investment analysis for government IT: A public value framework.* Center for Technology in Government, University at Albany.

Cyert, R. M., & Kumar, P. (1994). Technology management and the future. *IEEE Transactions on Engineering Management, 41*(4), 333-334.

Dawes, S. (2008). An exploratory framework for future e-government research investments. In *Proceedings of the 41st Hawaii International Conference on System Sciences (Hicss).*

De Marco, M., & Sorrentino, M. (2007). Sowing the seeds of IS cultivation in public service organisations. *Journal of Information Technology, 22*(2), 184-194.

De', R. (2006). Evaluation of e-government systems: Project assessment vs. development assessment. In M. A. Wimmer, H. J. Scholl, A. Grönlund, & K.V. Andersen (eds.), *Electronic government, Proceedings of the 5th International EGOV 2006 Conference,* Krakow, Poland (pp. 317-328). Berlin Heidelberg: Springer-Verlag.

Dunleavy, H. P., Margetts, H., Bastow, S., Callaghan, R., & Yared, H. (2002). Progress in implementing e-government in Britain: Supporting evidence for the National Audit Office Report "Government on the Web II."

EITO. (2007). *European Information Technology Observatory 2007*, Frankfurt: EITO-EEIG.

Fear, W. J. (2007). Programme evaluation theory, the next step toward a synthesis of logic models and organisational theory. *Journal of MultiDisciplinary Evaluation*, *4*(7), 13-25.

Flamholtz, E. G. (1996). *Effective management control: Theory and practice.* Norwell: Kluwer Academic Publishers.

Gregory, D., & Martin, S. (1994). Crafting evaluation research in the public sector: Reconciling rigour and relevance. *British Journal of Management, 5*(Special Issue), S43-S52.

Griffin, D., & Halpin, E. (2005). An exploratory evaluation of UK local e-government from an accountability perspective. *The Electronic Journal of e-Government*, *3*(1), 13-28.

Grimsley, M., Meehan, A., & Tan, A. (2005, September 13). Capital accounting: Evaluating e-government projects from a community development perspective. In Z. Irani, T. Elliman, & O. D. Sarikas (Eds.), *Proceedings of the eGovernment Workshop '05 (eGOV05)*, Brunel University, UK.

Gupta, M. P., & Jana, D. (2003). Government evaluation: A framework and case study. *Government Information Quarterly*, *20*(4), 365–387.

Heeks, R., & Bailur, S. (2007). Analysing e-government research: Perspectives, philosophies, theories, methods, and practice. *Government Information Quarterly*, *24*, 243-265.

Heintze, T., & Bretschneider, S. (2000). Information technology and restructuring in public organizations: Does adoption of information technology affect organizational structures, communications, and decision making? *Journal of Public Administration Research and Theory*, *10*(4), 801-830.

Hirschheim, R., & Smithson, S. (2000). Evaluation of information systems: A critical assessment. In L.P. Willcocks, & S. Lester (Eds.), *Beyond the productivity paradox* (pp. 381-409). Chichester: Wiley.

Hopwood, A. G., & Miller, P. (1994). *Accounting as social and institutional practice.* Cambridge University Press.

Irani, Z., Love, P., Elliman, Jones, S., & Themistocleous, M. (2005). Evaluating e-government: Learning from the experiences of two UK local authorities. *Information Systems Journal*, *15*(1), 61-82.

Janssen, D., Rotthier S., & Snijkers, K. (2004). If you measure it they will score: An assessment of international e-government benchmarking. *Information Polity*, *9*, 121–130.

Kaylor, C., Deshazo, R., & van Eck, D. (2001). Gauging e-government: A report on implementing services among American cities. *Government Information Quarterly*, *18*, 293-307.

Klecun, E., & Cornford, T. (2005). A critical approach to evaluation. *European Journal of Information Systems*, *14*, 229-243.

Kraemer, K., & Dutton, W. (1979). The interests served by technological reform. *Administration and Society*, *11*(1), 80-106.

Kumar, K. (1990). Post implementation evaluation of computer-based information systems: Current practices. *Communications of the ACM*, *33*(2), 203-212.

Lim, J. H., & Tang, S. (2008). Urban e-government initiatives and environmental decision performance in Korea. *Journal of Public Administration Research and Theory*, *18*(1), 109-138.

Lindblom, C. (1964). *The intelligence of democracy: Decision making through mutual adjustment.* New York: The Free Press.

Lippi, A. (2007). *La valutazione delle politiche pubbliche*. Bologna, Italy: il Mulino.

Lipsky, M. (1980). *Street-level bureaucracy. Dilemmas of the individual in public services*. New York: Russell Sage Foundation.

Löfstedt, U. (2007). E-government services in local governments—a study of development in Swedish municipalities. *Journal of Organisational Transformation and Social Change, 4*(2), 157-176.

Maggi, B. (1990). *Razionalità e benessere. Studio interdisciplinare dell'organizzazione, 3rd ed.* Milano: Etaslibri.

Maggi, B. (2003). *De l'agir organisationnel. Un point de vue sur le travail, le bien-être, l'apprentissage*. Toulouse, France: Octarès.

Maggi, B., & Albano, R. (1997). La teoria dell'azione organizzativa. In G. Costa, & R. C. D. Nacamulli (Eds.), *Manuale di organizzazione aziendale, 2nd ed.* (Vol. 1, pp. 220-249). Torino, Italy: Utet.

Marra, M. (2004). Alcuni aspetti e problemi della valutazione nella PA. *Rassegna Italiana di valutazione, VIII*(29), 41-58.

Moon, M. J. (2002). The evolution of e-government among municipalities: Rhetoric or reality. *Public Administration Review, 62*(4), 424-33.

Newcomer, K., & Caudle, S. (1991). Evaluating public sector information systems: More than meets the eye. *Public Administration Review, 51*(5), 377-384.

OECD. (2004). *The e-government Imperative*. Paris: OECD.

OECD. (2005). *E-Government Studies: Norway*. Paris: OECD.

OECD. (2007). *E-Government Studies: The Netherlands*. Paris: OECD.

Pardo, T., & Scholl, H. J. (2002). Walking atop the cliffs: Avoiding failure and reducing risk in large scale e-government projects. In *Proceedings of the 35th Hawaii International Conference on System Sciences (Hicss).*

Peters, R. M., Janssen, M., van Engers, T. M. (2004). Measuring e-government impact: Existing practices and shortcomings. In *Proceedings of ICEC'04, Sixth International Conference on Electronic Commerce* (pp. 480-489).

Petrakaki, D., Hayes, N., & Introna, L. D. (2008). Performance monitoring and accountability through technology: E-Government in Greece. In *Proceedings of the 41st Hawaii International Conference on System Sciences (Hicss).*

Picci, L. (2006). Misurare l'e-government: Il caso italiano, *ASTRID-Rassegna n. 2*. Retrieved from http://mpra.ub.uni-muenchen.de/3343/

Pina, V., Torres, L. & Royo, S. (2007). Are ICTs improving transparency and accountability in the EU regional and local governments? An empirical study. *Public Administration, 85*(2), 449-472.

Pressman, J., & Wildavsky, A. (1973). *Implementation*. Berkeley, CA: University of California Press.

Rebora, G. (1999). *La valutazione dei risultati nelle amministrazioni pubbliche*. Milano, Italy: Guerini e Associati.

Regonini, G. (2001). *Capire le politiche pubbliche*. Bologna, Italy: il Mulino.

Schick, A. (1971). From analysis to evaluation. *Annals of the American Academy of Political and Social Science, 394*, 57-71.

Scholl, H. J. (2003). E-Government: A special case of business change. In *Proceedings of the 36th Hawaii International Conference on System Sciences (Hicss).*

Scholl, H. J. (2005). Organizational transformation through e-government: Myth or reality? In

M. A. Wimmer, R. Traunmueller, A. Grönlund, & K. V. Andersen (Eds.), *Electronic Government, Proceedings of the 4th International EGOV 2005 Conference*, Copenhagen, Denmark (pp. 1-11). Berlin Heidelberg: Springer-Verlag.

Scholl, H. J. (2006). Is e-government research a flash in the pan or here for the long shot? In M. A. Wimmer, H. J. Scholl, A. Grönlund, & K. V. Andersen (Eds.), *Electronic Government, Proceedings of the Fifth International EGOV 2006 Conference*, Krakow, Poland (pp. 13-24). Berlin Heidelberg: Springer-Verlag.

Seddon, P. B., Staples, S., Patnayakuni, R., & Bowtell, M. (1999). Dimensions of information systems success. *Communications of the AIS, 2*(November), Art. 20.

Simon, H. A. (1947). *Administrative behavior.* New York: Mac Millan.

Simon, H. A., Thompson, V. A., & Smithsburg, D. W. (1991). *Public administration.* New Brunswick: Transaction Publishers.

Sorrentino, M. (2006). E-Government research: Time to switch direction. In A. Grönlund, H. J. Scholl, K. V. Andersen, & M. Wimmer (Eds.), *Electronic Government, Communication Proceedings of the Fifth International EGOV Conference*, Krakow, Poland (Vol. 18, pp. 17-24). Linz: Universitätsverlag Rudolf Trauner.

Sorrentino, M. (2007). Interpreting e-government: Implementation as the moment of truth. In A. Grönlund, H. J. Scholl, K. V. Andersen, & M. Wimmer (Eds.), *Electronic Government, Communication Proceedings of the Sixth International EGOV 2007 Conference*, Regensburg Germany (pp. 281-292). Berlin Heidelberg: Springer-Verlag.

Sorrentino, M., & Ferro, E. (2008). Does the answer to e-government lie in intermunicipal collaboration? An exploratory Italian case atudy. In M. Wimmer, J. H. Scholl, & E. Ferro (Eds.), *Electronic Government, Communication Proceedings of the Fifth International EGOV 2008 Conference*, Turin, Italy (pp. 1-12). Berlin Heidelberg: Springer-Verlag.

Stame, N. (Ed.) (2007). *Classici della valutazione.* Milano: Franco Angeli.

Stewart, J., & Walsh, K. (1994). Performance measurement: When performance can never be finally defined. *Public Money and Management, April-June*, 45-49.

Stowers, G. N. L. (2004, March). *Measuring the performance of e-government.* IBM Center for the Business of Government.

Symons, V. (1991). A review of information systems evaluation: Content, context, and process. *European Journal of Information Systems, 1*(3), 205-21.

Symons, V., & Walsham, G. (1991). The evaluation of information systems: A critique. In R. Veryard (Ed.), *The Economics of Information Systems and Software* (pp. 71-88). Oxford: Butterworth-Heinemann.

Thompson, J. D. (1967). *Organizations in action.* New York: McGraw Hill.

Vann, J. L. (2004). Resistance to change and the language of public organizations: A look at "clashing grammars" in large-scale information technology projects. *Public Organization Review, 4*, 47-73.

Walsham, G. (1993). *Interpreting information systems in organizations.* Chichester: Wiley.

Weiss, C. H. (1998). *Evaluation: Methods for studying programs and policies.* Englewood Cliffs: Prentice Hall.

West, D. M. (2005). *Digital government.* Princeton: Princeton University Press.

West, D. M. (2006). *Global e-government.* Retrieved on June 1, 2007, from http://www.InsidePolitics.org/egovtdata.html

Willcocks, L. P., & Lester, S. (Eds.) (2000). *Beyond the Productivity Paradox*. Chichester: Wiley.

Wong, W., & Welch, E. (2004). Does e-government promote accountability? A comparative analysis of Web site openness and government accountability. *Governance, 17*(2), 275-297.

KEY TERMS

Bounded Rationality: Conceptual model that assumes individuals are intentionally rational, i.e. they try to maximize their decisions. However, this ideal model is almost impossible to apply in practice: actions and decisions are taken and performed by individuals whose knowledge of the alternatives and the consequences is incomplete; in addition, preferences are subject to change and are not always clearly orderable.

E-Government Evaluation: The concepts, methods and techniques used for assessing the results of e-government programs. The evaluation can be carried out at any time (before, during, or after the implementation process) according to the different mindsets: organisational, economical, sociological, human empowerment or other.

Implementation: The process whereby the adopted ICT-based solutions (hardware, software platforms, procedures) become operational in the organization.

Interdisciplinary Approach: A study approach that integrates concepts from a variety of disciplines. Analysis techniques, methodologies, taxonomies and evaluation schemes can be taken from different branches of learning with the goal of building a theoretical framework that surpasses the constraints of individual disciplinary interpretations.

Organizational Change: Change that has significant effects on the formal configuration of the organizational setting and on the coordination and control processes that take place within it.

Public Policy: Program of action incepted and implemented by a public institution to respond to a socially perceived problem.

Technological Change: Change triggered by the introduction, adoption and widespread application of a new technology or the upgrading of a technology already used by an organisation.

Theory of Organisational Action (TOA): Theoretical perspective that translates the organisation into processes of bounded rational actions and decisions and is mindful of the individuals and the relational structures that these produce and reproduce unceasingly.

Chapter XVII
The Myth of E-Government

Katarina Lindblad-Gidlund
Midsweden University, Sweden

Katarina Giritli-Nygren
Midsweden University, Sweden

ABSTRACT

The idea of e-government is spread at a rapid rate. In almost the entire world governments are attempting to adapt to the suggested changes which implies that e-government has become a global phenomenon. We suggest that the idea of e-government is best understood as a mythologised megatrend. It has become a symbol for the modernised government of today. A symbol which, in some sense, has to be demythologized in order to to be able to be realised. It is argued that it is possible to gain further insights into, and tools to cope with, the gap between myth and reality by differentiate between general and specific interpretations of the idea. By analysing these interpretations the myth can be partially unravelled, which is illustrated by a large scale study based on 2,624 employees in public administration. The result indicates a loose coupling between the general and the specific level.

INTRODUCTION

During the last decade computerised technology and advanced information systems in public administration has increased. Today these implementations in public sector are often part of the overarching idea of e-government. Included in the e-government concept there is also an expectation of an organizational redesign and a rethinking of public administration work in general. Lenk & Traunmuller (2000) points out that if the guiding vision 'e-government' should be realised, the public administration has to go through an institutional change. This is, as many researchers (Fountain 2001, Lin & Conford 2000, and Lenk & Traunmuller 2000) have noticed, not something that happens automatically. The public sector has a long institutional memory with ingrained habits which are embedded in routines, norms and bureaucratic politics. These institutional settings are carried by both individuals, cultures and structures within the organization and will of course influence the transformation process, and to be able to achieve institutional change the electronic government has to bring about adjustments of the whole set of institutional entities (Yang 2003).

As all-embracing ideas such as that of e-government begin to be adopted in different parts of the world, they have to be translated in order to suit the local context (Bekker & Homberg 2007, Czarniawska & Joerges 1996). In this chapter we focus on the complex relationship between the general and specific translations or interpretations regarding the myth of e-government. We assume that myths are interpreted differently according to the general and specific point of reference and that the knowledge regarding how these interpretations differ provides valuable insights into the demythologization of a realisable e-government.

In order to gain knowledge with regards to the concerns of general and specific interpretations of e-government we put forward the Relation with technology-model (Lindblad-Gidlund 2005) as an analysis strategy. It highlights the importance of creating a more in-depth understanding of the reference point from which myths such as e-government are translated. The objective here is to show how general and specific points of references could enhance the understanding of the gap between the rhetoric and the reality of e-government implementation. We consider the general level to be more closely related to the all-embracing idea of e-government and the specific level to be more closely related to the employees' understanding of the implementation of the e-government with reference to their daily work life praxis.

The chapter will take its starting point in a general description about the idea of e-government to then move forward by analysing e-government through a discussion about mythologization. While doing so, the quality of individualisation is especially focused upon. To further illustrate the process of individualisation the Relation with technology-model is used as an analysis strategy to go deeper into the relation between the idea of transformation and the praxis of the same.

The linkage between the arguments is explored with the help of a large scale study. And the results give at hand that it is important to investigate the coupling between the general level (the idea of transformation) and the specific level (the praxis) to gain further insight about how the myth is actually embedded.

BACKGROUND

Since e-government has, in many respects, become a global symbol for a new and modern government we found it rewarding to view the idea of e-government as a megatrend. In order to do this, our starting point was the Scandinavian version of neo institutionalism as presented by Røvik (2002) and Czarniawska & Joerges (1996). From this perspective megatrends are seen as travelling ideas which have to be translated into local contexts.

Ideas that have been selected and entered the chain of translations acquire almost physical, objective attributes; in other words, they become quasi-objects, and then objects. (Czarniawska & Joerges, 1996, p. 32)

For an idea to achieve the status of a "megatrend" it has to be unison with the dominant discourse of the time. Homogenisation is deemed to be taking place when an organisational concept becomes a symbol for modern society. In becoming a symbol, the idea gains a penetrating power and is legitimated as the "best" or "only" way to reform and modernise an organisation. A common feature for all-embracing megatrends (Røvik 2002, Anttiroikko 2002, Czarniawska & Joerges 1996) is their global sphere of action and that they are associated with basic modern values such as rationality, efficiency, science and progress. At the point when different sectors, in order to achieve credibility and to become socially accepted and legitimised, are adjusting to the same organisational reform, they become more alike and such a process could be described as a process of isomorphism (Powell & DiMaggio 1983, Røvik 2002).

According to Czarniawska and Joerges (1996), as travelling ideas become more harmonised, they obtain their power by being mythologized. To mythologize and strengthen its existence, the origin and description of a megatrend idea often remains unknown and occurs as the result of a rhetorical strategy:

When the translation of ideas into action is well advanced, the actors involved feel a need to mythologize by dramatizing origins. (Czarniawska & Joerges, 1996, p. 26)

To be able to identify whether an idea has achieved the status of a myth (or institutionalised organisational recipe) some crucial common qualities have been outlined. They should have undergone and indeed have successfully proceeded with *social authorisation, universalising, comodification, timing, harmonising, dramatising and individualising* processes (Røvik 2002). To be *socially authorised* means that the organisational idea is legitimised through social authorisation and to be *universalised* means that the idea has a universal relevance. *Comodification* refers to the process through which the idea is transformed into a recipe (object), ready to be used in every single organisation. To be *timed* has to do with how the idea responds to other ongoing changes. When an idea is *harmonised* it is "neutral" and neither provokes nor strengthens existing conflict dimensions and when it is *dramatised* it is joined together by means of dramatic elements and histories. Finally, when it is *individualised,* the individual organisational members perceive it as an embodied change considering both their organisation and their personal adjustments (ibid).

If it is possible to consider e-government as a megatrend with the capability of reflecting the institutionalised norms and values of modern life, then its status to the above mentioned requirements should be investigated. In addition, the ability of the idea to travel increases according to the number of requirements fulfilled and if the concept has not been successful in proceeding with some of these factors then its ability to travel will be limited (ibid). Our aim, in the following section, is to examine, according to previous research, how e-government is fulfilling the requirements to be called a megatrend.

The Megatrend of E-Government

The idea of e-government is often described (Löfgren 2007, Moon & Norris 2005, Yildiz 2007, Bekker & Homberg 2007) as an object or the "the principal tool" by which public administrations can improve their governmental activities both internally, for improved efficiency and effectiveness, and externally for improved relations with their stakeholders. The idea of e-government therefore consists of different processes which, with the assistance of ICT, are supposed to increase: accountability, quality delivery of service, efficient delivery of service, transparency, access, political participation of citizens and data transfer services (information exchange) (Yildiz 2007, Bekker & Homberg 2007, Löfgren 2007, Grönlund 2002 among others).

The e-government idea has passed through a *social authorisation* phase, which means that the organisational idea has been legitimated by means of social authorisation. Social authorisation is thus a question of being related to instances perceived as authoritative within the field (Røvik 2002). The concept of e-government has been spread throughout the world by policy documents referring to the vision associated with e-government from both national and supranational agencies. During the 1990s supranational agencies (EU, UN, IMF, OECD and the World Bank) declared e-government to be a core issue on their agenda (de Senarclens 2004). A myth was being created; the only chance for a democratic government to survive in the future, as social and economic advancement has become more and more bound to technology creation, was to invest in e-government (Kakabadse & Kouzmin 2003).

For the idea to become *universalised* it has to be described as universal, which means that it should not be limited to one particular type of organisation (Røvik 2002). According to Jaeger (2003) the idea of e-government could be described as an idea embraced with great enthusiasm by many governments. It should also be relevant to many different sectors since a universalised idea has a universal relevance. This universality is normally (Røvik 2002) accumulated by means of a very general and abstract description of the concept. According to Czarniawska & Joerges (1996) global ideas or megatrends are to be regarded as solutions of problems. The implication behind the consideration that e-government is the solution to governmental problems is that, at present, the means of increasing certain aspects does not exist. This, in turn, implies that there are governmental shortcomings in several areas including; low accessibility, effectiveness, transparency and satisfactory service to citizens. As no standard definition exists regarding the exact nature of e-government (Yildiz 2007, Bekker & Homberg 2007), the idea gaining ground is that it is both a general and abstract common set of beliefs.

The *comodification* process refers to the process through which the idea is transformed into something, often presented as an object. The idea is described in terms similar to that of a recipe and with obvious positive effects ready to be used in every single organisation (Røvik 2002). Firstly, the presence of the prefix "e" indicates a comodification i.e. that e-government is something other than or something more specific than the more general concept of government. A characteristic of the rhetoric of e-government is the citizen perspective/approach, which focuses on how governments, by adopting e-government, will be able to provide better and faster services to its citizens and businesses (Bekker & Homburg 2007). This is also something which appears to be rather general and easy to adopt. By adopting a "scientific" rhetoric the concept becomes an "object" with a rational logic. This criterion is almost related to the others because it is part of the process causing the idea to appear as being general, easy to adopt and usable in many respects.

The idea should also be properly *timed* "as a new, modern and future oriented answer to ongoing processes of environmental change" (Røvik 2002). It is obvious that the rhetoric of e-government rests heavily upon a belief in both scientific and technological progress and could therefore be readily connected to the discourse of modernity. At a later stage, these ideas are often suggested to be the organisational answer to ongoing societal changes or paradigm shifts and are the "only way" to deal with future challenges. Since the "myth" of e-government is closely linked to the "myth" of technological progress and rationalism it reviews many of the major trends and issues in public administration and governance which have occurred over the previous decades. From such a perspective, e-government is certainly "properly timed". It is suggested as being the solution to a host of diverse problems and has strong connotations with ongoing societal changes.

The general objective of e-government has, since the 1990s, focused on the reform of core state functions and the building of state capacity for development and progress, described as liberalization, customer orientation and unfiltered integration in the world economy (Bekkers & Homburg 2007, Amoretti 2007). The rethinking of the state's role in development is perceived as being a prerequisite for the e-government idea. In this phase states are committed to the redefinition of the government's economic priorities (Amoretti 2007). The state delegates its accountability to its citizens while the global neoliberal political development continues to be the guiding principle of international organizations' policies and strategies as far as e-government rhetoric is concerned. Therefore, the idea of e-government travels into the local agencies as a new and refined technology of administration described with words such as rationalisation, cost effectiveness and customer orientation, which are not contradictory to the contemporary all-embracing neoliberal discourse. And, the idea receives the status of a megatrend after being considered as being the only way of dealing with future challenges (such as the age of globalization).

When a concept is so general and non-specific such that different groups (with for example different political views) can commit to the reform, it has been *harmonised*. The concept should be "neutral" and not provoke or strengthen existing conflict dimensions (Røvik 2002). The concept of e-government is generally not considered as being either a political tool or a question of party politics; it is presented as being ideologically neutral, with positive outcomes for all and in such a way that it would be unthinkable to view it otherwise (Ilshammar, Bjurström & Grönlund 2005). At a later stage, the e-government concept is sufficiently flexible to be adopted at different levels by governments possessing differing political views and can be adopted by both the developed and developing nations. It is not merely a transformation taking place in the Anglo-Saxon part of the world (Kakabadse & Kouzmin 2003)

The statement is frequently cited that it will be impossible to face future challenges such as ageing, climate change and terrorism (i2010 e-government action plan) without there being an e-government transformation. For example, the September 11, 2001 attack is sometimes mentioned as having made it necessary to share information among agencies (Halchin 2004) as a means of increasing security. To present the idea closely linked with such challenges could be seen a step toward dramatising the concept, since an idea has to be successfully *dramatised*, which means that it must be joined with dramatic elements and histories. However, this criterion is not as clearly fulfilled as the others.

If we now have examined the status of e-government as a "mythologized" megatrend according to the processes of social authorisation, universalisation, comodification, timing, harmonisation and dramatisation, there is still one criterion to be dealt with namely, the *individualisation*. As mentioned above, individualisation has to do with the organisational members' interpretations of the megatrend and this is the focus of the next section of the article i.e. how the relation between the myth of e-government and its realisation could be analysed by the use of general and specific interpretations.

MAIN FOCUS OF THE CHAPTER

When a concept is *individualised* it means that the individual organisational members perceive it as an embodied change, considering both their organisation and their personal adjustments i.e. it is not something above and far away, it is connected and related to some extent (Røvik 2002). This could be considered as organisational members' general and specific interpretations of the idea which is something we, in this article, aim to investigate. In addition, by distinguishing between general and specific interpretations we want to analyse the degree to which and the manner in which the concept of e-government is individualised. Our starting point is that the general level is more closely related to the all-embracing idea of e-government and the specific level more closely related to the employees understanding of e-government implementation in their daily work life praxis. The analysis within this article takes it starting point in such an argumentation; gaining insight concerning the organisational members' general and specific relations with the megatrend, and how these relations correspond to each other and how these will create valuable knowledge about the transformation process of e-government.

General and Specific Relation with e: An Analysis Strategy

In order to gain further understanding of the process of individualisation the relation with technology (RwT)-model by Lindblad-Gidlund (2005) is used as an analysis strategy since it provides tools to go deeper into the relation between the idea of transformation and the praxis of the same. To be able to do so the RwT-model highlights the importance of being sensitive to the reference point when analysing our relation with different forms of technology related change.

It does this by separating the general and specific points of reference. In this context, the general level is more closely related to the all-embracing idea of an e-government transformation and, as such, to the rhetorical strategy. In this regard, the specific level is, on the other hand, more closely related to the enacted idea i.e. to the understanding by the employees of the e-government transformation within their daily work life/praxis.

Another part of the model involves the combination of subject positioning and action strategy to illustrate and formulate the perceived ability to make a change. The combination of this pair of concepts provides the possibility of recognising whether the all-embracing idea and the enacted idea is perceived as being subordinate or dominant and whether they are subject to alterations. The argument, in this case, is that as long as we are unaware of our relation with technology we could hardly, at least not with any precision, make decisions as the result of conscious thoughts. We require mental pictures to assist us to see and acknowledge our relation. In this regard, the model could be used as a basis for a mutual understanding and could also inspire us into having further discussions. The model could be illustrated as shown in Figure 1.

Figure 1. The relation with technology-model by Lindblad-Gidlund 2005

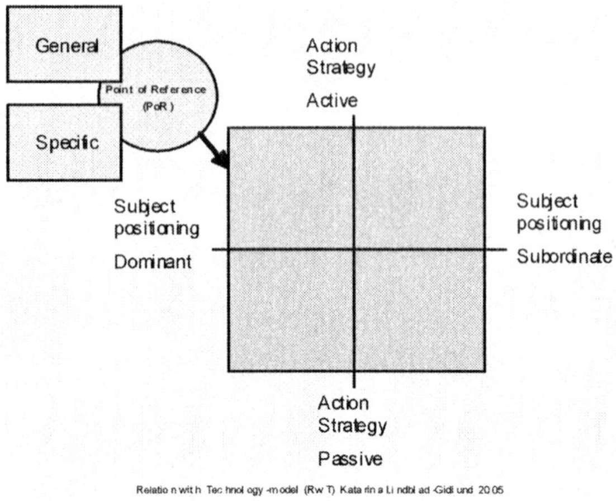

In the model, the *point of reference* symbolises the need for the employee to have a point of reference in order to be able to describe his or her relation with technology, which in this context is the e-government transformation. The reference point also serves as a distinction between general and specific relations with the concept. The general apprehension is seldom a thought, which is either particularly elaborated or analysed and often refers to a general perception about the concept. The specific point of reference, on the other hand, is generally elaborated to a greater extent and is also more often considered to be an object of change and is, finally, referring to a more specific situation of information technology implementation. The two dimensions *subject positioning* (dominant-subordinate) and *action strategies* (active-passive) illustrate different ways of describing ones relation with the electronic transformation both to make it clear and conscious for the respondent him/herself but also for others.

Method

The choice of the RwT-model as the analysis strategy meant that several other steps were implied, but it was still possible to perform both a qualitative and quantitative study. In this case a quantitative and extensive study was chosen in order to create an as overall picture as possible of the perceptions among the employees in the municipal administration. Our data has therefore been collected from a local municipality (medium-sized with 95 000 inhabitants). We are, in more general terms, following a local Swedish municipality's transformation and its implementation of e-government from several perspectives.

The empirical analysis presented in this paper is therefore based on a survey given to the entire body of employees in the municipal administration (2624 employees). To manage such a large quantity, a web inquiry tool (eval) was used and to be able to distribute the inquiry to the total mailing list of all those employed at the municipal administration, we were provided with a set of given prerequisites. One of these stated that the inquiry should not take more than approximately five minutes to answer. It should also be noted that in this specific municipality the concept of 24-hour government was the most frequently used term in different policy documents, which caused the choice of this term rather than e-government.

The structure of the inquiry relies heavily upon the RwT-model with three questions directed towards each level, namely the general and specific. The three questions concern (i) the primary aim related to the idea and (ii) the problem identifier and finally (iii) how the idea is perceived, as either subordinate or dominant, in combination with whether or not it is subject to alterations. Each question had four fixed answer alternatives. By altering the reference point the respondents were asked to change their perspective between the general (24-hour municipality) and specific (IT implementation) level.

The first question, primarily aimed at the idea of a 24-hour municipality, asked the respondents to relate the idea to the concepts; *efficiency, democracy (transparency, participation), service* or other. These three alternatives were chosen as they are the prevailing incentives which have been identified as the reasons for e-government transformation1. For the second question, the problem identifier, the respondents were asked to reflect upon whether it was primarily the *politicians/managers, administration, citizens* or others who had identified a need for this transformation. With regards to the general level, politicians are considered to be important actors due to the Swedish duality system. Finally, since the idea of e-government has been stated, over and over, as being a citizen-driven project, it was interesting to determine whether this corresponds to the understanding of those involved in actually conducting the transformation.

From the total of 2624 employees, a response rate of 48.4%, was achieved, i.e. 1270 answers were received within two weeks (with a reminder after one week). It was not possible to determine the reasons for all the non-answers, but some involved automatic mail replies (stating holidays, maternity leave, sick leave) while others contacted us and said that they could not answer the inquiry since they did not know what we meant by '24-hour municipality' (we intentionally did not provide an explanation for this term as the idea was to receive responses which were not affected by a definition given by us but by the one given by the municipality, and, additionally, if such a reaction would come, our intentions were to follow up in a separate study).

The empirical findings are divided into two parts; general and specific relations. These will be analysed at a later stage in relation to each other and some conclusions will be suggested.

General Relation with 24-Hour Government

In accordance with the theoretical basis and the analytical model, our first question is related to the all-embracing idea of e-government transformation and, as such, to the rhetorical strategy. The respondents were asked to reflect upon the idea of a 24-hour government and given three fixed alternatives and, in addition, the option of

Table 1.

1. In many situations it is often talked about a 24-hour government and expectations exist that the XX municipality should strive towards such a direction. According to you, do these thoughts primarily aim at:

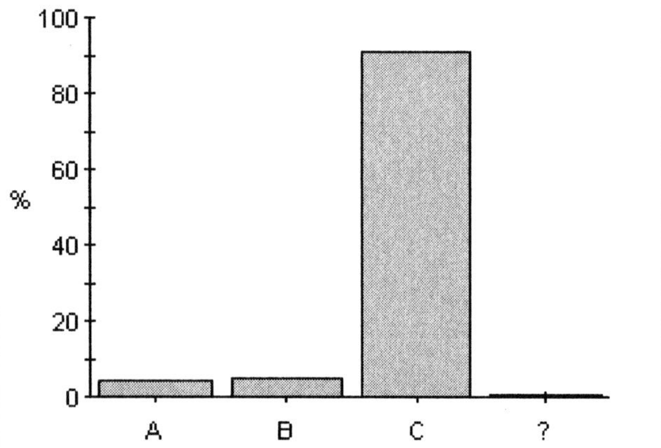

	%	#
A) Increase internal efficiency	4.09%	52
B) Increase transparency and participation	4.8%	61
C) Increase the municipality's service (quicker and better services)	90.7%	1152
D) Other	0.394%	5
Total	100%	1270

answering 'other', for what they perceived to be the primary aim of such a transformation (see Table 1). However, it is important to note that it is not suggested that it is possible to totally separate between these three options as they do connect to each other and are intertwined to a large extent. The aim of the question is rather to investigate what kind of picture is perceived as being the most prominent and suggested most often.

As the table shows, according to the employees in the municipal administration, the predominant aim of 24-hour government transformation is that it should increase the municipality's service (quicker and better services). As 90.7% of the respondents provided such an answer, question two became even more interesting; who did they think identified the need for such an increase in the municipality's service?

The response to the second question, whether the idea of a 24-hour municipality is able to provide solutions to problems primarily identified by politics, administration or citizens (or other), did not display such a dominant response as for question one. However, it was found that as many as 47.5% saw the municipal citizens as being the primary identifiers with regards to the

Table 2.

2. Do you think that the idea of an 24-hour municipality holds solutions to problems primarily identified by:

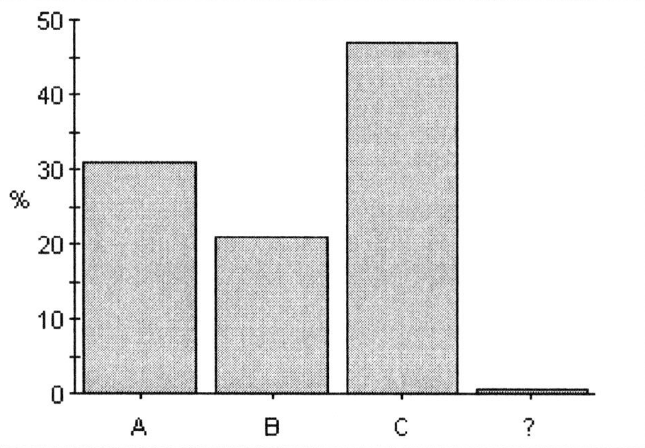

	%	#
A) Politics	30.8%	391
B) Administration	21%	267
C) Citizens	47.5%	603
D) Other	0.709%	9
Total	100%	1270

necessity for increased service (see Table 2). If the 'problem' was felt to be a lack of service, an increase in service was perceived to be what the citizens wanted.

The third question was a combination of two dimensions; (i) whether they thought that the transformation should serve the citizens or if the citizens should adjust to the transformation and (ii) whether or not they thought that if it did not serve the citizens they could do something about it. The response shows that the majority (50.1%) of the employees in the municipal administration thought that the idea of 24-hour government should serve the citizens (i.e. the citizens were in a dominant and active position). and that it was not the transformation itself that was important for any reason (such as image or ratings). In addition, that if it did not do so, the citizens could do something about it and create a change.

But, at the same time, as many as 20.9% of the respondents (the combination of 12.4% and 8.5%) placed themselves in a subordinate relation where the idea of 24-hour government where perceived as dominant (see Figure 2). And additionally 27.7% respondents placed themselves in the complicated position were they perceived the idea of 24-hour municipality as something that should serve the citizens, but if it did not, the citizens could not to anything to change it.

Figure 2. Relation with technology model (RwT)

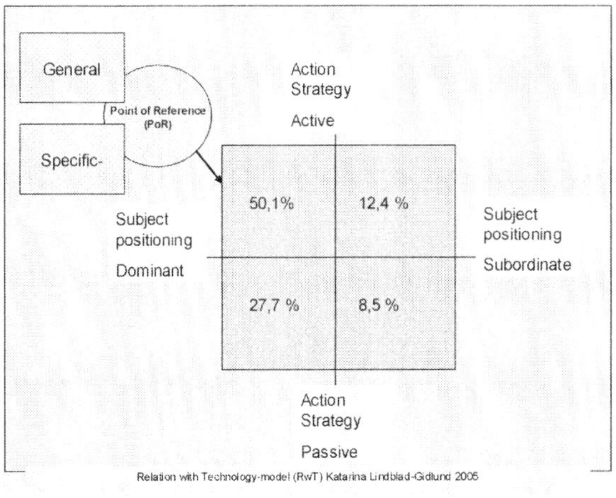

This is rather remarkable in what is put forward as a citizen-driven transformation and, what is further interesting is that the idea of 24-hour municipality seems to have reached the status of something that is accepted as "the only way forward".

The Specific Relation

In a similar structure to the three questions about the 24-hour municipality, the respondents were asked to reflect upon the implementation of IT-solutions into their daily work situation. The reason for focusing on the implementation of IT-solutions on the specific level is simple; our point of departure is that the prefix 'e' in e-government refers to ICT enabled transformation. If not, another prefix would be more suitable. And in relation to how the idea of e-government is put forward today the starting point seems reasonable. However, this should not be seen as a declaration in one direction or the other, but in a study of the idea of e-government the above starting point is relevant.

The respondents were again given three fixed alternatives plus the additional option of answering 'other'. The three fixed alternatives related to those used concerning the 24-hour municipality, but were expressed in a more concrete manner in accordance with the division between general and specific.

It showed that what the respondents perceived to be the primary aim of such a transformation (information technology implementation process i.e. the specific level), differs somewhat with the aim with reference to the general level i.e. to increase the municipality's service. Only 30.9% answered that they wanted the implementation of IT-solutions to increase their options to provide a better service. Instead they chose (66.5%) the first alternative, to increase effectiveness and facilitate their daily work. See Table 3.

Table 3.

3. When different forms of IT-solutions are implemented into you daily work situation, do you primarily want them to:

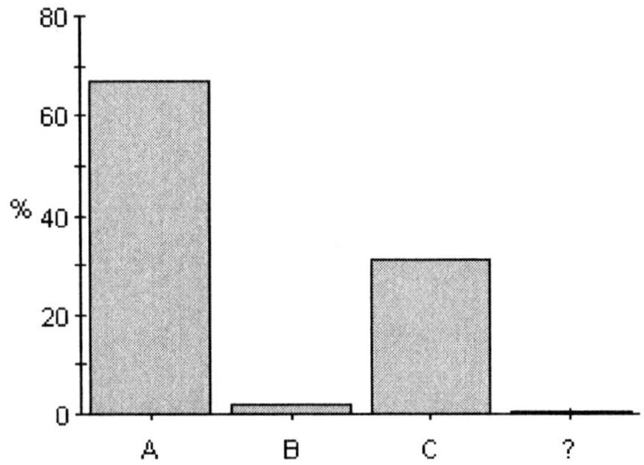

	%	#
A) Increase effectiveness and facilitate your daily work	66.5%	845
B) Increase the possibility for others to get insight and acquaint themselves with your work	1.97%	25
C) Increase the possibilities for you to provide better service	30.9%	392
D) Other	0.63%	8
Total	100%	1270

The results might be interpreted as, that there exists a causal relationship between internal efficiency and ability to provide external service, where internal efficiency is closely related and maybe even seen as a prerequisite for the ability to provide external service. This alternative interpretation might however be more suitable in the private market but in public sector the relationship between the two is not that obvious and certainly needs to be more closely analysed (which we will come back to later on).

The response to the second question on the specific level, whether the implementation of IT-solutions offers solutions to problems primarily identified by the management, public administrators or citizens (or other) did not show a similar domination as the related question for the general level. Instead, the answers given were that IT-solution implementation offer solutions to problems primarily identified by the management (42%), secondly by the public administrators (30.4%) and thirdly, the citizens (26.1%). In the same manner as for the question above (table 3), the results indicate a loose coupling between the general and the specific level. In their daily work situation the results indicate that they do not

Table 4.

4. Do you think that when different forms of IT-solutions are implemented into your daily work the reason is that they hold solutions to problems primarily identified by:

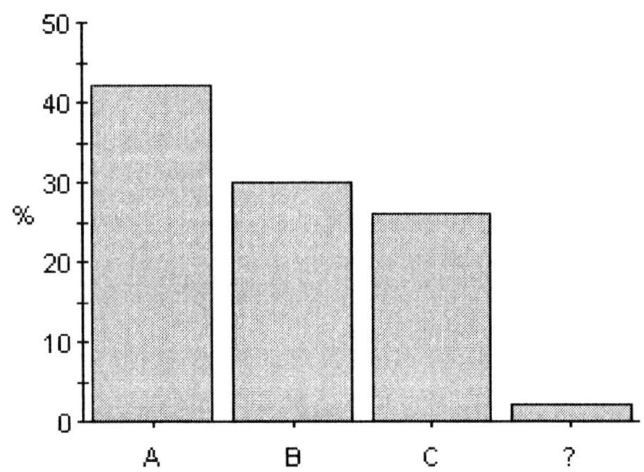

	%	#
A) Management	42%	533
B) Public administrators	30.4%	386
C) Municipal citizens/ clients/ users	26.1%	331
D) Others	1.57%	20
Total	100%	1270

Figure 3. Relationship with technology model (RwT)

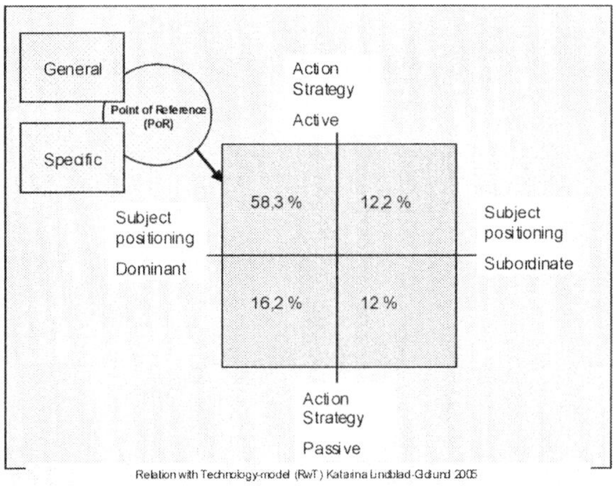

strongly relate the increased use of IT-solutions as something rewarding for the citizens. It is mostly a solution for problems identified by the management. See Table 4.

The third question referring to the specific level was (in a similar manner to that for the general level) a combination of two dimensions; (i) whether they thought that the implementation of IT-solutions should serve them, or if they were under the impression that they should adjust to the implemented IT-solutions and (ii) whether they thought that if it did not serve them they could do something about or not. The response shows that the majority (58.3%) of the employees in the municipal administration thought that IT solutions were implemented to support their daily work (i.e. a dominant relation) and if it did not do so they could do something about it and create a change (an active action strategy).

It is however noticeable that as many as 24.2% (the combination of 12.2% and 12%) described their relation with the implementation of IT-solutions as subordinate (i.e. the IT-implementation in itself were dominant) and 16.2% described a dominant relation but with no possibility to make a change if needed.

The Relation Between General and Specific Interpretations

To consider the degree to which the concept of e-government is *individualised,* the question is whether the employees perceived the transformation as an embodied change when considering both their organisation and their personal adjustments (Røvik 2002). And it appears to be since 50.1% at the general level and 58.3% at the specific level showed a dominant and active relation i.e. the transformation were supposed to support them and they could influence it if they thought it to be necessary. In this sense it could be argued that the concept is, to some extent, individualised, the employees had embraced the idea of transformation. Our results also show that the respondents saw a slightly lower possibility with regards to changing the transformation process for the general rather than for a specific level (which is quite natural and also implied by the RwT-model).

In addition, it is interesting to further analyse the how the results on each level correspond to each other. A characteristic of the rhetoric of e-government, as we have touched upon above, is the citizen perspective, which focused on how governments (by adopting e-government) would be able to provide both better and faster services to their citizens and businesses (Bekker & Homburg 2007). What is noticeable is however that their understanding of the all-embracing idea of e-government transformation appears to be have been formed in a somewhat unreflected manner, or at least is very similar to the existing public discourse, and their interpretations of the more tangible transformation of IT-implementation (in their daily work situation) are not that closely related to the actual idea.

They do not relate the increased use of IT-solutions as something primarily rewarding for the citizens (the answer from an internal office perspective was chosen ahead of the two alternatives based on a more external starting point). It is mostly perceived as a solution to problems identified by management i.e. they are not under the impression that the implemented IT-solutions are able to solve those problems identified and experienced by citizens. This could indicate that the implementation of IT-solutions is perceived as the answer to other types of questions, which are more typically associated with internal office questions such as internal efficiency and financial budget.

So, the relation between enhanced service towards citizens through improved efficiency in their daily work situation is a bit complicated. However, the same loose coupling has strong support in the popular rhetoric regarding e-government transformation and the results of this study shows that further analysis is needed. Not only to understand the relationship in between the general and specific level but also to be able to manage this relation into realisable processes.

Moreover, the response to the second question, whether the idea of e-government municipality has the ability to provide solutions to problems primarily identified by politics, administration or citizens, 47.5% saw the municipal citizens as the primary identifier while they, with regards to the specific level, mainly envisaged the management as being the primarily identifiers (42 %) and only 26.1% saw the citizens as identifier. This is quite interesting since it implies that the respondents separated between the general and specific level and not that strongly saw the citizens as the ones critically reviewing their daily work performance. If IT-solutions should be implemented in their daily work life it was not that strongly perceived as something the citizens would identify as needed.

Taken together, these results indicate a loose coupling between the general and the specific level and the results shows the complexity in how the coupling between the general and specific level is done. Such an analysis could provide valuable knowledge concerning the hindrances to the transformation process for the future since it might identify conflicts in goal perception and processes to achieve what is expected.

FUTURE TRENDS

As the idea of e-government continues its global journey, it simultaneously continues its local translation processes. These processes are being witnessed, at present, both nationally and regionally and several questions are arising during the process of actually trying to put the idea of e-government into practice. Of course these processes hold contextual prerequisites without generalisation possibilities but there are some shared features where generic analysis strategies could enhance the understanding of these local translation processes.

To this point we have examined to which degree e-government has received the status of a mega-trend. Our result shows that e-government to quite a high degree fulfil the criteria for being a mega-trend. Due to this, we argue that e-government is best understood as a mythologized managerial reform. The symbolic production of e-government on an ideological level is connected with words as liberalization, customer orientation and unfiltered integration in the world economy while the practical production of e-government, new IT-solutions, are mostly perceived as a solution to problems identified by management. This indicates that the practical production of e-government is connected with words as internal efficiency and financial budget. How the symbolic and practical production of e-government is connected to each other is still a question to discover.

What we have showed by arguing that e-government has become a mythologized managerial reform is that e-government heavily rests upon the global neoliberal political development as the guiding principle of international organizations' policies and strategies. However, from a transformational perspective, similar technology and organisational structure can serve different socio-economic aims and it might be the case, for good or bad, that the technological progression is impeded by existing socio-economic modes of production.

Furthermore, a well known insight from an institutional perspective is that the adoption of new ideas regarding administrative reforms often affects organisational talk but has less effect on practice. By contrast, some researchers warn against the conclusion about decoupling as the final outcome of a translation. Such a conclusion is often a result from a study without a time perspective and they suggest that organisational talk might cause changes in practice later on (see for example Brunsson and Sahlin Andersson 2000, and Røvik 2002). When an idea reaches the status of a mythologized megatrend it is necessary to remember that they are fabricated. They have gone through processes of comodification, harmonising, universalising and they have the power of a shared myth. They are to some degree taken for granted, without awareness, as a way of representing a unified and understood reality. They also have the power to render neutral what is in value. Therefore, we want to put attention to the important process trough which the myth is translated into different divisions of practice. It is necessary to analyse how different socio-economic modes of production are intermingled without taken into consideration if they are of contradictory nature or not.

When e-government appears in local policy statements the first translation has been taking place, and the first step in framing the transformation as organisational talk is done. In this semantic implementation process operative leaders are often left to play a specific role in translating the ideas into their own division's "language" (Røvik 2002, Latour 1987, Czarniawska & Joerges 1996). By attributing their subjective and intersubjective meaning to the idea they construct a meaningful way to use it which also can be seen as an activity of sense making (Weick 1995, Orlikowski & Gash 1994). In Grönlund et al., Anttiroiko (2002) states that local authorities are required to adjust to the external environment and adapt to so-called 'mega-trends'. According to Anttiroiko local decision makers deal with the ambiguity and/or uncertainty inherent in strategic decision making and as such, local authorities are placed in the role of institutional mediators between global mega-trends and local conditions.

For that reason, researchers, as well as local practitioners, could gain new insights by analysing the transformation of practice as an ongoing process characterised by micro-political processes (interplay or struggle between interests) among actors, actions and meanings.

CONCLUSION

In this article we have suggested that the idea of e-government is best understood as a mythologized megatrend, which has become a symbol for the present day modern government. By examining the concept of e-government, it has been noted that nearly all the criteria for mythologized megatrends have been fulfilled. The processes of social authorisation, universalisation, comodification, timing, harmonisation and dramatisation have been analysed theoretically, while the process of individualisation was investigated empirically. According to our empirical findings the idea of e-government appears to be individualised in such a way that the organisational members interpret the transformation at the general/organisational level as a means of increasing the municipality's service towards the citizen and at the specific/personal level as being able to increase the effectiveness and to facilitate their daily work. In addition, it also shows that the idea is individualised, to some extent, since the organisational members, on both levels, are under the impression that this is something they might be able to influence and positions themselves in a dominant position.

This indicates that the idea of e-government has become a myth, which, in some sense, has to be demythologized in order to be realisable, which is illuminated by the fact that, in this study, the relation between the general and the specific interpretations are loosely coupled and rather complex. In the introduction we said that the electronic government has to bring about adjustments of the whole set of institutional entities to achieve change. The concept of praxis has to be congruent with the concept of ideology and to be able to obtain legitimacy among the whole set of institutional entities it has to be congruent with broader social norms and values of government issues. In this article it is argued that it is possible to gain further insights about, and tools to cope with, the gap between myth and reality by means of the differentiation between the general and specific interpretations of the idea.

REFERENCES

Amoretti, F. (2007). International organizations ICTs policies: E-Democracy and e-government for political development. *Review of Policy Research, 24*(4), 331-344.

Anttiroiko, A. (2002). Strategic knowledge management in local e-government. In Grönlund (Ed.), *Electronic government – design, applications, and management*. Hershey, PA: Idea Group Publishing.

Bekkers, V., & Homberg, V. (2007). The myths of e-government: Looking beyond the assumptions of a new and better government. *The Information Society, 23*, 373-382.

Bertot, J. C., & Jaeger, P. T (2006). User-centered e-government: Challenges and benefits for government web sites. *Government Information Quarterly, 23*, 163-168.

Brunsson, N., & Sahlin-Andersson, K. (2000) Constructing organizations: The case of public sector reform. *Organization Studies, 21*, 721-746.

Cooper, R. B., & Zmud, R. W. (1990). Information technology implementation research: A technological diffusion approach. *Management Science, 36*(2), 123-139.

Czarniawska, B., & Joerges, B. (1996). Travels of ideas. In B. Czarniawska, & G. Sevon (Ed.), *Translating organizational change*. New York: Walter De Gryter.

DiMaggio, P. J., & Powell, W. (1983). The iron cage revisited, institutional isomorphism, and collective rationality in organizational fields. *American Sociological Review, 48*, 147-60.

Fountain, J. (2001). *Building the virtual state: Information technology and institutional change*. Washington, DC: Brookings Institution.

Grönlund, et al. (2002). *Electronic government – design, application, and management*. Hershey, PA: Idea Group Publishing.

Halchin, L. E. (2004). Electronic government: Government capability and terrorist resource. *Government Information Quarterly, 21*, 406-419.

i2010 eGovernment action plan. (2005, June). *Accelerating e-government in Europe for the benefit of all*. Communication from the council.

Ilshammar, L., Bjurström, A., & Grönlund, Å. (2005). Public e-services in Sweden. Old wine in new bottles? *Scandinavian Journal of Information Systems, 17*, 11-40.

Jaeger, P. T. (2003). The endless wire: E-Government as global phenomenon. *Government Information Quarterly, 20*, 323-331.

Kakabadse, A., Kakabadse, N., & Kouzmin, A. (2003). Reinventing the democratic governance project through information technology? A growing agenda for debate. *Public Administration Review, 63*(1), 44–60.

Lenk, K., & Traunmuller, R. (2000, February 10-11). *Presentation at the IFIP WG 8.5 Working Conference on Advances in Electronic Government*, Zaragoza.

Lin, A., & Conford, T. (2000). Framing implementation management. *ICIS 2000* (pp. 197-205).

Lindblad-Gidlund, K. (2005) *Techno therapy, a relation with technology.* Unpublished doctoral dissertation, Umeå University, Sweden.

Löfgren, K. (2007). The governance of e-government: A governance perspective on the Swedish e-government strategy. *Public, Policy, and Administration, 22*(3), 335-352.

Moon, M. J., & Norris, D. F. (2005). Does managerial orientation matter? The adoption of reinventing government and e-government at the municipal level. *Information Systems Journal, 15*, 43-60.

Orlikowski, W., & Gash, D. C. (1994). Technological frames: Making sense of information technology in organizations. *ACM Transactions on Information Systems, 12*(2), 174-207.

Røvik, K. (2002). The secret of the winners: Management ideas that flow. In K. Sahlin-Andersson, & L. Engwall (Eds.), *The expansion of management knowledge. Carriers, flows, and sources.* Stanford, CA: Stanford University Press.

Senarclens de, P. (2001). International organisations and the challenges of globalisation. *International Social Science Journal, 53*(170), 509–522.

Weick, K. E. (1995). *Sensemaking in organisations.* London: SAGE Publications.

Yang. (2003). Neoinstitutionalism and e-government: Beyond Jane Fountain. *Social Science Computer review, 4*(21), 432-442.

Yildiz, M. (2007). E-Government research: Reviewing the literature, limitations, and ways forward. *Government Information Quarterly, 24*(3), 646-665.

KEY TERMS

Comodification: One of the seven criteria an idea has to successfully pass to perceive the status of a super standard or megatrend. It refers to the process through which an idea (reform) becomes a product.

General and Specific Interpretations: Refer to a distinction between different reference points. The general (and primary) interpretation is seldom a particularly elaborated or analysed thought, and it often refers to a general perception about a concept. Specific (and secondary) point of reference on the other hand is more elaborated and is also, often to a higher degree, an object of change and finally, referring to a more specific situation of information technology implementation.

Individualisation: One of the seven criteria an idea has to successfully undergo to perceive the status of a super standard or megatrend. It has to be understood as something beneficent not only for the organisation also for their personal adjustments.

Myth: Something that is believed to be true by those who attach significance to it but could be questioned by others. In this context, a myth is considered as an institutionalised organisational recipe which is believed to cause certain effects if it is implemented.

Neo Institutionalism: An approach in social theory that focuses on the way that institutions interact and affect society. This perspective provides a way to explain and analyse why so many businesses end up having the same organizational structure (isomorphism) even though they evolved in different ways.

Relation with Technology: Highlights the importance of analysing technology related change as relationistic i.e. not perceive our relation as an attitude towards technology related change but an ongoing dialectical process. This process gains from being analysed with sensitivity to the starting point (point of reference) and a separation between the general and specific level.

Social Authorisation: One of the seven criteria an idea has to successfully pass to perceive the status of a super standard or megatrend. It refers to the process by which an idea is becoming legitimated and related to instances perceived as authoritative in the field.

Translation: Refers to the process through which an organisational recipe is adopted. It involves the process of interpretation, when making sense of an organisational change in order to change existing routines, norms and way of functioning.

Universalising: One of the seven criteria an idea has to successfully pass to perceive the status of a super standard or megatrend. It has to do with to which degree an idea has universal relevance. It should not be delimited to a certain type of organisation, field or country.

ENDNOTE

1 See for example: *Handlingsplan för eFörvaltning. Nya grunder för IT-baserad verksamhetsutveckling i offentlig förvaltning.* Regeringskansliet 2008 (*eGovernment Action Plan* the Swedish Government Offices 2008)

Chapter XVIII
Measurement of Transformational Government Strategies Using Balanced Scorecard Approach

Ivaylo Gueorguiev
European Software Institute Center, Bulgaria

ABSTRACT

This chapter puts forth some guidelines for transformational government strategy measurement using balanced scorecard. The complexity of transformational government strategy is rooted in the multistakeholder environment it is derived from. The citizens, the businesses, and the administration have different interests and finding the right balance of these interests would be a challenge for any initiative. Everyone is a stakeholder in the transformational government, since everyone participates in the decision making process through democratic elections, everyone contributes to the financing of the government by paying taxes, and finally everyone uses government services. In this multistakeholder environment the balanced scorecard methodology can provide tools for effective measurement and management of the transformation of public services. Planning and presenting the strategy in strategy maps and creating a system of performance measures in a number of perspectives can ensure a foundation for effective management system of the transformational government on the strategic level.

INTRODUCTION

The research approach in the current paper is broadly based on the conceptual analysis. The study is developed on the basis of detailed research of the transformational government area, including public services modernization, e-government concepts and balanced scorecard. The theoretical views have been examined through the research of books and reports related to balanced scorecard and transformational government. The practical aspects of transformational government introducing and using the principles of balanced scorecard have been studied as has been the available information and case studies, as well as the respective stakeholders in transformational government introduction and the service providers for transformational government and balanced scorecard. The author assumes that studying the literature and the case studies is a sufficiently reliable source of information for an area related on one hand side to public processes and on the other to the introduction of information technologies. Both factors support and encourage the stakeholders to share their achievements openly in the public space.

The information collected in the research process was used to perform a feasibility analysis of the introduction of the main principles and best practices of balanced scorecard in managing the transformational government strategy. The transformational government is a strategic initiative, which encompasses the interests of stakeholders different in type. The IT-based public services improvement strategies define three stakeholder groups: citizens, businesses and administration (Whitehouse, USA, 2003; Cabinet Office, 2005). The administration's role is twofold: it is both a party providing public services and a client of the strategy as well.

The needs and expectations of the different stakeholders are transforming with different dynamics. Preserving the balance between the needs and expectations is an important process in the transformational strategy execution. The success or failure of this balancing process is determined by the stakeholders' satisfaction and participation not only in the accomplishment of the strategic goals but also in the entire process of the strategy execution (Hopkins, 2005). Improving the public services by means of information technologies is a massive reform in the overall work of the administration. The success of this reform is not known in advance. International Institute of Administrative Sciences (1998, p. 6) defines six success factors that contribute to the successful implementation of public reforms programmes. They can be summarized in three groups:

Group 1: Political support and implementation capacity on strategic level

- explicit political support over an extended period to give the exercise credibility and create an acceptance
- an implementation body with sufficient power to put the program into effect, and intellectual and technical capacity for successful execution

Group 2: Effective communication with all stakeholders

- communication between all actors and stakeholders on the objectives and the strategies of the programs
- involvement of ministries and agencies in the identification of issues to be addressed and the development and implementation of programs

Group 3: Sound management on strategic and operational levels

- clearly defined goal and strategy for its achievement
- a feedback, monitoring and evaluation processes

Political Support and Implementation Capacity on Strategic Level

A strategy aimed at changing the way the administration works requires political will for change, commitment of high-level leaders, and significant capacity for implementing the change on the operational level. The political support is an important factor for ensuring sustainable development of the e-government initiatives (Heeks, 2006, p. 166). This political support can only be developed together by the highest levels of management through constant communication with all stakeholders. The effective rapport with the stakeholders is based on a clear intent, well-defined partnership goals, and courage for embarking on an initiative and taking the risks, as well as stakeholder communication which maintains learning and adaptation during the implementation of the entire initiative (Khosrowpour, 2005, p. 379).

Effective Communication with All Stakeholders

Feedback from the stakeholders is an important element of the successful transformation of the public services. Cultivating feed-back into two-way communication is an active learning process for the stakeholders and increases the effectiveness of the e-government (OECD e-Government Studies, 2005 pp 166-167).

Each stakeholder should have good understanding of the strategy and how it will benefit them. Stakeholders need to be certain that the expensive transformational government initiatives are continuously improving their lifestyle, businesses or operations.

The different stakeholders are interested in different aspects of transformational government strategy. For certain business segments, the government represents a significant client for their products and services, whereas for other segments transformational government is an opportunity for gaining competitive advantage through more efficient and effective transactions. The differences in the interests we find in the different segments of the society are even more considerable. Young people are more interested in using technologies to access government services than older people. People in urban areas have different interest then those living in the rural areas. From one hand side all of the stakeholders expect to benefit from the transformational government strategy, on the other, the strategy by itself cannot be successful without the contribution of all stakeholders.

Sound Management on the Strategic and Operational Levels

The scope of the strategy is so wide, that without clearly predefined goals, priorities and definitions, most maintenance and improvement activities performed by any administration can be considered as part of the transformational government. Without the leadership and the commitment of the highest political level the effort on the operational level might eventually prove unfocused, the budget insufficient, and the services provided - administration-centric instead of citizens -centric.

In these conditions the administrations need a universal mechanism for definition and communication of clear objectives and measuring the success of different initiatives. The Balanced scorecard approach, developed by Kaplan and Norton, has proven its efficiency in planning and execution of strategies, mostly in corporations but also in a large number of government and non-profit organizations. It is a powerful methodology for definition, measurement and control of complex strategies.

Another important characteristic of the balanced scorecard is that it is an effective tool for communication of the main strategy elements among the various stakeholders (Niven, 2003). The representation of the strategy through strategy maps ensures a common language, understood by each stakeholder involved in the process. This shared language could be the basis for transparency and effective participation of stakeholders in the strategic management. The use of perspectives for representation and modeling of the activities and the IT processes helps people intuitively accept the entire e-government concept and implement it better (Plunkett, 2004).

Measuring the results of the strategy is a precondition for its effective management. Kaplan & Norton identify the insufficient measurement as a managerial rather than informational problem (1996, p. 231). Measuring the execution progress of the transformational government not only ensures its good governance, but with good communication can achieve a significant marketing effect for the stakeholders. Short response time to any change in the environment, ensured by the ongoing communication between the stakeholders, could significantly increase the effectiveness and efficiency of the transformational government. Constant feedback, proactive decision making and participation of all stakeholders in each phase of development and execution of the transformational government strategy could guarantee the long term success of transformational government (Culbertson, 2005, pp 145- 146).

The purpose of this Chapter is to offer some directions for using the balanced scorecard as a system for measuring and managing the progress of the transformational government strategy. Measuring the implementation of the strategy through balanced scorecard is observed both as a mechanism for measuring and managing the transformational government strategic plan and as a means of communication between the different stakeholders. In this context the balanced scorecard can impact positively most of the aspects of the transformational government through the entire implementation cycle: from the initiation of the change, through its planning and implementation, and the communication of its benefits. The focus of this paper is on defining a possible indicators structure for measuring the transformational government strategy; the paper does not cover the full process of creating and managing the transformational government strategy through balanced scorecard.

BACKGROUND

The Transformational Government Concept

Transformational government draws on and further develops the e-government and e-governance ideas, successfully implemented in various countries such as the USA, New Zealand, Australia, a number of the EU member states and others. In the e-government strategies the predominating principle is one of using information technologies for offering administrative services directed to the needs of the citizens. For example President's Management Agenda (Whitehouse, 2003), Initiated in July 2001, adheres to three guiding principles:

- Citizen-centered, not bureaucracy or agency-centered;
- Results-oriented, producing measurable improvements for citizens; and
- Market-based, actively promoting innovation.

Transformational government is a strategic initiatives proposed by former Prime Minister Tony Blair (Cabinet Office, 2005, pl), who described the challenges facing the government as defined by the constantly advancing technologies. „This process can either overwhelm us, or make our lives better and our country stronger... Government has to respond to keep up with the hopes and aspirations of citizens and business, to remain efficient and trustworthy." The initiative sets the ambitious goal of using technology to change the way of providing services.

The transformational government strategy aims at achieving excellent results in three main directions (Cabinet Office, 2005, p. 2):

- The transformation of public services for the benefit of citizens, businesses, taxpayers and front-line staff.
- The efficiency of the corporate services and infrastructure of government organisations, thus freeing resources for the front-line.
- The steps necessary to achieve the effective delivery of technology for government.

The Balanced Scorecard Model

Robert S. Kaplan and David P. Norton developed the balanced scorecard concept in the 90s when they were working with a dozen of companies to establish a system of performance-measurement (Kaplan & Norton, 1996, p. vii-xi). They proposed a performance-measurement model, which plots the formulation and measurement of the company strategy in a strategic map, containing four perspectives: Financial, Customers, Internal Business Processes, and Learning & Growth. The Financial perspective contains the goals related to the company shareholders or what the shareholders would consider a company success. The main question in the Customers perspective is how the company should look in the eyes of its customers in order to achieve its vision and goals in the financial perspective. The Internal Business Processes perspective defines the key business processes necessary for the company to satisfy the needs of its clients. The fourth perspective: Learning & Growth should define goals of how the company should acquire knowledge and maintain growth in order to ensure the goals in the other perspectives for achieving its vision. The company goals are structured in these perspectives and linked with cause-and-effect relationships. The accomplishment of each goal is measured with expressly selected, limited number of indicators. The model suggests a balanced approach, which enhances the traditional financial indicators with measurements in the other perspectives. Thus it compensates for one of the main shortcomings of the financial performance measures, the fact that they are lagging indicators and do not offer many opportunities for a proactive approach in the management decision-making, while the measurements related to knowledge, the internal processes and clients are usually characterized as leading. Hence it could be suggested that their accomplishment will impact the success of the company and the achievement of the goals in the financial perspective in the following period.

Adapting the Balanced Scorecard to the Transformational Government Specifics

The concepts and strategies for e-government and for transformational government are focused on the needs of the citizens and the businesses. They both use technology to provide for the needs and requirements of the two groups of stakeholders. Unlike the business strategies the transformational government strategies are being implemented in the conditions of administrative monopoly, which could make their sponsors and end-users more passive. In this case it is important for the effectiveness of the strategy to define, measure and communicate the stakeholder-related goals. On one hand side these are „end-users": citizens, business and administration, and on the other these are the direct sponsors of the transformational government – the government or the high-level administration. In the strategic plan, the needs satisfaction of the citizens and the businesses is essential. Unlike the clients of a corporation who impact the corporate strategies through their purchasing decisions for goods and services, the citizens and the businesses impact the choice of sponsor for the strategy – the government or the parliament during elections – and finance the transformational government implementation through taxes. These stakeholders are very sensitive about the end benefits and the cost of the transformational government initiative. In order to satisfy them the government needs to establish realistic and measurable expectations. On the operational level, the initiative for transformation of the administrative services is managed by the governments and the respective agencies. The agencies are considerably interested in facilitating their work through technology, but they do not always put forth the benefits for the end-client.

The agencies and the government need serious argumentation in order to secure budget and commitment to the transformational government initiative. There is a necessity for clear goals and performance measures to create realistic expectations for all stakeholders and ensure their commitment in the long term.

In this organizationally complex environment, the classic balanced scorecard perspectives can hardly provide the necessary scope.

The transformational government needs to adapt and transform the classic corporate balanced scorecard model. The fundamental change would be in the arrangement and allocation of the perspectives. The main challenge for balanced scorecard in the government organizations is to direct them outward, toward the clients, and not inward, towards the internal needs and processes of the government. Kaplan & Norton conclude (2006, p.2) that most governmental organizations use the balanced scorecard methodology as a performance management tool rather than a strategy management and measurement tool.

Niven (2003) rearrange the classic balanced scorecard perspectives for business organizations by putting the mission of the organization and the customers at the front. The financial perspective is presented as a means for achieving the mission and the goals or as a restrictive condition in a limited budget.

Kaplan and Norton in collaboration with Leonard (2006) propose a modified version of the Financial perspective merged with the Customer perspective, suitable for governmental organizations. In the version suggested in collaboration with Leonard (2006, p.136) the Financial and the Clients perspective are subdivided into 3 parts, defining: the value that the services create for their clients; implementation costs and support for the strategy.

We have already mentioned that in order to find and sustain the balance of the interests of the stakeholders, it is necessary to plan and implement the communication and transparency among them. In our previous works (Gueorguiev, Dimitrova, Komitska, Traykov, & Spassov, 2005) on this subject we have suggested the description of a separate communication-related perspective. Combining the transformational government with the principles and the instruments of the administrative reform and using balanced scorecard could have a positive effect for the entire transformational government strategy implementation.

PRINCIPAL MODEL: MEASURING TRANSFORMATIONAL GOVERNMENT STRATEGY THROUGH BALANCED SCORECARD

The introduction of balanced scorecard can take place at different stages of the strategy development. At the very initiation of the strategy, the balanced scorecard can provide a structured communication platform for the different stakeholders. It evolves into a solid base for the development of a strategy measurement system and cause-and-effect-based communication. Established in this way, the strategy would be easier to measure, and hence easier to manage.

The balanced scorecard can also be build around an already existing strategy. In such a case the goals and the performance measures of the strategy are distributed in predefined perspectives and if necessary additional cause-and-effect relationships and measurements are inserted.

A sample balanced scorecard model of the transformational government strategy can be created and the respective measurement model can be applied to it on the basis of the experience and the literature studied.

Measurements and metrics analysis is at the heart of the balanced scorecard, but it is not a process as an end in itself. The main function of the measurement and analysis is to assist the management decision-making process and to maintain the continuous transformational government strategy improvement process and the management information system supporting it.

The performance measures should completely reflect the goals of the transformational government strategy and should ensure a high level of objectivity of the measurement data.

A multitude of sample performance measures have been suggested in this Chapter as an illustration, but in creating each and every strategic map it is reasonable to use a limited number of performance measures, in order for the system to be effective on the strategic management level. Niven, (2003) recommends no more than 20-25 performance measures in a single map are recommended in creating balanced scorecard on the strategic level. This number of performance measures can be sufficient for the transformational government strategic management, but will most probably appear insufficient if we observe the management on the services level. In this case the use of cascading balanced scorecards and performance measures is recommended, briefly discussed further in this Chapter.

The balanced scorecard is to be managed as a transformational government measurement and control process at different levels. At the very initiation of the balanced scorecard, the process should be well-provided-for with the necessary resources for executing the activities related to planning, training of all employees, building and maintaining the system in accordance with the goals of the transformational government strategy.

The very establishment of the system for performance measurement and management of the transformational government strategy is a project complex enough to be considered priority project when providing for the resources for transformational government.

Structure of the Model

The measuring transformational government strategy through balanced scorecard concept presented in the following section is a set of specially selected perspectives and sample metrics, which cover the transformational goals to a great extent.

The basic structure used in this Chapter includes mission, three financial and customer-related perspectives, internal processes perspective and knowledge and growth perspective.

The principal difference in the model structure, compared to the traditional Balanced Scorecard model for companies, is the substitution of the financial and customer perspectives with three new perspectives:

- Stakeholders Benefits and Values
- Political Support and Implementation Capacity on Strategic Level
- Transparency and Communication with the Stakeholders

The introduction of these three perspectives aims to address better the transformational government specifics related to answering the transformational government service needs of the different stakeholders, measuring and maintaining sustainable results.

The remaining two perspectives: the Internal Processes Perspective and the Knowledge and Growth Perspective highly correspond to the traditional Balanced Scorecard model.

The focus is on measuring the perspectives. The presentation of each perspective includes goals and main characteristics of the perspective and how it relates to the success factors that contribute to the successful implementation of public reforms programmes (International Institute of Administrative Sciences 1998, p. 6) and to the Balanced Scorecard model for governmental organizations proposed by Kaplan and Norton in collaboration with Leonard (2006, p.136); specific characteristics of the perspective related to the opportunity to measure it through the Balanced Scorecard as well as a set of sample metrics to be used for measuring the perspective.

Mission

The mission of the strategy is the significance of its development, implementation and the value it creates. In a broader perspective the missions of transformational government and E-government strategies are to ensure more transparent and more valuable service for all stakeholders through the means of information technology. This mission has been accepted for this paper in order to develop the sample transformational government strategy management and measurement model through the balanced scorecard tools.

Financial and Customer-Related Perspectives

The perspectives for transformational government, which we are suggesting to replace the traditional perspectives, related to customers and finance in the corporate balanced scorecard are:

1. Benefits and values for the stakeholders, including potential benefits related to decreasing the direct or indirect costs providing services to stakeholders.
2. Political support and implementation capacity on the strategic level, including commitment to potential future investment for transformational government development.
3. Transparency and communication with stakeholders.

The perspectives defined above originate from the essence of transformational government, the balanced scorecard model for the government sector suggested by Kaplan and Norton in collaboration with Leonard (2006 p.136), and four of the six success factors of the administrative reform (International Institute of Administrative Sciences 1998, p. 6) related to Political support and implementation capacity on strategic level and Effective communication with all stakeholders.

Stakeholders Benefits and Values

Stakeholder benefits and values is a results-oriented perspective, which contributes the most to the mission of the transformational government strategy. This perspective covers goals and performance measures for e-services for stakeholders and their contribution to improving the quality of life and business effectiveness. This perspective covers one of the perspectives suggested by Kaplan and Norton in collaboration with Leonard (2006 p.136) related to the value of the services for their clients. It is similar to the classic balanced scorecard customer perspective for commercial organizations.

The goals and performance measures define the success or failure of the transformational government. A lot of the businesses and the citizens are not likely to be very eager to learn how many services are offered by the e-government or how many citizens have used the on-line environment to communicate with the government or other such „boring statistics." The citizens and the businesses would like to experience the impact of the transformation – to get their jobs done better with less effort, to obtain services with added value etc. It is then that the stakeholders will support the initiative and will assist in its development.

Defining clear performance measures at this level is made difficult by the large scope of the services provided by different stakeholders and the blend of direct and indirect benefits for the stakeholders. For example, performance measures such as decreasing the execution time of certain services impact the direct cost for the stakeholder, when using those services. If we take for instance the registration of certain commercial activity, these performance measures are related to the time and resources spent by the businessmen related to the registration as well as the respective benefits of quicker market entry. Indirectly, these benefits contribute to the benefits for the government such as higher support for the government as well as higher fiscal proceeds from the respective businesses.

Measuring the services does not always directly impact the benefits of those services. A significant part of the services offered by the government are not optional, they are mandatory, such as the registration or licensing of a certain kind of activity. With the technology development it may appear that some of these services are no longer necessary, i.e. they can be either fully automated or altogether discontinued. In such a case, the decrease of the implementation time does not carry a significant benefit when compared to the option for termination.

With the transformation of government services and the orientation to „citizen and business centric e-government" it can be expected that the role of additional value–added services, offered or supported by government, will increase.

It appears that at this level it is more important to examine "Life events", covering a number of services, rather then observe specific services. In the example above, such a life event is the registration of a commercial activity, and the services it covers will most likely be related to tax, sanitation requirements, construction and/or environmental standards and other similar administrative services.

An example of a „life event" is a citizen changing residence. In this case the services used for facilitation and the mandatory services are offered by different governmental and municipal institutions. Measuring the real benefit is related to decreasing the cost associated with using the service (in the case of mandatory services such as the registration with various agencies) and increasing the benefit from the services (for example services related to providing information about the living areas, childcare facilities, health centers etc.).

This perspective is directly related to the "external" stakeholders such as business and citizens, but it could define and measure benefits and value for the administration, which are consequence of the better satisfaction of the citizens and the businesses. Such benefits can take the form of higher motivation of the employees in the respective administrations, decreased effort for processing complaints, better image for the respective administration.

Creating a benefits measurement system on the basis of life events in these perspectives is a complicated process, which could require resource-intensive research and analysis. The actual "life events" should be defined as well as the services and systems related to them, and then reference values of the performance measures should be estimated. This task becomes relatively easier when it is about measuring the direct costs and resources for achieving the respective goal. It is much more difficult to estimate or measure the benefits of the added-value services and the improved service during the end-client and service provider interaction. Much like the corporations in balanced scorecard, the governments can include in the measurement process methods such as the "mystery shopper" or surveys for citizen and business satisfaction.

When using the mystery shopper method, specially trained interviewers go through the different stages or the entire process of the service whilst filling in a ready structured questionnaire. As a result we can have information from the point of view of the client and compare it with the initially set service standards.

The transition to life events requires time, that is why in the beginning we can start by measuring the benefits of the transformation of individual services and their aggregation and analysis in groups of services and at a later stage full transition to life events.

An important element which can define the effectiveness of this perspective and hence turn into a prerequisite for the success of the entire strategy is the good knowledge about the needs and requirements of the stakeholders. When developing a measurement system for the Stakeholder Benefits and Values Perspective the metrics used should correlate with the needs and requirements of the stakeholders. In this way we can have a "live system", which is at the pulse of the society and the business and can direct the management of the strategy.

The entire cycle of the transformation implementation is a long-term process. That is why the goals for service improvement should come considerably before the current needs and expectations of the stakeholders, so that the transformational government can implement these expectations in due time. Forecasting the development of the citizens and business expectations in an area heavily dependant on technologies such as transformational government is a challenge for every government. If we were to draw a parallel with other sectors, a similar challenge is the forecast of the development of technology and science. The developed, industrial countries use specialized methods for long-term planning and forecasting the technology development, such as the foresight initiatives.

OECD defines the technology foresight (OECD, 1998, p. 20) as a systematic attempt to see far in the future of technology and science, economy and society, with the purpose of defining the emerging technologies, which are most likely to bring the greatest economic and social benefits.

Lau, Daglio, & Dragsted provide the example with the technology foresight in Finland (2004, p.43), which impacts the e-government implementation positively by foreseeing the significance and the development of public registers.

Measuring the transformational government strategy in the Stakeholders Benefits and Values Perspective should be in accordance with the specific scope and the concrete goals set in the perspective. The basic function of the metrics and the analysis methods is to provide information about the progress of the strategy implementation, but nevertheless we can recap a set of sample performance measures valid for this perspective:

- Number of services/ life events planned/ number of services life events transformed in the transformational government strategy implementation
- Extent of services integration: information supplied one-way communication, two-way communication, full coverage of all service operations including payment, offering services grouped according to the needs of the client (life events)
- % of transformed services against the total number of services
- % transformed services used by the clients against the total number of the services used by clients.
- Client satisfaction by the transformed services
- Number of clients using value-added services
- % clients using value-added services
- Number of users of e-services
- Share of clients using e-services
- Costs of the service / "life event" for the client
- Time spent for the service / "life event" for the client
- Planned against actual benefits for the client related to the service / "life event"
- Service capacity: ability to service a number of clients per unit of time.
- Number of defined and resolved problems in working with clients
- Number of inconsistencies between planned service standards and actual client service.

The above are just part of the possible performance measures in the Stakeholders Benefits and Values Perspective. Depending on the concrete strategy, part of them can be selected and additional metrics can be set.

We should have in mind that the performance measures in this perspective reflect the end result of the transformational government introduction and much like the Financial Perspective in the corporate balanced scorecard can be defined as lagging. These performance measures are a result of past activities and cannot provide adequate direction for the actions to be taken in the present moment with a view to achieving strategy success in the future.

Political Support and Implementation Capacity on Strategic Level

This perspective and the related goals and performance measures should ensure the political support for transformational government and the appropriate capacity for the implementation of the goals. The perspective covers two of the six key success factors of Political support and implementation capacity on strategic level (International Institute of Administrative Sciences 1998, p. 6) related to the explicit political support and an implementation body with sufficient power to put the program into effect. At the same time covers two of the perspectives suggested by Kaplan and Norton in collaboration with Leonard (2006 p.136) related to the implementation costs of the public services and the support provided by the donors.

The purpose of this perspective is to define goals and performance measures for strong political leadership in the process of the transformational government strategy implementation.

Firstly, this should be ensured by a strong political sponsorship of the highest level. The experience and the practice of the leading transformational government and e-government strategy countries (for example Whitehouse, USA, 2003; Cabinet Office, 2005) shows that these strategies have been developed as a comprehensive framework for the work of the government and there is a substantial support on the part of the legislative power. This process is expressed by the direct commitment of the Prime Minister or the President to the transformation of the public services.

Secondly, a strategy with such a scope needs a solid organizational foundation to ensure sustainability and resources in the long-term period. The strategy needs to be supported by an organizational capacity, which will maintain its development and will provide the necessary expert and executive resource.

Thirdly, transformational government is an expensive process, both from the point of view of IT resources, and from the point of view of planning and change implementation. In order to secure the budget for financing the transformational government, solid arguments are necessary to prove the feasibility of the program. Furthermore, the benefits of the transformational government shouldn't be measured just in terms of saved resources by the administration from the optimization of the service provision. The mission of the transformational government is to provide better services to the stakeholders hence the main results of the strategy implementation are measured in the Stakeholder Benefits and Values Perspective.

The goals and metrics in this perspective reflect the commitment of the stakeholders to the process. This includes their readiness and capacity to invest in services transformation. In the short-term, this investment can be accepted as political decisions for budget allocation. In the mid-term and long-term the taxpayers can seriously impact these decisions.

The capacity to plan, communicate and implement the set goals can strongly influence the sustainability and the development of the transformational government initiative. These factors and the potential cause-and-effect relationships on the macro level will be discussed in the other balanced scorecard perspectives.

The Political Support and Implementation Capacity on Strategic Level Perspective is to provide metrics, which will convince the sponsors of the program in its usefulness and benefits and will measure the commitment and the resource availability for its implementation. Sample performance measures for this perspective are:

- Average period for discussion and reporting of the transformational government introduction progress with participation of the highest level of strategy planning and management
- Number of critical decisions escalated to higher management/number of decisions made at the highest management level
- Number of meetings at the highest level at which the transformational government introduction has been discussed
- Number of suggestions for amendments in the legal framework related to the transformational government introduction
- Number of normative acts, adapted to the transformational government needs
- Number of specialists employed in the management and introduction of the transformational government
- Budget allocated for the transformational government introduction
- Administration support budget share for transformational government services transformation
- ICT budget related to transformational government introduction. (for example as a share of the total ICT budget)
- Number of administrative and organizational units included in the administrative services transformation program
- Share of civil servants participating in the implementation of the transformed administrative services
- Increase in the administrative services budget

Combined metrics can be used from the Stakeholder Benefits and Values Perspective related to resources necessary for program implementation.

Use and analysis of such combined performance measures is to include the difference in the timeframe of the two groups of performance measures. Unlike the performance measures in the Stakeholder Benefits and Values Perspective, the performance measures in the Political Support and Implementation Capacity on the Strategic Level perspective are rather leading, than lagging. The goals in this perspective provide the basic financial and political resource for the strategy implementation by forming the foundation, on which its success can be built. Without this foundation the transformational government cannot start or continue its positive development. For example, increasing the investment at the present moment can result in benefits for the stakeholders no sooner than when the investment is absorbed.

Transparency and Communication with the Stakeholders

Transparency and Communication with the Stakeholders is the perspective, which effectively supports all the other perspectives and mainly the perspectives related to the stakeholders: citizens, business, administration and transformational government sponsors.

Transparency and Communication with the Stakeholders complies with two of the six key success factors of effective communication with all stakeholders (International Institute of Administrative Sciences 1998, p. 6) related to communication between all actors and stakeholders and involvement of ministries in the development and implementation of programs.

As a whole the perspective promotes active participation in the transformation of the administrative services by informing the stakeholders about the progress on mission, goals and tasks of the transformational government and providing a feed-back channel and participation in the respective decision-making.

The different stakeholders have different motivation for participation in the transformational government. This assumption entails different communication strategies for the different stakeholders. The services are to be transformed on the basis of studying and forecasting the needs of the stakeholders relating to the scope and means of providing the respective services. The discussion itself and involving the stakeholders in the definition of the needs and requirements for transformational government is already a premise for their active participation in the transformation process.

While in the Stakeholder Benefits and Values and in the Political Support and Implementation Capacity on Strategic Level perspectives we discuss the results and the resources for the transformational government, in this perspective we include entire performance measures related to support of effective communication among all stakeholders. Thus the perspective "translates" the performance measures and results of the transformational government into a language for each stakeholder and maintains the communication.

First of all, through communication with stakeholders directly involved with the transformational government planning and introduction, the goals in the Political Support and Implementation Capacity on Strategic Level perspective are maintained. The exchange aims at providing sufficient information for ensuring political commitment of the sponsors and the direct transformational government implementers. In the context of this perspective, stakeholders directly involved in the transformational government management are the political sponsor of the transformational government, the administrations who run and implement the strategy, and the citizen and business organizations who are directly involved in the transformational government decision-making process.

The sponsors of the initiative on the highest political level will most likely be interested in the aggregate performance measures about the extent of the constituency support they will receive as a result of the administrative services transformation, as well as performance measures related to the benefits from the transformation. Such argumentation would confirm the position of the transformational government leaders and would provide them with grounds for continuing and even expanding the scope of this expensive investment.

On the operative management level, the interest would lie in the performance measures related to definition and alignment of the needs for service transformation, so that the goals are prioritized and thus the high effectiveness of the entire transformational government is sustained. Even in the USA, one of the leaders in the e-government introduction, communication focus on the budget rather than the better service for the citizens is considered an obstacle (Whitehouse, 2007)1 to higher e-government effectiveness.

Focused communication of the performance measures related to the budget of the initiative and the financial benefits of its implementation would guarantee transparency and foresight. An important performance measure related to the effectiveness of the initiative is the use of the budget indicators by the stakeholders providing resources and participating in its implementation.

Secondly, through communication with the stakeholders, who are transformational government clients, the goal is to provide information exchange relating to forecasting the transformation needs. The already transformed services should be promoted among potential users and realistic expectations about the transformational government benefits should be developed. Stakeholders in this group can be defined as the citizens, businesses or administrations who are direct users of the services as well as companies and organizations, representing the interests of certain groups of citizens, businesses and administrations.

The end-users of the transformed services would be interested in the performance measures on the level of service or life event as well as opportunities for utilizing value-added services.

The transformational government has exceptionally extended scope of services. It is not possible to introduce all of them at once. Maintaining an effective and efficient process of transformation would require studying the constantly developing needs of the clients and prioritizing and planning the activities on the basis of the study. This is relevant both for developing the already transformed services or life events further and for including new services and life events in the transformational government scope. The analysis and collection of such information is subject to the perspectives Stakeholder Benefits and Value and Political Support and Implementation Capacity. For the Transparency and Communication with Stakeholders Perspective it is important to plan goals and maintain performance measures, which provide information and communication channels for the process study and analysis for the needs and effectiveness of the communication with stakeholders.

A significant part of the transformational government services can be defined as supply-driven, due to the fact that they are mandatory when certain life events occur. Hence the goal of the transformational government promotion campaign is to inform citizens and business about the services and convince them in the value of the transformation. The information of potential clients is not only conducive to the full utilization of the transformation services, but can significantly contribute to the support for the transformational government strategy. Such campaign can compensate the lack of interest in those users of transformational government services, who have been in a passive position until this moment and have only used the mandatory services.

Last but not least, the goals and performance measures of the Transparency and Communication with Stakeholders Perspective should provide the basis for formulation and analysis of the expectations of the stakeholders about the transformational government strategy implementation. A significant mismatch between transformational government strategy target results and actual expectations of the stakeholders would be a clear signal either for goals to expectations alignment or for additional promotion activities, which will communicate the goals in a way that will create realistic expectations with the potential clients.

The two main target groups for communication: participants in the management and implementation of the transformational government strategy and users of transformed administrative services is only provisory and aims to illustrate the different roles of the citizens, businesses and the administrations. Messages and communication channels are to be selected according to these roles in order to optimize the transformational government strategy communication so that it is conducive to the stakeholders making informed decisions, facilitating the more effective transformational government development.

Sample performance measures for this perspective are:

- Share of high-level managers, connected to the transformational government strategy implementation, who periodically use transformational government progress information (for example the system for the strategy progress measurement)
- Share of civil servants who know the mission, vision and strategy for transformational government
- Share of civil servants who approve of and commit to the mission, vision and strategy for transformational government
- Share of civil servants whose expectations correlate with the transformational government goals
- Number of regular users of the transformational government progress measurement system

- Number of publications, analyses, etc. quoting data from the transformational government progress measurement system
- Regularity or number of the management decisions or improvements resulting from using data of the transformational government measurement
- Number of improvement suggestions or complaints received by the administration or the civil servants participating in the transformational government implementation
- Share of the potential transformed administrative services users, who are informed about the transformational government strategy
- Share of the representatives of the stakeholders using the services, who regularly receive and use transformational government progress information (for example the transformational government progress measurement system)
- Share of the representatives of the stakeholders using the services, who know the mission, vision and strategy for transformational government
- Share of transformational government services users, who approve of and commit to the mission, vision and strategy for transformational government
- Share of transformational government services users, whose expectations correlate with the transformational government goals
- Number of improvement suggestions or complaints received by the transformational government users

In conclusion we should have in mind that the performance measures in this perspective measure the effectiveness of the communication with the transformational government stakeholders and not the effects of the transformational government application. These effects are to be measured in the Stakeholder Benefits and Value and Political Support and Implementation Capacity perspectives.

The performance measures in this perspective are lead rather than lag indicators. They influence a great share of the performance measures in the other perspectives related to the customers and finance.

Internal Processes Perspective

Internal Processes Perspective should suggest goals and performance measures, which define and measure the processes, in which we should invest and improve so that we can attain the goals in the customer and finance related perspectives.

This perspective is the connection unit between the strategy with its vision and values, goals and benefits for the society, defined in the finance and clients related perspectives and the perspective for knowledge and development, covering goals and performance measures related to human resource, information technology and knowledge, which will be reviewed later in the Knowledge and Growth perspective.

The Internal Processes Perspective complies with two of the six key success factors of sound management on the strategic and operational levels (International Institute of Administrative Sciences 1998, p. 6) related to clearly defined goal and strategy and a feedback, monitoring and evaluation processes.

The improvement of the internal processes is a factor of critical importance for the transformational government Strategy implementation. The diffusion of technology in the administrative services without change of processes would accelerate their implementation, but would not significantly contribute to their efficiency. New technologies offer vast opportunities for process optimization and their reorientation from administration-centric to customer-centric design and implementation. This transformation, though aided by the technology will not automatically happen with their application. Prior to the introduction of the technologies and in parallel, it is necessary to reorganize the processes so that they prioritize the client needs, design new processes and finally use technologies as an instrument for fullest satisfaction of those needs.

Due to the general character of the balanced scorecard-based transformational government strategy measurement model suggested in this Chapter, many different groupings of the processes in this perspective are possible. In order to simplify the model we can group the internal processes in the way the financial and clients perspectives are grouped. Thus we will have the following groups of processes:

- Processes creating stakeholder benefits and values, related to planning and providing transformed services
- Processes related to the strategic and operative management of the transformational government strategy
- Processes providing the stakeholder communication

The processes creating value and benefits for the stakeholders are the processes of administrative services implementation. In most cases, before their transformation they are suited to make it easier for the administration. A clear, distinctive mark of the administration-centric processes is when the client needs to communicate with numerous administrative and organizational structures and needs to provide information already available, or generated from one administration unit to another and receives as a result one single administrative service or part of such. If we use as an example the company registration, then the citizen needs to communicate with the tax offices, social security services, statistic services and other administrative structures and at the end of the process a business will be registered. The citizen will not be significantly relieved if this entire series of communications is transformed form presence in the respective institution into information technology base communication. The real value for the client in this case would be the opportunity to register the business with all the types of services with one single communication with the administration. This mandatory part of the service can be accompanied by a number of added-value services, for example giving information to the company about the specific market conditions on which it will operate. In this case the client will save time from routine tasks, which he can invest in developing their business.

In addition to the technological aspects of the reengineering of the processes and automation of the operations, the example given above has significant organizational and managerial aspects. Political will and sufficient power resources are necessary in order to transform the legal framework so that the operations are optimized and the use of different channels is possible for certain service or life event. That is why it is necessary to set and support processes ensuring political support and implementation capacity of the transformational government strategy.

The transformation of services is a complex initiative for the implementation of which many projects are being managed and implemented. Building capacity for the management of the different projects as well as the entire projects portfolio is a serious challenge for transformational government. Cabinet Office (2005) discusses the projects portfolio management as a key competence for the transformational government Strategy implementation in the UK, which is included in the goals and strategies for transformational government.

Therefore the balanced scorecard should define indicators that measure the efficiency and effectiveness of the project and portfolio management.

Sample performance measures for this perspective are:

- Budget and human resource used in the service

- Number of operations or services implemented in the framework of the preliminary planned budget against the total number of operations and services
- Number of operations and services implemented without deviation from their requirements against the total number of operations or services
- Funds used for strategic and operative management
- Downtime
- Number of optimized processes included in the transformed services against the total number of processes
- Number of defects in the systems or processes found during their development
- Number of defects in the systems or processes found after deployment
- Number of services clients
- Total working hours used for the development and implementation of processes against working hours for rework
- Number of tasks completed on time against the total number of tasks/projects
- Number of tasks or projects completed on planned budget against the total number of tasks/projects
- Number of tasks or projects completed according to initial requirements against the total number of tasks or projects
- Number of organizational units who have introduced and complied with formal quality assurance systems
- Number of certified systems
- Strategic goals implementation progress
- Budget spent on stakeholder communication
- Number (or share) of potential transformational government clients covered by the information campaign
- Information service capacity – for example: number of information offices
- Number of administrative services, which allow interactive stakeholder communication: call centers, Q&A, complaints and others
- Number of target clients serviced by the planned information channels

As a whole the performance measures of the processes are lead indicators. The quality of the internal processes has a direct impact on the quality of the services being provided.

Knowledge and Growth Perspective

The Knowledge and Growth Perspective has the purpose of structuring goals and performance measures related to the knowledge necessary for the transformational government strategy implementation. The goals need to create the key intangible assets, which will provide support and development of the internal processes necessary for the transformation of the administrative services. Kaplan & Norton (2004, p.200) define three components of the intangible assets related to the Knowledge and Growth Perspective: human resource, information capital and organizational capital, which are to be aligned with the internal processes and internally integrated.

The processes creating value and benefits for the stakeholders serve the transformational government end-client. That is why the intangible assets here are related to knowledge, skills and motivation of the staff to provide the transformational government services. This is also relevant for the communication skills with different end-clients, the competences related to the essence of the administrative services, including their implementation and competences for providing quality service. It is necessary to organize and maintain a knowledge management system, which support the processes of service and communication with the end client. It is of utmost importance for this group of processes the staff to develop client-oriented values and organizational structure.

The processes related to the strategic and operative development of the transformational government strategy are provided by the management and operative teams of the transformational government. The knowledge and skills of the employed in management should cover a large scope of expertise, which starts with strategic management, includes project and services portfolio management and covers projects and team management. The integration of the information of the management levels requires complex information provision and well-defined management models as well as quality assurance. The management of such a complex strategy as the transformational government strategy requires development of leader-oriented values and organizational structure for risk taking and risk-sharing and team work.

The executive teams should develop and maintain competencies both in the specific areas in which they are employed and in the process modeling and ICT introduction.

The processes ensuring stakeholder communication require market and management communication skills. The structuring of this information by groups of stakeholders depends to a great extend on the specific transformational government strategy. Generally speaking the target communication groups cover: citizens, business, administration and civil servants. Communication and information channels are to reflect the needs and requirements of each and every group or subgroup of stakeholders. In order to maintain the effective communication between the stakeholders, the employees responsible for this group of processes should develop values and organizational culture of openness, objectivity in communication as well as observing the needs and requirements of the different stakeholders.

Sample performance measures for this perspective are:

- Number of trained employees by type of training
- Number of trained employees in specific competence against the total number of employees
- Number of certified employees by area of knowledge
- Share of employees with post-graduate degree
- Length of service of the employees in the respective administration
- Length of service of the employees in the respective competence field
- Attrition rate / number of employees leaving the administration
- Willingness to work in the administration – for example number of candidates per open position
- Level of knowledge of the transformational government strategy
- Level of knowledge of the transformational government processes
- Level of knowledge of the transformational government plans
- Number of days spent on training
- Share of employees who have appositive attitude to the transformational government introduction processes
- Share of employees who have planned goals and responsibilities in accordance with the goals set in the balanced scorecard
- Level of accomplishment of preliminary set goals for the employees
- Employee satisfaction
- Leadership
- Innovation
- Number of violations of the rule and the ethics accepted in the administration
- Level of introduction and use of knowledge management systems
- Level of introduction and use of information technologies
- IT needs identified: Information systems introduced ratio

Alignment of the Transformational Government Strategy Balanced Scorecard at the Organizational and Personal Levels

Balanced scorecard is not just a measurement instrument, it can be considered as comprehensive management philosophy for the transformational government strategy. The transformational government introduction will impact many administrations positioned at different levels of the state governance and in the service provision. The management of this system requires a high level of synergy in the strategies, plans, goals and activities on the entire management and service chain. It is not possible to measure and represent this complex system through one single strategy map. The strategic map on the level of transformational government strategy supports the management of the strategy and would contain strategic goals measured on the basis of aggregated performance measures for the progress of this strategy's implementation.

The goals implementation on the strategic level reflects in goals on the organizational-operative level. In this transition from level to level the administrations and the other organizations providing the various administrative services can organize their strategies, goals, and measurements in strategic maps with the same or similar structure in order to „translate"the goals of higher level into strategic goals, Objectives and measurements valid for their activities. In this way a cascade of strategic balanced scorecard maps is defined, which can even go down to the level of personal goals for the employees and the specialists responsible for the respective activities.

Finally, as a result for the administration we can expect a synergy between strategy and operation plans and clearer understanding of the roles and significance of the different units, included in the services transformation.

Organized in this way the balanced scorecard cascade would provide opportunity for fast and effective feed-back and continuous improvement of the transformational government strategy. In the case of significant deviations in some of the performance measures on the strategic level an in-depth analysis of the added-value chain could suggest the right and timely change solutions for the strategy or correction activities for problem resolution.

Another important benefit of the balanced scorecard cascades is that through the similar structure, defining the cause-and-effect relationships and goal performance measures they provide the opportunity to structure the communication on the basis of objective criteria. The aligned structure would facilitate the exchange and the distribution of best practices.

At the level of employees, every employee can connect their goals and work to the transformational government strategy goals and thus focus on the activities with highest value-added.

From the point of view of users and sponsors of the transformational government, the opportunity of two-way tracking of the goals and their measurement from strategic to operational level can guarantee transparency of the entire process and allow for better management. The transformational government can take better advantage of the participation of each stakeholder in the process of strategy implementation, and the stakeholders will have the opportunity for better and fuller benefits and values from the transformed services.

The more organizations and individuals participate in the process of defining the strategic maps and their components, the more stakeholders will commit to the transformational government strategy implementation process and support its development.

FUTURE TRENDS

The transformational government mission expresses the willingness of the administration and society to focus on the needs of the citizens and thus move them closer to the service levels of the private sector. With the development of this process we see the technologies and models successfully used by the big corporations for the measurement and management of their own strategies coming forth. Together with the transformation of the administrative services, the state organizations should transform the way they manage their strategies related to providing services to the citizens and businesses. All these factors are conducive to the use of balanced scorecard as a tool for measurement and management of the transformational government strategy. There is abundance of information about the use of balanced scorecard in a number of administrations and there is a significant potential for a number of advantages of this model in managing on the level of transformational government strategies with multi-stakeholder and multi-organizational participation. The use of the structure of the balanced scorecard for further study of the successful introduction of transformational government and e-government strategies could result in a generic transformational government and e-government measurement and management model and thus contribute to their benchmarking and improvement.

CONCLUSION

The Balanced scorecard method provides guidelines and good practices for effective measurement, management and control. Such an approach is used by corporations, non-profit organizations and government agencies.

In the management of the transformational government strategy a number of specifics can be defined in contrast with the corporate or agency strategies. A key difference is the presence of a greater number and greater diversity of stakeholders expressing different interests and being at a different level in the value-added chain in the transformational government service transformation. A number of potential perspectives and performance measures were provided for measuring the strategy progress, adapted to the transformational government specifics.

They are defined on the basis of the key success factors that contribute to effective implementation of public reforms programmes defined by the International Institute of Administrative Sciences (1998, p. 6), balanced scorecard perspectives for governmental organizations substituting the Financial and Clients perspectives, suggested by Kaplan and Norton in collaboration with Leonard (2006 p.136) and the transformational government main principles. As a result we have proposed a structure of a strategy map with new perspectives including Stakeholder Benefits and Values, Political Support and Implementation Capacity, Transparency and Communication with Stakeholders as well as the classic balanced scorecard perspectives of Internal Processes and Knowledge and Growth. For each perspective we have defined a number of potential performance measures of the results of the transformational government.

In order to align the administration and the other organizational goals in the transformational administrative services chain, it is necessary to cascade the system in the administrations on the operative and executive level.

The balanced scorecard success depends on the training of the individuals and on its actual use for the transformational government strategy management at the highest level.

The adaptation of the strategic map and the perspectives included in it to the specifics of the administrative services transformation ensures a reliable management information system and provides mechanisms for its effective development and continuous improvement.

REFERENCES

Barbara, A., Juliet, L., Paquet, G., & Roy, J. E-Government and public private partnership. In

M. Khosrowpour (Ed.), *Practicing e-government: A global perspective.* Hershey, PA: Idea Group Inc.

Cabinet Office. (2005). *Transformational government enabled by technology.* Crown Copyright 2005.

Corkery, J., Daddah, T., O'Nuallain, C., & Land, T. (Eds.). (1998). *Management of public service reform: A comparative review of experiences in the management of programmes of reform of the adminitrative arm of central government.* International Institute of Administrative Sciences, IOS Press.

Culbertson, S. (2005). Transformed government. In M. Khosrowpour (Ed.), *Participating e-government: A global perspective.* Hershey, PA: Idea Group Inc.

Garson, D. (2003). *Digital government: Principles and best practices.* Hershey, PA: Idea Group Inc.

Gueorguiev, I., Dimitrova, S., Komitska, M., Traykov, H., & Spassov, K. (2005). Balanced scorecard based management information system – A potential for public monitoring and good governance advancement. *Electronic Journal on E-Government, 3*(1) , 29-38.

Heeks, R. (2006). *Implementing and managing e-government: An international text.* SAGE.

Hopkins, A. (2005). E-Government trick or treat. In M. Khosrowpour (Ed.), *Participating e-government: A global perspective.*

Kaplan, R. S., & Norton, D. P. (2004). *Strategy maps: Converting intangible assests into tangible outcomes.*

Kaplan, R. S., & Norton, D. P. (2006). *Strategy scorecards in nonprofit ,government, and health care organizations.* Harvard Business School Press.

Kaplan, R. S., & Norton, D. P. (1996). *The balanced scorecard: Translating strategy into action.* Harvard Business School.

(2004). Chapter 2: The case of e-government. In E. Lau, M. Daglio, & S. Dragsted (Eds.), *Finland.* OECD.

Niven, P. R. (2003). *Balanced scorecard step-by-step for government and nonprofit agencies.* John Wiley and Sons.

OECD. (1998). *Science, Technology and Industry Outlook.* OECD.

OECD E-Government Studies. (2005). *E-Government for better government.* OECD Publishing.

Plunkett, P. (2004). *Lessons learned on information technology performance management: Applying the balanced scorecard and applied information economics to federal information technology initiatives.* Federal Chief Information Officers Council.

Whitehouse. (2007, March 23). *Obstacles to greater effectiveness* . Retrieved on April 12, 2008, from Results.gov: http://www.whitehouse.gov/results/obstacles/index.html

Whitehouse, (2003). *E-Government strategy: Implementing the president's management agenda for e-government.*

KEY TERMS

Goal: Briefly presents what is to be achieved.

Performance Measure: Generic term representing the level of performance of a goal. Often its value is compared to target parameters.

Life Event: A specific everyday situation for the citizen or business in which they naturally use a number of administrative services in order to complete it.

Mission (mission statement): Explains in a summarized fashion why the strategy has been developed and why the organization exists.

Perspective: In the balanced scorecard context this is a category of goals and performance measures related to the goals of the organization.

Strategic Map: In the balanced scorecard context, it is introduced by Kaplan и Norton to present the goals, performance measures ordered by perspectives and related through cause-and-effect linkages.

Strategy: Presents the goals of an organization or group of organizations on the highest level in order to complete a certain mission. In the context of transformational government, the mission is related to using ICT for providing better administrative services to the citizens and businesses. An example of a transformational government strategy can be found in the Cabinet Office (2005).

Transformational Government or E-Government Stakeholder: An individual, group of individual or an organization, which is affected by the transformational government or E-government or is in some way responsible for the results of transformational government or E-government. Stakeholders are the citizens, businesses, NGOs, administrations and agencies, government employees and others.

Transformational Government or E-government User/Client: Each individual or organization using administrative services.

ENDNOTE

1 "Congress and the press critique how much money is spent from year-to-year on important programs, rather than on what we actually purchase with the money we do spend. They suggest that an increase or decrease in funding means we care more or less about the programs' beneficiaries, without focusing on whether or not the target group is being well served by the money we do spend."

Chapter XIX
Measuring Transformational Use of ICTs at Regional Level

Karsten Gareis
empirica, Germany

Tobias Hüsing
empirica, Germany

ABSTRACT

The experience of recent years has shown that take-up of ICT, for example within strategies to implement online public services, is a necessary but not sufficient condition for making progress towards regional development goals. What is of interest is not ICT use per se, but applications of technology which exert a transformational impact on users, that is which support people, firms, and the public sector by opening up new, more effective ways for achievement of goals rather than simply making existing structures and processes more efficient. This chapter focuses on use of ICT by individuals in their roles as citizens, workers, learners, patients, consumers, and so forth. We argue that here, the transformational potential of ICTs is rooted in its effect in terms of empowerment of users, that is, "the process of granting people the power to take responsible initiatives to shape their own life and that of their community or society in economic, social, and political terms." The chapter presents a conceptual framework for analysing ICT-enabled empowerment. It also presents some results of an Internet user survey conducted in early 2008 in 12 selected regions in the EU.

INTRODUCTION

One of the clearest challenges which Europe faces in the context of the development towards a knowledge-based society (KBS) is to improve the performance of its diverse regions. As the European Commission's strategic framework "i2010" (CEC, 2005c) has made clear, the avoidance of a regional digital divide is desirable on the grounds of both equity (social cohesion and inclusion) and of improving the overall economic competitiveness of Europe. It is increasingly accepted that bringing about an KBS will not be achieved by the market alone, but that policy intervention will be required in a number of areas—especially if the goal is to develop a KBS in which all participate in line with their needs and abilities.

Among decision-makers in EU regions, there is still confusion about how they can best tap the full potential of ICT and the knowledge economy. Likewise, most region are uncertain about how to react adequately to the challenges arising from recent paradigmatic developments such as globalisation, the network society and the new international division of labour, all of which are directly related to applications of ICT. Until now, most efforts by regional policy-makers have focussed on laying the infrastructure for ICT deployment, and on fostering the uptake of key ICTs such as the Internet by private households, businesses, the civic sector and government. Across the EU territory, significant progress has been made on both accounts. Most available evidence, however, suggests that the success in translating ICT investments into real progress in economic and social development varies considerably across regions. It remains a challenge to explain why this is the case, and what can be done about it. It is often assumed that such difference have something to do with the extent to which regions and their inhabitants are able to make *transformational* use of ICTs.

What do we mean by transformational uses of ICT? By means of a broad literature analysis, it was possible—in spite of the overall rather elusive way the term is used—to identify a number of core characteristics of ICT-enabled, transformational change (Cornford et al., 2006). "Transformational" is often understood as uses of ICT that open up substantially new ways for individuals, firms and governments to make progress in achieving their goals. In many cases, this refers to activities which would not have been possible without ICTs. In particular, three themes appear to be of key importance for the notion of transformational use of ICTs:

1. It appears that the transformational potential of the Internet, mobile telephony and other ICTs resides mainly in the way these technologies enable network creation at a scale and depth not possible before. The specific properties of networks (such as network externalities), in combination with the particularities of (digital) information goods when compared to tangible goods, imply that network creation is one of the main underlying principles for ICT-enabled, paradigmatic change. In the social domain, network creation is related, in particular, to the notion of social capital (see Field, 2003).
2. Given today's volatile economic and technological environment, it is of key importance to recognise and react to emergent change through the ability to exploit new opportunities. This implies the key role played by lifelong learning as a continuous, often collective learning process embracing the entire population, and innovation (including social innovation) for transformational change (Tuomi, 2006).
3. Transformational use of ICTs, in particular at the level of individuals and communities, is often understood to be related to empowerment. The European Commission (CEC, 2005b) defines empowerment as "the process of granting people the power to take responsible initiatives to shape their own life and that of their community or society in economic, social and political terms" (p. 32).

In order to demonstrate the difference between transformational and non-transformational uses of ICT, it appears useful—at the risk of oversimplification—to think of ICT diffusion as a two-phase process (see Figure 1): In a first phase, ICT is adopted to better do what has been done before already, i.e. to increase efficiency (i.e. speed,

Figure 1. Conceptualising ICT diffusion as a two-phase process

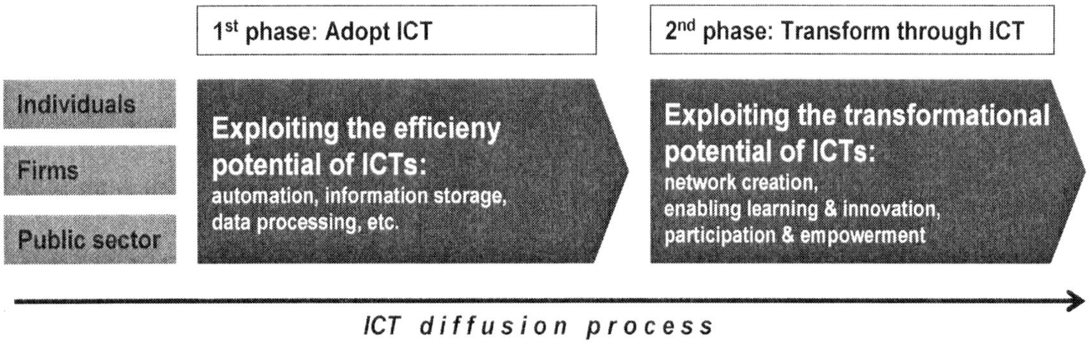

throughput, output, variety, productivity). While significant improvements can be obtained this way, the true potential of ICTs to enable new, effective ways of doing things is not being exploited. This is what the second phase is about: Questioning traditional processes and means of achieving the fundamental goals of stakeholders, and making progress towards stronger social and networking capital, continuous learning and innovation, and empowerment of people as citizens, consumers, patients, learners and creators, to name only the most obvious roles.

The purpose of this chapter is to briefly present a conceptual framework for understanding and measuring transformational use of ICTs. We will focus on use of ICT *by individuals* in their manifold roles. In the last part of the chapter, some results of an Internet user survey are presented which was conducted in early 2008 in 12 selected regions in the EU in order to develop insight into and to pilot indicators for capturing transformational use of ICTs by individuals. The survey data can be used to explore perceptions about the transformational effect of the Internet on individuals and the regions they are residing in. The analysis also sought to assess the extent to which certain statistical measures can be applied for the purpose of benchmarking regions according to individuals' transformational use of ICT.

STATUS QUO

A number of benchmarking mechanisms have been put in place in order to monitor the progress towards the KBS in the European Union (CEC, 2005a; 2006). Benchmarking is a central component of the Open Method of Coordination and, as such, an important policy tool for EU policy-making on Information Society related issues.

The first benchmarking frameworks for ICT-related statistics were developed within the original eEurope 2002 initiative, and then further refined during eEurope 2005. Whereas most of the statistics in this early phase were still based on Eurobarometer surveys, one-off research studies or poorly harmonised national sources, lately more and more of the data have been collected by the National Statistical Institutes under the guidance of Eurostat.

The most important instrument for this purpose are the annual Information Society surveys, established in 2002 by the European Commission in view of an increasing demand for official statistics on ICT related issues within the EU (Eurostat; 2006). Indicators derived from the data were used to benchmark ICT-driven developments in enterprises and by individuals. Eurostat developed two model surveys, one on enterprises, one on individuals, in close collaboration with Member States and in coordination with initiatives within the OECD Working Party on the Information Society (OECD, 2008). These model instruments are regularly adapted to the changing needs of users and policy makers. They are composed of model questionnaires and accompanying methodological guidelines for their implementation. In 2004 the European Parliament and the Council adopted Regulation (EC) No 808/2004 covering the above mentioned surveys. As a framework regulation, it allows flexibility to adapt the surveys to newly evolving needs by users and decision makers. Annual implementing measures are forming the basis for the Eurostat model surveys and will ensure harmonized data for all EU Member States for the upcoming years.

Within the i2010 policy process, a revised set of benchmarking indicators was agreed upon in 2006 to measure progress towards achieving the i2010 goals (i2010 HLG, 2006). Indicators are grouped into nine themes: Development of broadband; Advanced services; Security; Impact; Investment in ICT research; Adoption of ICT by businesses; Impact of adoption of ICT by business; Inclusion; and Public services.

The development of indicators to benchmark the KBS on a consistent basis across the European territory marks a significant step in the evolution of European policy in the area. For the purpose, however, of benchmarking European regions' success in building up a KBS, the indicators developed to date have a number of limitations. First, they are overwhelmingly technology focused. They relate principally to the supply of and demand for ICTs and selected electronically-delivered services. Only in some cases are these supplemented by other indicators setting out the purposes for which technologies are used. Even here the indicators are usually not informed by current scientific knowledge of the determinants of (regional) social and economic development. Second, they tend to reflect an assumption that ICTs will automatically lead to economic and social development. However, we do not know that this is the case and the indicators developed to date in order to monitor ICT take-up are not sufficiently sophisticated to allow us to test this. Third, although the i2010 strategic framework acknowledges that ICTs do not diffuse uniformly across all regions and socio-demographic groups and that e-inclusion and the regional digital divide is a concern across Europe, the benchmarking exercise foreseen barely addresses the issue of regional imbalances, even within the context of the narrow technological approach outlined above. Only in the case of individuals' access to and use of the Internet are sub-national differences considered at all, and this is confined to differences between Objective 1 and non-Objective 1 regions.

TOWARDS A FRAMEWORK FOR MEASURING TRANSFORMATIONAL USE OF ICT BY INDIVIDUALS

For a meaningful analysis of transformation in the form of individual empowerment, a recourse to theories of human and social development is required. This bring us to Nobel price winning economist Amartya Sen. He suggests that policy-making, as far as it is concerned with social and economic development, should focus on the "capabilities" which people have (i.e. "entitlements based on legal rules but also socially-enforced moral rules which enable or constrain the ability to do or be certain things"), their relation to the "functionings" which they "have reason to value", and how both are affected by policy choices (Sen, 1999).

A number of authors have stressed the high relevance of Amartya Sen's work for policy choices surrounding implementation of ICTs (Mansell, 2002; Alampay, 2006). As Bianchi et al. (2006) point out, Sen's work "can substantially enrich the debate on ICT for growth and cohesion. In a nutshell, he shows that mere aggregate numbers about availability of resources, such as Internet connections, do not say much about effective empowerment of the individual and thus the productive use of the technology at societal level. Sen's normative framework therefore prompts us to switch from a technology-centred to a people-centred take on inclusion". Sen's concept for the analysis of ICT-related policies forces policy stakeholders to revisit the whole premise of why people's access to ICTs such as the Internet is deemed essential.

How, then, can we identify and conceptualise activities which are potentially transformed by ICTs, and how can we make sense of their 'empowering impact'? A useful starting point is the work of Nurmela et al. (2004), who have developed a framework for the analysis of individuals' use of ICT based on extensive empirical research with focus groups. The authors distinguish seven spheres of application of ICTs by private households/individuals.

For the purpose of analysing the utility which individuals derive from these activities, application of the media-system dependency goals identified by Ball-Rokeach (1985) appears to be of special interest.

Jung et al. (2001) based their "Internet Connectedness Index" on this approach. They came up with six main goals with regard to the use of Internet and other ICTs:

- Two understanding goals: to stay on top of events and groups that you care about (social understanding); to express yourself or your opinions (self-understanding);
- Two orientation goals: to accomplish business, financial, or work tasks (action orientation); to get advice on how to deal with other people, such as doctors and other health professionals (interaction-orientation);
- Two play goals: to play or amuse yourself (solitary play); for social reasons like making new friends (social play).

For the purpose of the present paper, we define these six goals as "objective functions". Based on

Table 1. Spheres of ICT application by individuals

Activity	Applications of ICT (Examples)	Users' Objective Function
Communicate (social interaction)	e-Mail, mobile phone, SMS, messaging services, IRC chat, social network services, location-based services, and so forth	• Social play; • Social understanding; • Self understanding • Interaction-orientation • Action orientation
Receive & process information, and learning	Passive: PC and mobile device, Digital /interactive TV and radio, Internet information portals, streaming radio, podcasting, blogging Active: search engine, discussion boards, communities of interest, eLearning services, location-based services, and so forth	• Social understanding; • Interaction-orientation; • Action orientation; • Self-understanding
Take care of personal business, transactions and requests for assistance	PC and/or mobile device, Internet, mobile phone, SMS, 3G-phone, online banking software, spreadsheet programme, security software, patient-sided eHealth services, location-based services, and so forth	• Action orientation
Entertainment	Latest generation PC or mobile device, gaming software, multimedia software, broadband Internet, peripherals	• Solitary play; • Social play
Generate and distribute own content	PC, digital camera, Internet, multimedia software, publishing software, podcasts, blogging	• Self-understanding; • Solitary play; • Social play
Participate in policy-making and public life	PC and mobile device, Internet, discussion boards on communities of interest, IRC chat, social network services	• Self-understanding; • Social understanding
Employment-related activities	Office applications, specialist software, Internet, Intranet, communities of practice, peripherals, CSCW tools, social network services, PDA, mobile telephony, location-based services, and so forth	• Action orientation

these and other similar categorisations, we identified seven areas of 'everyday life activities' which are directly affected by key applications of ICT (see Table 1). These are: to communicate (social interaction); to receive & process information and to learn; to take care of personal business, transactions and requests for help; to enjoy entertainment; to generate and distribute own content; to participate in policy-making and public life; and to engage in employment-related activities. Each of these activities is associated with one or several objective functions as described above.

It is now possible to show for each of these activity areas to what extent ICTs—in the form in which they have developed, which itself is a socially constructed process, see MacKenzie & Wajcman, 1999)—have the inherent potential to offer fundamentally new ways for achieving the objective functions associated with particular activities. For the purpose of benchmarking, we need to ask for each of the seven spheres of activities to what extent certain uses of the Internet and other ICT constitute a transformational use of technology, according to our understanding of the term as outlined above.

Communication and Social Interaction

Techno-social innovations which give rise to fundamentally new communication channels and tools can be expected to play a potentially transformational role, simply because of the essential role which communication plays for human society. Without any doubt, the Internet belongs into this category, as does mobile telephony (which tends to be less often acknowledged, see Tuomi, 2002; Sheller & Urry, 2006). Both of these technologies are in the process of becoming ubiquitous, which Castells et al. (2004) argue means nothing less than a homogenisation of space: "being ubiquitous means transcending space" (p. 236). Obviously, this has far-reaching consequences for social interaction.

Katz & Rice (2002) define social interaction as "focused on individual relations and goals", in contrast to civic and community involvement ("participation in a jointly produced social, civic, or community activity"). Social interaction "entails interaction with specific others whom one either knows initially or eventually comes to know. This interaction is likely to involve dyadic, familial, friendship, romantic, and group relations. [Compared to social participation] it speaks less directly to the interests and goals of collectives" (p. 32).

Analysis of the effect of technology on patterns of social interaction is related, of course, with the debate about *social capital*. Social capital is sensibly defined by Field (2003) as follows: "By making connections with one another, and keeping them going over time, people are able to work together to achieve things that they either could not achieve by themselves, or could only achieve with great difficulty. People connect through a series of networks and they tend to share common values with other members of these networks; to the extent that these networks constitute a resource, they can be seen as forming a kind of capital" (p. 7).

Whereas the notion of social capital has generally being considered in the policy process as something positive for those who are endowed with it (CEC, 2005b), closer analysis reveals the need for distinguishing between three different types (Nahapiet & Ghoshal, 1998):

- bonding social capital, i.e. strong ties between like people (or organisations) in similar situations;
- bridging social capital, i.e. more distant or "weak ties" of like persons (or organisations);
- linking social capital, i.e. weak ties which reach out to unlike people/organisations, such as those which are entirely outside of the community or in a different sector.

Some authors have suggested, based on the seminal work of Granovetter (1973), that it is the latter two types of social capital which appear to be of most importance as determinants of success in the knowledge-based economy and society (Boase et al., 2006).

Against this background, an increasing number of commentators and researchers have pointed out that the Internet can play a decisive role in transforming access to social capital as well as the capability to translate stocks of social capital into personal benefits.

Among the ICTs which are being discussed in this context are simple applications such as e-mail—one of the Internet's killer applications, as it has been driving people online just to be able to participate in electronic communication—but also "virtual communities" (Rheingold, 2000) and participative web services, usually subsumed under the term Web 2.0. It describes applications of the Internet which comprise a strong degree of user involvement, such as in the case of the popular social networking sites which combine traditional means of online communications (discussion boards, online chat, e-mail) with the possibility to upload and share (often self-created) content, to identify people with similar interests, and to easily find content or users which is likely to be relevant, for example by implementation of rating and "tagging" of pieces of content. In spite of the criticism which the hype around the Web 2.0 applications has attracted, there is widespread consensus that the Internet has indeed become a powerful instrument for user involvement and an outlet for creativity (Benkler, 2006; OECD, 2007; Tapscott & Williams, 2007). The rapid diffusion of such applications point towards an increasing range of possibilities for Internet-based social innovations to transform patterns of sociability.

In a similar way, the diffusion of mobile telephony has exceeded all expectations as users have quickly grasped the possibilities which it offers them to do things they value highly, but could not do before (Castells et al., 2004; Ling, 2008). Most importantly, users of mobile phones are independent from stationary connections, i.e. they can make phone calls and send text messages from practically anywhere. The implication is that people enjoy considerably enhanced control over the communication process. But this is far from the only major transformational effect which is ascribed to wireless communication systems. The arrival of the third generation of mobile telephony, especially of fast UMTS-connections and the increasing functionality of mobile phones (integrating features of personal information managers, cameras, digital music players, and so forth) will also open up new possibilities and further heighten the transformational potential of this kind of applications.

In order to analyse the transformational impact of these ICTs with regard to activities related to communication and social interaction, we need to ask whether these technologies have exerted a significant influence on the quality and quantity of social interaction. More concretely, transformation could be linked to evidence of significant increases in:

- the number of weak ties between individuals (bridging social capital);
- the diversity of social ties between individuals (linking social capital);
- levels of social capital as measured by belonging to social groups as well as active participation in discussions and decision-making within social groups;
- the creation of new weak ties among those who traditionally suffered from low levels of social capital;
- the degree to which individuals are able to benefit from their social ties by gaining access to resources when these are needed (Dutton, 2005).

For the discussion of the social impacts of ICT, it is necessary to take into account that ICT-enabled "networked individualism" (Castells,

2001) is developing as part of longer-term trend, by which the community as a social construct—based primarily on face-to-face interaction and as such bound to a limited geographical territory, such as a neighbourhood—has been loosing much of its relevance. This process started long before the advent of ICTs and the Internet (Wellman, 2001).

Reception and Processing of Information, and Learning

The perception of information from the mass media remains one of the basic purposes of media consumption, including use of the Internet. Increasingly, however, the progressive convergence between previously separated media spheres, strongly influenced by the further development of the Internet, has made traditional distinctions, such as mass media versus individual/personal media, more and more meaningless. Today, most experts observe a gradual shift towards what is called "meso-media" (Feldmann & Zerdick, 2005), with mass media becoming more personalised (e.g. though increasing number of specialist channels, digital television with heightened interactivity) and personal media being opened up to larger numbers of the public (e.g. through online chats, discussion forums, blogging).

Concerning information offered for active retrieval by individuals, it is safe to say that the Internet has made a huge difference to the accessibility of information. People who are equipped with the adequate skills in identifying, selecting and processing information enjoy the benefits of almost instant access to an incredible wealth of data on the Internet. As opposed to the pre-Internet era when most mediated information was transmitted through the mass media, the Internet enables high degrees of personalisation of information retrieval. The huge leaps in performance which search engine technology have made in recent years have provided users with adequate tools to exploit this richness of information.

The question is now whether these developments constitute a transformation of previous practice, or simply an acceleration. It is certainly true that just enabling people from different backgrounds (e.g. different nations, cultures) to exchange information freely between each other will not necessarily yield meaningful outcomes. Many Internet users might be much less interested in learning new things, but in finding confirmation for opinions they already hold and in contacting people which they feel are "like them" (Katz & Rice; 2002). It has been noticed that the possibility for personalising the information which one is exposed to may lead to narrow-mindedness and social fragmentation. Indeed, Katz & Rice (2002) report from a evidence that levels of selective exposure to news are significantly higher for Internet users than for newspaper readers and viewers of TV news. As a consequence, Hill & Hughes (1998) claim that "people go on-line to find out more information about a subject, not to be transformed".

There are, however, also many signs of truly transformational practice. Online communities of practice are of particular importance in this regard. The experience of recent years certainly gives credibility to the claim of Manuel Castells (2001) who states that virtual communities of practice are an expression of the latent existence of common interests and/or values between people who do not know each other, but who could derive personal utility from interaction. This suggests that there are good reasons to use engagement in online communities of interest and participation in social network platforms as indicators for transformational use of ICTs. More research is, however, certainly needed before such indicators can be used for benchmarking.

A more obvious incidence of transformational use of technology is ICT-enabled participation in lifelong learning. The case for transforming structured learning and training into a lifelong activity has been made powerfully by academics and policy-makers alike (e.g. OECD, 2001).

Evidence of this happening is, unfortunately, very limited indeed. In particular, there is little progress in achieving higher rates of participation in lifelong learning within those sub-groups of the population which are at risk of social exclusion (van Dijk, 2005). Any use of ICT which achieves engagement in lifelong learning by those who otherwise would not participate in such activities can without doubt be called "transformational".

With regard to the traditional obstacles which affect people who are willing to engage in learning activities, eLearning applications offer a lot of potential. Data from a representative survey conducted by eUSER (2006) suggest that a sizeable minority of people currently engaged in online eLearning courses would not have been able to engage in training if it was not for the possibility to do this online—again, an example of truly transformational application of ICTs.

Personal Business, Transactions and Requests for Assistance

Instrumental uses of ICTs in the private domain include transactions such as online banking, online ordering and reservations, as well as many e-government applications. In general, we can observe increases in control of consumers over activities of a transactional nature, reaching from simple personalisation of products enabled by Internet technologies to instances of full-fletched co-development of goods and services, in which consumers become "prosumers" who have a strong influence on how the products they purchase look like and work.

ICTs have opened up a whole range of new possibilities for people whose ability to take care of personal business and transactions used to be constrained—for example because of lack of time, because of individual functional restrictions, or because of geographical location in a peripheral or otherwise disadvantaged region of Europe.

While increased convenience alone should not be confused with transformational change, in some cases such changes may exert a strong impact on the ability of people to lead a self-determined life. It appears futile to try to draw a clear line between non-transformational and transformational applications of ICT in this area.

One of the more fascinating effects of the Internet has been the evolution of online trading and selling between private households through the Internet, mainly by means of online auctions. The Internet, together with other ICTs, has made a big impact on the ease and flexibility with which such tasks can be carried out. The basic underlying reason can be found in transaction cost theory. As was noted by the early transaction cost theorists already, transaction costs can be altered by technological progress. ICTs in general, and the Internet, in particular, have been shown to reduce the costs of many types of transactions (Malone et al., 1987; Picot et al., 2003; Cordella, 2006). An important component of the transaction costs that are incurred by activities for acquiring information are search costs. These arise when market participants have to invest in activities to find the information they need to decide how to behave on the market, e.g. to take part in the labour market or stay out. Search costs are determined by the nature, number and intensity of search activities, but also by the technique and technology used for investigating information. For this reason, ICTs have a major influence on search costs, not only on their overall level, but also on their composition and the relative costs of different search techniques. In that way, the Internet has transformed the marketplace by enabling the emergence of new markets which have not been sustainable before, because transaction costs were prohibitive—a typical example of market failure which the Internet and other ICTs were able to abolish.

"Requests for assistance" here refers to instrumental use of the ICT in cases of need or emergencies. Any improvements in access to health and emergency related services are obviously of highest relevance to the capability of people to lead a self-determined and healthy life (Murero et al., 2006).

Entertainment

"Users have a tendency to twist new technology to fulfil their interests or desires", as Castells (2001, p. 54) writes. The Internet, mobile telephony and the other new ICTs are certainly no exceptions in this regard. Because of our focus on uses of ICT relevant for regional development and society at large, entertainment applications are of less interest to us. Note, however, that boundaries between ICT-based entertainment activities and other domains, such as learning, social interaction and communication, distribution of own content, and even employment, are becoming increasingly blurred (Castronova, 2005). Of special relevance are gaming applications which help overcome barriers to engagement in lifelong learning, especially among those people which are generally considered to be averse to formal education and training courses. Such "serious games" (Annetta, 2008) have attracted a lot of interest by practitioners in the adult education domain. If such online games are taken up by parts of the population which are unlikely to be reached by traditional training offers, we can speak of a transformational impact.

Generation and Distribution of User-Created Content

The Internet and (increasingly) also mobile networks offer unprecedented possibilities for the distribution of user-created content (OECD, 2007). This appears—in contrast to other uses of the Internet such as information retrieval and one-to-many entertainment—to represent a fundamentally new way of people to interact with public media (Zittrain, 2006).

In the early years of this decade, many experts shared the observation by Nurmela et al. (2004) that "the need now is for various kinds of forums where citizens could build up the courage they need to put up their own production on display" (p. 14). Castells (2001) wrote "the most important latent demand [is] for interactive free expression and autonomous creation—nowadays largely stymied by the sclerotic vision of the traditional media industry" (p. 200).

Since then, the runaway success of Internet services such as MySpace, Linked-In and YouTube has confirmed that there is a big interest from users in publishing self-created content on the Internet (Benkler, 2006). Open source systems, decentralised broadcasting, serendipitous interaction, common-interest communication, and co-creation have all become mainstream uses of ICTs. In this context, Katz & Rice (2004) apply the term "Internet enabled expression" which "refers to the material that is created by individuals or groups to reflect their views, interests, or talents. These materials are produced for the observation, interest, or response of their creators and, usually, others" (p. 5). This definition clearly points towards the overlap between self-generated content and civic and political participation (see below).

For the moment, it appears that indicators which measure active contribution to social network services and similar applications can be good proxies of transformational use of ICT in the form of exchange of user-created content.

Participation in Policy-Making and Public Life

From early on, there have been claims that the Internet would play a considerable role in fostering democracy through enhanced participation of citizens in the policy-making process—especially at the local and regional levels of government. As a number of leading scholars (e.g. Tuomi, 2002) have shown, the development of the Internet itself owes much to a fundamentally open, democratic process of social production. It is hardly surprising, then, that futurist authors have seen in the Internet a potentially giant step forward towards a truly democratic society.

Only in recent years, however, e-participation emerged on the public agenda, itself drawing on three developments: (a) Development and implementation of CSCW (Computer Supported Cooperative Work) and groupware, which make use of latest-generation ICTs to enable and support collaborative human interaction; (b) Increasing interest in what is termed e-democracy (earlier: tele-democracy) since the late 1990s, when the focus shifted rapidly from eVoting to several forms of ICT-supported and ICT-enabled interaction between governments and citizens; (c) The evolution of e-government developments towards increasingly complex service delivery.

While the issue of e-voting has all but disappeared from the political agenda in most EU countries, the pace of techno-economic change, as indicated by the rapid diffusion of broadband access to the Internet, and the spread of online social networking mean that the possibilities to let citizen participate in policy-making have, arguably, never been as good as today. At the same time, concerns about increasing numbers of citizens becoming disengaged with the political process have been growing in recent years.

As in the case of e-learning, we can distinguish between two types of transformational use with regard to online participation in policy-making: First, people who are already interested in politics and society at large may be offered tools for higher-quality participation in policy-making: Second, and even more importantly, citizens who up to now have not been willing to engage in civic participation may be stimulated to take an active role.

Care needs to be taken, however, for benchmarking activities concerning political participation. Judgemental and normative statements about the relationship between Internet usage and the democratic process need to be based on a common understanding of the meaning of the term "democracy". The existence of such a consensus cannot be taken for granted. Dahlberg (2001) distinguishes between three idealised forms of democracy (liberal individualism, communitarism and deliberate democracy) and shows that, depending on the interpretation of democracy a person subscribes to, she or he will judge the potential and actual impact of the Internet on democracy in very different terms.

Worker Empowerment and Organisational Change

We can sketch the development of the public debate about transformational impact of ICTs in organisations as follows: Starting from an early phase in which the focus was on technology per se, via a backlash phase in the aftermath of the dot.com crash, in which the positive effect of ICT on performance was put in doubt in general, the scientific and public debate has now reached a consensus that ICT does indeed matter, but that its introduction needs to be embedded in a wider strategy of organisational change. Confirmation comes from a rich body of research which has appeared since the mid 1990s (OECD, 2001, 2004; Smith & Fingar, 2003).

This means that, while most models of ICT-enabled progress in companies focus on how ICT 'drives' organisational change, complementary organisational change is required to 'unlock' the powers of ICT. Such a strategy needs, more than anything else, take full account of the central role which the workforce plays in making successful change happen (Malone, 2004).

For analysing such processes of organisational change (and the degree to which they amount to "transformational change"), it appears useful to refer to the research about what has been called "new forms of work organisation", "new organisation of work" or "modernisation of work organisation" (Nordflex, 1999). A widely used definition for these was adopted by the European Work Organisation Network (Savage, 2001): "New Work Organisation is the application of principles and practices within enterprises which aim to capitalise on, and develop the creativity and commitment of employees at all levels in achieving competitive advantage and in meeting the business and service challenges posed by the social, economic and technological environment in which the enterprise exists" (p. 5).

We can observe transformational use of ICT within the domain of work and employment in cases where the implementation of ICT systems significantly increases the extent to which workers are participating in decisions about their working conditions. Indicators measuring characteristics of workplaces, including participation in such decisions, are collected in many countries through national employee surveys (Huys & Ramioul, 2007). Comparisons across countries are possible in Europe by using the data from the European Working Conditions Survey (Parent-Thirion et al., 2007).

SOME EVIDENCE FROM A 12-REGION INTERNET USER SURVEY IN EUROPE

As discussed above, most existing statistics on the use of ICTs by households—especially those few ones which are available at the regional level within Europe—focus on basic readiness and uptake of ICTs rather than the value which people and organisations derive from using the Internet, mobile telephony, and other ICTs. In recent years, however, scientific research including work at publicly funded research centres such as the Oxford Internet Institute (Dutton & Helsper, 2007) and the Pew Internet & American Life Project (Boase et al., 2006), as well as research by National Statistical Institutes (e.g. Harper & Kelly, 2003; Nurmela, 2006) has made progress in identifying and measuring the ways in which the Internet and other ICTs exert a direct, and arguably transformational, influence on people's lives. This is the background against which in the following results from an indicator piloting survey are presented. The survey has provided data with which some of the issues surrounding transformational use of ICT in the seven areas of 'everyday life activities' introduced in the previous section can be explored in more depth.

Methodology for Data Collection

The data were obtained through an online survey of Internet users in 12 NUTS2 regions in 7 countries of Europe (Germany, Italy, Poland, Slovakia, Spain, Sweden and United Kingdom). Data collection was centrally managed and programmed, and made use of the Ipsos Online Access Panel and equivalent panels of partner institutes. The Ipsos Access Panels comprise more than 1 million consumers in over 20 countries, and are in full compliance with the international standards for online access panels defined within EFAMRO, the international federation of market research agency associations.

For the survey, a stratified random sample was drawn, with quotas being applied to make sure that certain types of individuals are adequately represented in the sample. For building the sample, a quota sampling approach was used in order to create a sample representative for the target group, i.e. regular Internet users aged 18-64 regarding age, gender and region. The quotas were created by obtaining the universe figures from two sources; Eurostat 2006 for Slovakia, Poland and Sweden and offline representative studies (CAPIBUS) that were provided by partner institutes of Ipsos in United Kingdom, Spain and Italy as well as used for Germany. In case of over/under-achievement of quotas, ex-post weighting of cased was used to correct for the deviation.

The questionnaire included a larger number of questions grouped into six modules: socio-demographics, entrepreneurial experience, Internet use, ICT skills & training, social activities & civil participation; social ties & networking. The instrument was pre-tested in the laboratory and in the field prior to start of the data gathering phase.

The data gathered were then analysed using the SPSS software package in order to assess the validity of measurement, comparability across cultures (i.e. countries, language areas), statistical relevance (explanatory power) and cost efficiency.

Note that the sizable differences regarding the share of regular Internet users within the population aged 18-64 between the countries covered by the survey—in particular, between the Old and the New Member States—imply that the socio-demographic composition of the universe (i.e. age, employment and social status distribution) also differs quite extensively between the countries in the sample. In general, the universe in the countries with comparatively low Internet diffusion (Italy, Poland, Slovakia) tends to be younger and better educated compared to the other countries. This needs to be taken into account when comparing the results between regions.

Table 2 includes a number of key indicators which describe the regions selected for the survey.

How Important are Different Uses of the Internet for the Lives of People?

The extent to which the Internet "makes a real difference" to people's lives can be explored by looking at people's perceptions. Whereas most indicator systems which are currently in use attempt to measure whether individuals have used certain applications of the Internet, the survey presented respondents with a list of possible uses of the Internet and then asked how important these are perceived to be for (a) their private life and (b)—using a somewhat different list of items—their ability to carry out their job (if in employment). Table 3 presents the results for importance for private life.

We found that the majority of Internet users consider many of the uses they make of the Internet as being of essential or at least high importance. Commercial functions such as online-banking and pre-purchase information seeking about products and services are among the uses considered as most important, which suggests that applications which mainly increase the convenience of

Table 2. Key indicators on regions covered by survey[1] (Data source: Eurostat REGIO database)

Region	Country	Population		GDP/head in PPS		Unemployment rate (%, 2005)	HRST (%, 2005)
		Total (2004)	Density (2003)	EU25=100 (2003)	% Change 1999-2003		
Pomorskie	PL	2191.5	120	46.3	-0.2	18.9	29
Malopolskie	PL	3256.6	214	40.4	0.5	15.2	31
Bratislavsky Kraj	SK	600.5	292	115.9	13.9	5.3	55
Východné Slovensko	SK	1565.6	99	38.8	3.5	23.1	27
Schleswig-Holstein	DE	2826.0	179	98.3	-7.5	10.3	46
Thüringen	DE	2364.2	147	75.2	0.1	17.2	53
Mellersta Norrlland	SE	371.7	5	105.5	-1.5	8.2	43
Emilia Romagna	IT	4080.4	191	137.0	-8.8	3.7	31
Navarra	ES	576.8	55	123.1	9.0	5.6	53
Extremadura	ES	1067.5	26	63.8	3.6	15.8	33
South Yorkshire	UK	1278.8	816	89.4	6.7	5.3	32
East Anglia	UK	2239.9	176	106.8	6.0	4.1	39

Table 3. The perceived importance of the Internet for private life (Data source: TRANSFORM 12 Region Internet User Survey)

	Percent saying this Internet use is of *essential* importance for their lives[2]	Percent saying this Internet use is of high importance for their lives[3]	Importance of this Internet use for private life: Mean on 10-point scale
To use your bank's online services	44.1	66.1	3.44
To communicate with people outside of the region	38.0	63.2	3.49
To communicate with people in the region	35.4	58.9	3.72
To communicate with people abroad	34.2	52.9	4.28
For educational and learning purposes	28.1	57.4	3.70
To find info about sth. you consider buying locally	27.4	62.1	3.49
To work at home	26.3	47.2	4.67
To look for career related information in general	21.4	49.0	4.32
To look for career related info from region or city	19.4	46.5	4.48
To look for news about region or city	17.7	46.2	4.30
To buy or order goods and services	17.3	49.5	4.16
To obtain info about events in region or city	17.1	48.6	4.13
To find info about health issues in general	14.4	41.2	4.49
To find info about health services in region or city	13.6	36.9	4.80
To play online games	9.4	21.4	6.67

transactions—i.e. not considered as transformational in the previous section—are perceived by Internet users as highly relevant.

Information sources which are specific to the resident region are given—on average—roughly the same weight as non-region specific information sources. While it can be assumed that there are big differences between the quality of region-specific information made available online, which includes online public services, our data suggest that Internet users tend not to distinguish between region-specific and non-specific information sources.

By means of a factor analysis4, the 15 items could be reduced to four factors, each of which represents types of Internet usage which are typically given roughly the same importance by respondents. The four factors are:

- "To play online games" appeared as a separate factor [Online gaming];
- A second factor includes "To buy or order goods and services", "To use your bank's online services" and "To find information about goods or services which you consider buying at shops in your region or city". These are instrumental uses with a clear focus on commercial transactions [Commercial];
- A third factor includes "To communicate with people located in the same region", "To communicate with people located outside of the region but inside country", "To communicate with people located abroad", "To work at home" and "For educational and learning purposes". These uses relate to online communication and to instrumental uses concerned with work and learning [Communication, work & studies];
- The final factor includes "To find information about health and medical care services in your region, city or neighbourhood", "To find information about health issues in general",

"To look for news about your region, city or neighbourhood", "To obtain information about events in your region, city or neighbourhood", "To look for career related information from your region, city or neighbourhood" and "To look for career related information (jobs, information related to your work) in general". These are uses which have to do with information that in earlier times would have been sought in newspapers, specialist magazines and reference books. [General information search].

Subsequently, these factors were used as independent factors in a regression analysis (see below).

In order to explore whether the Internet has made a difference to the ease of maintaining weak ties, the survey asked respondents directly whether they think that the Internet has had an effect on the number of people they communicate with at least occasionally. This is a very simple operationalisation of the notion of "weak ties" as suggested by Granovetter (1973). In line with the theory-based assumptions according to which the Internet is likely to increase the number of weak ties by diminishing the costs of keeping in (loose) contact with a large number of people (Boase et al., 2006), the data shows that one in two respondents felt the Internet has increased their number of private weak ties within the region as well as within the country. 46% also felt an increase in occasional contacts with people abroad. For all of these types of contacts, the share of respondents who perceive a strong increase as a consequence of the Internet is between one in four and one in five.

For another piece of analysis, we applied a methodology developed by the Pew Internet & American Life Project (Boase et al., 2006): Interviewees were presented with a list of items describing what can be termed "major decisions in life" (see Table 4). For each of these decisions, we first enquired whether respondents had to deal with it in the reference period, in which case they were then asked what role the Internet played for dealing with the decision.

The results clearly show how that the Internet does indeed play a highly significant role in decisions which are transformative in character. About one in four Internet users who have been face with major decisions about financial issues, education & training for themselves or their children, moving place or changing jobs state that the Internet was of essential importance for dealing with the issue. Somewhat less than one in five of those

Table 4. The role of the Internet for major decisions in life (Data source: TRANSFORM 12 Region Internet User Survey)

	Percent of Internet users who dealt with this issue in last 3 years	Percent of those who dealt with issue for which Internet played an *essential* role[5]	Percent of those who dealt with issue for which Internet played an *important* role[6]	Importance of the Internet for dealing with issue: Mean on 10-point scale
Made a major investment or financial decision	46.1	25.1	50.8	4.43
Gotten additional education or training for your career	48.4	25.3	51.7	4.27
Chosen a school or college for yourself or your child	32.9	28.4	53.6	4.25
Helped another person deal with a major illness	38.0	19.3	39.4	5.21
Moved into a new place to live	31.1	23.1	38.9	5.47
Changed jobs	34.5	29.5	48.8	4.71

who have been helping another person deal with a major illness or health condition considered the role of the Internet as essential. If considering all of those who indicated a high importance of the Internet in the process, figures are around 50% for all listed "major decisions" with the exception of "helping another person deal with a major illness" and "moved into a new place to live", for which somewhat less than 40% indicate that the Internet was of major importance. These results also indicate that local and regional public agencies can indeed play a powerful role in helping citizens deal with potentially transformational decision in life, by offering online public services (in key areas such as health, education & training, jobs and accommodation) which meet the needs and preferences of users.

Participative Web Applications

Our survey included a question on what are sometimes advanced Internet services, or Web 2.0 applications. The results (see Figure 2) suggest that the share of Internet users who actively contribute to the Internet, including uploading of user-created content, is indeed considerable.

57% have, in the 3 months prior to the survey, posted messages to chat sites, newsgroups or online discussion forums—arguably one of the more established activities on the Internet.

The share of Internet users who have uploaded self-created text, images, photos, videos, or music to any website to be shared, is equally impressive with 42% (in the total sample). 22% have designed or maintained an own website, and 14% run their own blog.

Taken together, Internet users who have contributed user-created content in the 3 months prior to the survey make up 51% of the sample. If engagement on chat sites, newsgroups or discussion forums and creating a profile on a social networking site are added, the share (which may be dubbed "participative web users", see OECD, 2006) rises to 74%.

Figure 2. Uptake of advanced Internet applications (Data source: TRANSFORM 12 Region Internet User Survey)

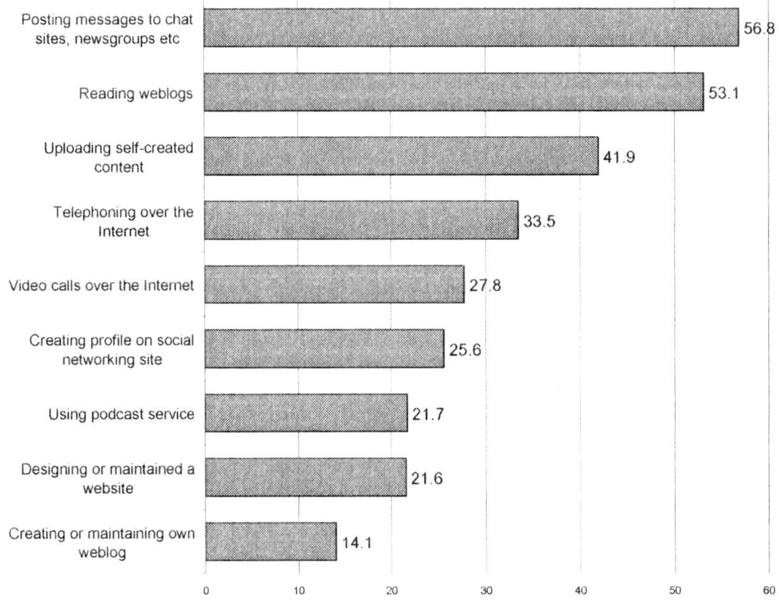

In percentage, multiple answers. Base: All Internet users; n=3363

Further research is needed to explore whether such participative behaviour is novel in the sense that the Internet (and increasingly also mobile networks, see Ling, 2008) liberates creativity which before was unable to find expression.

ICTs and Active Participation in Civil Society

Research into social capital is concerned, among other things, with group membership as an indicator for civil participation and individual-level investment in social capital, usually outside the sphere of work. The survey explored group membership as well as the ways in which respondents communicate with other people in the group(s) they are member of. According to the results, 65% have been members of any type of group (business or professional association; a sport club or league; a religious organization; a hobby group or club; a neighbourhood, school, charity, voluntary or any other local group; a political or activist group; or any other group or organization) in the three years prior to the survey. Once we check whether respondents have *actively taken part in decision-making and discussion* within any group they are member of, we find that one in four in the total sample is a passive group member only; only 13% of the total sample are frequently participating in decision-making and discussions (at least 2-3 times per week).

What is the influence of using ICT on active group membership? It has been argued that extensive use of ICTs is detrimental for civil participation, as face-to-face contacts are replaced by media-poor ICT-mediated contacts, such as via e-mail, chat or instant messaging (e.g. Putnam, 2000). Our findings, however, show that strong use of e-mails and other ICT for making contacts within groups goes hand-in-hand with a stronger participation in day-to-day decision-making within these groups (see Table 5).

What is more, additional analysis showed that this correlation is stronger than the association between face-to-face meetings within groups and participation in day-to-day decision-making within these groups. This suggests that e-mail is indeed a powerful tool for active participation in civil society.

Other research has suggested that it is "those who tend to be introverted [who] find their social contacts expanded via the information relative to their nonsurfing counterparts.[...] This means that being an Internet user is itself a source of online sociability" (Katz & Rice, 2002, p. 264). Evidence for this proposition was recently

Table 5. Relationship between active group membership and ICT use (% of those with group membership) (Data source: TRANSFORM 12 Region Internet User Survey)

	Use of e-mail, etc for contacting group members				Total sample
	Never	**Several times per year to once a month**	**About once a fortnight to once a week**	**At least 2-3 times a week**	
Passive group membership only	74.6	36.3	22.8	15.2	*37.6*
Active group membership (participation in decision making) several times per year to once a month	14.6	44.9	27.5	13.0	*21.3*
Active group membership (participation in decision making) about once a fortnight to once a week	7.7	13.5	35.9	28.1	*21.5*
Active group membership (participation in decision making) at least 2-3 times a week	3.1	5.2	13.8	43.7	*19.6*
Total	100	100	100	100	100

provided by Hampton (2007) who carried out longitudinal research in four Boston (USA) neighbourhoods. Transformational impact could therefore be diagnosed in cases where ICT use is associated with civil participation, and where such participation would not, or only to a lesser extent, take place through traditional ways of communication only.

According to our own survey data, 8% of respondents who are *active* members of a group meet with other people in these groups less often than "several times per year". Of these (n=106), more than one in three has e-mail contact with other group members at least 2-3 times per week, and more than one in two have such e-mail contact at least once a fortnight.

Perceptions About the Effect of the Internet on Living Conditions in Regions

The TRANSFORM survey attempted to gauge whether applications of the Internet are perceived as having had a positive effect on living conditions within regions, and whether there are differences in this regard between regions which may be explained by different ICT-related regional policies. For this purpose two questions with similar sets of items were applied:

- A question on perceived conditions in the NUTS2 region for a) Finding a good job, (b) Getting high-quality education, (c) Engaging in adult/further education and lifelong learning, (d) Setting up an own business, (e) Making your voice heard in regional politics and public life, (f) Enjoying leisure time, (g) Enjoying a high quality of life;
- And a second question as follows: "Some people think that the Internet has an influence on the living and working conditions in Europe's regions, others think that this is not the case. In the past three years, what kind of influence would you say the Internet has had on the general conditions in your region regarding ...", then using the same set of items as above.

Results from the first question (Table 6) suggest that there are indeed significant differences in living conditions between regions as perceived by the resident population. In general, these differences confirm what is to be expected from the differences as they show up in general regional development indicators. For example, in most regions with unemployment rates much above the EU average (Extremadura, Thüringen, Vychodne Slovensko) the perceived conditions for finding a good job are worse than average. An exception here are the Polish regions, which may reflect the fact that respondents can be expected to have—when compared to the rest of the population—very good ICT skills, the labour market for which is much more favourable than for low-qualified Polish workers.

Apart from the difficult situation in some regions with regard to job availability, the most problematic area of the ones included in the question appears to be political and civil participation, i.e. "making one's voice heard in regional politics and public life". In two countries there are marked differences between regions in this regard: In Germany, where the less favourable score for Thüringen reflects the wide-spread disengagement with politics to be found in Eastern Germany, and in Slovakia, where the much more favourable value for the capital region is indicative of the fact that Bratislava is the clear centre of policy-making for the whole country.

Against this background, how do Internet users in the 12 regions perceive the influence of the Internet in their particular region so far?

As Table 7 shows when compared to Table 6, those aspects of living conditions which are currently perceived, on average, to be most positive (education and training, enjoying leisure time) are also those where the highest share of respondents think that the Internet has made things better in

Table 6. Perceived living conditions in own region (means on 10-point scale with 1=very good, 10 = very bad) (Data source: TRANSFORM 12 Region Internet User Survey)

		Finding a good job	Getting good education	Engaging in lifelong learning	Setting up an own business[7]	Making one's voice heard	Enjoying leisure time	Enjoying quality of life
Schleswig-Holstein	DE	5.61	4.03	4.36	5.01	4.97	2.85	3.32
Thüringen	DE	6.60	4.63	5.04	5.64	5.79	3.97	4.84
Emilia-Romagna	IT	4.55	4.00	4.23	4.76	5.11	3.86	4.27
Malopolskie	PL	4.26	2.48	3.23	3.94	5.24	3.07	3.50
Pomorskie	PL	3.87	2.75	3.41	3.77	5.05	3.24	3.49
Bratislavsky Kraj	SK	2.65	2.27	2.59	2.82	3.00	2.72	3.00
Vychodne Slovensko	SK	7.08	3.90	4.72	5.61	5.41	4.40	6.10
Navarra	ES	4.29	3.20	3.92	4.43	5.82	3.67	3.39
Extremadura	ES	6.06	4.77	5.13	5.39	5.40	4.20	4.08
Mellersta Norrlland	SE	5.49	4.00	3.92	4.06	4.87	2.73	3.01
South Yorkshire	UK	5.17	4.49	4.13	4.79	6.22	4.12	4.73
East Anglia	UK	5.41	4.31	4.22	4.55	6.06	3.87	4.04
Total sample		5.13	3.79	4.12	4.54	5.31	3.57	3.96

Table 7. Perceived effect of the Internet on living conditions in own region (Very positive or positive effect8 in % of total sample per region) (Data source: TRANSFORM 12 Region Internet User Survey)

		Finding a good job	Getting good education	Engaging in lifelong learning	Setting up an own business	Making one's voice heard	Enjoying leisure time	Enjoying quality of life
Schleswig-Holstein	DE	52.9	48.2	50.7	42.3	30.7	58.9	45.8
Thüringen	DE	47.2	42.8	39.7	44.1	29.2	60.0	42.8
Emilia-Romagna	IT	59.4	65.2	62.7	54.2	48.1	70.7	49.1
Malopolskie	PL	74.6	85.6	67.5	61.8	44.5	81.4	63.4
Pomorskie	PL	75.0	78.4	69.3	59.0	48.9	79.2	66.5
Bratislavsky Kraj	SK	86.9	80.4	76.2	77.4	56.0	84.0	66.4
Vychodne Slovensko	SK	64.2	70.4	58.2	54.7	38.6	68.3	46.7
Navarra	ES	49.3	52.1	44.2	43.4	36.8	67.0	50.2
Extremadura	ES	44.8	48.2	45.7	46.4	40.8	61.9	47.8
Mellersta Norrlland	SE	57.3	58.9	57.5	56.6	50.6	52.7	51.4
South Yorkshire	UK	48.0	51.1	49.1	49.5	27.5	51.5	38.3
East Anglia	UK	50.9	52.5	51.0	52.8	28.7	61.0	49.0
Total sample		58.1	60.1	55.0	53.4	39.5	65.9	51.0

their region. This pattern shows throughout, with the exception of conditions for "finding a good job", where the current situation is considered, on average, as quite bad, but where the Internet is perceived as having had a significant positive effect by 58% of all respondents.

While much has been made of the Internet's potential to improve direct participation of citizens in day-to-day policy-making and in civil society, the results from the survey indicate that it is proving difficult to translate such potential into reality. Only 40% of respondents think that the Internet has improved conditions for this in their region—much less than for all the other aspects of living conditions listed. It appears that those regions, in particular, which suffer from wide-spread disengagement with politics, such as Thüringen in Eastern Germany, are also the least successful in applying the Internet for the purpose of improving the situation. In contrast, every second respondent from the Swedish region Mellersta Norrlland states that the Internet has improved conditions for political participation—roughly the same share than those who see a positive effect for the other aspects of living conditions.

A multivariate OLS regression was carried out to analyse the factors which explain differences in the extent to which individuals have experienced a positive effect of the Internet on overall living conditions in their region.

The dependent variable is:

- Factor score constructed from seven items asking about the perceived effect of the Internet on: a) Finding a good job, (b) Getting high-quality education, (c) Engaging in adult/further education and lifelong learning, (d) Setting up an own business, (e) Making your voice heard in regional politics and public life, (f) Enjoying leisure time, (g) Enjoying a high quality of life in the resident NUTS2 region.

As independent variables, three groups of variables were considered:

- Socio-demographic variables (age, gender, region, still studying yes/no, educational attainment, employment status, household type);
- Social context (trust; active group membership; size of network of personal ties; diversity of network of personal ties; first-hand experience with self-employment);
- Internet experience variables (year started using Internet, hours Internet use per day, multi-location Internet use, providing help about computers to others);
- Type of Internet usage (Importance of different uses of the Internet for private life, uptake of participative web services).

The results are presented in Table 8.

Controlling for contextual factors such as socio-demographics, we find a significant positive influence of uptake of participative Internet services (typically referred to as Web 2.0 applications), here defined as comprising: Posting messages to newsgroups; Creating or maintaining own weblog; Uploading self-created text, images, photos, videos, music and so forth to any website to be shared; Creating a profile on a social networking site; and designing or maintained a website.

Among the social context variables, a significant explanatory factor is trust in people in the neighbourhood and trust in the willingness of people in the region to help each other (but **not** general trust).

Of the socio-demographic variables, the results indicate that the following groups are significantly more likely to perceive a positive impact of the Internet on living conditions within their NUTS2 region: people who are not unemployed; men; and—in particular—Internet users in the Polish regions in the sample, Emilia-Romagna and the Bratislava region, and also— to a lesser

Table 8. Association between Internet's perceived effect on living conditions within the NUTS2-region, other ICT-related, social and contextual factors (OLS Regression) (Data source: TRANSFORM 12 Region Internet User Survey)

Dependent Variable: Influence of Internet on life					
	B	**Std. Error**	**Beta**	**t**	**Sig.**
(Constant)	11.64	11.74		0.99	0.32
qs1_1 Age	0.00	0.00	-0.06	-2.43	0.02
qs2 Gender	0.17	0.04	0.09	4.41	0.00
Region (reference Thuringia)					
SchleswigH	0.13	0.09	0.04	1.52	0.13
EmiliaRomagna	0.54	0.09	0.16	6.19	0.00
Malopolskie	0.65	0.09	0.20	7.16	0.00
Pomorskie	0.60	0.09	0.18	6.62	0.00
BratislavskyKraj	0.82	0.10	0.19	7.93	0.00
VychodneSlovensko	0.30	0.11	0.07	2.78	0.01
Navarra	0.20	0.09	0.06	2.25	0.02
Extremadura	0.12	0.09	0.04	1.40	0.16
MellerstaNorrland	0.29	0.09	0.08	3.04	0.00
SouthYorkshire	0.20	0.09	0.06	2.26	0.02
EastAnglia	0.29	0.09	0.08	3.19	0.00
Still studying	0.13	0.07	0.05	1.76	0.08
Education: reference=lower secondary and less					
Upper secondary education	0.04	0.06	0.02	0.56	0.57
Tertiary / other 21+ education	0.01	0.07	0.00	0.10	0.92
Employment status: reference=inactive					
Employee (incl. family workers)	-0.14	0.08	-0.07	-1.75	0.08
Self-employed	-0.16	0.10	-0.05	-1.64	0.10
Unemployed	-0.27	0.10	-0.07	-2.74	0.01
Student (not in the labour force)	-0.24	0.11	-0.09	-2.14	0.03
Household type: reference=single household					
2+ person household, no kids <16	0.05	0.06	0.02	0.71	0.48
Household with children <16	0.03	0.07	0.02	0.48	0.63
Agreement: Generally speaking, most people can be trusted.	0.00	0.01	0.00	-0.01	0.99
Agreement: Most people in my neighbourhood can be trusted.	0.05	0.01	0.13	4.19	0.00
Agreement: People around here are really willing to help each other out.	0.05	0.01	0.13	4.30	0.00
Active group membership	0.09	0.04	0.05	2.33	0.02
Sum social ties (classes)	0.00	0.01	-0.01	-0.36	0.72
Diversity: Number of different occupations + ethnicity + languages among social ties	0.02	0.01	0.06	2.18	0.03

continued on following page

Table 8. continued

	B	Std. Error	Beta	t	Sig.
Propinquity to self-employment	0.11	0.05	0.05	2.35	0.02
Year started using Internet	-0.01	0.01	-0.02	-1.01	0.31
Duration Internet per Day in Minutes	0.00	0.00	0.04	2.05	0.04
Frequent multi-location Internet use	0.11	0.04	0.06	2.49	0.01
Providing help to others than friends/family	0.06	0.04	0.03	1.41	0.16
Number of Web 2.0 uses	0.05	0.02	0.07	3.01	0.00

ANOVA(b)	Sum of Squares	df	Mean Square	F	Sig.
Regression	468.5	33.0	14.2	20.0	0.000
Residual	1440.3	2032.0	0.7		
Total	1908.9	2065.0			

Model Summary

R	R Square	Adjusted R Square	Std. Error of the Estimate
0.50	0.25	0.23	0.84

extent—the Mellersta Norrland, Eastern Slovakia and East Anglia, when compared to the rest of the regions.

The data indicate a significant degree of variation concerning the extent to which people feel that the Internet has made a real difference to living conditions in their resident region. In most cases, these differences appear to be between countries rather than between regions within the same countries—although care must be taken as the number of regions covered by the analysis is too small to allow generalisation. The effect of the Internet is felt most strongly by Internet users in the New Member States, especially in the Bratislava region which has seen spectacular growth rates in recent years. Among regions from the Old Member States, there is some evidence that Emilia Romagna has succeeded better than the other regions in perceivably improving living conditions with the help of ICT. Mellersta Norrland and East Anglia also emerge as "good performers", although the evidence is weaker (but still significant).

The role of trust is found to be of special relevance for the extent to which a positive impact of the Internet is felt within regions. This does not apply to general trust, but to trust in people in the immediate region and the belief that people are willing to help each other out. It appears that the Internet requires a certain degree of community-level social capital (as indicated by high levels of trust) in order to yield the positive effects on living conditions which are hoped for by policy-makers.

Finally, the extent to which individuals have taken up participative Web2.0 applications is significantly and positively associated with perceived Internet-enabled improvements in living conditions. It can be assumed that people who believe in the power of the Internet to make a difference are also more enthusiastic about new Internet services, and that—vice versa—experience of advanced Internet applications is likely to make people more aware of the difference which the Internet has already made to living conditions. It follows that activities which strengthen awareness among regional stakeholders, including society at large, about the possible benefits to be derived from latest-generation ICTs can exert a positive influence on regional development.

CONCLUSIONS AND OUTLOOK

This chapter has attempted to present a concept for the analysis and measurement of transformational uses of ICT, mainly at the sub-national (e.g. regional) level. The chapter focused on use of ICT by individuals in their roles as citizens, workers, learners, patients, consumers, and so forth. We have argued that here, the transformational potential of ICTs is rooted in its effect in terms of empowerment of users, i.e. "the process of granting people the power to take responsible initiatives to shape their own life and that of their community or society in economic, social and political terms" (CEC 2005b, p. 32). Finally, the chapter discussed some results of an Internet user survey which was conducted in early 2008 in 12 selected regions in the EU, and which was used to pilot indicators for capturing transformational use of ICTs by individuals and to gain insight into perceptions and determinants of such transformational usage.

Our own analysis of the survey data supports the claim that the Internet is indeed having a tangible, and arguably transformative, impact" on users. This effect makes itself felt through an instrumental, and often essential, role of the Internet in major, transformative decisions in life; through Internet-enabled participation in forms of creativity and socialising; through easier, frequent participation in decision-making within social groups; and through improvement in living conditions in EU regions, especially with regard to the ability to find a good job.

With regard to the measurement of transformational use of ICT—in particular as far as the regional level is concerned—currently available indicators in the EU are not sufficient for benchmarking purposes. The obvious first step must be to make progress towards availability of basic indicators of ICT infrastructure, uptake and use for all NUTS2 regions. Eurostat, National Statistical Institutes and the regions need to join together and explore ways in which the data can be supplied in a cost-effective and reliable way. Financial support should be given to regions that participate on their own initiative in harmonised data collection. If needed, options should be explored to cut down the level of detail in other areas of statistical measurement to free up funds needed for the collection of KBS statistics at regional level.

Once such basic indicators are available—as they are already in a small number of EU regions which have set up their own KBS observatories (cf. UNDERSTAND 2006)—there is an obvious need to supplement indicators which mainly focus on technology (such as the i2010 benchmarking indicators) with measures which focus on impacts. In particular, new indicators are needed for benchmarking the capacity (of individuals, firms and regions) to 'unlock' the transformational potential of ICTs, and the actual practice in doing so.

For capturing transformational uses, we have suggested to group individuals' uses of ICT according to a classification of spheres of everyday life activities. This enables a better informed analysis of changes caused or enabled by the application of ICTs. In each of these spheres, transformational use of technology can be operationalised as applications for purposes which have a significant importance for the lives of people, and which would not have been possible without the help of ICTs such as the Internet. In particular, this refers to uses which increase the capability of people to build and maintain social ties (network capital and social capital), to continuously engage in learning and activities related to innovation, and to get empowered by having a bigger say in decision-making which is likely to concern their lives.

In key areas where transformational use of ICT can play a significant role in fostering social and economic development in regions—such as those related to the notion of social capital—the current status of evidence and theory building is not, however, robust enough to allow for the definition of benchmarking indicators in the sense of statistical measures where "more" is always "better". This means that there is a need for more research into the soft factors (including social capital) underlying success in regional development, and the way such factors are associated with patterns of use of ICTs.

ACKNOWLEDGMENT

The research was carried out in the context of a project (TRANSFORM) within the EU's 6th Framework Programme. The project consortium gratefully acknowledges funding by the European Commission, DG Information Society & Media. All views expressed in this document, however, are those of the author and do not necessarily reflect the views of the European Commission. More information about the project can be found at www.transform-eu.org.

REFERENCES

Alampay, E. A. (2006). Beyond access to ICTs: Measuring capabilities in the information society. *International Journal of Education and Development using Information and Communication Technology (IJEDICT), 2*(3), 4-22.

Annetta, L. A. (Ed.) (2008). *Serious Educational Games: From Theory to Practice*. Rotterdam: Sense.

Ball-Rokeach, S.J. (1985). The origins of individual media-system dependency: A sociological framework. *Communication Research, 12*(4), 485-510.

Benkler, Y. (2006). *The wealth of networks: How social production transforms markets and freedom*. New Haven, CT, & London: Yale University Press.

Bianchi, A., Barrios, S., Cabrera, M., Cachia, R., Compañó, R., Malanowski, N., Punie, Y., Turlea, G., Zinnbauer, D., & Centeno, C. (2006). *Revisiting e-inclusion: From vision to action. Working paper.* Sevilla, Spain: Institute for Prospective Technology Studies.

Boase, J., Horrigan, J. B., Wellman, B., & Rainie, L. (2006). *The strength of Internet ties. Report.* Washington, DC: Pew Internet & American Life Project.

Castells, M. (2001). *The Internet galaxy—reflections on the Internet, business, and society.* Oxford, UK, & New York: Oxford University Press.

Castells, M., Fernandez-Ardeval, M., Linchuan Qiu, J., & Sey, A. (2004). *The mobile communication society—a cross-cultural analysis of available evidence on the social uses of wireless communication technology. Report.* Annenberg Research Network on International Communication.

Castronova, E. (2005). *Synthetic worlds: The business and culture of online games.* Chicago: University of Chicago Press.

Commission of the European Communities (CEC). (2005a). *Information society benchmarking report.* Brussels, Belgium: European Commission.

Commission of the European Communities (CEC). (2005b). *Proposal for a recommendation of the European Parliament and of the Council on Key Competences for Lifelong Learning.* Brussels, Belgium: European Commission.

Commission of the European Communities (CEC). (2005c). *i2010—A European information society for growth and employment.* Communication from the Commission to the European Parliament, the European Economic and Social Committee, and the Committee of the Regions, COM(2005) 229 final, Brussels, Belgium: European Commission.

Cordella, Antonio (2006). Transaction costs and information systems: Does IT add up? *Journal of Information Technology, 21*, 195–202.

Cornford, J., Richardson, R., Sokol, M., Marques, P., & Gillespie, A. (2006). *Transformation of regional societies through ICTs: State(s) of the art(s)—a discussion document*. Bonn, Germany: TRANSFORM Consortium.

Dahlberg, L. (2001). Democracy via cyberspace: Mapping the rhetoricsand practices of three prominent camps. *New Media and Society, 3*(2), 157-177.

Dutton, W. H. (2005). The Internet and social transformation: Reconfiguring access. In W. H. Dutton, B. Kahin, R. O'Callaghan, & A. W. Wyckoff (Eds.), *Transforming enterprise: The economic and social implications of information technology* (pp. 375-397). Cambridge, MA, & London: MIT Press.

Dutton, W. H., & Helsper, E. J. (2007). *The Internet in Britain: 2007.* Oxford, UK: Oxford Internet Institute, University of Oxford.

Eurostat. (2006). *Methodological manual for statistics on the information society, survey year 2006, v2.1.* Luxembourg: Eurostat.

eUSER Consortium. (2006). *Report on current demand/supply match and relevant developments. Project deliverable.* Bonn, Germany: Empirica.

Feldmann, V., & Zerdick, A. (2005). E-Merging media: The future of communication. In A. Zerdick, et al. (Eds.), *E-Merging media: Communication and the media economy of the future* (pp. 19-29). Berlin, Heidelberg, & New York: Springer.

Field, J. (2003). *Social capital.* London, & New York: Routledge.

Granovetter, M. (1973). The strength of weak ties. *American Journal of Sociology, 91*, 1360-1380.

Hampton, K. N. (2007). Neighborhoods in the network society—the e-neighbors study. *Information, Communication & Society, 10*(5), 714-748.

Harper, R., & Kelly, M. (2003). *Measuring social capital in the United Kingdom.* London: ONS.

Hill, K. A. & Hughes, J. (1998). *Cyberpolitics: Citizen activism in the age of the Internet.* New York: Rowman and Littlefield.

Huys, R., & Ramioul, M. (2007). Measuring the degree of organisational transformation, a methodological benchmark of organisation surveys. *Sotziologuicheski problemi, 40*, 58-80.

i2010 High Level Group (i2010 HLG) (2006). *i2010 benchmarking framework, issue no. 1.* Brussels, Belgium: European Commission.

Jung, J.-Y., Qiu, J. L., & Kim, Y.-C. (2001). Internet connectedness and inequality: Beyond the "divide." *Communication Research, 28*(4), 507-35.

Katz, J. E., & Rice, R. E. (2002). *Social consequences of Internet use—access, involvement, and interaction.* Cambridge, MA, & London: MIT Press.

Ling, R. (2008). *New tech, new ties: How mobile communication is reshaping social cohesion.* Cambridge, MA, & London: MIT Press.

MacKenzie, D., & Wajcman, J. (Eds.) (1999). *The social shaping of technology, 2nd edition.* Buckingham, UK: Open University Press.

Malone, T. W. (2004). *The future of work.* Boston: Harvard Business School Press.

Malone, T. W., J. Yates, & Benjamin, R. I. (1987). Electronic markets and electronic hierarchies. *Communications of the ACM, 30*, 484-497.

Mansell, R. (2002, July 4-7). New media and the power of networks. In *Proceedings of DSIage2002, Cork* (pp. 21-28).

Murero, M., Rice, R. E., Katz, J. E., Dutta-Bergman, M., & Banerjee, I. (Eds.) (2006). *The Internet and health care: Theory, research, and practice*. Philadelphia, PA: Lawrence Erlbaum Associates.

Nahapiet, J., & Ghoshal, S. (1998). Social capital, intellectual capital, and the organizational advantage. *Academy of Management Review 23*(2), 242-266.

Nordflex Group. (1999) *Flexibility matters—flexible enterprises in the nordic countries*. Stockholm: NUTEK.

Nurmela, J. (2006). Does the use of communication media add to social capital? In L. Iisakka (Ed.), *Social capital in Finland—statistical review* (pp. 63-72). Helsinki, Finland: Statistics Finland.

Nurmela, J., et al. (2004). *Finnish people's communication capabilities in interactive society of the 2000s (Reviews 2004/7)*. Helsinki: Statistics Finland.

OECD. (2001). *Knowledge, work organisation and economic growth, labour market, and social policy (Occasional Papers No. 50)*. Paris: OECD.

OECD. (2004). *The economic impact of ICT—measurement, evidence, and implications*. Paris: OECD.

OECD. (2007). *Participative Web: User-created content. Working party on the information society, online document.* Paris: OECD.

OECD. (2008). *Guide to measuring the information society. Working party on the information society, online document.* Paris: OECD.

Parent-Thirion, Agnès; Fernández Macías, Enrique; Hurley, John; Vermeylen, Greet (2007). *Fourth European Working Conditions Survey.* Luxembourg: Office for Official Publications of the European Communities.

Picot, A., Reichwald, R., & Wigand, R. T. (2003). *Die grenzenlose unternehmung, 5th edition*. Wiesbaden: Gabler.

Putnam, R. (2000). *Bowling alone. The collapse and revival of American community.* New York: Simon & Schuster.

Rheingold, H. (2000). *The virtual community—homesteading on the electronic frontier, 2nd edition*. Cmabridge, MA, & London: MIT Press.

Savage, P. (2001). *New forms of work organisation—the benefits and impact on performance.* Paper presented to DG Employment & Social Affairs by The European Work Organisation Network (EWON). Brussels, Belgium: European Commission.

Sen, A. (1999). *Development as freedom*. Oxford, UK, & New York: Oxford University Press.

Sheller, M., & Urry, J. (2006). The new mobilities paradigm. *Environment and Planning A, 38*, 207-226.

Smith, H., & Fingar, P. (2003). *IT doesn't matter—business processes do: A critical analysis of Nicholas Carr's IT article in the Harvard Business Review*. Tampa, FL: Meghan-Kiffer Press.

Tapscott, & Williams. (2007). *Wikinomics—how mass collaboration changes everything.* New York: Portfolio.

Tuomi, I. (2002). *Networks of innovation: Change and meaning in the age of the Internet*. Oxford, UK, & New York: Oxford University Press.

Tuomi, I. (2006). The future of learning in the knowledge society—disruptive changes for Europe by 2020. In Y. Punie, et al. (Eds.), *The future of ICT and learning in the knowledge society.* Luxembourg: Office for Official Publications of the European Communities.

UNDERSTAND Consortium. (2006). *Methodology handbook. Project report*. Swansea, UK: University of Wales.

van Dijk, J. A. G. M. (2005). *The deepening divide—inequality in the information society.* London, & Delhi, India: SAGE.

Wellman, B. (2001). Computer networks as social networks. *Science, 293*, 2031-2034.

Zittrain, J. (2006). *The generative Internet (Working Paper 28/2006).* University of Oxford, Faculty of Law.

KEY TERMS

Empowerment: "The process of granting people the power to take responsible initiatives to shape their own life and that of their community or society in economic, social and political terms" (CEC 2005b, p. 32).

Participative Web: "The 'participative Web' is the most common term and underlying concept used to describe the more extensive use of the Internet's capabilities to expand creativity and communication. It is based on intelligent web services and new Internet-based software applications that enable users to collaborate and contribute to developing, extending, rating, commenting on and distributing digital content and developing and customising Internet applications" (OECD 2007, p. 17).

Social Capital: "By making connections with one another, and keeping them going over time, people are able to work together to achieve things that they either could not achieve by themselves, or could only achieve with great difficulty. People connect through a series of networks and they tend to share common values with other members of these networks; to the extent that these networks constitute a resource, they can be seen as forming a kind of capital" (Field, 2003, p.5).

Social Networking: The term is used here for desribing users of social network services, which are applications for building online communities of people who share interests, preferences or activities. Typically, social networking makes use of web based tools which provide a variety of ways for users to interact, such as e-mail and instant messaging services.

Transformational Change: Change processes which are establishing fundamentally new ways to achieve progress towards achieving the basic goals of an agent, such as a private household, worker, business, or regional government. As such, transformational change is the opposite of incremental change. Transformational change can also be understood to be about effectiveness rather than about efficiency.

Transformational Uses of ICT: Applications of ICT which enable users to obtain goals which would be unobtainable without these technologies. This refers, in particular, to uses which have an empowering effect on users in their role as citizens, workers, learners, patients, consumers, and so forth.

User-Created Content: A term which is used in connection to the notion of the "participative Web". The OECD (2007, p. 18) proposes three central characteristics as defining properties of user-created content: publication requirement (the work is made publically available rather than exchanged between individuals); a minimum degree of creative effort; and creation outside of professional routines and practises.

ENDNOTES

1 Indicator definitions: Annual average population in 1000, 2004; Population density: Inhabitants per km^2 in 2003; GDP per inhabitant (in PPS), EU25=100, 2003; Change of GDP per inhabitant (in PPS) in percentage points of the average EU25, 2003 as compared with 1999; Unemployment rate, 2005; Human Resources in Science and Technology (HRST) in percent of labour force 2005.

[2] Value "1" on 10-point scale (1 = essential, 10 = not important at all)

[3] Values "1" to "3" on 10-point scale (1 = essential, 10 = not important at all)

[4] The factor analysis was done using the SPSS statndard procedure, extraction method: principal components, varimax rotation and using the eigenvalue > 1 criterion. Factor scores were calculated using regression method.

[5] Value "1" on 10-point scale (1 = essential, 10 = not important at all)

[6] Values "1" to "3" on 10-point scale (1 = essential, 10 = not important at all)

[7] Only respondents who have made some first-hand experience with self-employment (i.e. either considered self-employment for themselves, or knowing somebody personally who started a business in last 3 years)

[8] Values "1" and "2" on 5-point-scale from "very positive" to "very negative"

Chapter XX
Evaluating IT-Enabled Transformation in Public Services:
A Case Study on Assessing Information Systems Effectiveness in a Government Organization in Turkey

Sevgi Ozkan
Middle East Technical University, Turkey

Murat Cakir
Middle East Technical University, Turkey

ABSTRACT

While the paradigm for organizations evolves into an information perspective and information systems' (IS) role shifts from efficiency to effectiveness, among the top issues of IS management is measuring and improving IS effectiveness. This chapter offers an IS effectiveness evaluation methodology applied on a government organization in Turkey. IS maturity is taken as a reference for determining independent variables of the research. The chapter supports that "IS effectiveness" is a relative term conceptualized by organizational features. The case study suggests future research areas. A number of findings and propositions have been presented, including the alignment of technology and business process, integrating stakeholders' trust and commitment, the significance of top management support, top-down vs. bottom-up approaches, which can enhance the adoption and institutionalization of information systems implementations within a government organization.

INTRODUCTION

The adoption of Information Systems (IS) represents significant financial investments, with alternative perspectives to the evaluation domain coming from both the public and private sectors (Sahraoui, Ghoneim, Irani and Ozkan, 2008). As a result of increasing IS budgets and increasing expenditures on computers and computer based information systems and the emphasis shift from "doing things right" to "doing the right things", assessment of the value added to organizations by IS assets, namely the effectiveness of information systems, has become a perennial issue for practitioners, researchers and managers (Ozkan, Bilgen, Hackney, 2007; Srinivasan, 1985; Scott, 1995; Yuthas and Eining, 1995; Seddon 1999; Kumar, 1990; Khalil and Elkordy, 1996; Ferrat and Agarwal, 1996, Malik and Goyal, 2001). Rau (2004) goes further and states that: "*never has demonstrating the value of IT to an organization been as imperative as today*". Despite the need for IS effectiveness evaluation, an agreement does not occur on a well-defined, deterministic and commonly acknowledged success framework for all systems and organizations. In addition to the motives for the IS effectiveness assessment, it should be highlighted that it is more urgent for developing countries as confined financial resources have been allocated for the expensive information technology instead of providing food and education even vaccine for the babies. It is evident from the literature that research on the implementation of information systems in government is rather limited, which could be due to the general misconception of the public sectors as rigid and risk-averse establishments (Kim, Pan and Pan, 2007).

The majority of the findings on information systems effectiveness and the correlated aspects are generally derived from the research in developed countries. These findings are required to be analyzed by cross-cultural studies to be operated in other countries which have different characteristics (Khalil and Elkordy, 1996). While communication means increase global perspectives, local approaches are also getting importance more than ever. Success stories and frames can not be replicated considering that the same outputs will be gained without country-specific adjustments (Sahay and Avgerou, 2002). As a consequence, with globalization, researchers have begun to analyze the aspects to adapt management practices across physical and cultural distances (Teng et.al, 1997).

For developing countries, information technology involves challenges as well as advantages. In developing countries, it is often experienced that computer systems may be used only for automation of existing business processes without their optimization resulting in gross inefficiencies (Yahya, 1993). The reason that developing countries have problems in IT use is that, in so-called "developing" countries IT investments may be realized without considering the reasonable needs of organization because of the general problematic political atmosphere surrounding the organization and country (Yahya, 1993; Sahay and Avgerou, 2002). Although it is not necessarily reasonable to allege that Turkey is experiencing the same problems in the same degree as presented above, it may be argued that Turkey still has some problems in exploiting the full potential of computer-based systems, particularly in the public sector. It enhances the objectivity of assessment to notice whether some organizational transformation practices like business process reengineering or total quality management is performed to make use of IS effectively or not. In other words, despite the wide usage of IS development methods and project management tools and techniques, an information system whose effectiveness is to be evaluated may have development phase problems like insufficient requirement analysis, problematic business process modeling or implementation fallacies.

Since there is no explicit formulation to assess effectiveness in complex socio-technical systems, usually the methodology can not be clearly and explicitly explained. In almost every IS effectiveness research, organizational characteristics are pointed as one of the most important aspects of assessment. In the case study reported in this chapter, an attempt is made to clarify and explicitly integrate the relations between tangible and intangible elements affecting assessment.

INFORMATION SYSTEMS IN THE PUBLIC SECTOR

DeLone and McLean's Model has been accepted as an significant phase to combine former research in IS effectiveness and has been justified as the basis (Kappelman, 1997; Seddon, 1999). The model is based on the work of Shannon and Weaver (1949) and on a study of 180 published empirical and theoretical papers which address the issue of IS success. In their construction of the model, DeLone and McLean(1992; 2003) argue that: "*...investigations determine the IS effectiveness frameworks for specific contexts...*", and they state that: " *The structure of systems success is composed of a set of factors common to all systems plus a set of factors unique to each individual system*". There are two main streams in IS effectiveness assessment literature. The first one focuses on measuring impacts of IS on organizational performance, whereas the second one focuses on easily measurable variables like user satisfaction or system use to appreciate the effectiveness in a subjective way. The organizations with concrete goals like a certain amount of profit or product prefer the first way. Cost-benefit analysis may be used only if benefits are quantified realistically. At this point, it is imperative to highlight the main difference between public and private organizations, namely the economic character. A service oriented public organization's benefits cannot be priced in the market in that reduced cost may not mean improved performance. Considering those, for this case, attempting to assess effectiveness by cost benefit analysis would be problematic.

Another route is measuring the perceived effectiveness in order to capture the outcomes of information systems. User satisfaction, which is prone to users' attitudes, is still a good surrogate for IS effectiveness measurement (DeLone and McLean, 2003). In this technique, users' perceptions are evaluated by questionnaire surveys about the perceived usability of the system (Yuthas and Eining, 1995). It should be noted that this way has some inherent theoretical problems because of users' inconsistent attitudes. Melone (1990) argues that subjectivity of people may cause the researcher to reach incorrect results like effective IS leading to unsatisfied users or ineffective IS leading to satisfied users if only questionnaires are used to obtain responses from users. In addition to that, rational perception of organizational goals is also vital for user-centered evaluations because outcome of an information system, which satisfies the user, may not correspond with the organizational aim (Davis, 1985). Also, public employees believe in that they have less job autonomy compared to people working for business firms (Gauch, 1993). So, users' general dissatisfaction may inhibit the objectivity of measurement. In addition, validity of an IS effectiveness assessment performed by only questionnaire document sent through and collected via formal channels may be in doubt. Because documents processed in the formal channels are generally perceived as ineffectual in bureaucratic organizations.

Another measure of system effectiveness for information systems is system usage (Khalil and Elkordy, 1996), on the other hand, the environment of a public organization is rather bureaucratic and officials in a public organization have to follow some fixed procedures. System usage may be mandatory and employees may not have autonomy in performing their jobs; so as Srinivasan (1985) argues, "*while in some classes of systems, strong positive correlations may exist between system use and system effectiveness, in some other types of systems these two may not point out the same phenomena.*" For a non-profit public organization, system usage may not be the proper measurement technique for IS effectiveness because of its bureaucratic nature. In addition to that, rules and regulations may impose to use manual information systems along with the computer based systems. Furthermore, since in a public organization management has greater impact on subordinates' performance more than any other private one, management support in terms of permission and authorization for evaluation may augment the strength of the research and researcher.

Rationale and Methodology

Within the IS research literature, qualitative research is advised in order to interpret the underlying issues within the assessment context. In qualitative research, researcher performs detailed observation within the ecology of the target system like a common inhabitant without making any theoretical implication or hypotheses before gathering data (Kaplan and Duchon, 1988). Considering the aforementioned factors stated in previous section, case study research was chosen as a qualitative approach allowing researchers to study in a natural environment interpreting the phenomena by observations and interviews. Prior to the case study, to have formal consent for observation and interviews with the users, a letter of application involving the purpose of the research and interview topics was sent to the head of the organization. This permission enabled the cooperation with IS department's and other department's employees. In addition, a contact person was assigned for the coordination by IS department. Processing of obtaining formal consent enabled to diffuse "IS effectiveness phenomena" to some extent, so one of the intention of the IS evaluations was realized. Semi-structured interviews have been conducted for data collection. There were a number of predetermined questions and these questions were directed to each interviewee in a systematic and consistent order, but the interviewers were allowed freedom to digress in order to explore far beyond the answers to the prepared and standardized questions. Table 1 depicts the framework that comprises 39 interview questions systematically classified under seven categories of IS success. Since there was less a priori knowledge of what the variables of interest would be and how they would be measured, variables were determined during the case study.

Observations within the organization on various information systems are useful before conducting the interviews. During observation, it has been found out that there is at least one PC for every member of staff and these computers are linked via a network. In other words, every department/unit is connected with each other. Despite the physical integration of computers, there is not a top-down or organizational computer based information system involving all the sub-functions or departments. This reveals that IS planning within this organization is not an overall effort but rather local or function specific automation implementations by the IS department. Although there are some subsystems working collectively managing the same data/information, it is common that the identical data would be produced, saved or replicated in various departments of the organization without considering the integration. From the current IS discipline perspective, information system under the observation may be categorized as "ineffective" because there is no top-down approach, business processes are not optimized but only some of them automated and these automated sub-functions or applications seem as archipelago with limited integration. However, making such a categorization is always problematic. Therefore, at this stage, more IS literature focusing on other countries' or organizations' IT/IS diffusion practices and experiences were studied in depth.

IS effectiveness definition compels us determine "overall organizational goals". We may infer from the definition that the effectiveness of an

Table 1. Framework for IS effectiveness evaluation

System Quality
Ease of use: Do you find it easy to use the IS? ***Ease of Learning:*** Is it easy to learn how to use the IS? ***Convenience of access***: Is it convenient to access to the IS? Is it easy to get authorization? ***System Accuracy:*** Are you satisfied with the accuracy of the system? ***System Flexibility:*** Is the IS capable to change or to adjust in response to new conditions, demands, or circumstances? ***System Reliability:*** Is the IS available when you need it? ***Integration of systems:*** When it's necessary to compare or consolidate data from different sources, do you find any inconsistencies? ***Response/turnaround time:*** Is the elapse time between your initiated request for service or action and a reply to that request short?
Information Quality
Relevance: Does the system provide reports that seem to be just about exactly what you need? ***Usefulness:*** To what extent does this system provide reports to you that seem to be just about exactly what you need? ***Clarity:*** Is the information clear? ***Format:*** Do you think the output is presented in a useful format? ***Accuracy:*** To what extent do the data that you receive from this system require correction? ***Precision:*** Does the system provide the precise information you need? ***Conciseness:*** To what extent does this system overload you with more data than it seems you can possibly use? ***Sufficiency:*** Does the information content meet your needs? ***Completeness:*** Is the output information complete? ***Reliability:*** Is the output information consistent and dependable? ***Currency***: Does the system provide up-to-date information? ***Timeliness:*** Do you get the information you need in time?
Service Quality
Tangibles: Does IS have up-to-date hardware and software? ***Reliability:*** When IS promises to do something by a certain time, does it do so? ***Responsiveness:*** Does the IS tell users exactly when services will be performed? ***Assurance:*** Do you think the IS personnel is technically competent? ***Empathy:*** Does the IS help you solve your problems within the organization?
Use
Use: Do you actually use this system fully compared to your original expectations?
User Satisfaction
Overall Satisfaction: Would you like this system to be modified or redesigned all over again from the beginning? ***Information Satisfaction:*** Are you satisfied with the IS?
System/Subsystem Benefits
Decision Effectiveness: Has the utilization of IS improved the quality of decisions you make in the organization? ***Improved Individual Productivity:*** Have you personally benefited from the existence of IS in this organization? ***Task Performance:*** Does the system assist you in performing your job better? ***Individual Power or Influence:*** Does the system assist you in being seen more valuable in the organization?
Organizational Factors
Top Management Support: Does top management support for the system and show positive degree of interest, enthusiasm, support, or participation? ***Organizational Adaptation:*** Is the organization content with the IS unit? ***Organizational Resources***: Are there policies and procedures which establish precedence for the allocation of IS resources and services between different organizational units and their requests? ***Psychological Climate***: Are the expectations from the IS realistic within the organization? ***Human Resources:*** Is there sufficient training provided for the users? ***IS Management***: Is there an hierarchical relationship of the IS function to the overall organizational structure?

information system can be assessed by measuring the degree of contribution of IS to organizational goals. After performing the first observation, we may say that IS in the target organization is ineffective because there is no top down approach regarding the organizational goals. The question in mind in this section is that "Is it reasonable to categorize an IS as ineffective if the approach is not top-down?" Top-down implementation methodologies require the context to be analyzed carefully and goals determined by experts exactly before commitment of the management (Sacco, 1994). For example, Business Process Re-engineering (BPR), by designing the business processes from scratch, enables organization to have a great performance gain by using IT.

It is evident from the IS evaluation literature that information system's contribution to organizational performance requires the consideration of some other organizational factors. Because, in general, studies attempt to find correlations between organizational output and IS contribution instead of observable and minimal impacts (Kanungo et. al, 1999). Besides the difficulty of measuring the contribution of IS to organizational performance, public organizations can not rely on market indicators as private business organizations. This reality causes not to be able to set BPR objectives by a top-down approach determining tangible targets of organization rationally. Another problem is that since public organization have to comply with legal regulations, it is almost impossible to redesign the processes without the formal consent of the authority. Consequently, public organizations may not have chance to gain the full benefits of BPR and rather just have to automate the processes by IT resulting very limited performance increase (Thong et.al, 2000). In addition to the top-down and structured implementations in the literature, there are loosely structured, bottom-up methodologies letting individuals to implement the applications in an agile manner themselves (Sacco, 1994). However, as Sacco (1994) emphasized, these type of loosely structured causes to appear archipelago like information systems which are very challenging to integrate with each other. Considering those perspectives, it can be argued that, individual or island-like IS efforts cannot or should not be evaluated as "not effective" despite the lack of top-down approach, at the first shot. The realistic view may be to evaluate every organization and IS implementation effort by determination of a reference within the context of organization itself and this approach may enhance the validity of assessment.

Information Systems Maturity as a Reference for Evaluation

Within the information system development, there have been efforts merging the top-down and the bottom-up approaches (Gibson and Nolan, 1974, McKenney and McFartlan, 1982). These researchers suggest that the early stages of adopting information technologies are typically unstructured and experimental. According to Nolan's Stage Hypothesis Model (1973) an information system may be placed in different stages. It should be pointed out that there is no clear-cut or rigid line between the stages, but this taxonomy may help us to understand the "growing IS" matter namely IS Maturity. Mahmood and Becker (1985) state that information system maturity plays an important role in IS effectiveness. They refer to Nolan's (Nolan, 1973) Stage Model to explain maturity and claim that it is the best-known and widely accepted model for growth and management. They assume that as an IS move from stage I to stage VI, it becomes more mature. Nolan's model (Nolan, 1973) includes six growth stages (see Table 2).

Within the IS effectiveness literature, it has been argued that as the organization's IS move on to higher stages, effectiveness increases. However, how the term "effectiveness" change according to the stages is not explicitly defined. In other words, an IS is accepted as more effective

Table 2. Nolan's six stages of growth

Stage I Initiation	Control of the computer resources is presumed to be lax, planning is almost nonexistent, and only few applications are installed.
Stage II Contagion	Organization encourages innovation and extensive applications by maintaining low control and high slack. Nevertheless, lack of planning brings in poorly designed systems.
Stage III Control	The problems arising from bad design and rising costs create difficulties for users and management, and a basic shift in orientation from management of the computer to management of data resources occur. This stage is also characterized by initial confusing attempts to develop user accountability for the expenditure incurred.
Stage IV Integration	Database and data communication technologies are applied to several key application areas. This stage is also characterized by the level of high quality services. The users demand increased support, and as a result cost continues to increase. Control and planning system proves to be ineffective because of the redundancy of data. Demands grow for better control and more efficiency.
Stage V Data administration	Data administration is introduced in which control of computing resources is tight; however, low slack is maintained in the development of new systems.
Stage VI Maturity	The application portfolio, whose structure now mirrors the organization and information flows in the company, is completed. High slack is still maintained over the development of systems and control of computing resources is still very tight. At this point maturity is achieved.

than the one which is not mature. Organizations should persist with the requisite investments in IT in the initial stages to experience significant benefits of information systems in the end. In general, organizations need to reach the stage 5, or beyond to experience IT enabled advantages that enhance organizational effectiveness as opposed to increasing efficiency only.

DeLone and McLean (1992) has pointed out that without a well-defined dependent measure, researchers cannot be confident in their results and much of the research is indeed purely speculative, establishing finer theoretical formulations for concepts of IS success should be strongly advocated. Although conceptual definitions of IS effectiveness are relatively consistent, pragmatic definitions have been lacking. In view of the Nolan's stage hypothesis, the information systems in the case study are between the third and fourth stages. In other words, sub-systems are needed to be integrated and a higher service quality is vital. Considering these issues, dependent variable of the research would be "moving to next phase" in terms of IS maturity and our independent variables would be "flexibility of systems" and "system integration" which are asserted in Delone and Mclean (1992-2003) model but they are mentioned with other arbitrarily selected measures. The definition and conceptual refinement of a dependent variable is the vital issue for IS field. On the other hand, determining a few criteria does not mean for the researcher to measure using these but rather to investigate the mutual dependencies with other criteria. Although this phase was asserted before the interview phase, as mentioned in method rationale, qualitative methods require detailed observation in the in the natural setting without committing any theoretical constructs or to hypotheses before collecting any data. In other words, some of these findings appeared after performing several interviews; in fact, the collection and the analysis of the data obtained have gone hand-in-hand as theories and themes have come out during the study.

CASE STUDY: A GOVERNMENT ORGANISATION IN TURKEY

Research has been conducted in a government organization in Turkey. In the case study, IS applications serving to various functional areas and different subsystems of the public organization have been evaluated in order to ensure capturing the big picture. In this study, relevant criteria have been selected from the DeLone and McLean model and while doing this, as DeLone and McLean (1992) argue: "*structure, size, mission and environment of organization*" have been taken into consideration. Observation and semi-structured interviews were chosen as data collection methods. In order to have valid and reliable questions, selected criteria were mapped to questions (Table 1) from nine of the instruments (Baroudi and Orlikowski, 1988; Sanders, 1984; Goodhue,1995; Davis, 1989; Doll and Torzadeh,1988; Franz and Robey 1986; Raymond, 1985; Bailey and Pearson, 1983; Pitt. et al,1995) which are accepted as the most valid and reliable ones. Replications were excluded; different scales and question forms were arranged according to qualitative research techniques. Then the questions were re-worded as probing questions and an interview form with 39 questions has been developed.

Hofstede's (1980) work has been accepted to comprehend Turkish Society's specific-to-herself traits in order to determine the possible effects of national characteristics on evaluation. It is accepted that these dimensions may have changed by the time; on the other hand, they still constitute somewhat relative evidence as a reference. It has been claimed that power distance is higher in the Turkish Society, meaning that people are not likely to voice their feelings freely. Therefore, the evaluator preferred to do one-to-one interviews with individuals in order to receive better contributions. The Turkish Society has also been categorized as more collectivist in general, in that personnel may tend to refrain from exhibiting objective comments about IS. Therefore the evaluator let the interviewees digress from the subject to explore the matter and capture the issue. Another characteristic of the Turkish Society has been identified as strong uncertainty avoidance. Therefore it had been assured that the questions in evaluations conveyed the meaning without conflicts and uncertainties.

A number of information systems operational at various departments within the organization have been observed. After the observation phase, IS literature concerning IS/IT practices were examined in order to conceptualize the current situation. Considering IS maturity, dependent and independent variables of the evaluation were determined and interviews were held with some of the system users selected with the cooperation of the IS department. As the nature of the case study calls for an integrative approach, analysis and data collection activities have been performed concurrently throughout the study. The case evaluation process consisted of four-steps: (1) Observation of the system, (2) Definition of the dependent and independent success variables according to maturity level, (3) Interviewing the users/stakeholders using the customized interview form, (4) Qualitative analysis of the collected data. Constant comparison method, established by Glaser and Strauss (1967), has been utilized throughout the case study for data analysis. In this research, following this method, the relevant IS literature has been reviewed continuously throughout data collection and collected data have been compared continuously with other data to detect emerging categories and to direct the data collection process recursively.

Findings

It has been observed that if the IS is not mature, then IS assessment cannot be performed following a top-down approach by determining the system's contribution to organizational effectiveness.

Proposition 1: *Information systems and their users are not apt to implement just goal based top-down cost-benefit analyses or quantitative user perceived effectiveness assessments based on generic instruments.*

The case also revealed that assessments just performed by user-satisfaction questionnaires may be prone to errors because end users are not responsive enough to get reliable results. Their perceptions are still challenging. However, interviews were successful in getting the information from the users.

Proposition 2: *Observations and semi-structured interviews are the favorable data collection methods for the IS evaluation in a non-profit public or government organization.*

If a manual system exists along with the computer-based system, users tend to use the manual system that they are used to. Since there is an alternative system, users do not notice their evolving needs and do not feedback to IS department, so the system does not evolve and some users prefer manual system because of inefficiency of the system. In a larger scale, because some users do not use the system, there may be some inconsistencies which lead to integrity problems. Eventually the system becomes "useless" and diminishes as observed in an information system within this case.

On the other hand, if the system does not have a manual alternative and if the system is flexible then the subsystems are integrated, in other words the system grows and the organization's IS move to higher maturity stages. At the end, organizational benefits may occur.

Proposition 3: *Manual alternatives for the computer based information systems inhibit the growing of the computer based system and in the long term.*

Another finding is that there is a necessity of revision of formal regulations and rules for the users to make them leave the manual system.

It has also been observed that users in hierarchically higher levels enhance the prospect of system's success. In addition, user expectations have been found to be shaped by previous systems, however, if a system is used without an alternative, users convey their needs to IS departments for modifications for their evolving needs.

Finally, it has been observed that technological infrastructure i.e. network and personal computers, are sufficient but inflexibility of some applications hinder to respond the evolving needs of users.

Proposition 4: *"Dependent variable" of IS success in this case study is "growing and moving to next stage" in terms of maturity. Independent variables are "flexibility" in "System Quality" and "processing of change requests" in "Service Quality".*

DISCUSSION

A common definition of information system effectiveness is related to its contribution to organizational effectiveness (Thong et.al, 1993; Yuthas and Eining, 1995; Malik and Goyal, 2001). Following this definition IS researchers have tried to formulate some techniques to assess effectiveness. In other words, it may be investigated whether an information system is effective or not by measuring the contribution of the information system to the organization. For private organizations, this is rather applicable, because it is not impossible to compare the indicators of a company before and after IS implementation, or it is likely to have benchmarks from other companies in the same sector, but for a government organization it rather needs intricate investigations to have reliable data to evaluate effectiveness. Because there is no market indicator, and that there is no other organization performing in the same sector and the government organization in this case study has some diverse and intangible goals. This case organization is (1) a public organization, (2) comprised of Turkish people, and (3) an active government organization having relations with other countries' similar government organizations worldwide.

Impact of Public Organizations' Characteristics on IS Effectiveness Assessment

Studies comparing private and public organizations take those organizations into consideration with different duties or business aims. Public sector organizations have been represented mostly by not-for-profit government agencies that have either a social service or a regulatory orientation; the private ones are for profit and market oriented "business firms", "manufacturing concerns", or "private enterprises" (Lachman, 1985).

Determining an information system's impact on organizational effectiveness is a very complex issue for public organizations (Newcomer and Caudle, 1991). Many of the IS effectiveness measures appropriate for business may be exploited for public organizations; but public organizations' information systems require some different measures and shifts in emphasis (Bozeman and Bretschneider, 1986). On the other hand, as pointed out by Henry (1987), the distinction between private and public organizations may also be drawn from ideological beliefs rather than empirical research.

These criticisms emphasize the need for objectivity of the research in a way that the researcher gets rid of biases. These biases generally impose the opinion that public organizations are generally managed irrationally, they are ineffective and inefficient. The source of those prejudices may be the debate between political disciplines but this epistemological debate is beyond the scope of this study. The borders of the discussion area are drawn by the IS measurement perceptions and techniques which are dealt with in the previous chapter. In this section, differences are classified under the categories of economic characteristics, personnel attitudes, and management issues.

Economic Characteristics of Public Organizations

The main difference between public and private organizations is the economic character of respective sectors and the means and services they deliver. The primary characteristic of a public service is that usually its benefits cannot be priced in the market. In private organizations organizational performance is measured in terms of reduced costs and increased quality; but reduced cost does not exactly imply better performance for public organizations (Bozeman and Bretschneider, 1986).

In general, the benefits of a regulatory government agency cannot be priced in the market. Although it may be attempted to quantify benefits for cost-benefit analysis of information systems like decision analysis, cost displacement/avoidance, cost effectiveness analysis, time savings time salary, and work value model; such analyses may not point out the effectiveness of information systems in public organizations. Therefore, cost benefit analysis may be used in a government organization only if the benefits are quantified realistically.

Personnel Attitudes in Public Organizations

Government employees classify themselves as less autonomy, less motivated and less advantageous than their private counterparts (Gauch, 1993). Because of the formal and rigid environment of the public organizations, officials have tendency to perceive themselves as less innovative (Thong et.al, 2000).

User satisfaction is still a good substitute for IS effectiveness measurement (DeLone and McLean, 2003). In this technique, people are in the center of the evaluation and it is implemented by questionnaire surveys. Satisfaction questionnaires aim to understand the effectiveness by the perceived usefulness of system by users (Yuthas and Eining, 1995). The problem is that user based assessments are shaped by perceptions and attitudes. Melone (1990) claims that subjectivity of people derived from organization type may cause researcher to acquire wrong results like effective IS leading to unsatisfied users or ineffective IS leading to satisfied users if only questionnaires are used to get responses from users. In addition to that, rational perception of organizational goals is also vital for user-centered evaluations because outcome of an information system, which satisfies the user, may not coincide with the organizational aim (Davis, 1985).

In government organizations in Turkey, information technologies are mostly used in routine and programmable managerial tasks, they are rarely used in non-programmable managerial tasks and functions. It may be interpreted from his statement that the people in the government organizations in general may recognize information systems as the low-level data processing systems. So this may affect the results of the questionnaires performed for IS assessments which need users' awareness of differences between 'information system' and 'information technology'. In other words, in a government organization in Turkey, personnel may tend to perceive IS effectiveness as 'level of technology'. For example answer to a questionnaire element like "are you satisfied with new IS?" may not reflect the satisfaction derived from the IS but the answer may be the expression of the enchantment of a new computer system. So, this may affect the results of IS evaluations which are generally constructed on the basis of capturing the people's perceptions like user satisfaction, service quality or usefulness.

Management in Public Organizations

Because of legal frames and bureaucratic structure, managers in public organizations do have less autonomy and they are less flexible in contrast with the private managers (Thong et. al, 2000; Gauch, 1993; Bozeman and Bretschneider, 1986; Lachman, 1985)

System usage is widely accepted as a measure of system effectiveness for information systems (Khalil and Elkordy, 1996), on the other hand, as asserted in previous paragraph, the environment of a public organization is rather bureaucratic and officials in a public organization have to follow some fixed procedures. Therefore system usage may be mandatory and employees may not have autonomy in performing their jobs; so as Srinivasan (1985) argues, while in some classes of systems, strong positive associations may exist between system use and system effectiveness, in some other classes of systems these two may indicate two entirely different phenomena. For a government organization in Turkey, system usage may not be the proper measurement technique for IS effectiveness because of its bureaucratic nature. In addition to that, rules and regulations may impose to use manual information systems along with the computer based systems.

Documents processed in the formal channels are generally perceived as just papers and the personnel state that they deal with the formal documents just not to interfere with rules because of the bureaucracy. People working in government organizations in Turkey generally use informal and oral communication for imperative issues. In other words, whatever its content, a document coming from the formal channels may be recognized as a stack of paper. So, validity of an IS effectiveness evaluation performed by only questionnaire documents sent through and collected via formal channels may be in doubt.

Although the mere usage of formal communication channels may decrease the validity of IS effectiveness assessment, formal permission for evaluations may augment the strength of the research and researcher; because As Thong et.al (2000) asserted, visible top management support encourages positive attitudes both in bureaucratic and informal means, and enhance the achievement of the assessment.

Impact of Local Attributes on IS Effectiveness Assessment

Little et al (2000) claim that cultural issues are becoming more important as the world moves toward increased communication and globalization, therefore information systems solutions from the developed world, cannot be replicated in the developing world with the expectation that similar results would come; local adaptations are required considering the local and country-specific features (Sahay and Avgerou, 2002).

Since this study proposes and adopts an IS effectiveness assessment framework for a government organization in Turkey, a comparison between Turkey and other countries may enable us to declare some specific arguments and adaptations on IS effectiveness assessment perceptions and techniques.

Turkey as a Developing Country

Ceyhun and Çağlayan (1996) state that Turkey did not experience the industrial age and now is trying to take advantage of the information age but the perceptions are still conventional and these perceptions are standing on short term profits; therefore Turkey will not be able to exploit the benefits of information technology. Uçkan (2003) states that Turkey needs a "paradigm shift" in order to overcome difficulties experienced in information technology. While IT products open new opportunities for developing countries, they also pose a set of new challenges (Yahya, 1993). These challenges are:

- In developing countries, information systems are just automation of manual procedures, so they may not enable the required leverage for an organization.
- IT based information systems and manual systems may be used concurrently which may decrease the potential emphasis on the will of evolving IS.
- Managers' decisions may be more political than rational.
- IS departments may be settled in low layer of the organization and they may be perceived as only service suppliers rather than business enabler cooperatives.

Although it is not sensible to claim that Turkey is experiencing the same problems in the same degree as presented above, it may be argued that Turkey still has some problems in exploiting the full potential of computer-based systems. It may enhance the objectivity of assessment to notice if some organizational transformation practices like business process reengineering or total quality management is performed or not to exploit IS effectively. In other words, despite the wide usage of IS development methods and project management tools and techniques, target information system to evaluate may have development phase problems like insufficient requirement analysis, problematic business process modeling or implementation problems. So, before IS effectiveness assessment, the evaluator may investigate those aspects to perform a realistic assessment for the system that may involve inherent development problems.

Cultural Dimensions of the Turkish Nation

Based on a study of 50 nations, Hofstede (1980) argues that national cultures differ mainly along four dimensions:

- **Individualism:** "The extent to which people of a country show a propensity to see themselves as self-sufficient individuals(individualist) as compared to a propensity to see themselves primarily as an integral part of a social group(collectivist)."
- **Uncertainty avoidance:** "The extent to which people of a country show a tendency to maintain a status quo when feeling uneasy or threatened by situations those are uncertain or ambiguous."
- **Power distance:** "The extent to which people of a country show inclination to accept unequal distributions of power, such as between senior managers and operational level employees."
- **Masculinity and femininity:** "The extent to which the dominant values in society are "masculine" that is assertiveness, the acqui-

sition of money and things, and not caring for others, the quality of life, or people."

Hofstede, in his empirical research, scores countries according to dimensions given. He claims that:

- Power distance in Turkey is higher than the average
- Collectivism in Turkey is higher than the average
- Uncertainty avoidance in Turkey is stronger than average
- Femininity in Turkey is higher than average

Although Hofstede's work is widely accepted, it should be noted that he ranked 50 countries more than 20 years ago, those dimensions are relative and not absolute, and his results are subjected to change over time There is a time lag between the original study and the present time, so especially changes in 1980's have influenced the cultural dimensions of the Turkish society. In addition to possible obsoletion, it would be very unrealistic to claim that the original sample can give definite characteristics of Turkish community, because the sample of people chosen by Hofstede have considerably higher standards than average Turkish people, both in education and the other indicators of lifestyle. Hoftstede's sample group consisted of employees in an international computer company. Though there have been changes in the culture of Turkish people with respect to 1980, in this research, those findings are accepted as baseline.

Since "power distance" is higher in the Turkish society, managers may not take into consideration subordinate's perceptions because in "high power distance" societies, superiors (managers) consider subordinates as a 'potential threat to one's power' and 'people to blame'. Another factor related to "power distance" is that in high "power distance" cultures like Turkey, subordinates intend to believe that 'their perceptions are not worth to assert', therefore effectiveness assessment techniques including subordinates' perceptions may be constructed accordingly. In addition, because of "high power distance" in the Turkish society, senior level managers generally perceive firm criteria like system or information quality measures more seriously than their subordinates' perceptions. Yeo (1998) claims that in organizations in which the power distance is high, when people of differing status are put in a room together, subordinates talk very little. Therefore, researcher should prefer to conduct person-to-person interviews.

Since the Turkish society is more "collectivist", employees may not behave independently by not reflecting their observations freely. Also in "collectivist" cultures, 'value standards differ for in-groups and outer groups' (Hofstede, 1980). Because of these two reasons, employees may not be objective in their attitudes. For example, an employee may not assert his negative ideas about the system, because he may have a close friend in IS department. So while implementing surveys or interviewing with users to assess effectiveness, evaluation objectivity may be enhanced considering these points. Another point is that assessment techniques namely observations involving objective criteria are important for collectivist cultures because 'there is emotional dependence of individual on organization and institutions' so employees may not criticize their organization's other departments objectively by surveys conducted generally for "user satisfaction", "system usage", "service quality" measurements.

Since "uncertainty avoidance" is stronger in Turkey, it may be asserted that Turkish people try to 'refrain from conflicts and uncertainties' and they 'search for the absolute truths and values', so managers in the government organizations prefer somewhat tangible and concrete measures in assessment of IS effectiveness.

"Femininity" is higher in Turkish Society. It should be pointed out that masculinity and femininity are terms that do not represent gender issues in this context. For example, aid for weak is popular in Turkey, which is a strong sign for a feminine culture. Hence, in the government organizations in Turkey ROI (Return on investment) or other cost-benefit evaluations may not be the proper techniques for IS effectiveness assessment, because Turkish people may not think or behave within the context of financial rationality when constructing a system. Therefore, assessment of investments may indicate inefficiency but in general, it can be claimed that effectiveness does not require efficiency.

CONCLUSION

This chapter presents an adoption of a proposed evaluation instrument and methodology on a case study, for IS effectiveness assessment in a government organization in Turkey. The applied methodology is the compound of user-centered and goal-based evaluations so it has been assumed that the methodology surpasses the limitations of goal-based and user-centered evaluations and makes use of the advantages of both approaches in a qualitative manner. Meanings and areas of interest have been explored and hence key findings of IS success have been determined in order to develop an evaluation methodology that could be implemented in any subunit of the public organization. The case study is not just an implementation of an instrument but rather it helps to develop hypotheses for IS effectiveness and its assessment in a public organization in Turkey.

REFERENCES

Bailey, J. E., & Pearson, S.W. (1983). Development of a tool for measuring and analyzing computer user satisfaction. *Management Science, 29(*5), 530-545.

Baroudi, J. J., & Orlikowski, W. J. (1988). A short-form measure of user information satisfaction. *Journal of Management Information Systems, 4*(4), 44-59.

Benbasat, I., Goldstein, D. K., Mead, M. (1987). The case research strategy in studies of information systems. *MIS Quarterly*, 368-386.

Bozeman, B., & Bretschneider, S. (1986). Public management information systems. *Public Administration Review, Special Issue*, 475-487.

Ceyhun, Y., & Çağlayan, M. U. (1996). *Bilgi teknolojileri türkiye için nasıl bir gelecek hazırlamakta?* Türkiye İş Bankası Kültür Yayınları.

Davis, J.G. (1985). A typology of management information systems users and its implications for user information satisfaction research. *ACM.*

Davis, F. D. (1989). Perceived usefulness, perceived ease of use, and user acceptance of information technology. *MIS Quarterly, 13*(3), 319-340.

DeLone, W. H., & McLean, E. R. (1992). Information systems success: The quest for the dependent variable. *Information Systems Research,* 60-95.

DeLone, W. H., & McLean, E. R. (2003). The DeLone and McLean model of information systems success: A ten-year update. *Journal of Management Information Systems,* 9-30.

Doll, W. J., & Torzadeh, G. (1988). The measure of end-user computing satisfaction. *MIS Quarterly, 12*(2), 259-274.

Ferrat, T. W., & Agarwal, R. (1996). Toward managing information systems professionals better. *SIGCPR/SIGMIS*, 268-275.

Franz, C. R., & Robey, D. (1986). Organizational context, user involvement, and usefulness of information systems. *Decision Science,17*(3), 329-356.

Gauch, R. R. (1993). Differences between public and management information systems. *CPR*, 385-399.

Gibson, C. F., & Nolan, R.L. (1974). Managing the four stages of EDP growth. *Harvard Business Review*, 20-29.

Glaser, B., & Straus, A. L. (1967). *The discovery of grounded theory: Strategies for qualitative research*. Chicago: Adline.

Goodhue, D. L. (1995). Task-technology fit and individual performance. *MIS Quarterly*, *19*(2), 213-236.

Hofstede G. (1980). Motivation, leadership, and organization: Do American theories apply abroad? *Organizational Dynamics*, 42-63.

Kanungo, S., Duda, S., & Srinivas,Y. (1999). A structured model for evaluating information systems effectiveness. *Systems Research and Behavioral Science*, *16*, 495-518.

Kappelman, L. A. (1997). Measuring information systems service quality: Concerns on the SERVQUAL questionnaire. *MIS Quarterly*, 195-208.

Kaplan, B., & Duchon, D. (1988). Combining qualitative and quantitative methods in information systems research: A case study. *MIS Quarterly*, 570-586.

Khalil, O. E. M., & Elkordy, M. M. (1996). The relationship between some decisions and task environment characteristic and information systems effectiveness: Empirical evidence from Egypt. *SIGCPR/SIGMIS, Colorado*, 125-137.

Kim, H. J., Pan, G., & Pan, S. L. (2007). Managing IT-enabled transformation in the public sector: A case study on e-government in South Korea. *Government Information Quarterly*, *24*, 338-352.

Kumar, K. (1990). Post implementation evaluation of computer based information systems: Current practices. *Communications of the ACM*, *33*(4), 203-212.

Lachman, R. (1985). Public and private sector differences: CEO's perceptions of their role environments. *Academy of Management Journal*, *28*(3), 671-680.

Little, J. C., Granger, M., Adams E. S., Holvikivi, J., Lippert S. K., Walker, H. M., & Young, A. (2000). Integrating cultural issues into the computer and information technology curriculum. *ITICSE 2000 Working Group Reports*, 136-154.

Mahmood, M. A., & Becker, J. D. (1985). Impact of organizational maturity on user satisfaction with information systems. *ACM*, 134-151.

Melone, N. P. A. (1990). Theoretical assessment of the user satisfaction construct in information systems research. *Management Science*, *36*(1), 76-90.

Malik, K., & Goyal, D. P. (2001). Information systems effectiveness: An integrated approach. *IEEE*, 189-194.

McKenney, J., & McFarlan, F. (1982). The information archipelago--maps and bridges. *Harvard Business Review*, 109-119.

Nolan, R. L. (1973). Managing the computer resource: A stage hypothesis. *Communication of the ACM*, 399-405.

Ozkan, S., Hackney, R., & Bilgen, S. (2007). PB-ISAM: A process based framework for information systems effectiveness assessment. *Journal of Enterprise Information Management*, *20*(6), 700-725.

Pitt, L. F., Watson, R. T., & Kavan, C. B. (1995). Service quality: A measure of information systems effectiveness. *MIS Quarterly*, 173-186.

Rau, K. (2004). The CIO dashboard performance management program: Measuring and managing the value of IT. *Information Strategy: The Executive's Journal*, 6-17.

Raymond, L. (1985). Organizational characteristics and MIS success in the context of small business. *MIS Quarterly*, *9*(1), 7-52.

Sacco, J. F. (1994). Implementing microcomputers in local government: A case study of loosely structured approach. *SiGCPR 94-3 Virginia*, 261-270.

Sahay, S., & Avgerou, C. (2002). Introducing the special issues on information and communication technologies in develeoping countries. *The Information Society,* 73-76

Sahraoui, S., Ghoneim, A., Irani, Z., & Ozkan, S. T-Government for benefit realization: A research agenda. In Z. Irani, & P. Love (Eds.), *Evaluating information systems: Public and private sector.* London, UK: Elsevier.

Sanders, G. L. (1984). MIS/DSS success measure. *Systems,Objectives & Solutions*, *4*, 29-34.

Scott E. J. (1995). The measurement of information systems effectiveness: Evaluating a measuring instrument. *Database Advances*, *26*(1), 43-61.

Seddon P. B., Staples, S., Patnayakuni, R., & Bowtell, M. (1999). Dimensions of information systems success. *Communications of the Association for Information Systems, 2.*

Shannon, C. E., & Weaver, W. (1949). *The mathematical model theory of communication.* Urbana, IL: University of İllinois Press.

Srinivasan, A. (1985). Alternative measures of system effectiveness: Associations and implications. *MIS Quarterly*, 243-253.

Teng, James T. C., Calhoun, K. J., Cheon, M. J., Raeburn, S., & Wong, W. (1997). Is the east really different from the west: A cross cultural study on information technology and decision making. *MIS Quarterly,* 40-46.

Thong, Y. L., Yap, C., & Kin-Lee, S. (2000). Business process reengineering in the public sector: The case of the housing development board in Singapore. *Journal of Management Information Systems*, *17*(1), 245-271.

Uçkan, Ö. (2003). E-Devlet , e-demokrasi ve Türkiye, literatür yayıncılık, İstanbul.

Yahya, A. H. (1993). On the problems of information technology management in developing nations. *CPR*, 349-355.

Yeo, A. (1993). Cultural effects in usability assessment. *ACM Doctoral Consortium*, 74-75.

Yuthas, K., & Eining, M. (1995). An experimental evaluation of measurements of information system effectiveness. *Journal of Information Systems*, *9*(2), 69-84.

KEY TERMS

Context: Represents a designation or description of the information systems application environment.

IT-Enabled Transformation: Involves understanding the benefits and implementation issues of IT solutions used to transform organizations.

Perceived Effectiveness: Presents the effectiveness as perceived by the user of the information system.

Socio-Technical System: Recognizes the interaction between people and technology. A Socio-technical system is about the social aspects of people and society and technical aspects of machines and technology. Socio-technical refers to the interrelatedness of *social* and *technical* aspects of an organisation.

User-Centered Evaluation: Presents evaluation the information systems focusing on the users of the system.

Section V
T-Government Adoption and Acceptance

Chapter XXI
A Cost Model of Open Source Software Adoption

Barbara Russo
Free University of Bolzano-Bozen, Italy

Giancarlo Succi
Free University of Bolzano-Bozen, Italy

ABSTRACT

A limited budget for IT may lock public bodies in obsolete inefficient solutions slowing down their process of innovation. Various actions of estimating, controlling, and reducing IT costs have been already performed at national and European levels and Open Source Software (OSS) has been often pointed as a promising alternative that may also render public services and the underlying business processes more transparent and accessible to citizens. In this chapter, we propose a model of cost of a migration to OSS as a decision making instrument that helps public bodies being autonomous and independent in the IT adoption. The model is empirically validated in the real daily operations of more than 3,500 users. If adopted systematically our model might be a powerful tool to support transformational government and to establish an empirical open knowledge base on the economic advantages of OSS on which to found future strategies of OSS adoption.

INTRODUCTION

Transformational governance supports new technologies that better increment the quality of the services and save resources[1]. In this perspective, Open Source Software (OSS) appears to be an appealing solution. It is a technology free of charge, easy to get, transparent to the user, and ready for first use. As such, it has a big potential to support shared services (Janssen, Joha, & Weerakkody, 2007) within and among public bodies. Namely, shared services can benefit of open common standards and community development for interoperability, easy access, and maintenance.

Furthermore, OSS is readily available with little initial expense and therefore it is an opportunity for public organizations that have limited budget and resources.

Embedding OSS in an existing system / environment is not always an easy task tough. Selection of the appropriate OSS, data conversion, and software configurations and customizations for a given operational environment are time-consuming activities that often result impracticable in public bodies by the limited resources. Furthermore, at our knowledge, there is still no established process with a clear sequence of steps that guides to a successful deployment of OSS. Altogether, the assimilation gap (Fichman & Kemerer, 1997) between the acquisition and making a system really operational could be quite significant in the case of OSS. Therefore moving towards OSS becomes a risky decision that requires a deep investigation on the future financial engagement of an organization (Arthur, 1989; Federal Financial Institution Examination Council, 2004; Katz, 1994).

In addition, like for any adoption of a new technology, migrating to a new software solution increases the uncertainty of the future economic asset of an organization. Costs of adoption, assimilation, and ownership are hard to forecast, may drastically vary over time and tend to stabilize only in the long term[2]. In the specific case of a migration to OSS, the uncertainty is further amplified by the lack of empirical evidence of any positive return (Chau & Tam, 1997). The little understanding of the effects of a transition to OSS adds variability and unpredictability to any decision making process based on a direct economic evaluation. For these reasons, a migration toward OSS often does not follow a proper strategy of IT innovation but rather it is initiated by a need of compliance with new regulations and it is then let to the initiative of individual OSS promoters.

Moving to a new software configuration has further critical economic aspects. The theory of the increasing returns (Arthur, 1989) explains that the success of a product does not depend only on its technical superiority. A network effect occurs when the value of a product depends not only on its intrinsic technical value but also on the number of identical or compatible products already in use. A typical example of a network effect is the telephone—having the only telephone in the world would have been less valuable (who one could call?) than having a telephone in a network of 1 billion telephones already installed. In particular "network effects," often cause "lock-in" situations (Katz & Shapiro, 1994; Economides 2000). More generally, an organization is locked into using a product by a complex combination of technical connectivity issues and liability and contractual agreements that bind it to a specific supplier, brand, or vendor even for future investments. An organization experiences software switching costs when is locked in a specific software configuration and decides to break it to move to a different solution.

Switching costs may become evident for a long time after a transition. As a migration to a new technology does not take place in isolation, switching costs are also experienced maintaining and supporting the infrastructures throughout its lifecycle.

Therefore, to determine whether migrating to OSS paybacks, we need to consider not only the zero costs of licenses purchasing, but also all the costs occurring in the adoption and maintenance of this software. Typical questions are "How much does it cost to make the open source system integrated in existing proprietary software? Will the open source solution work also with the new versions of the operating system? Are training materials and technical support available now and will they be available in the future? Will my staff suffer a loss of productivity due to the introduction of OSS? Are there hidden costs in the migration to OSS? After all, if all the previous answers encourage migrating to OSS, how do I perform an effective transition?" Clearly, the uncertainty caused by the lack of evidence of economic benefits of OSS on the long terms does not help in answering such questions.

For these reasons, it is of paramount importance to define a cost model that predicts which costs occur and when these costs are relevant in the economy of a transition toward OSS.

At the current state, it is still not clear what model of costs can be used in the case of the open source technology (Lerner & Tirole, 2000). There might be significant differences with proprietary software. For example, in (Glynn, Fitzgerald, & Exton, 2005) the adverse attitude toward OSS of employees is a critical factor. In such article, interviewees considered the transition to OSS a sign that their manager under-valued their work, as they felt that managers have reduced the budget allocated for their working environment. Therefore, such employees started to complain and to reduce their enthusiasm in their work, which clearly resulted in lower quality and productivity. As such, an adverse attitude might convert in loss of productivity and dissatisfaction, causing costs.

Our research aims at shedding some light on the economic aspect of a transition toward OSS providing a model of costs and its application to five European organizations. We adopt the concept of total cost of ownership[2], and we introduce a clear separation line between tangible and intangible costs, migration and ownership costs, cost of initial purchasing and other cost factors. To derive a cost model, we adopt a twofold approach: 1) a top-down analysis that derives costs factors in a given context 2) a bottom-up inference that defines the nature of the costs. We base our study on data effectively collected during the daily activities of the European organizations, including 3884 workplaces in two years. Data on costs has been collected with several budget inspections and periodic interviews. Data on productivity has been collected automatically. In particular, we used a tool that registers time of work—with second precision—on any single document in any personal computer[3].

With this work, we do not pretend to give a final answer to the question whether migrating to OSS benefits to the society. This would include research in too many dimensions. We rather want to contribute to this issue in the economic aspect proposing an instrument that helps managers predicting, monitoring, and controlling costs to migrate to OSS.

Moreover, it is our opinion that there cannot be a single answer to how / whether migrating to OSS is feasible for all kind of software needs and in any environment. In our case study, we focus on software for personal productivity used in large public organizations, as it is the most distributed software used by generic users. We believe that this is a suitable choice to exemplify the advantages of using any OSS in public organizations.

Our paper is organized as follows. In section 2, we provide some background on cost modelling. In section 3—the focus of the chapter—we introduce the proposed cost model, the validation of the model on our sample data, and the data analysis. In section 4, we briefly discuss future trends. In section 5, we conclude on the findings of our work. At the end, we include two appendices for the reader's sake: (a) the questionnaire used to collect cost in the OSS migration and (b) the detailed description of the cost categorization.

BACKGROUND

Modelling IT Costs to Support Transformational Government

Transformational government aims at getting the best out of available technologies. It is an evolution of the concept of e-government, for which the major goal is enabling electronic services. Transformational government focuses on how technology improves the business of the public bodies with respect to the citizens' needs, the front and back-office optimization, and the professionalism of the management.

In this perspective, open technologies are an opportunity of growing the professionalism of public officers and management. Within its limited budget, a public organization has the chance to innovate its IT infrastructure and digital services with a higher control on what is getting. Namely, open technologies are anytime available and testable, transparent on how they manage information, sharable as they are based on Open Data Standards[4] (ODS), and affordable as they have no initial cost of purchasing. Namely, mangers in public organizations are aware that ODS—as for example the Adobe Acrobat[5] files—allow higher interoperability between services and offices and enable easy access to public services for citizens. In this sense, with open technologies, the IT management of public organizations can increase its level of professionalism having access to the inner structure of software in use. The IT infrastructure is not a black box anymore; it can be tested and modified on demand. Thus, the IT department becomes a shared service within the organization serving as internal consultant for other public services.

As such, why aren't open technologies and in specific OSS adopted extensively yet?

There is a problem of choice and trust. Public offices do not have enough resources to take a decision on the best IT configuration for their needs. Although a culture on OSS has been growing, OSS communities—the ones creating and maintain OSS—are more interested in technical than business consultancy. Therefore, few decisional instruments can help the public management to choose in the large IT market. In addition, OSS does not follow traditional methods of production and distribution as these are based on communities of developers that, in general, do not refer to a specific software company. This does not help the trust in OSS and increase the uncertainty in the decision to adopt it.

A wrong decision can waste many resources and dissatisfy citizens and employees. The opportunity to reduce waste and to increase efficiency with open technology is appealing, but can be a risk. Managers in the public sector still need suitable instruments to decide in terms of IT. One crucial factor is the cost. It is not clear what would be the public spend when migrating and using open technologies like OSS. It is also not clear whether adopting open technologies will supply the same level of quality of the services and a stable IT infrastructure. It might be that open technologies require more cost for maintenance of the IT infrastructure.

In this chapter we propose an instrument to support managers of public bodies in their decision making process toward innovation with OSS. We propose a cost model that takes into account cost for the migration and cost for the ownership of OSS.

A systematic use of the model will help public managers to keep under control the public spend in IT maintaining the appropriate level of quality of their services. Managers can use it as a prediction instrument to schedule future investments and maintain up to date the current infrastructure.

Cost Models

A cost model is a method that defines a set of cost factors describing the financial impact of a strategic decision made or to be made. For example, a cost factor is "cost of purchasing software" that in general refers to the contractual cost to buy software from a vendor. However, there are other cost factors less obvious like "cost for software training," which might include, for example, the time spent to learn a software application.

The two major cost models used in literature are Return on Investment (ROI) and Total Cost of Ownership (TCO).

The ROI (Putnam & Meyers, 1991) model includes both an investment and a return perspective. The authors define the return as the payback of funds allocated also for other purposes than only the investments. The return should equal the earnings foreseen for the original purposes plus the costs of the risk. On the return side, organizations look at reducing operating costs, predicting savings, determining a payoff, and computing the cost of applying new technologies. When benefits are computed, those benefits are by any large converted into money. On the investment side of the ROI equation, organizations look at the costs involved in introducing new technologies and service improvement initiatives. In addition, effort is a primary input. Effort does not translate to money for budgeting purposes, but it is seen as a precious commodity in those organizations in which, on the return side, the satisfaction of the employees and the citizens is of great importance.

The TCO model acknowledges factors of cost emerging in a time window of at least five years after the purchase of a new technology[2]. Unlike the ROI model, the TCO model captures better the intangible (or hidden) costs (Brynjolfsson & Hitt, 2003) and the propagation of the effects of a transition to a new IT solution in the long term. Namely, a new IT product is embedded in a "cluster" of related innovations that involves the whole organization for a long period after the initial migration (Brynjolfsson & Hitt, 2003).

Relying on models of monetary returns—like ROI—does not explain completely the financial engagement on the long term in particular in those organizations like public bodies. Namely, public bodies have little interest in a monetary return, whereas they principally care of the quality of their services and the productivity of the internal staff. In public administrations, economic decisions are made not to justify monetary earnings, but rather to reduce current costs, to maintain the quality of the services, and to increase the satisfaction of the internal staff. Moreover, since OSS has little costs of purchasing, speaking of monetary returns in the case of OSS has, in general, no real meaning, as no initial investment is needed in practice.

We call *cost categorization* the set of cost factors defined by a given cost model for a given context. A simple example of cost categorization differentiates between tangible and intangible (or hidden) costs. Intangible costs are costs difficult to trace and measure and in general, they are not foreseen in a budget plan. They often refer to investments on human resources and their impact on the overall organization's productivity. Temporary productivity loss due to lack of skills / knowledge of new technologies are examples of intangible costs. Recent estimates allocate to intangible costs the 75% of the IT investments (Brynjolfsson & Hitt, 2003) in a period of five years. Therefore, ignoring intangible costs affects the overall economy of an organization, (Brynjolfsson & Hitt, 2003). The extent of use and dependency of a software application may also determine unexpected costs in a software migration. A data-entry or structured-task worker who uses only a few applications may be the best candidate to move to a new IT solution. Using fewer applications means fewer applications to rewrite or replace, so migration costs may be low. An expert worker who uses a variety of applications will be more problematic to move because the migration costs may be extremely high. How the company uses its software has a great impact on these figures (Bozman, Gillen, Kolodgy, Kusnetzky, Perry, & Shiang, 2002). Dependency on other software applications is called network externality. Costs due to network externality may be relevant in specific contexts amplifying also the costs of searching for documentation and the costs for consultancy.

In the case of OSS, examples of cost model/ categorizations are not frequent or exhaustive. Alan MacCormack reviewed 84 studies on TCO of a transition to OSS (MacCormack, 2003). MacCormack's results suggest that many studies suffer from a lack of reliable data on which to base conclusions, as well as a lack of consistency in the approach taken to calculate the cost model. Furthermore, few studies use data from a sample large enough to be representative of a broader population.

In a migration cost factors relevant to proprietary software might become meaningless for open source technologies. For example, the absence of up-front license fees and the availability of community-based support can reduce or even eliminate the initial costs of OSS deployment. On the other hand, with OSS, additional outlays for maintenance and support may reduce the benefits of any saving on licenses. Moreover, license fees look like a more relevant cost factor in economies where labor and support costs are much lower (De Azevedo Filho, 2003; Kshetri, 2004). But they are even less significant in countries in which piracy of proprietary software is endemic.

Other costs might rise when switching from proprietary to open source technologies. For example, adverse attitude of the employees toward OSS may also cause cost because of loss of productivity. In general productivity loss causes costs when the new technology is not stable or stably understood (Arthur, 1989).

Examples of Existing Cost Categorizations

The major effort to define a cost categorization is identifying the correct cost factors compounding it. In general, the identification is performed in three steps: finding a source of candidate factors, defining causes of costs in a given context, and finally selecting the appropriate cost factors in the list of candidates.

In 2003 the national center for the IT of Germany (KBSt) has published a broad list of categories of costs for software and hardware migrations, the WiBe21 (KBSt, 2003). The WIBe21 represents a good source of candidate measures. The widest-known cost categorizations are included in this list. In the following sections, we discuss three most significant categorizations for OSS.

The Cost Categorization of Linuxvalue.Com[6]
Linuxvalue.com proposes the following cost categories for a server side Linux migration: 1) Downtime; 2) Software; 3) Hardware; 4) Storage; 5) Services; 6) Facilities.

The interesting aspect of this model is that takes into account downtime costs that lead to unproductive labor and loss of e-business transactions and stalls of revenue generating activities specific to a server side transition such as e-commerce business applications. Although they do not specify it, downtown costs are an example of hidden costs.

The Cost Categorization of CyberSource[7]
CyberSource instead, proposes a TCO model that considers a migration to open source from scratch—that is with no previous software setting. To this end, it also considers costs such as the acquisition of hardware and primary services like broadband internet connections. In this categorization also costs for Office productivity applications play a crucial role, in particular for interoperability with data standards.

Also in this case hidden costs are not explicitly mentioned but productivity loss is another example of hidden costs. In our empirical analysis, we also found this cost as we are similarly dealing with desktop migrations.

The Cost Categorization of eGep Project[8]
A different perspective is taken in the categorization defined in the project e-Government Economics Project (eGep), a project of the European Commission's Modinis programme. In public administrations, costs are justified against the improvement of the quality of the services they provide. At a European level, services and their quality are part of an ongoing discussion on e-Government in terms of their type of availability. For this purpose, the eGEP's model includes costs of setting up, providing and maintaining e-services collected with use the Activity Based Costing method (ABC). ABC method is a process-driven full costing system that presupposes a thorough analysis and mapping of the work processes and activities needed for the provision of the service for which the assessment of cost is sought.

eGep has very much discussed the issue of hidden costs, which also explains the use of the ABC method. Namely, this type of costs can cause serious impediments to provide and maintain quality e-services, in particular in those organizations that have limited budget.

All these categorizations are based on empirical evidence and this makes them closer to our approach. All of them lack of a method to define the costs, though. They all start from known and conceivable costs in the specific context they focus on. In this way, they can hardly be extended to other contexts. The solution is including a rigorous method to derive the appropriate measures of cost and their nature from the analysis of the strategy and business goals of an organization. As such, the categorization resulting from the application of method gives different cost factors in different contexts (Table IV), which is what one expects.

MAIN FOCUS OF THE CHAPTER

Our goal is to define a clear procedure that identifies costs to adopt OSS, their nature, and their relevance over time. The major novelty of our approach is the use of the Goal Question Metric paradigm (Basili, Caldiera, & Rombach, 1994), a deductive instrument commonly used in software measurement.

The model of costs we define has three views: 1) the temporal view, that describes costs occurring over time (Figure 1), 2) the logical view that describes the way costs items are derived, and 3) the object view that correspond to the categorization of costs in a given context (Table I and Table II).

The Model of Cost for the Adoption of Open Source Software

The Temporal View

Costs to adopt and maintain a new technology vary over time. It is a fact that introducing a new technology perturbs the regular pace of job activities and causes an increase of the overall initial expenditure. Depending on the degree of use of the technology, the effects might be more or less pervasive. Personnel need to be trained, the infrastructure needs to be re-configured, and the knowledge of the new system needs to be achieved at various levels of use. After this initial phase, costs tend to standardize and stabilize. At this point, old and new technology can be fairly compared.

In the temporal view of our cost model (Figure 1), we call migration the phase to reach this stability and we determine the extent of this phase with the level of productivity reached by the end-users with the new technology (until the dotted

Figure 1. The temporal view of our method

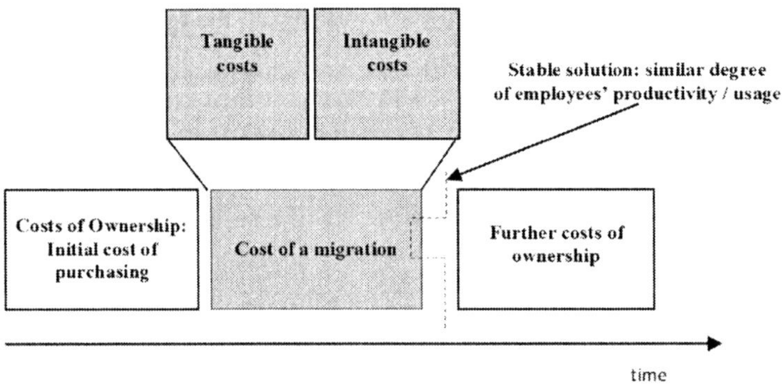

line in Figure 1). Once the end-user is able to work with a comparable productivity[9], the migration phase ends and the use of the new technology can be considered stable (Arthur, 1989).

The phase of proper ownership starts soon after (after the dotted line in Figure 1). In the ownership phase, employees are used to the new technology and work with comparable productivity. The dotted line in Figure 1 is not a straight line to indicate that the ownership phase can even start a bit before the employee's productivity reaches a comparable productivity. This may happen for internal strategic reasons of an organization

The types of costs that can be collected in the overall process of transition to OSS depend on the phase.

Migration costs (grey area) are the volatile costs that pertain to the specific phase of adoption and first general use of the new software configuration, the migration phase. As such, they measure the monetary effort that managers need to invest temporary to migrate to a new technology. Migration costs might be considerably high and may lock the organizations in with previous suppliers and IT legacy systems (Arthur, 1989): loss of benefits or interoperability with obsolete technologies may be too expensive hampering any migration process.

Ownership costs (white areas) are instead costs that refer to the use and the maintenance of a technology during its stable operational life. Costs of ownership are monitored over a period of at least five years and are budgeted yearly. They may also be substantial high and not affordable in the long term (Sanders, 1998). In this phase, the major investments concern periodical activities and support often regulated by contractual agreements.

In our model, we include initial cost of purchasing among the costs of ownership although they are budgeted at the early stages of the migration phase. This is because the cost of purchasing is often included in a long-term contract together with traditional ownership costs like costs of support or update. In Figure 1, we also subdivide migration costs into tangible and intangible. In general, intangible costs have more impact in the migration phase. Namely, in the ownership phase, the software configuration is stable and we do not expect to have peculiar fluctuations.

At this point, it is clear that an answer to a question regarding the benefits of transitioning to OSS needs to address two different issues:

Issue_1: *Does an organization have the economic resources to introduce OSS?—migration to OSS*

Issue_2: *Does the transition to OSS pay-off?—ownership of OSS.*

The Logical View

In this section, we present the logical view of our model (Figure 1). The logical view explains how the cost factors are derived from the context. In the following, we describe it sequentially.

First, we select four macro categories of costs of the WiBe21 list that are in common with several existing categorizations and that suit better our context[10]: 1) Software, 2) Support, 3) Learning/ Training, and 4) Staffing.

Then we break out the four categories into subcategories (Table I and Table II). For this, we use the Goal Question Metric (GQM) paradigm (Basili, Caldiera, & Rombach, 1994) to identify the suitable factors of costs in the WiBe21, which meet the local business, the IT strategy, and the context of the organizations under study. The GQM paradigm is a deductive instrument that derives from a given business goal the suitable measurement framework for a given context enabling the achievement of the business goal itself. The GQM requires a deep understanding of the context. We shall introduce the GQM paradigm with a brief exemplification of its use in our case. The interest reader can find the proper definition in (Basili, Caldiera, & Rombach, 1994). We apply the GQM paradigm starting from the two business goals determined by our two issues:

Business Goal_1: *Understand the economic resources needed to introduce OSS*

Business Goal_2: *Understand whether the transition to OSS pays-off*

With the GQM we then define a set of measurement goals derived from Business Goal_1 and Business Goal_2 and a set of questions and the relative cost factors derived from the measurement goals (Appendix A and Appendix B). The questions have been included in a questionnaire administrated to the employees of the organizations under study (Appendix A). Thank to the context analysis foreseen in the GQM, cost factors are also collected and categorized by their tangible/intangible nature.

For example, to understand the Business Goal_1 we define the following measurement goal[11]:

Analyze the migration effort to characterize it in terms of "costs for searching" from the point of view of the IT staff at the early phase of the migration phase in the public organization under study.

Effort, here, will be measured as time spent by the IT staff to search for available OSS and its documentation. It does not include any preliminary use or test of OSS. In a public administration that occasionally migrates to new software, this effort is not regularly budgeted; as such, it is a clear example of hidden cost.

With the rules defined by the GQM, we can derive the questions to collect measure of cost in the macro category "Support":

1. What are the costs of IT staff for searching for OSS alternatives?
2. What are the costs of IT staff for searching for documentation for the chosen OSS?

We can answer the questions, for example, computing the measure "days spent by the IT employees times their daily salary" for the two different activities "searching for OSS alternative" or "searching for documentation...". In general, these costs are intangible.

After applying the GQM, we prune duplicate costs factors. At the end, we get the lists of cost factors fitting our context (the object view).

The Object View

The object view of our model describes the concrete costs factors determined applying our method to real cases. Factors are classified as migration or ownership and tangible or intangible costs (Table 1 and Table 2). The set of cost factors here represents the union set of the costs derived from the case study.

Table 1. Categories in the migration cost model

Category		Intangible?
Software	Pilot projects	Y
	Data conversion tools	
	Interfacing to legacy software	
	Software add-ons	
	Security tools	
	Upgrades	
Support	Search for alternatives	Y
	Search for documentation	Y
	Data compliance	
	Search for new support contracts	Y
	External support fees	
Training/ Learning	IT staff formal training	
	IT staff self-learning	Y
	Employees' formal training	
	Employees' self-learning	Y
	Lack of productivity	Y
Staffing	Employees' extra hours/ bonus	
	Salary of temporary employees	
	Installation and deployment	Y
	Overheads and bonus	Y

Table 2. Categories in the ownership cost model

Category	
Software	Acquisition (licenses)
	Updates
	Upgrades
	Software add-on
	Security (explore vulnerability)
Support	Maintenance (internal)
	Maintenance (support contracts)
	Consultancy
Training	Employees' regular training
	IT staff regular training
Staffing	Lack of productivity
	Salary of employees

Table 1 shows the costs for a migration. It gives a measure of the effort that an organization temporary needs for migrating to OSS. These costs might be significant as they are often underestimated given that their intangible part is not collected or considered. Table 2 shows costs for the ownership of OSS. A complete overview of the ownership costs needs a long period of monitoring that might be hard to perform specially for recent technologies. In our organizations, we are able to compute these costs mainly with predictions based on the first one/two years of ownership of OSS.

Costs factors in Table 2 and 3 are derived speculating on causes that determine them—see the logic view. Same causes of costs relate to different factors depending whether they refer to migration or ownership costs.

For example, in our context "Lack of productivity" is classified as "Training/Learning" in the migration whereas is classified as "Staffing" in the ownership phase. Namely, in the first case lack of productivity is due to the time spent in specific training during office hours. In the second case, lack of productivity refers to the usage of the software application accelerating ore decelerating the work of the employee.

The Case Study

Brief Review of the Context

The context of a migration highly influences the categorization and the cost nature. Costs that might be relevant for a given organization may not be significant for another one.

In this section, we briefly give an overview of the software configurations of the five organizations we studied. We use fictitious acronyms to identify them throughout the paper.

These organizations have initial software settings and experience in the adoption of OSS that has led to different types of migration. Table III summarizes the migration settings in each public organization.

In Table 3, no partial migration from mixed software (proprietary and open source software) or complete migration (all the software applications are migrated) has been reported. *Migration from scratch* means that initially only a restricted number of people uses computers and software.

In our study, the migration is a unique process involving different types of OSS, but in our analysis, we use only data on the desktop migration[12]. We believe that this data is a good indicator of

Table 3. Description of the migration

Organization	Type of migration	The magnitude of the desktop migration, June 2006
SGV	Partial migration from proprietary software	238 servers and about 3,000 PCs.
PP	Partial migration from proprietary software	120 workstations and about 450 PCs.
SK	Migration from scratch	about 60 PCs.
TO	Migration from scratch	44 PCs
BH	Partial migration from proprietary software	210 PCs

the magnitude of the overall OSS transition given that desktop applications are the most deployed, distributed and used programs.

Table 3 also shows that we had at disposal a significant set of data.

The Data Collection

The in field investigation lasted two years, the data collection was performed mostly during the first year. We analyzed a rich variety of data collected through various means: questionnaires and interviews—subjective data—and data automatically gathered with PROM[13]—objective data. We performed several interviews and refinements of the data collected. First, we collected data on software configuration settings, experience in the OSS sector, policies and strategies in place, and attitude towards OSS. Then we administrated the questionnaire about the causes of costs. We analysed the causes and we administrated again a refined questionnaire that highlighted the intangible and tangible nature of the migration costs. At the end, results were sent back to the organizations for validation. This procedure is displayed in Figure 2.

Administering the questionnaires was not straightforward. The employees interviewed have been selected on the base of the GQM; depending on the type of measurement goal, different stakeholders have been identified and contacted. To get the best quality for the data we visited each interviewee explaining the meaning of the questions—in particular giving examples of hidden costs they might have incurred during the migration.

Overview of the Findings

In this section, we summarize the findings of the study. We have applied our cost model to five European public organizations. The application of the model returns for each organization a set of values of costs for the migration, for the initial purchasing, and for the ownership of software. The migration costs are labelled as tangible or intangible and they are subdivided into four macro categories. The ownership costs are computed on annual base and, when data was not available, by a computational prediction based on the first one / two years of monitoring. In Table 4, we summarize the cost factors of the migration phase identified in four of five organizations. The grey cells indicate no cost retrieved.

In the following, we briefly discuss Table 4 per organization under study.

SGV. The high costs for frequent upgrades are the major reason that motivated the transition. The migration to OSS started with a pilot project on 10 PCs. This had been foreseen in the budget of the migration, so SGV did not claim it under hidden cost. Initially, the migration was conducted with no real training, as the majority of the employees were part-time. The lack of training and immedi-

Figure 2. Data collection—one year

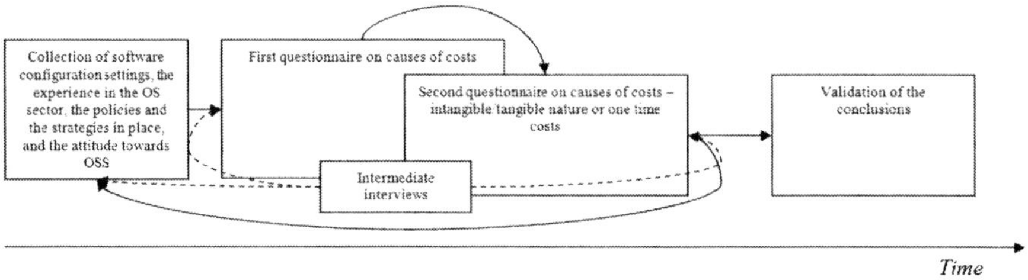

Table 4. Costs of migration in the organizations studied (Y = hidden costs)

Category	Subcategory	SGV	PP	SK	TO
Software	Pilot projects		Y		Y
	Data conversion tools				
	Interfacing to legacy software				
	Software add-ons				
	Security tools				
	Upgrades				
Support	Search for alternatives	Y	Y	Y	Y
	Search for documentation	Y		Y	Y
	Data compliance				
	Search for new support contracts				
	External support fees				
Training /Learning	IT staff formal training				
	IT staff self-learning	Y	Y	Y	Y
	Employees' formal training				
	Employees' self-learning	Y	Y	Y	
	Lack of productivity		Y	Y	
Staffing	Employees' extra hours/ bonus			Y	
	Salary of temporary employees				
	Installation and deployment	Y	Y	Y	Y
	Overheads and bonus		Y	Y	

ate support causes the failure of this first attempt. For the proper migration, a well-defined strategy was put in place: extensive training, complete replacement with the open source software, and no maintenance of the previous old solution kept just for external exchanges. To facilitate the migration the organization also hired a person to follow the migration in all the offices and developed software to nightly convert documents in the open format. Few technical impediments have occurred. For example, the migration of the database and its interfaces has resulted unfeasible.

In SGV, most of the hidden costs occurred because the management decided to allocate only internal personnel to manage the migration process. IT staff spent a considerable amount of time in searching and writing OSS documentation and external support. On the other hand, the management recognized the high importance of training as a critical factor for a successful migration and included these costs into the annual cost balance.

PP. This organization adopted a local law that recommended the use of OSS. Before the migration, the organization has performed two pilot projects: 1) re-engineering a piece of legacy software replacing the old proprietary version with an in-house new version of it. PP modified the contract to have the ownership of the code and the right to distribute it freely to other organizations and 2) adoption of OSS supported by a yearly contract with five external consultants. In this case, the organization has saved on licenses and wages for in-house IT staff, but has paid for the external consultancy coordinated by two internal employees. Both projects caused a non-expected cost.

In the migration, costs for software relate to several tools implemented as add-ons, plug-ins, and security tools. There was an unexpected little cost for searching for alternatives.

Training for non-IT end-users was provided in three different ways:

- For generic requests, technicians tried to solve users' problems. The cost of this training was estimated at one day per month
- IT staff have written internal manuals and short references guide. For example, to manage the introduction of digital signatures in some business processes, the IT staff wrote 10 different references guides to help employees using smart cards with certificates
- Training for software developed by external suppliers was provided by an external instructor

SK. In 2005, the migration started with a three months pilot project to investigate the feasibility of a migration to OSS. At the beginning of the migration neither the IT personnel (7 people), nor the employees participating in the tests (initially 60 people) were prepared, i.e. properly trained, to work with OSS. During the first days, some issues about computers' configurations arose (i.e. small RAM capacity on old machines that triggered unexpected crashes of the software). Consequently, some PCs were dropped from the experimentation. In general, the personnel were favourable to switch to Open Source products, as it was aware that such migration would solve many problems with the software licenses and related cost.

The organization has not performed an extensive migration. By its explicit decision, the management did not allocate any specific budget for the migration. Mainly costs were due to unforeseen small support needs or training. Thus, hidden costs resulted proportionally significant, although the small amount of the overall expenditure did not add a particular contribution to our original research question on migration costs. In particular self-training for the IT experts and help desk for the generic user accounted as the major cost in the migration.

TO. The management decided to migrate to OSS as it received European funding to cover most of the costs. Before the migration, employees used old computers. No LAN was used and the network was used only for external communication. No other specific software was generically deployed.

In the migration, a help desk was installed but as users did not have complex requests, no extensive use for such support was experienced. No external support was needed and all the work related to the transition was done internally.

Figure 3 and Table 5 report the cost of migration in four organizations. As for Table 4, this table does not display the result of the fifth organization since the transition to OSS was already mature.

The major fact in Table 5 concerns the costs for staffing. They are classified as intangible for all the organizations (Table 4) and in general, they represent the lowest share among all the categories of cost. In our cost factor definition, this means that almost no incentives or extra resources have been allocated for the migration. The totals also show an interesting fact: in three organizations, intangible costs almost equal their tangible counterpart. In the case of TO, this is due to the little

Figure 3. Overall effort for the migration among the organizations (2006)

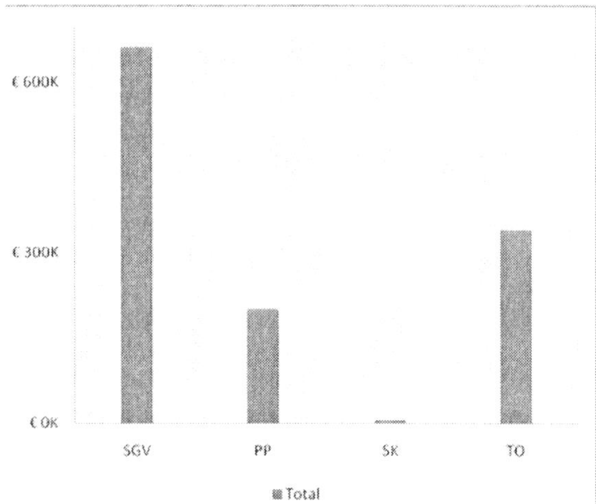

Table 5. The model of migration costs by category in each organization

	Software Tang. | Intang.	Support Tang. | Intang.	Training/Learning Tang. | Intang.	Staffing Tang. | Intang.	Total Tang. | Intang.
SGV	6.0%	12.4%	44.3%	37.3%	100%
	82% | 18%	40% | 60%	92% | 8%	0% | 100%	51% | 49%
PP	5.9%	15.6%	68.8%	9.7%	100%
	0% | 100%	62% | 38%	57% | 43%	0% | 100%	49% | 51%
SK	49.6%	16.3%	30.6%	3.5%	100%
	96% | 4%	77% | 23%	0% | 100%	0% | 100%	60% | 40%
TO	0.3%	20.8%	77.0%	1.9%	100%
	100% | 0%	28% | 72%	27% | 73%	0% | 100%	27% | 73%

investment foreseen for the migration. In the two more complete transitions,—SGV and PP- the reason may be found in the underestimation of the effort for the internal resources, which was not accounted before our interview.

Figure 4 shows the annual monetary engagement for software ownership among the organizations. Here also BH is included as most mature migration among all the five organizations. The major costs of ownership for BH was for developing and maintaining the proprietary and in-house software that involved a ¾-time job of a junior developer and ¼-time of the IT expert. Moreover, with the migration BH permanently hired an IT expert. Figure 4 does not include initial costs of

Figure 4. A comparison of the annual ownership cost including initial costs

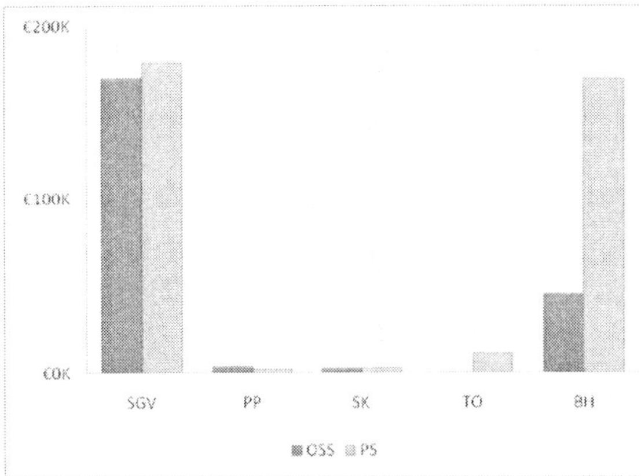

purchasing. Specifically, the organizations are divided into two classes: BH and SGV, which—at the end of this study—almost completed the migration, and PP, SK, and TO, which were a bit behind the schedule. SGV, TO, and BH show some savings with the new OSS solution. SK has equal costs for the new and the old solution and PP reports of higher costs in the new open source settings.

If we isolate the initial costs of purchasing (Figure 5 and Figure 5: Initial cost of purchasing (IC) and annual ownership costs (OC) for open source (OSS) and proprietary software (PS)), we see a peculiar behaviour: all the organizations reduced substantially their initial costs and all of them increased their ownership costs with OSS. The more mature organizations about doubled their ownership costs while PP and SK experienced with OSS more than five times the ownership of proprietary software. Despite the big difference, for PP and SK the result is not so critical giving the size of their migration and the relative monetary engagement (Figure 5). TO did not foresee any cost of ownership with OSS. This might be because of the five years ownership period was not concluded at the time of the interview.

Summarizing the findings, we conclude that:

- In the two more IT mature organizations, SGV and BH, we found a higher financial

Figure 5. Initial cost of purchasing (IC) and annual ownership costs (OC) for open source (OSS) and proprietary software (PS)

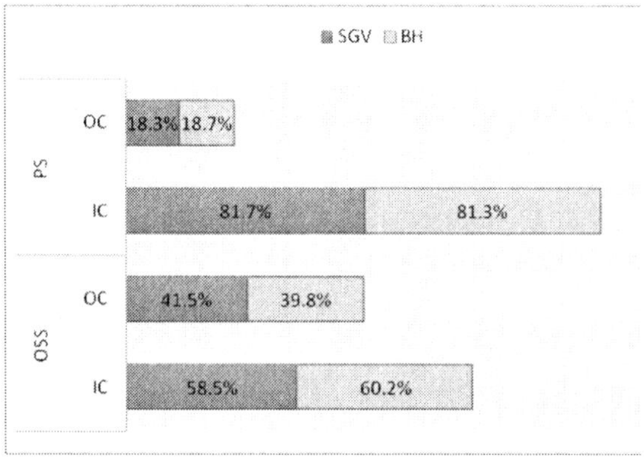

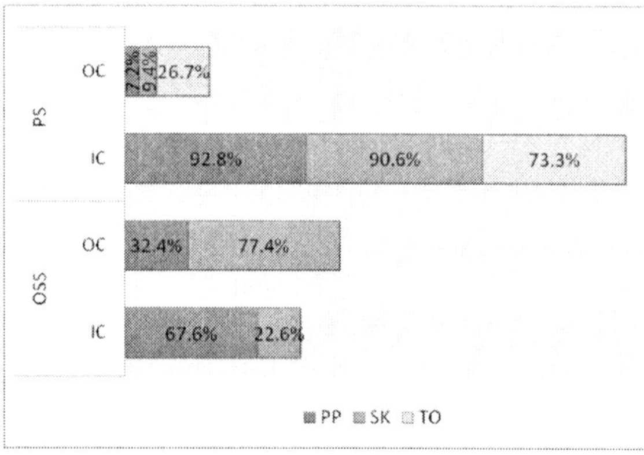

engagement. This might be obvious as organizations with more experience might have a better-defined strategy to migrate to OSS and therefore they might have finer financial plan to perform a large migration (Table III).

Costs of a Migration

- Intangible costs definitely affect costs in a migration. We have seen that they are in general half of them. In our definition, they are mostly Staffing costs.
- The cost of training is generically high. This may be an indicator of a successful transition. Three out of four organizations reported training as hidden cost. This is a sign of a poor upfront strategy. SGV understood this after a first initial unsuccessful pilot project. In its case, training is mostly a tangible cost.

Initial Costs

- Initial costs of purchasing are definitely higher for proprietary software. This was not a surprise.
- Initial cost of purchasing for OSS was not zero. This may be due to localizations, customizations or interfacing with legacy systems

Cost of Ownership

- Costs of migration are significant and comparably higher than the annual costs of ownership—migration costs also occurred in a shorter period (Figure 3 and Figure 4). This means that the transition requires a first exceptional monetary effort.
- Costs of ownership are higher for proprietary software. Excluding initial costs, they are higher for OSS, though. Initial costs reported are on annual base and distributed over a period of five years.

Discussing the Findings Against Maccormack's Survey on TCO

As we already mentioned, Alan MacCormarck (MacCormarck, 2003) performed a deep review of studies on the TCO for software platforms. In his work, he found that calculating the TCO is a complex matter that depends on the local context and strategies to deploy software. He also found very different cost categorizations across the studies and use of inadequate data to support the analysis.

Aware of MacCormack's findings, in our work we have managed the complexity of calculating the TCO with the use of a well-defined deductive process to derive measures of cost (the

GQM), a well-known categorization of cost factors (WiBe21), and an automated tool to collect measures of employees' productivity.

We have not adopted the ROI model. This is because in our settings the ROI model has little relevance, as our organizations are public bodies or work exclusively for public bodies that do not base their decision process on the monetary return[14].

As MacCormack suggested, we have considered the Value Delivered (VD) in addition to the TCO model. This is for capturing the variations in functionalities needed or the customizations preferred by the end-users.

VD is based on two main factors, *differences in product features* to accommodate needs of different users and the *option value*, which is the freedom to have options among which to choose. In our case studies, we have simply non-expert users with homogeneous software needs. Thus, our work does not provide any finding in the variation of product features; instead, it contributes to the discussion of the option value as the end-users can freely choose between open and closed software solutions.

Our results also differ from the MacComarck's in the discussion about the most relevant category of cost. For MacCormack this was "staffing." We must say that in our study we differentiate between the pure migration and the stable ownership phase. With this distinction, we have seen that in our organizations "training" is the most relevant macro category of cost in the migration phase and "support"—that includes consultancy for maintenance and documentation of the OSS—in the ownership phase while "staffing" is not as relevant as "support."

FUTURE TRENDS

Despite the valuable contribution of the open source communities in technical issues, the state of the practice for evaluating business advantages and methods of adopting OSS is rather poor. Specifically, the economic value of open technologies is still a Babel of non-formalized case studies (MacCormack, 2003). This does not help the adoption of such software. While ODS are considered a key means to release public governance from legacy systems[14] the use of OSS is still under discussion. The UK Government itself in the implementation plan of transformational government[1] mentioned OSS only as an alternative to commercial of the shelf software. There is still a need of trust on OSS although there are examples that those technologies provide superior technical advantage at least in terms of interoperability and transparency.

The way to establish trust is evidence organized and elaborated with a rigorous approach. In particular, there is a need of evidence of the economic advantages of OSS. Scientists need to commit and supply economic instruments to help managers of public organizations that do not have the resources to investigate the matter. In this perspective, we believe that the cost model introduced in this chapter helps providing a well-defined method that could be easily replicated by other researchers to establish an open empirical knowledge base on the economic assessment of OSS adoption and ownership.

Of course, the economic one is not the only aspect to consider in a cost / benefit analysis of migration toward OSS. Social, legal, and technological aspects have great importance in the decision process of technology adoption (Glynn, Fitzgerald, & Exton, 2005; Rogers, 2003). We believe that the uncertainty that harms the diffusion of OSS in public bodies can be overcome with a combined analysis of all the aspects, economic, legal, social, and technical and a strong political support at European level. Nevertheless, since OSS is technological competitive and many legal issues do not affect any basic adoption, we think that the next step missing is a proper assessment of the costs of OSS adoption.

We believe that future research needs to establish a trustable knowledge on the (economic) benefits of adopting OSS, on which further strategies can be explored at managerial level and new research orisons can be opened. For example, we have seen that hidden costs have a great impact in the migration phase. Thus we can pose several questions, such as: Is there any suitable strategy that a public manager can implement to prevent intangible costs? Can be this the "pure service" strategy? Does a public body really need to own its software, or can it simply purchase its services and not the application as in the well-known case of SAP[15] or the open source software Funambol[16]? It seems that this will reduce the cost of deployment. Can this release public bodies from other hidden costs? Can this facilitate the adoption of OSS? Or would this lock the administration in more than it used proprietary software?

CONCLUSION

One of the responsibilities of the government toward citizens is to balance service quality with public spend. Transformational government evolves from e-government stressing this fact. Specifically, transformational government focuses on professionalism's increase and service sharing as a means to enhance the quality of the electronic services and the wise management of the public money. To achieve the objectives of transformational government public managers need instruments that help them in their decision making process, particularly for the selection and maintenance of the IT infrastructure. They need to provide services supported by the most adequate and modern technologies. Moreover, The public investment in IT does not generate any revenue; rather, the investment obtains benefits for the whole of society.

We believe that among software technologies, OSS and ODS are a promising means to achieve the quality of services controlling for costs in a transparent way. In addition, OSS allows shared services to be created and maintained as any expert can easily access to the software code and understand the flow of data that the software application shares with external parties.

As pointed out in the introduction there is a lack of knowledge on the benefit of OSS, though. To contribute to fill this gap we have proposed a rigorous economic assessment of OSS in this chapter. In the following, we describe the most crucial aspects of our work that we recommend researchers and practitioners to consider in any further investigation.

Our model differentiates between cost of migration and costs of ownership to respond better to the managers' needs. The former involves high investment for a shorter period, while the latter foresees expenditure for maintenance over a period of at least five years. We also focus on the tangible / intangible nature of the costs finding that in a migration, intangible costs are significant and it would be an error to ignore them.

We also investigate the impact of the initial costs of purchasing as OSS promises no cost for licensing. We realized that it is not always justified to base the migration to OSS on the promise of lower license costs. First, because past costs of purchasing of proprietary software are too much influenced by factors like inflation and market flow that they are not a means of comparison at the moment of a transition to any new software, second because they often include costs for deployment and customization, which come up as unexpected for OSS too. Thus to have a better understanding of any saving with the adoption of OSS, we propose to include any purchasing cost into the total ownership cost computation spreading it in a period of at least five years.

Another crucial aspect we consider is the context of the migration. Our cost model has been applied to five European organizations that have followed different types of migration on the base of their IT environment. We found that the types of costs in a cost model differ in the five organizations by their nature (tangible / intangible), by the phase of the transition (migration /ownership), and of course by their value. With the analysis of the context, we performed a facilitator / inhibitor analysis. We found that the top motivations to transit to OSS are: 1) exchanging of documents in an open shared format (ODS), 2) reusing old hardware in some cases, and 3) being independent of software vendors even when creating a distribution or an application for local needs. We found that some pre-conception or adverse attitudes hamper the process of transition to OSS, but may be bypassed a policy of both ad hoc and periodic training to fill the lack of knowledge / experience in relation to what OSS products are appropriate and how they might be deployed. We measured the adverse attitude toward OSS with the application's usage and consequently with the employees' productivity. In our case studies, we have sampled the usage with the office suites, Microsoft office and OpenOffice.org as they represent an instrument widely used by the most heterogeneous people in our case study. The productivity rate would have determined the beginnings of the ownership phase and revealed possible intangible costs due to lack of productivity. As result, we found that in our five organizations there was no lack of productivity with the use of the OpenOffice.org in the ownership phase.

In conclusions, our study aims at contributing at professionalism's increase and service sharing in the public sector. To build such a culture public officers need suitable instruments and resources. Specifically, they need to get the best out of technologies' offer. They also need economic tools to be autonomous in their decision process toward innovation. We think that open technologies and specifically OSS would help in giving more competence and knowledge both in IT and economics representing thus an opportunity toward implementing transformational government in public offices.

In this respect, we expect that future research will further test our approach on real case studies to consolidate our findings and create a knowledge base. To this end, we see OSS communities as the best place to develop and maintain trustable open information about the (economic) aspects of adopting OSS.

ACKNOWLEDGMENT

The data collection has been partially supported by the COSPA project—VI European Framework Contract no.: IST-2002-2164. We also thank all the organizations participating in this study.

REFERENCES

Arthur, W. B (1989). Competing technologies, increasing returns, and lock in by historical events. *Economic Journal, 99*(394), 116-131.

Basili, V. R., Caldiera, G., & Rombach, H. D, (1994). Goal question metric paradigm. In J. J. Marciniak (ed.), *Encyclopedia of Software Engineering volume 1*(pp. 528-532). John Wiley and Sons.

Bozman, J., Gillen, A., Kolodgy, C., Kusnetzky, D., Perry, R., & Shiang, D. (2002). *Windows 2000 vs. Linux in Enterprise computing: An assessment of business value for selected workloads. IDC, sponsored by Microsoft Corporation. White paper.* Retrieved from www.idc.com

Chau, P. Y. K., & Tam, K. Y. (1997). Factors affecting the adoption of open systems:aAn exploratory study. *MIS Q., 21*(1), 1-24.

De Azevedo Filho, W. A, (2003). *Using open source in community based projects. Gartner group.* Retrieved from http://www.gartner.com/DisplayDocument?doc_cd=114394

Economides, N. (2000). Durable goods monopoly with network externalities with application to the PC operating systems market. *Quarterly Journal of Electronic Commerce, 1*(3), 193-201.

Federal Financial Institution Examination Council. (2004). *Risk management of free and open source software. Financial Institution Letter.* Retrieved October 2004, from http://www.fdic.gov/news/news/financial/2004/FIL11404a.html

Fichman, R. G., & Kemerer, C. F. (1997). The assimilation of software process innovations: An organizational learning perspective. *Manage. Sci., 43*(10), 1345-1363.

Glynn, E., Fitzgerald, B., & Exton, C. (2005). Commercial adoption of open source software: An empirical study. *Empirical Software Engineering, 200,* 225-234.

Hitt, L., & Brynjolfsson, E. (2003). Computing productivity: Firm level evidence. *Review of Economics and Statistics, 85*(4), 793-808.

Janssen, M., Joha, A., & Weerakkody, V. (2007). Exploring relationships of shared service arrangements in local government. *Transforming Government: People, Process and Policy, 1*(3), 270-284.

Katz, M. L., & Shapiro, C. (1994). Systems competition and network effects. *Journal of Economic Perspectives, 8*(2), 93-115.

KBSt (German Federal Government Coordination and Advisory Agency). (2003, July). WiBe21: A guide to migrating the basic software components on server and workstation computer. KBSt Publication Service.

Kshetri, N. (2004). Economics of Linux adoption in developing countries. *IEEE Software, 21*(1), 74-81.

Lerner, J., & Tirole, J. (2002). Some Simple economics of open source. *Journal of Industrial Economics, 50*(2), 197-234.

MacCormack, A, (2003). Evaluating total cost of ownership for software platforms: Comparing apples, oranges, and cucumbers. *AEI-Brookings Joint Center for Regulatory Studies Series,* No. 03-7.

Putnam, L. H., & Meyers, W. (1991). *Measures for excellence: Reliable software on time, within budget* (Facsimil., p. 400). Prentice Hall PTR.

Rogers, E. M. (1995). *Diffusion of innovations, (fourth edition).* Free Press.

Sanders, J. (1998). Linux, open source, and software's future. *IEEE Software, 15*(5), 88-91.

KEY TERMS

Cost Model: A method that defines a set of cost factors—possibly interdependent—describing the financial impact of a strategic decision made or to be made. Its application results in a categorization of cost factors that suit a specific context and for a specific business.

GQM: The Goal Question Metric paradigm. A deductive instrument to derive the appropriate measures from a measurement goal (Basili *et al.*, 1994).

Hidden costs: See intangible costs.

Intangible costs: Costs that are not foreseen. They are hidden in the sense that they are not budgeted or predictable.

OSS: Open Source Software. Software whose code is available and accessible to anyone.

Productivity: The rate of work output in time. In this paper, this is measured in documents created per unit of time.

Proprietary Software: Software that are legal property of a party. Typically, the source code is not available. The use of them is in general under contractual agreements.

ROI: Return on Investments. A model of costs based on the payback of funds allocated for the investments. In the extension of (Putnam *et al.*, 1991) the return concerns funds also allocated for other purposes than a specific investment.

Tangible costs: Costs that are budgeted and foreseen by the management. They are predictable. The opposite of intangible costs

TCO: Total Cost of Ownership. The annual costs of ownership of a product averaged in a period of at least five years.

ENDNOTES

1 Transformational Government—implementation Plan. Chief Information Officer Council. Retrieved April, 2008, from http://www.cio.gov.uk/documents/pdf/transgov/transgovt.pdf

2 Gartner Group, (2003). Distributed Computing Chart of Accounts. Retrieved December 2003 from http://www.gartner.com/4_decision_tools/modeling_tools/costcat.pdf

3 PROMetric. A tool to collect software metrics, http://www.prom.case.unibz.it/

4 According to ISO data standards are "documented agreements containing technical specifications or other precise criteria to be used consistently as rules, guidelines, or definitions of characteristics, to ensure that materials, products, processes and services are fit for their purpose." Open Data standards are data standards that are standards for ensuring interoperability between different solutions that need to operate on the same data, written by super partes organizations, publically documented and freely available for adoption.

5 www.adobe.com

6 Linux ROI Return on Investment on Linux Migration/Purchase" www.linuxvalue.com/linux.xls. Retrieved in May 2007

7 http://www.cybersource.com.au/about/linux_vs_windows_tco_comparison.pdf Retrieved 16th May 2006

8 http://82.187.13.175/egep/asp/E_Home.asp

9 We measure productivity with the number of documents created per day.

10 Winslow, M., (2004). Evaluating the ROI of Open Source on the Desktop. Enterprise Linux Today. Retrieved April 2008, from http://www.linuxtoday.com/it_management/2004021902126OPBZDT%20%20com/read/43720.htm

11 This is one of the many measurement goals derivable from the business goal. The structure of the measurement goal follows the one of the GQM approach (Basili *et al.*, 1994)

12 i.e. a migration of the desktop applications

13 PROMetric. http://www.prom.case.unibz.it/

14 Transformational Government—enabled by Technology. Chief Information Officer Council. Retrieved April, 2008, from http://www.cio.gov.uk/transformational_government/strategy/

15 http://www.sap.com/index.epx

16 Capobianco, F., A Successful Business Model for Open Source Systems, keynote of the 4th International Conference on Open Source Systems (OSS 2008), Retrieved in September 2008 from http://oss2008.dti.unimi.it/.

APPENDIX A

Template questionnaire for investigating OSS migration costs. Questions in the questionnaire are determined by the Measurement Goals derived from the Business Goal_1 stated in section 3.1.1 with the use of the GQM (Basili *et al.,* 1994).

Support * *everything that is NOT software!*
1. What was the cost for searching for OSS alternatives?
2. What was the cost for searching for documentation for the chosen OSS?
3. What was the cost for installation and deployment of the OSS?
4. What was the cost for achieving technical and data compliance and interoperability of the OSS?
5. What was the cost for searching for new support contracts?
6. What was the cost for external support during the migration?

Software
7. What was the cost of the pilot project(s) (Spike solutions, feasibility analysis, ...)?
8. What was the cost for data conversion tools?
9. What was the cost for interfacing to legacy software?
10. What was the cost for software add-ons?
11. What was the cost for security tools?
12. What was the cost for upgrades (if easily traceable in the contract)?
13. Were there other costs caused by the introduction of OSS?

Staffing
14. What are the salaries of employees (by categories)?
15. What was the cost for salaries of temporary employees?
16. What was the cost for staff extra hours and bonuses caused by the migration?

Learning/Training
17. What was the cost for the IT training for the new solution?
    differentiated between guided and self learning
18. What was the cost for employees' training for the new solution?
    differentiated between guided and self learning
19. What was the cost caused by the lack of productivity?

APPENDIX B

The table below the complete lists of factors of costs whose measurement will give the answer to the questions related to migration and ownership costs. The factors of costs are the derived with the GQM from the Business Goals of section 3.1.1.

Cause	Description	Cost
Attitude	Attitude is in this study represented through the impact of user acceptance. This is the degree of perceived usefulness and ease of use with the new software applications. User acceptance is acknowledged to have a significant impact on end-users adoption of the new application and the training/learning period, thus affecting the total learning/training costs	**Learning/ Training**
Unproductive labor	Unproductive labor is defined as the learning/training period where the *end-user* as well as *IT-staff* has not received a sufficient level of knowledge to be fully productive. Unproductive labor impacts on the costs during the learning period.	
Internal training methods	Internal training methods includes conventional procedures like internal training sessions and training groups, but also peer support where the users with better knowledge of the software helps their colleagues.	
Acquisition	This is related to the full acquisition costs of the license and possible add-ons that are required throughout the product life time. This is highly specific to each organization.	**Software**
Maintenance	Maintenance is a service provided by the vendor to keep the product working during its life time. Include all costs related to the license's ongoing maintenance requirements, including annual maintenance fees and other direct expenditures towards the *vendor/producer*	
Future development path	Future development path identifies uncertainty regarding the future development of the software product. This ensures software compliance with future standards and requirements.	
Operational interoperability	A description (often graphical) of the operational elements, assigned tasks, and information flows describing the system. It defines the type of information exchanged, the frequency of the exchange, and what tasks are supported by these information exchanges. Costs here are driven by keeping the same operational interoperability after the transition.	
Technical compliance	A minimal set of rules governing the arrangement, interaction, and interdependence of the parts or elements whose purpose is to ensure that a conformant system satisfies a specific set of requirements. It identifies system services, interfaces, standards, and their relationships. Costs here are driven by keeping the same technical interoperability after the transition.	
Security	Security is the ability of a system to protect information and system resources with respect to confidentiality and integrity. Costs here are related to measure vulnerability of the system and to add security protocols/applications to the system.	
Customer loyalty programs & Contracts	Customer loyalty programs are referred to deliberate company strategy of rewarding repeat purchase and contractual agreements are referred to the legal contract set up by two partners. The cost of switching from proprietary solutions to OSS ones due to customer loyalty program and contractual agreements	
Salary	The full loaded salaries for IT-staff, including possible overhead and bonuses. Supplying competent IT staff may differ between proprietary software and Open Source. This may impact on costs.	**IT-staffing**
Attitude	Attitude is in this study represented through the impact of user acceptance. User acceptance is acknowledged to have a significant impact on end-users adoption of the new application. Reluctance here may have a big impact on costs related to the technical decision making process.	

continued on following page

APPENDIX B. CONTINUED

Cause	Description	Cost
External Fees	Fees for all external support during the adoption and use of the OSS applications.	**Support**
Search for support	All expenses included in finding suitable support for training, education, and other possible services that require external expertise.	
Specialized suppliers	Demand for new suppliers; may increase over time if capabilities are hard to find/maintain. Costs here include unpredictable external fees	
Search for alternatives	It includes the internal and external effort involved in finding alternative, suitable applications for the specific needs of the organization	
Search for documentation	It includes the internal and external effort involved in finding and creating the documentation to support OSS	

Chapter XXII
Citizen's Acceptance of Electronic Services:
A Qatari Perspective

Shafi Al-Shafi
Brunel University, UK

Vishanth Weerakkody
Brunel University, UK

ABSTRACT

The Qatari government has launched Wireless Internet Parks (iPark) concept under their national electronic government (e-government) initiative with a view of providing free internet access for all citizens while enjoying the outdoors. By offering free wireless Internet access, the Qatari government hopes to increase accessibility of e-government services and encourage their citizens to actively participate in the global information society with a view of bridging the digital divide. This research proposes an extended unified theory of acceptance and use of technology (UTAUT) model for examining the adoption and diffusion of iPark services in Qatar. A pilot survey was conducted of iPark users using an extended version of the UTAUT model to explain the intention to use. The results of a multiple regression analysis are consistent with our predictions that effort expectancy, perceived technology, and Wireless Internet trust significantly influence intention to use. Implications of these results for practice and research are discussed.

INTRODUCTION

The wireless free internet park (iPark) concept was launched in 2007 by the government of Qatar under the banner of e-government to make public services more accessible to citizens. The iPark initiative is implemented in a number of public parks and provides free connection to the citizens' Internet ready devices such as, laptop and PDA's any time of day. The first such initiative launched in the Western Asia region. The primary goal of the initiative is to increase internet usage by establishing "hot spots" in public parks (IctQATAR, 2008). There are currently three designated wireless internet hotspots throughout selected public parks in the city (ibid). This paper explores citizens' acceptance of the iPark concept as part of the e-government initiative in Qatar.

The Qatari E-government initiative was launched in 2000. In global terms the UN E-government readiness report (2008) ranked Qatar's e-government project as number 53 worldwide. As in many countries, the national e-government focus in Qatar is to achieve the highest performance in executing governmental transactions electronically, through streamlined business processes and integrated information technology solutions (IctQATAR, 2008). Moreover, the Qatari government hopes that free internet access offered through the iPark concept will encourage more citizens to use e-government services and help bridge the digital divide.

The Internet while being the primary mode of access to e-government services has not been adapted globally at the same time or rate; some countries are considered as leaders (such as the US, UK and Singapore) and others simply follow (i.e. the Arabian Gulf region) (Gupta and Gupta, 2005). More recently, wireless technologies have become a useful means of internet connectivity and access to electronic services (e-services). Wi-Fi for 'Wireless Fidelity' is a set of standards for wireless local area networks (WLAN) and provides wireless access to the Internet (Lehr and McKnight, 2003). Hotspots providing such access include Wi-Fi-cafes where services may be free to customers. In fact, a hotspot need not be limited to a confined location; as illustrated in this paper, public parks can be used to offer free wireless internet access to citizens.

In particular, Wi-Fi has opened up new opportunities for electronic commerce (e-commerce) and e-government by allowing citizens to build connectivity 24/7. Moreover, it helps to increase accessibility of services and to expand social, government and business networks. The European Commission estimated Wi-Fi users to be around 125 million worldwide in the year 2006, and that there will be more than 500 million Wi-Fi users worldwide by 2009 (JiWire, 2006). However, wireless security remains mostly important factor that challenges wireless internet hot spots. As Wi-Fi grows the security threat also increases rapidly and therefore the need to protect information becomes imperative (Peikari and Fogie, 2003). The security risk remains largely from hackers, who are individuals, that access into the system without any authorization and for personal gain.

Given the above context, the rationale for this research is to gain a better understanding about the free wireless internet park "iPark" initiative in Qatar. Using a pilot survey questionnaire, this study aims to explore the intention of citizens to use iPark services in Qatar. This is achieved by examining their perceptions of 'Ease of Use' and 'Usefulness' in relation to internet access in the iPark. To pursue this line of inquiry, this research uses Unified Theory of Acceptance and Use of Technology (UTAUT). UTAUT theorizes that an individual's behavioural intention to use a technology is determined by performance expectancy, effort expectancy, social influence, and facilitating conditions (Venkatesh et al., 2003).

The paper is structured as followed. In the next section a literature perspective of e-government is offered followed by an outline of the theoretical model used for the research. Then the empirical background to the research is presented. This is followed by the methodology used for the research and a presentation of the empirical results. Finally the paper concludes by analyzing the empirical results, discussing the research implications and identifying areas for future research.

E-GOVERNMENT ADOPTION AND DIFFUSION: A LITERATURE PERSPECTIVE

With the popularity of e-government growing, various researchers have offered different definitions to explain the concept (Seifert and Petersen, 2002). However, these definitions differ according to the varying e-government focus and are usually centered on technology, business, citizen, government, process, or a functional perspective. (Wassenaar, 2000; Wimmer and Traunmuller, 2000; Bonham *et al.*, 2001; Seifert and Petersen, 2002; Zhiyuan, 2002; and Irani *et al.*, 2006). The definition considered to be most suitable for the purpose of this paper is one that defines e-government as making full use of the potential of technology to help put its citizens at the centre of the e-services provided and which makes its citizens its intention (Waller *et al.*, 2001)

Like e-business, e-government promises to deliver a number of benefits to citizens, businesses and governments. The most significant benefits of e-government, according to the literature, are delivering electronic and integrated public services through a single point of access to public services 24 hours a day, seven days a week (Reffat, 2003); bridging the digital divide so that every citizen in society will be offered the same type of information and services from government (InfoDev, 2002); rebuilding customer relationships by providing value-added and personalized services to citizens (Davison et al., 2005); fostering economic development and helping local businesses to expand globally; and creating a more participative form of government by encouraging online debating, voting and exchange of information (Reynolds and Regio, 2001; Bonham et al., 2001; InfoDev, 2002; and Davison, et al., 2005).

Like any other new technology or organisational concept, the introduction of e-government to a country will also result in a number of challenges for the citizens and the government alike (Margetts and Dunleavy, 2002; Seifert and Petersen, 2002; Zakareya and Irani, 2005). Lack of access to e-services (Chircu and Lee, 2005), security concerns (Harris and Schwartz, 2000), trust (Al-Sebie and Irani, 2005), individual differences (Reffat, 2003) and digital divide (Carter and Bèlanger, 2005; Chen et al., 2006) are challenges that can impact on participation and thereby obstruct the further take-up of e-government services.

From the aforementioned, this research will focus particularly on the influence that technology complexity and Wireless Internet trust have on the intention to use a new technology, in this instance iPark. Similarly it will also examine the influence performance expectancy and effort expectancy that have on the intention to use such services.

In terms of adoption and diffusion, several studies have explored e-government acceptance in the United States (Carter and Belanger, 2005; Carter et al., 2008) and the U.K (Choudrie and Dwivedi, 2005). However, no studies exist that examine factors that influence Qatari citizens' adoption of e-government services. In this respect Lee et *al.*, (2005) state that cross-national research on e-government is sparse in the literature and Dwivedi et *al.*, (2006) highlights the need for studies that investigate the adoption rate and behaviour of e-services. Given this context, this study attempts to address this gap in a Qatari perspective by integrating the aforementioned constructs from the Unified Theory of Acceptance and Use of Technology (UTAUT).

TECHNOLOGY ADOPTION: A THEORETICAL BACKGROUND

Researchers in the field of Information Systems and Technology have for long been interested in investigating the theories and models that have the power in predicting and explaining behaviour (Venkatesh et al, 2003). Within this extensive area of research, some literature focuses on intention to use technology. Venkatesh et al., (2003) introduced the Unified Theory of Acceptance and Use of Technology (UTAUT) model and the aim of the model was to understand intention/usage as the dependent variable.

The UTAUT model consists of eight theoretical models: the theory of reasoned action (Davis et al. 1989) , the technology acceptance model (Davis ,1989) , the motivational model(Davis et al., 1992), the theory of planned behaviour (Ajzen, 1991), a model combining the technology acceptance model and the theory of planned behaviour(Taylor and Todd 1995)., the model of PC utilization(Thompson et al., 1991), the innovation diffusion theory(Rogers, 1995) , and the social cognitive theory(Compeau and Higgins, 1995) . The UTAUT model combine of the previous eight theoretical models and is made up of four core determinants of usage intention (Venkatesh et al., 2003). Venkatesh et al., (2003) have tested the unified theoretical model in four different organizational settings for a period of six months and the study showed significant predicts intention (performance expectancy, effort expectancy, social influence, and facilitating conditions), Whereas attitude toward using technology, self-efficacy, and anxiety are theorised not to be direct determinants of intention.

CONCEPTUAL MODEL AND HYPOTHESIS

From the aforementioned factors that make up UTAUT, this research utilized two independent variables (performance expectancy, effort expectancy) together with two additional independent factors (technology complexity and wireless internet trust) and one dependant factor (intention to use) to formulate the research model used for the study.

Performance expectancy is defined as the degree to which individuals believe that using a system will help them improve their job performance and contains five variables: Performance Expectancy, extrinsic motivation, job-fit, relative advantage, and outcome expectations (Venkatesh et al., 2003).

Effort expectancy is the degree of ease associated with the use of the system (Venkatesh et al., 2003). Venkatesh et al., (2003) identify three constructs from the eight models that make up the concept of effort expectancy: perceived ease of use, complexity, and ease of use.

Technology complexity in terms of this research is defined as wireless internet speed or response time. The adoption and diffusion of Wireless hotspots will depend very much on the speed of Internet connection. Moreover, according to Pew Internet and American Life Project (2006), Wi-Fi has the potential to reshape customers' needs and conversely customers can reshape the technology.

Wireless Internet trust according to June et al., (2003) refers to a complex social phenomenon that reflects technological, behavioural, social, psychological, and organisational aspects. In this context, security and privacy are two key factors that influence Wireless Internet trust. Wireless internet security will be of greater threat compared to wired internet (ibid). Therefore, a high level of confidence and trust among all users about the Wireless Internet security will be the basis of a successful iPark initiation; in this context, ensuring the privacy of individuals will be a salient issue).

Based on the aforementioned and the theoretical context offered, this paper will test the strength of the hypothesized relationships mentioned in

Figure 1. Proposed research model

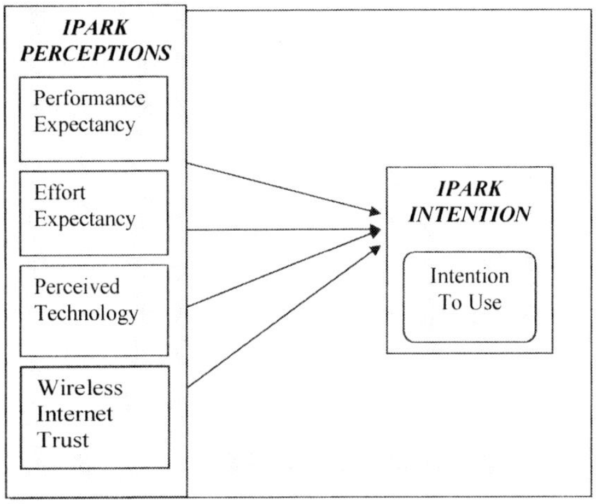

Table 1. Research hypothesis

NO.	Hypothesis
H1:	Effort Expectancy (EE) will have a positive effect on intention to use.
H2:	Performance Expectancy (PE) will have a positive effect on intention to use.
H3:	Perceived Technology will have a positive effect on intention to use.
H4:	Wireless Internet trust will have a positive effect on intention to use.

the theoretical model outlined in Figure 1 and the appropriateness of the model in predicting users' intention to use iPark in the State of Qatar.

RESEARCH METHODOLOGY

To explore the argument set out above and understand the context of the iPark initiative in Qatar, brief informal open-ended interviews (Yin, 1994) were conducted with three citizens and one Academic in the last quarter of 2007. The interviews lasted around 30 minutes and provided the context to formulate a detailed survey questionnaire that was to be used to investigate the citizens' perceptions of iPark in Qatar.

After the questionnaire was designed, a limited testing was done using one researcher and four practitioners. This was important to improve the questions and to test respondents' comprehension and clarity before the actual survey was administered (Saunders *et al.*, 2002). The pilot testing led to the removal of one question and modification to another.

The protocol followed for data collection was as follows. First, one of the researchers approached the iPark users, identified himself and provided a brief description of the research and the main purpose of the questionnaire. Then, the process of completing the questionnaire began by distributing the questionnaire to users and briefly explaining the contents of the questionnaire. Thereafter the questionnaires were collected after a period of around 20 to 30 minutes.

The survey questionnaire was distributed to a total of 55 iPark users between the period of November and December 2007; 54 usable responses were obtained. Overall, a survey questionnaire approach was selected as it is inexpensive, less time consuming and has the ability to provide both quantitative scale and qualitative data from a large research sample (Cornford and Smithson, 1997). The questionnaire used had 26 closed-ended questions and used likert scale type (5-point scale) questions (Saunders et al., 2002). Questions were compiled from (IT) adoption literature to represent the constructs in the proposed research model (fig. 2) and wording of the questionnaire was modified to fit the research context.

DATA ANALYSIS

The proposed model consists of four independent variables, Performance Expectancy; Effort Expectancy, Wireless Internet Trust and Technology complexity in terms of Internet speed/response time and one dependent variable, intention to use.

To check the responses of these questions, the first stage consisted of checking the responses and tagging them with a unique number.

The authors generated the descriptive statistics (percentage and tables) and used Linear Regression analysis by utilising SPSS (Version 15.0). Descriptive data analysis provides the reader with an appreciation of the actual numbers and values, and hence the scale that researchers are dealing with (Dwivedi and Weerakkody, 2007).

RESEARCH FINDINGS

The State of Qatar where this research was conducted is a peninsula with a strategic position at the centre of the west coast of the Arabian Gulf. The total land area is approximately 11,437 sq km. The population estimated to be around 1,500,000 (The Peninsula, 2008); however, only a minority of the population is citizens by birth, while the rest are residents who live or work in Qatar and are not Qatari's by birth (Al-Shafi and Weerakkody, 2008). Of these 54 usable respondents, 15% were females while 85% were males. Also, of the 54 respondents, 74% had internet connections in their home/work or both.

When examining the 'Effort Expectancy' of iPark services, 85% of the respondents mentioned that they found the service was easy for them, while 15% thought otherwise.

In terms of education, the majority of respondents (38%) hold postgraduate degrees (Masters and PhD), 36% hold undergraduate level qualifications and 26% hold secondary school certificates.

As far as age, the results revealed that the majority of respondents (38%) were found in the age group of 31-45, followed by the age group of 19-30 constituting around 32% of the total respondents. In contrast, the younger groups (less than 18) and older age groups (46-60) consisted together of 30% of the total respondents.

Additionally, the study shows that the majority of respondents used iPark for: emails (76%); chat (35%); e-government services (22%); Fun (43%); Research (22%); News (56%); Enquiry (26%); Downloading Information (54%); and other (6%).

As found in the study, the average scores for respondents' Effort Expectancy ranged from 4.07 to 4.37. Descriptive statistics show that these scores are quite high. For Performance Expectancy, the score ranged from 3.85 and 4.54, which is quite high. Concerning technology complexity and wireless Internet trust, the score ranged from 2.87 to 3.70, indicating that the scale is average. The last score ranged from 3.30 to 3.72 for intention to use, indicating that the scale is average.

RELIABILITY TEST

Cronbach's coefficient alpha values were chosen to examine the internal consistency of the measure (Hinton et al., 2004) (table 2). Cronbach's results varied between 8.26 for the intention to use and 8.40 for the Technology complexity and also for the Wireless Internet trust.

Hinton et al., (2004) have suggested four different points of reliability, excellent ranges (0.90 and above), high (0.70- 0.90), high moderate (0.50-0.70) and low (0.50 and below). The previous mentioned values show that all of the constructs got high reliability within Table 2. The high Cronbach's values of the constructs means that constructs were internally consistent and the reliability is measuring the same construct.

Table-3 also shows that the correlation is significant to these key factors, *Effort expectancy (0.417), perceived technology (0.405), and Wire-*

Table 2. Reliability of measurements

Constructs	Number of items	Cronbach's Alpha (a)
Effort Expectancy	4	0.83
Performance Expectancy	4	0.83
Technology Complexity	1	0.84
Wireless Internet trust	1	0.84
Intention To Use	2	0.83

Table 3. Correlations

Key Factors		Intention To Use
Effort expectancy	Pearson Correlation	.417(**)
	Sig. (2-tailed)	.002
Performance Expectancy	Pearson Correlation	.258
	Sig. (2-tailed)	.060
Perceived Technology	Pearson Correlation	.405(**)
	Sig. (2-tailed)	.002
Wireless Internet trust	Pearson Correlation	.455(**)
	Sig. (2-tailed)	.001

** Correlation is significant at the 0.01 level (2-tailed).
* Correlation is significant at the 0.05 level (2-tailed).

less Internet trust (0.455). Whereas, the fourth key factor Performance Expectancy (0.258) was found to have insignificant impact.

REGRESSION ANALYSIS: FACTORS INFLUENCING THE INTENTION TO USE IPARK.

A regression analysis was conducted with the use of iPark channels as dependant variable and Effort Expectancy, Performance Expectancy, perceived technology, and Wireless Internet trust as predictor variables. From a total of 54 cases that were analysed a significant model emerged {F (4, 54) =7.101, p < .001} (Table-4). The second significant statistic that was obtained from the analysis is the R^2, which ranges from 0 to 1, with 1 being a perfect fit model. It was found that R^2= 0.377 for this analysis. This factor explains 38% of the changes in the intention to use iPark. Other unidentified factors account for the remaining 62%. The R^2 of 38 (38%) is considered as a good value for a cross-sectional data involving many predictor variables.

Also, Table 4 shows that of all the factors, the following have no significant impact on intention to use iPark: Effort Expectancy (β = 0.093, p= 0.489); Performance Expectancy (β = 0.171, p= 0.243); perceived technology (β = 0.262, p= 0.041); and Wireless Internet trust (β = 0.362, p= 0.005).

FUTURE TRENDS

This research describes an early attempt to study the adoption of the iPark initiative by Qatari citizens and thus represents only the views of a limited sample of users (54). To ensure more thorough testing of the hypothesis proposed in this research, the authors have planned future research to survey a larger number of iPark users.

DISCUSSION AND CONCLUSION

This paper discussed the results of a survey targeted towards iPark users in Qatar and it provides a representative account of the citizens' perceptions of the iPark project. While the availability and use of Wi-Fi networks continue to increase, for users, Wi-Fi facilitates greater mobility, information access, and flexibility in connectivity, improved efficiency, low cost, ease of use, and new applications, which could change the way they access electronic services.

The results of this research showed that the correlation is significant to three key factors: Effort expectancy, perceived technology, and

Table 4. Regression analysis results

			ANOVA			
Model		Sum of Squares	df	Mean Square	F	Sig.
1		25.266	4	6.317	7.101	.000(a)
			Regression	Model		
Model	R	R Square	Adjusted R Square			
1	.614(a)	.377	.324		1	
	Factors	Affecting	Intention To Use	iPark		
Intention To Use iPark Factors		Beta	Standardised Beta		T Statistics	Significance
(Constant)		.069			.083	.934
Effort Expectancy		.103	.093		.697	.489
Performance Expectancy		.244	.171		1.183	.243
Perceived Technology		.312	.262		2.100	.041
Wireless Internet trust		.330	.362		2.979	.005

Predictors: (Constant), Effort Expectancy, Performance Expectancy, Perceived Technology, and Wireless Internet trust
Dependent Variable: Intention To Use.

Wireless Internet trust. Whereas, the fourth key factor Performance Expectancy was found to have insignificant impact with the Intention to use. Also, the research showed that Effort Expectancy, Performance Expectancy, Perceived Technology, and Wireless Internet trust have a positive relationship with the Intention to use. Given these findings, it can be concluded that the iPark initiative in Qatar has been successful initially in promoting wider access to the Internet. This is encouraging from an e-government perspective. The authors suggest that public parks (iParks) can be used to advertise and market the Qatari e-government national website and raise e-government awareness among Qatari citizens. While the research findings are encouraging from a practical perspective for the Qatari government, from a theoretical perspective these results reconfirm that technology acceptance is influenced by key constructs such as Effort Expectancy, technology complexity, and Wireless Internet trust aspects of the services used.

REFERENCES

Ajzen, I. (1991). The theory of planned behavior. *Organizational Behavior and Human Decision Processes, 50*(2), 179-211.

Al-Shafi, S., & Weerakkody, V. (2008). *Adoption of wireless internet parks: An empirical study in Qatar.* Paper presented at the Proceedings of the European and Mediterranean Conference on Information systems (EMCIS08), Dubai, UAE.

Al-Sebie, M., & Irani, Z. (2005). Technical and organisational challenges facing transactional e-government systems: An empirical study. *Electronic Government, An International Journal, 2*(3), 247–276.

Bonham, G., Seifert, J., & Thorson, S. (2001). *The transformational potential of e-government: The role of politic leadership.* Paper presented at the 4th Pan European International Relations Conference of the European Consortium for Political Research, University of Kent, Canterbury, UK.

Carter, L., & Bélanger, F. (2005). The utilization of e-government services: Citizen trust, innovation, and acceptance factors. *Information Systems Journal, 15*, 5-26.

Carter, L., Schaupp, L., & Evans, A. (2008). Antecedents to e-file adoption: The U.S. perspective. *Hawaii International Conference on System Sciences, Proceedings of the 41st Annual* (216-216).

Chen, C., Tseng, S., & Huang, H. (2006). A comprehensive study of the digital divide phenomenon in Taiwanese government agencies. *International Journal of Internet and Enterprise Management, 4*(3), 244-256.

Chircu, A. M., & Lee, D. H-D. (2005). E-Government: Key success factors for value discovery and realisation. *E-Government, an International Journal, 2*(1), 11-25.

Choudrie, J., & Dwivedi, Y. (2005). A survey of citizens adoption and awareness of e-government initiatives. The government gateway: A United Kingdom perspective. E-Government workshop. Brunel University, West London.

Compeau, D. R., & Higgins, C. A. (1995). Computer self-efficacy: Development of a measure and initial test. *MIS Quarterly, 19*(2), 189-211.

Cornford, T., & Smithson, S. (1997). *Project research in information systems: A student's guide*. London: Macmillan Press.

Davis, F. D., Bagozzi, R. P., & Warshaw, P. R. (1992). Extrinsic and intrinsic motivation to use computers in the workplace. *Journal of Applied Social Psychology, 22*(14), 1111-1132.

Davis, F. D. (1989). Perceived usefulness, perceived ease of use, and user acceptance of information technology. *MIS Quarterly, 13*(3), 319-339.

Davis, F. D., Bagozzi, R. P., & Warshaw, P. R. (1989). User acceptance of computer technology: A comparison of two theoretical models. *Management Science, 35*(8), 982-1003.

Davison, R. M., Wagner, C., & Ma, L.C. (2005). From government to e-government: A transition model. *Information Technology & People, 18*(3), 280-299.

Dwivedi, Y., & Weerakkody, V. (2007). Examining the factors affecting the adoption of broadband in the Kingdom of Saudi Arabia. *Electronic Government, an International Journal, 4*(1), 43-58.

Dwivedi, Y., Papazafeiropoulou, A., & Gharavi, H. (2006). Socioeconomic determinants of adoption of the government gateway initiative in the UK. *Electronic Government, 3*(4), 404-419.

Gupta, V., & Gupta, S. (2005). Experiments in wireless Internet security. *Statistical Methods in Computer Security.*

Harris, J. F., & Schwartz, J. (2000, June 22). Antidrug Web site tracks visitors. *Washington Post*, 23.

Hinton, P. R., Brownlow, C., McMurvay, I., & Cozens, B. (2004). *SPSS explained*. East Sussex, England: Routledge Inc.

IctQatar. (2008). *Free wireless internet in Qatar's public parks*. Retrieved from http://www.ict.gov.qa/output/page422.asp

InfoDev. (2002). The e-government handbook for developing countries. Retrieved from http://www.cdt.org/egov/handbook

Irani, Z., Al-Sebie, M., & Elliman, T. (2006). *Transaction stage of e-government systems: Identification of its location & importance*. Paper presented at the Proceedings of the 39th Hawaii International Conference on System Science, Hawaii.

Jiwire (2006). JiWire launches worldwide point-of-connection wi-fi hotspot advertising network. Retrieved from http://www.jiwire.com/about/announcements/press-advertising-network.htm

June, L., Chun-Sheng, Y., Chang, L., & James, E. (2003). Technology acceptance model for wireless

Internet. *Internet Research: Electronic Networking Application and Policy,13*(3), 206-222.

Lee, S. M., Tan, X., & Trimi, S. (2005). Current practices of leading e-government countries. *Communications of the ACM, 48*(10), 99-104.

Lehr, W., & McKnight, L. W. (2003). Wireless Internet access: 3G vs. WiFi? *Telecommunications Policy, 27*, 351-370.

Margetts, H., & Dunleavy, P. (2002). *Cultural barriers to e-government. Working Paper.* University Collage of London and London School of Economics for National Audit Office.

Peikari, C., & Fogie, S. (2003). *Maximum wireless security.* Retrieved from http://www.berr.gov.uk/files/file9972.pdf

Pew Internet & American Life Project. (2006). Home broadband adoption. Retrieved from http://www.pewinternet.org/pdfs/PIP_Broadband_trends2006.pdf

Reffat, R. (2003). *Developing a successful e-government. Working Paper.* University Of Sydney, Australia.

Reynolds, M. M., & Regio-Micro, M. (2001). *The purpose of transforming government: E-Government as a catalyst in the information age. Microsoft E-Government Initiatives.* Retrieved from http://www.netcaucus.org/books/egov2001/pdf/EGovIntr.pdf

Rogers, E. (1995). *Diffusion of innovations.* New York: Free Press.

Saunders, M., Lewis, P., & Thornhill, A. (2002). *Research methods for business students,Third edition.* Harlow: Prentice Hall.

Seifert, J., & Petersen, E. (2002). The promise of all things E? Expectations and challenges of emergent e-government. *Perspectives on Global Development and Technology, 1*(2), 193-213.

Taylor, S., & Todd, P. A. (1995). Assessing IT usage: The role of prior experience. *MIS Quarterly, 19*(2), 561-570.

The Peninsula Newspaper. (2008). Bursting at the seams. Retrieved from http://www.thepeninsulaqatar.com/Display_news.asp?section=Local_News&month=January2008&file=Local_News200801296298.xml

Thompson, R. L., Higgins, C. A., & Howell, J. M. (1991). Personal computing: Toward a conceptual model of utilization. *MIS Quarterly, 15*(1), 124-143.

UN. (2008). *World public sector report: UN e-government survey: From e-government To connected governance.* New York.

Venkatesh, V., Morris, M., Davis, G., & Davis, F. (2003). User acceptance of information technology: Toward a unified view. *MIS Quarterly, 27*(3), 425-478.

Waller, P., Livesey, P., & Edin, K. (2001). E-Government in the service of democracy. *ICA Information, 74.*

Wassenaar, A. (2000). E-Governmental value chain models. *DEXA* (pp. 289-293). IEEE Press.

Wimmer, M., & Traunmuller, R. (2000). *Trends in e-government: Managing distributed knowledge.* Paper presented at the Proceedings from 11th International Workshop on Database and Expert Systems Applications, New York.

Yin, R. K. (1994). *Case study research - design and methods, second edition.* London: Sage Publications.

Zakareya, E., & Irani, Z. (2005). E-Government adoption: Architecture and barriers. *Business Process Management Journal, 11*(5), 589-611.

Zhiyuan, F. (2002), E-Government in digital era: Concepts, practice, and development. *International Journal Of The Computer, The Internet and Management, 10*(2), 1-22.

Chapter XXIII
E-File Adoption:
Diffusion, Experience, and Trust

Lemuria D. Carter
North Carolina A&T State University, USA

Ludwig Christian Schaupp
West Virginia University, USA

ABSTRACT

In the United States (U.S.), Congress has set ambitious goals for the diffusion of several e-government initiatives. One of congress' recent goals was to significantly increase the percentage of tax and informational returns filed electronically. This chapter proposes a model of e-file adoption that integrates diffusion of innovation theory, online trust, and e-government experience into a comprehensive view of e-file acceptance. To test the model we administered a survey to 260 graduate and undergraduate students. The results of multiple linear regression analysis indicate that the proposed model explains 76% of the variance in intention to use an e-file system. Relative advantage, compatibility, trust of the government, trust of the Internet, e-filing in the past year, and previous completion of an e-government transaction all had a positive impact on e-file adoption. Implications for practice and research are discussed.

INTRODUCTION

An enormous amount of money has been spent on e-government services worldwide. However, to date the results have been hard to measure and disappointing by most measures. One thing that has become inherently clear is that setting up e-government systems simply to duplicate brick and mortar equivalents is a tremendous waste of citizens' time and money. An efficient effective e-government service is designed with the user in mind, not the bureaucrat. E-government is not all about the technology, it involves rethinking and redesigning the way government operates. One issue that has continued to elude government agencies in their quest for e-government adoption is the need for cohesive multi-channel distribution. It should not make a difference whether a citizen contacts the government agency via the internet, telephone, in person, or in writing; they outcome should be the same and it should be done in an efficient and effective manner (Economist 2008).

To date, e-government websites have been more about quantity than they have about quality. In contrast, e-commerce has been a resounding a success by any measure of success. E-commerce has transformed industries, such as travel. However, in contrast e-government initiatives have not seen nearly the success and to date has only proven to be extremely expensive. The underlying issue to date has not necessarily been a problem of design, but utilization. The key to successful e-government, are systems that are utilized and meet users' needs. Several countries are making efforts to meet these needs through transformational government. According to the Transformational Government Annual Report published by the Cabinet Office in the United Kingdom (UK), public services are being redesigned to enhance Website rationalization, shared services and customer satisfaction. Regarding Website rationalization, more than 900 government websites have been scheduled for closure to make it easier for people to find information online. In terms of shared services, over half of UK government employees participate in shared corporate services. Finally, the public sector has adapted new best practice standards to improve customer satisfaction (Cabinet 2008).

One of the greatest benefits of e-government is convenient access to information and services. It just as well could be referred to as i-government, where "i" stands for information. Before the Internet, getting information from any aspect of the government could prove to be quite a feat. Getting the right form and finding out how to fill it out almost always involved going to the post office, writing a letter, enclosing a self-addressed stamped envelope, or even going to a government office and waiting in line to speak to someone. The information came at a cost, paid for by your time, effort, and in some cases fees.

Today, governments in almost all advanced countries house virtually all documents intended for the public online (somewhere in cyberspace). This gives the citizen access to almost anything they might want. It goes without saying that simply providing information online is no guarantee of good e-government (being able to download a form does not mean that it gets filled out correctly and sent to the right place). Making the right forms readily available is only part of it, getting citizens to adopt the e-services has proven to be the real challenge.

According to Brown University's annual Global e-Government Study the United States (U.S.) ranked fourth out of 198 countries surveyed in global e-government (Fletcher 2002). A flagship project in the U.S. is usa.gov, which is critically acclaimed as the best single e-government website in the world. Its sole purpose is to provide information to citizens including links to over 100 online services, including links to renew a passport, download visa forms, etc. One electronic service that is receiving a great deal of attention beyond simply posting information on the web: e-filing. The electronic filing of income tax returns (the e-file program) has grown into a Congressional initiative, however, its outright adoption by citizens has not yet been fully achieved. E-filing has the potential to improve the overall process of tax filing for the individual filer while at the same time reducing the cost to both taxpayers and tax collection agencies (Fu, Farn et al. 2006).

E-file services have been implemented with the goal of easing the burden on the taxpayer and increase compliance through the innovative use of technology (IRS 2004). The Internal Revenue Service (IRS) has a documented goal in which any exchange or transaction that currently occurs in person, over the phone or in writing can be accomplished electronically. In response, congress set a goal of having 80% of all tax and informational returns filed electronically by 2007 (IRS 2004). The use of IRS endorsed e-file systems has continued to grow over the last couple of years with 52.9 million individual returns being filed in 2003, approximately 68 million in 2005 (VanDenburgh and Harmelink 2006), and approximately 73 million in 2006 (Cornish 2007). However, this still only accounts for a little more than 50% of the total number of returns. Thus, the government has fallen well short of the 80% goal and outright adoption by citizens remains elusive for the IRS.

For all practical purposes the e-file program has largely been considered to be an e-government success story. The e-file program began in 1986 as a pilot project by the IRS and H&R Block in three cities: Cincinnati, Phoenix, and Raleigh-Durham, NC. 25,000 tax returns were filed electronically that year. In 1990, the e-file program went nationwide and has enjoyed tremendous growth. Yet, despite the impressive growth the IRS and Congress have not reached their published goal of 80% of all returns being filed electronically. In fact we are still well short of that goal.

The objectives of this chapter are:

1. To identify the impact of diffusion of innovation factors on e-file adoption
2. To identify the impact of online trust perceptions on e-file adoption
3. To identify the impact of e-experience factors on e-file adoption

Building on previous technology acceptance studies, we develop a model aimed at further understanding U.S. taxpayers' intention to use an e-file system. Specifically, a survey is conducted to examine taxpayers' intentions to use an IRS endorsed e-file system. This study posits that by integrating literature on diffusion of innovation, online trust and e-experience researchers can gain a more comprehensive understanding of e-file adoption. In particular, we explore the impact of adoption factors, online trust factors and e-experience factors on intention to e-file. The remainder of this paper is organized as follows: first, the background literature is presented; then, the research model and hypotheses are illustrated; next the methodology is discussed; finally the results, implications and suggestions for future research are presented.

BACKGROUND

Technology Adoption

Davis' (1989) technology acceptance model (TAM) and Rogers' (2003) diffusion of innovation theory (DOI) are two models commonly used to study user adoption of information systems. TAM, which is based on the theory of reasoned action (TRA), has two major constructs: perceived usefulness (PU) and perceived ease of use (PEOU)—which influence one's intention to use a system. Perceived usefulness was originally defined by Davis as the belief that using a particular system would enhance one's job performance. Perceived ease of use refers to one's perceptions of the amount of effort required to use the system. The model predicts that higher perceptions of usefulness and ease of use will increase intention to use a system. All other things being equal, perceived ease of use is predicted to influence perceived usefulness, since the easier a system is to use, the more useful it can be (Davis, 1989).

Unlike TAM, which refers specifically to technology adoption, Rogers (2003) conceptualizes a generic theory of adoption: the diffusion of innovation theory (DOI). An innovation refers to a new idea, concept, object, or in this case, I-voting. Diffusion refers to the dissemination of an innovation into society. Rogers' theory identifies five constructs that influence a potential adopter's decision: relative advantage, complexity, compatibility, trialability and observability. Relative advantage refers to the belief that a new system has benefits above and beyond the current system. Complexity refers to perceptions of difficulty associated with adopting a system. Compatibility posits that one will be more likely to adopt an innovation if it is consistent with his values, views, beliefs, and customs. Trialability posits that one will be more likely to adopt an innovation if he/she can try it out before actually committing to it. And observability suggests that one will be more likely to adopt an innovation if its benefits are visible and tangible. TAM constructs are included in the DOI model. Perceived ease of use is represented by complexity and perceived usefulness is captured by relative advantage (Plouffe, et al., 2001; Venkatesh, et al., 2003). Venkatesh et al. (2003) introduces UTAUT—the unified technology acceptance and usage theory—which combines eight behavioral models, including TAM and DOI. In their study, Venkatesh et al. test each model individually and report that both TAM and DOI (referred to as IDT in their study) explain 38 percent of the variance in intention to use an information system in a voluntary setting.

Venkatesh et al. (2003) also compare the constructs of TAM and DOI in the Unified Theory of Acceptance and Use of Technology (UTAUT). The UTAUT model is comprised of eight theoretical models: the theory of reasoned action (TRA), the technology acceptance model (TAM), the motivational model, the theory of planned behavior (TPB), a model combining the technology acceptance model and the theory of planned behavior, the model of PC utilization, the innovation diffusion theory, and the social cognitive theory.

Regarding the plethora of adoption models, the IS literature posits that three adoption constructs -relative advantage, compatibility and complexity—are among the most relevant constructs to technology adoption research (Agarwal, 1998; Benbasat and Barki, 2007; Tornatzky and Klein, 1982; Van Slyke, et al., 2004). Hence, we include the aforementioned diffusion factors in our model.

Online Trust

Definitions of trust abound in the literature. One frequently utilized definition is that presented by Rotter (1967). The author draws from social learning theory and defines trust as an expectancy that the promise of another can be relied upon. Rotter's research is referenced in numerous studies of trust (Mayer et al. 1995; Zucker, 1986). Trust of electronic services has been explored extensively in both e-commerce (Gefen and Straub, 2002; Gefen et al., 2003; Jarvenpaa et al., 2000; McKnight et al. 2002; Pavlou 2003; Tan and Theon, 2001; Van Slyke et al., 2004) and e-government (Carter and Bélanger, 2005; Gefen et al. 2005; Welch et al., 2004; Warkentin et al. 2002).

It has been suggested that there are two targets of trust: the entity providing the service (party trust) and the mechanism through which it is provided (control trust) (Tan and Theon, 2001). Thus, users should consider both the characteristics of the Web vendor and characteristics of the supporting technological infrastructure before using an electronic-service (Pavlou 2003). Trust in e-government is therefore composed of the traditional view of trust in a specific entity (trust of the government) as well as trust in the reliability of the enabling technology (trust of the Internet) (Carter et al. 2005; Pavlou 2003).

E-Experience

In addition to the aforementioned factors, the literature indicates that demographic variables also have an important impact on technology adoption (Corey and Garand 2002; Venkatesh et al. 2003). Research suggests that frequency of Internet use and previous completion of electronic transactions can have a positive impact on one's intention to use an e-government transaction (Belanger and Carter 2006). We posit the three electronic experiences will have a significant impact on e-file adoption; e-filing in the past year, previous completion of an e-commerce transaction and previous completion of an e-government transaction.

MAIN FOCUS OF THE CHAPTER

Research Model & Hypotheses

Based on the aforementioned literature, we propose the following research model (see Figure 1). Intention to use an e-file system is influenced by three technology adoption factors—relative advantage, compatibility and complexity–three e-experience factors—e-commerce, e-government, and e-file usage—and two trust factors—trust of the government and trust of the Internet.

The research hypotheses are presented in Table 1.

Methodology

To obtain study participants, an e-mail announcement was sent to MBA students, masters' level and upper level accounting students. Each survey participant was provided a link to a Web-based survey, which provided data validation controls ensuring a selection was made for all questions. To encourage participation an mp3 player was

Figure 1. Proposed e-file adoption model

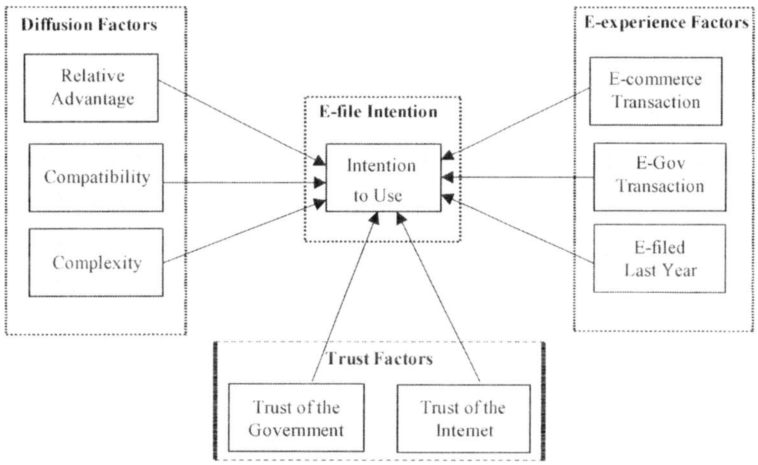

Table 1. Research Hypotheses

No.	Hypothesis
Diffusion of Innovation	
H1.	Relative Advantage (RA) will have a positive effect on intention to use.
H2.	Compatibility (CMP) will have a positive effect on intention to use.
H3.	Complexity (CLX) will have a negative effect on intention to use.
Online Trust	
H4.	Trust of the Government (TOG) will have a positive effect on intention to use.
H5.	Trust of the Internet (TOI) will have a positive effect on intention to use.
E-experience	
H6.	Previous completion of an e-commerce transaction (Ecom) will have a positive effect on intention to use.
H7.	Previous completion of an e-government transaction (Egov) will have a positive effect on intention to use.
H8.	Previous completion of an e-file transaction (Efil) will have a positive effect on intention to use.

randomly given away to a participant. The survey questions were aimed at assessing their perceptions of the dependent and independent variables. Demographic questions were included last on the survey, as fatigue effects would have less influence on them. All surveys were confidential and no identifying personal information was required. The results were analyzed using multiple linear regression in SPSS 15.0.

Sample

The survey was completed by 260 MBA, upper level and graduate accounting students. 53 % of the participants were female. The sample's age ranged from 18-54; 83% of the sample was in the 18-24 age group. 89% were Caucasians. 93% have completed an e-commerce transaction and 71% have completed an e-government transaction. 34% of the respondents used an e-file system last year.

Instrument Development

To investigate users' intentions to use an IRS endorsed e-file system, a questionnaire based data gathering technique was utilized. Questions were compiled from validated instruments (Carter and Belanger 2005, Fu et al. 2006, Pavlou 2003). Wording was modified to fit the e-filing context. The resulting items for each construct were then included in random order on the survey instrument. Questions were measured on a 7-point Likert-type scale, ranging form 1 (strongly disagree) to 7 (strongly agree). The instrument is available from the authors upon request.

Items were tested for reliability using Cronbach's alpha. The reliability analysis is presented below in Table 2.

Factor analysis was conducted using principal component analysis with promax rotation. Items loaded on the proper factors. The loadings are presented in Table 3.

Table 2. Reliability analysis

Construct	# Items	Reliability
Relative Advantage (RA)	3	.764
Compatibility (CMP)	4	.893
Complexity (CLX)	3	.845
Trust of the Government (TOG)	5	.884
Trust of the Internet (TOI)	4	.828
Intention to Use (USE)	5	.892

Table 3. Factor Loadings

Item	RA	CMP	CLX	TOG	TOI	USE
RA1	.888					
RA2	.754					
RA3	.601					
CMP1		.780				
CMP2		.709				
CMP3		.631				
CMP4		.700				
CLX1			.874			
CLX2			.844			
CLX3			.720			
TOG1				.880		
TOG2				.803		
TOG3				.874		
TOG4				.726		
TOG5				.800		
TOI1					.885	
TOI2					.768	
TOI3					.829	
TOI4					.713	
USE1						.894
USE2						.912
USE3						.889
USE4						.608
USE5						.855

Data Analysis

The research model was tested using multiple linear regression analysis. Regression analysis is used to relate a dependent variable to a set of independent variables. The goal of this study is to determine the relationship between use intentions (dependent variable) and citizens' perceptions of electronic filing systems (independent variables). The model includes eight independent variables relative advantage, compatibility, complexity, trust of the government, trust of the Internet, and previous use of e-commerce, e-government and e-file. The dependent variable is intention to use.

Table 4. Hypotheses testing

Hypoth.	Coeff.	t-val.	Sig.	Supported
H1(RA)	.218	3.859	.000	YES***
H2 (CMP)	.429	6.545	.000	YES***
H3 (CLX)	-.036	-.610	.542	NO
H4 (TOG)	.137	3.089	.002	YES**
H5 (TOI)	.105	2.394	.017	YES**
H6 (Ecom)	.021	.623	.534	NO
H7 (Egov)	.071	2.091	.038	YES**
H8 (Efil)	.160	4.475	.000	YES***

*p < 0.10, **p < 0.05, ***p<.001

Results

The model explains a large percent of the variance in citizen adoption of e-filing systems; adjusted R Square equals 0.769. Since the overall model was significant (F=104.080 p=.000), we tested the significance of each variable. Six of the eight hypotheses are supported. Relative advantage, compatibility, trust of the government, trust of the Internet, and previous use of e-government and e-file all have a significant impact on intention to e-file (see Table 4). Interestingly, complexity and previous use of e-commerce did not have a significant impact on one's intention to use an e-file system. Implications for practice and research are provided in the discussion section.

The resulting model is presented in Figure 2.

Implications for Practice and Research

This chapter's overall purpose was to investigate users' intention to file there taxes online via an IRS endorsed e-file system. The study focused on building an integrated model that identifies the impact of diffusion factors, e-experience factors, and trust factors on U.S. taxpayers' intention to use an IRS endorsed e-file system. To

Figure 2. Significant results

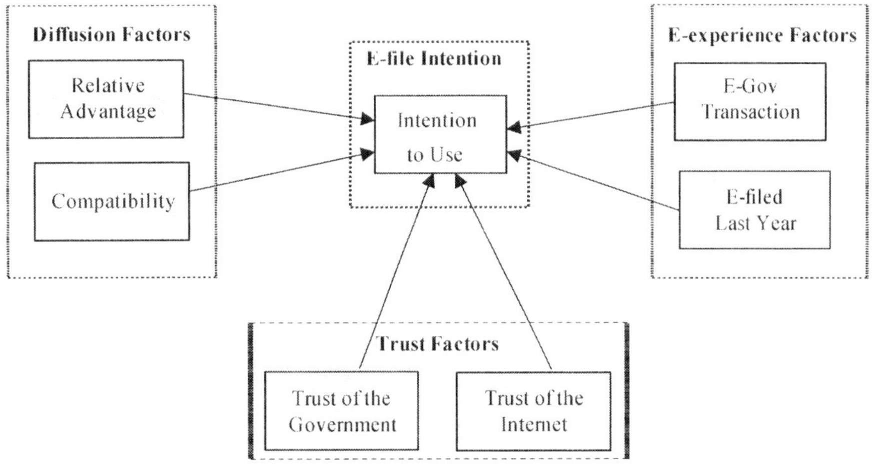

investigate the research question, we proposed a model of e-file adoption to be investigated. The results provide support for the research model. Eight independent variables (relative advantage, compatibility, complexity, previous e-commerce transaction, previous e-government transaction, previous e-file transaction, trust of the government, and trust of the Internet) were investigated and six were shown to be significant predictors of intention to use an e-file system.

Relative advantage was shown to be a significant predictor of intention to use in this study. This finding is not unexpected, having been identified as a predictor of intention to use in previous IT adoption literature. This highlights the necessity for an e-file system to be easy to use and effective in order to present taxpayers with a quicker, more efficient manner of filing their taxes. This is perhaps the most relevant aspect for most U.S. taxpayers. Promoting the benefits of e-filing will be imperative to achieve the 80% adoption goal. The relative advantage of e-file adoption over traditional means of filing taxes must be realized by taxpayers, in order to achieve adoption. The ultimate goal of using an e-file system form the user perspective is whether or not they accomplished their task of filing their taxes and it was quicker and more efficient than traditional means.

Compatibility was also shown to be a significant predictor of intention to use in the study. This finding highlights the necessity for an e-file system to fit into U.S. taxpayers' lifestyles. This fit will be imperative to achieve the 80% e-file adoption goal set forth by Congress. This is perhaps the most important aspect of an e-file system in order to initially capture the non-traditional e-filers.

Complexity was not found to be a significant predictor of intention to use in this study. However, one possible explanation is that in this study, the sample was comprised primarily of experienced users of technology, which is a likely explanation as to why complexity was not found to be significant. One could also argue that with the act of filing taxes the importance is in conducting the transaction, not in the ease of use.

Trust of the government was shown to be a significant predictor of usage. This finding was also expected in this study. Trust of the government has also been found to be significant in predicting usage in previous e-government research. Trust is at the forefront of all transactions, whether it be monetary in nature or other. If there is not trust between the user and the government agency adoption will not occur, as was shown in this study.

Trust of the Internet was also shown to be a significant predictor of intention to use in this study. This finding is not unexpected, having been identified as a predictor of intention to use in previous e-government and e-commerce studies. This finding provides evidence that indeed citizen's trust of the Internet significantly influences e-file usage. Trust of the Internet is paramount for e-file adoption

Previous e-commerce transaction experience did not significantly influence intention to use the e-file system. Although, interestingly well over 90% of the sample reported previous e-commerce transaction experience. However, previous e-government transaction experience and whether or not the citizen e-filed last year were both found to significantly influence intention to e-file in this study. This finding highlights the fact that an e-government transaction does not mimic an e-commerce transaction. There are unique elements involved with an e-government transaction as opposed to a simple e-commerce transaction. As a result there are added barriers to adoption.

One surprising finding was that in this study 71% of respondents reported having conducted some kind of e-government transaction previously, however, only 34% of respondents said they had e-filed their taxes. This is surprising given that around 50% of all returns in the U.S. our e-filed presently and with an experienced user base such as the subjects were in this study it would seem logical that they would at least be on par with the national average. This is especially surprising given the fact that so many of the respondents,

71%, had conducted some type of e-government transaction prior. Based on the results of this study, the IRS should attempt to influence citizen perceptions of the relative advantage of e-filing in order to increase adoption. Multiple linear regression allows us to analyze the magnitude of the coefficient for each independent variables. According to Table 3, relative advantage and compatibility have the highest impact on the intention to use. This suggests the IRS should highlight the advantages of filing taxes electronically, such as quicker returns, as compared to traditional methods. An emphasis on the relative advantages of e-filing should have a notable impact on citizen adoption.

FUTURE TRENDS

Future research should attempt to validate the findings of this study by testing a more diverse array of participants to increase the variance on some variable dimensions. The sample was composed of graduate and undergraduate students. Previous research suggests that students have a higher affinity towards and access to technology than the average citizen. While valid results were produced from testing, there was limited diversity in the sample.

Future research should also consider using multiple-methods to collect and analyze data to test the proposed model. Data for this study was collected through surveys, therefore allowing a potential of self-report bias from respondents. The survey was administered online which may also bias the results by capturing the views of those who may be more knowledgeable and comfortable with technology than the average citizen.

This study explores strategies used to increase e-file adoption. Future research should evaluate these strategies from the government perspective. For instance, what type of information sharing or third party partnerships can be used to enhance e-filing? What customer service standards should be implemented? What impact will these initiatives have on government human and capital resources?

CONCLUSION

In conclusion, this chapter presents a comprehensive yet parsimonious view of e-file adoption. It integrates adoption, trust, and experience factors to explain over seventy-six percent of the variance in intention to use an e-file system. The proposed e-file model can serve as a building block for future studies of e-file adoption. The constructs in the model are also applicable to other e-government systems, such as online license renewal. The proposed model adds to the current discourse on the evolution of e-government by presenting a very focused yet explanatory model of e-file utilization. The diffusion of e-filing is consistent with the goals of transformational government: it enables the seamless completion of a government services using technology.

REFERENCES

Agarwal, R., & Prasad, J. (1999). Are individual differences germane to the acceptance of new information technologies? *Decision Sciences*, *30*(2), 361-391.

Agarwal, R., Sambamurthy, V., & Stair, R. (2000). The evolving relationship between general and specific computer self-efficacy: An empirical investigation, *Information Systems Research*, *11*(4), 418-430.

Becerra, M., & Gupta A. K. (1999). Trust within the organization: Integrating the trust literature with agency theory and transaction costs economics. *Public Administration Quarterly*, *23*(2), 177-203.

Belanger, F., & Carter, L. (2006). *The effects of the digital divide on e-government: An empiri-*

cal evaluation. Paper presented at of the Hawaii International Conference on System Sciences, Kauai, HI.

Benbasat, I., & Barki, H. Quo vadis TAM. *Journal of the Association for Information Systems, 8*(4), 211-218.

Cabinet Office. (2008, July 16). Latest report shows transformational government has brought major improvements to public services. London: Cabinet Office Press Office.

Carter, L., & Belanger, F. (2005). The utilization of e-government services: Citizen trust, innovation, and acceptance factors. *Information Systems Journal, 15*(1), 2—25.

Chau, Y. K., & Hu, J. H. (2001). Information technology acceptance by individual professionals: A model comparison approach. *Decision Sciences, 32*(4), 699-718.

Corey, E. C., & Garand, J.C. Are government employees more likely to vote? An analysis of turnout in the 1996 U.S. national election. *Public Choice, 111*, 259-283.

Davis, F. D. (1989). Perceived usefulness, perceived ease of use, and user acceptance of information technology. *MIS Quarterly, 13*(3), 319-340.

Eastin, M. A., & LaRose, R. L. (2000). Internet self-efficacy and the psychology of the digital divide. *Journal of Computer Mediated Communication, 6*(1).

Economist, The. (2008, February 28). The good the bad and the inevitable. A special report on government and technology.

Evans, K. (2006, December). Expanding e-government: Making a difference for the American people using information technology. Executive Office of the President, Office of Management and Budget.

Fletcher, P. D. (2002). E-File: Electronic tax administration in the United States.

Fu, J.-R., Farn, C.-K., & Chao ,W.-P. (2006). Acceptance of electronic tax filing: A study of taxpayer intentions. *Information & Management, 43*, 109-126.

Ganesan, S., & Hess, R. (1997). Dimensions and levels of trust: Implications for commitment to a relationship. *Marketing Letters, 8*(4) 439-448.

Gefen, D., Karahanna, E., & Straub, D. W. (2003). Trust and TAM in online shopping: An integrated model. *MIS Quarterly, 27*(1), 51-90.

Gefen, D., Rose, G., Warkentin, M., & Pavlou, P. (2002). Cultural diversity and trust in IT adoption: A comparison of potential e-voters in the USA and South Africa. *Journal of Global Information Management, 13*(1), 54-78.

Gefen, D. (2000). E-Commerce: The role of familiarity and trust. *Omega: The International Journal of Management Science, 28*(6), 725-737.

Hart, P., & Saunders, C. (1997). Power and trust: Critical factors in the adoption and use of electronic data interchange. *Organizational Science, 8*(1) 23-42.

Hsu, M. H., & Chiu, C. M. (2004). Internet self-efficacy and electronic service acceptance. *Decision Support Systems, 38*, 369-381.

IRS. (2004). IRS e-strategy for growth.

Jarvenpaa, S. L., Knoll, K., & Leidner, D. E. (1984). Is anybody out there? Antecedents of trust in global virtual teams. *Journal of Management Information Systems, 14*(4), 29-64.

Lee, M. K. O., & Turban, E. (2001). A trust model for consumer Internet shopping. *International Journal of Electronic Commerce, 6*(1) 75-91.

Marakas, G. M., Yi, M. Y., & Johnson, R. D. (1998). The multilevel and multifaceted character of computer self-efficacy: Toward clarification of the construct and an integrative framework for research. *Information Systems Research, 9*(2), 126-163.

Mayer, R. C., Davis, J. H., & Schoorman, F. D. (1995). An integrative model of organizational trust. *Academy of Management Review, 20*(3), 709-734.

McKnight, D. H., Choudhury, V., & Kacmar, C. (2002). Developing and validating trust measures for e-commerce: An integrative approach. *Information Systems Research, 13*(3), 334-359.

McKnight, D. H., Cummings, L. L., & Chervany, N.L. (1998). Initial trust formation in new organizational relationships. *Academy of Management Review, 23*(3), 473-490.

Moore, G., & Benbasat, I. (1991). Development of an instrument to measure the perceptions of adopting an information technology innovation. *Information Systems Research, 2*(3), 192-222.

Pavlou, P. (2003). Consumer acceptance of electronic commerce: Integrating trust and risk with the technology acceptance model. *International Journal of Electronic Commerce, 7*, 69-103.

Plouffe, C. R., Hulland, S. J., & Vandenbosch, M. (2001). Research report: Richness vs. parsimony in modeling technology adoption decisions--understanding merchant adoption of a smart card-based payment system. *Information Systems Research, 12*(2), 208-222.

Rogers, E. M. (2003). *Diffusion of innovation*. New York: The Free Press.

Rotter, J. A new scale for the measurement of interpersonal trust. *Journal of Personality, 35*, 651-665.

Szajna, B. (1996). Empirical evaluation of the revised technology acceptance model. *Management Science, 42*(1), 85-92.

Tan, Y. H., Theon, W. Toward a generic model of trust for electronic commerce. *International Journal of Electronic Commerce, 5*(2) 61-74.

Thompson, R., Higgins, C., & Howell, J. (1991). Personal computing: toward a conceptual model of utilization. *MIS Quarterly, 15*(1), 124-143.

Thompson, R., Higgins, C., & Howell, J. (1994). Influence of experience on personal computer utilization: Testing a conceptual model. *Journal of Management Information Systems, 11*(1), 167-187.

Tornatzky, L. & Klein, K. Innovation characteristics and innovation adoption implementation: A metaanalysis of findings. *IEEE Transactions on Engineering Management, 29*, 28-45.

VanDenburgh, W. M., & Harmelink, P. J. (2006). The IRS's lack of support for direct, free e-Filing. *Tax Notes, 112*, 171-182.

Van Slyke, C., Belanger, F., & Comunale, C.L. Factors influencing the adoption of Web-based shopping: The impact of trust. *Database for Advances in Information Systems, 35*(2), 32-49.

Venkatesh, V., Morris, M. G., & Davis, G. B. (2003). User acceptance of information technology: Toward a unified view. *MIS Quarterly, 27*(3), 425-478.

Wang, Y., & Emurian, H. (2005).Trust in e-commerce: Consideration of interface design factors. *Journal of Electronic Commerce in Organizations, 3*(4), 42-60.

Warkentin, M., & Gefen, D. (2002). Encouraging citizen adoption of e-government by building trust. *Electronic Markets, 12*(3), 157-162.

Welch, E.W., Hinnant, C. C., & Moon, M. J. (2005). Linking citizen satisfaction with e-government and trust in government. *Journal of Public Administration Research and Theory, 15*(3), 371-391.

Zucker, L. G. (1986). Production of trust: Institutional sources of economic structure, 1840-1920. *Research in Organizational Behavior,* (8), 53-111.

KEY TERMS

Compatibility: The belief that an innovation is consistent with one's values, views, beliefs, and customs

Complexity: An assessment of the difficulty associated with adopting a new system

Diffusion of Innovation: The dispersion of a new idea, product or system

E-Government: The delivery of government services and information via the Internet

Relative Advantage: The belief that a new system has benefits above and beyond the current system

Trust of the Internet: Level of confidence one has in the reliability of the Internet

Trust of the Government: Level of confidence on has in the ability of a government agency to provide accurate and secure electronic services

Transformational Government: The use of Internet-based technology to make government information and services seamlessly available to agencies, businesses and citizens

Chapter XXIV
E-Government Implementation in Transition Countries

Mysore Ramaswamy
Southern University and A&M College, USA

ABSTRACT

The implementation of e-government is a challenging task in any developed political context, but all the more uniquely so in the postcommunist transitioning countries. These factors surpass the indubitable benefits of automation as an output and information technology as a tool, and take into account elements of context and capacity that should not be overlooked. The degree of resistance to change due to organizational, structural, and social factors varies depending upon differences in each of these critical dimensions. In postcommunist countries such as Armenia, e-transformation is considered in some quarters as a second disruption, the first being the fall of the Soviet rule. In this chapter, we develop a comprehensive framework which is needed for successful implementation of e-government initiatives. This framework combines not only the critical dimensions of e-government interactions but also the various sociotechnical aspects that are particularly relevant to the special challenges of transitioning countries.

INTRODUCTION

Innovations in information and communication technology (ICT) have dramatically influenced the nature and quality of government-to-constituent interactions all over the world. However the underlying structural, organizational and institutional components upon which technological innovation is superimposed are as widely divergent as the cultures from which they derive. As a result, the successes of such implementations are widely divergent, and the means by which their effectiveness can be assessed are as of yet in nascent form. Electronic government (e-government) can be defined as the use of information and communication technologies (ICT) by government to deliver information and services to its constituents. Gronlund (2005) states that while government organizations have succeeded in achieving more efficient operations and better services at the national level, progress is slow to emerge at the local level. In spite of the considerable literature on digital or e-government, there is no general agreement on good measures for digital government or what we should be measuring (Carbo & Williams, 2004). Some studies have focused on availability, cost, and quality of ICT networks and equipment. Another stream of research looks at digital government as a special case of ICT-enabled business process change (Scholl, 2003). Factors such as societal readiness for e-government have also to be taken into account (Moon, 2005), in tandem with countless assessments of e-readiness as undertaken by various international organizations specialized in "ICT for development" work. In addition to the above, a clearer understanding of the organizational and structural changes that precede the transformation to e-governance is necessary; such analysis is heretofore largely lacking. With the filling of these gaps as a main objective, we take a bottom-up approach and analyze the actual interactions that occur between entities in an e-governance context.

In this chapter, we use the term "e-governance" in a broad sense to include a deeper understanding of the way ICTs impact the existing (and potential future) interactions between a government and its constituents. In other words, e-governance goes beyond the 'what' of an e-government interaction that presumably delivers service to a constituent - and includes rather an analysis of the 'how' and 'why'. We note that one cannot improve upon something in automation that is not already rational and functional in its current daily practice. In spite of tremendous innovations in the field of information technology (IT), the benefits of this progress have not reached all segments of our society, particularly in the case of developing and transition countries (Carbo & Williams, 2004; Ramaswamy & Selian, 2007). Most governments across the world desire their citizens and businesses to interface with them through electronic means for the obvious reasons of efficiency in cost-saving and effectiveness. It is less obvious whether the transparency in process and information-sharing that this presupposes is also an equally important objective for all leaders. As Jane Fountain (2001) states in her work, there is a certain element of the 'perversity of incentives' to acknowledge here; Kedzie calls this the "Dictator's Dilemma" in the state (Allison, 2002) – where increased efficiency and political efficacy (brought about by ICTs) are positively related to each other, and negatively related to authoritarian and highly centralized control. That said, of course, the clear exponential increases in numbers of Internet users around the world during the last two decades (Scholl, 2003; Wimmer, 2001) are a strong indicator of the likelihood of increases in demand for such ICT-enabled services within the confines of respective political systems.

The rest of this chapter is organized as follows. In the next three sections, we discuss the following e-Government models respectively: Design Reality Gap Model, Agent-Service-Discretion Model, and E-Governance Cube. This is followed by a discussion of socio-technical challenges in transition countries such as Armenia. In the subsequent section, we develop a comprehensive framework that aids in the implementation of e-government initiatives by taking a holistic approach that effectively responds to the socio-technical challenges encountered in transition countries. The conclusions and future research directions are presented in the last section.

DESIGN-REALITY GAP MODEL

The objective of Design-Reality Gap Model proposed by Heeks (2003) is to evaluate the amount of change between 'where we are now' and 'where the e-government project wants to get us.' The structure of this model is indicated in Appendix I. In this approach, e-government projects are analyzed along the following seven dimensions:

- Information,
- Technology,
- Processes,
- Objectives and Values,
- Staffing and Skills,
- Management Systems and Skills, and
- Other Resources: Time and Money.

Using each of the seven dimensions, the following two factors are analyzed: first, the organizational reality relating to the dimension that exists right now at the time of analysis (i.e. current snapshot); and second, the requirements within the design of the e-government application.

The next step is to give a numerical rating to each of the above dimensions in order to indicate the size of the design-reality gap on that dimension. For example, taking the first dimension – information – 0 would indicate that the information used in the e-government application was exactly the same as the information currently being used in the given organization. 5 would indicate that the information used in the e-government application was somewhat different from the information currently really being used. 10 would indicate that the information used in the e-government application was completely and radically different from the information currently really being used.

Putting the above seven dimensions together with the notion of gaps produces a model capable of understanding the relative success or failure of e-government initiatives. In its simplest form, the Design-Reality-Gap model yields a cumulative score based on the rating numbers for all the seven dimensions. A more complex variation would involve two rounds. To begin with, the risk assessment team would assign a weight to each of the dimensions. Then the weighting score would be multiplied by the rating to give an overall set of weighted ratings, the sum of which is used as an indicator of success or failure.

If nothing else, this is a valuable tool and method for assessing whether the current institutional capacity of a given organization is capable of living up to its own service mandate. This is assuming, of course, that any large discernible gaps between 'design' and 'reality' are reflective of an absolute commitment of e-government application designers to the development of clear, effective automated solutions, without bias. This is in contrast perhaps to what some believe are the natural, gravitational tendencies of government-supported/subsidized human organization (particularly in developing countries) to subvert the simplicity of service delivery in a quagmire of bureaucratic and corrupt activity for personal gain. This makes sense insofar as it reflects a phenomenon to be observed in most places where human resource incentives structures are too weak to ensure the contrary (that is, a smaller gap between design and reality).

AGENT-SERVICE-DISCRETION MODEL

Naarmala (2004) has proposed an Agent-Service-Discretion Model to cover all scenarios of e-Government interactions. This is a variation of the e-commerce model proposed by Choi (1997). The three axes in that model refer to player, product and process.

In the model proposed by Naarmala as shown in Appendix II, the x-axis refers to an agent of e-government interaction (e-interaction). This entity can be a public officer, either physical or online. The y-axis represents the presence of service including delivery. The range extends from the mostly physical, to the mostly online. The z-axis refers to discretion or the degree of freedom over decision-making. Nearer to the origin indicates highly structured or rule-bound procedures, whereas farther from the origin refers to interactions that invoke a high degree of discretion. This type of analysis provides a way to compare e-government interactions with that of classical e-commerce interactions.

This model provides a way to analyze various activities based on the degree of the three dimensions required to execute that particular activity. For example, a case where a customer is dealing with an officer face-to-face and the actual decision made is strictly rule bound and regulated indicates a situation where all the three dimensions (agent, service, and discretion) are physical. Different scenarios that occur due to different mixes of the three dimensions can be viewed as development phases from traditional administrative services towards pure, virtual public e-services.

Several semi-stages on the way towards pure public e-services can be analyzed using this framework. These interactions include both service and agent being online, and the degree of discretion occurring in various degrees.

The main advantage of this model is that it presents a more nuanced way of analyzing government-constituent interactions, taking into consideration the element of 'degrees of freedom' over decision-making. This critical aspect of measurement is missing in the previous model.

E-GOVERNANCE CUBE

Government-to-citizen (G2C) interactions of e-Government comprise a very significant component in the formation of a truly inclusive and functioning e-society. In this context, we need to address the following questions:

- How can we make e-Government truly citizen-centric?
- Do we have objectives that are realistic?
- How well are we achieving these objectives fully and cost-effectively?
- Are these objectives jointly determined and agreed upon by citizens and their government agencies?

We need better models to plan, fund, develop, implement, operate, and evaluate successful e-Government across various political and social, cultural, and economic contexts (Carbo & Williams, 2004). Above all is the necessity for such models to be able to acknowledge and adjust to the idiosyncrasies of specific cases.

Some of the above concerns are addressed by the e-Governance cube model. Ramaswamy and Selian (2007) propose the formation of an e-Governance cube with the following three axes: *interaction class* on the x-axis, *processing complexity* on the y-axis, and *perceived value* on the z-axis as shown in Appendix III. These parameters are based on the principles that define quality of information (Zmud, 1978). E-interactions are analyzed along these three dimensions.

In the e-Governance cube, government-to-constituent interactions are categorized into three groups: government-to-government (G2G), government-to-business (G2B), and government-to-citizen (G2C). This categorization is useful for analyzing differences in the types of information needs typically necessary for the successful execution of specific types of service delivery. The interaction class is represented on the x-axis.

Processing complexity is represented on the y-axis. The processing complexity of an interaction is a function of the information available as to how to execute that task. Focusing on the information required for processing an e-governance transaction, we can combine relevance, accuracy and precision, and define correctness as an attribute that refers to the accuracy and relevance of the information provided, while adding in some way to the successful execution of the task. In addition to correctness, we find that the following three attributes are necessary and sufficient to capture its utility: completeness, clarity, and ease of accessibility. The adequacy of available information to process the task is captured by the term 'completeness'. 'Clarity' is the expectation that the information provided is in a form that is easy to understand. 'Ease of accessibility' indicates the ease with which people who need it can find and access that information. Each attribute is measured in turn on the binary basis of values set between 0 and 1, 0 referring to the absence of these attributes, and 1 referring to their presence.

Users' or constituents' perceptions of the value of e-governance interactions play a key role in assessing the level of resistance in government to restructuring, and the subsequent automation of bureaucratic procedures already in place. This dimension of perceived value is represented on the z-axis. The range of this axis is divided into three simple parts: low (L), medium (M) and high (H). Thus, the e-interactions towards the top of the cube have a higher perceived value. Accordingly, the volume of government-constituent interactions will increase when the perceived value of such interactions is deemed higher, or more 'valuable'. Defining these ranges for the axes in this way enables the division of the e-governance cube into 27 sub-cubes. Appendix III indicates a government-to-citizen interaction of processing complexity β, and of perceived value of medium range (C, β, M) being transformed to an interaction of lesser processing complexity α.

The e-governance cube provides a means of evaluating an extensive (if not comprehensive) series of government-constituent interactions. Depending upon which of the 27 sub-cubes contains the given transaction of interest, we are now able to make inferences on the potential of that transaction for its ease of conversion to e-governance. This naturally opens up a wide arena of analysis, particularly for others who wish to specialize and focus specifically on the dynamics and characteristics of very specific e-governance transactions. In the context of the e-governance cube model, the further one moves away from the origin, the more resistance one is likely to encounter to automation. From the e-inclusion point of view, the processes that are valued high on the z-axis (perceived value) need to be addressed first.

SOCIO-TECHNICAL CHALLENGES

To derive a more comprehensive perspective of the context in which the e-governance transformation in Armenia is being attempted, it is necessary to undertake a brief analysis of the period of Soviet domination. This period was characterized by a highly centralized political culture and a well defined bureaucracy. There was minimal G2C interaction and hardly any effective mass political participation - or the demand for it. All of this changed after the collapse of the Soviet Union.

The sharing of information or information integration is at the core of any e-government implementation program (Klischewski and Scholl, 2006); especially at the G2G level. The e-Governance cube can be used to identify tasks for the suitability for automation. In addition, it also illustrates areas of resistance to change based on the types of entities involved, processing complexity, and perceived value of transaction.

Referring to Appendix III, as we move away from the origin of the e-governance cube in y and z axes, (sub-cubes towards the top and back of the cube) there is an increase in processing complexity, and perceived value. Typically, this movement indicates an associated increase in the levels of resistance in government to restructuring and automation. Therefore, interactions in the sub-cubes towards the top and back should be analyzed carefully as they are likely to encounter resistance to restructuring and automating. This is true for all the three entity types.

The post-independence or transition period of Armenia started with the disruption of institutional stability and resulted in a deterioration of existing bureaucratic procedures. This has resulted in an environment of ill defined and poorly-adhered to protocols for government-to-constituent interactions. Before we can identify areas suitable for e-governance implementations, it is vital to ensure that a clearly defined and understandable procedure for reform is in place. Process restructuring becomes critical in this context.

Barriers to change are identified in the following four areas: Organizational Characteristics, Human Capacity, Financial Capacity, and Technical Infrastructure. Organizational characteristics such as the existence of local information technology (IT) departments that address questions of automation, and the existence of collaboration between IT and public relations (PR) departments which results in the availability of streamlined public information are vital to the transformation process. As Dawes and Prefontaine (2003) point out, data-intensive collaborations at some point involve the issue of data ownership. Such issues in a fledgling bureaucracy can be a potential stumbling block especially in G2G transactions. In addition, it is important to determine whether there is any institutionalized means of process review and opportunities for constituents to address their grievances. By helping to provide local service and service delivery, e-government can become a mechanism for spurring community involvement and thus become a catalyst for direct political and/or e-participation (Komito, 2005). Naturally, this may be viewed with skepticism by various parts of the bureaucracy. In the context of post-communist societies, this is further exacerbated by the subservience of bureaucracy to political authority.

The human capacity component in an institution is critical to the ability and capacity of that institution to evolve. For the purposes of this analysis, this component can be used interchangeably with the notion of social capital – even in the limited parameters of a single institution. Social capital refers to the 'stock' that is created when a group of departments or divisions develop the ability to work together for mutually productive gain. Actors in a collaborative network, even within one institution, learn of new technologies, opportunities, challenges, and the outcome of transactions more quickly because of the density of interaction within the network. Vertically organized networks, like the kind we find in the case of Armenia, tend toward characteristics that adversely affect learning of information processing capacity.

The financial barrier is a critical one to the emergence of innovation and institutional transformation. This is in part a matter of creating incentives for people to innovate. As it stands, the average salaries in IT departments of ministries in Armenia are quite low compared to the comparable private sector jobs, and do not create an environment conducive to innovation. The most critical element here is a lack of commitment – strategic and financial – to the objectives of institutional transformation. The status quo suits the purposes of many.

Barriers posed by technical infrastructure refer to problems of depreciating equipment, lack of standardization and interoperability, an overall disregard for licenses, etc. This creates an environment where change is not a priority.

A COMPREHENSIVE FRAMEWORK

We propose a comprehensive framework which first looks at the macro level. Here we are concerned with overcoming the socio-technical barriers. Either a two-phased approach or hybrid approach can be used to overcome some of the barriers mentioned in the previous section. In the two-phased approach, we introduce structural changes and later follow them up with technological changes which include automation. In the hybrid approach, we introduce automated solutions alongside existing processes and roles that may not be easily dispensed with given various levels of necessity for personnel/civil servant employment. The objective here is to not undermine the relevance of social networks. The effects of synergy that follow when G2B interactions such as procurement are improved can have secondary/tertiary effects on G2C transactions. Although bottom-up change is undoubtedly important, the most important factor in overcoming the barriers to transformation in the post-Communist context is support and commitment from the top. This is especially relevant as the socio-technical challenges have to be overcome. A guided strategic government plan fully supported at the top levels will serve as a catalyst for real transformation particularly in places where bottom-up attempts are unable to attain critical mass and or achieve necessary momentum.

The second part of our comprehensive framework looks at the micro level. The main objective of analyzing the dimensions of e-government interactions is to improve the effectiveness of e-governance as a system. It is to be noted that placing an IT layer over and automating a faulty bureaucratic system may yield a more efficient system, but will certainly not be one desired by or responsive to its core constituents. The analysis as undertaken by using the e-governance models described in this paper will yield a better understanding of the government-constituent interaction in terms of processing complexity, as well as the degree of importance attached to that interaction by the constituent.

By integrating key elements of the three models described in the preceding sections, the following framework can be used to initiate the process chain that transforms conventional bureaucratic tasks to e-government interactions:

- **Step 1:** Using the design-reality-gap model, ascertain the gap that exists between the status quo and the ideal design in critical areas such as information, technology, and processes.
- **Step 2:** Using the agent-service-discretion model, identify the task to be automated in terms of agent (physical or online), service (physical or online), and discretion (degree of freedom over decision making).
- **Step 3:** Using the e-governance cube, identify the e-governance potential of the subject task by considering the dimensions of interaction class, processing complexity and perceived value to the constituent.

The range of government-constituent interactions is indeed very large as evidenced by the three stakeholder groups of constituents (citizen, business, and government). The gamut of interactions is also very diverse. It is critical that these interactions are properly restructured before being automated (Homburg & Bekkers, 2002; Ramaswamy & Selian, 2007).

One of the major advantages of analyzing the e-interactions from the dimensional perspective – irrespective of the specific model used – is the help this lends to the process of restructuring. For example, using the e-Governance Cube, restructuring a process that is at a distance from the x-axis (higher complexity as well as perceived value) requires far more attention than a process that is less complex and having lower perceived value.

CONCLUSION

In the context of transition countries such as Armenia, the implementation of e-government must be achieved in several stages. The first stage addresses steps necessary for the realization of the transformation from a pre-bureaucratic governmental structure to a citizen-friendly, service-delivery oriented bureaucracy. Support from the top levels of administration is critical for the achievement of this change. The second set of actions pertains to the actual implementation of e-government which entails automating key government-to-constituent transactions. The transactions that are optimally suitable (i.e., low-hanging fruit) should be implemented first, provided they are supported by real organizational change and a correlated improvement in human capacity to support it from beneath.

Interactions between the government and its constituents are the basic building blocks of e-government. In this chapter, we have presented and analyzed differing modeling techniques that shed light on diverse aspects of these interactions.

The several dimensions of the Design-Reality Gap Model set a contextual framework under which we need to build improvements. The Agent-Service-Discretion Model focuses on the degree of discretion that is required from the governmental agent – whether physical or online – and thus provides a needed perspective. The essentials of information processing are embedded in the e-governance cube and this modeling technique provides an easy approach towards process restructuring. However, a comprehensive modeling framework that incorporates all critical dimensions discussed above and also facilitates process restructuring is still lacking.

The future work in this area focuses on integrating the three modeling techniques to one comprehensive framework. Such a framework will enable policy makers and researchers to point out the potential priority areas that need to be automated first and also yield a realistic estimate of resources needed to achieve such transformation. In addition, such an approach will also help process restructuring.

REFERENCES

Allison, J. E. (2002). *Technology, development, and democracy: International conflict and cooperation in the information age*. Albany, NY: State University of New York Press.

Carbo, T., & Williams, J. G. (2004). Some determinants of user perceptions of information quality on the World Wide Web. *Electronic Journal of E-Government, 2*(2), 94-105.

Choi, S., et al. (1997). *The economics of electronic commerce*. Indianapolis, IN: Macmillan Technical Publishing.

Dawes, S. S., & Prefontaine, L. (2003). Understanding new models of collaboration for delivering government services. *Communications of the ACM, 46*(1), 40-42.

Fountain, Jane E. (2001). *Building the virtual state: Information technology and institutional change*. Washington, DC: Brookings Institution Press.

Gronlund, A. (2005). What's in a field – exploring the e-government domain. In *Proceedings of the 38th Hawaii International Conference on System Sciences* (8 pages).

Heeks, R (2003). Causes of e-government success and failure: Design reality gap model. Retrieved on February 22, 2007, from http://www.e-devexchange.org/ eGov/ causegap.htm

Homburg, V., & Bekkers, V. (2002). The back-office of e-government. In *Proceedings of the 35th Hawaii International Conference on Information Systems* (9 pages).

Klischewski, R., & Scholl, H. J. (2006). Information quality as a common ground for key players in e-government integration and interoperability. In *Proceedings of the 39th Hawaii International Conference on System Sciences* (10 pages).

Komito, L. (2005). E-Participation and governance: Widening the net. *The Electronic Journal of E-Government, 3*(1), 39-48.

Moon, M. J., et al. (2005). What drives global e-governance? An exploratory study at a macro level. In *Proceedings of the 38th Hawaii International Conference on System Sciences* (10 pages).

Naarmala, J. (2004). Going digital – explaining dimensions of e-government. Retrieved on February 20, 2007, from www.ebrc.info/ pages_ C86FCC04-3314-4DF9-9AE2-138286 0CB17F.asp

Ramaswamy, M., & Selian, A. (2007). E-Government in transition countries: Prospects and challenges. In *Proceedings of the 40th Hawaii International Conference on Information Systems* (10 pages).

Scholl, H. J. (2003). E-Government: A special case of ICT-enabled business process change.

In *Proceedings of the 36th Hawaii International Conference on System Sciences* (12 pages).

Wimmer, M. R., et al. (2001). Electronic business invading the public sector: Considerations on change and design. In *Proceedings of the 34th Hawaii International Conference on System Sciences* (10 pages).

Zmud, R. W. (1978). An empirical investigation of the dimensionality of the concept of information. *Decision Sciences* (9), 187-195.

KEY TERMS

E-Governance: Conceptual study of utilizing digital technologies in governance at all levels.

E-Government: Tactical implementation of ICT in government-constituent interactions.

E-Inclusion: Expanding the benefits of ICT to the overall population.

E-Readiness: Degree of preparedness of a country for implementing e-governance.

E-Society: A community where most of the transactions can be executed digitally.

Information and Communication Technologies (ICT): Networked computer technologies for processing and communication of information.

Transition Countries: Countries undergoing transformation from authoritarian systems.

APPENDIX A. DESIGN-REALITY GAP MODEL (ADAPTED FROM HEEKS, 2003)

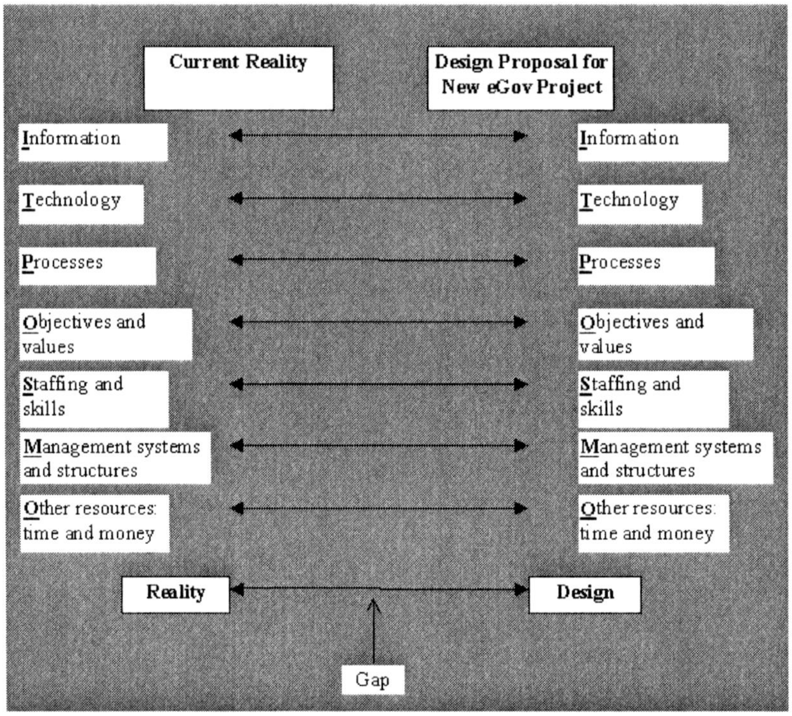

APPENDIX B. AGENT-SERVICE-DISCRETION MODEL (ADAPTED FROM NAARMALA, 2004)

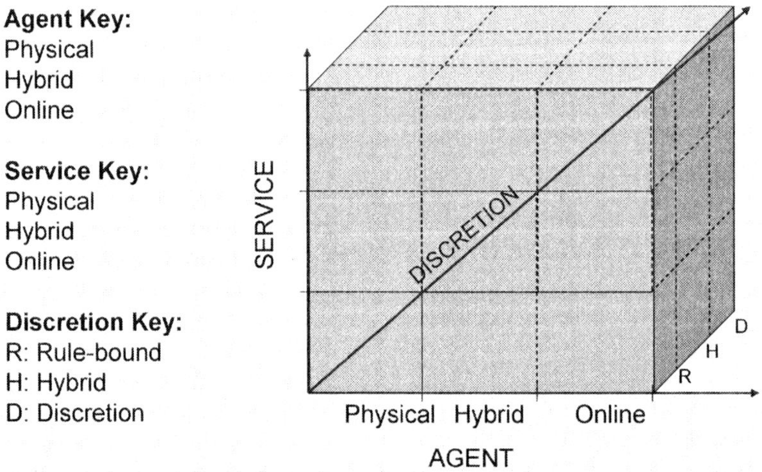

APPENDIX C. E-GOVERNANCE CUBE (ADAPTED FROM RAMASWAMY AND SELIAN, 2007)

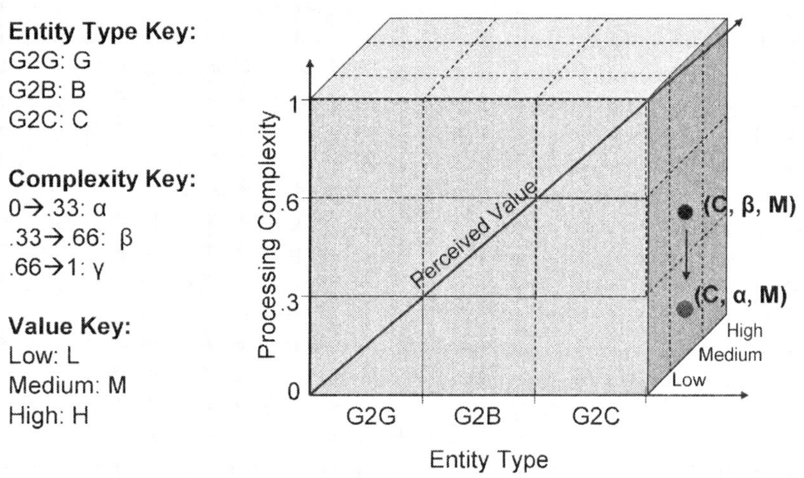

Chapter XXV
IT Governance in the Public Sector in a Developing Country

Edephonce N. Nfuka
Stockholm University and Royal Institute of Technology, Sweden

Lazar Rusu
Stockholm University and Royal Institute of Technology, Sweden

ABSTRACT

This chapter focuses on IT governance in the public sector organizations in a developing country like Tanzania. Today in many organizations in the public sector, the use of IT has become crucial in sustaining and extending the organizations' strategies and objectives. This pervasive use of technology has caused a critical dependency on IT that calls for a specific focus on IT governance. In this chapter, we provide its overview and, based on the analysis of five case studies indicate the current practices, problems, and consequences in the Tanzanian public sector environment. Moreover, we reveal twelve key issues to consider for effective IT governance together with the trends and future research in improving ICT-enabled transformational government in public service delivery in this environment. In this context, the chapter contributes to an understanding of the IT governance practices and related ICT-enabled transformational government issues and complexities involved in the transformational phase for better public service delivery in a developing country like Tanzania.

INTRODUCTION

Many organizations today, including public sector organizations, rely on Information and Communication Technology (ICT) and continue to make significant IT-enabled business investments (ITGI, 2006). This is due to, among other things, the constantly increasing demand for more efficient and cost-effective services for citizens (G-C)[1], businesses (G-B)[2] and among public sector organizations themselves (G-G & G-E)[3] (Amaravadi, 2005; Brown, 2003), and the continued effort to embrace e-government[4] or lately its advanced context of transformational government. This has led to pervasiveness and dependency on IT in current dynamic and often turbulent multiservice provision environments where effective management of IT and its alignment with business goals is essential for success. This required management is also because increasingly there is an integration of ICT evolving challenges related to IT and business strategic alignment, project execution, security assurances, sustainability and handling intra- and inter-organizational relationships and synergies (ITGI, 2007). For example, in a survey conducted by the IT governance Institute (ITGI and PwC, 2006) it was found that the top ten management problems include inadequate view on how well IT is performing, non-alignment between IT and business strategies and the higher cost of IT with low return on investment. Prudent management of such IT environment calls for IT governance, which is the organizational capacity to plan and control the formulation and implementation of IT strategy to ensure fusion of business and IT (Van Grembergen *et al.*, 2003). For example a study at the Centre of Information Systems Research of Massachusetts Institute of Technology (MIT-CISR) on IT governance related issues, indicated that there is a 20% better return on IT-enabled business investments when effective IT governance is in place (Weill & Ross, 2004).

The need for effective IT governance is also becoming essential in the public sector in developing countries, in which increasingly we see a variety of fragmented IT initiatives and activities, with loss of synergies and exploitation of economies of scale. The need is equally amplified by, alongside resources constraints, relatively lower IT literacy, culture and leadership, basic citizens competing needs and priorities. Also on the fact that the sector is complex and its effectiveness is characterized by a need for intra and inter-organizational synergies that call for common and effective strategies, services, communication, collaboration and accountability to multiple stakeholders (Weill and Ross, 2004). These problematic governance related issues in the sector stem from IT strategic planning and implementation to management, support and monitoring (Ndou, 2004; ITGI and PwC, 2006; ITGI & PwC, 2006a; Bakari, 2007). As a result effective integration of ICT and indeed ICT-enabled transformational government in these environments needs consistent strategic alignment of IT and business goals in order to increase efficiency in public service delivery and meet stakeholders' expectations (Moyo, 1996; Duffy, 2002; Guldentops, 2003).

This chapter therefore looks into these concerns from an IT governance viewpoint, specifically in the public sector in a developing country, as a contribution to the understanding and nurturing of ICT-Enabled Transformational Government for efficient and cost-effective public service delivery. It mainly covers an overview of IT governance and based on five case studies, describes its current practices, problems encountered and consequences in the sector. Moreover, it looks at the key issues to consider for effective IT governance in Tanzanian environment and finally the trends and future research in this area.

IT GOVERNANCE OVERVIEW

This section provides an overview to IT governance. The focus is on the strategic alignment between business and IT and its approaches for better value delivery. The first part provides insight into what IT governance entails, while the rest covers the elements for its implementation, metrics and frameworks in practice.

Defining IT Governance

IT and its use in business environments have experienced several turbulences and fundamental transformations in the past decades leading to a new area of IT governance. To date professionals and academics have conducted a number of researches and developed theories and best practices in this emerging knowledge domain (Peterson, 2003). This also has resulted in a variety of IT governance definitions defined in different ways in the numerous articles and books (Simonsson & Johnson, 2005). The most prevalent include the following: *"IT governance is defined as specifying the decision rights and accountability frameworks to encourage desirable behavior in using IT"* (Weill & Ross, 2004), which is from decision rights viewpoint, while from business and IT fusion viewpoint *"IT governance is the organizational capacity exercised by the board, executive management and IT management to control the formulation and implementation of IT strategy and in this way ensuring the fusion of business and IT"* (Van Grembergen, 2002). Also from an enterprise viewpoint it is defined as "an integral part of enterprise governance and *consists of the leadership and organizational structures and processes that ensure the enterprise's IT sustains and extends the organization's strategies and objectives"* (ITGI, 2003).

Although the definitions differ on some aspects, mainly all focus on same issues, such as strategic link between business and IT, integral part of enterprise governance and encouraging desirable behavior in using IT. As indicated by all them, IT governance is situated at multiple levels in the organization, i.e. strategic for board or other governing bodies, management for executives and operational for line management involvement (Figure 1). This implies that in all these levels, business and IT people need to be involved in the IT governance process and understand their individual roles and responsibilities.

Key IT Governance Focus Areas

The IT Governance Institute states that fundamentally, IT Governance is concerned about two outcomes: IT's delivery of value to the business

Figure 1. The three layers of IT governance responsibility (© 2003 by Van Grembergen, De Haes, & Guldentops. Used with permission.)

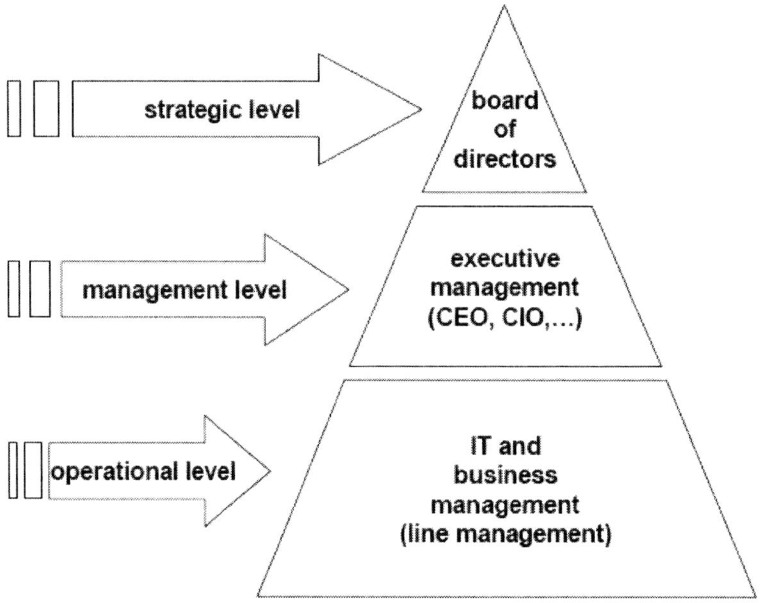

Figure 2. Focus areas of IT governance (ITGI, 2003) (Source: COBIT 4.1© 1996-2007 ITGI. All rights reserved. Used with permission.)

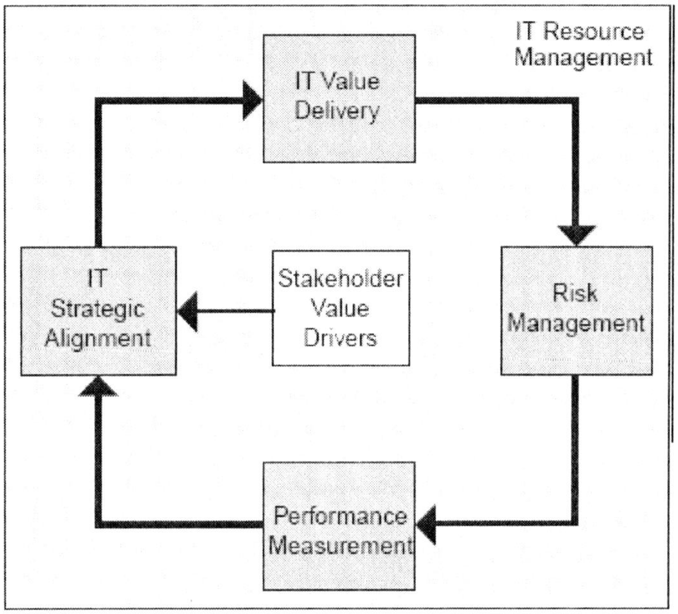

and mitigation of IT risks (ITGI, 2003). The first is driven by strategic alignment of IT and business and the second by embedding accountability into the enterprise. Both need to be managed and measured adequately. This leads to five focus areas for IT Governance: Strategic alignment, Value delivery, Risk management, Resource management and Performance management. Stakeholder value drivers (Figure 2) drive all these.

Key IT Governance Decisions

As earlier indicated IT governance is also about specifying the decision rights and accountability frameworks. From this viewpoint an effective IT governance must address three issues, i.e. the decisions to be made to ensure effective management and use of IT; who should make such decisions (Weill & Ross, 2004); and how these decisions will be made and monitored (Duffy, 2002b; Broadbent, 2003). These decisions to be made with regard to IT governance are *IT Principles* that clarify the business role of IT; *IT Architecture* which defines the integration and standardization requirements; *IT Infrastructure* that determines shared and enabling services; *Business Application Needs* which specify the business requirements for purchased or internally developed IT applications; and *IT Investment and Prioritization* that chooses initiatives to fund and how much to spend (Figure 3). How these decisions are practiced in the organization is likely to affect the functioning and integration of ICT in the organizational strategies and goals.

IT Governance Structures, Processes, and Relational Mechanisms

Now that we have a better understanding of IT governance, the question is on the kind of mechanisms that we can implement in an organization to bring the benefits it promises. Holistically, IT governance can be deployed using a mixture of various structures, processes and relational mechanisms (Weill & Woodham, 2002; Peterson, 2003). Structures involve the organization of the

Figure 3. Key IT Governance Decisions (Adapted from Weill & Ross, 2004)

IT Principle Decision High – levels statements about *how IT is used in the business.*		
IT architecture decision	**IT infrastructure decision**	**IT investment and prioritization decision**
Organizations logic for data, applications, and infrastructure capture in a set of policies, relationships, and technical choice to achieve *desired business & technical standardization and integration.*	Centrally coordinated *shared IT services that provide the foundation for the enterprise's IT capability.* **Business applications need decision** Specifying the *business need for purchases* or *internally development of IT applications.*	Decisions about how *much and where to invest in IT*, including project approvals and justification technology.

IT function, clearly defined roles and responsibilities and a diversity of IT/business committees. Processes refer to the strategic decision-making and monitoring. Relational mechanisms are the catalyst for attaining and sustaining business-IT alignment, even when structures and processes are in place. These mechanisms form the IT governance implementation framework (Figure 4). However, as we will see in the cases, the decision on what to implement depends on the context and contingencies in organization and the interacting environment as whole (Schoderbek *et al.*, 1998; Ribbers *et al.*, 2002).

Measuring the IT Governance Process

In recent years, many organizations have been in the process of implementing a combination of IT governance mechanisms, some directly as specific IT governance projects and others indirectly as part of general organizational improvements. An important aspect of the IT governance implementation is the performance measurement. Balanced Scorecard (BSC), a performance measurement framework originally developed by Kaplan and Norton (1992), is one of the frequently used per-

Figure 4. Necessary elements of an IT governance framework (© 2008 by Van Grembergen & De Haes Used with permission)

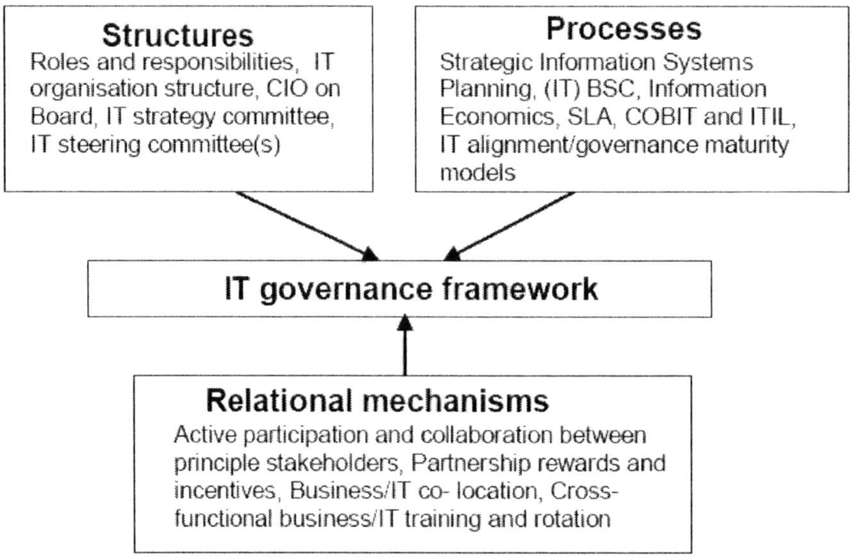

formance measurement tools today. Based on the latter and earlier version of IT BSC (ITGI, 2003), a specific BSC for IT governance was developed (Van Grembergen & De Haes, 2005). Its four dimensions with original BSC in brackets are corporate contribution perspective (financial), stakeholders perspective (customer), operational excellence perspective (internal processes), and future orientation perspective (learning and growth) (Figure 5). BSC is not only a performance measuring system but also provides a management system when causal relationships between metrics are implemented.

The ultimate goal of instituting IT governance is the attainment of better IT value delivery and consequently achievement of higher corporate contribution. It therefore starts with a corporate contribution perspective, then to other three scorecard dimensions with cause-and-effect relationships among each other (Figure 5). As observed in Figure 5, the metrics of the main elements of IT governance, i.e. structures, processes, and relational mechanisms is in the operational excellence and future orientation dimensions. This also applies to the maturity level of an organization that we can measure from processes perspective, for example based on the generic maturity model with selected or all 34 COBIT IT Processes (ITGI, 2007a). We can also measure IT governance performance with a relatively quicker performance assessment developed out of MIT-CISR research work in 256 firms worldwide on IT governance strategies and implementation issues (Weill & Ross, 2004).

IT Governance Frameworks in Practice

There are several established standards and best practices essential to the process of IT governance in an organization. One of the most internationally deployed best practices and fully-fledged IT governance framework is COBIT. COBIT framework is based on the premise that IT resources need to deliver the information that an enterprise requires to achieve its objectives and this need to be managed by a set of naturally grouped IT processes. To date COBIT framework has 34 IT processes (ITGI, 2007a).

Figure 5. Metrics for an IT governance balanced scorecard (© 2005 by Van Grembergen & De Haes Used with permission)

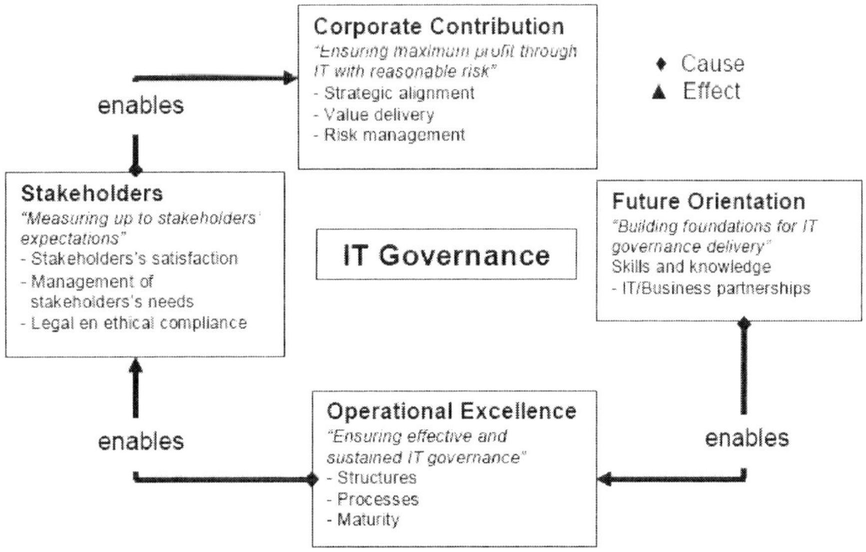

Recently, ISACA has released Val IT, a new framework that enables the creation of business value from IT-enabled investments, designed to align with and complement COBIT (ITGI, 2007). In addition, it has released a reduced version of COBIT, i.e. COBIT QuickStart. This is on the premises that the breadth and depth of the COBIT guidance are overwhelming for SMEs and other entities where IT is not mission-critical or essential for survival. It can also serve as a starting point for enterprises like public sector organizations, in their move towards an appropriate level of control and governance of IT (ITGI, 2007b).

Several standards, frameworks and best practices issued by both international standardization and other organizations, exist in addition to COBIT, for managing different aspects of IT that altogether might be useful when embarking on IT governance related implementation or research work. These include ITIL for IT Service Management, ISO 17799 for IT Security Management, PRINCE2 for Project Management, and ISO 38500 for Corporate Governance of IT (ITGI, 2006a; Brand & Boonen, 2007; ISO, 2008).

STATE OF IT GOVERNANCE IN THE PUBLIC SECTOR IN A DEVELOPING COUNTRY

As indicated in the introduction to the chapter, the public sector in developing countries has already made considerable investment in ICT and this is the case for Tanzania. Though the first use of computers in Tanzania dates back to the seventies, the significant achievement of ICT can be traced back to the early nineties after various adjustments of regulatory and commercial policies, both macroeconomic and within ICT's converging sector (Bakari, 2007). Since then the country and the public sector in particular have experienced dramatic changes in the use of ICT. Today we have general use of computers, some specific business applications and a variety of IT organization in many public sector organizations. However, like in many developing economies this usage is coupled with limited IT knowledge, infrastructure, harmonization, and management (Ndou, 2004; Bakari, 2007).

In this section we describe the state of IT governance in such environment as part of the results of ongoing research that in this case, and based on a broader IT governance Assessment Process (ITGAP) Model (Peterson, 2004), investigated the current state of IT governance in the public sector in Tanzania. This had three main aspects, first, to assess the current state of IT governance mainly on mechanisms (Van Grembergen and De Haes, 2008) and key decisions (Weill & Ross, 2004) practices along IT governance key focus areas (ITGI, 2003) and how they contribute to business performance in the sector. The second aspect was to uncover IT governance related problems and potential consequences in the studied organizations. The third aspect was to explore key issues to take into account for effective IT governance in public sector organizations, from the perspective of ICT-enabled transformational government and improvement of public service delivery.

In order to understand the practices in the sector mainly in ministries, departments and agencies (MDAs), we applied the case study research method (Yin, 2003) and selected five cases based on the level of IT deployment in the organization, and its multiplier effect on the services provided to the public and related organizations in the sector. These five cases are Tanzania Revenue Authority (TRA), Medical Stores Department (MSD), Prime Minister's Office-Regional Authority and Local Government (PMO-RALG), President's Office-Public Service Management (PO-PSM), and Ministry of Finance and Economic Affairs (MoFEA). In this case study research, we have gathered data by conducting face-to-face in-depth interviews, alongside structured questionnaires. This applied to both IT (IT department) and business (user departments) representatives, mainly directors, managers, key personnel, chief executives and in some applicable cases, board members.

Table 1. Distribution of respondents in the case studies

Respondents\Organizations	TRA	MSD	PMO-RALG	PO-PSM	MoFEA	Total
IT Management	8	5	5	6	7	31
Business Management	6	6	6	5	6	29
Total	14	11	11	11	13	60

Five interview questionnaires were developed, two for IT management (Chief Information Officer (CIO) known as Director of IT, IS or MIS in the studied environment and IT line managers or supervisors). The rest were for Business Management groups: Directors/Managers, Chief Executives and where applicable, board members. The interviews and overall data collection were undertaken between March and November 2008. Table 1, provides interviewees distribution in the five case studies.

Case Study: TRA

Introduction

TRA is an agency responsible for administration of central government revenues. Through its 1st, 2nd and 3rd corporate strategic plans, various initiatives including IT have been implemented towards the more efficient and cost-effective revenue collection. For example, while in 2003/2004 TRA collected about 1.4 billion US$ with close to 3,457 employees, in 2007/08 financial year, it expects to exceed the planned budget of about 3.3 billion USD with almost the same number of employees, 46 being IT staff. In addition, the authority has an organization-wide operating budget estimated at 115US$ million with an IT department using 1.3 US$ million. The decision-making structures of TRA are organized according to their function. Four core departments are headed by commissioners and seven support departments including IT are headed by directors. The top most level is managed by a Commissioner General under the supervision and control of Board of Directors (TRA, 2008).

IT Related Governance Context

In the survey, it was indicated that the Tanzanian government depends on the tax collected and therefore TRA has embarked on a major tax administration improvement including use of IT to provide services in a transparent manner, flexibility, ease of interaction and certainty to improve revenue collection and cost-effectiveness without increasing tax rates (Ruparel, 2006). Together with these, its vision is to be a modernized tax administrator, where well governed IT is a key integrator for the efficient realization of higher revenue collection. In addition, as *the Director of ICT* indicated, *the realization of ISO 9000 standard on quality management, to which TRA has recently embarked, triggered the need of several IT processes and governance improvements to achieve the required quality in the public services delivery.* Similarly, the Director indicated that *the required strategic alignment between business and IT was yet another motive given the intensive integration of IT in the process of integrating various functions across the departments.* This included the Integrated Income Tax Information System (ITAX) and Customs Management Information System (ASYCUDA). In order to realize these IT governance related drivers, the authority has been improving on structures, processes and relational mechanisms as per subsequent sections.

IT Governance Structures

The survey indicated that the IT department is at the same level as other business and support departments. It is headed by a Director who reports to the CEO. The director is part of the executive management team and attends the Board. The IT function is also supported by an Information Systems Steering Committee (ISSC) that has members both from IT and business departments (Figure 6). It meets quarterly and oversees the IS investment and specifically it provides strategic leadership for IS operations.

Moreover, survey indicated the authority to have several committees at project level to oversee the IT activities. These also include IT and business people to increase partnership and acceptability. The committees at this level are normally called project boards and are chaired by the head of the business department concerned. Also at the lower levels there are implementers and technical teams all comprising IT and business people. One of the projects, for example, is the Drivers' Licenses System (DLS) that manages the processing and issuing of Drivers' licences across the country. The other is Central Motor Vehicle Registration System (CMVRS) that manages the registration and issuing of motor vehicle cards. Both have the Project Board as well as implementation and technical teams.

The IT structure in place and the described committees, among others, have increased the alignment between IT and business, making it strategic. In fact, when the *modernization programme manager* was interviewed said, "*I work closely with IT people through IT structure and I am member of some committees.*" This structures have reduced duplication of efforts and increased awareness and ownership of IT-enabled projects.

IT Governance Processes

The survey indicated that the authority has several processes including elements of ITIL, a framework for IT service management (OGC, 2008), which currently only looks into problems and incidents management, to ensure that best practices are instituted to serve IT users better. In addition, it has an IT project life cycle that uses PRINCE2, a worldwide project management methodology (ITGI, 2006a). As it was indicated by *the manager responsible with systems practices, this practice in combination with the earlier mentioned project committees and respective project managers provide consistency across the organization and ensure success in the whole project life cycle from the request for pre-study, idea processing and validation, prioritizing up to development or acquisition and maintenance.* He also added that

Figure 6. TRA IS Steering Committee (Adopted from TRA, 2008)

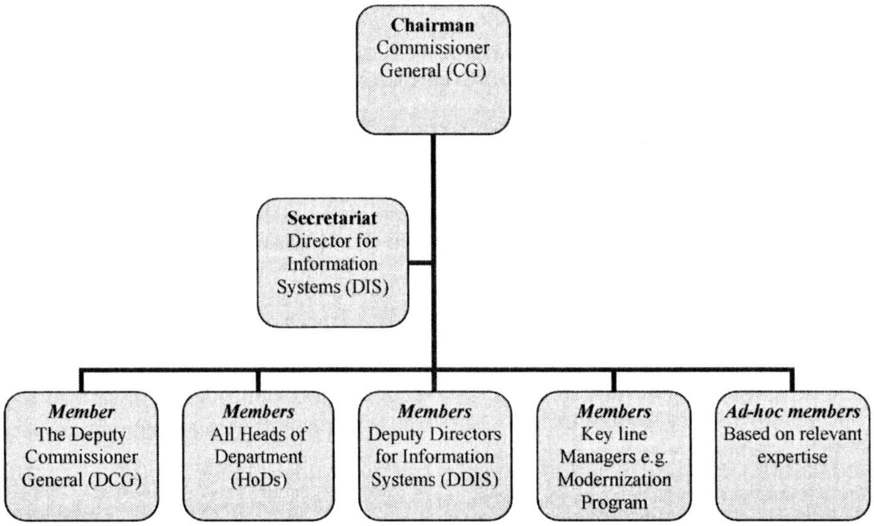

if there is a problem at any stage of the project, it is likely to be captured earlier and mitigation prompted thus avoiding investment loss and late delivery.

Recently, the authority has also introduced the balanced scorecard (BSC) at corporate level and cascaded it down to departments including IT (Figure 7). *When the chairperson of the board* was interviewed said *BSC enables her to see the overall performance of the authority including IT much easier than before.* This also applies to the *Director of ICT* when was interviewed he enthusiastically indicated *BSC to have increased the alignment between IT and business including improvement in the reporting mechanisms and track of the IT achievement back to business goals.* Finally, it is worth noting that the authority expects to deploy some elements of COBIT. It is likely that a modest deployment of such IT governance framework together with present best practices will improve further the governance of IT.

IT Governance Relational Mechanisms

Relational mechanisms are a catalyst of IT uptake in an organization and this is even more important in an environment where the culture of using IT is relatively new. During the survey, the majority

Figure 7. TRA IT balanced scorecard (Adopted from TRA, 2008)

Perspective	Corporate Strategic Goal	Strategic Initiative	Strategic Measure
Financial	Increase revenue in a cost effective way	Growth	Contribution towards reaching revenue targets
		Manage costs	Costs/budget
Customer	High quality and responsive customer service	Continually delight the targeted customer	Customer satisfaction index
			% of Satisfied customers
		Ensure customer friendly and support	Average time taken to fix a problem
		Manage customer enquiries (help desk)	Time taken to respond to customers
Internal Processes	Increase revenue in a cost effective way	Enhancement of Financial system (Epicor). Enhancement of ITAX Implementation of ASYCUDA++.	Realize deliverables
			New modules acceptance rate
			System downtime rate
			Number of new modules developed
			Application portfolio developed
	Integrate TRA operations	CMVRS enhancement Drivers licence system (DLS) development Payroll & HR system enhancement	Realize deliverables
			New modules acceptance rate
			System downtime rate
			Number of new modules developed
			Application portfolio developed
Learning and Growth	Improve staff competence, motivation, etc	Develop strategic competencies	Strategic competence availability
		Develop skills that enhance customer service delivery	Customer complaints
		Develop skills that enhance process improvement	Number of process improvement
		Attract & retain top talents	Key employee turnover
		Motivate staff	Employee satisfaction index
			Number of new modules developed
			Application portfolio developed

both IT and business people seemed to be aware of practices related to shared understanding of business/IT goals, shared learning and dialogue, informal meeting between business and IT and cross-functional business and IT training. For example, *one of the commissioners* said *regular training takes place for IT people in business issues like tax administration and vice versa*; while *Director of ICT* indicated *a practice on operational meetings like the case of using annual managers meetings to introduce new IT developments.*

Case Study: MSD

Introduction

The MSD is an autonomous body established with the objective to develop, maintain and manage an efficient and cost-effective system of procurement, storage and distribution of approved essential drugs and other medical supplies required for use across the country. It has a countrywide distribution network with nine zones and total customer base of over 4,000 health facilities. It serves all district, regional, specialized and referral hospitals. Through a corporate strategic plan, highly organized processes and ever expanding infrastructure, MSD services have been expanding from about US$14 million in 1998 to US$100 million during 2006/07 financial year, managed by over 350 employees, 9 of them being IT staff (MSD, 2008). The decision-making structure of MSD is organized around three core and two support directorates including IT, both headed by Directors. The highest position is occupied by a Director General, under supervision and control of a Board of Trustees.

IT Related Governance Context

The survey across the organization indicated that the context of governance of IT is due to the need to ensure timely availability of supplies for quality medical services where increasingly IT systems are seen as a backbone. Several sources showed an example of these IT systems in place to be ORION that manages procurement, storage and distribution and recently the Integrated Logistics System (ILS) that manages varied health supplies using a single set of procedures. When *Director of IS* interviewed said, *having governance over these IT systems that handle large transactions of stocks and connects all nine zones is essential for consistency, economies of scale and effective management of business information required for quality of service.* Others included the need of strategic alignment and accountability of IT and business people to keep improving service delivery. It is in this perspective that MSD has been improving IT governance related mechanisms as described in subsequent parts.

IT Governance Structures

The survey across the organization indicated IT Directorate to be at the same level as other director-

Figure 8. MSD information security committee (Adopted from MSD, 2008)

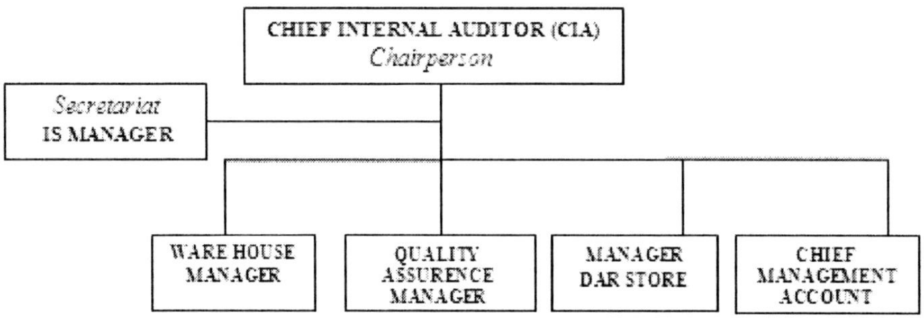

ates. It is headed by a Director and reports to the CEO. In addition, the head is part of the executive management team and attends the Board. While there is no IT steering committee at MSD, IT functions are supported by several other committees. An example of these is the Information Security Committee that oversees security related policies and procedures; and the Chief Internal Auditor is the chairperson with other members from IT and business (Figure 8). Others are project-based committees, for example, when *Information systems manager* interviewed indicated *the Integrated Logistic System (ILS) committee that oversees the project conceptualization and implementation, chaired by the directorate concerned.*

IT Governance Processes

The survey indicated that they do not have an IT strategic plan. When *Director of IS* interviewed on this said, "*we have commissioned consultants in developing it, but have been slow, meanwhile we have IT plans incorporated in corporate strategic plan.*" He adds, "*however there are also good elements of governance like use of a performance based yearly business plan that indicates objectives to achieve and KPIs for monitoring and evaluation.*" Moreover, several respondents indicated to apply ROI in appraisal of new or upgrading IT investment.

IT Governance Relational Mechanisms

These mechanisms are essential at MSD and according to the survey, the majority indicated to be aware of the ones related to understanding of business and IT goals e.g. formulating and deploying IT plans in consultation with management and committees. Others are informal meetings between business and IT e.g. in discussing business logic related issues during planning and implementing IT initiative. Cross-functional business and IT training are also practiced in several IT/Business themes for example when one of the directors interviewed said, "*IT/Business training in supported infrastructure and applications like efficient use of IT in communication and customer care training have been essential in improving services to the public.*" These mechanisms ensure subsequent accountability in implementation and use.

Case Study: PMO-RALG

Introduction

PMO-RALG is the ministry responsible for coordinating regional and local government affairs to facilitate the empowerment of Tanzanians through autonomous local government institutions geared to reducing poverty. Through various ministry strategic plans and the Local Government Reform Programme (LGRP), the ministry has been improving its coordinating functions of about 21 regional secretariats (RSs) and 133 Local Government Authorities (LGAs) to provide public services in their localities (PMO-RALG, 2008).

The decision-making structure of the ministry is organized in eight divisions, including an IT Division, all headed by Directors. At the top level it is led by the Minister and managed by the Permanent Secretary. Currently, it is supported by 250 staff, 6 of them are IT staff. Moreover, there is one IT staff at each RS that provides assistance to the LGAs in the area.

IT Related Governance Context

The survey across the organization indicated that the need of governance of IT in the ministry is because of required coordination and Information management between LGAs, regional administration and MDAs. However, when the *Director of MIS* was interviewed said, *these developments especially in IS have been achieved but rarely coordinated among sectors and vertical programmes that work at regional and local government levels.* For example, *the ICT analyst* and *coordinator of one of the five zones* (Figure 9) said, *systems like Integrated Financial Management Information System (IFMIS), Planning and Reporting (PLAN-REP), Local Government Monitoring Database (LGMD) and sector based as Health Management Information System (HMIS) and Education Management Information System (EMIS), have been introduced by different actors in the same area but most of them used uncoordinatedly.*

PMO-RALG being the coordinating ministry perceives that improving governance over these IT resources and associated organizations that promote, fund, support and manage them is vital for consistency, organizational performance, quality of services, sustainability, and reducing duplication of efforts and overburdening of the end-users. Other drivers as per survey include having a managed and faster IT services among the user departments and a need of the holistic but realist approach instead of a limited view that only solves the immediate problem like the case of IFMIS that is able to provide financial control but missing adequate reporting tools. It is in this perspective the MIS directorate action plan has specifically included a key result area on IS Governance as a contribution to improve further governance of IT related mechanisms that are described in the subsequent parts.

IT Governance Structures

The survey and document collected like the ministry strategic plan indicated IT division to be at the same level as other divisions and is headed by a Director who reports to CEO. When *Director of MIS* interviewed in relation to other possible

Figure 9. Governance structure: committees & groups (Adopted from PMO-RALG, 2008)

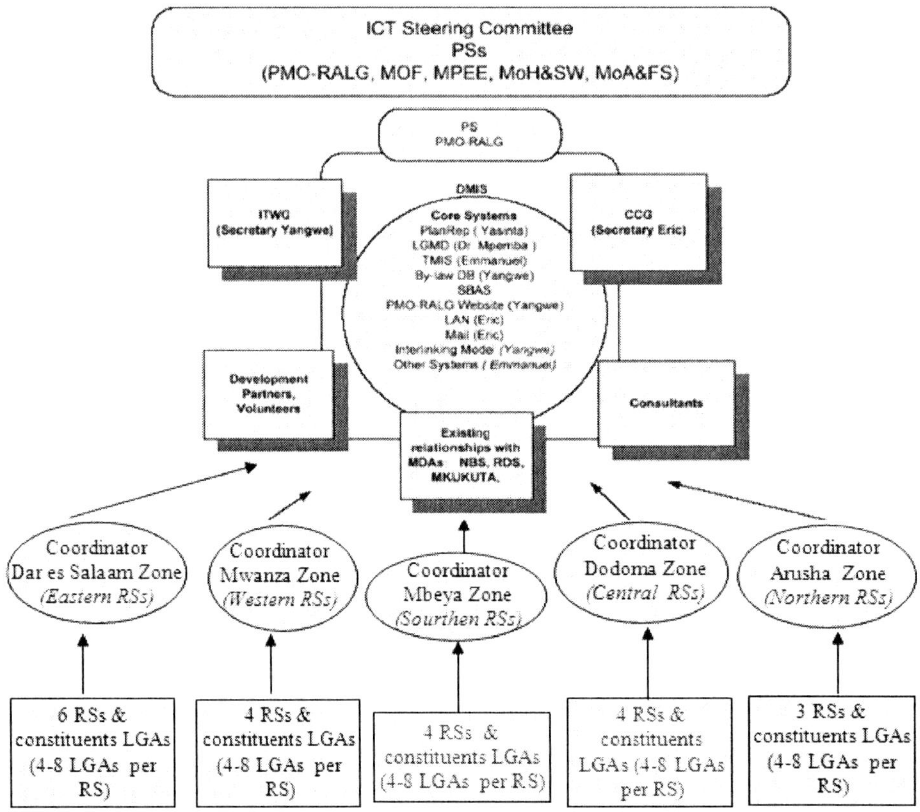

IT structure in place he said, *we do not have IT steering committee, however recently we have proposed a high-level ICT steering committee (Figure 9) to cut across the ministries that are heavily interacting with the LGAs through various IT applications*. He continues, *this is in order to minimize duplication of efforts and improve information flow*. In addition, *he indicated that several other committees called groups support the IT function including IT specialists Working Group (ITWG) that comprises of them (21 RSs), Zone coordinators, Director MIS, Manager LGRP and Change Control Group (CCG) that involves relevant ministries and IS supporting organizations*.

Figure 9 indicates these setups including five zonal coordinators, each coordinating several RSs that in turn support LGAs in their respective areas. One quick observation is that with these setups in place governance is becoming better and certainly earlier indicated duplication of efforts will slowly decrease especially if higher levels and business people in the ministry and in those RSs and LGAs continuously get feedback and kept engaged in the process.

IT Governance Processes

The survey indicated that the ministry only has IT plans embedded in the ministry strategic plan. However, when *M & E expert and coordinator of one of the five zones* interviewed said, *we have developed a comprehensive IT operational plan based on previous MIS strategies and current ministry strategic plan*. He continues, *this Operational plan has Key Result Areas (KRAs) that include IS governance, which is also linked to the targets of the ministry strategic plan thus will facilitate strategic decision-making, monitoring, evaluation and contribution to the organization goal*.

IT Governance Relational Mechanisms

Having relational mechanisms is vital in a government institution like this given its distribution across several coordinating functions and levels. The survey through questionnaire and interviews of business/IT people indicated practices such as shared understanding of business and IT goals. For example when *Permanent secretary* interviewed said, *major IT initiatives and subsequent implementation are presented and discussed in the management meetings, which comprise directors of business/IT departments thus assisting the joint understanding of these initiatives, however I would like to see more use among us*. Others are shared learning and dialogue through workshop; informal meeting between Business and IT management during project initiation and implementation; and Cross-functional business and IT training on leadership and supported information systems. These together with structures and processes mentioned earlier ensure alignment and accountability in IT enabled projects thus increasing IT contribution and achievement of the ministry goals.

Case Study: PO-PSM

Introduction

The President's Office, Public Service Management is a Ministry in charge of public service management with the mission to ensure that the Public Service is effectively and efficiently managed through improved human resources management, systems and structures. Through various ministry strategic plans and the Public Service Reform Programme (PSRP), the ministry has been improving its role as a ministry and as a facilitator of the latter with a view to improving public service delivery as a whole. This way as a ministry, among others, has put in place Human Capital Management Information Systems (HCMIS) that manage all government employees, currently about 400,000. As a facilitator of the reforms, Ministries, Departments and Agencies (MDAs) have been empowered in various aspects to improve public service delivery, including putting in place several ICT facilities, applications, Information Systems Strategic Plan (ISSP) and capacity building. The decision-making structure of the ministry is organized into seven divisions (including MIS Division), all headed by Directors. At the top, the ministry is led by the Minister and managed by the Permanent Secretary. Currently, it is supported by 300 staff, and 15 of these are IT staff. In addition, the overall number of the MDAs facilitated is about 72 (PO-PSM, 2008).

IT Related Governance Context

The survey across the organization indicated that the context of governance of IT is due to the required effective management of ICT in the ministry and empowering other MDAs to advance ICT for improving public service delivery. This includes ensuring that HCMIS, mentioned earlier, is managed and used effectively in all these MDAs.

Other drivers as per survey include the increasing demand from public for better service delivery as also indicated in the ministry customer satisfaction survey (PO-PSM, 2008). In addition, during interviews, for example *Assistant MIS director for government business services* said, *one of the drivers for governance of IT in this environment is the required harmonization of IT initiatives to allow better information flows across a variety of stakeholders. He* continues, *also PSRP that looks for increasing efficiency and effectiveness of the public services delivery is another driver.* In order to achieve these, PO-PSM has been improving structures, processes and relation mechanisms explained in the subsequent parts.

IT Governance Structures

The survey in the ministry indicated the IT division to be at the same level as others and its head, Director of MIS, to report to the CEO. It also indicated that there is no IT steering committee; however, executive and operational management meetings make the ICT related decisions. Also for major projects in the ministry, there are project committees with the chairperson from the business department concerned and members from business and IT. For example, when *senior computer system analyst* and *the Principle administration officer* interviewed said, *HCMIS is one of such projects, its members represent IT/Business from two ministries given its use for both HR (PO-PSM) and Payroll (MoFEA) functions* (Figure 10).

Figure 10. HCMIS project committee, PO-PSM and MoFEA: An example of governance of ICT based projects (Adopted from PO-PSM, 2008)

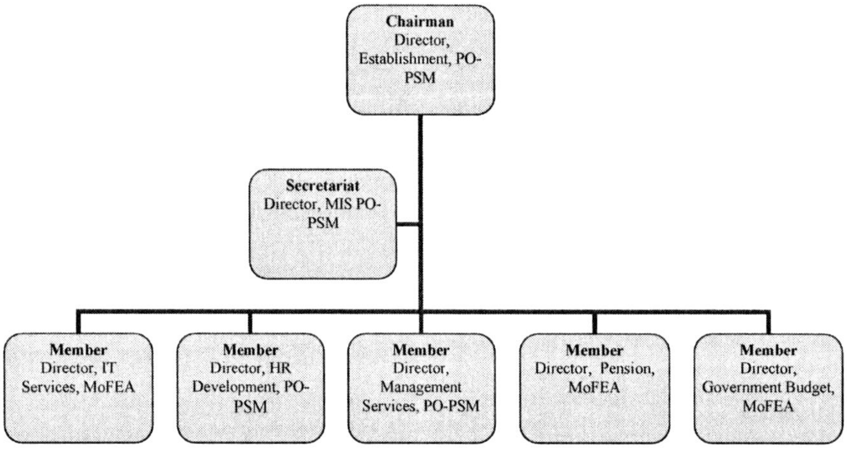

IT Governance Processes

The survey indicated that there is no strategic plan rather IT plans are embedded in the ministry strategic plan. It also indicated some elements of best practices like SWOT analysis used to prepare IT plan and ROI in appraisal of Major IT investment. Apart from that, when MIS director interviewed said, *the directorate has created a client charter as part of SLA for user departments, though recently introduced, it allows measuring and improving IT service*. These altogether make the process of decision-making, monitoring and evaluation efficient.

IT Governance Relational Mechanisms

The survey indicated consistency in practices related to shared understanding of business and IT goals, shared learning and dialogue, informal meetings and cross-functional business and IT training. For example, when *Assistant MIS director for government business services* interviewed said, *some awareness and training sessions have been held jointly and usefully on e-government and public service reforms*. In addition, when *senior e-government expert* interviewed said, *the meetings are one of the major practices spanning from formal ones (like the executive, operational and project-based management meetings) to the ad-hoc ones*. These practices have assisted the ministry to integrate IT that apparently has impact in the constantly increasing quality in the public service delivery (PO-PSM, 2008).

Case Study: MoFEA

Introduction

The ministry is responsible for managing the overall revenue, expenditure and financing of the government. It also provides advice on financial and economic affairs in support of the government's economic and social objectives (MoFEA, 2008). Through various ministry strategic plans and the Public Financial Management Reform Programme (PFMRP) the ministry improved its public services delivery. It has also introduced several IT systems to facilitate its role. These systems include Integrated Financial MIS (IFMIS) that manages the budget and expenditure of the country, rolled-out countrywide. Also together with PO-PSM, it has established HCMIS that, among others, runs payroll for all the government employees.

The decision-making structure of the ministry is organized in 10 divisions, including the IT division, headed by commissioners or directors. The top most position is held by the Minister and the Permanent Secretary manages day-to-day activities. Currently, the ministry is supported by 1,200 staff, 100 of whom are IT staff.

IT Related Governance Context

The ministry is a key organ in directing the socio-economic development of the country, as it manages both revenue and expenditure. Also being in a developing country with a budget that depends outside support of about 40% (MoFEA, 2008) there is a need of ensuring that sources of aid are coordinated with respective programmes and that appropriate reporting is done. In order to make sure that the IT deployed is used efficiently, effectively and responsibly, MoFEA has been improving its approaches to IT services, for example when *Assistant IT services director for systems development and administration* interviewed said, *the ministry have recognized the need of effective management of IT and included efficiency and effectiveness of IS as part of its eight's ministry objectives*. Mechanisms in the ministry are indicated in subsquent sections.

IT Governance Structures

The survey indicated that the head of IT function is the Director of IT Services Division, who reports to the CEO and is part of the executive management. It also indicated that there is no IT steering committee; however, they have a Website Board that oversees content matters and the members are IT and business people with Information and Communication Unit as secretariat (Figure 11). When *one of the assistants of director of IT services interviewed said this board seems to contribute to the state of the art and updated website. He also adds, as it relates to committees, we also participate in the HCMIS project committee from payroll viewpoint together with PO-PSM that deals with other HR aspects, thus more accountability* (Figure 10).

IT Governance Processes

The survey indicated only IT plans to be embedded and tracked from within the ministry strategic plan. When *IT personnel/MTEF account* interviewed said, *the plan is also tracked from the expenditure point of view where MTEF, which is standardized across the government, is used.* This is good as such tracking, if is enforced, can be viewed through strategic plan and expenditure point of views.

IT Governance Relational Mechanisms

In the survey the majority said to be aware of the shared understanding of business and IT goals, informal meeting between business and IT and cross-functional business and IT training. The practices for the first two include management and project meetings, and strategic planning and budgeting processes. The last one, as for example said by *the assistant treasury registrar on reforms* is *practiced through joint awareness and training related to IT systems in place and area of business applications.* An example is the case of IFMIS among IT and accountants where general knowledge in accounts and IT are given and then the actual use and management of the system. Though the ministry has a long way to effective IT governance, these mechanisms have increased IT contribution to its organizational goals.

Summary and Discussion of IT Governance Mechanisms Across Studied Organizations

The practice on IT governance mechanisms spanning from structure, processes to relational

Figure 11. MoFEA Website board, governance of the ministry website content and development (Adopted from MoFEA, 2008)

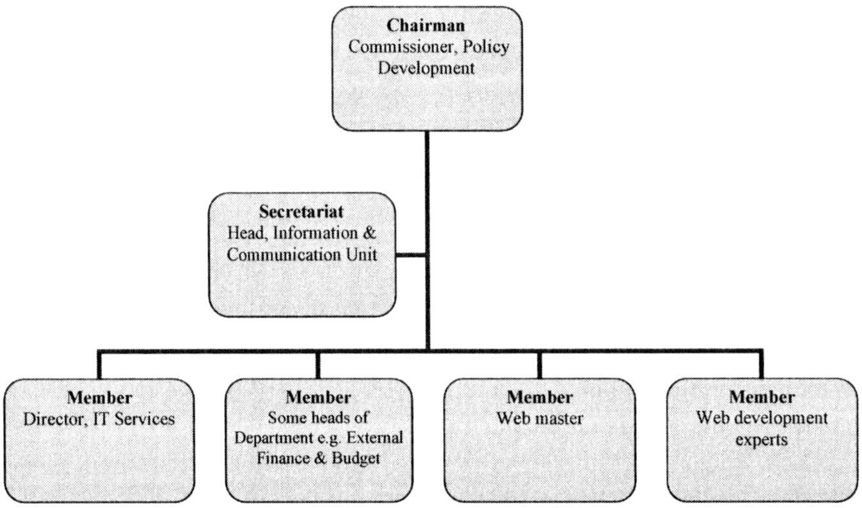

mechanisms found earlier in each case are summarized and discussed in the perspective of the commonality or differences in practices across studied organizations (Table 2, 3 and 4).

Generally, in the analysis of IT governance mechanisms across the studied organizations we found that the studied environments undertake several useful practices, some being specific to their environment like MTEF and IT Plans. In addition, we found a number of unpracticed mechanisms in each category like IT Steering/ Strategy committees, IT governance frameworks and Knowledge management. However, more weaknesses seem to be on the processes where internationally recognized best practices and standards are rarely applied. In addition, we found that there have been improvements due to the practiced mechanisms, though not undertaken as specific IT governance projects but rather as routine improvement in governance of IT to further increase IT contribution in meeting the organizational goals.

Table 2. IT governance mechanisms across the studied organizations: Structures

Structures		
Type of Practice		How Practiced across Studied Organizations
1	Organizational structure of IT function	All are ***headed by CIO*** (Director of IT, MIS or IT services in the studied environment), ***report*** to CEO, ***part of the executive management*** and ***attend the board*** in the applicable cases.
2	How is IT instituted in the organization	***Mostly centralized,*** with cases staff distributed to work directly in specific user departments thus ***elements of decentralization***.
3	Committees	Generally, ***no IT steering Committees,*** except in one of them.
		Generally, ***at major projects level mostly business applications***, there are committees established to oversee their implementations and in most cases with IT and business people.
		Also in some of them there are ***several other committees*** handling cutting-across issues like security, change controls, website content management and technology management.

Table 3. IT governance mechanisms across the studied organizations: Processes

Processes		
Type of Practice		How Practiced across Studied Organizations
1	Strategic Information Systems Planning	***Not directly*** applied, with exception of one case that have IT Strategy. However, there are elements of its application in developing IT Plans as part of the corporate strategic planning.
2	SWOT Analysis	***Mostly applied across studied organizations in different magnitude;*** lower when preparing IT plans that are incorporated in the corporate strategic plan and higher in the IT strategic plan process practiced in only one of the studied organizations.
3	Balanced scorecard	***Generally not applied,*** except in one of the studied cases, which applies it in performance management from corporate level down to departments. Meanwhile in the other organizations there are locally developed M & E based on corporate strategic plans.
4	ROI calculation and measurements	***Not directly applied.*** However, major IT investment needs analysis of non-financial and financial benefits like the case of HCMIS project cited earlier that its justification was to reduce ghost workers and increase efficiency to manage government employees.
5	COBIT or related IT Governance framework	***Not applied.*** However, one of the studied organizations has started implementing some modules of ITIL and looking forward to incorporate some aspects of COBIT.
6	Service Level Agreements (SLAs)	***Hardly applied*** with user departments. However, it is mostly applied for external service providers (third parties).
7	Activity Based Costing/ Budgeting (ABC)	***Mostly applied*** based on a Medium-Term Expenditure Framework (MTEF), a government wide tool for planning activities, resources, and associated performance.

Table 4. IT governance mechanisms across the studied organizations: Relational mechanisms

Relational Mechanisms		
Type of practice		How Practiced across Studied Organizations
1	Shared understanding of business/IT goals	***Widely practiced*** mostly through management meetings, project-based committees and other special IT programme committees that mostly comprise business and IT people.
2	Shared learning and dialogue	***Somehow practiced*** through meetings, workshops and training on issues pertaining to business and IT, in relation to Information Systems implementation and use.
3	Informal meeting between Business and IT management	***Widely practiced*** at different levels for example in clarifying some IT/business issues especially when new IT enabled projects are being initiated, implemented or enhanced.
4	Cross-functional business/IT training	***Somehow practiced through*** workshops and training on matters of interest among IT and business people like leadership and effective use of the supported infrastructure and applications.
5	Performance/ Partnership rewards and incentives	***Not systematically practiced.*** However, occasionally some people are rewarded like in the case of outstanding performance related to the development of innovative IT solution.
6	Cross-functional business/IT job rotation/ co-location	***Not widely practiced.*** However, in some cases co-location across the units and branches in one of the organizations has been applied and indicated to reduce the resistance to some IT related changes and thus increasing the performance.
7	"Virtual meeting points" for business and IT people	***Rarely practiced.*** Although there is already for example Intranet platform in many of these organizations, it is not used widely, among others, due to the culture and enforcement issues.
8	Knowledge management	***Rarely practiced*** in terms of having the knowledge base and access to them.

These results are in contrast with the related studies in the developed world, in this case firms in Belgium (Van Grembergen & De Haes, 2008), where several of them indicated to have specific IT governance projects and use of best practices like COBIT, ITIL and Balance Scorecard. This is in line with the level of the IT widespread in these two worlds.

IT Governance Key Decisions Across the Studied Public Sector Organizations

One of the key determinants of effective IT governance in the organization is where the IT decision-making authority is located (Weill and Ross, 2004) in relation to IT governance key decisions (Figure 3). We applied it in the studied organizations in terms of who provides the inputs and makes decisions, and found that both are distributed across the organization as indicated in Figure 12. However, the notable pattern indicates that IT provides most of the inputs except the business application needs, where inputs come from business related groups. The decisions indicate a different trend as mostly are made by the executive management team comprising IT and business people. If this is done well, it is likely to increase strategic alignment and smooth implementation and use of IT applications.

Looking at related studies elsewhere and taking the case of MIT-CISR work and specifically on the public sector (Weill and Ross, 2004), it is obvious that there are similarities in the pattern especially in taking decisions, where federal dominates in both cases. However, we noted the difference on decisions related to IT architecture and infrastructure where for their case is done by IT monarchy whiles ours is federal. When it comes to the inputs, the difference seems to be substantial because while IT monarchy dominates most of the inputs, in our case it is dominated by federal. Looking at the differences in both cases one might say that the mature IT governance practices especially on structures might be one of the determinants of these differences.

Figure 12. IT governance key decisions patterns in the studied public sector organizations in a developing country (Adopted from Weill & Ross, 2004)

Decision / Style	IT principles		IT architecture		IT Infrastructure strategies		Business applications needs		IT investment and prioritization	
	Input	Decision	Input	Decision	Input	Decision	Input	Decision	Input	Decision
A group of business executives *(Business Monarchy)*	1						2		1	
IT executives *(IT Monarchy)*	5		5	1	5	1	2		5	
Business unit leaders *(Feudal)*									2	
IT/Business executives and business unit leaders *(Federal)*	1	5	1	4	1	4	2	5	2	5
IT executives and a business group of a process to computerize *(Duopoly)*							2			
individual business process owner *(Anarchy)*				1			1			

...... *Input pattern* ▬▬ *Decision pattern*

Problems and Consequences Across the Public Sector in a Developing Country

Use of ICT in public sector organizations in a developing country is still a new culture and this contributes further to the problems encountered in this environment (Mhayaya, 2003; Ndou, 2004). These problems are discussed here based on the representative case studies earlier presented and discussed. In addition, the section indicates the consequences so that the implication for not taking necessary improvements is known and certainly this acts as a motivation for change.

Problems

As it was earlier indicated, one vital way of looking at IT governance issues in an organization is its key focus areas (ITGI, 2003) as applied by other earlier different studies (Supangkat *et al.*, 2006; Buckby *et al.*, 2008). This categorization, i.e. Strategic alignment, Value delivery, Risk management, Resource management and Performance management, we also apply it to discuss the problems in the sector. In addition, we rank the problems found in these categories according to their seriousness in the sector (Figure 13).

Strategic alignment focuses on ensuring the linkage of business and IT plans; on defining, maintaining and validating the IT value proposition; and on aligning IT operations with enterprise operations (ITGI, 2003). In the survey across the studied organizations, we found that there is no IT strategic plan in most of them that tie the business and IT activities more effectively although we noticed that there are IT plans incorporated within the corporate strategic plans. This, among others, lead to the problems we found to be among the highly rated including inadequate convincing competencies of IT management people; business people lower acceptance to the new IT applications; lack of business people ownership in IT-enabled projects and business people limited awareness on optimal use of IT (Figure 13). These, in some cases leads to MDAs being forced to allocate IT

Figure 13. Ranked IT Governance Related Problems Seriousness as a Result of the Survey in the Studied Organizations

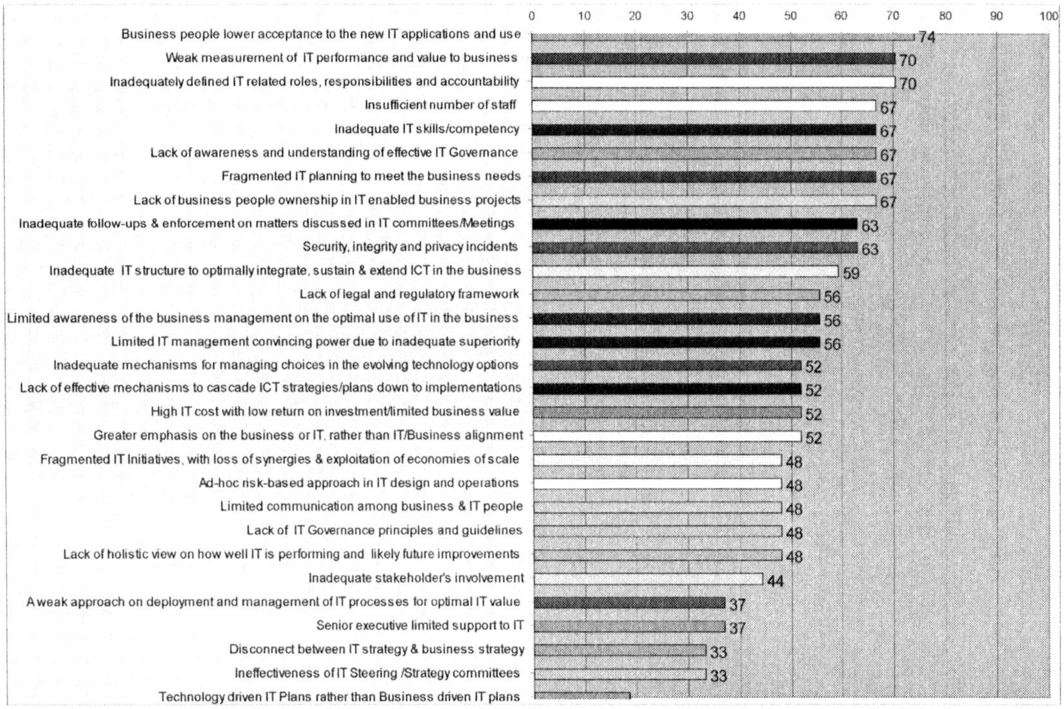

personnel to do what business people should do, rather than strategically and operationally supporting them.

The aspect of inadequate ICT policies, procedures and IT structure to optimally integrate, sustain and extend ICT in the business is other problem that we found consistent across most of them. They hamper consistency in ICT use and associated management, which is yet seen as another serious problem. While it appears that there are some mechanisms to communicate ICT plans and goals, e.g. through meetings and workshops, inadequate mechanisms and enforcements to cascade them down to implementation still hamper the widespread use of ICT and promised benefits. An example is the Intranet, which we found to be in place in many of them and can really increase IT/business partnership and internal efficiency but still not widely used, as *Principle administration officer* quoted saying, *the Intranet is in place and training have been provided to us but we have not seen it being used.*

Value delivery is one of the IT governance outcomes and is about value proposition throughout the delivery cycle, ensuring that IT delivers the promised benefits against the strategy or plans (ITGI, 2003). In the survey we found that despite the high cost of IT there is still a lower return or business value. This is due to missing synergies and inadequate enforcement for a widespread optimal use. For example when *one of the Assistant treasurer registrars* in MoFEA interviewed said, *apart from various IT applications that have been deployed and in use some offices are still using computers merely as fast type-writers.*

Risk management requires awareness by senior and operational officers and embedding of risk management responsibilities in the organisation (ITGI, 2003). The survey results indicate that generally there is a weak risk-based approach in designing and operating IT services and presence of several security incidents which is also in consistent with earlier studies on security management in the environment (Bakari, 2007). In addition, lack of the legal framework contributes to the difficulties in managing the risk and to some extent the widespread use of IT (Mollel & Lukumay, 2007). For example, when Director of finance and administration at *MSD interviewed said we are accountable to parliament and subject to Auditor general, such auditing could be done using audit trail in a PC but we are forced to do some manual work again. This aspect need legal and regulatory framework for enforcing it so that such uses are legally allowed, thus increasing value of IT.*

Resource Management ensures optimal investment and proper management of critical IT resources (ITGI, 2003) and is yet another problematic area in the sector. The issue of attracting and sustaining skilled and competent IT personnel is still a nightmare to solve, despite the efforts made. Lack of IT governance awareness and certainly some guidelines together with HR related problem on lack of clear roles, responsibilities and accountability are other problems that lead to ad-hoc practices. Availability of adequate budget for the required IT resources is yet another problem, which gets worse as you cascade down the organization and to the branches and regions. Together with these, is the case of fragmented IT initiatives with a loss of synergies and exploitation of the economies of scale. For example, in some of them and as said by *one of the Assistant commissioners* at MoFEA, *you still find heavy-duty printers or photocopiers with the capacity to serve a number of employees or offices, only serving a single person or office, thus mostly staying idle.*

Performance management tracks and monitors strategy and implementation plans, and benefits accrued and measured beyond the conventional accounting (ITGI, 2003). Although there is progress in this direction, like the recently use of the balanced scorecard in one of the organizations or metrics embedded in the corporate strategic plans, we generally found that there is weak measurement of IT performance and value to business (Figure 13). Others are inadequate follow-ups and enforcement on the matters agreed in the IT related committees and other meetings. For example when *modernization programme manager* at TRA interviewed said, *here we have a number of committees, though have helped to advance IT decisions and operations, the seriousness on schedules and timely following-up of issues agreed can still be improved.* This indicates that having IT structures is not enough; we must go beyond to implement processes and relational mechanisms to ensure promised returns.

The results indicated in Figure 13 are comparable to other related studies like the ones produced by the IT Governance Institute (ITGI and PwC, 2006; ITGI and PwC, 2008) on global IT governance status and MIT-CISR (Weill and Ross, 2004) on IT governance study on 256 organizations worldwide. While there are some similarities with them like staff problems, weak measurement of IT performance, high cost of IT but low ROI and security incidents, we also found some differences. These include lower acceptance of new IT applications, lack of ownership of IT projects, fragmented IT initiatives and inadequate enforcement mechanisms that hamper governance of IT and improvement of public services.

Consequences

Several studies indicate possible consequences for not having effective IT governance in place, as it relates to the public sector (Weill and Ross, 2004) and in a developing country (Mhayaya, 2003). Based on these and preliminary survey in the sector we found that there are serious consequences (Figure 14) due to the problems and challenges related to IT governance practices in the sector and can be detrimental to the efforts towards ICT-enabled transformational government and the improvement in the public service delivery as a whole.

The most experienced consequences in the sector include difficulty in holding individuals accountable for their results. Others are ad-hoc solutions due to user and management frustrations as people finds own solutions and sometimes take the advantage to misuse the IT resources. There are also traditional consequences as IT investment loses, which given the magnitude of systems put in place in these organizations, we are talking about huge losses of funds and efforts when a project fails to deliver its promises. Similarly, there is damage to reputation. Knowing consequences related to IT governance practices, can assist to focus on important issues for effective IT governance and consequently improving service delivery.

KEY ISSUES TO CONSIDER FOR EFFECTIVE IT GOVERNANCE IN THE PUBLIC SECTOR ORGANIZATIONS IN A DEVELOPING COUNTRY

In this section, we discuss the key issues considered important for effective IT governance in the public sector organizations in a developing country. While there is no unified framework or key issues for IT governance, the concern is on two things: IT's delivery of value to the business i.e. value creation and mitigation of IT risks i.e. value preservation (ITGI, 2007). The IT governance focus areas provide this approach where the former is driven by strategic alignment of IT with the business, while the latter is driven by embedding accountability into the enterprise. It is in this perspective together with consideration of other studies (Luftman *et al.*, 2004; Van Grembergen & De Haes, 2008) that we consider IT governance key focus areas (ITGI, 2003) a benchmark for bringing together key issues relevant to such environment for effective IT governance.

In the case studies, we equally took into account the fact that IT Value to be achieved due to effective IT governance is also in relation with IT delivery that ensures efficient IT utilities mainly on provision and management of reliable and cost-effective infrastructure. Also, IT innovation that focuses on ensuring timely and cost effective delivery of IT applications; and business impact

Figure 14. Ranked inadequate IT governance related consequences as a result of the survey in the studied organizations

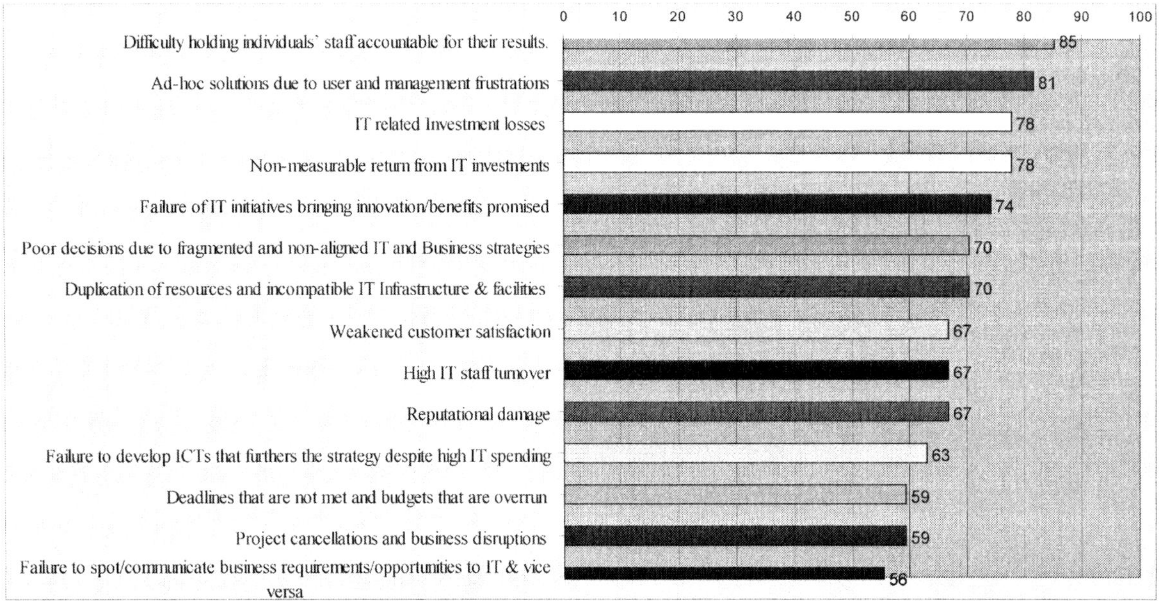

that lends itself more on ways IT leverages business competencies and relationships (Peterson, 2004).

Based on the above literature and preliminary survey in the environment we identified issues to survey (Figure 15) for consideration to effective IT governance in these organizations.

Taking into account this ranking (Figure 15), interviews made and current state of IT governance as indicated in earlier section, we briefly discuss 12 key issues that we found to be vital for the effective IT governance in the studied environment (Table 5). As earlier indicated the discussion focuses on IT governance key focus areas, i.e. strategic alignment, value delivery, risk management, resource management and performance management.

Strategic Alignment Related Issues

IT Leadership Understanding of Business Goals and IT Contribution and Bringing it to the Management Attention

The survey shows 93% of the respondents indicated its importance in this environment (Figure 15). In addition, the interviews across these organizations indicated this concern. For example, when *one of the assistant directors of IT services* at MoFEA interviewed said, *our organization and government institutions in general are still characterized by relatively lower awareness on the available ICT opportunities.* He continues *IT management competencies to bring such understanding and required actions convincingly to the management is vital but apparently still*

Figure 15. Respondents based ranking of key issues to consider for effective IT governance in public sector organizations from a developing country

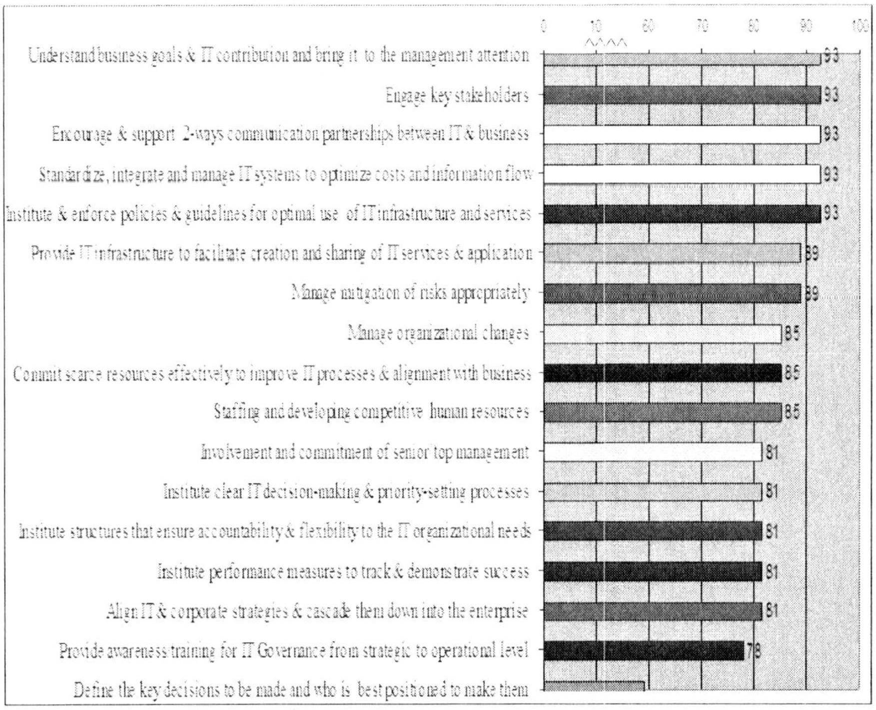

inadequate. In addition, findings in earlier section on state of IT governance support it. For example in most of them, there are no IT strategy plans and steering committees to bring the contribution more comprehensively to the management. Also in terms of problems a limited IT management people convincing competencies (Figure 13) was indicated to be scored by majority (56%) with a consequence on people finding own solutions (Figure 14) and some taking advantage to misuse the IT resources.

Generally, this key issue is vital in the studied environment due to the government efforts to integrate IT in its reforms and development agenda. However, for this to happen a good understanding of IT contribution and buy-in by the management team in each of these organizations is required. Further improvement in this issue will likely increase such alignment (Luftman *et al.*, 2004) and contribution of IT in the public service delivery.

Involvement and Support of Senior Management

The survey indicated 81% of the respondents to support the importance of this key issue (Figure 15). Also in the interviews across the organizations, we found that while support of senior management was important, equally was their involvement in some action-oriented improvements for widespread use of IT. For example, when *senior computer systems analyst* at PO-PSM interviewed said, *senior management willingness and support to IT is important for widespread use in the organization*. She continues, *also we should see them using email to call meetings, Intranet to access internal documents and likes*. In addition, findings in earlier section support it. For example among the problems highly rated in this study is the business people lower acceptance to the use of IT with 74% (Figure 13). An increase in their involvement and support could minimize such weaknesses that among others leads to IT related investment loses rated 78% (Figure 14).

Table 5. Key Issues to Consider for Effective IT Governance (ITG) in the Public Sector Organizations from a Developing Country

No.	Key issues arranged as per ITG key focus areas	ITG Focus Area
1	IT leadership understanding of business goals and IT contribution and bringing it to management's attention	Strategic Alignment
2	Involvement and support of senior management	
3	Encouragement and support of IT/Business communication and partnership	
4	Engagement of key stakeholders	
5	Consolidation of IT structures to ensure responsiveness and accountability	
6	Defining and aligning IT strategies to corporate strategies and cascade them down in an organization	
7	Consolidating, communicating and enforcing policies and guidelines for cost-effective acquisition and use of IT across the organization	Value Delivery
8	Consolidating IT risk mitigation strategies	Risk Mgt.
9	Consolidating, standardizing and managing IT infrastructure to optimize costs and information flow	Resource Management
10	Providing IT governance awareness & training for optimal use of IT	
11	Attracting and retaining competitive IT professionals	
12	Consolidating and benchmarking IT performance measurable beyond the conventional accounting	Performance Management

Moreover, the studied environment is still characterized by a relatively lower IT culture and knowledge, which needs closer support and direct involvement of senior management for a substantial and consistent use of IT. Further improvement in this key issue will advance business value derived from IT investment (Weill & Ross, 2004; Nfuka & Rusu, 2007).

Encouragement and Support of IT and Business Communication and Partnership

The survey shows 93% of the respondents indicated its importance (Figure 15). Also in interviews, several respondents indicated that not only encouragement is required for smooth IT/Business cooperation but also support of these communication and partnership between IT (IT department) and business (user departments). For example when *Director of MIS* at PMO-RALG interview said, *communication and partnership is crucial here, should be encouraged and supported given the wide coordination function of the ministry and the fact that the practices as informal meetings, mailing lists etc increases the projects ownership right from the beginning.* Additionally, earlier findings in previous section also support it. For example, a problem on avoiding greater emphasis on the business or IT rather than IT/Business alignment (Figure 13) scored by majority of respondents (52%) could be minimized. This also applies to the problem on awareness and understanding of the business people on the IT opportunities and IT people on business imperatives that could be increased.

Generally, the studied environment is characterized by lateral and vertical complex relationships that not only require IT structures and processes but also some relational mechanisms to encourage and support the communication and partnership between business and IT and therefore a need of further improvement in this key issue. Such improvement is also vital due to its effectiveness as perceived in some studies on IT governance design (Van Grembergen & De Haes, 2008) and strategic alignment (Luftman *et al.*, 2004).

Engagement of Key Stakeholders

The survey indicated 93% of the respondents to support this key issue (Figure 15). The interviews also indicated its importance in this environment. For example when *chairperson of TRA Board* interviewed said, *such engagement if done from early stage assists, as we have seen in some of our projects.* She continues, *this helps to determine broader view of the need and appropriate approach for the solution and given the widespread of the public sector organizations like TRA any improvement in this area will leapfrog the use of IT.*

Generally, the studied public sector organizations are characterized by mutual dependence for the success of each of them and therefore a need for further improvement of this key issue within an organization and related organizations. Such improvement is also vital due to the required alignment as indicated by Luftman *at el.*, (2004) and earlier study in the latter organization (Nfuka & Rusu, 2007).

Consolidation of IT Structures that Ensure Responsiveness and Accountability

The survey indicated 81% of the respondents to support its importance in this environment (Figure 15). The need of such consolidation is also indicated by findings in the earlier section on state of IT governance practices. For example, though the findings showed several IT governance elements including formal IT positions, roles and some committees to be in place, most of them don't have necessary elements like IT steering committees to effectively and comprehensively handle integration of ICT into their corporate strategies and operations. The interviews also indicated a similar trend. For example, when *Director of ICT* at TRA interviewed said, *though we have structures like IT steering and other committees we are still working on improving further accountability issues including effectiveness in timely follow ups and reporting back and forth.* On the other hand when *one of the assistant directors of IT* services at MoFEA interviewed said, *there are inadequate official and salary linked professional categorization of the IT staff especially in ministries, sometimes with inadquite stated roles and responsibilities.* Some interviewees also indicated that in some cases, IT people have been found doing work belonging to other departments that in their view are probably pressing, leaving less attention to the IT matters which again hamper the IT contribution in these organizations.

Generally, the studied environment is characterized by complex and multiple levels of IT responsibility and decision making therefore a need of further improvement of this key issue at each level and in between them. Such improvement is also vital as per other studies that indicated the responsiveness and accountability to be at the heart of the improved governance structures (Peterson, 2003).

Defining and Aligning IT Strategies to Corporate Strategies and Cascading them Down in an Organization

The survey indicated 81% of the respondents to support the importance of this key issue (Figure 15). Its importance is also seen in the findings of the IT governance practices in the earlier section, which indicated most of them not having IT strategic plan, rather they had IT plans that are part of the overall organization strategic plan. So the first matter seen here is to consolidate those existing plans so that they take into consideration other missing parts of a reasonable IT strategic plan to support IT infrastructure and business applications. The other part of this key issue is on the fact that having an IT strategic plan is not enough. For example when *Director of ICT* at TRA interviewd said, *we have learnt that having IT strategic plan is not effective if not cascaded down to the departments, branches and individuals and then a feedback loop and short-term action plans.* He continues, *the recently deployed Balance scorecard has assisted us in this underouver and we expect that further consolidations in the use and rollout given the number of departments, branches and staff involved country-wide, will further help in the alignment.*

Generally, the studied organizations are characterized by use of corporate strategic plans to budget, implement and monitor its activities. Further improvement on having and aligning IT strategies to such corporate strategic plans and making them known and used downwards in an organization is vital. Such improvement is also important as indicated by Duffy (2002) and Henderson & Venkatraman (1993). Can provide a more widespread use and contribution of IT.

Value Delivery Related Issues

Consolidating, Communicating and Enforcing Policies and Guidelines for Cost-Effective Acquisition and Use of IT Across the Organization

The survey indicated 93% of the respondents to support its importance (Figure 15). The key issue is equally important due to the findings in the IT governance practices, which indicated that not all cases have these management instruments but even where are in place, they have not been used consistently. For example when *information systems manager* at MSD interviewed said, *this issue is central to the success and widely use of IT so apart from the required strong management support, communication and enforcement of policies with mechanisms for reward and punishment is vital.* This was also expressed in an interview with one of the *Assistant commissioner* at MoFEA, who said, *some kind of enforcements are required and can increase widespread use of IT even with the existing IT infrastructure, facilities and applications, for example in calling meetings, access to shared files or direct access to applications rather than requesting from subordinates while also having access that provides even more flexibility.*

Given the widespread nature of the studied organizations, having strategies in place is not enough for a meaningful and consistent contribution of IT in business as also indicated by Duffy (2002a). It needs to be complemented by policies, procedures and guidelines to communicate and enforce the optimal use of IT across the organization. Further improvement along this key issue will allow consolidation and ensure such communication and enforcement, resulting into a more widespread use and contribution of IT.

Risk Management Related Issues

Consolidating IT Risk Mitigation Strategies

The survey indicated 89% of the respondents to support its importance (Figure 15) with a decreased support in the validation process. However, this issue is highly supported in various findings related to state of practices in this study. For example, one of the highly rated problems indicated to be security, integrity and privacy incidents with 63% and lack of legal and regulatory framework with 56% (Figure 13). Its importance and need to be consolidated is even growing further in this environment as indicated in an interview with *one of the assistants director of IT services at MoFEA*, who said, *IT risk mitigation consideration here is due to lower IT security awareness and ever-increasing deployment of open standards, web-based systems, and handling critical business applications like HCMIS and IFMIS that have even caused presence of three different physical networks in the same organization and therefore duplication of resources.*

Generally, the studied environment indicates a need of IT risk related assurance and IT resources protection given different required levels of access and confidentiality within the government cycles and therefore importance of further improvement on this key issue. Such improvement is also important due the need of value preservation along value creation (ITGI, 2007) and a recent study, which pointed out security concerns in this environment (Bakari, 2007).

Resource Management Related Issues

Consolidating, Standardizing and Managing IT Infrastructure to Optimize Costs and Information Flow

The survey indicated 93% of the respondents to support its importance (Figure 15). This is also supported by the findings on the state of IT governance in this environment that indicated lack of standards and best practices for process of IT decision making and monitoring. Further support is also indicated in the interviews. For example when *Director of MIS* at PO-PSM interviewed said, *we have several fragmented and duplicated IT initiatives in and across our government institutions some efforts are required to minimize the trend for economies of scale and better information flow.* In addition, when Director of ICT at PMO-RALG interviewed said, *the infrastructure available needs to be extended and facilities like PCs added to increase inclusiveness, thus facilitating enforcement across the board.* Further improvement on this key issue is also important, as one of the aspects in IT delivery in this widespread environment is to ensure efficient IT utilities mainly on provision and management of the reliable and cost effective infrastructure in an organization as also sited by Peterson (2004). Other key issues (Table 5) to consider as part of resource management is attracting and retaining competitive IT professionals that was supported by 85% of the respondents. Another is providing IT governance awareness and training for optimal use of IT that was supported by 78% of the respondents. These two issues were also supported by the state of IT governance presented in the earlier section and are also considered critical by Luftman *et al.* (2004) and Warland & Ridley (2005) respectively.

Performance Management Related Issues

Consolidating and Benchmarking IT Performance Measurable Beyond the Conventional Accounting

The survey indicated 93% of the respondents to support its importance (Figure 15). The importance of this key issue is also seen in the findings of the studied practices in the earlier section, For example, one of the top most rated problems indicated to be weak measurement of IT performance and value to business with 70% (Figure 13) and a corresponding consequences like non-measurable return from IT investment also highly rated at 78% (Figure 14).

In addition, the findings indicated processes to be the weakest IT governance practices in this environment. Such processes include non-existence of the comprehensive performance management system like balance scorecard in most of them that provides performance measures beyond the conventional accounting. Further improvement along this key issue is important for performance measurable beyond conventional accounting. This is also indicated by the inventors of the practice (Kaplan & Norton, 1992) and related studies (Van Grembergen, 2000; Van Grembergen & De Haes, 2005) also given the nature of the public sector (Sethibe et al., 2007).

Generally, IT governance can greatly improve with consideration of these 12 key issues across IT governance focus areas in line with local practices like medium-term expenditure planning and experience from organizations already applying elements of best practices such as ITIL and balanced scorecard. This will lead to effective IT governance, thus contributing to the ICT-enabled transformational government and public service delivery in general.

TRENDS AND FUTURE RESEARCH FOR EFFECTIVE IT GOVERNANCE IN THE PUBLIC SECTOR IN A DEVELOPING COUNTRY

This section provides the current trends on IT governance that are applicable to the public sector in a developing country and it looks into future research taking into consideration the particular characteristics in the environment. Looking at the efforts put into the integration of ICT in the public sector, in a developing country like Tanzania and the current researches perspectives in the area, we see two main areas to concentrate in the future i.e. intra- and inter-organizational. These areas are also stressed in a different context by Ryan Peterson (2003), while discussing the design of effective IT governance architectures.

Intra-organizational, looks at IT governance diffusion from individual organizations point of view, concentration being on differentiation and integration of IT decision making and monitoring. This looks at IT function localizations and the mechanisms that can help it to bring aboard the business and IT people working together in IT decision making and monitoring. Also looking at what can be innovated to improve the integration of ICT in the strategic plans and cascading mechanisms to the individuals, taking into account organizations culture and bureaucracy that characterizes the sector.

Inter-organizational looks into IT governance issues from the public sector as whole, mainly from e-government point view, with concentration on core competencies and strategic collaborations. This is on the fact that there are several efforts in these countries to put in place e-government strategies and appropriate mechanisms with the view of ICT-enabled transformational government. Given the nature of the required participation from creation of the strategies to implementation, management and monitoring, the IT governance should bring-in best ways for effective collaboration and coordination mechanisms (Peterson,

2003) as well as competency and enforcement, while allowing encouragement and facilitation.

These two research considerations depend on each other (Figure 16); for example, the coordination at the e-government level requires a well organized IT function in the organizations concerned and therefore any effective IT governance at the organization level is a good foundation to the effectiveness of the e-government. On the other hand, some of the problems mostly faced at the organization level, like the inadequate inter-organization synergies and economies of scale seen earlier, a well-governed e-government in place can minimize them thus bringing effectiveness in individual organizations. These researches if set well, taking into consideration holistic view or individual focus area of IT governance (Buckby *et al.*, 2008), will contribute to the improvement of the governance in the sector and facilitate the ICT-enabled transformational government and improvement of the services.

CONCLUSION

In this chapter, we have presented an IT governance overview, and based on case study in five organizations from Tanzanian public sector, we found the current practices, and the problems encountered together with the potential consequences of not having IT governance in place. Moreover, we have identified the key issues to take into account for effective IT governance and presented our suggestions for future research in this environment.

A combination of a broader IT Governance Assessment Process (ITGAP) Model together

Figure 16. The Research Areas to be Studied Concerning IT Governance in the Public Sector in a Developing Country

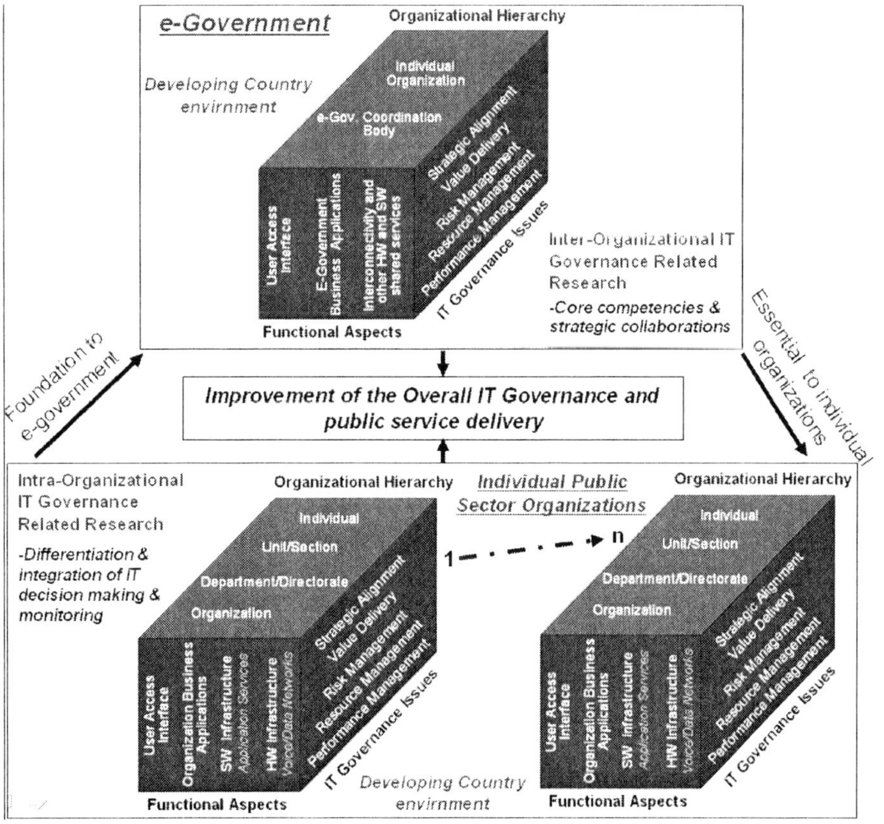

with IT governance mechanisms, IT governance key focus, and IT governance decision areas provided the means for a thorough look into the studied environment. We found a combination to be useful in uncovering practices of interest in this environment, where on the one hand, IT resources are scarce and its development and management relatively less established, and on the other hand, the use of ICT in provision of public services is gaining momentum due to the continued demand from public on better services.

In the analysis of IT governance practices in the studied environment, we found a diverse mix of structures, processes and relational mechanisms some being specific to this environment like MTEF and IT plans. However, in contrast with the developed world; we found the practices to be relatively immature, especially in the application of internationally recognized best practices and standards in the processes. Similarly, we noted that improvements on these practices are on going processes not as a specific IT governance project but rather as routine improvements on governance of IT to increase the IT contribution to organizational goals.

The analysis also revealed several problems and their consequences in the organizations. These problems, categorized in IT governance key focus areas, include the lack of a specific IT strategic plan in most of them; lack of business people ownership in IT-enabled projects; inadequate or absent ICT policies and guidelines; lack of IT governance awareness and guidelines; inadequate follow-up and enforcement mechanisms; and lack of clear roles, responsibilities and accountability. Others are weak risk-based approach in designing and operating IT related services; weakness in attracting and sustaining skilled and competent IT personnel; limited budget for required IT resources; fragmented IT initiatives with a loss of synergies and exploitation of the economies of scale; high cost of IT with lower return or business value; and weak measurement of IT performance and value to business.

In addition, based on problems and challenges in the sector, we revealed several consequences that can be detrimental to the efforts towards ICT-enabled transformational government and hence improvement in the public service delivery. The most common include the difficulty of holding individuals accountable for their results; ad-hoc solutions due to user and management frustrations; and traditional but costly consequences in such environment like IT investment losses and reputation damage.

The use of the findings from these case studies, analyzed previously, apart from revealing the current IT governance practices, previously unexplored, will help the IT decision makers and researchers in the public sector in a developing country like Tanzania on key issues to consider for effective IT governance in this and similar environment/settings.

The key issues we found out include IT leadership understanding of business goals and IT contribution and bringing it to management attention; involvement and support of senior management; engagement of key stakeholders; consolidation of IT structures to ensure responsiveness and accountability; defining and aligning IT strategies to corporate strategies and cascading them down in an organization; attracting and retaining competitive IT professionals; consolidating, standardizing and managing IT infrastructure to optimize costs and information flow; and consolidating IT risk mitigation strategies. Other key issues are consolidating, communicating and enforcing policies and guidelines for cost-effective acquisition and use of IT across the organization; encouragement and support of IT/Business communication and partnership; providing IT governance awareness and training for optimal use of IT; and finally yet importantly consolidating and benchmarking performance measurable beyond the conventional accounting.

Looking at these revealed key issues and the continuous efforts put in the integration of ICT in individual organizations and the public sector as whole one in a developing country like Tanzania, two main research areas have been identified also for a further research in the near future. One area is concerning intra-organizational that looks IT governance diffusion at organization level with focus on differentiation and integration of IT decision making and monitoring; and the other is inter-organizational, that looks at the public sector as a whole one, mainly on e-government with focus on core competencies and strategic collaboration.

REFERENCES

Amaravadi, C. S. (2005). Digital repositories for e-government. *E-Government, 2(*2), 205-218.

Bakari, J. B. (2007). *A holistic approach for managing ICT security in non-commercial organizations: A case in a developing country.* Unpublished doctoral dissertation, Stockholm University, Stockholm.

Brand, K., & Boonen H. (2007). IT governance based on COBIT 4.1 - *a management guide, 3rd rev.edition*. Van Haren Publishing.

Broadbent, M. (2003). Understanding IT governance. *CIO Canada*, *11*(4), 13-14.

Brown, M. M. (2003). Electronic government. In J. Rabin (Ed.), *Encyclopedia of public administration and public policy.* Marcel Dekker.

Buckby S., Best, P., & Stewart, J. (2008). The current state of information technology governance literature. In A. Cater-Steel (Ed.), *Information technology governance and service management: Frameworks and adaptations*. Hershey, PA: Idea Group Publishing.

Duffy, J. (2002). *IT/Business alignment: Is it an option or is it mandatory?* IDC document # 26831, IT and Business Alignment Advisory service.

Duffy, J. (2002a). *IT governance and business value part 1: IT governance - an issue of critical importance*. IDC document # 27291.

Duffy, J. (2002b). *IT governance and business value part 2: Who's responsible for what?* IDC document # 27807.

Guldentops, E., Van Grembergen, W., & De Haes, S. (2002). Control and governance maturity survey: Establishing a reference benchmark and a self-assessment tool. *Information Systems Control Journal*, *6*, 32-35.

Guldentops, E. (2003). Governing information technology through COBIT. In W. Van Grembergen (Ed.), *Strategies for information technology governance*. Hershey, PA: Idea Group Publishing.

Henderson, J. C., & Venkatraman, N. (1993). Strategic alignment: Leveraging information technology for transforming organizations. *IBM Systems Journal, 32*(1), 4-16.

ISO. (2008). ISO/IEC standard (ISO/IEC 38500:2008) for corporate governance of information technology. Retrieved in June 2008, from http://www.iso.org/iso/pressrelease.htm?refid=Ref1135

ITGI. (2003). *Board briefing on IT governance, 2nd ed.* Retrieved in May 2008, from www.itgi.org

ITGI. (2006). *Enterprise value: Governance of IT investments, the Val IT framework*. Retrieved in May 2008, from www.itgi.org

ITGI. (2006a). *COBIT mapping: Overview of international IT guidance, 2nd ed.* Retrieved in May 2008, from www.itgi.org

ITGI & PwC. (2006). *IT governance global status report*. Retrieved in May 2008, from www.itgi.org

ITGI & PwC. (2006a). *IT governance in practice. Insight from leading CIOs*. Retrieved in May 2008, from www.itgi.org

ITGI. (2007). *IT governance implementation guide: Using COBIT and Val IT, 2nd edition.* IT Governance Institute.

ITGI. (2007a). COBIT 4.1. IT governance institute. Retrieved in May 2008, from www.itgi.org

ITGI. (2007b). *COBIT quickstart, 2nd Edition*. IT Governance Institute. Retrieved in June 2008, from www.itgi.org

ITGI & PwC. (2008). *IT governance global status report*. Retrieved in May 2008, from www.itgi.org

Kaplan, R., & Norton, D. (1992). The balanced scorecard: Measures that drive performance. *Harvard Business Review, 70*(1), 71-79.

Luftman, J. N., Bullen, C. V., Liao, D., Nash, E., & Neumann, C. (2004). *Managing the information technology resource: Leadership in the information age*. Pearson Prentice Hall.

Mhayaya, S. G. (2003). *A study of the potential usage of ICT (e-government) in improving efficiency and effectiveness of 'executive functions' of the government including delivery of public services, Case of Tanzania*. A dissertation for degree of MEM at University of Dar Es Salaam, Tanzania.

Mollel, A., & Lukumay, Z. (2007). *Electronic transactions and law of evidence in Tanzania*. Iringa University College: Peramiho Printing Press.

MoFEA. (2008). *About Ministry of Finance and Economic Affairs (MoFEA) and related statistics in the case study*. Retrieved in May 2008, from www.mof.go.tz

Moyo, L. (1996). *IT strategies for Africa's survival in the twenty-first century: IT all pervasive in IT for development v7n1 PP: 17-27*. Retrieved in May 2008, from www.itgi.org

MSD. (2008). *About medical stores department (MSD) and related statistics in the case study*. Retrieved in May 2008, from www.msd.or.tz

Ndou, V. (2004). E-Government for developing countries: Opportunities and challenges. *The Electronic Journal on Information Systems in Developing Countries (EJISDC)*.

Nfuka E. N., & Rusu L. (2007). Management of IT-enabled change in a public organization in Tanzania. *International Journal of Information Systems and Change Management, 2(*4), 334-349 .

Peterson, R. R. (2003). Integration strategies and tactics for information technology governance. In W. Van Grembergen (Ed.), *Strategies for information technology governance*. Hershey, PA: Idea Group Publishing.

Peterson, R. R. (2004). Crafting information technology governance for today's turbulent environment. *Information Systems Management, 21*(4), 7-21.

PMO-RALG. (2008). *About prime minister's office regional authority and local government (PMO-RALG) and related statistics in the case study*. Retrieved in May 2008, from www.pmo-ralg.go.tz

PO-PSM. (2008). *About president office, public services management (PO-PSM) and related statistics in the case study*. Retrieved in May 2008, from www.utumishi.go.tz

Ribbers, P. M. A., Peterson, R. R., & Parker, M. M. (2002). Designing information technology governance processes: Diagnosing contemporary practices and competing theories. In *Proceedings of the 35th Hawaii International Conference on System Sciences, IEEE Computer Society*.

Ruparel, R. (2006). Project appraisal document for tax modernization project in Tanzania. *World Bank, Volume 1, Report No. 36221–TA*. Retrieved in May 2008, from http://www-wds.worldbank.org

Schoderbek, P., Schoderbek, C., & Kafalas, A. (1998). *Management systems, Custom edition*. Primus Global Solutions Pvt. Ltd.

Sethibe, T., Campbell, J., & McDonald, C. (2007). IT governance in public and private sector organizations: Examining the differences and defining future research directions. In *Proceedings of 18th Australasian Conference on Information Systems*.

Simonsson, M., & Johnson, P. (2005). *Defining IT governance – a consolidation of literature, industrial information and control systems. Working paper*. KTH, Royal Institute of Technology. Retrieved in May 2008, from www.ics.kth.se

Supangkat, S. H., Rahmat, B., & Sembiring, J. (2006). *IT governance for developing countries*. School of Electrical Engineering and Informatics, Institute of Technology Bandung. Engage Indonesia.

TRA. (2008). *About Tanzania revenue authority (TRA) and related statistics in the case study*. Retrieved in May 2008, from www.tra.go.tz

Yin, R. (2003). *Case study research design and methods, third edition*. Sage Publications.

Van Grembergen, W. (2000). The balanced scorecard and IT governance. *Information Systems Control Journal, 2*, 40-43.

Van Grembergen, W., De Haes, S., & Guldentops, E. (2003). Structures, processes, and relational mechanisms for IT governance. In W. Van Grembergen (Ed.), *Strategies for information technology governance*. Hershey, PA: Idea Group Publishing.

Van Grembergen, W., & De Haes, S. (2005). Measuring and improving IT governance through the balanced scorecard. *Information Systems Control Journal, 2*, 35.

Van Grembergen, W., & De Haes, S. (2008). *Implementing information technology governance: Models, practices, and cases*. Hershey, PA: IGI Publishing.

Warland, C., & Ridley, G. (2005). Awareness of IT control frameworks in an Australian state government: A qualitative case study. In *Proceedings of the 38th Hawaii International Conference on System Sciences*.

Weill, P., & Woodham, R. (2002). *Don't just lead, govern: Implementing effective IT governance*. (CISR WP No.326). Cambridge, MA: MIT Sloan School of Management.

Weill, P., & Ross J. W. (2004). *IT governance: How top performers manage IT decision rights for superior results*. Harvard Business School Press.

KEY TERMS

Developing Countries: A broad range of countries that generally lack a high degree of industrialization, infrastructure, and other capital investment, sophisticated technology, widespread literacy, and advanced living standards among their populations as a whole.

E-Government: The use of Information Technology to provide delivery of public services to citizen, business partners, and those working in the public sector. It provides citizen and organizations a more convenient access to government information and services.

IT Governance: An integral part of enterprise governance and consists of the leadership and organizational structures and processes that ensure the enterprise's IT sustains and extends the organization's strategies and objectives.

IT Governance Processes: Are part of the IT governance mechanisms that refers to formalization and institutionalization of strategic IT decision-making and monitoring procedures like the IT balanced scorecard.

IT Governance Relational Mechanisms: Are part of the IT governance mechanisms that are the catalyst for attaining and sustaining business-IT alignment, even when structures and processes are in place. They are about the active participation of, and collaborative relationship among, corporate executives, IT management, and business management.

IT Governance Structures: Are part of the IT governance mechanisms that involve structural (formal) devices and mechanisms for connecting and enabling horizontal, or liaison, contacts between business, and IT decision-making functions. It includes clearly defined roles and responsibilities and a diversity of IT/business committees like the IT steering committee.

IT Value Delivery: One of the IT governance focus areas that execute the value proposition throughout the delivery cycle, ensuring that IT delivers the promised benefits against the strategy, concentrating on optimizing costs & proving the intrinsic value of IT.

Performance Management: Is one of the IT governance focus areas that tracks and monitors strategy implementation, project completion, resource usage, process performance and service delivery, using, for example, balanced scorecards that translate strategy into action to achieve goals measurable beyond conventional accounting.

Public Sector: The part of the economy and administrative life that deals with government services delivery by and for the government, whether national, regional or local/municipal.

Resource Management: Is one of the IT governance focus areas about optimal investment in, and the proper management of, critical IT resources i.e. applications, information, infrastructure and people. Key issues relate to the optimization of knowledge and infrastructure.

Risk Management: Is one of the IT governance focus areas that require risk awareness by senior corporate officers, a clear understanding of the enterprise's appetite for risk, understanding of compliance requirements, transparency about the significant risks to the enterprise, and embedding of risk management responsibilities in the organization.

Strategic Alignment: Is one of the IT governance focus areas that optimizes the relational mechanisms between the business and IT organization by working on the IT effectiveness of the organization in order to maximize the business value from IT. It aims at establishing relationship between the business and IT in which IT becomes a strategic enabler for business growth.

ENDNOTES

1 G-C : Government to Citizen
2 G-B: Government to Business
3 G-G: Government to Government and G-E: Government to Employee
4 e-Government refers to government's use of information technology to exchange information and services with citizens, businesses, and other arms of government.

Compilation of References

Accenture. (2006). Shared Services: Government shared services model for high performance. Retrieved June 23, 2006, from http://www.accenture.com/Global/Services/By_Industry/Government/R_and_I/DrivingServices.htm.

ACSI. (2006). ACSI methodology. About ACSI. American consumer satisfaction index. Retrieved April 26, 2008, from http://www.theacsi.org/index.php?option=com_content &task=view&id=48&Itemid=41

Adams, S. (2005). Learning the lessons of Katrina for the unexpected tomorrow. *Risk Management, 52*(12), 24-29.

Adler, M., & Henman, P. (2005). Computerizing the welfare state: An international comparison of computerization in social security. *Information, Communication, and Society, 8*(3), 315-342.

Affisco, J. F., & Soliman, K. S. (2006). E-Government: A strategic operations management framework for service delivery. *Business Process Management Journal, 12*(1), 13–21.

Agarwal, R., & Prasad, J. (1998). The antecedents and consequents of user perceptions in information technology adoption. *Decision Support Systems, 22*(1), 15-29.

Agarwal, R., & Prasad, J. (1999). Are individual differences germane to the acceptance of new information technologies? *Decision Sciences, 30*(2), 361-391.

Agarwal, R., Sambamurthy, V., & Stair, R. (2000).The evolving relationship between general and specific computer self-efficacy: An empirical investigation, *Information Systems Research, 11*(4), 418-430.

Agile Alliance. (2008). Retrieved on September 15, 2008, from http://www.agilealliance.org

Agwunobi, Adm. J. O. (2007). Ideas are welcome. *Pandemic Flu Leadership Blog, United States Department of Health and Human Services, May 22–June 27, 2007.* Retrieved April 27, 2008, from http://blog.pandemicflu.gov/indexc728.html?cat=7

Ajzen, I. (1991). The theory of planned behavior. *Organizational Behavior and Human Decision Processes, 50*(2), 179-211.

Akbulut, A. Y. (2002). An investigation of the factors that influence electronic information sharing between state and local agencies. In *Proceedings of the 8th Americas Conference on Information Systems*, (pp. 2454-2460). Dallas, TX.

Alampay, E. A. (2006). Beyond access to ICTs: Measuring capabilities in the information society. *International Journal of Education and Development using Information and Communication Technology (IJEDICT), 2*(3), 4-22.

Alford, J. (1998). A public management road less travelled: Clients as co-producers of public services. *Australian Journal of Public Administration, 57*(4), 128-137.

Algermissen, L., Delfmann, P., & Niehaves, B. (2005). Experiences in process-oriented reorganisation through reference modelling in public administrations: The case study regio@KomM. In *Proceedings of the 13th European Conference on Information Systems (ECIS 2005).* Regensburg, Germany.

Allen, B. A., Juillet, L., Paquet, G., & Roy, G. (2001). E-Governance & government on-line in Canada: Partnerships, people, & prospects. *Government Information Quarterly, 18,* 93-104.

Allison, J. E. (2002). *Technology, development, and democracy: International conflict and cooperation in the information age.* Albany, NY: State University of New York Press.

Al-Mashari, M., & Zairi, M. (1999). BPR implementation process: An analysis of key success and failure factors. *Business Process Management Journal, 5*(1), 87-112.

Al-Sebie, M., & Irani, Z. (2005). Technical and organisational challenges facing transactional e-government systems: An empirical study. *Electronic Government, An International Journal, 2*(3), 247–276.

Al-Shafi, S., & Weerakkody, V. (2008). *Adoption of wireless internet parks: An empirical study in Qatar.* Paper presented at the Proceedings of the European and Mediterranean Conference on Information systems (EMCIS08), Dubai, UAE.

Alter, S. (1996). *Information systems: A management perspective.* Menlo Park: The Benjamin/Cummings.

Alvesson, M. (2004). *Knowledge work and knowledge-intensive firms.* Oxford, UK: Oxford University Press.

Amaravadi, C. S. (2005). Digital repositories for e-government. *E-Government, 2(*2), 205-218.

AMCIS. (2008). E-Government: Past, present, and future. Conference mini-track description. Retrieved April 26, 2008, from http://www.business.mcmaster.ca/amcis2008/MT/amcis-pr-069-2008-File001.pdf

Amoretti, F. (2007). International organizations ICTs policies: E-Democracy and e-government for political development. *Review of Policy Research, 24*(4), 331-344.

Andersen, E. A., Grude, K. V., & Hague, T. (2004). *Goal directed project management.* Kogan Page.

Andersen, K. V., & Henriksen, H. Z. (2006). E-government maturity models: Extension of the Layne and Lee model. *Government Information Quarterly, 23*(2), 236–248.

Andrews, T., Curbera, F., Dholakia, H., Goland, Y., Klein, J., Leymann, F., Liu, K., Roller, D., Smith, D., Thatte, S., Trickovic, I., & Weerawarana, S. (2003). *Business Process Execution Language for Web Services – Version 1.1.* Retrieved April 28, 2006 from http://dev2dev.bea.com/techtrack/BPEL4WS.jsp

Ang, P. H. (1999). Information highways policy and regulation: The Singapore experience. In V. Iyer (Ed.), *Media regulations for new times*, (pp. 97-114). Singapore: Asian Media Information and Communication Centre.

Annetta, L. A. (Ed.) (2008). *Serious Educational Games: From Theory to Practice.* Rotterdam: Sense.

Anon. (2006). *Traffic and transport: Metro rail taking shape.* Dubai, UAE: Al Nisr Publishing LLC. Retrieved on July 28, 2008 from http://archive.gulfnews.com/indepth/dubaimetro/more_stories/10050775.html, accessed 28 July 2008.

Anttiroiko, A. (2002). Strategic knowledge management in local e-government. In Grönlund (Ed.), *Electronic government – design, applications, and management.* Hershey, PA: Idea Group Publishing.

Archibugi, D., & Bengt-Ake, L. (2001). *The globalizing learning economy.* Oxford, UK: Oxford University Press.

Arens, Y., & Rosenbloom, P. S. (2003). Responding to the unexpected. How IT can help prepare for the future attacks and disasters. *Communications of the ACM Journal, 46*(9), 33-36.

Arthur, W. B (1989). CompetingTtechnologies, Iincreasin gRreturns, andLlockIin byHhistoricalEevents. *Economic Journal, 99*(394), 116-31.

Australian Business Foundation. (1997). Sydney, Australia: Australian Business Foundation.

Australian Government Information Management Office. (2005a). Australian government technical interoperability framework, version 2. Retrieved on April 3, 2008. from http://www.agimo.gov.au/publications/2005/04/agtifv2

Australian Government Information Management Office. (2005b). Australian government architecture reference models, version 1.0, June 2007. Retrieved on March 14, 2008, from http://www.agimo.gov.au/__data/assets/pdf_file/0007/57517/AGA_Reference_Models_Version_1.0.pdf

Australian Government. (2005). *'Australians' use of and satisfaction with e-government services*. Barton, Australia: Commonwealth of Australia.

Avgerou, A., Ciborra, C., Cordella, A., Kallinikos, J., & Longshore Smith, M. (2006, May). *E-Government and trust in the state: Lessons from electronic tax systems in Chile and Brazil*. LSE Working Paper Series No. 146.

Avison, D., & Fitzgerald, G. (2008). *Information systems development*. McGraw-Hill.

Avison, D., Lau, F., Myers, M., & Nielsen, P. A. (1999). Action research. *Communications of the ACM, 42*(1), 94-97.

Axelrod, R. (2006). *The evolution of cooperation*. New York: Perseus Books Group.

Baacke, L., Fitterer, R., Mettler, T., & Rohner, P. (2008). A methodology for ICT impact analysis based on semantic process models. In *Proceedings of the 7th International EGOV Conference*. Torino, Itay.

Baacke, L., Rohner, P., & Winter, R. (2007). Aggregation of reference process building blocks to improve modeling in public administrations. In A. Grönlund, H. J. Scholl, & M. A. Wimmer (Eds.), *Proceedings of the Electronic Government, 6th International EGOV Conference* (pp. 149-156).

Baacke, L., Rohner, P., Winter, R., & Fitterer, R. (2009). Component-based distributed modeling of collaborative service processes: A methodology for the identification of reference process building blocks. In *Proceedings of the Forty-Second Annual Hawaii International Conference on System Sciences (HICSS-42)*.

Baark, E. (2005). Innovation policy forensics: An analysis of biotechnology in Hong Kong. Systems of innovation, institutions, and public policies. *DRUID Tenth Anniversary Summer Conference 2005 on Dynamics of Industry and Innovation: Organizations, Networks and Systems*, Copenhagen, Denmark.

Backhouse, J. (Ed.). (2005). Structured account of approaches on interoperability D4.1 v1.0. FIDIS. Project, December 2005. Retrieved on March 12, 2008, from http://www.fidis.net/fileadmin/fidis/deliverables/fidis-wp4-del4.2.set_of_requirements.pdf

Bailey, J. E., & Pearson, S.W. (1983). Development of a tool for measuring and analyzing computer user satisfaction. *Management Science, 29(5*), 530-545.

Baird, S. A. (2007, December 10—13). Government role in developing an interoperability ecosystem. In *Proceedings of the 1st international Conference on Theory and Practice of Electronic Governance, ICEGOV '07*, Macao, China (Vol. 232, pp. 65-68). New York: *ACM*.

Bakari, J. B. (2007). *A holistic approach for managing ICT security in non-commercial organizations: A case in a developing country*. Unpublished doctoral dissertation, Stockholm University, Stockholm.

Ball-Rokeach, S.J. (1985). The origins of individual media-system dependency: A sociological framework. *Communication Research, 12*(4), 485-510.

Balutis, A. P. (2001). E-Government 2001, part I: Understanding the challenge and evolving strategies. *The Public Manager, 30*(1), 33–37.

Bangeman, E. (2007). Adobe to make PDF an open standard. Retrieved on October 2, 2007, from http://arstechnica.com/news.ars/post/20070129-8724.html

Banipal, K. (2006). Strategic approach to disaster management: Lessons learned from Hurricane Katrina. *Disaster Prevention and Management, 15*(3), 484-494.

Barbara, A., Juliet, L., Paquet, G., & Roy, J. E-Government and public private partnership. In M. Khosrowpour (Ed.), *Practicing e-government: A global perspective*. Hershey, PA: Idea Group Inc.

Barley, S. R. (1996). Technicians in the workplace: Ethnographic evidence for bringing work into organization studies. *Administrative Science Quarterly, 41*(8), 404-441.

Barney, J. B. (1986). Types of competition and the theory of strategy: Toward an integrative framework. *Academy of Management Review, 11*, 791-800.

Barney, J. B. (1991). Firm resources and sustained competitive advantage. *Journal of Management, 17*(1), 99-120.

Barney, J. B. (1995). Looking inside for competitive advantage. *Academy of Management Executive, 9*(4), 49-61.

Barney, J. B. (2001). Is the resource-based "view" a useful perspective for strategic management research? Yes. *Academy of Management Review, 26*(1), 41-56.

Barney, J. B. (2001). Resource-based theories of competitive advantage: A ten year retrospective on the resource-based view. *Journal of Management, 27*(643), 650.

Baroudi, J. J., & Orlikowski, W. J. (1988). A short-form measure of user information satisfaction. *Journal of Management Information Systems, 4*(4), 44-59.

Barrett, S., & Fudge, C. (Eds.) (1981). *Policy and action: Essays on implementation of public policy.* London: Methuen.

Bartlett, L., & Kinney, J. (2005). *Latino youths in California have lower health care coverage rates than non-Hispanic whites. UCLA study finds investing in health care for youths may lead to stronger future workforce.* California, USA: UCLA News.

Barua, A., Sophie Lee, C. H., & Whinston, A. B. (1996). The calculus of reengineering. *Information Systems Research, 7*(4), 409–428.

Barzelay, M. (2001) *The new public management: Improving research and policy dialogue.* Berkeley, CA: University of California Press.

Basili, V. R., Caldiera, G., & Rombach, H. D, (1994). GoalQquestionMmetricPparadigm. In J. J. Marciniak eEd.), *Encyclopedia of Software Engineering 1*(pp. 528-532). John Wiley and Sons.2

Bass, C. & Lee, J. M. (2002). Building a business case for EAI. *EAI Journal*, 18-20.

Bass, L., Clements, P., & Kazmann, R. (2006). *Software Architecture in Practice. Second Edition.* Addison Wesley.

Basu, S. (2004). E-Government and developing countries: An overview. *International Review of Law Computers, 18*(1), 109-132.

Batini, C., Lenzerini, M., & Navathe, S. B. (1986). A comparative analysis of methodologies for database schema integration. *ACM Computing Surveys, 18*(4), 323-364.

Baum, C., & DiMaio, A. (2000). Gartner's four phases of e-government model. Gartner, Inc. Research Note (Tutorial TU-12-6113).

Beath, C. M. (1991). Supporting the IT champion. *MIS Quarterly, 15*(3), 355-72.

Beaumaster, S. (2002). Local government IT implementation issues: A challenge for public administration. In *Proceedings of the 35th Annual Hawaii International Conference on System Sciences*, (pp. 1725-1734). IEEE Computer Society.

Becerra, M., & Gupta A. K. (1999). Trust within the organization: Integrating the trust literature with agency theory and transaction costs economics. *Public Administration Quarterly, 23*(2), 177-203.

Beck, K. (1999). *Extreme programming explained: Embrace change.* Addison Wesley.

Becker, J., & Niehaves, B. (2007). Epistemological perspectives on IS research: A framework for analysing and systematizing epistemological assumptions. *Information Systems Journal, 17*, 197-214.

Becker, J., Kugeler, M., & Rosemann, M. (2003). *Process management: A guide for the design of business processes.* Berlin, Germany: Springer.

Becker, S. N., & Whisler, T. L. (1967). The innovative organisation: A selective view of current theory and research. *The Journal of Business, 40*(4), 462-469.

Bekkers, V. J. J. M. (1998). Wiring public organizations and changing organizational juridisctions. In I. T. M. Snellen & W. B. H. J. v. d. Donk (Eds.), *Public administration in an information age* (pp. 57-77). Amsterdam: IOS Press.

Bekkers, V. J. J. M., & Homburg, V. M. F. (Eds.). (2005). *The Information Ecology of E-Government*. Amsterdam: IOS Press.

Bekkers, V., & Homberg, V. (2007). The myths of e-government: Looking beyond the assumptions of a new and better government. *The Information Society, 23*, 373-382.

Bekkers, V., & Homburg, V.(2005). E-Government as an information ecology: Backgrounds and concepts. In V. Bekkers & V. Homburg (Eds.), *The information ecology of e-government: E-government as institutional and technological innovation in public administration* (pp. 1-20). Amsterdam: IOS Press.

Belanger, F., & Carter, L. (2006). *The effects of the digital divide on e-government: An empirical evaluation.* Paper presented at of the Hawaii International Conference on System Sciences, Kauai, HI.

Belanger, F., & Hiller, J. S. (2006). A framework for e-government: Privacy implications. *Business Process Management Journal, 12*(1), 48–60.

Bellamy, C., & Taylor, J. (1997). Transformation by stealth: The case of the UK criminal justice system. In J. Taylor, I. T. M. Snellen & A. Zuurmond (Eds.), *Beyond BPR in public administration.* Amsterdam: IOS Press.

Benbasat, I., Goldstein, D. K., Mead, M. (1987). The case research strategy in studies of information systems. *MIS Quarterly*, 368-386.

Benkler, Y. (2006). *The wealth of networks: How social production transforms markets and freedom.* New Haven, CT, & London: Yale University Press.

Benner, M. J., & Tushman, M. L. (2003). Exploitation, exploration, and process management: The productivity dilemma revisited. *Academy of Management Review, 28*(2), 238-256.

Benyon-Davies, P. & Williams, M. D. (2003). Evaluating electronic local government in the UK. *Journal of Information Technology, 18*, 137-149.

Benyon-Davies, P. (2005). Constructing electronic government: The case of the UK inland revenue. *International Journal of Information Management, 25*(1), 3-20.

Berg, M., & Goorman, E. (1999). The contextual nature of medical information. *International Journal of Medical Informatics, 56*, 51-60.

Bergeron, B. (2003). *Essentials of shared services.* New York: John Wiley & Sons.

Berkman Center for Internet & Society at Harvard Law School. (2005). *Roadmap for open ICT ecosystems.*

Bertot, J. C., & Jaeger, P. T (2006). User-centered e-government: Challenges and benefits for government web sites. *Government Information Quarterly, 23*, 163-168.

Bertot, J.C., & Jaeger, P. T. (2008). The e-government paradox: Better customer service doesn't necessarily cost less. *Government Information Quarterly, 25*, 149-154.

Beynon-Davies, P. (2005). Constructing electronic government: The case of the UK inland revenue. *International Journal of Information Management, 25*, 3-20.

Beynon-Davies, P., & Williams, M. D. (2003). Evaluating electronic local government in the UK. *Journal of Information Technology, 18*, 137-149.

Bhagat, R. S., Kedia, B. L., Harveston, P. D., & Triandis, H. C. (2002). Cultural variations in the cross-border transfer of organizational knowledge: An integrative framework. *Academy of Management Review, 27*(2), 204-221.

Bharosa, N., Janssen, M., Rao, H. R., & Lee, J. (2008, May 4-7). *Adaptive information orchestration: Architectural principles improving information quality.* Paper presented at the 5th International Conference on Information Systems for Crisis Response and Management (ISCRAM2008), Washington, DC, USA.

Bhatnagar, S. (2002). E-Government: Lessons from implementation in developing countries. *Regional Development Dialogue, 24.*

Bianchi, A., Barrios, S., Cabrera, M., Cachia, R., Compañó, R., Malanowski, N., Punie, Y., Turlea, G., Zinnbauer, D., & Centeno, C. (2006). *Revisiting e-inclusion: From vision to action. Working paper.* Sevilla, Spain: Institute for Prospective Technology Studies.

Blackler, F. (1993). Knowledge and the theory of organizations: Organizations as activity systems and the reframing of management. *Journal of Management Studies, 30*(6), 863-884.

Blackler, F. (1995). Knowledge, knowledge work, and organizations: An overview and interpretation. *Organization Studies, 7*(2), 277-300.

Blair, T. (2007). Chief information officer council: Foreword. *Transformational Government: Enabled by Technology.* Retrieved April 26, 2008, from http://www.cio.gov.uk/transformational_government/strategy/contents/foreword.asp

Boase, J., Horrigan, J. B., Wellman, B., & Rainie, L. (2006). *The strength of Internet ties. Report.* Washington, DC: Pew Internet & American Life Project.

Bogdanor, V. (2005). Introduction. In B. Vernon (Ed.), *Joined-up government* (pp. 1-18). Oxford, UK: University Press.

Bogenrieder, I., & Nooteboom, B. (2004). Learning groups: What types are there? A theoretical analysis and an empirical study in a consultancy firm. *Organization Studies, 25(*2), 287-313.

Boland, R. J., & Tenkasi, R. V. (1995). Perspective making and perspective taking in communities of knowing. *Organization Science, 6*(4), 350-372.

Bonham, G., Seifert, J., & Thorson, S. (2001). *The transformational potential of e-government: The role of politic leadership.* Paper presented at the 4th Pan European International Relations Conference of the European Consortium for Political Research, University of Kent, Canterbury, UK.

Booz Allen Hamilton (2005). *Beyond e-government: The world's most successful technology-enabled transformations* (Report). Retrieved March 20, 2008 from http://www.boozallen.com/media/file/151607.pdf

Borins, S. F. (2007). *Digital state at the leading edge.* Toronto, Canada: University of Toronto Press.

Bosilj-Vuksic, V., Indihar Stemberger, M., Jaklic, J., & Kovacic, A. (2002). Assessment of e-business transformation using simulation modelling. *Simulation, 78*(12), 731-744.

Bouchard, L. (1993). Decision criteria in the adoption of EDI. In *Proceedings of the 14th International Conference on Information Systems*, Orlando, Florida, USA (365-376).

Boujraf, A. D. A., & Noble, M. (2007). *Delivery of final master case study. Towards e-administration in the large (R4eGov).* Deliverable WP3-D7. R4eGov—Towards e-Administration in the large (Proposal/Contract no.: IST-2004-026650).

Bourgeois, L. J. I., & Eisenhardt, K. M. (1988). Strategic decision processes in high velocity environments: Four cases in the microcomputer industry. *Management Sciences, 14*(816), 835.

Bovens, M., & Zouridis, S. (2002). From street-level bureaucracy to system-level bureaucracy: How information and communication technology is transforming administrative discretion and constitutional control. *Public Administration Review, 62*(2), 174-184.

Bowman, C., & Ambrosini, V. (2003). How the resource-based and the dynamic capability views of the firm inform corporate-level strategy. *British Journal of Management, 14*, 289-303.

Bozeman, B., & Bretschneider, S. (1986). Public management information systems. *Public Administration Review, Special Issue*, 475-487.

Bozman, J., Gillen, A., Kolodgy, C., Kusnetzky, D., Perry, R., & Shiang, D. (2002). *Windows 2000 us. Linux in EnterpriseCcomputing: An assessment of business value for selected workloads. IDC, sponsored by Microsoft Corporation. White paper.* Retrieved from www.idc.com

Bradford, M., & Florin, J. (2003). Examining the role of innovation diffusion factors on the implementation success of ERP systems. *Inter. JAIS, 4*(3), 205-225.

Bradner, S. (1996). RFC 2026: The Internet standards process—revision 3. Retrieved on February 2, 2002, from http://www.ietf.org/rfc/rfc2026.txt

Braganza, A., & Lambert, R. (2000) Strategic integration: Developing a process-governance framework. *Knowledge and Process Management,* 7, 177-186.

Brain, D., Seltsikas, P., & Tailor, D. (2005). Process modelling notations for e-government: An assessment of modelling notations for identity management. In *Proceedings of the BLED 2005*.

Brand, K., & Boonen H. (2007). IT governance based on COBIT 4.1 - *a management guide, 3rd rev.edition*. Van Haren Publishing.

Branscomb, L., & Florida, R. (1997). *Challenges to technology policy in a changing world economy. Investing in innovation: Creating a research and innovation policy that works*. USA: MIT Press.

Brint, S. (2001). Knowledge society and the professions. Professionals and the 'knowledge economy': Rethinking the theory of postindustrial society. *Current Sociology, 49*(4), 101-132.

Brito, J. (2006). Public safety interoperability. *Regulation, 29*(3), 6-7.

Broadbent, M. (2003). Understanding IT governance. *CIO Canada, 11*(4), 13-14.

Brown, J. S., & Duguid, P. (1991). Organizational learning and communities-of-practice: Towards a unified view of working, learning, and innovation. *Organization Science, 2*(1), 40-57.

Brown, J. S., & Duguid, P. (1998). Organizing knowledge. *California Management Review, 40*(3), 90-111.

Brown, J. S., & Duguid, P. (2001). Knowledge and organization: A social-practice perspective. *Organization Science, 12*(2), 198-213.

Brown, J. S., Collins, A., & Duguid, P. (1989). Situated cognition and the culture of learning. *Education Researcher, 18*(1), 32-42.

Brown, M. M. (2003). Electronic government. In J. Rabin (Ed.), *Encyclopedia of public administration and public policy*. Marcel Dekker.

Brudney, J. L., & Seldon, S.C. (1995). The adoption of innovation by smaller local governments: The case of computer technology. *American Review of Public Administration, 25*(1), 71-87.

Bruijn, J. A. d., & Heuvelhof, E. F. t. (2000). *Networks and decision making*. Utrecht, The Netherlands: Lemma.

Bruijn, J. A. d., Heuvelhof, E. F. t., & in 't Veld, R. J. (2002). *Process management: Why project management fails in complex decision making processes*. Boston: Kluwer Academic Publishers.

Bruijn, J. A. d., Wagenaar, R. W., Voort, H. G. v. d., & Joode, R. v. Wendel d. (2004). *Shared services in de overheid*. Report Atos KPMG.

Brunsson, N., & Sahlin-Andersson, K. (2000) Constructing organizations: The case of public sector reform. *Organization Studies, 21*, 721-746.

Brusa, G., Caliusco, M. L., & Chiotti, O. (2007). Enabling knowledge sharing within e-government back-office through ontological engineering. *Journal of Theoretical and Applied Electronic Commerce Research, 2*(1), 33-48.

Bryson, J. M., & Anderson, S.R. (2000). Applying large-group interaction methods in the planning and implementation of major change efforts. *Public Administration Review, 60*(2), 143-162.

Buckby S., Best, P., & Stewart, J. (2008). The current state of information technology governance literature. In A. Cater-Steel (Ed.), *Information technology governance and service management: Frameworks and adaptations*. Hershey, PA: Idea Group Publishing.

Burn, F. & Robins, G. (2003). Moving towards e-government: A case study of organisational change processes. *Logistics Information Management, 16*(1), 25-35.

Butler, P., & Collins, N. (2004). Citizen as consumer. In N. Collins and T. Cradden (Eds.), *Political issues in Ireland today* (pp. 135–148). Manchester, UK: Manchester University Press.

Cabinet Office (2005). *Transformational Government Enabled by Technology*. London: The Stationery Office, Crown Copyright.

Cabinet Office. (2006). Retrieved from http://www.cio.gov.uk/documents/annual_report2006/trans_gov2006.doc

Cabinet Office. (2008, July 16). Latest report shows transformational government has brought major improvements to public services. London: Cabinet Office Press Office.

Cabrera, A., & Cabrera, E. F. (2002). Knowledge-sharing dilemmas. *Organization Studies, 23*(5), 687.

Capgemini (2007). *The User Challenge Benchmarking: The Supply Of Online Public Services, 7th Measurement.* Retrieved March 20, 2008 from http://ec.europa.eu/information_society/eeurope/i2010/docs/benchmarking/egov_benchmark_2007.pdf

Carbo, T., & Williams, J. G. (2004). Some determinants of user perceptions of information quality on the World Wide Web. *Electronic Journal of E-Government, 2*(2), 94-105.

Carroll, A. B. (1993). *Business and society:Ethics and stakeholder management.* Cincinnati, OH.

Carter, F. J., Jambulingham, T., Gupta, V. K., & Melone, N. (2001). Technological innovations: A framework for communicating diffusion affects. *Information and Management, 38*, 277-287.

Carter, L. & Belanger, F. (2005). The utilization of e-government services: Citizen trust, innovation, and acceptance factors. *Information Systems Journal, 15*(1), 5-25.

Carter, L., Schaupp, L., & Evans, A. (2008). Antecedents to e-file adoption: The U.S. perspective. *Hawaii International Conference on System Sciences, Proceedings of the 41st Annual* (216-216).

Carver, L., & Turoff, M. (2007). Human-computer interaction: The human and computer as a team in emergency management information systems. *Communications of the ACM, 50*(3), 33-38.

Castells, M. (2001). *The Internet galaxy—reflections on the Internet, business, and society.* Oxford, UK, & New York: Oxford University Press.

Castells, M., Fernandez-Ardeval, M., Linchuan Qiu, J., & Sey, A. (2004). *The mobile communication society—a cross-cultural analysis of available evidence on the social uses of wireless communication technology. Report.* Annenberg Research Network on International Communication.

Castronova, E. (2005). *Synthetic worlds: The business and culture of online games.* Chicago: University of Chicago Press.

Cats-Baril, W., & Thompson, R. (1995). Managing information technology projects in the public sector. *Public Administration Review, 6*(55), 559-566.

CEN/ISSS. (2005). E-Health Standardization Focus Group. Current and future standardization issues in the e-health domain: Achieving interoperability. Retrieved on April 5, 2008, from http://www.i2-health.org/ehealth-iop/eHealthStandardizationExecutive%20summaryFinal-version2005-02-21.pdf

Ceyhun, Y., & Çağlayan, M. U. (1996). *Bilgi teknolojileri türkiye için nasıl bir gelecek hazırlamakta?* Türkiye İş Bankası Kültür Yayınları.

Chamberlain, J. & Castleman, T. (2005). Moving personal tax online: The Australian taxation office's e-tax initiative. *International Journal of Cases on Electronic Commerce, 1*(3), 54-70.

Chan, C. M. L., Lau, Y., & Pan, L. (2008). E-Government implementation: A macro analysis of Singapore's e-government initiatives. *Government Information Quarterly, 25*, 239-255.

Chancellor of the Duchy of Lancaster. (2005). *Transformational government enabled by technology.* UK: HM Government.

Chau, P. Y. K., & Tam, K. Y. (1997). Factors affecting the adoption of open systems:aAn exploratory study. *MIS Q., 21*(1), 1-24.

Chau, Y. K., & Hu, J. H. (2001). Information technology acceptance by individual professionals: A model comparison approach. *Decision Sciences, 32*(4), 699-718.

Chen, C., Tseng, S., & Huang, H. (2006). A comprehensive study of the digital divide phenomenon in Taiwanese government agencies. *International Journal of Internet and Enterprise Management, 4*(3), 244-256.

Chen, D., & Vernadat, F. (2003). Enterprise interoperability: A standardisation view. In *Proceedings of the IFIP TC5/WG5.12 International Conference on Enterprise Integration and Modeling Technique* (pp. 273-282). B.V. Kluwer.

Chen, H. (2003). Digital government: Technologies and practices. *Decision Support Systems, 34*(4), 223–227.

Chen, H. (2005). *Adopting emerging integration technologies in organisations*. Unpublished doctoral thesis, Brunel University, London, UK.

Cheng, J., Cheng, S., & Yang, M. (2007). *Evaluating the e-government based on BSC. Integration and Innovation Orient to E-Society, Vol. 2*. Boston: Springer.

Chesbrough, H. W., & Teece, D. J. (1996). When is virtual virtuous? Organizing for innovation. *Harvard Business Review, 74*(1), 65-73.

Chief Information Officer Council. (2007). Strategy: Citizen and business centred services. *Transformational Government: Enabled by Technology, created 01 Nov 2005, updated 23 May 2007*. Retrieved April 26, 2008, from http://www.cio.gov.uk/transformational_ government/strategy/contents/strategy_2.asp

Chief Information Officer Council. (2007). Transformational government. Retrieved on September 9, 2007, from http://www.cio.gov.uk/transformational_government/strategy/

Chircu, A. M., & Lee, D. H-D. (2005). E-Government: Key success factors for value discovery and realisation. *E-Government, an International Journal, 2*(1), 11-25.

Chisholm, D. (1989). *Coordination without hierarchy*. Berkeley, CA: University of California Press.

Choi, S., et al. (1997). *The economics of electronic commerce*. Indianapolis, IN: Macmillan Technical Publishing.

Choudrie, J., & Dwivedi, Y. (2005). A survey of citizens adoption and awareness of e-government initiatives. The government gateway: A United Kingdom perspective. E-Government workshop. Brunel University, West London.

Christie, C. A. (2003). Understanding evaluation theory and its role in guiding practice: Formal, folk, and otherwise. *New Directions for Evaluation, 97*(Spring), 91-93.

Ciborra, C. U., Braa, K., Cordella, A., Dahlbom, B., Failla, A., Hanseth, O., Hepsø, V., Ljungberg, J., Monteiro, E., & Simon, K. A. (2000). *From control to drift: The dynamics of corporate information infrastructures*. Oxford, UK: Oxford University Press.

Clark, J., Casanave, C., Kanaskie, K., Harvey, B., Clark, J., Smith, N., Yunker, J., & Riemer, K. (2001). *ebXML business process specification schema version 1.01*. UN/CEFACT and OASIS.

Clark, R., & Chopeta, L. (2004). Graphics for learning: Proven guidelines for planning, designing, and evaluating visuals in training materials. Jossey-Bass/Pfeiffer.

Clarkson, M. B. E. (1995). A stakeholder framework for analyzing and evaluating corporate social performance. *Academy of Management Review, 20*, 92-117.

CNIPA. (2007). *Linee strategiche volte ad indirizzare le amministrazioni nella predisposizione del piano triennale per l'informatica 2008-2010*. Rome.

Cohen, S., & Eimicke, W. (2003). *The future of e-government: A project of potential trends and issues*. In *Proceedings of the 36th Hawaii International Conference on System Sciences*. IEEE Computer Society.

Cohen, W. M., & Levinthal, D. A. (1990). Absorptive capacity: A new perspective on learning and innovation. *Administrative Science Quarterly, 35*, 128-152.

Comfort, & Hasse. (2006). Communication, coherence, and collective action: The impact of Hurricane Katrina on communications infrastructure. *Public Works Management & Policy, 10*(4), 328-343.

Comfort, L. K., & Kapucu, N. (2006). Interorganizational coordination in extreme events: The World Trade Center attacks, September 11, 2001. *Natural Hazard Journal, 39*, 309-327.

Commission of the European Communities (CEC). (2005a). *Information society benchmarking report*. Brussels, Belgium: European Commission.

Commission of the European Communities (CEC). (2005b). *Proposal for a recommendation of the European Parliament and of the Council on Key Competences for Lifelong Learning.* Brussels, Belgium: European Commission.

Commission of the European Communities (CEC). (2005c). *i2010—A European information society for growth and employment.* Communication from the Commission to the European Parliament, the European Economic and Social Committee, and the Committee of the Regions, COM(2005) 229 final, Brussels, Belgium: European Commission.

Committee for Economic Development. (2006). *Open standards, open source, and open innovation: Harnessing the benefits of openness.* Washington, DC: Committee for Economic Development.

Commonwealth of Massachusetts, I. T. D. (2004). *Enterprise open standards policy* (No. ITD-APP-01).

Compeau, D. R., & Higgins, C. A. (1995). Computer self-efficacy: Development of a measure and initial test. *MIS Quarterly, 19*(2), 189-211.

Cooper, R. B., & Zmud, R. W. (1990). Information technology implementation research: A technological diffusion approach. *Management Science, 36*(2), 123-139.

Cordella, A. (2006). Transaction costs and information systems: Does IT add up? *Journal of Information Technology, 21,* 195–202.

Corey, E. C., & Garand, J.C. Are government employees more likely to vote? An analysis of turnout in the 1996 U.S. national election. *Public Choice, 111,* 259-283.

Corkery, J., Daddah, T., O'Nuallain, C., & Land, T. (Eds.). (1998). *Management of public service reform: A comparative review of experiences in the management of programmes of reform of the adminitrative arm of central government.* International Institute of Administrative Sciences, IOS Press.

Cornford, J., Richardson, R., Sokol, M., Marques, P., & Gillespie, A. (2006). *Transformation of regional societies through ICTs: State(s) of the art(s)—a discussion document.* Bonn, Germany: TRANSFORM Consortium.

Cornford, T., & Smithson, S. (1997). *Project research in information systems: A student's guide.* London: Macmillan Press.

Cresswell, A. M., Burke, G. B., & Pardo, T. A. (2006, September). *Advancing return on investment analysis for government IT: A public value framework.* Center for Technology in Government, University at Albany.

Cresswell, A. M., Pardo, T. A., Canestraro, D. S., Dawes S. S., & Juraga, D.(2005). *Sharing justice information: A capability assessment toolkit* (p. 116). Albany, NY: Centre for Technology in Government.

Crocker, D. (1993). Making standards the IETF way. *Standardview, 1*(1), 48-56.

Cross, R., Parker, A., Prusak, L., & Borgatti, S. P. (2001). Knowing what we know: Supporting knowledge creation and sharing in social networks. *Organizational Dynamics, 30*(2), 100-120.

Crossrail. (2006). *About us.* London: Cross London Rail Links Limited. Retrieved on July 28, 2008, from http://www.crossrail.co.uk/pages/aboutus48.html, accessed 28 July 2008

Culbertson, S. (2005). Transformed government. In M. Khosrowpour (Ed.), *Participating e-government: A global perspective.* Hershey, PA: Idea Group Inc.

Currion, P., Silva, C. d., & Walle, B. V. d. (2007). Open source software for disaster management. *Communications of the ACM: SPECIAL SECTION: Emergency Response Information Systems: Emerging Trends and Technologies Table of Contents, 50*(3), 61-65.

Cyert, R. M., & Kumar, P. (1994). Technology management and the future. *IEEE Transactions on Engineering Management, 41*(4), 333-334.

Czarniawska, B., & Joerges, B. (1996). Travels of ideas. In B. Czarniawska, & G. Sevon (Ed.), *Translating organizational change.* New York: Walter De Gryter.

Daft, R. L., & Lengel, R. H. (1996). Organizational information requirements, media richness and structural design. *Management Science, 3,* 554-571.

Daft, R. L., & Weick, K. E. (1984). Toward a model of organizations as interpretation systems. *Academy of Management Review, 9*(2), 284-295.

Dahlberg, L. (2001). Democracy via cyberspace: Mapping the rhetoricsand practices of three prominent camps. *New Media and Society, 3*(2), 157-177.

Daniel, K., Aart, K., & Massimo, M. (2008). Governance matters VII: Aggregate and individual governance indicators, 1996-2007. *World Bank Policy Research Working Paper No. 4654.*

Danziger, J. N., & Andersen, K. V. (2002). Impacts of IT on politics and the public sector: Methodological, epistemological, and substantive evidence from the Golden Age of transformation. *International Journal of Public Administration, 25*(5), 591–627.

Danziger, J. N., & Kraemer, K. L. (1986). *People and computers: The impacts of computing on end users in organisations.* New York: Columbia University Press.

Darmawan, I. G. N. (2001). Adoption and implementation of information technology in Bali's local government: A comparison between single level path analyses using PLSATH 3.01 and AMOS 4 and multilevel path analyses using MPLUS 2.01. *International Education Journal, 2*(4), 100-23.

Davenport, T. H. (1993). *Process innovation: Reengineering work through information technology.* Boston: Harvard Business School Press.

Davenport, T. H. (1998). Putting the Enterprise into the Enterprise System. *Harvard Business Review, 76*(4), 121-131.

Davenport, T. H., & Prusak, L. (1998). *Working knowledge: How organizations manage what they know.* Boston: Harvard Business School Press.

Davenport, T. H., & Short, J. E. (1990). The new industrial engineering: Information technology and business process redesign. *Sloan Management Review, 31*(4), 11–27.

Davis, F. D. (1989). Perceived usefulness, perceived ease of use, and user acceptance of information technology. *MIS Quarterly, 13*(3), 319-340.

Davis, F. D., Bagozzi, R. P., & Warshaw, P. R. (1989). User acceptance of computer technology: A comparison of two theoretical models. *Management Science, 35*(8), 982-1003.

Davis, F. D., Bagozzi, R. P., & Warshaw, P. R. (1992). Extrinsic and intrinsic motivation to use computers in the workplace. *Journal of Applied Social Psychology, 22*(14), 1111-1132.

Davis, J.G. (1985). A typology of management information systems users and its implications for user information satisfaction research. *ACM.*

Davison, R. M., Martinsons, M. G., & Kock, N. (2004). Principles of canonical action research. *Information Systems Journal, 14*(1), 65-86.

Davison, R. M., Wagner, C., & Ma, L.C. (2005). From government to e-government: A transition model. *Information Technology & People, 18*(3), 280-299.

Dawes, S. (2002). *The future of e-government.* Albany, NY: Center for Technology in Government. Retrieved on March 10, 2008, from http://www.ctg.albany.edu/publications/reports/future_of_egov/future_of_egov.pdf

Dawes, S. (2008). An exploratory framework for future e-government research investments. In *Proceedings of the 41st Hawaii International Conference on System Sciences (Hicss).*

Dawes, S. S., & Pardo, T. (2002). Building collaborative digital government systems. In W. J. McIver, & A. K. Elmagarmid (Eds.), *Advances in digital government. Technology, human factors, and policy.* Norwell, MA: Kluwer Academic Publishers.

Dawes, S. S., & Prefontaine, L. (2003). Understanding new models of collaboration for delivering government services. *Communications of the ACM, 46*(1), 40-42.

Day, G. S. (1994). The capabilities of market-driven organizations. *Journal of Marketing, 58*, 37-52.

DCITA. (2000). GovernmentOnLine—The commonwealth government's strategy. *The Australian Government Information Management Office, Canberra, Australia April 2000.* Retrieved on July 24, 2008, from http://

www.agimo.gov.au/archive/publications_noie/2000/04/govonline#Contents, accessed 24 July 2008

De Azevedo Filho, W. A, (2003). *UsingOopen Source inCcommunityBbasedPprojects. Gartner group*. Retrieved from

de Long, D. W., & Fahey, L. (2000). Diagnosing cultural barriers to knowledge management. *Academy of Management Executive*, *14(*4), 113-128.

De Marco, M., & Sorrentino, M. (2007). Sowing the seeds of IS cultivation in public service organisations. *Journal of Information Technology, 22*(2), 184-194.

De', R. (2006). Evaluation of e-government systems: Project assessment vs. development assessment. In M. A. Wimmer, H. J. Scholl, A. Grönlund, & K.V. Andersen (eds.), *Electronic government, Proceedings of the 5th International EGOV 2006 Conference*, Krakow, Poland (pp. 317-328). Berlin Heidelberg: Springer-Verlag.

DeLone, W. H., & McLean, E. R. (1992). Information systems success: The quest for the dependent variable. *Information Systems Research,* 60-95.

DeLone, W. H., & McLean, E. R. (2003). The DeLone and McLean model of information systems success: A ten-year update. *Journal of Management Information Systems,* 9-30.

DeNardis, L., & Tam, E. (2007). *Interoperability and democracy: A political basis for open document standards.* Paper presented at the 5th International Conference on Standardization and Innovation in Information Technology. Retrieved on October 28, 2008 from http://www.krechkin.com/siit2007/program.html

Denison, D. R., Hart, S. L., & Kahn, J. A. (1996). From chimneys to cross-functional teams: Developing and validating a diagnostic model. *Academy of Management Journal*, *39*(4), 1005-1023.

Denning, J. P., & Hayes-Roth, R. (2006). Decision making in very large networks. *The Profession of IT, 49*(11), 19-23.

Department of Information Resources (2000). Seamless government issues: State of Texas. Updated Apr 17, 2003, http://www.dir.state.tx.us/egov/report/seamless.htm. In M.H. Fagan. (2006). Exploring city, county, and state e-government initiatives: An east Texas perspective. *Business Process Management Journal, 12*(1), 101–112.

Deprest, J., & Robben, F. (2003). *E-government :the approach of the Belgian federal administration.* Brussels, Belgium: FEDICT.

Devadoss, P. R., Pan, S. L., & Huang, J. C. (2002). Structural analysis of e-government initiatives: A case study of SCO. *Decision Support Systems, 34*, 253-269.

DeVol, R., Klowden, K., Collins, J., Wallace, L., Wong, P., & Bedroussian, A. (2004). *Arkansas' position in the knowledge-based economy: Prospects and policy options.* Santa Monica, USA: Milken Institute.

Dewett, T., & Jones, G. R. (2001). The Role of Information Technology in the Organization: A Review, Model, and Assessment. *Journal of Management, 27*(3), 313-346.

Diedrich, E., Wimmer, M., Schmidt, D., Mondorf, A., Matheis, T., Ziemann, J., & Freiheit, J. (2007). *Analysis of R4eGov scenarios for interoperability.* Deliverable WP4-D3. R4eGov—Towards e-Administration in the large (Proposal/Contract no.: IST-2004-026650).

Dierick, I., & Cool, K. (1989). Asset stock accumulation and sustainability of competitive advantage. *Management Science*, *35*(12), 1504-1511.

DiMaggio, P. J., & Powell, W. (1983). The iron cage revisited, institutional isomorphism, and collective rationality in organizational fields. *American Sociological Review*, *48*, 147-60.

Dingsøyr, T., Røyrvik, E., & Djarraya, H. K. (2005). Supporting organizational learning: The contribution of a technical skills management tool. *Communications of the ACM, 12*, 96-100.

Ditch, W. (2007). XML-based office document standards. *JISC Technology & Standards Watch.*

Dixon, R. D. (1999). The behavioural side of information technology. *International Journal of Medical Informatics*, *56*(1-3), 117-23.

Doll, W. J., & Torzadeh, G. (1988). The measure of end-user computing satisfaction. *MIS Quarterly, 12*(2), 259-274.

Dougherty, D. (2001). Reimagining the differentiation and integration of work for sustained product innovation. *Organization Science*, *12*(5), 612-631.

Drabek, T. E. (1985). Managing the emergency response. *Public Administration Review, 45*, 85.

Drucker, P. (1993). *Postcapitalist society.* New York: Harper Business.

Drucker, P. F. (2004). The age of social transformation. *The Atlantic Monthly, 274*(5), 53-80.

Duffy, J. (2002). *IT/Business alignment: Is it an option or is it mandatory?* IDC document # 26831, IT and Business Alignment Advisory service.

Duffy, J. (2002). *IT governance and business value part 1: IT governance - an issue of critical importance*. IDC document # 27291.

Duffy, J. (2002). *IT governance and business value part 2: Who's responsible for what?* IDC document # 27807.

Dunleavy, H. P., Margetts, H., Bastow, S., Callaghan, R., & Yared, H. (2002). Progress in implementing e-government in Britain: Supporting evidence for the National Audit Office Report "Government on the Web II."

Dunleavy, P. (2006). *Digital era governance : IT corporations, the state, and e-government*. New York: Oxford University Press.

Dutton, W. H. (2005). The Internet and social transformation: Reconfiguring access. In W. H. Dutton, B. Kahin, R. O'Callaghan, & A. W. Wyckoff (Eds.), *Transforming enterprise: The economic and social implications of information technology* (pp. 375-397). Cambridge, MA, & London: MIT Press.

Dutton, W. H., & Helsper, E. J. (2007). *The Internet in Britain: 2007.* Oxford, UK: Oxford Internet Institute, University of Oxford.

Dwivedi, Y., & Weerakkody, V. (2007). Examining the factors affecting the adoption of broadband in the Kingdom of Saudi Arabia. *Electronic Government, an International Journal, 4*(1), 43-58.

Dwivedi, Y., Papazafeiropoulou, A., & Gharavi, H. (2006). Socioeconomic determinants of adoption of the government gateway initiative in the UK. *Electronic Government*, *3*(4), 404-419.

Eastin, M. A., & LaRose, R. L. (2000). Internet self-efficacy and the psychology of the digital divide. *Journal of Computer Mediated Communication*, *6*(1).

Ebrahim, Z., & Irani, Z. (2005). E-Government adoption : Architecture and barriers. *Business Process Management*, *11*(15), 589-611.

Ebrahim, Z., Irani, Z., & Sarmad, S. (2004). Factors influencing the adoption of e-government in public sector. *European & Mediterranean Conference on Information Systems*, Tunis, Tunisia.

Ecma International. (2006). Ecma international approves office open XML standard.

Ecma International. (2007). Office open XML overview. Retrieved on November 1, 2007, from http://www.ecma-international.org/news/TC45_current_work/OpenXML%20White%20Paper.pdf

Economides, N. (2000). Durable goods monopoly with network externalities with application to the PC operating systems market. *Quarterly Journal of Electronic Commerce*, *1*(3), 193-201.

Economist, The. (2008, February 28). The good the bad and the inevitable. A special report on government and technology.

Edmiston, K. D. (2003). State and Local E-Government. *American Review of Public Administration, 33*(1), 20-45.

E-Europe. (2005). *An information society for all: E-Government.* Retrieved August 14, 2006, from http://europa.eu.int/information_society/eeurope/2005/all_about/action_plan/index_en.htm

E-Government Task Force (2002). E-government strategy: Simplified delivery of services to citizens. *Office of Management and Budget, United States Federal Government.* Retrieved April 26, 2008, from http://www.whitehouse.gov/omb/inforeg/egovstrategy.pdf

E-Government Unit, Cabinet Office. (2005). E-Government interoperability framework, version 6.1, 18th March 2005, London, UK. Retrieved on April 10, 2008, from http://www.govtalk.gov.uk/schemasstandards/egif_document.asp?docnum=949

eircom. (2000). *Ennis information age town: A connected community.* Ireland: eircom.

Eisenhardt, K. M. (1989). Building theories from case study research. *Academy of Management Review, 14*(4), 532-550.

Eisenhardt, K. M. (1989). Building theories from case study research. *Academy of Management Review, 14*(4), 532-550.

Eisenhardt, K. M., & Martin, J. A. (2000). Dynamic capabilities: What are they? *Strategic Management Journal, 21*(10), 1105-1121.

EITO. (2007). *European Information Technology Observatory 2007,* Frankfurt: EITO-EEIG.

Ellingsen, G., & Monteiro, E. (2003). Mechanisms for producing a working knowledge: Enacting, orchestrating, and organizing. *Information and Organization, 13,* 203-229.

Elnaghi, M., AlShawi, S., & Missi, F. (2007). A leadership model for e-government transformation. *Proceedings of European and Mediterranean Conference on Information Systems* (EMCIS2007). June 24-26, Polytechnic University of Valencia, Spain.

EU. (1999). eEurope: An information society for all-Communication on a commission initiative for the special European Council of Lisbon, 23 and 24 March 2000, Commission of the European Communities, Brussels. COM/99/0687 final. 2002. Retrieved from http://europa.eu.int/information_society/eeurope/news_library/pdf_files/initiative_en.pdf.

European Commission, Commission of the European Communities. (2003). *Linking-up Europe: The importance of interoperability for e-government services.* Staff Working Document.

European Commission. (2004). *European interoperability framework for pan-European e-government services. European communities.* Retrieved August 14, 2006, from http://europa.eu.int/idabc

European Public Administration Network (EPAN). (2004). Key principles of interoperability. Architecture, Ireland: European Union.

Eurostat. (2006). *Methodological manual for statistics on the information society, survey year 2006, v2.1.* Luxembourg: Eurostat.

eUSER Consortium. (2006). *Report on current demand/supply match and relevant developments. Project deliverable.* Bonn, Germany: Empirica.

Evans, G. (2003). *Implementing e-government: An executive report for civil servants and their advisors.* Hampshire, England: Gower Publishing Limited.

Evans, K. (2006, December). Expanding e-government: Making a difference for the American people using information technology. Executive Office of the President, Office of Management and Budget.

Fahey, L., & Prusak, L. (1998). The eleven deadliest sins of knowledge management. *California Management Reveiw, 40*(3), 265-275.

Fanderi, H., Fischer, K., & Kamper, J. (1992). The open document architecture: From standardization to the market. *IBM Systems Journal, 31*(4), 728-754.

Fang, Z. (2002). E-Government in digital era: Concept, practice, and development. *International Journal of the Computer, the Internet, and Management, 10*(2), 1–22.

Feagin, J., Orum, A., & Sjoberg, G. (1991). *A case for case study.* Chapel Hill, NC: University of North Carolina Press.

Fear, W. J. (2007). Programme evaluation theory, the next step toward a synthesis of logic models and organisational theory. *Journal of MultiDisciplinary Evaluation, 4*(7), 13-25.

Federal Financial Institution Examination Counci,. (2004). *RiskMmanagement of Free andOopen SourceS-software. Financial Institution Letter,*. Retrievediin October 2004, from http://www.fdic.gov/news/news/financial/2004/FIL11404a.html

Feldman, M. (2005). *The importance of proximity and location. Knowledge and place: Proximity, mobility, clusters, and institutions: Advancing knowledge and the knowledge economy.* U.S. National Science Foundation.

Feldmann, V., & Zerdick, A. (2005). E-Merging media: The future of communication. In A. Zerdick, et al. (Eds.), *E-Merging media: Communication and the media economy of the future* (pp. 19-29). Berlin, Heidelberg, & New York: Springer.

Fenger, H. J. M. (2006). Shifts in welfare governance: The state, private, and non-profit sectors in four European countries. In P. Henman & H. J. M. Fenger (Eds.), *Administering welfare reform* (pp. 73-92). Bristol, UK: The Policy Press.

Ferrat, T. W., & Agarwal, R. (1996). Toward managing information systems professionals better. *SIGCPR/SIGMIS*, 268-275.

Fichman, R. G., & Kemerer, C. F. (1997). The assimilation of software process innovations:aAn organizational learning perspective. *Manage. Sci.*, *43*(10), 1345-1363.

Field, J. (2003). *Social capital.* London, & New York: Routledge.

Flamholtz, E. G. (1996). *Effective management control: Theory and practice.* Norwell: Kluwer Academic Publishers.

Fletcher, P. D. (2002). E-File: Electronic tax administration in the United States.

Florida, R. (2002). The economic geography of talent. *Annals of the Association of American Geographers*, *92*(4), 743-755.

Florida, R. (2002). *The rise of the creative class–and how it's transforming work, leisure, community, and everyday life.* New York: Basic Books.

Florida, R., & Gates, G. (2001). *Technology and tolerance: The importance of diversity to high-tech growth.* Washington, D.C.: Center for Urban and Metropolitan Policy.

Ford, T. C., Colomb, J., Grahamr, S. R., & Jacques, D. R. (2007, June). A survey on interoperability measurement. In *Proceedings of 12th International Command and Control Research and Technology Symposium*, Newport, RI.

Fornell, C. (2007). Government satisfaction scores: ACSI scores and commentary. Retrieved April 26, 2008, from http://www.theacsi.org/index.php?option=com_content& task=view&id=176&Itemid=62

Fountain, J. (2001). *Building the virtual state: Information technology and institutional change.* Washington, DC: Brookings Institution.

Fountain, J. (2001). The virtual state: Transforming American government? *National Civic Review, 90*(3), 241–251.

Frambach, R. T., & Schillewaert, N. (2002). Organisational innovation adoption: A multi-level framework of determinants and opportunities for future research. *Journal of Business Research*, *55*(2), 163-76.

Franz, C. R., & Robey, D. (1986). Organizational context, user involvement, and usefulness of information systems. *Decision Science, 17*(3), 329-356.

Freeman, R. E. (1984). *Strategic management: A stakeholder approach.* Boston: Pitman

Friedman, T. (2005). *The world is flat: A brief history of the twenty-first century.* New York: Farrar, Straus & Giroux.

Fu, J.-R., Farn, C.-K., & Chao ,W.-P. (2006). Acceptance of electronic tax filing: A study of taxpayer intentions. *Information & Management*, *43*, 109-126.

Gallivan, M. J. (2001). Organisational adoption and assimilation of complex technological innovations: Development and application of a new framework. *The DATABASE for Advances in Information Systems*, *32*(3), 51-85.

Gandhi, S., & Cross, C. (2001). E-Government initiative at city of Orlando: Current trends and future directions. *Proceedings of the URISA conference, October 1-12.*

Ganesan, S., & Hess, R. (1997). Dimensions and levels of trust: Implications for commitment to a relationship. *Marketing Letters, 8*(4) 439-448.

Garfield, M. (2000). Critical success factors for the state telemedicine policy. In *Proceedings of the 6th Americas Conference on Information Systems*, Long Beach, California, USA (pp. 1573-1578).

Garson, D. (2003). *Digital government: Principles and best practices.* Hershey, PA: Idea Group Inc.

Garud, R., & Nayyar, P. R. (1994). Transformative capacity: Continual structuring by intertemporal technology transfer. *Strategic Management Journal, 15*, 365-385.

Garud, R., & Rappa, M. A. (1994). A socio-cognitive model of technology evolution: The case of cochlear implants. *Organization Science*, *5*, 344-362.

Gates, W. (1995). *The road from here*. New York: Viking.

Gauch, R. R. (1993). Differences between public and management information systems. *CPR*, 385-399.

Gefen, D. (2000). E-Commerce: The role of familiarity and trust. *Omega: The International Journal of Management Science, 28*(6), 725-737.

Gefen, D., Karahanna, E., & Straub, D. W. (2003). Trust and TAM in online shopping: An integrated model. *MIS Quarterly*, *27*(1), 51-90.

Gefen, D., Rose, G., Warkentin, M., & Pavlou, P. (2002). Cultural diversity and trust in IT adoption: A comparison of potential e-voters in the USA and South Africa. *Journal of Global Information Management*, *13*(1), 54-78.

Gherardi, S., & Nicolini, D. (2000). The organizational learning of safety in communities of practice. *Journal of Management Inquiry*, *9*(1), 7-18.

Gibson, C. F., & Nolan, R.L. (1974). Managing the four stages of EDP growth. *Harvard Business Review*, 20-29.

Gilbert, D., Balestrini, P. & Littleboy, D. (2004). Barriers and benefits in the adoption of e-government. *The International Journal of Public Sector Management*, *17*(4), 286-301.

Gil-Garcia, J. R., & Martinez-Moyano, I. (2007). Understanding the evolution of e-government: The influence of the systems of rules on public sector dynamics. *Government Information Quarterly*, *24*(2), 266-290.

Gil-Garcia, J. R., & Pardo, T. A. (2005). E-Government success factors: Mapping practical tools to theoretical foundations. *Government Information Quarterly, 22*(2), 187-216.

Gil-Garcia, J. R., Canestraro, D., Costello, J., Baker, A., & Werthmuller, D. (2006). Fostering innovation in electronic government: Benefits and challenges of XML for web site management. Paper presented at the 67th ASPA National Conference, organized by the American Society for Public Administration, Denver, CO.

Gil-Garcia, J. R., Chengular-Smith, I., & Duchessi, P. (2007). Collaborative e-government: Impediments and benefits of information-sharing projects in the public sector. *European Journal of Information Systems*, *16*(2), 121-133.

Gillies, J., & Cailliau, R. (2000). *How the web was born.* Oxford, UK: Oxford University Press.

Glaser, B., & Straus, A. L. (1967). *The discovery of grounded theory: Strategies for qualitative research.* Chicago: Adline.

Glynn, E., Fitzgerald, B., & Exton, C. (2005). Commercial adoption of open source software:aAn empirical study. In *Empirical Software Engineering, 200. (pp.* 225-234).

Godin, B. (2003). The knowledge-based economy: Conceptual framework or buzzword. *Canadian Project on History and Sociology of S&T Statistics. Working Paper No.24.*

Goodhue, D. L. (1995). Task-technology fit and individual performance. *MIS Quarterly*, *19*(2), 213-236.

Goodland, M., & Slater, C. (1995). *SSADM version 4.* McGraw-Hill Publishing Co.

Gopalakrishnan, S., & Damanpour, F. (1997). A review of innovation research in economics, sociology, and technology management. *Omega, 25*(1), 15-28.

Gore, A. (1997). Introduction: Access America: Reengineering through information technology. *Report of the National Performance Review and the Government Information Technology Services Board.* Retrieved April 30, 2008, from http://govinfo.library.unt.edu /accessamerica/docs/intro.html

Government of India. (1989). Central motor vehicles rules, 1989. Retrieved on March 1, 2007, from http://www.morth.nic.in/index3.asp?sublink2id=280&langid=2

Granovetter, M. (1973). The strength of weak ties. *American Journal of Sociology, 91*, 1360-1380.

Grant, G., & Chao, D. (2005). Developing a generic framework for e-government. *Journal of Global Information Management, 13*(1), 1–30.

Grant, G., McKnight, S., Uruthirapathy, A., & Brown, A. (2007). Designing governance for shared service organizations in the public service. *Government Information Quarterly, 24*, 522-538.

Grant, R. M. (1996). Toward a knowledge-based theory of the firm. *Strategic Management Journal, 17*(109), 122.

Grant, R. M. (1997). *Contemporary strategy analysis.* Cambridge, MA: Blackwell.

Green, P., & Rosemann, M. (2000). Integrated process modeling: An ontological evaluation. *Information Systems, 25*(2), 73-87.

Gregory, D., & Martin, S. (1994). Crafting evaluation research in the public sector: Reconciling rigour and relevance. *British Journal of Management, 5*(Special Issue), S43-S52.

Greiner, U., Lippe, S., Kahl, T., Ziemann, J., & Jaekel, F. (2006). *Designing and implementing cross-organisational business processes – description and application of a modelling framework.* I-ESA Conference, France, Bordeaux.

Griffin, D., & Halpin, E. (2005). An exploratory evaluation of UK local e-government from an accountability perspective. *The Electronic Journal of e-Government, 3*(1), 13-28.

Grimsley, M., Meehan, A., & Tan, A. (2005, September 13). Capital accounting: Evaluating e-government projects from a community development perspective. In Z. Irani, T. Elliman, & O. D. Sarikas (Eds.), *Proceedings of the eGovernment Workshop '05 (eGOV05)*, Brunel University, UK.

Groklaw. (2007). Expert testimony of Ronald Alepin in Comes v. Microsoft - Embrace, Extend, Extinguish—Updated. Retrieved on October 22, 2007, from http://www.groklaw.net/article.php?story=20070108020408557

Gronlund, A. (2005). What's in a field – exploring the e-government domain. In *Proceedings of the 38th Hawaii International Conference on System Sciences* (8 pages).

Grönlund, et al. (2002). *Electronic government – design, application, and management.* Hershey, PA: Idea Group Publishing.

Groth, L. (1999). Future organizational design. In L. Groth (Ed.), *Future organizational design* (pp. 325-344). Chicester, England: John Wiley & Sons.

Gruhl, D., Guha, R., Liben-Nowell, D., & Tomkins, A. (2004). Information diffusion through blogspace. *WWW Conference* (pp. 491–501). New York: ACM. Retrieved April 27, 2008, from http://citeseer.ist.psu.edu/cache/papers/cs2/24/http:zSzzSzwww.www2004 .orgzSzproceedingszSzdocszSz1p491.pdf/gruhl04information.pdf

Gueorguiev, I., Dimitrova, S., Komitska, M., Traykov, H., & Spassov, K. (2005). Balanced scorecard based management information system – A potential for public monitoring and good governance advancement. *Electronic Journal on E-Government, 3*(1) , 29-38.

Guijarro, L. (2004, August 30-September 3). Analysis of the interoperability frameworks in e-government initiatives. In R. Traunmüller (Ed.), *Electronic Government: Third International Conference, E-Gov 2004*, Zaragoza, Spain (Vol. 3183, pp. 36-39). New York: Springer-Verlag Berlin Heidelberg.

Guijarro, L. (2007). Interoperability frameworks and enterprise architectures in e-government initiatives in Europe and the United States. Government Information Quarterly, 24(1), 89-101.

Guizzardi, G., Pires, L. F., & Sinderen, M. J. v. (2002). On the role of domain ontologies in the design of domain-specific visual modeling languages. In *Proceedings of the 2nd Workshop on Domain-Specific Visual Languages, 17th ACM Conference on Object-Oriented Programming, Systems, Languages and Applications (OOPSLA 2002)*. Seattle,WA.

Guldentops, E. (2003). Governing information technology through COBIT. In W. Van Grembergen (Ed.), *Strategies for information technology governance*. Hershey, PA: Idea Group Publishing.

Guldentops, E., Van Grembergen, W., & De Haes, S. (2002). Control and governance maturity survey: Establishing a reference benchmark and a self-assessment tool. *Information Systems Control Journal, 6*, 32-35.

Gupta, M. P. & Jana, D. (2003). E-Government evaluation: A framework and case study. *Government Information Quarterly, 20*, 365-387.

Gupta, M., Kumar, P., & Bhattacharya, J. (2004). *Government online opportunities and challenges*. Tata McGraw-Hill Publishing Company Limited.

Gupta, V., & Gupta, S. (2005). Experiments in wireless Internet security. *Statistical Methods in Computer Security*.

H. Lee, H., & Luedemann, H. (2007). *A lightweight decentralized authorization model for interdomain collaborations*. ACM Workshop on Secure Web-Services.

Haag, S., Cummings, M., & McCubbrey, D. (2003). *Management information systems for the information age*. McGraw-Hill Companies.

Hackman, J. R. (1990). *Groups that work (and those that don't)*. San Francisco: Jossey-Bass.

Halchin, L. E. (2004). Electronic government: Government capability and terrorist resource. *Government Information Quarterly, 21*, 406-419.

Hamel, G., & Prahalad, C. K. (1994). *Competing for the future*. Boston: Harvard Business School Press.

Hammer, M. & Champy, J. (1993). *Reengineering the corporation: A manifesto for business revolution*. New York: Harper Collins Publishers, Inc.

Hammer, M. (1990). Reengineering work: Don't automate, obliterate. *Harvard Business Review, 68*(4), 104–112.

Hammer, M. (1996). *Beyond reengineering: How the process-centered organization is changing our work and our lives*. London: HarperCollins Business.

Hammer, M. (2004). Deep Change. *Harvard Business Review, 82*(4), 84-93.

Hammer, M. H., & Champy, J. (1993). *Reengineering the corporation: A manifesto for business revolution*. New York: Harper Business.

Hampton, K. N. (2007). Neighborhoods in the network society—the e-neighbors study. *Information, Communication & Society, 10*(5), 714-748.

Hansard. (1990). Lord Brabazon of Tara in response to the Queen's speech. *The Parliamentary Debates (Hansard) House of Lords Official Report Monday, 12th November 1990. Fifth Series-Volume DXXIII: col 122.* Retrieved from http://www.hansard-archive.parliament.uk/The_Official_Report,_House_of_Lords_1909_to_2004/S5LV0523P0.zip.

Hansard. (2008). Mr. Deputy Speaker (Sir Alan Haselhurst) notice of royal assent. *Hansard (House of Commons Daily Debates) 22 July 2008. 479 Part No. 133: col 761.* Retrieved from http://www.publications.parliament.uk/pa/cm200708/cmhansrd/cm080722/debtext/80722-0019.htm#08072274000781.

Hansen, M. T. (2002). Knowledge networks: Explaining effective knowledge sharing in multiunit companies. *Organization Science, 13*(3), 232-248.

Hardar, I., & Soffer, P. (2006). Variantions in conceptual modeling: Classification and ontological analysis. *Journal for the Association of Information Systems 7*(8), 568-592.

Harmon, P. (2007). *Business process change: A guide for business managers and BPM and six sigma professionals, 2nd ed.* Amsterdam: Elsevier/Morgan Kaufmann Publishers.

Harper, R., & Kelly, M. (2003). *Measuring social capital in the United Kingdom*. London: ONS.

Harris, J. F., & Schwartz, J. (2000, June 22). Antidrug Web site tracks visitors. *Washington Post*, 23.

Harrison, T., Gil-Garcia, J. R., Pardo, T. A., & Thompson, F. (2006). *Learning about interoperability for emergency response: Geographic information technologies and the World Trade Center crisis*. Paper presented at the Proceeding of the 39th Hawaii International Conference on System Sciences.

Hart, P., & Saunders, C. (1997). Power and trust: Critical factors in the adoption and use of electronic data interchange. *Organizational Science*, *8*(1) 23-42.

Heeks, R. (2001). *Reinventing government in the information age*. New York: Routlage.

Heeks, R. (2003). *Most eGovernment for Development Projects Fail: How Can Risks be Reduced?*. iGovernment Working Paper Series, IDPM. University of Manchester, UK.

Heeks, R. (2003). *Causes of e-government success and failure: Factor model*. Institute for Development Policy and Management. University of Manchester, UK.

Heeks, R. (2003). *eGovernment for Development, The Impact of eGovernment Failure*. University of Manchester, UK: Institute for Development Policy and Management.

Heeks, R. (2006). *Implementing and managing e-government: An international text*. SAGE.

Heeks, R., & Bailur, S. (2007). Analysing e-government research: Perspectives, philosophies, theories, methods, and practice. *Government Information Quarterly*, *24*, 243-265.

Heintze, T., & Bretschneider, S. (2000). Information technology and restructuring in public organizations: Does adoption of information technology affect organizational structures, communications, and decision making? *Journal of Public Administration Research and Theory*, *10*(4), 801-830.

Henderson, J. C., & Venkatraman, N. (1993). Strategic alignment: Leveraging information technology for transforming organizations. *IBM Systems Journal*, *32*(1), 4-16.

Hendrick, R. (1994). An Information Infrastructure for Innovative Management of Government. *Public Administration Review*, *6*(54), 543-550.

Hendriks, P. (1999). Why share knowledge? The influence of ICT on the motivation for knowledge sharing. *Knowledge and Process Management*, *6*(2), 91-100.

Hernon, P., Reylea, H. C., Dugan, R. E., & Cheverie, J. F. (2002). *United States government information: Policies and sources*. Westport, CT: Libraries Unlimited.

Heutschi, R., Österle, H., Winter, R., & Brenner, W. (2007). *Serviceorientierte architektur: Architekturprinzipien und umsetzung in der praxis*. Berlin, Germany: Springer.

Hevner, A. R., March, S. T., Park, J., & Ram, S. (2004). Design science in information systems research. *MIS Quarterly*, *28*(1), 75-105.

Hill, C. W. L., & Jones, T. M. (1992). Stakeholder-agency theory. *Journal of Management Studies*, *29*, 131-154.

Hill, K. A. & Hughes, J. (1998). *Cyberpolitics: Citizen activism in the age of the Internet*. New York: Rowman and Littlefield.

Hinsz, V. B. (2001). A groups-as-information-processors perspective for technological support of intellectual teamwork. In M. D. McNeese, E. Salas, & M. Endsley (Eds.), *New trends in cooperative activities: System dynamics in complex environments* (pp. 22-45). Santa Monica, CA: Human Factors and Ergonomics Society Press.

Hinton, P. R., Brownlow, C., McMurvay, I., & Cozens, B. (2004). *SPSS explained*. East Sussex, England: Routledge Inc.

Hirschheim, R., & Klein, H. K. (1994). Realizing emancipatory principles in information systems development: The case for ETHICS. *MIS Quarterly, 18*(1), 83–109.

Hirschheim, R., & Smithson, S. (2000). Evaluation of information systems: A critical assessment. In L.P. Willcocks, & S. Lester (Eds.), *Beyond the productivity paradox* (pp. 381-409). Chichester: Wiley.

Hitt, L., & Brynjolfsson, E. (2003). ComputingPproductivity: FirmLlevel Evidence. *Review of Economics and Statistics, 85*(4), 793-808.

Ho, A. T. H. (2002). Reinventing local governments and the e-government initiatives. *Public Administration Review, 62*(4), 434-444.

Hofstadter, D. R. (1983). Computer tournaments of the prisoner's dilemma suggest how cooperation evolve. *Scientific American, 248*(5), 14-23.

Hofstede G. (1980). Motivation, leadership, and organization: Do American theories apply abroad? *Organizational Dynamics*, 42-63.

Hofstede, G. (2003). *Geert Hofstede™ cultural dimensions*. Stockholm: ITIM International. Retrieved on July 28, 2008, from http://www.geert-hofstede.com/hofstede_dimensions.php, accessed 28 July 2008

Homburg, V. (2004). E-Government and NPM: A perfect marriage? In *Proceedings of the 6th International Conference on Electronic Commerce (ICEC'04)* (pp. 547-555). ACM Press.

Homburg, V. M. F. (1999). *The political economy of information management: A theoretical and empirical analysis of decision making regarding interorganizational information systems*. Capelle aan de IJssel, The Netherlands: Labyrinth.

Homburg, V. M. F. (2000). Politics and Property Rights in Information Exchange. *Knowledge, Policy, and Technology, 13*(3), 13-22.

Homburg, V. M. F. (2007). A Comparative Account of Joined-Up Government Initiatives in Dutch and Belgian Social Security. *International Journal of Cases on Electronic Commerce, 3*(2), 1-12.

Homburg, V. M. F. (2008). *Information systems and public administration: Understanding e-government*. London: Routledge.

Homburg, V., & Bekkers, V. (2002). The back-office of e-government. In *Proceedings of the 35th Hawaii International Conference on Information Systems* (9 pages).

Hong, K. K., & Kim, Y. G. (2002). The critical success factors for ERP implementation: An organisational fit perspective. *Information and Management, 40*(1), 25-40.

Hopkins, A. (2005). E-Government trick or treat. In M. Khosrowpour (Ed.), *Participating e-government: A global perspective*.

Hopwood, A. G., & Miller, P. (1994). *Accounting as social and institutional practice*. Cambridge University Press.

Horst, M., Kuttschreuter, M. & Gutteling, Jm. (2007). Perceived usefulness, personal experiences, risk perception, and trust as determinants of adoption of e-government services in The Netherlands. *Computers in Human Behavior, 23*(4), 1838-1852.

Houghton, J., & Sheehan, P. (2000). *A primer on the knowledge economy*. Melbourne City, Australia: Center for Strategic Economic Studies, Victoria University.

Hsu, M. H., & Chiu, C. M. (2004). Internet self-efficacy and electronic service acceptance. *Decision Support Systems, 38*, 369-381.

Hu, P. J., Cui, D., & Sherwood, A. C. (2006, January 4-7). Examining cross-agency collaborations in e-government initiatives. In *Proceedings of the 39th Annual Hawaii international Conference on System Sciences—Volume 4 (HICSS)*. Washington, DC: IEEE Computer Society.

Hu, P., Cui, D., & Sherwood, A. (2006). Examining cross-agency collaborations in e-government initiatives. *Proceedings of the 39th Hawaii International Conference on System Sciences*.

Humphreys, P. C. (1998). Improving public service delivery. *Committee for Public management Research, Discussion Paper 7*. Dublin: Institute of Public Administration. Retrieved April 27, 2008, from http://www.

cpmr.gov.ie/publications/discussion-papers/improving-public-service-delivery.pdf/

Hutchins, E. (1995). *Cognition in the wild.* Cambridge, MA: MIT Press.

Huys, R., & Ramioul, M. (2007). Measuring the degree of organisational transformation, a methodological benchmark of organisation surveys. *Sotziologuicheski problemi, 40*, 58-80.

Hyde, R. (2003). *Art of assembly language*. San Francisco, CA: No Starch Press.

i2010 eGovernment action plan. (2005, June). *Accelerating e-government in Europe for the benefit of all.* Communication from the council.

i2010 High Level Group (i2010 HLG) (2006). *i2010 benchmarking framework, issue no. 1.* Brussels, Belgium: European Commission.

IctQatar. (2008). *Free wireless internet in Qatar's public parks.* Retrieved from http://www.ict.gov.qa/output/page422.asp

IDABC. (2004). European interoperability framework for pan-European e-government services, version 1.0, Brussels. Retrieved on January 3, 2008, from http://europa.eu.int/idabc/en/document/3761

IDABC. (2005). *The IDABC program (2005-2009).* Retrieved on August 14, 2006, from http://europa.eu/scadplus/leg/en/lvb/l24147b.htm

IEEE. (1990). *IEEE standard computer dictionary.* New York: IEEE.

Ilshammar, L., Bjurström, A., & Grönlund, Å. (2005). Public e-services in Sweden. Old wine in new bottles? *Scandinavian Journal of Information Systems, 17*, 11-40.

Indihar Štemberger, M., & Jaklič, J. (2007). Towards e-government by business process change-a methodology for public sector. *International Journal of Information Management*, *27*(4), 221-232.

InfoDev. (2002). The e-government handbook for developing countries. Retrieved from http://www.cdt.org/egov/handbook

Information Systems Audit and Control Association (ISACA). (2003). *System development life cycle (SDLC) review document G23.* USA.

Information Technology Standards Committee. (2003) Singapore IT standards. Retrieved on March 20, 2007, from http://www.itsc.org.sg/index.htm

International Telecommunication Union. (2005). Ubiquitous network societies. The case of the Republic of Singapore. *ITU Workshop on Ubiquitous Network Societies.* International Telecommunication Union.

IPS. (2008). IPS online passport pre-application site. *UK Home Office: Identity and Passport Service (IPS).* Retrieved on July 24, 2008 from https://www.ips.gov.uk/epa1r1a/about.aspx, accessed 24 July 2008.

Irani, A., Love, P. E. D., Elliman, T., Jones, S., & Themistoleous, M. (2005). Evaluating e-government: Learning from the experiences of two UK local authorities. *Information Systems Journal, 15*, 61-82.

Irani, Z., Al-Sebie, M., & Elliman, T. (2006). *Transaction stage of e-government systems: Identification of its location & importance.* Paper presented at the Proceedings of the 39th Hawaii International Conference on System Science, Hawaii.

Irani, Z., Al-Sebie, M., & Elliman, T. (2006, January 4-7). Transaction stage of e-government systems: Identification of its location and importance. In *Proceedings of the 39th Annual Hawaii international Conference on System Sciences—Volume 4 (HICSS).* Washington, DC: IEEE Computer Society.

Irani, Z., Elliman, T. & Jackson, P. (2007). Electronic transformation of government in the UK: A research agenda. *European Journal of Information Systems,* (October).

Irani, Z., Love, P., Elliman, Jones, S., & Themistocleous, M. (2005). Evaluating e-government: Learning from the experiences of two UK local authorities. *Information Systems Journal*, *15*(1), 61-82.

Irani, Z., Ozkan, S. G. A., & Elliman, T. (2007). T-Government for benefit realisation. *Proceedings of European and Mediterranean Conference on Information Systems (EMCIS2007) June 24-26*. Polytechnic University of Valencia, Spain.

Irani, Z., Sahraoui, S., Ozkan, S., Ghoneim, A., & Elliman T. (2007). T-Government for benefit realisation. In *Proceedings of European and Mediterranean Conference on Information Systems 2007 (EMCIS2007), June 24-26* (pp. 22-1-22-11). Polytechnic University of Valencia, Spain.

Irani, Z., Sharif, A., Love, P.E.D., & Kahraman, C. (2002). Applying concepts of fuzzy cognitive mapping to model: The IT/IS investment evaluation process. *International Journal of Production Economics, 75*, 199-211.

Ireland Offline. (2006) Campaigning for affordable, unmetered, and broadband internet access in Ireland. Retrieved on March 9, 2007, from http://www.ireland-offline.org/

IRS. (2004). IRS e-strategy for growth.

ISO. (2008). ISO/IEC standard (ISO/IEC 38500:2008) for corporate governance of information technology. Retrieved in June 2008, from http://www.iso.org/iso/pressrelease.htm?refid=Ref1135

ITGI & PwC. (2006). *IT governance global status report*. Retrieved in May 2008, from www.itgi.org

ITGI & PwC. (2006). *IT governance in practice. Insight from leading CIOs*. Retrieved in May 2008, from www.itgi.org

ITGI & PwC. (2008). *IT governance global status report*. Retrieved in May 2008, from www.itgi.org

ITGI. (2003). *Board briefing on IT governance, 2nd ed.* Retrieved in May 2008, from www.itgi.org

ITGI. (2006). *Enterprise value: Governance of IT investments, the Val IT framework*. Retrieved in May 2008, from www.itgi.org

ITGI. (2006). *COBIT mapping: Overview of international IT guidance, 2nd ed.* Retrieved in May 2008, from www.itgi.org

ITGI. (2007). *IT governance implementation guide: Using COBIT and Val IT, 2nd edition*. IT Governance Institute.

ITGI. (2007). COBIT 4.1. IT governance institute. Retrieved in May 2008, from www.itgi.org

ITGI. (2007). *COBIT quickstart, 2nd Edition*. IT Governance Institute. Retrieved in June 2008, from www.itgi.org

ITIL Website. (2008). http://www.itil-officialsite.com

Jacobs, J. (1961). *The death and life of great American cities*. New York: Random House.

Jacobsen, I., Booch, G., & Rumbaugh, J. (1999). *The unified software development process*. Boston: Addison-Wesley.

Jaeger, P. T. (2002). Constitutional principles and e-government: An opinion about possible effects of federalism and the separation of powers on e-government policies. *Government Information Quarterly, 19*(4), 357-368.

Jaeger, P. T. (2003). The endless wire: E-Government as global phenomenon. *Government Information Quarterly, 20*, 323-331.

Jaffee, D. (2001). *Organization theory, tension, and change*. Singapore: McGraw-Hill International Edition.

Jaklič, J, Groznik, A., & Kovačič, A. (2003). Towards e-government: the role of simulation modelling. In: Verbraeck, A., Hlupic, V. (Eds.). *Simulation in industry: October 26-29, 2003, Delft, Netherlands. Delft: SCS, 2003* (pp. 257-262). Delft, The Netherlands: SCS – Europe BVBA.

Janssen, D., Rotthier S., & Snijkers, K. (2004). If you measure it they will score: An assessment of international e-government benchmarking. *Information Polity, 9*, 121–130.

Janssen, M., & Cresswell, A. (2005). Enterprise architecture integration in e-government. In *Proceedings of the 38th Hawaii International Conference on System Sciences*, Hawaii, USA (pp. 1-10).

Janssen, M., & Hjort-Madsen, K. (2007). Analyzing enterprise architecture in national governments: The cases of Denmark and The Netherlands. 40th Annual Hawaii International Conference (HICSS 2007) (p. 218a). System Sciences.

Janssen, M., & Joha, A. (2006). Motives for establishing shared service centers in public administrations. *International Journal of Information Management, 26*(2), 102-116.

Janssen, M., & Scholl, H. J. (2007, December 10-13). Interoperability for electronic governance. In *Proceedings of the 1st International Conference on Theory and Practice of Electronic Governance (ICEGOV '07),* Macao, China (Vol. 232, pp. 45-48). New York:ACM.

Janssen, M., Joha, A., & Weerakkody, V. (2007). Exploring relationships of shared service arrangements in local government. *Transforming Government: People, Process and Policy, 1*(3), 27 284.

Jarvenpaa, S. L., Knoll, K., & Leidner, D. E. (1984). Is anybody out there? Antecedents of trust in global virtual teams. *Journal of Management Information Systems, 14*(4), 29-64.

Jawahar, I. M., & McLaughlin, G. L. (2001). Toward a descriptive stakeholder theory: An organizational life cycle approach. *Academy of Management Review, 26*(3), 397-414.

Jefferson, T. L. (2006). Evaluating the role of information technology in crisis and emergency management. *The Journal of Information and Knowledge Management Systems, 36* (3), 261-264.

Jefferson, T. L. (2006). Using the internet to communicate during a crisis. *The Journal of Information and Knowledge Management Systems, 36*(2), 139-142

Jennex, M. (2004). Emergency response systems: The utility Y2K experience. *Journal of Information Technology Theory and Application, 6*(3), 85-102.

Jensen, J. (2007). Comment #3, under P. Omidyar (2007). Thank you for the conversation. *Pandemic Flu Leadership Blog, United States Department of Health and Human Services, May 22–June 27, 2007.* Retrieved April 27, 2008, from http://blog.pandemicflu.gov/?p=109#comments

Jiwire (2006). JiWire launches worldwide point-of-connection wi-fi hotspot advertising network. Retrieved from http://www.jiwire.com/about/announcements/press-advertising-network.htm

Johannessen, J. A. (1994). IT and innovation: Identifying critical innovation factors. *Information Management & Computer Security, 2*(2), 4-9.

Jones, S., & Hughes, J. (2001). Understanding IS evaluation as a complex social process: A case study of a UK local authority. *European Journal of Information Systems, 10*, 189-203.

June, L., Chun-Sheng, Y., Chang, L., & James, E. (2003). Technology acceptance model for wireless Internet. *Internet Research: Electronic Networking Application and Policy, 13*(3), 206-222.

Jung, J.-Y., Qiu, J. L., & Kim, Y.-C. (2001). Internet connectedness and inequality: Beyond the "divide." *Communication Research, 28*(4), 507-35.

Kahin, B. (1995). The Internet and the national information infrastructure. In B. Kahin & J. Keller (Eds.), *Public access to the Internet* (pp. 3-23). Cambridge, MA: The MIT Press.

Kakabadse, A., Kakabadse, N., & Kouzmin, A. (2003). Reinventing the democratic governance project through information technology? A growing agenda for debate. *Public Administration Review, 63*(1), 44–60.

Kallinikos, J. (2004). Deconstructing information packages: Organizational and behavioural implications of ERP systems. *Information and Organization, 17*(1), 8-30.

Kamal, M. M. (2004). Integrating e-government through EAI. In *Proceedings of the 10th* Americas *Conference on Information Systems,* New York, USA (pp. 1143-1149).

Kamal, M. M. (2006). IT innovation adoption in government sector: Identifying the critical success factors. *Journal of Enterprise Information Management, 19*(2), 192-222.

Kamal, M. M., & Themistocleous, M. (2006). A conceptual model for EAI adoption in an e-government environment. *European and Mediterranean Conference on Information Systems (EMCIS)*, Costa Blanca, Spain (pp. 1-11).

Kamal, M. M., & Themistocleous, M. (2007). Investigating EAI adoption in LGAs: A case study based analysis. In *Proceedings of the 13th Americas Conference on Information Systems*, Keystone, Colorado (pp. 1-13).

Kamal, M. M., Themistocleous, M., & Elliman, T. (2008). Extending IT infrastructures in the local government authorities through enterprise application integration. In *Proceedings of the 14th Americas Conference on Information Systems – AMCIS'08*, Toronto, Canada.

Kamal, M. M., Themistocleous, M., & Elliman, T. (2008). Mapping factors influencing EAI adoption in the local government authorities on different phases of the adoption lifecycle. *European and Mediterranean Conference on Information Systems*, Dubai, UAE.

Kanungo, S., Duda, S., & Srinivas,Y. (1999). A structured model for evaluating information systems effectiveness. *Systems Research and Behavioral Science, 16*, 495-518.

Kaplan, B., & Duchon, D. (1988). Combining qualitative and quantitative methods in information systems research: A case study. *MIS Quarterly*, 570-586.

Kaplan, R. S., & Norton, D. P. (1996). *The balanced scorecard: Translating strategy into action.* Harvard Business School.

Kaplan, R. S., & Norton, D. P. (2004). *Strategy maps: Converting intangible assests into tangible outcomes.*

Kaplan, R. S., & Norton, D. P. (2006). *Strategy scorecards in nonprofit ,government, and health care organizations.* Harvard Business School Press.

Kaplan, R., & Norton, D. (1992). The balanced scorecard: Measures that drive performance. *Harvard Business Review, 70*(1), 71-79.

Kappelman, L. A. (1997). Measuring information systems service quality: Concerns on the SERVQUAL questionnaire. *MIS Quarterly*, 195-208.

Kapucu, N. (2006). Interagency communication networks during emergencies: Boundary spanners in multiagency coordination. *American Review of Public Administration, 36*(2), 207.

Karagiannis, D. (1995). BPMS: Business process management systems. *ACM SIGOIS Bulletin 16*(1), 10-13.

Karahanna, E., Straub, D. W., & Chervany, N. L. (1999). Information technology adoption across time: A cross-sectional comparison of pre-adoption and post-adoption beliefs. *MIS Quarterly, 23*(2), 183-213.

Kashyap, V., & Sheth, A. (1996). Semantic and schematic similarities between database objects: A context-based approach. *The International Journal on Very Large Data Bases (VLDB), 5*(4), 276-304.

Kasunic, M., & Anderson, W. (2004 April). *Measuring systems interoperability: Challenges and opportunities* (Tech Rep. CMU/SEI-2004-TN-003). Carnegie Mellon University, Software Engineering Institute.

Katz, J. E., & Rice, R. E. (2002). *Social consequences of Internet use—access, involvement, and interaction.* Cambridge, MA, & London: MIT Press.

Katz, M. L., & Shapiro, C. (1994). SystemsCcompetition andNnetworkEeffects. *Journal of Economic Perspectives, 8*(2), 93-115.

Kaylor, C., Deshazo, R., & van Eck, D. (2001). Gauging e-government: A report on implementing services among American cities. *Government Information Quarterly, 18*, 293-307.

KBSt, Federal Government C-ordination and Advisory Agency, German,. (2003, July). WiBe21Aa guide to migrating the basic software components on server and workstation computer. KBSt Publication Service, ISSN 0179-7263, 53.

Kean, T. H., & Hamilton, L. H. (2004). *The 9/11 report.* New York: St. Martin's Press.

Keating, M. (1995). Size, efficiency, and democracy: Consolidation, fragmentation, and public choice. In D. Judge, G. Stoker, & H. Wolman (Eds.). *Theories of urban politics* (pp. 117–134). Thousand Oaks, CA: Sage Publications.

Kelly, S., & Tolvanen, J.-P. (2000). Visual domain-specific modelling: Benefits and experiences of using metaCASE tools. In J. Bézivin, & J. Ernst (Eds.), *Proceedings of the 1st International Workshop on Model Engineering. 14th European Conference on Object-Oriented Programming (ECOOP 2000).* Cannes, France.

Kenis, P., & Schneider, V. (1991). Policy networks and policy analysis: Scrutinizing a new analytical toolbox. In B. Marin & R. Mayntz (Eds.), *Policy networks, empirical evidence and theoretical considerations* (pp. 26-59). Frankfurt am Main, Germany: Campus Verlag.

Kennedy, J. F. (1962). The space effort. *Speech at Rice University, Houston, TX*. Rice Webcast Archive. Retrieved April 30, 2008, from http://webcast.rice.edu/speeches/19620912kennedy.html

Kerr, J., & Hunter, R. (1993). *Inside RAD: How to build fully functional computer systems in 90 days or less.* McGraw-Hill.

Kettinger, W.J., Teng, T.C., & Guha, S. (1997). Business process change: A study of methodologies, techniques, and tools. *MIS Quarterly*, *21*(1) 55-81.

Khalaf, R. (2005). *From RosettaNet PIPs to BPEL processes: A three level approach for business protocols.* 3rd International Conference, BPM 2005, Nancy, France.

Khalil, O. E. M., & Elkordy, M. M. (1996). The relationship between some decisions and task environment characteristic and information systems effectiveness: Empirical evidence from Egypt. *SIGCPR/SIGMIS, Colorado*, 125-137.

Khoumbati, K. (2005). *Evaluating the adoption of enterprise application integration in healthcare organisations.* Unpublished doctoral dissertation, Brunel University, London, UK.

Khoumbati, K., & Themistocleous, M. (2007). Application of fuzzy simulation for the evaluation of enterprise application integration in healthcare organisations. *Transforming Government: People, Process, and Policy*, *1*(3), 230-241.

Khoumbati, K., Themistocleous, M., & Irani, Z. (2006). Investigating enterprise application integration benefits and barriers in health care organisations: An exploratory case study. *International Journal of Electronic Healthcare*, *2*(1), 66-78.

Kim, H. J., & Bretschneider, S. (2004). Local government information technology capacity: An exploratory theory. In *Proceedings of the 37th Annual Hawaii International Conference on System Sciences* (pp. 121-130).

Kim, H. J., Pan, G., & Pan, S. L. (2007). Managing IT-enabled transformation in the public sector: A case study on e-government in South Korea. *Government Information Quarterly, 24*, 338-352.

Kinder, T. (2003). Mrs. Miller moves house: The interoperability of local public services in Europe. *Journal of European Social Policy, 13*(2), 141-157.

Kirch Foundation. (2005) San Joaquin Valley air quality. Retrieved on February 18, 2007, from http://www.kirschfoundation.org/who/ar2005/ar2005_04.html

Klecun, E., & Cornford, T. (2005). A critical approach to evaluation. *European Journal of Information Systems, 14*, 229-243.

Klein, H. K., & Myers, M. D. (1999). A set of principles for conducting and evaluating interpretive field studies in information systems. *MIS Quarterly, 23*(1), 67-93.

Klein, P. (2008). How Web 2.0 can reinvent government (interview with Anthony Williams). *CIO Insight Weekly Report*. Retrieved April 21, 2008, from http://www.cioinsight.com/c/a/Expert-Voices/Web-20-Reinventing-Democracy/

Klischewski, R. (2004). Information integration or process integration? How to achieve interoperability in administration. In R. Traunmüller (Ed.), *Proceedings of EGOV 2004,* (LNCS 3183, pp. 57-65).

Klischewski, R., & Scholl, H. J. (2006). Information quality as a common ground for key players in e-government integration and interoperability. In *Proceedings of the 39th Hawaii International Conference on System Sciences* (10 pages).

Knaack, I. (1999). *Die Einführung von vorgangsbearbeitungssystemen in der öffentlichen verwaltung als*

IT-organisatorischer gestaltungsprozeß. Berlin, Germany.

Knorr-Cetina, K. (1999). *Epistemic cultures: How the sciences make knowledge*. Cambridge, MA: Harvard University Press.

Kogut, B. (2000). The network as knowledge: Generative rules and the emergence of structure. *Strategic Management Journal, 21*, 405-425.

Kogut, B., & Zander, U. (1992). Knowledge of the firm, combinative capabilities, and the replication of technology. *Organization Science, 3*(3), 383-397.

Komito, L. (2005). E-Participation and governance: Widening the net. *The Electronic Journal of E-Government, 3*(1), 39-48.

Kraemer, K., & Dutton, W. (1979). The interests served by technological reform. *Administration and Society, 11*(1), 80-106.

Krechmer, K. (2006). The meaning of open standards. *The International Journal of IT Standards and Standardization Research, 4*(1), 43-61.

Kruchten, P. (2003). *The rational unified process: An introduction (3rd edition)*. Addison-Wesley Professional Management Institute.

Kshetri, N. (2004). Economics of LinuxAadoption inDdevelopingCcountries. *IEEE Softw., 21*(1), 74-81.

Kubicek, H., & Cimander, R. (2007, September 11). *Three dimensions of organisational interoperability*. Paper presented at eGovInterop'07 Conference, Paris, France.

Kubicek, H., & Hagen, M. (2000). One stop government in Europe: An overview. In M. Hagen & H Kubicek (Eds), *One stop government in Europe: Results from 11 national surveys* (pp. 1-36). University of Bremen, Bremen.

Kumar, K. (1990). Post implementation evaluation of computer based information systems: Current practices. *Communications of the ACM, 33*(4), 203-212.

Kumar, V., Maheshwari, B., & Kumar, U. (2002). ERP systems implementation: Best practices in Canadian government organizations. *Government Information Quarterly, 19*, 147–172.

Lachman, R. (1985). Public and private sector differences: CEO's perceptions of their role environments. *Academy of Management Journal, 28*(3), 671-680.

Lam, A. (2000). Tacit knowledge, organizational learning, and societal institutions: An integrated framework. *Organization Studies, 21*(3), 487-513.

Lam, W. (2005). Barriers to e-government integration. *The Journal of Enterprise Information Management, 18*(5), 511-530.

Lam, W. (2005). Investigating success factors in enterprise application integration: A case-driven analysis. *European Journal of Information Systems, 14*(2),175-187.

Lam, W., & Shankararaman, V. (2004). An enterprise application integration methodology. *IT Professionals, 6*(1), 40-48.

Landsbergen, Jr., D., & Wolken, Jr., G. (2001). Realizing the promise: Government information systems and the fourth generation of information technology. *Public Administration Review, 61*(2), 206-220.

Lapré, M. A., & Van Wassenhove, L. N. (2003). Managing learning curves in factories by creating and transferring knowledge. *California Management Review, 46*(1), 53-71.

Latour, B. (1987). *Science in action: How to follow scientist and engineers through Society*. Cambridge, MA: Harvard University Press.

Laughlin, R. C. (1991). Environmental disturbances and organizational transitions and transformations: Some alternative models. *Organization Studies, 12*(2), 209-232.

Lave, J. (1998). *Cognition in practice: Mind, mathematics and culture in everyday life*. New York: Cambridge University Press.

Lave, J., & Wenger, E. (1991). *Situated learning: Legitimate peripheral participation*. Cambridge, MA: Cambridge University Press.

Lave, J., & Wenger, E. C. (1990). *Situated learning: Legitimate peripheral participatory* (IRL Report 90-0013). Palo Alto, CA: Institute of Research and Learning.

Lawrence, R., & Barker, K. (2001). Integrating relational database schemas using a standardized dictionary. In *Proceedings of the 16th ACM Symposium on Applied Computing*. Las Vegas, NV.

Layne, K., & Lee, J. (2001). Developing fully functional e-government: A four-stage model,. *Government Information Quarterly, 18*(2), 122–136.

Leavitt, M. O. (2007). Closing thoughts. *Pandemic Flu Leadership Blog. United States Department of Health and Human Services, May 22–June 27, 2007*. Retrieved April 27, 2008 from http://blog.pandemicflu.gov/?p=8

Lee, A. S., & Baskerville, R. L. (2003). Generalizing generalizability in information systems research. *Information Systems Research, 14*(3), 221-243.

Lee, C. S., Chandrasekaran, R., & Thomas, D. (2003). Examining IT usage across different hierarchical levels in organisations: A study of organizational, environmental, and IT factors. In *Proceedings of the 9th AMCIS* (pp. 1259-1269).

Lee, J., & Rao, H. R. (2007). Perceived risks, counterbeliefs, and intentions to use anti/counterterrorism Web sites: An exploratory study of government-citizens online interactions in a turbulent environment. *Decision Support Systems, 43*(4), 1431-1449.

Lee, M. K. O., & Turban, E. (2001). A trust model for consumer Internet shopping. *International Journal of Electronic Commerce, 6*(1) 75-91.

Lee, S. M., Tan, X., & Trimi, S. (2005). Current practices of leading e-government countries. *Communications of the ACM, 48*(10), 99-104.

Lehr, W., & McKnight, L. W. (2003). Wireless Internet access: 3G vs. WiFi? *Telecommunications Policy, 27*, 351-370.

Lenk, K., & Traunmuller, R. (2000, February 10-11). *Presentation at the IFIP WG 8.5 Working Conference on Advances in Electronic Government*, Zaragoza.

Leonard, D. (1998). *Wellsprings of knowledge: Building and sustaining the sources of innovation*. Boston: Harvard Business School Press.

Lerner, J., & Tirole, J. (2002). Some SimpleEeconomics ofOopenSsource. *Journal of Industrial Economics, 50*(2), 197-234.

Lesser, E. (2004). *Communities of practice: Making the most of intellectual capital*. IBM Corporation.

Liebeskind, J. P. (1996). Knowledge, strategy, and the theory of the firm. *Strategic Management Journal, 17*(Special Issue), 93-107.

Liedtka, J. (1999). Linking competitive advantage with communities of practice. *Journal of Management Inquiry, 8*(1), 5-16.

Lim, J. H., & Tang, S. (2008). Urban e-government initiatives and environmental decision performance in Korea. *Journal of Public Administration Research and Theory, 18*(1), 109-138.

Lin, A., & Conford, T. (2000). Framing implementation management. *ICIS 2000* (pp. 197-205).

Lindblad-Gidlund, K. (2005) *Techno therapy, a relation with technology*. Unpublished doctoral dissertation, Umeå University, Sweden.

Lindblom, C. (1964). *The intelligence of democracy: Decision making through mutual adjustment*. New York: The Free Press.

Ling, R. (2008). *New tech, new ties: How mobile communication is reshaping social cohesion*. Cambridge, MA, & London: MIT Press.

Ling, T. (2002). Delivering Joined-up Government in the UK: Dimensions, Issues and Problems. *Public Administration, 80*(4), 615-642.

Linthicum, D. (2000). *Enterprise application integration*. Massachusetts: Addison-Wesley.

Lippi, A. (2007). *La valutazione delle politiche pubbliche*. Bologna, Italy: il Mulino.

Lippman, S. A., & Rumelt, R. (1982). Uncertain imitability: An analysis of interfirm differences in efficiency under competition. *The Bell Journal of Economics, 13*(2), 418-438.

Lipsky, M. (1980). *Street-level bureaucracy. Dilemmas of the individual in public services.* New York: Russell Sage Foundation.

Little, J. C., Granger, M., Adams E. S., Holvikivi, J., Lippert S. K., Walker, H. M., & Young, A. (2000). Integrating cultural issues into the computer and information technology curriculum. *ITICSE 2000 Working Group Reports*, 136-154.

Livingston, B. (2000). Is Microsoft's change in Kerberos security a form of 'embrace, extend, extinguish'?. Retrieved on September 17, 2007, from http://www.infoworld.com/articles/op/xml/00/05/15/000515oplivingston.html

Lockamy, A., & McCormack, K. (2004). The development of a supply chain management process maturity model using the concepts of business process orientation. *Supply Chain Management: An International Journal, 9*(4), 272-278.

Löfgren, K. (2007). The governance of e-government: A governance perspective on the Swedish e-government strategy. *Public, Policy, and Administration, 22*(3), 335-352.

Löfstedt, U. (2007). E-government services in local governments—a study of development in Swedish municipalities. *Journal of Organisational Transformation and Social Change, 4*(2), 157-176.

Luftman, J. N., Bullen, C. V., Liao, D., Nash, E., & Neumann, C. (2004). *Managing the information technology resource: Leadership in the information age.* Pearson Prentice Hall.

MacCormack, A, (2003). Evaluating TotalCcost ofOownership for Software Platforms: ComparingAapples,Ooranges, andCcucumbers. *AEI-Brookings Joint Center for Regulatory Studies Series*, No. 03-7.

MacKenzie, D., & Wajcman, J. (Eds.) (1999). *The social shaping of technology, 2nd edition.* Buckingham, UK: Open University Press.

Maggi, B. (1990). *Razionalità e benessere. Studio interdisciplinare dell'organizzazione, 3rd ed.* Milano: Etaslibri.

Maggi, B. (2003). *De l'agir organisationnel. Un point de vue sur le travail, le bien-être, l'apprentissage.* Toulouse, France: Octarès.

Maggi, B., & Albano, R. (1997). La teoria dell'azione organizzativa. In G. Costa, & R. C. D. Nacamulli (Eds.), *Manuale di organizzazione aziendale, 2nd ed.* (Vol. 1, pp. 220-249). Torino, Italy: Utet.

Mahmood, M. A., & Becker, J. D. (1985). Impact of organizational maturity on user satisfaction with information systems. *ACM*, 134-151.

Mahoney, J. T., & Pandian, R. J. (1992). The resource-based view within the conversations of strategic management. *Strategic Management Journal, 13*, 363-380.

Makolm, J. (2002, September). Best practice in e-government. In R. Tranmüller & K. Lenk (Eds.), In *Proceedings of the First International Conference on Electronic Government, EGOV 2002, Aix-en-Provence* (pp. 370–374). Berlin, Germany: Springer.

Malik, K., & Goyal, D. P. (2001). Information systems effectiveness: An integrated approach. *IEEE*, 189-194.

Malone, T. W. (2004). *The future of work.* Boston: Harvard Business School Press.

Malone, T. W., J. Yates, & Benjamin, R. I. (1987). Electronic markets and electronic hierarchies. *Communications of the ACM, 30*, 484-497.

Malotaux, M., van der Harst, G., Achtsivassilis, J., & Hahndiek, F. (2007). Preparation for update European interoperability framework 2.0--final report, 4.6.2007, for the interoperable delivery of European e-government services to public administrations, businesses and citizens. Retrieved on April 1, 2008, from http:// ec.europa.eu/idabc/servlets/Doc?id=29101

Manoj, B. S., & Baker, A. H. (2007). Communication challenges in emergency response. *Communications of the ACM, 50*(3), 51-53.

Mansell, R. (2002, July 4-7). New media and the power of networks. In *Proceedings of DSlage2002, Cork* (pp. 21-28).

Mantzana, V. G. (2006). *Investigating the adoption of enterprise application integration in healthcare organisations using an actor-oriented approach*. Unpublished doctoral dissertation, Brunel University, London, UK.

Marakas, G. M., Yi, M. Y., & Johnson, R. D. (1998). The multilevel and multifaceted character of computer self-efficacy: Toward clarification of the construct and an integrative framework for research. *Information Systems Research*, *9*(2), 126-163.

March, J. G. (1989). *Decisions and organizations*. Oxford, UK: Blackwell Publishers.

Margetts, H., & Dunleavy, P. (2002). *Cultural barriers to e-government. Working Paper.* University Collage of London and London School of Economics for National Audit Office.

Markus, L. (2004). Technochange management: Using IT to drive organizational change. *Journal of information Technology 19*(1), 4-20.

Markus, L., & Bashein, R. (2006). *Interorganizational tecnochange: How to make successful choices in electronic partner integration*. Society for Information Management, Advanced Practices Council.

Markus, L., & Robey, D. (1988). Information technology and organizational change: Causal structure in theory and research. *Management Science*, *34*.

Marra, M. (2004). Alcuni aspetti e problemi della valutazione nella PA. *Rassegna Italiana di valutazione*, *VIII*(29), 41-58.

Martin, J. (1991). *Rapid application development*. Macmillan Coll Div.

Masud, S. (2003). *Use RosettaNet-based Web Services, Part 1: BPEL4WS and RosettaNet, 2003.* Retrieved April 28, 2006, from http://www-128.ibm.com/developerworks/webservices/library/ws-rosel/

Matheis, T., Ziemann, J., Diedrich, E., Schmidt, D., & Wimmer, M. (2007). *Methodical interoperability requirements for e-government*. Deliverable WP8-D1. R4eGov—Towards e-Administration in the large (Proposal/Contract no.: IST-2004-026650).

Maxwell, E. (2006). Open standards, open source, and open innovation: Harnessing the benefits of openness. *Innovations: Technology, Governance, Globalization, 1*(3), 119.

May, C. (2006). Escaping the TRIPs' trap: The political economy of free and open source software in Africa. *Political Studies, 54*(1), 123-146.

Mayer, R. C., Davis, J. H., & Schoorman, F. D. (1995). An integrative model of organizational trust. *Academy of Management Review*, *20*(3), 709-734.

Mayer, R. J., Menzel, C. P., Painter, M. K., deWitte, P. S., Blinn, T., & Perakath, B. (1995). *Information Integration for Concurrent Engineering (IICE) IDEF3 Process Description Capture Method Report*.

Mc.Quillan, H. (2000). *Ennis information age town: A connected community*. Ireland: Eircom.

McCormack, K., & Johnson, W. (2001). *Business process orientation: Gaining the e-business competitive advantage*. Delray Beach, FL: St Lucie Press.

McInerney, C. (2003). Wired Ennis: Learning and technology in an informaion age town. *Information Technology, Education and Society, 4*(2), 9-34.

McIvor, R., McHugh, M., & Cadden, C. (2002). Internet technologies supporting transparency in the public sector. *The International Journal of Public Sector Management*, *15*(3), 170-187.

McKenney, J., & McFarlan, F. (1982). The information archipelago--maps and bridges. *Harvard Business Review*, 109-119.

McKnight, D. H., Choudhury, V., & Kacmar, C. (2002). Developing and validating trust measures for e-commerce: An integrative approach. *Information Systems Research*, *13*(3), 334-359.

McKnight, D. H., Cummings, L. L., & Chervany, N.L. (1998). Initial trust formation in new organizational relationships. *Academy of Management Review, 23*(3), 473-490.

Meissner, A., Luckenbach, T., Risse, T., Kirste, T., & Kirchner, H. (2002, June 24). *Design challenges for an integrated disaster management communication and information system.* Paper presented at the The First IEEE Workshop on Disaster Recovery Networks (DIREN 2002), New York City, co-located with IEEE INFOCOM 2002.

Melitski, J. (2003). Capacity and e-government performance. *Public Performance and Management Review, 26*(4), 376-390.

Melone, N. P. A. (1990). Theoretical assessment of the user satisfaction construct in information systems research. *Management Science, 36*(1), 76-90.

Mendonça, D., Jefferson, T., & Harrald, J. (2007). Collaborative adhocracies and mix-and-match technologies in emergency management. *Communications of the ACM, 50*(3), 44-48.

Meyer, A. D., Goes, J. B., & Brooks, G. R. (1995). Organizations reacting to hyperturbulence. In G. P. Huber & W. H. Glick (Eds.), *Organizational change and redesign: Ideas and insights for improving performance* (pp. 66-111). New York: Oxford University Press.

Meyer, J. W., & Rowan, B. (1977). Institutional organizations: Formal structures as myth and ceremony. *American Journal of Sociology, 80*, 340-363.

Mhayaya, S. G. (2003). *A study of the potential usage of ICT (e-government) in improving efficiency and effectiveness of 'executive functions' of the government including delivery of public services, Case of Tanzania.* A dissertation for degree of MEM at University of Dar Es Salaam, Tanzania.

Miles, M., & Huberman, A. (1994). *Qualitative data analysis: An expanded sourcebook.* Newbury Park, CA: Sage.

Millar, J., Demaid, A., & Quintas, P. (1997). Trans-organizational innovation: A framework for research. *Technology Analysis & Strategic Management, 9*(4), 399-418.

Millard, J., Iversen, J. S., Kubicek, H., Westholm, H., & Cimander, R. (2004). *Reorganisation of government back-offices for better electronic public services—European good practices (back-office reorganisation).* Brussels: EU DG Information Society.

Miller, D., Eisenstat, R. A., & Foote, N. (2002). Strategy from the inside out: Building capability-creating organizations. *California Management Review, 44*(3), 37-54.

Miller, E. (2007, February). OpenCongress.org. *SunSpots: The Sunlight Foundation blog.* Retrieved April 27, 2008, from http://www.sunlightfoundation.com/node/2202

Miller, P. (2000). Interoperability: What it is and why should I want it. *Ariadne, 24.* Retrieved on April 5, 2008, from http: //www.ariadne.ac.uk/issue24/ interoperability/intro.html

Mintzberg, H. (1983). *Structure in fives: Designing effective organizations.* Englewood Cliffs, NJ: Prentice Hall.

MODINIS. (2005). *MODINIS program: Follow-up of e-Europe 2005 action plan.* Retrieved on August 14, 2006, from http://europa.eu/scadplus/leg/en/lvb/l24226c.htm

Moe, T. L. (2006). An integrated approach to natural disaster management: Public project management and its critical success factors. *Disaster Prevention and Management, 15*(3), 396.

MoFEA. (2008). *About Ministry of Finance and Economic Affairs (MoFEA) and related statistics in the case study.* Retrieved in May 2008, from www.mof.go.tz

Mollel, A., & Lukumay, Z. (2007). *Electronic transactions and law of evidence in Tanzania.* Iringa University College: Peramiho Printing Press.

Montagna, J. M. (2005). A framework for the assessment and analysis of electronic government proposals. *Electronic Commerce Research and Applications, 4*, 204-219.

Moon, J., & Bretschneider, S. (1997). Can state government action affect innovation and diffusion. *Technology Forecasting and Social Change, 54*, 57-77.

Moon, M. J. (2002). The evolution of e-government among municipalities: Rhetoric or reality? *Public Administration Review, 62*(4), 424-433.

Moon, M. J., & Norris, D. F. (2005). Does managerial orientation matter? The adoption of reinventing government and e-government at the municipal level. *Information Systems Journal, 15*, 43-60.

Moon, M. J., et al. (2005). What drives global e-governance? An exploratory study at a macro level. In *Proceedings of the 38th Hawaii International Conference on System Sciences* (10 pages).

Moore, G., & Benbasat, I. (1991). Development of an instrument to measure the perceptions of adopting an information technology innovation. *Information Systems Research, 2*(3), 192-222.

Morgan, G. (1986). *Images of organizations*. London: Sage.

Morris, E., Levine, L., Meyers, C., Plakosh, D., & Place, P. (2004). Systems of systems interoperability (CMU/SEI-2004-TR-004). Software Engineering Institute, Carnegie Mellon University.

Moyo, L. (1996). *IT strategies for Africa's survival in the twenty-first century: IT all pervasive in IT for development v7n1 PP: 17-27.* Retrieved in May 2008, from www.itgi.org

MSD. (2008). *About medical stores department (MSD) and related statistics in the case study.* Retrieved in May 2008, from www.msd.or.tz

Mukand, S. W., & Rodrik, D. (2002). In search of the holy grail: Policy convergence, experimentation, and economic performance. *American Economic Review, 95*(1), 374-383.

Mumford, E. (1983). *Designing human systems for new technology: The ETHICS method.* Manchester, UK: Manchester Business School. Retrieved April 27, 2008, from http://www.enid.u-net.com/C1book1.htm

Munkvold, B. E., Eim, K., & Husby, O.S. (2006). A case study of information systems decision-making: Process characteristics and collaboration technology support. *International Journal of Cooperative Information Systems, 15*, 179-203.

Murero, M., Rice, R. E., Katz, J. E., Dutta-Bergman, M., & Banerjee, I. (Eds.) (2006). *The Internet and health care: Theory, research, and practice*. Philadelphia, PA: Lawrence Erlbaum Associates.

Murphy, J. (MP Parliamentary Secretary Cabinet Office Report). (2005). Beyond e-government the world's most successful technology-enabled transformations, executive summary. *INSEAD the business school for the world* (pp.1-124). Retrieved from www.localtgov.org.uk

Myers, M. D. (1994). A disaster for everyone to see: An interpretive analysis of a failed IS project. *Accounting, Management, and Information Technology, 4*(4), 185-201.

Myers, M. D. (1997). Qualitative research in information systems. *MIS Quarterly, 21*(2), 241–242. MISQ Discovery, archival version, June 1997, http://www.misq.org/discovery/ MISQD_isworld/. Retrieved September 21, 2008, from http://www.qual.auckland.ac.nz.

Naarmala, J. (2004). Going digital – explaining dimensions of e-government. Retrieved on February 20, 2007, from www.ebrc.info/ pages_ C86FCC04-3314-4DF9-9AE2-138286 0CB17F.asp

Nahapiet, J., & Ghoshal, S. (1998). Social capital, intellectual capital, and the organizational advantage. *Academy of Management Review, 23*(2), 242-266.

Nanda, A. (1996) Resources, capabilities, and competencies. In B. Moingeon & A. Edmondson (Eds.), *Organizational learning and competitive advantage.* London: Sage.

NAO. (2002). E-Revenue. *The National Audit Office, London, UK. HC 492 14 February 2002.* Retrieved on July 24, 2008 from http://www.nao.org.uk/publications/nao_reports/01-02/0102492es.pdf, accessed 24 July 2008

National Informatics Centre. (2004). IFEG—interoperability framework for e-governance: Technical standards, version 2.0.

National IT Architecture Committee. (2006). The interoperability framework, version 1.2.14, Retrieved on March 14, 2008, from http://standarder.oio.dk/English/

NCC. (2005). *PRINCE2 manual (managing successful projects with PRINCE2).*

Ndou, V. (2004). E-Government for developing countries: Opportunities and challenges. *The Electronic Journal on Information Systems in Developing Countries (EJISDC).*

Nelson, R. R., & Winter, S. (1982). *An evolutionary theory of economic change.* Cambridge, MA: Harvard University Press.

Newcomer, K., & Caudle, S. (1991). Evaluating public sector information systems: More than meets the eye. *Public Administration Review, 51*(5), 377-384.

Newel, S., Huang, J. C., Galliers, R. D., & Pan, S. L. (2003). Implementing enterprise resource planning and knowledge management systems in tandem: Fostering efficiency and innovation complimentary. *Information and Organization, 13*, 25-52.

Newman, J. (2003). Issue brief: Electronic government. *Bureau of Information and Telecommunications, State of South Dakota, Nov 2003.* Retrieved April 26, 2008, from http://www.state.sd.us/bit/Services/MGMTInfo/IssueBriefs/documents/Egovt-issue-brief.htm

Nfuka E. N., & Rusu L. (2007). Management of IT-enabled change in a public organization in Tanzania. *International Journal of Information Systems and Change Management, 2*(4), 334-349.

Ngai, E. W. T., & Gunasekaran, A. (2004). Implementation of EDI in Hong Kong: An empirical analysis. *Industrial Management & Data Systems, 104*(1), 88-100.

Niven, P. R. (2003). *Balanced scorecard step-by-step for government and nonprofit agencies.* John Wiley and Sons.

Nolan, R. L. (1973). Managing the computer resource: A stage hypothesis. *Communication of the ACM*, 399-405.

Nonaka, I. (1994). A dynamic theory of organizational knowledge creation. *Organization Science, 5*(1), 14-37.

Nonaka, I., & Takeutchi, H. (1995). *The knowledge-creating company : How Japanese companies create the dynamics of innovation.* Oxford, UK: Oxford University Press.

Nordflex Group. (1999) *Flexibility matters—flexible enterprises in the nordic countries.* Stockholm: NUTEK.

Norris, D. F. (1999). *Leading edge information technologies and their adoption: Lessons from US cities.* Hershey, PA: Idea Group Publishing.

Norris, D. F. (2005). E-government at the American grassroots: Future trajectory. *Proceedings of the 38th Annual Hawaii International Conference on System Sciences.* Retrieved 2008.09.19 from http://www.umbc.edu/mipar/documents/HICSSpaper.pdf

Nurmela, J. (2006). Does the use of communication media add to social capital? In L. Iisakka (Ed.), *Social capital in Finland—statistical review* (pp. 63-72). Helsinki, Finland: Statistics Finland.

Nurmela, J., et al. (2004). *Finnish people's communication capabilities in interactive society of the 2000s (Reviews 2004/7).* Helsinki: Statistics Finland.

Nye, Jr., J. (1999). *Information technology and democratic governance: Governance in networked world.* NH: Hollins Publishing Company.

Object Management Group. (2006). BPMN Final Adopted Specification 1.0. Retrieved on April 30, 2006, from http://www.bpmn.org/Documents/OMG%20Final%20Adopted%20BPMN%201-0%20Spec%2006-02-01.pdf

OECD E-Government Studies. (2005). *E-Government for better government.* OECD Publishing.

OECD Forum. (2006). *Balancing globalisation.* Retrieved from http://www.oecd.org/site/0,3407,en_21571361_35842076_1_1_1_1_1,00.html

OECD. (1998). *Science, Technology and Industry Outlook.* OECD.

OECD. (2001). *Knowledge, work organisation and economic growth, labour market, and social policy (Occasional Papers No. 50)*. Paris: OECD.

OECD. (2003). Checklist for e-government leaders. Retrieved from http://www.oecd.org/publications/pol_brief

OECD. (2004). *The economic impact of ICT—measurement, evidence, and implications*. Paris: OECD.

OECD. (2004). *The e-government Imperative*. Paris: OECD.

OECD. (2005). *E-Government Studies: Norway*. Paris: OECD.

OECD. (2007). *E-Government Studies: The Netherlands*. Paris: OECD.

OECD. (2007). *Participative Web: User-created content. Working party on the information society, online document*. Paris: OECD.

OECD. (2008). *Guide to measuring the information society. Working party on the information society, online document*. Paris: OECD.

Office of Government Commerce. (2004). *Open source software:Use within UK government*.

Opdahl, A. L., & Henderson-Sellers, B. (2002). Ontological evaluation of the UML using the Bunge–Wand–Weber model. *Software and Systems Modelling, 1*(1), 43-67.

OpenCongress.org (2008). About Open Congress. Retrieved April 27, 2008, from http://www.OpenCongress.org/about

Organisation for Economic Co-operation and Development (OECD). (2006). OECD e-government studies: Denmark. OECD.

Organization for Economic Cooperation and Development, OECD. (2001). *The hidden threat to e-government: Avoiding large government IT failures*.

Organization for Economic Cooperation and Development, OECD. (2003). *The e-government imperative*.

Organization for the Advancement of Structured Information Standards. (2007). Open by design: The advantages of the opendocument format (ODF). Retrieved on September 12, 2007, from http://www.oasis-open.org/committees/download.php/21450/oasis_odf_advantages_10dec2006.pdf

Orlikowkski, W. J., & Barley, S. R. (2001). Technology and Institutions: What Can Research on Information Technology and Research on Organizations Learn From Each Other? *MIS Quarterly, 25*(2), 145-165.

Orlikowski, W. (1992). The duality of technology: Rethinking the concept of technology in organizations. *Organization Science*.

Orlikowski, W. U. (2002). Knowing in practice: Enacting a collective capability in distributed organizing. *Organization Science, 13*(3), 249-273.

Orlikowski, W., & Gash, D. C. (1994). Technological frames: Making sense of information technology in organizations. *ACM Transactions on Information Systems, 12*(2), 174-207.

Orr, J. (1987). Narratives at work: Story telling as cooperative diagnostic activity. *Field Service Manager*, 47-60.

Orr, J. (1990). Sharing knowledge, celebrating identity: War stories and community memory in a service culture. In D. S. Middleton & D. Edwards (Eds.), *Collective remembering: Memory in society* (pp. 169-189). Newbury Park, CA: Sage.

Osborne, D., & Gaebler, T. (1992). *Reinventing government: How the entrepreneurial spirit is transforming the public sector*. Reading, MA: Addison-Wesley.

Ostroff, F. (1999). *The horizontal organization*. New York: Oxford University Press.

Overhage, S., & Turowski, K. (2007). Service-orientierte architekturen – konzept und methodische herausforderungen. In V. Nissen, M. Petsch, H. Schorscht (Hrsg.), *Service-orientierte architecturen – chancen und herausforderungen bei der flexibilisierung und integration von vnternehmensprozessen*. Deutscher Universitätsverlag.

Ozkan, S., Hackney, R., & Bilgen, S. (2007). PB-ISAM: A process based framework for information systems effectiveness assessment. *Journal of Enterprise Information Management, 20*(6), 700-725.

Palmer, S. R., & Felsing, J. M. (2002). *A practical guide to feature-driven development*. Prentice Hall.

Pappa, D., & Makropoulos, C. (2004). Designing a brokerage platform for the delivery of e-government services to the public. In M. Wimmer (Ed.), *Knowledge Management in Electronic Government: 5th IFIP International Working Conference* (KMGov 2004).

Pardo, T. A., Cresswell, A. M., Dawes, S. S., & Burke, G. B. (2004). Modeling the social & technical process of interorganizational information integration. In Proceedings of the 37th Annual Hawaii International Conference on System Sciences (p. 8). IEEE.

Pardo, T., & Scholl, H. (2002, January 7-10). Walking atop the cliffs-avoiding failure and reducing risk in large-scale e-government projects. In *Proceedings of the 35th Annual Hawaii international Conference on System Sciences (Hicss'02)* (Vol. 5). Washington, DC: IEEE Computer Society.

Parent-Thirion, Agnès; Fernández Macías, Enrique; Hurley, John; Vermeylen, Greet (2007). *Fourth European Working Conditions Survey*. Luxembourg: Office for Official Publications of the European Communities.

Paul J-H. H., Chau, P. Y. K., & Sheng, O. R. L. (2000). Investigation of factors affecting healthcare organization's adoption of telemedicine technology. In *Proceedings of the 33rd Annual Hawaii International Conference on Systems Sciences* (pp. 1-10).

Pavlou, P. (2003). Consumer acceptance of electronic commerce: Integrating trust and risk with the technology acceptance model. *International Journal of Electronic Commerce, 7*, 69-103.

Pea, R. D. (1990). *Distributed cognition* (IRL Report 91-0015). Palo Alto, CA: Institute for Research and Learning.

Peikari, C., & Fogie, S. (2003). *Maximum wireless security*. Retrieved from http://www.berr.gov.uk/files/file9972.pdf

Penrose, E. T. (1959). *The theory of the growth of the firm*. New York: Wiley.

Peristeras, V., & Tarabanis, K. (2006). The connection, communication, consolidation, collaboration interoperability framework (C4IF) for information systems interoperability. *Interoperability in Business Information Systems (IBIS), 1*(1), 61-72.

Perry, J. L., & Danzinger, J. N. (1980). The adoptability of innovation: An empirical assessment of computer applications in local governments. *Administration and Society, 11*(4), 461-492.

Perry, W. R. (2003). Incident management systems in disaster management. *Disaster Prevention and Management, 12*(5), 405-412.

Peteraf, M. A. (1993). The cornerstones of competitive advantage: A resource-based view. *Strategic Management Journal, 14*, 179-191.

Peters, R. M., Janssen, M., van Engers, T. M. (2004). Measuring e-government impact: Existing practices and shortcomings. In *Proceedings of ICEC'04, Sixth International Conference on Electronic Commerce* (pp. 480-489).

Peterson, R. R. (2003). Integration strategies and tactics for information technology governance. In W. Van Grembergen (Ed.), *Strategies for information technology governance*. Hershey, PA: Idea Group Publishing.

Peterson, R. R. (2004). Crafting information technology governance for today's turbulent environment. *Information Systems Management, 21*(4), 7-21.

Petrakaki, D., Hayes, N., & Introna, L. D. (2008). Performance monitoring and accountability through technology: E-Government in Greece. In *Proceedings of the 41st Hawaii International Conference on System Sciences (Hicss)*.

Pew Internet & American Life Project. (2006). Home broadband adoption. Retrieved from http://www.pewinternet.org/pdfs/PIP_Broadband_trends2006.pdf

Pfeiffer, D. (2007). Constructing comparable conceptual models with domain specific languages. In H. Österle, J. Schelp, & R. Winter (Eds.), *Proceedings of the European Conference on Information Systems (ECIS 2007)*. St. Gallen, Switzerland.

Pfeiffer, D., & Gehlert, A. (2005). A framework for comparing conceptual models. In *Proceedings of the Workshop on Enterprise Modelling and Information Systems Architectures (EMISA 2005)* (pp. 108-122). Klagenfurt, Austria.

Phippen, A., Land, F. & Ward, A. (2006). Community information line – an evaluation of citizen engagement in local e-government. *E-Government Workshop '06 (eGOV06), Brunel University, West London, UB8 3PH [accessed September 11 2006].*

Picci, L. (2006). Misurare l'e-government: Il caso italiano, *ASTRID-Rassegna n. 2*. Retrieved from http://mpra.ub.uni-muenchen.de/3343/

Picot, A., Reichwald, R., & Wigand, R. T. (2003). *Die grenzenlose unternehmung, 5th edition*. Wiesbaden: Gabler.

PICTURE Consortium. (2006). *Report on current practice of process modeling projects & techniques in European public administrations* (Deliverable 1.1).

PICTURE Consortium. (2007). *ICT functionality groups specification* (Deliverable 2.6).

PICTURE Consortium. (2007). *PICTURE Impact measurement methodology* (Deliverable 3.4).

PICTURE Consortium. (2007). *Study on ICT value analysis concepts for European PA* (Deliverable 3.1).

Pina, V., Torres, L. & Royo, S. (2007). Are ICTs improving transparency and accountability in the EU regional and local governments? An empirical study. *Public Administration, 85*(2), 449-472.

Pinto, M. B., & Pinto, J. K. (1991). Determinants of cross-functional cooperation in the project implementation process. *Project Management Journal, 22*, 13-20.

Pitt, L. F., Watson, R. T., & Kavan, C. B. (1995). Service quality: A measure of information systems effectiveness. *MIS Quarterly*, 173-186.

Plate, H., & Huys, D. (2007). *Specification and design of an extensible execution environment for collaborative e-government processes*. Deliverable WP5-D8. R4eGov—Towards e-Administration in the large (Proposal/Contract no.: IST-2004-026650).

Plouffe, C. R., Hulland, S. J., & Vandenbosch, M. (2001). Research report: Richness vs. parsimony in modeling technology adoption decisions--understanding merchant adoption of a smart card-based payment system. *Information Systems Research, 12*(2), 208-222.

Plunkett, P. (2004). *Lessons learned on information technology performance management: Applying the balanced scorecard and applied information economics to federal information technology initiatives.* Federal Chief Information Officers Council.

PMO-RALG. (2008). *About prime minister's office regional authority and local government (PMO-RALG) and related statistics in the case study.* Retrieved in May 2008, from www.pmoralg.go.tz

Polanyi, M. (1966). *The tacit dimension.* New York: Doubleday.

Pollitt, C. P. (2003). Joined-up Government: A Survey. *Political Studies Review, 1*(1), 34-49.

Pollitt, C. P., & Bouckaert, G. (2000). *Public Management Reform: A Comparative Analysis*. Oxford: Oxford University Press.

Pollitt, C. P., Van Thiel, S., & Homburg, V. M. F. (2006). *The New Public Management in Europe: Adaptation and Alternatives*. Basingstoke, England: Palgrave MacMillan.

PO-PSM. (2008). *About president office, public services management (PO-PSM) and related statistics in the case study*. Retrieved in May 2008, from www.utumishi.go.tz

Powell, W. (1990). Neither market nor hierarchy: Network forms of organization. In B. M. Staw & L. L. Cummings (Eds.), *Research in organization behavior*. Greenwich, CT: JAI Press.

Powell, W. W., & Snellman, K. (2004). The knowledge economy. *Annual Review Sociology, 30*, 199-220.

Prescott, M. B., & Conger, S. A. (1995). Information technology innovations: A classification by IT locus of impact and research approach. *The DATA BASE for Advances in Information Systems, 26*(2/3), 20-41.

Pressman, J., & Wildavsky, A. (1973). *Implementation*. Berkeley, CA: University of California Press.

Project Management Institute, PMI. (2001). *The PMI project management fact book*.

Project Management Institute, PMI. (2006). *Government extension to the PMBOK guide, third edition*.

Public Policy Institute of California. (2004). *How is migration changing the central valley*. San Francisco: Public Policy Institute of California.

Putnam, L. H., & Meyers, W. (1991). *Measures ForEexcellence: ReliableSsoftwareOonTtime,Wwithin Budget* (Facsimil., p. 400). Prentice Hall PTR.

Putnam, R. (2000). *Bowling alone. The collapse and revival of American community*. New York: Simon & Schuster.

Quarantelli, E. L. (1996). Local mass media operations in disasters in the USA. *Disaster Prevention and Management, 5*(5), 5-12.

Quarantelli, E. L. (1997). Problematical aspects of the information/communication revolution for disaster planning and research: Ten nontechnical issues and questions. *Disaster Prevention and Management: An International Journal, 6*(2), 94-106.

Quigley, J. M. (1998). Urban diversity and economic growth. *Journal of Economic Perspectives, 12*(2), 127-138.

Raff, D. M. (2000). Superstores and the evolution of firm capabilities in American bookselling. *Strategic Management Journal, 21*, 1043-1060.

Ragin, C. C. (1999). The distinctiveness of case-oriented research. *Health Services Research*, 1137-1151.

Ramachandran, A. (2007, September 26). Write your own laws. *Sydney Morning Herald*. Retrieved April 27, 2008, from http://www.smh.com.au/news/web/write-your-own-laws/2007/09/26/1190486375202.html

Ramaswamy, M., & Selian, A. (2007). E-Government in transition countries: Prospects and challenges. In *Proceedings of the 40th Hawaii International Conference on Information Systems* (10 pages).

Rau, K. (2004). The CIO dashboard performance management program: Measuring and managing the value of IT. *Information Strategy: The Executive's Journal*, 6-17.

Raveedran, L. (1998). *ASEAN telecommunications regulations report. Media Regulations for New Times*. Bangkok, Thailand: Asian Media Information and Communication Centre (AMIC).

Ray, D., Dash, S. S., & Gulla, U. (2007). In J. Bhattacharya (Ed.), *Towards next generation e-government* (pp. 12-25). New Delhi, India: GIFT Publication.

Raymond, L. (1985). Organizational characteristics and MIS success in the context of small business. *MIS Quarterly, 9*(1), 7-52.

Rebora, G. (1999). *La valutazione dei risultati nelle amministrazioni pubbliche*. Milano, Italy: Guerini e Associati.

Reddick, C. G. (2004). A two-stage model of e-government growth: Theories and empirical evidence for U.S. cities. *Government Information Quarterly, 21*(1), 51–64.

Reffat, R. (2003). *Developing a successful e-government. Working Paper*. University Of Sydney, Australia.

Regonini, G. (2001). *Capire le politiche pubbliche*. Bologna, Italy: il Mulino.

Rehg, W., McBurney, P., & Parsons, S. (2005). Computer decision-support systems for public argumentation: Assessing deliberative legitimacy. *AI & Society,* (19), 203–229.

Reiersgaard, N., Salvesen, H., Nordheim, S., & Päivärinta, T. (2005). EAI implementation project and shakedown: An exploratory case study. In *Proceedings of the 38th Annual Hawaii International Conference on System Sciences (HICSS'05)*, (pp. 1-10).

Renkema, T. J. W., & Berghout, E. W. (1997). Methodologies for information-systems investment evaluation at the proposal stage: A comparative review. *Information and Software Technology, 39*(1), 1-13.

Reynolds, M. M., & Regio-Micro, M. (2001). *The purpose of transforming government: E-Government as a catalyst in the information age. Microsoft E-Government Initiatives.* Retrieved from http://www.netcaucus.org/books/egov2001/pdf/EGovIntr.pdf

Rheingold, H. (2000). *The virtual community—homesteading on the electronic frontier, 2nd edition.* Cmabridge, MA, & London: MIT Press.

Ribbers, P. M. A., Peterson, R. R., & Parker, M. M. (2002). Designing information technology governance processes: Diagnosing contemporary practices and competing theories. In *Proceedings of the 35th Hawaii International Conference on System Sciences, IEEE Computer Society.*

Rivals set their sights on Microsoft Office: Can they topple the giant? (2007). *Knowledge@Wharton.* Retrieved on October 3, 2007, from http://knowledge.wharton.upenn.edu/article.cfm?articleid=1795

Robey, D., & Holmström, J. (2001). Transforming municipal governance in global context: A case study of the dialectics of social change. *Journal of Global Information Technology Management, 4*(4), 19-32.

Robson, C. (2002). *Real world research.* Oxford, UK: Blackwell.

Rodrik, D. (2000). *Institutions for high quality growth: What they are and how to acquire them.* National Bureau of Economic Research, Inc.

Rogers, E. M. (1995). *Diffusion of innovations, 4th ed.* New York: Free Press.

Rogers, E. M. (2003). *Diffusion of innovation.* New York: The Free Press.

Rolland, K. H., & Monteiro, E. (2006). *When 'perfect' integration leads to increasing risk: The case of an integrated information system in a global company.*

Rothenberg, J., Botterman, M., & Oranje-Nassau, C. V. (2008). Towards a Dutch interoperability framework recommendations to the forum standaardisatie. Rand Corporation.

Rotter, J. A new scale for the measurement of interpersonal trust. *Journal of Personality, 35,* 651-665.

Røvik, K. (2002). The secret of the winners: Management ideas that flow. In K. Sahlin-Andersson, & L. Engwall (Eds.), *The expansion of management knowledge. Carriers, flows, and sources.* Stanford, CA: Stanford University Press.

Rowley, T. J. (2004). Moving beyond dyadic ties: A network theory of stakeholder influences. *Academy of Management Review, 22*(2), 867-910.

Rowley, T. J., & Moldoveanu, M. (2003). When will stakeholder groups act? An interest-and identity-based model of stakeholder group mobilization. *Academy of Management Review, 28*(2), 204-219.

Royce, W. (1987). Managing the development of large software systems: concepts and techniques. Proceedings of the 9th international conference on Software Engineering. IEEE Computer Society Press.

Ruh, W., Maginnis, F., & Brown, W. (2000). *Enterpriser application integration* (A Wiley Tech Brief). New York: John Wiley & Sons Inc.

Rumelt, R. (1984). Towards a strategic theory of the firm. In R. B. Lamb (Ed.), *Competitive strategic management* (pp. 556-570). Englewood Cliffs, NJ: Prentice-Hall.

Ruparel, R. (2006). Project appraisal document for tax modernization project in Tanzania. *World Bank, Volume 1, Report No. 36221–TA.* Retrieved in May 2008, from http://www-wds.worldbank.org

Ryan, N. (2001). Reconstructing citizens as consumers: Implications for new models of governance. *Australian Journal of Public Administration, 60*(3), 104–109.

Sacco, J. F. (1994). Implementing microcomputers in local government: A case study of loosely structured approach. *SiGCPR 94-3 Virginia*, 261-270.

Sahay, S., & Avgerou, C. (2002). Introducing the special issues on information and communication technologies in develeoping countries. *The Information Society,* 73-76

Sahraoui, S., Ghoneim, A., Irani, Z., & Ozkan, S. T-Government for benefit realization: A research agenda. In Z. Irani, & P. Love (Eds.), *Evaluating information systems: Public and private sector*. London, UK: Elsevier.

Salminen, A. (2005). *Building digital government by XML*. Paper presented at the Hawaii International Conference on System Sciences, Hawaii.

Sanchez, E., Beery, D., & Shehab, J. (2002). EAI systems bring IT together. *Network Computing.*

Sanders, G. L. (1984). MIS/DSS success measure. *Systems,Objectives & Solutions, 4*, 29-34.

Sanders, J. (1998). Linux,Oopen Source, andSsoftware'sFfuture. *IEEE Softw., 15*(5), 88-91.

Saudi e-Government Program. (2005). YEFI—yesser framework for interoperability. Retrieved on March 14, 2008, from http://www.yesser.gov.sa/english/YEFI.asp?id=item4

Saunders, M., Lewis, P., & Thornhill, A. (2002). *Research methods for business students,Third edition*. Harlow: Prentice Hall.

Savage, P. (2001). *New forms of work organisation—the benefits and impact on performance*. Paper presented to DG Employment & Social Affairs by The European Work Organisation Network (EWON). Brussels, Belgium: European Commission.

Schaad, A., & Rahaman, M. (2007). *Extended requirements analysis of a collaborative, interoperable, and secure document exchange system*. Deliverable WP3-D9. R4eGov—Towards e-Administration in the large (Proposal/Contract no.: IST-2004-026650).

Schaffroth, M. (2005). Paradigmenwechsel bei der Gestaltung von e-government-Prozessen? / Das generische Geschäftsmodell der Vorgangsbearbeitung—Ein Diskussionsbeitrag aus der Schweiz. In R. Klischewski, & M. Wimmer (Eds.), *Wissensbasiertes Prozessmanagement im E-Government*. Münster, Germany: LIT.

Scheer, A.-W. (1998). *ARIS– Vom Geschäftsprozess zum Anwendungssystem. 3. Edition*. Berlin: Springer.

Scheer, A.-W. (2000). *ARIS—Business process modeling*. Heidelberg, Germany: Springer Publishing.

Scheer, A.-W., Kruppke, K., & Heib, R. (2003). *E-Government. Prozessoptimierung in der öffentlichen Verwaltung*. Springer.

Schick, A. (1971). From analysis to evaluation. *Annals of the American Academy of Political and Social Science, 394*, 57-71.

Schmidt, D., Wimmer, M., Mondorf, A., Herborn, T., Dietrich, L., Matheis, T., & Ziemann, J. (2007). *Critical state of the art report on interoperability in the public sector*. Deliverable WP4-D2. R4eGov—Towards e-Administration in the large (Proposal/Contract no.: IST-2004-026650).

Schoderbek, P., Schoderbek, C., & Kafalas, A. (1998). *Management systems, Custom edition*. Primus Global Solutions Pvt. Ltd.

Scholl, H. J. (2003). E-Government: A special case of ICT-enabled business process change. In *Proceedings of the 36th Hawaii International Conference on System Sciences* (12 pages).

Scholl, H. J. (2005). Organizational transformation through e-government: Myth or reality? In M. A. Wimmer, R. Traunmueller, A. Grönlund, & K. V. Andersen (Eds.), *Electronic Government, Proceedings of the 4th International EGOV 2005 Conference*, Copenhagen, Denmark (pp. 1-11). Berlin Heidelberg: Springer-Verlag.

Scholl, H. J. (2006). Is e-government research a flash in the pan or here for the long shot? In M. A. Wimmer, H. J. Scholl, A. Grönlund, & K. V. Andersen (Eds.), *Electronic Government, Proceedings of the Fifth International*

EGOV 2006 Conference, Krakow, Poland (pp. 13-24). Berlin Heidelberg: Springer-Verlag.

Scholl, H. J., & Klischewski, R. (2007). E-Government integration and interoperability: Framing the research agenda. *International Journal of Public Administration*, *30*(8-9), 889-920.

Schudson, M. (1998). *The good citizen: A history of American civic life*. New York: The Free Press.

Schulz, K., & Orlowska, M. (2004). Facilitating Cross-Organisational Workflows with a Workflow View Approach. *Data & Knowledge Engineering, 51*, 109-147.

Schware, R. & Deane, A. (2003). Deploying e-government programs: The strategic importance of "i" before "e." *Emerald research*, *5*(4), 10–19.

Schware, R. (2004). *Seminar on e-governance: From successful pilot to sustainable implementation*. The World Bank Group, Global Information and Communication Technologies Department.

Scott E. J. (1995). The measurement of information systems effectiveness: Evaluating a measuring instrument. *Database Advances*, *26*(1), 43-61.

Seddon, P. B., Staples, S., Patnayakuni, R., & Bowtell, M. (1999). Dimensions of information systems success. *Communications of the AIS*, *2*(November), Art. 20.

Seifert, J., & Petersen, E. (2002). The promise of all things E? Expectations and challenges of emergent e-government. *Perspectives on Global Development and Technology, 1*(2), 193-213.

Sen, A. (1999). *Development as freedom*. Oxford, UK, & New York: Oxford University Press.

Senarclens de, P. (2001). International organisations and the challenges of globalisation. *International Social Science Journal, 53*(170), 509–522.

Senyucel, Z. (2005). Towards successful e-government facilitation in UK local authorities. *E-Government Workshop '05 (Egov05)* (pp. 1-16).

SEP-2004 (2001). *Strategy of E-commerce in Public Administration for the Period 2001-2004*. Ljubljana, Slovenia: Ministry of Information Society. Retrieved September 10, 2003 from http://mid.gov.si/

SEP-2010 (2006). E-Government Strategy of the Republic of Slovenia for the period 2006 to 2010 Ministry of Public Administration, Ljubljana, Slovenia: Ministry of Public Administration. Retrieved March 20, 2008 from http://e-uprava.gov.si/e-uprava/

Serian, D. (2002). *Middleware and enterprise application integration*. London: Springer Verlag.

Sethibe, T., Campbell, J., & McDonald, C. (2007). IT governance in public and private sector organizations: Examining the differences and defining future research directions. In *Proceedings of 18th Australasian Conference on Information Systems*.

Shah, R. C., & Kesan, J. P. (2007). *Open standards and the role of politics*. Paper presented at the International Conference on Digital Government Research, Philadelphia, PA.

Shah, R., & Kesan, J. (2008). *Evaluating the interoperability of software implementations for open standards: ODF and OOXML as examples*. Paper presented at the Telecommunications Policy Research Conference.

Shanks, G., Tansley, E., & Weber, R. (2003). Using ontology to validate conceptual models. *Communications of the ACM*, *46*(10), 85-89.

Shannon, C. E., & Weaver, W. (1949). *The mathematical model theory of communication*. Urbana, IL: University of Illinois Press.

Sheller, M., & Urry, J. (2006). The new mobilities paradigm. *Environment and Planning A, 38*, 207-226.

Shin, M., Holden, T., & Schmidt, R. A. (2001). From knowledge theory to management practice: Towards an integrated approach. *Information Processing and Management*, *37*, 335-355.

Signore, O., Chesi, F., & Pallotti, M. (2005). E-Government: Challenges and opportunities. *CMG Italy – XIX Annual Conference*, Florence, Italy.

Simon, H. A. (1947). *Administrative behavior*. New York: Mac Millan.

Simon, H. A., Thompson, V. A., & Smithsburg, D. W. (1991). *Public administration*. New Brunswick: Transaction Publishers.

Simonsson, M., & Johnson, P. (2005). *Defining IT governance – a consolidation of literature, industrial information and control systems. Working paper*. KTH, Royal Institute of Technology. Retrieved in May 2008, from www.ics.kth.se

Singapore Department of Statistics. (2007) *Key annual indicators*. Retrieved on March 30, 2007, from http://www.singstat.gov.sg/keystats/annual/indicators.html

Singh, P. J., & Craike, A. (2008). Shared services: towards a more holistic conceptual definition. *International Journal of Business Information Systems, 3*(3), 217-230.

Škrinjar, R., Dimovski, V., Škerlavaj, M., & Indihar Štemberger, Mojca (2006). Process maturity and organizational structure as a framework for performance improvements. In Nilsson, A. et al. (Eds.), *Bridging the gap between academia and industry, Vol. I.* (pp. 95-106). New York: Springer.

Smith, H., & Fingar, P. (2003). *IT doesn't matter—business processes do: A critical analysis of Nicholas Carr's IT article in the Harvard Business Review*. Tampa, FL: Meghan-Kiffer Press.

Snijkers, K. (2005). *E-Government in een interbestuurlijke context. Casestudie: OCMW's en de kruispuntbank van de sociale zekerheid*. Leuven: Steunpunt Beleirdsrelevant Onderzoek Bestuurlijke Organisatie Vlaanderen.

Snijkers, K. (2006, May 11-13). *Managing intergovernmental e-government projects*. Paper presented at NISPAcee Conference, Ljubljana, Slovenia.

Somers, T. M., & Nelson, K. (2001). The impact of critical success factors across the stages of enterprise resource planning implementations. In *Proceedings of the 34th Annual Hawaii International Conference on System Sciences* (pp. 1-10).

Song, X., & Osterweil, L. J. (1994). Experience with an approach to comparing software design methodologies. *IEEE Transactions on Software Engineering, 20*(5), 364-384.

Songini, M. L. (2004). Australian firm faces ERP implementation woes. *Computerworld*.

Soo, C., Devinney, T., Midgley, D., & Deering, A. (2002). Knowledge management: Philosophy, processes, and pitfalls. *California Management Review, 44*(4), 129-150.

Sorrentino, M. (2006). E-Government research: Time to switch direction. In A. Grönlund, H. J. Scholl, K. V. Andersen, & M. Wimmer (Eds.), *Electronic Government, Communication Proceedings of the Fifth International EGOV Conference*, Krakow, Poland (Vol. 18, pp. 17-24). Linz: Universitätsverlag Rudolf Trauner.

Sorrentino, M. (2007). Interpreting e-government: Implementation as the moment of truth. In A. Grönlund, H. J. Scholl, K. V. Andersen, & M. Wimmer (Eds.), *Electronic Government, Communication Proceedings of the Sixth International EGOV 2007 Conference*, Regensburg Germany (pp. 281-292). Berlin Heidelberg: Springer-Verlag.

Sorrentino, M., & Ferro, E. (2008). Does the answer to e-government lie in intermunicipal collaboration? An exploratory Italian case atudy. In M. Wimmer, J. H. Scholl, & E. Ferro (Eds.), *Electronic Government, Communication Proceedings of the Fifth International EGOV 2008 Conference*, Turin, Italy (pp. 1-12). Berlin Heidelberg: Springer-Verlag.

South Dakota Horizons (2008). About. Retrieved April 27, 2008, from http://southdakota.communityblogs.us/about/

South Dakota Horizons–Fruechte, K. (2007, August). Horizons sets up individual community blogs. Retrieved April 27, 2008, from http://southdakota.communityblogs.us/2007/08/16/ horizons-sets-up-individual-community-blogs/

South Dakota Horizons–Jacobs, C. (2007, October). Ideas... host a monthly blog night in your community. Retrieved April 27, 2008, from http://southdakota.communityblogs.us/ 2007/10/08/ideashost-a-monthly-blog-night-in-your-community/

Spadone, P. (2006). *Collaborative workflow requirements for e-government.* Deliverable WP5-D1. R4eGov—Towards e-Administration in the large (Proposal/Contract no.: IST-2004-026650).

Srinivasan, A. (1985). Alternative measures of system effectiveness: Associations and implications. *MIS Quarterly*, 243-253.

Stalk, G., Evans, P., & Shulman, L. E. (1992). Competing on capabilities: The new rules of corporate strategy. *Harvard Business Review, 70*(2), 57-69.

Stame, N. (Ed.) (2007). *Classici della valutazione*. Milano: Franco Angeli.

Stamper, R., Liu, K., Hafkamp, M., & Ades, Y. (2000). Understanding the roles of signs and norms in organizations—a semiotic approach to information systems design. *Behaviour & Information Technology, 19*(1), 15 -27.

State Services Commission. (2007). New Zealand e-government interoperability framework (NZ e-GIF), version 3.2, July 2007. Retrieved on April 7, 2008, from http://www.e.govt.nz/standards/e-gif

Steen, T., van den Berg, C., van der Meer, F., Overeem, P., & Toonen, T. (2005). *Modernising Governments in other countries.* The Hague, The Netherlands: Modernising Government Project, Ministry of the Interior and Kingdom Relations.

Stehr, N. (2002). *Knowledge and economic conduct. The social foundations of the modern economy.* Toronto, Canada: University of Toronto Press Incorporated.

Stewart, J., & Walsh, K. (1994). Performance measurement: When performance can never be finally defined. *Public Money and Management, April-June*, 45-49.

Stewart, T. A. (2000). Knowledge worth $1.25 billion. *Fortune, 142*(12), 120-121.

Stoltzfus, K. (2005). Motivations for implementing e-government: An investigation of the global phenomenon. In *Proceedings of the 2005 National Conference on Digital Government Research, ACM* (Vol. 89, pp. 333–338). Atlanta, Georgia.

Storck, J. & Hill, P. A. 2000, "Knowledge diffusion through 'strategic communities'", *Sloan Management Review* pp. 63-74.

Stowers, G. N. L. (2004). Measuring the performance of e-government. *E-Government Series, IBM Center for the Business of Government.* Retrieved April 27, 2008, from http://www.businessofgovernment.org/pdfs/8493_Stowers_Report.pdf

Strikwerda. (2005). *Shared service centers. Van kostenbesparing naar waardecreatie*. Assen, The Netherlands: Van Gorcum-Stichting Management Studies.

Stuver, P. (2006). Maximizing emergency communication. *Risk management, 53*(5), 30-35.

Supangkat, S. H., Rahmat, B., & Sembiring, J. (2006). *IT governance for developing countries*. School of Electrical Engineering and Informatics, Institute of Technology Bandung. Engage Indonesia.

Svensson, J. S. (2002). Legal Expert Systems in Social Administration: From Fearing Computers to Fearing Accountants. *Information Polity, 7*, 143-154.

Symons, V. (1991). A review of information systems evaluation: Content, context, and process. *European Journal of Information Systems, 1*(3), 205-21.

Symons, V., & Walsham, G. (1991). The evaluation of information systems: A critique. In R. Veryard (Ed.), *The Economics of Information Systems and Software* (pp. 71-88). Oxford: Butterworth-Heinemann.

Szajna, B. (1996). Empirical evaluation of the revised technology acceptance model. *Management Science, 42*(1), 85-92.

Szulanski, G. (1995). Unpacking stickiness: An empirical investigation of the barriers to transfer best practice inside the firm. *Academy of Management Journal, Best Papers Proceedings*, 437.

Szulanski, G. (1996). Exploring internal stickiness: Impediments to the transfer of best practice within the firm. *Strategic Management Journal, 17(*Winter Special Issue), 27-43.

Szulanski, G. (2003). *Sticky knowledge: Barriers to knowing in the firm.* Thousand Oaks, CA: Sage.

Takeda, H., Veerkamp, P., Tomiyama, T., & Yoshikawa, H. (1990). Modeling design process. *AI Magazine, 11*(4), 37-48.

Tambouris, E. (2001, September 3-7). An integrated platform for realising online one-stop government: The eGOV project. In *Proceedings of the 12th international Workshop on Database and Expert Systems Applications (DEXA)* (p. 359). Washington, DC: IEEE Computer Society.

Tan, Y. H., Theon, W. Toward a generic model of trust for electronic commerce. *International Journal of Electronic Commerce, 5*(2) 61-74.

Tapscott, & Williams. (2007). *Wikinomics—how mass collaboration changes everything.* New York: Portfolio.

Tapscott, D., & Williams, A. (2006). *Wikinomics: How mass collaboration changes everything.* New York: Penguin Group.

Tassey, G. (2005). Underinvestment in public good technologies. *Journal of Technology Transfer, 30*, 90-94.

Taylor, S., & Todd, P. A. (1995). Assessing IT usage: The role of prior experience. *MIS Quarterly, 19*(2), 561-570.

Teece, D. J., & Pisano, G. (1994). The dynamic capabilities of firms: An introduction. *Industrial and Corporate Change, 3*(3), 537-556.

Teece, D. J., Pisano, G., & Shuen, A. (1997). Dynamic capabilities and strategic management. *Strategic Management Journal, 18(*7), 509-533.

Teigland, R., & Wasko, M. (2001, August 3-8). Recombining knowledge through know-how trading: Examining the impact of informal boundary-spanning communication on individual performance. *Academy of Management Proceedings.*

Teisman, G. R. (1992). *Complexe besluitvorming: Een pluricentrisch perspectief op besluitvorming over ruimtelijke investeringen.* Den Haag, The Netherlands: Vuga.

Telemedicine Alliance. (2005, November). *Towards interoperable e-health for Europe. (BR 255).* Noordwijk, The Netherlands: ESA Publ. Div.

Tellis, W. (1997). Introduction to case study. *The Qualitative Report, 3*(2).

Teng, James T. C., Calhoun, K. J., Cheon, M. J., Raeburn, S., & Wong, W. (1997). Is the east really different from the west: A cross cultural study on information technology and decision making. *MIS Quarterly,* 40-46.

The Clare Champion. (1998) *Information age dawns in 2,500 Ennis homes.* Retrieved on March 9, 2007, from http://www.clarelibrary.ie/eolas/coclare/places/infoage/dawns.htm

The Peninsula Newspaper. (2008). Bursting at the seams. Retrieved from http://www.thepeninsulaqatar.com/Display_news.asp?section=Local_News&month=January2008&file=Local_News200801296298.xml

Themistocleous, M. (2004). Justifying the decisions for EAI implementations: A validated proposition of influential factors. *Journal of Enterprise Information Management, 17*(2), 85-104.

Themistocleous, M., & Irani, Z. (2001). Benchmarking the benefits and barriers of application integration. *Benchmarking An International Journal, 8*(4), 317-331.

Themistocleous, M., & Irani, Z. (2006). Towards a methodology for the development of integrated IT infrastructures. In R. J. Sprague (Ed.), *Proceedings of the 39th Annual Hawaii International Conference on System Sciences (HICSS'06)* (pp. 4-7). Hawaii, USA: IEEE Computer Society.

Themistocleous, M., Irani, Z., & Kuljis, J. (2004). Extending the information system lifecycle through enterprise application integration: A case study experience. In *Proceedings of the 37th Annual Hawaii International Conference on System Sciences (HICSS'04)(pp. 1-8) –Track 8*, Big Island, HI: IEEE.

Themistocleous, M., Irani, Z., & Love, P. E. D. (2005). Developing e-government integrated infrastructures: A case study. In *Proceedings of the 38th Annual Hawaii International Conference on System Sciences (pp. 1-10)*, Big Island, HI: IEEE.

Thomas, J. C., & Streib, G. (2003). The new face of government: Citizen initiated contacts in the era of e-government. *Journal of Public Administration Research and Theory, 13*(1), 83-102.

Thompson, J. D. (1967). *Organizations in action*. New York: McGraw Hill.

Thompson, J. R. (2000). Reinvention As Reform: Assessing the National Performance Review. *Public Administration Review, 6*(60), 508-521.

Thompson, M., & Walsham, G. (2004). Placing knowledge management in context. *Journal of Management Studies, 41*(5), 725-747.

Thompson, R. L., Higgins, C. A., & Howell, J. M. (1991). Personal computing: Toward a conceptual model of utilization. *MIS Quarterly, 15*(1), 124-143.

Thompson, R., Higgins, C., & Howell, J. (1991). Personal computing: toward a conceptual model of utilization. *MIS Quarterly, 15*(1), 124-143.

Thompson, R., Higgins, C., & Howell, J. (1994). Influence of experience on personal computer utilization: Testing a conceptual model. *Journal of Management Information Systems, 11*(1), 167-187.

Thong, Y. L., Yap, C., & Kin-Lee, S. (2000). Business process reengineering in the public sector: The case of the housing development board in Singapore. *Journal of Management Information Systems, 17*(1), 245-271.

TRA. (2008). *About Tanzania revenue authority (TRA) and related statistics in the case study*. Retrieved in May 2008, from www.tra.go.tz

Trauth, E. M. (2000). *The culture of an information economy. Influences and impact in the Republic of Ireland*. The Netherlands: Kluwer Academic Publishers.

Trkman, P., Indihar Stemberger, M., & Jaklic, J. (2005). Information transfer in supply chain management. In *Informing Science and IT Education Conference 2005 (InSITE 2005)*, Vol. 2, (pp. 559-573). Santa Rosa, CA: Informing Science Institute.

Tsoukas, H. (1996). The firm as a distributed knowledge system: A constructionist approach. *Strategic Management Journal, 17*, 11-25.

Tsoukas, H. (2005). *Complex knowledge: Studies of organizational epistemology*. Oxford, UK: Oxford University Press.

Tuffs, D., Stapleton, J., West, D., & Eason, J. (1999). Interoperability of DSDM with the rational unified process. *DSDM Consortium*, 1.

Tuomi, I. (2002). *Networks of innovation: Change and meaning in the age of the Internet*. Oxford, UK, & New York: Oxford University Press.

Tuomi, I. (2006). The future of learning in the knowledge society—disruptive changes for Europe by 2020. In Y. Punie, et al. (Eds.), *The future of ICT and learning in the knowledge society*. Luxembourg: Office for Official Publications of the European Communities.

Turban, E., Aronson, J. E., & Liang, T. (2005). *Decision support systems and intelligent systems, 7th edition*. Upper Saddle River, NJ: Pearson/PrenticeHall.

Turoff, M. (2002). Past and future emergency response information systems. *Association for Computing Machinery. Communications of the ACM, 45*(4), 29.

Turoff, M., Hiltz, S. R., Cho, H.-K., Li, Z., & Wang, Y. (2002). Social decision support systems (SDSS). *Proceedings of the 35th Hawaii International Conference on System Sciences, 2002* (pp. 81–90). Retrieved April 26, 2008, from http://www.hicss.hawaii.edu/HICSS_35/HICSSpapers/PDFdocuments/CLCSC03.pdf

U.S. Department of Justice. (1999). Microsoft engaged in a predatory campaign to crush the browser threat to its operating system monopoly. Retrieved on September 5, 2007, from http://www.usdoj.gov/atr/cases/f2600/v-a.pdf

Uçkan, Ö. (2003). E-Devlet , e-demokrasi ve Türkiye, literatür yayıncılık, İstanbul.

Ulbrich, F. (2006). Improving shared service implementation: Adopting lessons from the BPR movement. *Business Process Management Journal, 12*(2), 191-205.

UN. (2008). *World public sector report: UN e-government survey: From e-government To connected governance.* New York.

UNDERSTAND Consortium. (2006). *Methodology handbook. Project report.* Swansea, UK: University of Wales.

Undheim, T. (2008). Best practices in e-government: On a knife-edge between success and failure. *European Journal of E-Practice.*

United Kingdom Parliament. (2008). eConsultations. Retrieved April 27, 2008, from http://forums.parliament.uk/html/index.html

United Nations Development Programme. (2007). *E-Government interoperability: Guide.* Bangkok, Thailand: UNDP Regional Centre.

United Nations Economic Commission for Europe. (2002). *Concept, outline, benchmarking, and indicators.* New York & Geneva: United Nations Publications.

United Nations. (2008). *UN e-government survey 2008: From e-government to connected governance.* New York: United Nations. Retrieved August 2008, from http://unpan1.un.org/intradoc/groups/public/documents/UN/UNPAN028607.pdf

University Consortium for Geographic Information Science. (1996). Research priorities for geographic information science. *Cartography and Geographic Information Science, 23*(3), 115-127.

US Government, General Services Administration. (2003). *Federal e-government initiatives: Are we headed in the right direction?* Washington, DC.

Van De Walle, e. a. (2007). Emergency response information systems: Emerging trends and technologies. *Communications of ACM.*

van Dijk, J. A. G. M. (2005). *The deepening divide—inequality in the information society.* London, & Delhi, India: SAGE.

Van Grembergen, W. (2000). The balanced scorecard and IT governance. *Information Systems Control Journal, 2*, 40-43.

Van Grembergen, W., & De Haes, S. (2005). Measuring and improving IT governance through the balanced scorecard. *Information Systems Control Journal, 2*, 35.

Van Grembergen, W., & De Haes, S. (2008). *Implementing information technology governance: Models, practices, and cases.* Hershey, PA: IGI Publishing.

Van Grembergen, W., De Haes, S., & Guldentops, E. (2003). Structures, processes, and relational mechanisms for IT governance. In W. Van Grembergen (Ed.), *Strategies for information technology governance.* Hershey, PA: Idea Group Publishing.

Van Slyke, C., Belanger, F., & Comunale, C.L. Factors influencing the adoption of Web-based shopping: The impact of trust. *Database for Advances in Information Systems, 35*(2), 32-49.

VanDenburgh, W. M., & Harmelink, P. J. (2006). The IRS's lack of support for direct, free e-Filing. *Tax Notes, 112*, 171-182.

Vann, J. L. (2004). Resistance to change and the language of public organizations: A look at "clashing grammars" in large-scale information technology projects. *Public Organization Review, 4*, 47-73.

Veal, D. C. (2001). Techniques of document management: A review of text retrieval and related technologies. *Journal of Documentation, 57*(2), 192-217.

Venkatesh, V. & Davis, Fd. (2000). A theoretical extension of the technology acceptance model: Four longitudinal field studies. *Management Science, 46*(2), 186-204.

Venkatesh, V., Morris, M., Davis, G., & Davis, F. (2003). User acceptance of information technology: Toward a unified view. *MIS Quarterly, 27*(3), 425-478.

Vernadat, F., & Kosanke, K. (1992). CIMOSA: A reference architecture for CIM. In *Proceedings of the IFIP TC5/WG5.3 eight international PROLAMAT conference on human aspects in computer integrated manufacturing, FIP Transactions (Vol. B-3).* North-Holland.

Veugelers, R. (2005). *Assessing innovation capacity: Fitting strategy and policy to the right framework. Measuring knowledge and its economic effects: Advancing knowledge and the knowledge economy.* Washington, D.C.: National Academies.

Viaene, J., Robben, F., Lahaye, D., & Van Steenberge, J. (1986). Algemene schets van een rationele informatieverwerking in de sociale zekerheid. *Belgisch Tijdschrift voor de Sociale Zekerheid, 4*(5), 399-473.

Villa, M. (2005). Process modelling in the public administrations & e-government gateways: ICTE-PAN. In *Proceedings of the eGovInterop'05 Conference*. Geneva, Switzerland.

von Hipple, E. (1994). Sticky information and the locus of problem solving: Implications for innovation. *Organization Science, 40*(4), 429-439.

Wagenaar, R. W., Matthijsse, R., Bruijn, J. d., Voort, H. v. d., & Wendel de Joode, R. v. (2006). Implementation of shared service centres in public administration: Dilemmas and trade-offs. In *Information and Communication Technology and Public Innovation* (Vol. 12, pp. 141-158). Amsterdam: IOS Press.

Waller, P., Livesey, P., & Edin, K. (2001). E-Government in the service of democracy. *ICA Information, 74.*

Walsham, G. (1993). *Interpreting information systems in organizations.* Chichester: Wiley.

Walsham, G. (1995). Interpretive case studies in IS research: Nature and method. *European Journal of Information Systems, 4*, 74-81.

Walter, S. G., & Spitta, T. (2004). Approaches to the ex-ante evaluation of investments into information systems. *Wirtschaftsinformatik, 46*(3), 171-180.

Wang, Y., & Emurian, H. (2005).Trust in e-commerce: Consideration of interface design factors. *Journal of Electronic Commerce in Organizations, 3*(4), 42-60.

Warkentin, M., & Gefen, D. (2002). Encouraging citizen adoption of e-government by building trust. *Electronic Markets, 12*(3), 157-162.

Warland, C., & Ridley, G. (2005). Awareness of IT control frameworks in an Australian state government: A qualitative case study. In *Proceedings of the 38th Hawaii International Conference on System Sciences.*

Wasko, M. M., & Faraj, S. (2000). It is what one does: Why people participate and help others in electronic communities of practice. *Journal of Strategic Information Systems, 9*, 155-173.

Wassenaar, A. (2000). *E-Governmental value chain models* (289-293). DEXA, IEEE Press.

Wastell, D., Kawalek, P., Langmead-Jones, P., & Ormerod, R. (2004). Information systems and partnership in multiagency networks: An action research project in crime reduction. *Information & Organization, 14*, 189-210.

Watson, E. E., & Schneider, H. (1999). Using ERP systems in education. *Communications of the Association for Information Systems*, February 1, 9.

Waugh, W. L. J., & Streib, G. (2006). Collaboration and leadership for effective emergency management. *Public Administration Review, 66*(Special Issue on Collaborative Public Management).

Webster, J. (1995). Networks of Collaboration of Conflict? Electronic Data Interchange and Power in the Supply Chain. *Journal of Strategic Information Systems, 5*(1), 31-42.

Weerakkody, V., Baire, S. & Choudrie, J. (2006). E-Government: The need for effective process management in the public sector. In *Proceedings of the 39th Hawaii International Conference on System Sciences.*

Weerakkody, V., Janssen, M. & Hjort-Madsen, K. (2007). Realising integrated e-government services: A European perspective. *Journal of Cases in Electronic Commerce, 3*(2), 14-38.

Weick, K. E. (1995). *Sensemaking in organisations.* London: SAGE Publications.

Weill, P., & Ross J. W. (2004). *IT governance: How top performers manage IT decision rights for superior results.* Harvard Business School Press.

Weill, P., & Woodham, R. (2002). *Don't just lead, govern: Implementing effective IT governance.* (CISR WP No.326). Cambridge, MA: MIT Sloan School of Management.

Weiser, P. J. (2007). Communicating during emergencies: Toward interoperability and effective information management. *Federal Communications Law Journal, 59*(3), 547-573.

Weiss, C. H. (1998). *Evaluation: Methods for studying programs and policies.* Englewood Cliffs: Prentice Hall.

Welch, E.W., Hinnant, C. C., & Moon, M. J. (2005). Linking citizen satisfaction with e-government and trust in government. *Journal of Public Administration Research and Theory, 15*(3), 371-391.

Wellman, B. (2001). Computer networks as social networks. *Science, 293*, 2031-2034.

Wenger, E. C. (2000). Communities of practice and social learning systems. *Organization, 7(*2), 225-246.

Wenger, E. C., & Synder, W. (2000). Communities of practice: The organizational frontier. *Harvard Business Review,* 139-145.

Wernerfelt, B. (1984). A resource-based view of the firm. *Strategic Management Journal, 5(*2), 171-180.

West, D. M. (2005). *Digital government.* Princeton: Princeton University Press.

West, D. M. (2006). *Global e-government.* Retrieved on June 1, 2007, from http://www.InsidePolitics.org/egovtdata.html

West, J. (2004, May 13). *What are open standards? Implications for adoption, competition, and policy.* Paper presented at the Standards and Public Policy, Federal Reserve Bank of Chicago, Chicago, IL.

West, J. (2007). The economic realities of open standards: Black, white, and many shades of gray. In S. Greenstein & V. Stango (Eds.), *Standards and Public Policy* (pp. 87-122). Cambridge: Cambridge University Press.

Whitehouse, (2003). *E-Government strategy: Implementing the president's management agenda for e-government.*

Whitehouse. (2007, March 23). *Obstacles to greater effectiveness* . Retrieved on April 12, 2008, from Results.gov: http://www.whitehouse.gov/results/obstacles/index.html

Wideman, R. (2002). *Comparing PRINCE2 with PMBoK.* Vancouver, Canada: AEW Services.

Willaert, P., van der Bergh, J., Willems, J., & Deschoolmeester, D. (2007). The process-oriented organisation: A holistic view, developing a framework for business process orientation maturity. In Alonso G., Dadam P., Rosemann M. (Eds.), *Proceedings of 5th International BPM Conference, Brisbane, September 24-27* (pp. 1-15). Berlin, Heidelberg: Springer-Verlag.

Willcocks, L. P., & Lester, S. (Eds.) (2000). *Beyond the Productivity Paradox*. Chichester: Wiley.

Williams, R., & Edge, D. (1996). The Social Shaping of Technology. *Research Policy, 25*, 865-899.

Wimmer, M. (2004). A European perspective towards online one-stop government: The eGov project. *Electronic Commerce Research and Applications*, 92-103.

Wimmer, M. A. (2001). European development towards online one-stop government: The "eGOV" project. In *Proceedings of the International Conference of Electronic Commerce (ICEC2001)*, Vienna, Austria.

Wimmer, M. R., et al. (2001). Electronic business invading the public sector: Considerations on change and design. In *Proceedings of the 34th Hawaii International Conference on System Sciences* (10 pages).

Wimmer, M., & Traunmuller, R. (2000). *Trends in e-government: Managing distributed knowledge.* Paper presented at the Proceedings from 11th International Workshop on Database and Expert Systems Applications, New York.

Wong, W., & Welch, E. (2004). Does e-government promote accountability? A comparative analysis of Web site openness and government accountability. *Governance, 17*(2), 275-297.

Wood, J., & Silver, D. (1995). *Joint application development.* John Wiley & Sons Inc.

Wright, D. K. (2002). Examining how the 11th September, 2001 terrorist attacks precipitated a paradigm shift advancing communications and public relations into a more significant role in corporate America. *Journal of Communication Management, 6*(3), 280-292.

Yahya, A. H. (1993). On the problems of information technology management in developing nations. *CPR*, 349-355.

Yang, K. (2003). Neoinstitutionalism and e-government: Beyond Jane Fountain. *Social Science Computer Review, 21*(4), 432–442.

Yeo, A. (1993). Cultural effects in usability assessment. *ACM Doctoral Consortium*, 74-75.

Yildiz, M. (2007). E-Government research: Reviewing the literature, limitations, and ways forward. *Government Information Quarterly, 24*(3), 646-665.

Yin, R. (1994). *Case study research. Design and* methods. (2nd ed.). Beverly Hills, CA: Sage Publications, Inc.

Yin, R. (2003). *Case study research design and methods, third edition.* Sage Publications.

Yin, R. K. (1989). *Case study research. Design and methods.* USA: Sage Publications, Inc.

Yin, R. K. (1994). *Case study research - design and methods, second edition.* London: Sage Publications.

Yuthas, K., & Eining, M. (1995). An cxpcrimcntal cvaluation of measurements of information system effectiveness. *Journal of Information Systems, 9*(2), 69-84.

Zachman, J. A. (1987). A framework for information-systems architecture. *In IBM Systems Journal, 26*(3), pp. 276-292.

Zack, M. H. (1999). Managing codified knowledge. *Sloan Management Review, 40*(4), 45-58.

Zackary, P. G. (2000). *The global me: New cosmopolitans and the competitive edge - picking globalism's winners and losers.* New York: Perseus Books.

Zahra, S. A., & George, G. (2002). Absorptive capacity: A review, reconceptualization, and extension. *Academy of Management Review, 27*(2), 185-203.

Zakareya, E., & Irani, Z. (2005). E-Government adoption: Architecture and barriers. *Business Process Management Journal, 11*(5), 589-611.

Zeleny, M. (1987). Management support systems: Towards integrated knowledge management. *Human Systems Management, 7*(1), 59-70.

Zhang, J., Dawes, S. S., & Sarkis, J. (2005). Exploring stakeholders' expectations of the benefits and barriers of e-government knowledge sharing. *The Journal of Enterprise Information Management, 18*(5), 548-567.

Zhiyuan, F. (2002), E-Government in digital era: Concepts, practice, and development. *International Journal Of The Computer, The Internet and Management, 10*(2), 1-22.

Ziemann, J., & Mendling, J. (2005). *Transformation of EPCs to BPEL – A pragmatic approach.* 7th International Conference on the Modern Information Technology in the Innovation Processes of the industrial enterprises, Genoa, Italy.

Ziemann, J., Kahl, T., & Werth, D. (2007). Using view process models in collaborative business processes. In Putnik, G. D., Cunha, M. M. (Eds.), *Encyclopedia of networked and virtual organisations.* Hershey, PA: Idea Group Inc.

Ziemann, J., Leyking, K., Kahl, T., & Werth, D. (2006). Enterprise model driven migration from legacy to SOA. In R. Gimnich, & A. Winter (Eds.), *Workshop software-reengineering und services.* Passau, Germany: MKWI.

Zittrain, J. (2006). *The generative Internet (Working Paper 28/2006).* University of Oxford, Faculty of Law.

Zmud, R. W. (1978). An empirical investigation of the dimensionality of the concept of information. *Decision Sciences* (9), 187-195.

Zucker, L. G. (1986). Production of trust: Institutional sources of economic structure, 1840-1920. *Research in Organizational Behavior,* (8), 53-111.

Zuurmond, A. (1998). From bureaucracy to infocracy. In I. T. M. Snellen & W. B. J. H. van de Donk (Eds.), *Public Administration in an Information Age* (pp. 259-272). Amsterdam: IOS Press.

About the Contributors

Vishanth Weerakkody is a member of faculty in the Business School at Brunel University, UK. Weerakkody was previously a faculty member in the department of IS and Computing at Brunel University and he has held various IT positions in multinational organisations, including IBM UK. Weerakkody is a member of the British Computer Society, Chartered IT professional and a Fellow of the UK Higher Education Academy. He is the current editor-in-chief of the *International Journal of Electronic Government Research.*

Marijn Janssen is an associate professor within the information and communication technology section and director of the interdisciplinary SEPAM Master programme of the Faculty of Technology, Policy and Management at Delft University of Technology. He has been a consultant for the Ministry of Justice and received a PhD in information systems (2001). He serves on several editorial boards and is involved in the organization of a number of conferences. He published over 100 refereed publications.

Yogesh K. Dwivedi is a lecturer in the School of Business and Economics at Swansea University in the UK. He was awarded his MSc and PhD by Brunel University in the UK, receiving a *Highly Commended* award for his doctoral work by the European Foundation for Management and Development. His research focuses on the adoption and diffusion of ICT in organisations and in addition to authoring a book and numerous conference papers, has co-authored papers accepted for publication by journals such as *Communications of the ACM,* the *Information Systems Journal,* the *European Journal of Information Systems,* and the *Journal of the Operational Research Society.* He is Senior Editor of *DATABASE for Advances in Information Systems*, Managing Editor of *Journal of Electronic Commerce Research*, Assistant Editor *of Transforming Government: People, Process and Policy* and a member of the editorial board/review board of a number of other of other journals, and is a member of the Association of Information Systems, IFIP WG8.6 and the Global Institute of Flexible Systems Management, New Delhi.

* * *

Sarmad Alshawi has more than 15 years of academic experience and currently lectures Aviation Management and Business Intelligence at the Business School, Brunel University, UK. Dr Alshawi is an active member of research groups at Brunel, with research in Business Intelligence, Data Management, Data Warehousing, CRM and E-government. Dr Alshawi has written in internationally refereed journals, spoken at conferences world-wide, and has guest-edited special issue journals. He has participated in many research projects, and currently is a co-investigator on the EPSRC funded MATCH healthcare project.

Shafi H. Al-Shafi is a PhD researcher at the School of Information Systems, Computing and Mathematics, Brunel University, UK. He obtained his Master in business administration MBA, (information technology) from the Faculty of Engineering and Computing, Coventry University in the UK. His research interests include e-government, impact of integration technologies, strategic management and e-commerce.

Dimitris Askounis is an assistant professor of management information & decision support systems in the School of Electrical and Computer Engineering at the National Technical University of Athens (NTUA). Dr. Askounis has published over 80 papers in scientific journals and international conference proceedings.

Wael Aziz is head of eGovernment Strategy Unit in Dubai Municipality. He obtained his MBA from Strathclyde University, UK. He holds a BSc in systems and biomedical engineering from Cairo University, Egypt, and postgraduate studies in artificial intelligence from faculty of Engineering, Al-Azhar University, Cairo. He is a member of the Egyptian Society for Engineers, International Association of Business Leaders, Germany, the Egyptian Society of Language Engineering, Egypt, e-Learning Initiative, Ministry of Communication & Information Technology, Egypt, and Arabic Bolger's Association. His research interests include e-government, performance management, benchmarking, and excellence models.

Lars Baacke works as research assistant at the Institute of Information Management (http://www.iwi.unisg.ch) at the University of St. Gallen (Switzerland). During his studies of information management he continuously focused on e-government and process management. Since 2006, he works in the Competence Center Health Network Engineering (CC HNE) and is involved in the EU funded project PICTURE and other projects in the fields of public administration and public health research (http://ehealth.iwi.unisg.ch).

Jörg Becker is full professor for information systems and information management and head of the Department of Information Systems at the University of Muenster, Germany. In 2004 he was appointed as managing director of the European Research Center for Information Systems. Jörg Becker has written more than 350 publications. He works as editor-in-chief for the *Information Systems and e-Business Management Journal* and is editor of *Wirtschaftsinformatik*, the leading German IS journal. Jörg Becker studied business administration and economics at the University of Saarland, Germany and the University of Michigan, Ann Arbor. His research areas contain management information systems, information modeling, e-government, and data management.

Philipp Bergener works as PhD student and research assistant at the European Research Center for Information Systems in Münster, Germany since 2007. Before starting his PhD he worked 16 month as a student assistant on projects in the public-sector. Philipp Bergener holds a diploma degree in information systems (Wirschaftsinformatik) from the Westphalian Whilhelms-University (WWU) Münster, Germany. His research focuses on e-government, process management, data management, method engineering and e-inclusion.

Ashley Braganza is professor of organisational transformation and deputy director of Brunel Business School. His research interests encompass change management, strategy implementation, process and knowledge management and transformation enabled information systems. He has published over 150 papers and 3 books on these subjects. At Brunel, he is responsible for three strategic portfolios: executive development, alumni and student placements. He is the Director of nexus—The Knowledge Exchange. He is the founder and chair of the British Academy of Management Special Interest Group in Transformation, Change and Development. His publications appear in prestigious academic and practitioner journals such as *Communications of the ACM, Journal of Information Technology, Communications of the AIS, Information Systems Journal, Journal of Strategic Change, International Journal of Information Management, Integrated Manufacturing Systems, International Journal of Project Management, International Journal of Knowledge Management*, and *Knowledge and Process Management.*

Hans de Bruijn is professor of public administration at Delft University of Technology, The Netherlands. Most of his work is on multi-actor governance. Recent publications are *Management in Networks: On Multi-Actor Decision Making* (with Ernst ten Heuvelhof) (Routledge, 2007), and *Managing Performance in the Public Sector* (Routledge, 2007).

Murat Cakir is a PhD candidate at the Informatics Institute, Department of Information Systems at Middle East Technical University, Ankara, Turkey, from where he received his MSc. His current research interests are: information systems evaluation, simulation testing and verification, user based simulation systems assessment.

Lemuria D. Carter is an assistant professor at North Carolina Agricultural & Technical State University. Her primary research interests include e-government diffusion, internet voting, Web-based trust and risk perceptions. She has published in several top-tier journals including, *Journal of Strategic Information Systems, Information Systems Journal*, and *Communications of the ACM.*

Yannis Charalabidis is a computer engineer and holds a PhD in information systems engineering from National Technical University of Athens (NTUA). He has been employed for 8 years as an executive director in Singular IT Group, specializing in ERP applications in Southern Eastern Europe. Currently he is heading e-Government & eBusiness Research in the Decision Support Systems Laboratory of NTUA, planning and coordinating high-level policy making, research and pilot application projects for governments and administrations worldwide. He teaches e-government information systems, interoperability and standardization, e-participation and government transformation in NTUA and the University of Aegean.

Shefali S. Dash is working as a deputy director general at National Informatics Centre, New Delhi. Her areas of specialisation are planning and implementation of MIS, DSS, e-governance, large scale computer communication infrastructure projects for rural areas. Some of the large projects handled by her are computerization of Rajiv Gandhi National Drinking Water Mission ,Community Information Centre, GRAMSAT, Warana Wired Village, etc. She has been instrumental in preparing e-governance plans for various state governments in India as well as for the government of Lao People's Democratic Republic. She has authored number of articles which have appeared in various journals and conference proceedings.

Marco De Marco is professor of organisation at the Catholic University of Milan President elect of ItAIS, the Italian chapter of AIS, and serves as conference chair at ECIS2009. He is in the editorial boards of the *Information Systems Journal*, the *International Journal of Digital Accounting Research*, and *Information Systems and E-Business Management*. He serves as an expert in a government committee to evaluate ICT projects to be funded. His major interests are systems development e-government, programme evaluation and banking information systems. His latest works were published in the *European Journal of Information Systems* and in the *Journal of Information Technology*.

Torgeir Dingsøyr works with research on agile software development, software process improvement and knowledge management as a senior scientist at SINTEF Information and Communication Technology. He has published more than 50 refereed papers in this field, including articles in *IEEE Transactions on Software Engineering, IEEE Software, Communications of the ACM, Information and Software Technology* and *Empirical Software Engineering*. He is a co-author of the book *Process Improvement in Practice: A Handbook for IT Companies*, published by Kluwer Academic Publishers in 2004, and holds a position as adjunct associate professor at Norwegian University of Science and Technology.

Marwan Elnaghi is a researcher in e-government at the School of Information Systems, Computing and Mathematics, Brunel University, UK. He obtained his MSc in industrial and administrative sciences from City University in London, UK. He holds a BSc in electrical and electronics engineering from Nottingham University, a post graduate diploma in computing from Brunel University, and post graduate certificate in education from Institute of Education University of London, UK. He was a senior member of academic staff and a member of the academic advisory board. He was in charge of computing in general and curriculum development at the Technical Studies Institute GHQ Armed Forces UAE; where he was actively involved in developing e-learning. His research interests include e-government, e-business and e-learning. He is a member of the British Computer Society and a member of the Institution of Engineering and Technology, UK.

René Fitterer works as research associate at SAP Research Switzerland where he currently pursuits his PhD in management at the University of St. Gallen. His responsibilities include design and development of the process landscaping module in PICTURE. His current research focus is on enterprise value assessment of information systems in public organizations as well as business process management. René holds a Master's degree in information systems from Eastern Michigan University (USA)

Karsten Gareis is senior researcher at empirica, Bonn. His main fields of interest are the way information society technologies impact on ways of working, social inclusion, and regional development. In recent years he was responsible for research on user orientation of public online services in the European Commission funded eUSER project. As project coordinator he oversaw the BISER and TRANSFORM projects, which looked into transformational use of ICTs in EU regions and its relation to regional innovation cultures, economic performance and social cohesion.

Katarina Giritli-Nygren is a teacher and a PhD student in sociology at Midsweden University, lecturing on classical sociological theory. Her doctoral thesis focuses on the organisational consequences of, and the social meaning of "e", in a local governmental setting. The aim is to study e-government as an administrative reform, from the global creation of a 'superstandard' to the local practice of everyday work.

Ulrike Greiner works as senior researcher and project manager at SAP Research Switzerland. Before that she worked as researcher at SAP Research Center Karlsruhe (Germany) where she was mainly involved in research on enterprise interoperability. Her current responsibilities include project management for the PICTURE project, research on business process management, user-centric process modeling and ICT value engineering in particular in e-government. Ulrike holds a PhD in computer science from the University of Leipzig (Germany).

Ivaylo Gueorguiev has been involved in a broad range of projects such as the development of the Bulgarian electronic government strategy and technology and innovation foresight initiatives as well as the management of project portfolios and software process improvement initiatives in various organizations. Mr. Gueorguiev has gained substantial experience in planning, managing and participating in the implementation of process improvement initiatives employing software engineering, information security and business management methodologies. Since 2005 Ivaylo Gueorguiev has been a program manager in the European Software Institute Center Bulgaria.

Umesh Gulla is faculty with University School of Management Studies, GGS Indraprastha University, Delhi, India. His research interests are in information systems management, outsourcing, e-commerce, e-governance, and enterprise resource planning/CRM.

M.P. Gupta is professor & chair-Information Systems & Coordinator-Center for Excellence in E-gov at the Department of Management Studies, IIT Delhi. His research interests lie in the areas of IS/IT planning and e-government. Prof. Gupta has authored the acclaimed book *Government Online* and edited *Towards E-Government* and *Promise of E-Government*, published by McGraw Hill, 2005. His research papers have appeared in national and international journals/conference proceedings. He was the recipient of the prestigious Humanities & Social Sciences fellowship of Shastri Indo Canadian Institute, Calgary (Canada) and a Visiting Fellow at the University of Manitoba.

Cory Allen Heidelberger is a doctoral candidate at Dakota State University. Previously he has taught high school English, speech, algebra, and physics; coached debate and oral interpretation; and written and directed plays. His blog, the Madville Times, focuses on local and state politics in South Dakota. He is a lifelong resident of Madison, South Dakota.

Vincent Homburg (1970) is associate professor at the Faculty of Social Sciences, Erasmus University Rotterdam. His work has appeared in, among other journals, *Knowledge, Technology and Policy, Information Polity, The International Journal of Public Administration* and *The Information Society.* Vincent is the author of *Understanding E-Government: Information Systems in Public Administration* (Routledge, 2008). Furthermore, he has edited *The Information Ecology of E-Government* (with Victor Bekkers) (IOS Press, 2005) and *The New Public Management in Europe* (with Christopher Pollitt and Sandra van Thiel) (Palgrave MacMillan, 2007).

Tobias Hüsing is a researcher at empirica. His educational background is in economics and sociology. Tobias specialises in quantitative empirical research and has been responsible for survey methodology and statistical analysis in a variety of large scale pan-European projects. His work addresses all kinds of questions relating to gauging and benchmarking the information society from a policy perspective.

Recent work includes various perspectives of the information society: that of patients and health care providers, schools and teachers, senior citizens, regional development, specific industries and SMEs, and of citizens and users in general. In many of these, his specific interest has been in questions of e-inclusion, the digital divide. Apart from developing these for empirica projects, Tobias has worked on questionnaires and methodologies for Eurostat and the European Commission.

Mojca Indihar Štemberger is an associate professor of information management at the Faculty of Economics, University of Ljubljana, Slovenia. She has published more than 100 articles in scientific journals, books and conference proceedings mainly in the area of business process management, e-business and decision support systems. She has also been acting as a consultant or project manager of several business process change projects in Slovenian public and private sector. She is a member of program committee of some Slovenian and international conferences and has been a conference chair of InSITE 2007 conference.

Jurij Jaklic is an associate professor of information management at the Faculty of Economics, University of Ljubljana, Slovenia. His main research interests are business process renovation, business process simulation modelling, business intelligence, and data management. He has published around 100 articles in scientific journals, book chapters and conference proceedings. Since 2003, he is a member of editorial board of Slovene professional journal on information systems. He has been a consultant for business process change on several projects in public and private sector.

Muhammad Mustafa Kamal is a post-doctoral researcher at the Brunel Business School Brunel University in the UK. He received his PhD from Brunel University in the area of information systems, in addition, he holds two MSc's—distributed computing systems (Greenwich University, London) and computer sciences (Punjab Institute of Computer Science, Lahore, Pakistan) and Bachelor's degree in business administration (Punjab College of Business Administration, Lahore, Pakistan). His current research interest includes investigating enterprise application integration (EAI) adoption in the local government authorities (LGAs), electronic government (e-government) integration and IT infrastructure issues in LGAs. Dr. Kamal has acted as a business analyst in a research project that focused on the integration of customer relationship management (CRM) applications in the London Borough of Havering (co-funded by ORACLE UK). Dr. Kamal also worked as a post-doctoral research assistant on a European funded research project (Ref: proposal n° 2006/VP021/30137) namely—the REFOCUS (senior employees training on information and communication technologies) project. He has published in the *Journal of Enterprise Information Management*, and his forthcoming publications are in the *European Journal of Information Systems*, *Transforming Government: People, Process, and Policy*, *International Journal of Information Management*, *International Journal of Electronic Government Research*. He has several publications in international conferences such as AMCIS, EMCIS and HICSS and book chapters. Also, he acts as an international reviewer for conferences such as HICSS, AMCIS and EMCIS. Currently, Dr. Kamal is an active editorial review board member for *International Journal of Electronic Government Research* (IJEGR).

Jay P. Kesan received his JD summa cum laude from Georgetown University, where he received several awards including Order of the Coif, and served as associate editor of the *Georgetown Law Journal*. After graduation, he clerked for Judge Patrick E. Higginbotham of the U.S. Court of Appeals for the

Fifth Circuit. Prior to attending law school, Jay Kesan—who also holds a PhD in electrical and computer engineering—worked as a research scientist at the IBM T.J. Watson Research Center in New York.

JinKyu Lee is an assistant professor of management science and information systems in Spears School of Business, Oklahoma State University. He holds a PhD (2007) in MIS from School of Management, University at Buffalo, Master of information systems (1999) from Griffith University, Australia, and BBA (1996) from Yonsei University, Korea. His current research interest includes new technology applications for public/commercial services, information security and privacy, and inter-organizational information sharing. Lee has published research articles in various academic journals and conferences and been involved in several NSF/NSA/DOD funded projects in e-government and information assurance areas.

Katarina Lindblad-Gidlund is associate professor and senior lecturer in social informatics at Midsweden University where she is the leader of the CITIZYS Research Group. She is also director of the international master programme of public information systems and in the editorial board of the *International Journal of Public Information Systems.*

Peter Loos is director of the Institute for Information Systems (IWi) at the German Research Institute for Artificial Intelligence (DFKI) and head of the chair for business administration and information systems at Saarland University. His research activities include business process management, information modelling, enterprise systems, software development as well as implementation of information systems. Loos has written several books, contributed to 30 books and published more than 100 papers in journals and proceedings.

Edephonce N. Nfuka is currently a PhD student in the Department of Computer and Systems Sciences, at Stockholm University, Sweden and an employee at the University of Dar es Salaam Computing Centre, Tanzania. He received a BSc engineering in computer and systems automation from Jose Antonio Echeverria Higher Technical University, Havana and MSc in software engineering from Universitat Politècnica de Catalunya, Barcelona. He is a member of the Association for Information Systems (AIS) and Information Systems Audit and Control Association (ISACA). He has over seven years of industrial and academic experience in the area of IT Management. His current research focuses on IT governance, specifically in the public sector in a developing country's environment/setting.

Sevgi Ozkan is a lecturer at the Informatics Institute, Middle East Technical University, Turkey. She is a member of Information Systems Evaluation and Integration Research Group (ISEing) and a visiting research fellow at Brunel University, UK, and has a PhD in the area of information systems evaluation, with a particular focus on assessing success and effectiveness of information systems. She received her BA and her MA in engineering—electrical and information sciences from the University of Cambridge; her MSc in business information systems from the University of London, and her PhD from Middle East Technical University. She has published her work in well acclaimed journals as well as in international conferences. She is on the executive board of the European and Mediterranean Conference on Information Systems (EMCIS). She has worked for IBM UK and Motorola UK prior to her doctorate studies. Her research interests are information systems evaluation, information and communication technology management in the public sector, information technology governance, evaluation of e-government systems.

Michael Räckers works as a PhD student and research assistant at the European Research Center for Information Systems in Münster, Germany since 2006. Before starting his PhD he worked one year as a student assistant on projects in the public-sector. Räckers holds a master degree in information systems from the Westphalian Wilhelms-University (WWU) Münster, Germany. His research interests are in the field of process modeling in public and private organizations, e-government, e-inclusion and electronic service delivery.

Mysore Ramaswamy is a professor of information systems at Southern University and A&M College, Baton Rouge, Louisiana, USA. He received his PhD in information systems and decision sciences from the Louisiana State University. As a recipient of Fulbright Scholar Award for 2004-2005, he has taught a graduate course in electronic commerce at the State Engineering University of Armenia, Yerevan, Armenia and conducted research on the impact of recent innovations in information technology in emerging market economies. His research has been published in several journals including *Information Systems Research*, and *IEEE Transactions on Knowledge and Data Engineering.*

Ashwin Rao is an undergraduate student in the College of Human Ecology at Cornell University. He is an honors BS candidate in the department of Human Development. He has been an NSF funded REU fellow on the topic of disaster management since 2007 (Jin Kyu Lee, Oklahoma State University—PI). His current research interests include intelligent system designs, cross-cultural differences in perceptions of danger, and analysis of foreign disasters.

Dibakar Ray is currently working as Scientist 'E' at National Informatics Centre, New Delhi. His research interest is e-government and interoperability of information systems. He has experience of designing, developing and implementing various e-government applications for various levels of government. He has authored number of research papers, which have appeared in various journal and conference proceedings.

Peter Rohner heads the Competence Center Health Network Engineering (CC HNE) at the Institute of Information Management (http://ehealth.iwi.unisg.ch) and holds a lectureship at the University of St. Gallen (http://www.unisg.ch). Before, he studied information management at the University of St. Gallen (lic. oec. Inform. HSG) and received a PhD for his work about architecture and integration of distributed systems (Dr. oec. HSG). Currently, he is working in the fields of e-health (division of labor and networkability in public health) and e-government (networkability of public administrations). He is member of different expert panels (e.g. eCH and SwissICT).

Knut Rolland has over 10 years of experience from working within large organizations with collaboration technology both as a researcher and a consultant. His main interests include corporate-wide collaboration platforms, integrated operations, and the organizational dynamics involved in introducing such technologies in organizations. He is a principal consultant in the Norwegian consulting company Avenir, and holds a position as an adjunct associate professor at the department of computer and information science at the Norwegian University of Science and Technology. Dr. Rolland research has been published in numerous international conferences, books and journals, including *The Information Society* and *Ethics and Information Technology.*

Barbara Russo is an associate professor of the Faculty of Computer Science of the Free University of Bolzano-Bozen, Italy and a member of the Center for Applied Software Engineering. She has various publications on agile methods and open source development. She has participated to several national and international projects in software engineering. She has been program committee member or program chair of various conferences and referee of international journals in the sector. Her current research interests mainly focus on reliability analysis and software metrics in the agile and open source development.

Lazar Rusu is a senior lecturer in IT management in the Department of Computer and Systems Sciences at Stockholm University and Royal Institute of Technology Stockholm, Sweden. He holds a diploma in electrical engineering (MSc) from Cluj-Napoca Polytechnic Institute, a diploma in management (MSc) from Babes-Bolyai University Cluj-Napoca and a PhD in management from West University of Timisoara, Romania. Over his career, he has focused mainly in doing research on the management of information systems/information technology and has a professional experience of over 20 years both industrial and academic in the area of information technology.

Demetrios Sarantis holds an MSc in operational research and information system from London School of Economics and Political Science and he is a PhD student of decision systems at the National Technical University of Athens, Greece. His research interests include organization and implementation issues in transformational government, public sector management, process modelling and reengineering in the public sector. He gained practical experience in several multinational companies and government organizations in different countries.

Ludwig Christian Schaupp is an assistant professor at West Virginia University. His primary research interests include website success metrics, e-government adoption and diffusion, and REA. He has published in several top-tier journals including *Communications of the ACM*, *Journal of Computer Information Systems*, and *Information Systems Frontiers*. He has also presented at several international conferences including Americas Conference on Information Systems (AMCIS) as well as the Hawaiian International Conference on Systems Sciences (HICSS).

Rajiv C. Shah received his PhD from the Institute of Communications Research at the University of Illinois at Urbana-Champaign. Prior to that he earned a JD from the University of Illinois at Urbana-Champaign and a BS in electrical engineering from the University of Nebraska-Lincoln.

Maddalena Sorrentino researches in organization theory and organisational change, and is a professor of e-government at the University of Milan. She is the author and editor of seven books and more than 140 articles, essays, Italian and international conference communications and research reports. In 2006 Maddalena founded the ICONA Inter-departmental Centre along with a group of her university colleagues. ICONA is dedicated to organisational innovation in public administrations. Maddalena is member of the editorial boards of the *Government Information Quarterly* and *Information Systems and e-Business Management*. She is advisor to private and public institutions on themes related to organisational development.

Florian Stroh studied computer science and business administration between 2000 and 2006 at the Technische Universität München (Germany). Since 2006 he is working as a research associate at SAP Research and is involved in the EU-funded research project PICTURE. In addition, he is a research assistant at the institute of information management of the University of St.Gallen (Switzerland).

Giancarlo Succi is professor with tenure at the Free University of Bolzano-Bozen, Italy, where he directs the Center for Applied Software Engineering. He was professor with tenure at the University of Alberta, Edmonton, Alberta, associate professor at the University of Calgary, Alberta, and assistant professor at the University of Trento, Italy. He coordinated several European projects, has been chair of various international conferences and referee for various international journals in software engineering. His research interests include multiple areas of software engineering, including open source development, agile methodologies, and experimental software engineering. Giancarlo Succi is a Fulbright Scholar.

Nasrat M. Touqan is an undergraduate student in the Spears School of Business at Oklahoma State University. He is a BS candidate in the department of Management Information Systems. He has been an NSF funded REU fellow on the topic of disaster management since 2007 (Jin Kyu Lee, Oklahoma State University—PI). His current research interests include mobile government, information systems architecture, management science methods and forecasting techniques.

Eileen M. Trauth is associate dean and professor, College of Information Sciences and Technology, The Pennsylvania State University. Her research is concerned with socio-cultural influences on the global information economy with a special focus on the role of gender diversity and social inclusion within the field. She has received two Fulbright Awards and grants from the National Science Foundation and Science Foundation Ireland to support her research. In addition to her work on gender, she has published papers and books on qualitative research methods, global informatics, information policy, information management and information systems skills.

Haiko van der Voort is an assistant professor of public administration at Delft University of Technology. He studied public administration in Leiden. He teaches organization theory and decision making theory for bachelors, masters and elective students and for professionals. He studies regulation and multi actor governance in the public domain.

Jing Yang is a doctoral student of management science and information systems in Spears School of Business, Oklahoma State University. She holds a MS (2007) in statistics from Oklahoma State University and a BE (2001) in statistics from Zhongnan University of Economics and Law, China. Her current research interest includes inter-organizational information sharing, information security and training, and cross-cultural differences in deception detection.

Benjamin Yeo is a senior research analyst in regional economics at the Milken Institute. His expertise involves knowledge management for e-business and economic development; information systems management; and information policy studies. Some of his recent projects include *Pittsburgh's Technology Strategy: SWOT Analysis*, a study of Pittsburgh's technology strategy; and *Nemours Children's Hospital: Advancing Orlando's Life Science and Economic Development,* a research on Orlando's newly approved Nemours Children's Hospital. He received a PhD in information science from the College of Information Sciences and Technology at the Pennsylvania State University, USA.

Jörg Ziemann has studied at the University of Göttingen, the University of California (Irvine, USA) and the University of Hamburg, were he received a diploma in business computer science (Dipl.-Wirt.-Inf.). In 2004 he joined the Institute for Information Systems (IWi) at the German Research Center for Artificial Intelligence (DFKI) where he worked on various EU projects in the fields of collaborative business process management and e-government. In this area he published more then 30 articles in journals and proceedings. Currently, Jörg is working on his PhD thesis.

Index

E

F

G

H

M

N

O

P

Q

R

S

T

U

V

W

X